P9-DUM-170

SCIENTIFIC CHANGE

edited by A. C. Crombie

SCIENTIFIC CHANGE

Historical studies in the intellectual, social and technical conditions for scientific discovery and technical invention, from antiquity to the present

SYMPOSIUM ON THE HISTORY OF SCIENCE
UNIVERSITY OF OXFORD 9–15 JULY 1961

BASIC BOOKS INC., PUBLISHERS NEW YORK

Colloquium organized under the auspices of the Division of History of Science of the International Union of the History and Philosophy of Science.

Library of Congress Catalog Card Number 63-20581

Manufactured in the United States of America

Contents

PART THREE
SCIENCE AND TECHNOLOGY IN THE MIDDLE AGES

6 What was original in Arabic science? S. PINES *The Hebrew University, Jerusalem* 181

7 Al-Bīrūnī and the theory of the solar apogee: an example of originality in Arabic science: WILLY HARTNER and MATTHIAS SCHRAMM *Goethe University, Frankfurt* 206

8 Motives and opportunities for science in the medieval universities: GUY BEAUJOUAN *Archives de France, Paris* 219

9 The medieval language of proportions: elements of the interaction with Greek foundations and the development of new mathematical techniques: JOHN E. MURDOCH *Princeton University* 237

10 What accelerated technological progress in the Western Middle Ages? LYNN WHITE, JR. *University of California, Los Angeles* 272

Commentaries on part three by:
A. P. YUSHKEVICH *Institute of History of Science and Technology, Soviet Academy of Sciences, Moscow* 292
R. W. SOUTHERN *Oxford University* 301
L. MINIO-PALUELLO *Oxford University* 306
BERTRAND GILLE *University of Clermont* 311

Discussion of part three by: 315
O. Temkin, J. Millás-Vallicrosa, A. C. Crombie, R. W. Southern, H. L. Crosby, J. R. Ravetz, J. Needham, F. Greenaway, M. Daumas, E. Olszewski, S. Pines, W. Hartner, G. Beaujouan, J. E. Murdoch

PART FOUR
PROBLEMS IN THE SOCIOLOGY OF SCIENCE

11 The function of dogma in scientific research: THOMAS S. KUHN *University of California, Berkeley* 347

Commentaries on part four by:
A. RUPERT HALL *University of Indiana* 370
MICHAEL POLANYI *Oxford University* 375

Discussion of part four by: 381
B. Glass, S. E. Toulmin, E. F. Caldin, T. S. Kuhn

PART FIVE: THE MAKING OF MODERN SCIENCE: FACTORS IN PHYSICAL DISCOVERY

PART SIX: THE MAKING OF MODERN SCIENCE: FACTORS IN BIOLOGICAL DISCOVERY

continued overleaf

PART EIGHT
HISTORY OF SCIENCE AS AN ACADEMIC DISCIPLINE

PART NINE
PROBLEMS IN THE HISTORIOGRAPHY OF SCIENCE

Acknowledgements

THIS SYMPOSIUM, under the title *The Structure of Scientific Change*, was held at Oxford on the 9–15 July 1961 on the authority of the Oxford University Committee for the History and Philosophy of Science. The members of this committee were the Vice-Chancellor, the Proctors, the Representative of of the Women's Colleges, Mr. H. R. Harré and myself *ex officio*, and Professor C. D. Darlington (Biological Sciences), Professor E. F. Jacob (Modern History), Professor W. C. Kneale (Literae Humaniores), and Professor G. Temple (Physical Sciences), representing these faculties respectively. Generous financial support made it possible to invite scholars representing most of the main aspects of the history of science now being investigated, and to provide suitable accommodation in the pleasing atmosphere of Worcester College for the international body that assembled. On behalf of the Committee I should like to thank the benefactors who contributed so generously to the cost of the Symposium, in the first place the Bollingen Foundation, Pfizer Ltd., and the National Science Foundation of the United States of America, and also the International Union of the History and Philosophy of Science, U.N.E.S.C.O., the British Council, May and Baker Ltd., the American Council of Learned Societies, and the Warden and Fellows of All Souls College. The contributions made by these benefactors covered the entire cost of organization, travel, accommodation and entertainment and has made it possible to publish the discussion in full. It would be inappropriate to mention by name the many individuals connected with these bodies whose sympathetic response to the idea of the Symposium contributed something more than simply financial support, but I should like to record my particular gratitude to Mr. John Barrett and Mr. Huntington Cairns of the Bollingen Foundation, to the late Mr. Stephen Crozier of Pfizer Ltd., and to Mr. Albert Spaulding of the National Science Foundation. The Committee also owes a debt of gratitude to the Warden of Rhodes House for providing the hall for the meetings. The Symposium was held under the auspices of the International Union of the History and Philosophy of Science, to which the adhering body in this country is the Royal Society; it is a pleasing duty to record thanks to Sir Harold Hartley, chairman of the British National Committee, and to Professor Vasco Ronchi and Dr. René Taton, president and secretary-general respectively of the International Union, for their co-operation in the final stages of planning. I should also like to record my thanks to all those who in Oxford assisted with many different details of organization, in particular to my colleague Mr. H. R. Harré; to Mrs. Sylvia Selby and Mrs. Dorothy McLean, successively my secretary, who efficiently took over a large part of the routine of organization; to Mrs. Mary Holdsworth and Mr. J. E. Wall for their assistance with the Russian contributions; to Mrs. J. A. Z. Gardiner and Mrs. G. Kitchin for their assistance in translating the contributions in French and to Mr. H. Lawson and Mrs. L. Minio-Paluello for those in Italian; and to Mr. P. C. Masters of Hunts Ltd. for his very helpful co-operation in lithoprinting the papers for circulation not only with speed but also with elegance.

I am sure I speak for all members of the Symposium in recording thanks to those who helped to make known the richness of Oxford itself in historical scientific materials, in particular to Dr. John R. Baker for arranging a special exhibition of microscopes in the Museum of the History of Science, to Dr. Richard Hunt for arranging a special exhibition of early scientific books and manuscripts in the Bodleian Library, and to the librarians of Merton, Queen's and Corpus Christi Colleges and of Christ Church for showing examples of the scientific works in their collections.

Finally, I should like to thank Dr. M. A. Hoskin and Messrs. R. M. E. Williamson, A. Savile and D. M. Knight for reading the proofs, Professor D. Hawkes for checking the transliterations from Chinese, and Dr. S. Stern for checking those from Arabic.

A. C. CROMBIE
Director of the Symposium

EDITORIAL NOTE

All quotations have been placed between double inverted commas and quotations within quotations between single inverted commas. Technical and archaic terms and phrases which are not quotations have been placed between single inverted commas.

I

Introduction

A. C. CROMBIE

> Aussi bien cette solidarité des âges a-t-elle tant de force qu'entre eux les liens d'intelligibilité sont véritablement à double sens. L'incompréhension du présent naît fatalement de l'ignorance du passé. Mais il n'est peut-être pas moins vain de s'épuiser à comprendre le passé, si l'on ne sait rien du présent.
>
> Marc Bloch, *Métier d'historien*

It was Paul Tannery who established for our time the vision of an *histoire générale des sciences* that should be not merely the separate histories of the particular sciences but a history of scientific thought studied in the context of society and ideas. It was Tannery's view also, as it was Ranke's, that analytical research and general synthesis must advance together, each raising questions for the other. These ideas were not new, for in the *Advancement of Learning* Francis Bacon had already laid out a remarkable design for an intellectual history that should not only include the origin and development of scientific thought in different societies, but should also relate scientific progress and decay to the disposition of the people and their laws, religion, and institutions. Bacon had called for something which he found lacking in his time, a history of

> the general state of learning to be described and represented from age to age, as many have done the works of nature and the state civil and ecclesiastical; without which the history of the world seemeth to me to be as the statua of Polyphemus with his eye out; that part being wanting which doth shew the spirit and life of the person.

He wanted something more than the "small memorials of the schools, authors, and books" in the "divers particular sciences" and "barren relations touching the invention of arts or usages". He wanted from intellectual history "a just story of learning, containing the antiquities and originals of knowledges, and their sects; their inventions, their traditions; their diverse administrations and managings; their flourishings, their oppositions, decays, depressions, oblivions, removes". He wanted these studied "with the causes and occasions of them, and all other events concerning learning, throughout the ages of the world". And he continued:

> The use and end of which work I do not so much design for curiosity, or satisfaction of those that are the lovers of learning; but chiefly for a more serious and grave purpose, which is this in few words, that it will make learned men wise in the use and administration of learning.

Bacon's influence upon the analytical approach to intellectual history has been profound. To take an early example, it can be seen in Daniel Le Clerc's *Histoire de la médicine.*[1] "There is", he wrote,

> an abundance of difference between a History of Physick, that is, a collection of all that relates to their persons, the titles, and numbers of their writings, and a History of Physick, that is, to set forth the opinions of the Physicians, their Systems, and Methods, and to trace step by step all their discoveries. . . . This history . . . is obliged to penetrate into the very soul of every age, and every Author; to relate faithfully and impartially the thoughts of all, and to maintain everyone in his right, not giving to the Moderns what belongs to the Antients, nor bestowing upon these latter what is due to the former; leaving every body at liberty to make reflections for himself upon the matters of Fact as they stand related.

It can be seen also in Voltaire's first essays in history written *en philosophe*, history written to discover the causes of progress and decline and to teach by the results. Seventeenth-century science had provided models of analytical and comparative methods of investigation; in return, Voltaire included in his comparative history of civilization brief accounts of the history of science and technology and suggestions for an analysis of the causes of their progress and stagnation both in the West and in China, India, Islam and other societies of the East. Without stressing the "serious and grave" practical purposes for which Bacon thought history should be studied, the programme he laid down has to a remarkable extent been that of subsequent

[1] First edition, 1696; Preface. For the passage quoted, from the English translation by Drake and Baden, London, 1699, I am indebted to F. N. L. Poynter, "Medicine and the historian. The Fielding H. Garrison Lecture", *Bulletin of the History of Medicine*, XXX (1956) 524; cf. also W. Pagel, "Aristotle and seventeenth-century biological thought", in *Science, Medicine and History*. Essays . . . in honour of Charles Singer (Oxford, 1953) I, 509.

intellectual historians[1]. His vision was Tannery's. Both may stand as godfathers to the experiment attempted in this book.

The proposal that a Symposium on the history of science should be held in England was made in 1957 at a similar meeting at the University of Wisconsin at Madison[2]. When I undertook to organize the Symposium at Oxford it fell to me as its prospective director to choose a theme for it that was definite enough to provide a single subject for discussion, interesting at this stage of the development of history of science as a discipline of learning, and potentially fruitful in suggesting further problems for and approaches to research. One possibility would have been to make an investigation from as many points of view as possible of science and scientific activity (including medicine and technology) in a specific period and society such as seventeenth-century or nineteenth-century England or Europe. Another would have been to study the history of specific scientific problems as successive generations have dealt with them through different periods. But apart from certain limited periods such as the seventeenth century and branches of study such as the history of mechanics, both of which have already been the subjects of considerable recent discussion, it would have been difficult to bring together enough experts for a suitably thorough examination either of all the relevant aspects of scientific activity in a period or of the continuous history of specific scientific problems. Besides, to design the Symposium exclusively in terms either of period or of scientific subject would have impoverished the theme by excluding too high a proportion of available historians of science. On reflection a solution emerged that seemed to satisfy the most desirable criteria and allow for a combination of these two possibilities without their limitations. This was to make the theme of the Symposium a very general though definite historical problem

[1] Cf. Herbert Butterfield, "The history of science and the study of history", *Harvard Library Bulletin*, XIII (1959) 329–47; A. C. Crombie, "Historians and the scientific revolution", *Endeavour*, XIX (1960) 9–13.

[2] *Critical Problems in the History of Science*, Proceedings of the Institute for the History of Science at the University of Wisconsin, 1–11 September 1957, edited by Marshall Clagett (Madison, Wisc., 1959). Other recent symposia, held under the auspices of the International Union of the History and Philosophy of Science, have been published as *La science au seizième siècle*, Colloque international de Royaumont, 1–4 Juillet 1957 (Paris, 1960); and *Actes du Symposium International des sciences physiques et mathématiques dans la première moitié du XVIIe siècle*, Pise-Vinci, 16–18 Juin 1958 (Florence and Paris, 1960).

that could be investigated in terms of examples selected from various periods, societies and sciences, namely the conditions for, or ætiology of, scientific and technical change.

With this as its theme the Symposium began to take shape as an experiment in dealing with a characteristic of history of science that makes it both difficult and challenging as a field of study, namely that it requires expert knowledge of more than one conventional discipline. It became clear that the theme could best be developed as a comparative historical investigation of the structure of mind and society, of the intellectual, technical and social conditions, favouring or discouraging both the making of original scientific discoveries and technical inventions, and the use of discoveries and inventions. The most effective way of carrying this out was to invite specialists in several different fields of science, history and philosophy to come together to explore this common problem. A plan of sufficiently diverse subjects and of examples to be investigated as case studies was drawn up, and a final selection reached on the basis of the authors available. The papers and commentaries that follow are the answers to questions put to a variety of specialists on both sides of the Atlantic, of the English Channel, and of the Iron Curtain. Within each period considered, the papers deal with two main groups of questions, concerning (1) internal factors: the interaction of fundamental ideas and technical possibilities in scientific thinking; and (2) external factors: the role of the social context, motives, opportunities, and general ideas. In discussions of this kind questions of methods and problems of historical analysis are never far from the surface, especially those involved in interpreting and communicating the thought and motives of earlier periods and other cultures. The theme of the Symposium offered an opportunity to bring them into the open. The concluding discussions are devoted explicitly to some special problems of history of science as an academic discipline, and to these questions of interpretation lying at the root of any historical scholarship.

The goal of historical scholarship is said to be to reconstruct the past, but the only past available for reconstruction is that which we can see from the present. The nature of science as an analytical discipline, involved at one and the same time in the uncertainties of discovery and in the accumulation of a body of objective knowledge, raises some special problems of historical reconstruction. Looking back from the present we can see scientific inquiry as an activity yielding a progressively growing body of universally communicable knowledge, any part of which we, latest heirs of the tradition, can test by the stable criteria of logical consistency and comparison with observation. Knowing the whole history of the tradition to its latest point of success, we are in a position to judge the relative importance and influence in that history of different ideas, techniques and discoveries whose potentialities and limitations the development of the tradition has now revealed. Thus the analytical reconstruction of the history of science must at the same time involve an analysis of science, and the present throws light upon the past simply by the development of the tradition itself. Our superior knowledge enables us to see the problems and intellectual manœuvres of Archimedes, or Harvey, or Galileo, or Faraday in a field of possibilities vastly more extensive than was visible to them. In this sense we can know more about their situation than those at the actual frontiers of discovery knew themselves. This does not mean yielding to the unsophisticated temptation to read history backwards in terms of the standards and problems of the present; that would not be reconstruction but a form of evaluation. It means that the advance of knowledge, both in science itself and in related disciplines of logic and philosophy of science and the social sciences, provides us with instruments of analysis which we can apply as a means of comparison across different periods and situations. We are dealing with the constants of scientific thought and social behaviour as well as with scientific and social change. We are put into a position to see particular episodes in scientific history as examples of more general logical situations or social phenomena.

Conversely historical knowledge of the scientific tradition enriches these instruments of rational analysis. It displays the varieties of scientific method and intellectual manœuvre on which any properly inductive analysis of scientific thinking must be based, it exposes us to the surprise that effective scientific thinking could be based on assumptions and have objectives so various and often so different from our own, and it enables us to distinguish the historically accidental from the logically essential elements in the succession of scientific systems. Thus the reconstructed past throws light upon the present.

Because the relevance and the illumination between past and present, and between different kinds of sciences and societies, go in both directions, case studies for the Symposium were selected for comparison from as wide as practicable a range of periods, societies and sciences, from Babylon to the present day. Of particular interest are comparisons both between the sets of conditions found in widely divergent societies, and between the situations found within the same society and science before and after large-scale changes in scientific or technological ideas or practices. It was essential to the purpose of the Symposium that these comparisons should be analysed in discussion by practising scientists, medical men, philosophers, and economists as well as historians of science.

If, instead of looking backwards down the tradition of scientific success, we try in imagination to place ourselves with Archimedes or Harvey, Anaximander or Mendel at the frontiers of *their* knowledge as we reconstruct the circumstances of their discoveries, we obtain a view of the future lacking the logical appearance of events seen in reverse, and historically more authentic as a view of events as lived. They did not know for sure where science was going until they had taken it there. Perhaps most revealing of all is to try to see things through the eyes of someone of less than the highest originality but sensitive to the times, a Pappus, a Mersenne, a T. H. Huxley, or some lesser figure, most or all of whose endeavours have sunk forever below the scientific horizon into the realm of purely 'historical interest'. Very often an essential clue can be found in contemporary writings outside science; so for example theological writings in the Middle Ages and historical writings in the eighteenth century can show us how minds were working at the time. To understand events as experienced by actual men and institutions we must be concerned with the history of errors and false starts as well as successes — although we make this distinction on the basis of what we now know of the tradition of success. As we go back in time the uncertainty of the outlook and of the objectives of scientific inquiries increases. The essence of the scientific movement is research. The answers to the essential question, what to *do* in scientific research — what questions to put to nature, by what methods to get answers, what to count as satisfactory answers — became clear only by the accumulation of successes and the marking of failures. This question, as Bacon put it, "whether or no anything can be known, was to be settled not by arguing, but by trying".[1] And the answers were "a birth of Time" as well as "a birth of

[1] *Novum Organum*, Preface.

Wit".[1] Before the general direction of the route to scientific knowledge had been discovered in Antiquity, it was an open question what kind of world men found themselves inhabiting and almost any road might have turned out to be the right one. With all respect to our Orientalist colleagues, the evidence seems to show that this Greek discovery has been diffused with the diffusion of Western science, and it has not yet been diffused to the whole of mankind. But even in Greek science no set of generally accepted aims, methods, and criteria of cogency in scientific argument had yet become established for the *whole* scientific community. The establishment of general agreement on these basic principles, on what Gilbert called the "new sort of Philosophizing",[2] and indeed the establishment of a scientific community with conditions of communication and education within which agreement could be reached, was one of the achievements, perhaps the major achievement, of the scientific movement in the seventeenth century.

In order to reconstruct the past as lived, the historian of science needs to make use both of the arts of the intellectual historian in disentangling the notions held by past thinkers about method and cogency in argument, and of the arts of the social historian in discovering the motives and opportunities for and the value given to science, medicine and technology by the people and within the institutions of the period.

Problems as presented and explanations as offered in scientific documents of the past are more often than not made intelligible to us only by asking what their author thought he was doing: what he saw as a problem, how he conceived the method of finding a solution, what modes of explanation he regarded as satisfactory. The answers to these historical questions must be sought by a study of science in the context of thought in which it existed, resting on the firm basis of texts established by the critical techniques of philologists. They can be found and understood by discovering three things.

The first is the body of general doctrine held by an author, comprising on the one hand his beliefs about nature, and on the other his conception of the organization of science, which together regulate the questions he puts and the answers he finds adequate. Western science has been dominated by a succession of large general doctrines, with nature conceived, for example, as a sociological order among personified powers (as it seems

[1] Ibid. I, 78. [2] *De Magnete*, Preface.

that the ancient Babylonians and Egyptians conceived it), as the product of a divine mind and hence possessing appropriate characteristics such as simplicity and harmony of parts, as strictly a machine, as a product of evolution, as a continuum, as atomic, as a manifestation of probabilities. Similarly the dominant body of Greek men of science saw as their goal the organization of every field of inquiry on the axiomatic model which was their most powerful intellectual invention, while the natural philosophers of early modern times transformed this axiomatic, geometrical pattern by an increasing preoccupation with experimental analysis of causal connexions and functional relationships. Again, opinion has varied, between different forms of 'positivism' and more optimistic conclusions, about the capacity of science to discover a rational structure of nature as distinct from that of the organizing mind of the inquirer. Each of these general systems has had the effect of concentrating research on certain types of problem. This in turn reflects on the second element controlling scientific history, the scientific systems made up of the theories and laws providing particular explanations within the framework of general doctrine, and of the methods, both intellectual and experimental, with their various technical potentialities and limitations, by which men of science address their questions to nature and obtain their answers. It may be argued that the driving force of change throughout the Western scientific movement has been produced by the interaction between doctrines, theories and methods of inquiry in search of answers to the question: what should be done in research? And this includes what counts as a satisfactory explanation. Each of these elements in the science of a period may clearly promote discoveries in some directions, and in others make them virtually impossible. But there is a third element in the situation, the disposition to change, the readiness to reject theories when they are falsified and to re-think accepted beliefs when they become impotent or obstructive. Change comes more easily in some societies, periods and scientific situations than in others. It is easier to reject particular theories within an accepted system of doctrine than to take the drastic step of rejecting the whole doctrine. The disposition to change has been cultivated more conscientiously and with greater understanding from the seventeenth century than before that period. But it is a matter of individual as well as collective behaviour. Kepler possessed it in shining degree.

The legitimate criticism has been made of much contemporary work in the history of science that while concentrating on the purely intellectual and for the most part internal development of science, it has largely neglected to take account either of the motives and opportunities for science among the interests of a period, or of the diffusion and application of scientific discoveries and technical inventions beyond immediately scientific circles. It is only comparatively recently that science and technology have risen to their present position among the vastly various concerns and interests that throughout history have moved men to thought and action. What were the motives and opportunities for science and technology for the few who paid attention to them in earlier times, and why have their numbers increased? With science an interest only of a scattered minority, what opportunities were there in Antiquity for even maintaining continuity between the generations, to say nothing of establishing a general consensus of opinion about scientific principles and methods? By contrast the universities and scientific societies of medieval and early modern times seem to have provided opportunities for continuity in education and research that made the development of a scientific community possible. But what was the value given to scientific doctrine and scientific inquiry within a range of interests and activities so divergent as those indicated, for example, by a predominant concern with a theological scheme of human responsibility and destiny, the never-ceasing pressures of politics, the cultivation of literary learning, the great strides in logic and philosophy, the continuation of traditional technical practices? Who used the inventions described in recent histories of technology? What effect did they have on the economics of production and trade, on navigation, transport and war? What were the motives and opportunities for invention and for the application of inventions? These are the important questions for historians of society. Only in history of medicine has there been any extended attempt to relate men of science to the society in which they lived. If Bacon and Tannery were to be its godfathers — with perhaps Karl Sudhoff as a third — it was essential for the Symposium to do more than treat the history of science simply as the internal history of scientific thought, and the history of technology simply as the history of techniques. The most natural corrective was to invite a discussion of the external context of society and ideas by historians interested in the variety of the activities of a period, and by economic historians and other specialists who could see science and technology as parts of a different kind of enterprise.

The questions put to the contributors to the Symposium in the light of these considerations may be grouped under five general headings:

1. What is the available evidence on which historical reconstruction can be based, and what are the gaps?

2. Who were the people taking part in scientific activity? — What were their numbers, education, social position, means of livelihood, personal motives and opportunities, means of communication, institutions? What critical audience was there to be convinced by, use, transmit, develop, revise or reject their conclusions? What social pressures were there within the scientific community itself to affect the consensus of opinion in favour of the old or the new?

3. What were the essential changes in scientific thought and how were they brought about? — What was the part played in the initiation of change by mutations in fundamental ideas leading to new questions being asked, new problems being seen, new criteria of satisfactory explanation replacing the old? What was the part played by new technical inventions in mathematics and experimental apparatus; by developments in pure mathematics; by the refinement of measurement; by the transference of ideas, methods and information from one field of study to another? What significance can be given to the description and use of scientific methods and concepts in advance of scientific achievement? How have methods and conceptions of explanation differed in different sciences? How has language changed in changing scientific contexts? What parts have chance and personal idiosyncrasy played in discovery? How have scientific changes been located in the context of general ideas and intellectual motives, and to what extent have extra-scientific beliefs given theories their power to convince?

4. How have scientific and technical changes been located in the social context of motives and opportunities? — What value has been put on scientific activity by society at large, by the needs of industry, commerce, war, medicine and the arts, by governmental and private investment, by religion, by different states and social systems? To what external social, economic and political pressures have science, technology and medicine been exposed? Are money and opportunity all that is needed to create scientific and technical progress in modern society?

5. How do questions of interpretation based on assumptions

made about science and about societies enter into the analysis of the history of science?

The subjects investigated in terms of these questions are set out in the sessions that follow, the papers having been circulated in advance and those belonging to each session discussed together. It is not to be expected that these papers and discussions will answer all the questions asked. But "the art of discovery advances with every act of discovery".[1] Whether or not Bacon or Tannery would recognize this experiment in bringing some part of their vision to fulfilment, the most fruitful purpose of any such attempt to make a synthesis of problems of research will have been realized if this investigation of the ætiology of scientific change suggests to scholars fresh problems and approaches to pursue, and to the general reader a genuinely historical vision of science itself.

[1] *The Advancement of Learning*, II; cf. *Novum Organum*, I, 130.

PART ONE

The Establishment of Scientific Thinking in Antiquity

2

Motives and Incentives for Science in Antiquity

LUDWIG EDELSTEIN

The knowledge of the arts and crafts (the *technai*), derived from experience and employed for practical purposes, in the opinion of the ancients was coeval with man. Scientific knowledge (the knowledge of the *mathemata* or *epistemai*, or *scientiae* in the strict sense of the word) to them was a discovery of a relatively late period of history, the seventh and sixth centuries B.C. Then for the first time, they agreed, an attempt was made to give a consistently rational picture of nature, to classify phenomena systematically and to explain them, to establish a limited number of principles and to deduce their consequences. But the implications of this new enterprise were understood differently at different times during the thousand years or so that ancient science lasted. And as the meaning of science itself changed, motives and incentives for it changed too. It is therefore impossible to proceed as if there were one answer to the question at issue. One can but try to discuss the various positions that were taken and to indicate their relative importance within the development of ancient science.[1]

I

The science arising in the pre-Socratic age undoubtedly aimed at understanding, at contemplation of the truth, of the essence of things. This vaunted theoretical attitude is glorified in Democritus's saying that it is greater gain to find an ætiology than to become King of Persia[2]; it is caricatured in the Socrates of the Aristophanic *Clouds* who is made to pose the question, "How many times the length of its legs does a flea jump?"

[1] Little work seems to have been done on the topic here under investigation. Those studies I have found most helpful will be referred to in the course of my discussion. In the main my material is drawn from a history of ancient science which I am preparing, and from a book, *The Idea of Progress in Antiquity*, scheduled to appear shortly.

[2] 68B 118, *Die Fragmente der Vorsokratiker*, ed. H. Diels and W. Kranz (5th ed., Berlin, 1934–5).

(v. 145.) The investigations of problems which to the comic poet seemed useless and meaningless were to the adherents of science worth everything. They wished to know what it is all about, if I may use this expression. To be born seemed to them preferable to not being born, "for the sake of viewing the heavens and the whole order of the universe".[1]

Such an attitude of course includes traits noticeable even in earlier periods. To give a picture of the world 'as it is', to describe it 'objectively', without the intrusion of the observer as it were, is characteristic already of the Homeric epic. With his panoramic ability, the poet, clinging closely to reality, encompasses in his work great things and small. The Greek artist was the first to try to represent a body as it appears in nature, showing it not from the front or the side but plastically. Again, explanation, classification and systematization are not foreign to Homeric or Hesiodic mythology. The epic knows well that what is truly seducing in the song of the Sirens is "their professions of knowledge".[2]

But although the wish to see things as they are, to explain, to systematize, to find out, has its share also in the ideal of theoretical knowledge, there is in the latter from the beginning something other and new. A life devoted to science is considered a life of happiness. "Blessed is he", says Euripides, "who has taken knowledge of science . . . contemplating the ageless order of deathless Nature — how it came to be formed, its manner, its way."[3] And such 'beatitudes' recur again and again in later literature. They attest the belief that scientific inquiry is one form of the human quest for *eudæmonia*. The pleasure sought by all men, yet found by most in the enjoyment of the senses or in the winning of glory, is found by the man of science in knowledge itself.[4]

[1] Anaxagoras, 59A 30, Diels-Kranz. See in general F. Boll, "Vita Contemplativa", *Sitzungsberichte d. Heidelberger Akademie d. Wissenschaften*, Philol. Hist. Klasse, VIII (1920).

[2] Odyssey, XII, v. 189; cf. Cicero, *De finibus*, V, 18, 49. Concerning the Cicero passage see below p. 19, n. 1. The 'theoretical' character of the Homeric epic has been noted, e.g. by S. H. Butcher, "The Greek love of knowledge", in *Harvard Lectures on Greek Subjects* (London and New York, 1904) 82 ff., 86 ff.

[3] A. Nauck, *Tragicorum Graecorum Fragmenta* (2nd ed., Leipzig, 1889) Fr. 910.

[4] For these 'beatitudes' cf. G. L. Dirichlet ("De veterum macarismis", *Religionsgeschichtliche Versuche und Vorarbeiten* XIV, 4, Giessen, 1914, p. 66), who, however, in my opinion does not discriminate sharply enough between testimonies concerned with science and those concerned with philosophy.

Such an emotion must not be confounded with that which still today a scientist may experience in his work. He feels pleasure when he solves a particular problem with which he has wrestled for a long time, and things at last fall into place; he enjoys playing the game of science successfully. Such a feeling has subjective grounds. The pleasure which the ancient scientist experienced, as the beatitudes indicate, is objectively determined. It is derived from "contemplating the ageless order of deathless Nature".

What is here at stake can be elucidated I think by a famous statement of Kant. The discovery of order in nature, he says,

> is the business of the understanding, which is designedly borne toward a necessary purpose, viz. the bringing of unity of principles into nature, which purpose then the judgment must ascribe to nature, because the understanding cannot here prescribe any law to it. The attainment of that design is bound up with the feeling of pleasure. . . . We no longer find, it is true, any marked pleasure in the comprehensibility of nature and in the unity of its divisions into genera and species, by which all empirical concepts are possible, through which we cognize it according to its particular laws. But this pleasure has certainly been present at one time, and it is only because the commonest experience would be impossible without it that it is gradually confounded with mere cognition and no longer arrests particular attention.[1]

To put it differently, science whose aim it is to understand nature must start from the presupposition that nature can be understood by reason. When this hypothesis for the first time proved to be correct, when scientists as it were by "a lucky chance" favouring their design met under empirical laws with such a systematic unity as they had assumed to exist, they were "rejoiced".[2] Disorder became rational order; chaos, cosmos. Definitions, classifications, general rules of coming-to-be and passing-away, could be devised and could be shown to exist in nature. For those to whom the fact of science is self-evident,

[1] I. Kant, *Critique of Judgment*, trans. J. H. Bernard (The Hafner Library of Classics, New York, 1951) Introduction, VI, pp. 23 f. What Kant says here about the original scientific experience in terms of critical idealism, Darwin, the reflective empirical scientist, expresses in his observation that the relation of species to one another "is a truly wonderful fact, the wonder of which we are apt to overlook from familiarity" (*The Origin of Species*, London, 1859, Ch. 4, pp. 128 f.). On the identity of the point of view in the two statements see B. Bauch, *Immanuel Kant* (2nd ed., Berlin and Leipzig, 1921) 418 ff.

[2] Kant, op. cit. Introduction, V, p. 20.

a commonplace of their life, this is a truism evoking pleasure at most for the flash of a moment. For the ancients who started the scientific enterprise, it was a wonder to which they had not yet become accustomed.[1]

Moroever it would seem that the scientific analysis of data was thought to provide a short cut to insight and, even if no practical results followed from it, was considered the basis of superior knowledge. Theætetus, distinguishing rational and irrational numbers and setting forth their characteristics, emphasizes that he is thereby freed from the necessity of dealing empirically with each succeeding number.[2] With the magic wand of definition the infinity of instances is made finite, as it were. On the other hand, when the scientific physician, instead of judging that a certain remedy benefited Callias and similarly Socrates, comes to judge "that it benefits all persons of a certain type, considered as a class, who suffer from this or that disease", he may not be able to treat better, but he knows more.[3] When everything is understood as made up of elements changing from one form into another, the manifoldness of all appearances is reduced to unity and uniformity and thus becomes manageable by the intellect. "Learning increaseth wisdom."[4]

Finally, although truth is independent of the human mind and is not made by men, theoretical cognition is not passive. Contemplation is an "activity" of the mind, Aristotle says.[5] It is a "theoretical virtue", the highest virtue of man. Such a definition is to be found in all philosophical systems to which ancient scientists owed allegiance.[6] As Cicero puts it following Antiochus,

> it is therefore at all events manifest that we are designed by nature for activity. Activities vary in kind, so much so that the more important actually eclipse the less, but the most important are, first, . . . the contemplation and the study of the heavenly bodies

[1] In Greek philosophy one may for instance note a sentiment similar to that expressed by Kant and Darwin in Plato's theory of the κοινόν of the ideas, which is also concerned with the fact that if no identities could be found, if reality consisted of incomparable units, knowledge would be impossible (cf. Bauch, op. cit. p. 419).

[2] Plato, *Theætetus*, 147C ff.

[3] Aristotle, *Metaphysics*, I, 981a 7 ff.

[4] Empedocles, 31B 17, l. 14, Diels-Kranz. This sense of power over nature through mere cognition is, I suggest, part of the original scientific experience of which Kant and Darwin speak.

[5] *Nicomachean Ethics*, X, 7, 1177a 20.

[6] For the relation between philosophy and science cf. below p. 29 and p. 25, n. 1.

and of those secrets and mysteries of nature which reason has the capacity to penetrate; secondly, the practice and the theory of politics; thirdly, the principles of Prudence, Temperance, Courage and Justice, with the remaining virtues.[1]

Three factors then seem to constitute the ancient ideal of theoretical knowledge: objective pleasure; a sense of bringing to a sudden halt the rush of experience together with a sense of heightened insight; an experience of active accomplishment. This was the original ideal with which Greek science started and of which it never completely lost sight, although its various aspects had probably greater or lesser significance depending on the individual and also on the age in which he lived. While the activeness of reason appears to have been felt throughout Antiquity, joy in the order of the world and wisdom in its ways certainly meant something other to a scientist who sided with Plotinus than to a follower of Aristotle.[2] Moreover, the theoretical ideal and its motivating force soon merged with another ideal destined to become no less important for scientific research.

II

At the very beginning of Greek science, the individual scientist works in almost complete isolation and on his own. There is as yet no scientific dialogue. Other workers in the field are mentioned at most in order to reject summarily their point of view. The opening words of the oldest historical treatise — "Hecatæus of Miletus speaks thus: I put down things as they seem to me to be true: for the accounts given by the Greeks are manifold and ridiculous, as it appears to me"[3] — are symbolic of the early attitude of 'going it alone'.[4]

But by the time of Plato and Aristotle, an entirely different concept of research had taken shape. Xenophanes's theory of progress[5] is now more generally accepted and has changed the

[1] *De finibus*, V, 21, 58. The Ciceronian analysis of the theoretical ideal (V, 18, 48 – 21, 60), from which I have quoted, is perhaps the most explicit and most comprehensive which is preserved from Antiquity.

[2] Cf. below p. 21, n. 5.

[3] 1 F 1, *Die Fragmente der Griechischen Historiker*, ed. F. Jacoby (Berlin, 1923) I.

[4] The isolation of the early scientist has been stressed by W. A. Heidel, *The Heroic Age of Science* (Baltimore, 1933) 73. See also below p. 27.

[5] 21B 18, Diels-Kranz.

scientist's relation to his predecessors, his contemporaries, and his successors. The search for truth, he realizes, is a co-operative undertaking. Every step forward on the road to the solution of a problem presupposes those previously taken and prepares those to be taken in the future. At the height of the Hellenistic era the belief begins to spread that such progress must of necessity be infinite. The individual is no more than a link in the chain of generations working together for a common purpose. How much or how little insight he possesses depends also on the point of time at which he stands in the gradually unfolding process of discovery.[1]

This expectation of progress does not carry with it the conclusion that since later generations will know so much more, the present generation knows too little to lay hold on anything that could properly be called knowledge. Such a sceptical resignation, if I am not mistaken, was not to prevail before the nineteenth century.[2] Enjoyment of what has been accomplished is quite possible, for what will be known better in the future is essentially the same truth. And through the progressivist creed the personal motive for gaining insight is associated with another and ulterior motive: that of making a contribution to the life of others, of helping to build up an edifice that will outlast him and grow beyond what he himself is privileged to see and to enjoy.

As Seneca puts it, summarizing the development of thought down to his own time, science is an inheritance, a patrimony left to us by earlier generations. We administer it and should leave it enriched to those who come after us. As we are grateful to our predecessors for what they have done for us and this is their reward, so the gratitude of our successors for what we have done for them is our reward. It motivates our endeavour as much as does our wish to understand. At the same time science, growing out of the efforts of the past, added to by those now alive and to be increased further in the future, is no longer the property of an individual, but of all men, of mankind. Thus the scientist becomes a citizen of two cities, the one on

[1] That, contrary to the current view, the idea of scientific progress is not modern but ancient, I have pointed out in "Recent trends in the interpretations of ancient science", *Journal of the History of Ideas*, XIII (1952) 575 f. This article will be quoted in the following as "Ancient science".

[2] Cf. M. Weber, "Wissenschaft als Beruf", *Gesammelte Aufsätze zur Wissenschaftslehre* (Tübingen, 1922) 536 f., who illustrates his thesis by Tolstoy's analysis of modern life.

earth in which he happens to be born and which is perishable, the other imperishable and voluntarily chosen. As a member of that eternal community comprising men of all ages, he works not for the tasks of the day, for mundane affairs, but for the enlightenment of the world — for the growth of civilization, to put it in modern teminology.[1]

Through civilization, the Stoics asserted, man erects over nature a second nature as it were, an *altera natura*.[2] In the same way, one may say that the history of the sciences is an *altera historia* over political history. While the latter is filled with wars, with fights for power, with destruction, this second history, unstained by blood and human passions, is devoted to the realization of man's intellectual gifts. Science and its discoveries, together with poetry and the fine arts, are the subjects of this truly humane story in which man transcends himself, or as the ancients would say, becomes most like the divine.[3]

Also in another respect, however, does ancient science touch upon the divine — the divine not in man, but in nature itself. Whenever the Greek or Roman confronts phenomena that reflect eternal laws, he hears in the eternal the voice of the divine; "eternal" and "divine" are interchangeable expressions. In later stages of science the divine becomes its concern in a still more specific sense. Teleological thought leads everywhere to the discovery of the working of God. Aristotle, having treated of "things divine" — that is, astronomy — turns to biology and shows his students that in this field too the divine is not missing, though to be sure it is present only to a lesser degree: "Come in; don't be afraid; there are gods even here."[4] In the second century A.D. Galen the anatomist writes:

> This [book on the Use of Parts] is a sacred book which I composed as a true hymn of the god who has created us, in the belief that I am truly pious not if I sacrifice many hecatombs of oxen to him and burn thousands of talents of cassia, but if I first recognize myself and then explain also to the others the wisdom of God, his power, his excellence. (III, 10)[5]

[1] For Seneca see *Naturales quaestiones*, Praefatio and e.g. VI, 5, 3; VII, 25, 4 f.; 30, 5. His views reflect theories of the Middle Stoa, which is itself indebted to earlier doctrines.

[2] Cicero, *De natura deorum*, II, 60, 152.

[3] Cf. below p. 37.

[4] *De partibus animalium*, I, 5, 645a 22.

[5] Cf. L. Edelstein, "Greek medicine in its relation to religion and magic", *Bulletin of the Institute of the History of Medicine*, V (1937) 215 f. and also 229. The neo-Platonists too find God in nature. Their explanation may seem

It is sometimes claimed that it was seventeenth-century science which, imbued with the spirit of Protestantism and Puritanism, for the first time promised to lead men to God. But when Swammerdam proposed to show divine providence at work in the anatomy of the flea — an animal as insignificant as that for whose study Aristophanes had ridiculed Socrates — he was not doing anything new.[1] Long before, pagan science was a way to God and taught men to read the book of the world as a book written by a divine author and thus to understand its meaning rightly. This one must remember in order to grasp the full significance of the words in which Ptolemy sets forth the dignity and value of astronomy: "I know that I am mortal, a creature of a day; but when I search into the multitudinous revolving spirals of the stars, my feet no longer rest on the earth, but, standing by Zeus himself, I take my fill of ambrosia, the food of the Gods." The scientist of late centuries, just as he was a servant of mankind, was a servant and worshipper of the deity. Ancient science was not mere knowledge nor was it mere technique; it preserved an awareness of the meaning of the universe and retained a place for values within the world of facts.[2]

III

So far I have considered science merely as theoretical understanding and have left out of consideration its usefulness for practical ends. Of the applicability of their findings the scientists were of course quite conscious, as the testimony shows. Archytas's studies in the theory of mechanics led him to construct instruments and machines, and even a rattle, "a good inven-

unscientific to the modern interpreter even in comparison with Aristotle's physics and biology, but it was of course meant to be scientific and was considered so by those who accepted it; see below p. 38. About the early "science of the cosmos" and "Greek monotheism" see W. Dilthey, "Einleitung in die Geisteswissenschaften", *Gesammelte Schriften* I (Leipzig and Berlin, 1922) 165 ff.

[1] That Swammerdam's statement is at least indirectly influenced by Christian ideas current in his time has been suggested by Weber, op. cit. p. 539.

[2] For modern science and the concept of meaning cf. e.g. Weber, op. cit. pp. 539 ff. He identifies all Greek science with knowledge through concepts and thus knowledge of eternal truth, which is sought for the purpose of right political action. This to me seems a much too narrow definition of the Greek concept of science. For Ptolemy's epigram see *Anthologia Palatina*, IX, 577.

tion", Aristotle says, "which people give to children in order that while occupied with this they may not break any furniture, for young things cannot keep still."[1] Archimedes, the "geometrical Briareus" as the Roman aggressors called him, invented weapons for the defence of his native city. Astronomers and geographers applied their knowledge to drawing maps that could be used by sailors and travellers. It is true, scientists did not undertake their research with practical purposes in mind; they did not feel that their labours were more valuable or justifiable on account of the practical fruits they bore. The latter rather were by-products, so to say. Yet science did not shy away from technology, as is often assumed.[2]

On the other hand, one cannot deny that applied science, as all ancient technology, did not advance as far as it could conceivably have done. During the thousand years of scientific studies in which the intellect on its "flight through the universe" revolutionized man's understanding of nature and achieved ever greater triumphs, the forms of daily existence changed relatively little, less perhaps than during the later Middle Ages, surely much less than in some of the decades since the middle of the nineteenth century. That the usefulness of science in Graeco–Roman times was comparatively unexploited, that it was, strictly speaking, no motive for developing scientific knowledge, is due I think mainly to three factors.[3]

First, the 'empirical' scientists, who considered speculation and theory of less importance, if of importance at all, and who on account of their prevalent concern with reality might have

[1] *Politics*, 1340b 28.

[2] For the place of technology in antiquity cf. A. Rehm, "Zur Rolle der Technik in der griechisch-römischen Antike", *Archiv f. Kulturgeschichte*, XXVIII (1938) 135 ff. (on Archimedes and the various traditions on his work, p. 145, n. 27); see also "Ancient science", pp. 579 f. (The brief outline of the development of ancient science given in this article is taken as the starting point for my discussion of the topics dealt with in this and in the following section.) The modern attitude, so different from that of the ancients, is I think best illustrated by Pasteur's saying: "To him who devotes his life to science, nothing can give more happiness than increasing the number of discoveries, but his cup of joy is full when the results of his studies immediately find practical application" (René J. Dubos, *Louis Pasteur*, Boston, 1950, p. 85).

[3] That the technological shortcomings of ancient civilization were not the consequences of economic conditions, of the existence of slavery, I have tried to show: "Ancient science", pp. 580 ff. Here I am concerned mainly with those factors inherent in the nature of ancient science itself that appear to have limited the interest in applied science.

taken a special interest in applying their knowledge, were the ones to curtail research and thereby to curtail also the chances of mastering the phenomena. For in the Hellenistic theory of empiricism, the possibility of comprehending nature is severely narrowed down. Everything inaccessible to the senses is regarded as hidden from exploration and thus closed to scientific study. It was the empirical physician who denied that anatomy and physiology could become sciences and rendered useful for medical treatment. Also, reading of books — the treasured-up experience of the past — for him took precedence over making new experiments and accumulating more data. Extension of knowledge, the opening-up of new opportunities for applied science, was therefore left almost exclusively to the 'theoretical' scientists — the "dogmatists" as they were derisively called by their opponents, and yet in fact the only ones to venture beyond the already known. But with them, of course, knowledge for the sake of knowledge was the prime motive and the prime concern.[1]

Second, one must not forget that ancient sciences have by their very nature so to say a slant towards the theoretical rather than the practical. Some, physics and psychology for instance, were really 'philosophical' sciences. For they remained in the domain of the philosopher and were studied by him as part of his analysis of the physical world and of human nature. When the original unity of philosophy and all the sciences, obtaining in the pre-Socratic period, dissolved, and independent, particular sciences were established — sciences pursued by specialists — they still kept in close touch with philosophy. Their first principles, their methodology rested on philosophical grounds. The issue between mechanism and teleology, the controversy about the respective values of empirical observation and theoretical reasoning were fought not with scientific but with philosophical arguments, and these discussions occupied

[1] Medicine by chance of tradition best represents the type of ancient empirical science, and F. M. Cornford (*Principium Sapientiae*, Cambridge, 1952, pp. 31 ff.) ascribes to the very first physicians an empirical theory of knowledge (p. 42), an interrogation of Nature "prepared to accept the answers she gives" (p. 38), a theoretical science based on particular observations (p. 8). This I think could be asserted not even of Hellenistic medicine (see "Ancient science", pp. 576 f. and p. 596, n. 59). In the light of modern historical hindsight empiricism may seem to be the most promising method. In Antiquity paradoxically enough it proved no more fruitful than the seemingly sound atomic theory of Democritus and Epicurus (cf. Dilthey, op. cit. pp. 169 ff., and "Ancient science", pp. 594 ff.).

a much larger part of scientific writing than they would in later science. Not that the scientist slavishly followed the dictates of a philosophic law-giver. Rather he took an active interest in philosophy, he became himself a philosopher. The title of Galen's essay "That the best physician is also a philosopher" epitomizes the prevailing attitude.[1] On the other hand, there was a feeling that men of experience, as Aristotle[2] says, are better in practical matters, better equipped to handle particulars, than is the scientist who knows the universals. Thus the improvement of the technical apparatus remained largely in the hands of artisans and craftsmen, who changed things slowly and cautiously in their traditional conservative manner.[3]

[1] Modern interpreters assume the existence of independent sciences at least from Hellenistic times (e.g. W. Jaeger, *Aristoteles*, Berlin, 1923, pp. 431 f.; L. Robin, *La Pensée grecque et les origines de l'ésprit scientifique*, Paris 1923, p. 433). But the original connexion between philosophical and scientific thought continues not only in medicine (as Robin would admit, p. 434), but for instance also in astronomy. According to the Stoa, the school most influential on scientific research, the mathematician calculates the movements of the stars and so forth, but in questions of aetiology or hypotheses to be made he must cooperate with the "physicist", the philosopher (e.g. Diogenes Laertius, VII, 132–133). No outstanding ancient scientist took an attitude similar to that of the modern positivist, for whom the description of the phenomenal world in concepts and the proof of the validity of law and order through experiment are the whole content of science (W. Dilthey, "Das Wesen der Philosophie", *Gesammelte Schriften*, V, Leipzig and Berlin, 1924, pp. 358 f.), and who believes in a fundamental conflict between metaphysics and science. On the relation between philosophy and science see also "Ancient science", pp. 578 f.

[2] *Metaphysics*, I, 4, 981a 13 ff.

[3] It is as difficult to draw the demarcation line between science and the arts and crafts as between science and philosophy. The arts and crafts were so to say the laboratory of the scientist. The study of medical theories and the deductions drawn from them had to be checked by medical practice; one cannot write about warfare, Polybius says, without military experience (XII, 25g, cf. 25d). According to Hiero the science of mechanics has, as well as a theoretical part, a practical part, consisting of the study of "metal-working, architecture, carpentry, painting, and the manual activities connected with these arts". Skill in such arts makes "the ablest inventor" (Pappus, *Mathematical Collection*, VIII, 1 ff.). Clearly, then, the Aristotelian passage to which I have referred expresses the more general feeling that practical invention properly speaking comes from an experience outside science. But behind such an attitude, as Aristotle implies, there is also the recognition of a philosophical problem which throughout the development of Greek philosophy and science presented great difficulty, namely, how any law can do justice to the particularity, the ineffability of individual phenomena. The answer always seems to be that the handling of reality requires a certain 'tact'. In addition, it may be true that ancient scientific

Last though not least, the relative neglect of the practical must I think be viewed against the background of the ancients' general attitude towards life, of which it seems characteristic that they acknowledged and respected boundaries set to their actions. They would, to be sure, aim at perfection in rational insight and in right conduct; they would fashion their cities or states in accordance with political ideals; they would above all civilize human existence so that it became truly human. They did not feel that it was their business to take the world over altogether. Men no more claimed than did their gods to be creators out of nothing, to act with a free will that imposes its law on things that have no nature of their own. Rather did they feel called upon to shape matter that was given and, here below at any rate, refractory to reason. The gods but mould, or to use a Platonic phrase, persuade the physical universe to accommodate itself to their wishes as far as possible. It does not stand otherwise with that universe which men build. Having accomplished what appeared possible and essential, the pagans were satisfied to use knowledge mostly for taking care of their daily wants which were modest, for defending their country when there was need, for adorning temple services and festivals, for increasing pleasure through play and amusement.[1]

laws in general, no less than Aristotle's laws of motion, lacked the abstraction from actual conditions characteristic of modern scientific laws, and therefore were less serviceable for the mastery of phenomena. This whole issue, like the relation between philosophy and science, still needs further elaboration.

[1] "In themselves inventions are passive"; a force is needed "to set them working" (Brooks Adams, *The Law of Civilization and Decay*, New York, 1955, p. 256). If in the modern age inventions are promoted primarily by capitalistic interests, the situation was quite different in Antiquity. Although the capitalistic spirit was not absent altogether, the "element of play" was far stronger. Even definitions of mechanics always include references to the art of contriving "marvellous devices" (Pappus, loc. cit., and Geminus apud Proclus, *In Euclid.*, ed. Friedlein, p. 41, 8). On the other hand, it would seem to be true that the increase in practical inventions noticeable since the Renaissance is in part due to the fact that man wished to participate "in the creative passion" of his God (cf. A. O. Lovejoy, *The Great Chain of Being*, 3rd ed., Cambridge, Mass., 1948, p. 84, and in general on this and the previous topic "Ancient science", pp. 583–5). To the ancients, confronted with the teaching of Moses, its strangest aspect was that according to him God was a creator *ex nihilo*, in contrast to their gods; such a concept seemed irrational to them and irreconcilable with their philosophy (Galen, *De usu partium*, XI, 14). And this fundamental difference between pagan and Christian thought did not, in my opinion, remain without influence on the later attitude towards reality. The ancients' zest

It is mainly for such reasons, I think, that ancient science remained relatively useless, that changes which in principle were within reach were actually not made. But to a certain extent the ineffectiveness of science in altering conditions depended also on social factors, as should become clear from the discussion of the incentives for science, to which I shall now turn.

IV

The new venture of science which started in the pre-Socratic centuries was a venture undertaken by individuals; it lacked the support of society. In the opinion of the citizens of the Greek communities, the scientist's "activity" was "idleness" — indeed withdrawal from the realities of life. They neither cared to be like him nor had they any use for him. Why then should they have given support to science? Far from supporting it, they did not even pay homage to it, as they did honour and reward poets or athletes. One who wished to engage in scientific studies had to be a man of independent means, free to indulge his fancies. At most he might maintain himself by teaching converts to the new cause. He certainly had no other hope of making a living. There were no schools with which one could be associated, no careers that one could follow as a scientist. The few who favoured the scientific movement advocated redress of the situation, for they were well aware of the fact that what society does not pay for or prize does not flourish.[1] No one listened to their remonstrances. Throughout the classical age science remained beyond the pale of society.

Matters changed in the Hellenistic world only to a certain extent. For on the whole the cost for his own maintenance, for travelling and books[2] and all the paraphernalia of scholarship

for reshaping themselves rather than the world is well expressed by Socrates's saying that in human matters one argues in order to produce corresponding action, but no one would argue about winds, rains and seasons in the hope of "producing" winds and rains and seasons (Xenophon, *Memorabilia*, I, 1, 15). Empedocles's dream of achieving the latter feats (31 B 111, Diels-Kranz) is to my knowledge quite exceptional (contrary to what Heidel, *Heroic Age of Science*, p. 58, appears to think).

[1] E.g. Plato, *Republic*, VII, 528 C. Cf. in general "Ancient science", pp. 597 ff. For the ἀργία of the philosopher see e.g. Aristophanes, *Frogs*, v. 1498, and Boll, "Vita contemplativa", p. 30. That in the early centuries of science one cannot speak of schools but only of personal associations has been pointed out by Heidel, op. cit. pp. 73 f.

[2] Polybius, XII, 27–8.

had still to be paid for by the individual. It was but in a few institutions such as the Museion that scientists received yearly stipends, but in a few places that collections of material and libraries were put at their disposal. The limited number of schools which came into being, and in which the members probably shared the expenses of living and research, were private foundations and not publicly supported. Unless a scholar was willing to seek association with a court — to become "a friend of a king" as the phrase went — he had to fall back on his own fortune or to practise a profession. Lucky was he who could practise one related to his studies, as a biologist might practise medicine.[1]

Society then having at first completely disregarded the scientist, did offer him some incentives of material advantage and prestige in the Hellenistic age, but they were few indeed and ineffective. For improvements were localized and sporadic. As little as in classical centuries was science a career many could afford to pursue. Kings sometimes tried to win the acclaim of the intellectuals by supporting science; it may also have happened that one or other prince was genuinely interested in scientific endeavours. But for the princes or the rich who could be induced to give their assistance, their patronage of science was I think more often than not a kind of showpiece or a matter of pragmatic considerations. Geographical exploration and the construction of war implements, which they mostly financed, were useful. Of support for long drawn out inquiries without practical results one hears nothing. The theoretical sciences certainly continued to be the concern of private individuals. And to say it once more, any help given was intermittent, from case to case; there was no consistent plan of promoting science.[2]

Why did science fail to secure more recognition and encouragement? The responsibility certainly does not lie with distrust of science, with political schemes of any class of society designed

[1] Contrary to the assumptions of nineteenth-century scholars (e.g. E. Curtius, "Die öffentliche Pflege von Wissenschaft und Kunst", *Alterthum und Gegenwart*, Berlin, 1877, p. 123), often repeated even nowadays, the Hellenistic age did not open up a new era in the social organization of science; see "Ancient science", pp. 598 ff.

[2] For the royal support of work on war engines see Philo of Byzantium, *Mechanics*, IV, 3, 5. The later stories about the help provided by Alexander the Great for research have been shown to be exaggerated ("Ancient science", p. 598, n. 62), and the same is probably true of the tradition concerning the first Ptolemies.

to prevent science from becoming a weapon in the fight for freedom and enlightenment. If fear was felt regarding the relationship of society and science, it was the scientists who were suspicious. For they were well aware of the fact that royal support or support from any outside quarters was potentially a danger to the objectivity of their research, because favours might be expected in return, favours that could necessitate distortions of the truth or actions irreconcilable with their ideals.[1] The true explanation for the reaction of society is I think to be found first of all in the scientific situation as it had taken shape by the time of Hellenism.

It was a situation not dissimilar to that of modern philosophy. Rival systems of science were competing with one another, rival systems which were in fact rival sciences. For there was nothing one could call science in the modern sense of the term, a body of knowledge valid everywhere, a system of principles, of rules of procedure and of theories, well defined and generally accepted. With the exception perhaps of mathematics, there were but "sciences", the adherence to which was optional. A science of mathematical astronomy faced a science of empirical astronomy. Empirical medicine, discarding anatomy and physiology, opposed dogmatic medicine based on anatomy and physiology. Descriptive geography rejecting quantitative analysis stood against a highly mathematized geography. Each of these sciences of course in the opinion of its proponents was true, but their claim to this effect clashed with counter-claims. This "dissension" as the ancients called it — a dissension not concerning particular results but concerning the basic presuppositions and aims of the scientific enterprise as such — made it almost impossible for anyone not a partisan to say what science was and what it was about, let alone to decide which of the existing systems of science should be encouraged and rewarded.[2]

That science in general or science as the Greeks knew it begins one day, and that, after the liberating word has been

[1] With regard to the scientists' fear of state subventions or court favours see "Ancient science", p. 593. On the other hand, although occasional persecutions of scientists occurred one cannot speak of political oppression, as is so often done nowadays (op. cit. pp. 589 ff.). The State was uninterested in science unless historians touched on particular political issues.

[2] That ancient science was in a state of dissension threatening its survival was a criticism made by scientists, not only by sceptical philosophers, e.g. Galen, *On Scientific Demonstration* (J. von Müller, *Abhandlung Akademie München*, XX, 1894, p. 419, quoted in "Ancient science", pp. 602 f.).

spoken, everyone knows the right course to follow, seems an ineradicable historical prejudice. In fact, the history of Greek science, in addition to being the story of the discovery of true and false data — true and false from the modern point of view — is also the story of the gradual discovery of the meaning of science. The concept of science itself has a history. It took almost eight hundred years to work out the implications of the enterprise on which the ancients had ventured and to create general agreement on it. *Tantae molis erat Romanam condere gentem.* The last step was only taken in the second century A.D., when largely through the work of Galen and of Ptolemy—theoreticians of science no less than scientists — a *scientia aeterna* began to be built up, science as it was to be understood from then on.[1]

When this happened, society took a greater interest in science than the classical and Hellenistic ages had done, and treated it with more respect and consideration. Universities were founded, professorships were endowed, schools multiplied. The unified Roman Empire had a unified science. Instruction became standardized; it taught one scientific truth, be the teaching given in Rome or Alexandria or Athens: "empirical" and "dogmatic" science were fused into what Galen called the teaching of "the best sect", the sect which stands above all sects. But the attempted cure was after all merely a palliative; it came too late. Soon political destruction made all constructive endeavour illusory. The ancients created science; they also developed it to the point where it could be assimilated into the social fabric. To carry out this assimilation effectively was left to other ages and other cultures.[2]

[1] E. Zilsel ("The genesis of the concept of scientific progress", *Journal of the History of Ideas*, VI, 1945, p. 327), who first compared the state of ancient science with that of modern philosophy, believed that such a comparison held for Antiquity as a whole. That this is not the case I have shown in "Ancient science" (pp. 602–4), where I have also pointed out that one therefore can hardly talk of a decay of science in late centuries. Granted that the late scientists furthered actual research to a lesser degree than their predecessors, the unification of science by which the earlier optional sciences were superseded was of decisive importance.

[2] That the stage at which dissension about the various possible approaches of science ended was reached under the Roman Empire, was I think not unconnected with the political circumstances. Galen prided himself on having unified medicine just as Trajan with his roads had unified Italy (*Opera omnia*, ed. C. G. Kühn, Leipzig, 1821–33, X, 623 f.). One might then well speak of an incentive provided for his work by the prevailing temper of the time. But this incentive worked only indirectly. The state did not participate in the efforts of Galen and the others. They proceeded as individuals acting on their own.

Yet, one may object, if men had been wiser, if they had recognized the value of science, if they had encouraged it as so many of the ancients themselves desired, the "dissension" of which I spoke could have been resolved earlier, and science would then have become integrated into civilization in Antiquity as it was later on. In such an objection there is I think a kernel of truth. The neglect of science on the part of society was undoubtedly due also to the predominance of other intellectual and emotional concerns.

Even those friendly to science often did not accept it altogether. The pre-Socratics and most of the classical philosophers to be sure were its fervent devotees. But among the minor Socratics emphasis on ethics began to grow, not to mention the fact that with Cynicism a conscious revolt of the civilized against civilization set in, which, though never spectacularly successful, left its mark on subsequent thought. Primitivism, the dream of a Golden Age of the past or future, a Rousseauesque admiration for the "noble savage" who has not eaten from the tree of knowledge, was the shadow of ancient rationalism and progressionism. Hellenistic philosophies, Stoicism as well as Epicureanism, were interested in science; in their last phases they even showed a strong appreciation of the significance of science. But they were given to the study of moral values at least as much as to the study of brute facts; if to them God was visible in nature, he was even more manifest in man and his actions. Rhetorical training, whose hold was probably greater than that of philosophical education, never included more than the rudiments of science, for everything beyond them was considered useless. The so-called liberal arts led to the threshold of science but no farther. And education in general, being a matter of the individual's free choice, continued to consist mainly in the study of poetry and music. Centuries after the eclipse of the sun had been proved to be a natural, recurrent phenomenon, such an event was still taken even by men in prominent positions as a divine omen, without their incurring the least censure except from the *avant garde* of intellectuals. For not everybody was willing to resign himself to the disenchantment of the world which followed from the attempt to comprehend nature in rational terms. Without the pressure of a general school system through which the results of science would be filtered down to the people, they did not feel obliged to believe in the results of science and preferred to cling to the mythos, to live in it, to think in its categories. Science never succeeded in breaking the power of mythology. No less an achievement than art and poetry, it was in contrast to them but a thin layer over ancient civilization and not at all as important to the Greeks and Romans as it was destined to become to the future.[1]

It goes without saying that the lack of institutionalization of ancient science accounts for many of its shortcomings. Without adequate prestige and recognition, without promise of financial security, it did not attract many people, not as many at any rate as could profitably have worked on securing the terrain which had been laid out. On the other hand, what was accomplished seems even more impressive because it was done with so little outside assistance. Considering why "men originally instituted a prize for competitions of the body, but none for wisdom", a pupil of Aristotle considers it a satisfactory answer to the puzzle that "the prize must be more desirable than the competition"; and he adds that though in the case of athletic contests such a prize can be found, "what prize could be better than wisdom?"[2] It would be carrying flattery to extremes if one believed that ancient society failed to pay scientists because kings and citizens admiringly realized that wisdom is its own reward. But one may fairly say, I think, that in a world in which science was not a career, the overwhelming majority of those who studied science must have done so for the sake of science. This is perhaps not the least of the reasons for the strength and the survival of the ideal of the theoretical life in all periods of ancient history. For motives rather than incentives, desire for the truth rather than outward allurement, had to persuade men to enter the service of science.[3]

[1] It seems unnecessary here to substantiate my description of the intellectual trends facing science. The facts I have mentioned are well known. I am concerned only to point out that they must be taken into account for an appreciation of the position of science in ancient society.

[2] *Problemata*, XXX, 11.

[3] In the opinion of the ancients, the political situation had great bearing on the progress of science. Pliny expresses his admiration for the scientists who accomplished so much despite constant warfare reigning in the Hellenistic period (*Natural History*, II, 45, 117). The *Pax Romana* was considered to create particularly favourable conditions for scientific work, and to impose a kind of obligation to make further strides (loc. cit.; also XIV, *praefatio*). According to Polybius (III, 59; XII, 28), science could make especially great progress in his time because after the rise of Roman power, men whose lives had so far been spent in the administration of their respective cities could now devote themselves to scientific pursuits. Such verdicts are reminiscent of the eighteenth-century evaluation of the great

V

In ancient moral theory, from Plato down to the end of Antiquity, the ethics of the good and virtuous man, the sage, is the main topic. But there is also, from the time of the Sophists, an undercurrent of ethical thought concerned with the morality of the judge, the lawyer, the physician, in short with professional ethics. To speak in Stoic categories, man in his life plays among other roles one which he assumes through his choice of work. In order to act well, he must be thoroughly acquainted with the character of his role, a character that varies with the various professions. What is fitting for the lawyer does not behove the judge; what becomes the soldier is unbecoming to the physician. And these demands of the role are objective demands imposed by the profession itself and have to be met by its adherents; the rules they state are as it were motive and incentive at the same time. It seems necessary therefore that in conclusion I should attempt at least to outline the professional ethics of the scientist. The direct testimony preserved on the topic is scarce. But it can be rounded out and made to speak more clearly by parallels from the professional ethics of the philosopher, with whom the scientist in Antiquity had so much in common.[1]

I take my departure from that statement of scientific ethics which seems to be among all that are extant the most explicit and the richest in implications. "Those who are altogether unaccustomed to research," says the Hellenistic physician Erasistratus,

monarchies as guarantors of peace and thus of the development of civilization, and certainly attribute to the state 'support' of science. But like the unifying influence of the Roman Empire toward the end of Antiquity (see above p. 30, n. 2), the preservation of peace made but an indirect, though certainly an essential, contribution to science.

[1] Concerning the influence of the Stoa on the development of professional ethics, cf. L. Edelstein, "The professional ethics of the Greek physician", *Bulletin of the History of Medicine*, XXX (1956) 411 ff. Medical ethics, of which most is known, shows that the profession was personified and thought of as making demands upon her followers, demands which operate in a sense as incentives, although they are, of course, but the expression of motives. Professional ethics includes also what might be called rules of performance, such as that a method must be adequate to the particular subject (e.g. Aristotle, *Metaphysics* II, 3, 995a 12 ff.), or that the authority of a writer matters little compared to the demands of truth (*Nicomachean Ethics*, I, 3, 1096a 15 ff.; cf. Plato, *Phaedrus*, 270C). Important as these rules are, I do not consider them in this context.

are at the first exercise of their intelligence befogged and blinded and quickly desist owing to fatigue and failure of intellectual power, like those who without training attempt a race. But one who is accustomed to investigation, worming his way through and turning in all directions, does not give up the search, I will not say day or night, but his whole life long. He will not rest, but will turn his attention to one thing after another which he considers relevant to the subject under investigation until he arrives at the solution of his problem.[1]

The thesis underlying Erasistratus's comments clearly is that scientific investigation presupposes training like that of an athlete. Without it the scientist will not be equal to the fight that is ahead of him. Neither art nor science can be conquered, says Democritus, if one is not willing to learn,[2] and the noble things of life one learns only through hard work[3] without it one cannot even learn how to read or to write, or to be a musician or an athlete.[4] A Platonic metaphor expresses the same thought in a different way. He who does not learn "to work like a slave" for the possession of the truth will never reach it.[5] Instead of being a slave to the body and its lusts, as man is by nature,[6] the philosopher or scientist must become a slave to knowledge. And it is not only hard work that is required, but also a tireless effort that withstands disappointments. Failure of an argument, Plato contends,[7] must not delude one into disdain of reason, into misology. One must persevere in the search, and fight the pessimism of the present with optimism regarding the future, with the hope that in the end one will win out. It does not matter after how long a time the truth will be reached.[8]

In such a stubborn and unrelenting contest all leads have to be explored, everything relevant has to be scrutinized. Small

[1] Galen, *Scripta minora*, ed. I. Müller (Leipzig, 1891) II, 17. I am quoting the translation of B. Farrington, *Greek Science* (2 vols., Pelican Books, Harmondsworth, 1949) II, 36. He as well as Heidel (*Heroic Age of Science*, pp. 53 f.) implies that Erasistratus's ethos is characteristic of 'the experimenter'. This, as will be seen, is not the case.

[2] 68B 59, Diels-Kranz. [3] Ibid. B 182. [4] Ibid. B 179.

[5] *Republic*, VI, 494D.

[6] *Phaedo*, 66D; cf. Gorgias, 82B 11a (15), Diels-Kranz.

[7] *Phaedo*, 89D ff.

[8] Cleanthes (apud Sextus Empiricus, *Adv. Mathem.*, IX, 90, Fr. I, 529, *Stoicorum veterum fragmenta* I, ed. H. von Arnim, 2nd ed., Leipzig, 1921) expressed similar ideas about the long struggle through which man attains virtue at the end of his life.

and great things have, or can have, equal importance. The dialectician is not allowed to honour the noble more than the mean and ridiculous,[1] and that is why the aged Parmenides tells the young Socrates that when he is older and more mature, he will not despise "cases that might be thought absurd, such as hair or mud or dirt or any other trivial and undignified objects".[2] Or as Aristotle expresses it in the introduction to his course on natural science, the student of nature

> will not leave out any one of [the animals] be it never so mean; for though there are animals which have no attractiveness for the senses, yet for the eye of science, for the student who is naturally of a philosophic spirit and can discern the causes of things, Nature which fashioned them provides joys which cannot be measured.[3]

Finally, in searching high and low and "turning in all directions", the scientist must make sacrifices of time, of comfort, of ease. He must risk health, even life. "Willingly would I burn to death like Phaëthon," exclaimed the astronomer Eudoxus, "were this the price for reaching the sun and learning its shape, its size and its substance."[4]

These are the main demands of the profession of science as the Greeks came to understand them. It cannot have been easy, for men who loved leisure and had no concept of the "nobility of toil", to turn their free time into hard labour, labour even of a slave. Nor can it have been less difficult for them to master that native pessimism and scepticism which made them so often complain that life is too short to arrive at wisdom.[5] One

[1] Plato, *Sophist*, 227B. [2] Plato, *Parmenides*, 130C; cf. E.

[3] *On Parts of Animals*, I, 5, 645a 7 ff.

[4] Plutarch, *Non posse suaviter vivi secundum Epicurum*, 1094A–B. These words were perhaps spoken in the famous debate on pleasure in which Eudoxus upheld against the Platonists the thesis that pleasure is the basic principle of human action (E. Frank, "Die Begründung der mathematischen Naturwissenschaft durch Eudoxus", *Knowledge, Will and Belief*, ed. L. Edelstein, Zürich and Stuttgart, 1955, pp. 154 f.). However that may be, the statement is made in the spirit in which Plato (*Republic*, II, 361E–362A; X, 613A) demands that the virtuous man uphold virtue unto death, even if crucified, a conviction shared by Stoics and Epicureans (see Cicero, *De finibus*, III, 13, 42 ff; IV, 12, 31; and *Tusculanae disputationes*, II, 7, 17 ff.).

[5] Cf., e.g., Protagoras, 80B 1, Diels-Kranz, and the first of the Hippocratic *Aphorisms*: "Art is long, life is short". For the contrast between the classical and the modern attitudes toward work, see, e.g., H. Michell, *The Economics of Ancient Greece* (Cambridge and New York, 1940), p. 14, and for changes in the Hellenistic evaluation of work in professions, Edelstein, "The professional ethics of the Greek physician", pp. 399 ff. The early reaction to exactness in science, "which seems to some people to be mean, no less

sometimes has the impression that they were themselves astonished at what they had achieved, and that this is the reason why they were fond of talking of peoples in their climate as by nature "lovers of wisdom", in contrast to other races that by nature were given to making money or indulging in the pleasures of the body.[1] And undoubtedly a native love of knowledge must have been a driving force in their quest for knowledge. But I am persuaded that there was another factor also, more elemental as it were than the love of any particular thing, however great and lovable. Every man of creative gifts, Aristotle asserts, "loves the work of his hands". "The cause of this", he adds,

> is that existence is to all men a thing to be chosen and loved . . . and that the handiwork *is* in a sense the producer in activity; he loves his handiwork, therefore, because he loves existence. And this is rooted in the nature of things: for what he is in potentiality, his handiwork manifests in activity.[2]

The knowledge of the scientist — expressed in definitions, classifications, empirical laws — is himself; it is his being, no longer as possibility but as reality, no longer as perishable existence of the hour but as eternal existence in the contemplation of the truth.[3]

Now, if the scientist lives up to the demands of his profession, if he plays his role as he should, he will be — as Galen says in his *Protreptic to the Sciences* which summarizes the long tradition of professional ethics — a worthy member of the "brotherhood" of those who have dedicated themselves to the pursuit of truth: geometers, arithmeticians, philosophers, physicians, astrono-

in an argument than in a business transaction" (Aristotle, *Metaphysics*, 985a 10 ff.; [Boll, "Vita contemplativa", p. 30]; see also Plato, *Theætetus*, 184C), also betrays the originally aristocratic or rather gentleman's ethics of scholarship.

[1] Plato, *Republic*, IV, 435E.

[2] *Nicomachean Ethics*, IX, 7, 1167b 34 ff.

[3] *Nicomachean Ethics*, X, 1177a 27 ff. Aristotle (op. cit., IX) names as the outstanding case of love of one's "handicraft" the poet's love for his poems. Love of handicraft then may be asserted also of the scientist, whom he does not mention. Moreover, according to the Pythagoreans, "love for what is truly noble" manifests itself in practical pursuits and in the sciences (Aristoxenus, Diels-Kranz, I, pp. 478, 17 ff., and in general L. Edelstein, *The Hippocratic Oath*, Baltimore, 1943, p. 60). Xenophon in his *Oeconomicus* maintains too that without love for the object no worker can succeed. Perhaps not everyone would have agreed with Aristotle's contention that man through thought becomes immortal. But it was certainly the belief of most of the dogmatists, Platonists, Aristotelians and Stoics; see Ptolemy's epigram quoted above, p. 22.

mers and grammarians (Ch. 5). This brotherhood is presided over by the god Hermes, the "King of Reason" (Ch. 3) — while all ordinary men belong to the brotherhood over which blind Fortune rules (Ch. 3) — and it is not money (Ch. 6) or birth (Ch. 7) that here determines rank and dignity. The virtues of the father to be sure are "a fine treasure", but it is still better to be able to put against them the claim of Sthenelus: "We avow ourselves to be better men by far than our fathers were".[1] Thus it will be the son who gives glory to his ancestors and to his country (Ch. 7), not only through wisdom but also through his irreproachable life.

The followers of Hermes, Galen says, are "cheerful like their god", do not blame life as do the followers of Fortune, are steadfast and consistent in their actions (Ch. 3). Among them one finds no thieves, grave-robbers and murderers as in the rival brotherhood of common men (Ch. 4). Similarly, Euripides had praised him who contemplates the "ageless order of deathless Nature" as having "no care for deeds of shame" and "no impulse to his fellows' harm or unjust deeds".[2] And at the end of the Hellenistic era, when the possibility of the conflict of duties was better understood, Stoic philosophy had with intrepidity and forthrightness drawn the inevitable conclusion that "there are things so terrible and horrid that the wise man will not do them even to save his country".[3] For the sage, be he philosopher or scientist, lives in that *altera historia* which is not the history of a particular race or country or time, but the history of mankind.[4]

The true scientist, like the true poet or artist, one may say, chooses the role for which he is born. Granted that this is true, even the born actor has much to learn. Otherwise his natural talent may not be fully developed; it may even become spoiled

[1] *Iliad*, IV, v. 405. [2] Fr. 910, Nauck.

[3] Posidonius apud Cicero, *De officiis*, I, 45, 159.

[4] For the conflict between the physician's obligations as citizen and as member of the medical profession see L. Edelstein, *Bull. Hist. Medicine*, XXX (1956) pp. 409 f. Despite the rare attestation, the problem must have been of great importance, for the role of the "patriot" is distinguished from other professional roles even in Horace's cursory treatment of the subject (*Ars poetica*, v. 312). That the scientist's fatherland is the world is stated by Seneca (*De otio*, 4, 1–2, and see above, p. 20). The sordid reality of what actually happened all too often, then as now, comes to the fore in Seneca's protestation that "the wise man will do even things of which he does not approve in order to accomplish in this manner greater ends" (Seneca apud Lactantius, *Institut. Div.* III, 15).

in course of time. Only the one who studies his role will be able to say at the end that he has performed well in the "comedy of life", and can justly ask for applause.[1] The discovery of the "personality" (*πρόσωπον*, *persona*) of the scientist, of his character traits, is not the least significant discovery in the history of ancient science. It revealed the objective duties and the true rewards of the scientific life, thus supplementing the force of personal motives and providing a strong incentive where none was provided by society. It created an ideal through which the inquiring mind, perhaps the most important piece of apparatus for scientific investigation, acquired a fixed and settled form.

The analysis I have given obviously does not exhaust the subject. Much more could and must be said about each topic in order to do justice to it. My analysis, however, is incomplete also in another sense. I have omitted from consideration a number of issues that might profitably have been taken up, because their discussion would have led me too far astray.

Not all that the Greeks and Romans regarded as scientific knowledge would nowadays be classified as such. It was a knowledge which included such 'pseudo-sciences' as astrology, Pythagorean number-symbolism, the Platonic scale of music, intrusions of the occult, and theories which the modern scientist calls superstitious or religious.[2] Although this very fact may indeed be indicative of an as yet incorrect understanding of science, it points more importantly to a different under-

[1] Suetonius, *Divus Augustus*, 99.

[2] That in Greek thought the 'scientific' and 'other' requests for knowledge are still undistinguished, has been noted by S. E. Toulmin, *The Place of Reason in Ethics* (Cambridge, 1960) 211. The tendency of recent historical studies to isolate within Greek science what seems scientific as judged by modern standards is justifiable and natural but it should not preclude an interpretation which takes as their science what the ancients labelled as such, or in other words takes science as part of the particular civilization, the particular historical situation in which it flourished ("Ancient science", pp. 576 ff.). The latter approach I think L. von Ranke also had in mind when, following French examples, he asserted that it was impossible to write the history of a nation without taking account of its scientific development (*Sämmtliche Werke*, Leipzig, 1888, LI–LII, 490, 552). In science as well as in art, man transcends the boundaries of nationality. And yet, there is even in art a national element; art tells something about the nation that made it (G. Dehio, *Geschichte der Deutschen Kunst*, Berlin and Leipzig, 1930, I, 1^4, p. 15). The history of ancient science can come to be understood more adequately only, I believe, if the objective and the subjective approach are combined.

standing of its meaning: science was thought to comprise both 'exact' and 'inexact' knowledge and consequently had a wider range of motives and incentives than modern science. Moreover, the ancient terms *epistemai*, *mathemata*, *scientiae* covered any methodical investigation by human reason of the data of human experience, and comprised the humanities as well as what is called science in modern times. An investigation of the subject here at stake should therefore take account also of historical studies, political theories, and ethics, so closely connected in Antiquity with the natural sciences that they were often the domain of one scholar. If this unity were stressed, it would become clearer I think why the truly practical sciences were the humanities — men thought they could remake themselves, as I put it before — and why the physical sciences remained largely theoretical, why, to use a famous phrase, the instinct of workmanship predominantly informed humanistic rather than so-called scientific studies.[1] Upon this central issue, a discussion of the ancient debate concerning the origin of science would throw further light. In certain periods two theories opposed each other, the one maintaining that all knowledge originated from practical interest, the other that it arose from theoretical concern. History was written and rewritten from each of these points of view. As far as the natural sciences are concerned, the upholders of the theoretical ideal were I think right. But the arguments used on both sides tell a good deal about the general evaluation of the scientific enterprise, which is decisive also for the reaction of society to science and the scientists.[2]

Finally, a distinction has to be drawn between the Greek and Roman contributions to the scientific movement. Though ancient science is fundamentally a Greek creation, the Romans had a share in it also. The Greek confidence in reason, their desire to penetrate the surface of phenomena in order to reach the essence of things, their striving to find the meaning of existence, which pervades even their dramatic art and in part their fine arts, gave to science its basic character. But the

[1] On the definition of science which I have here adopted see W. G. DeBurgh, *The Legacy of the Ancient World* (Pelican Books, Harmondsworth, 1953) II, 490, n. 2.

[2] For the two historical interpretations of the past, see W. Jaeger, "Über Ursprung und Kreislauf des philosophischen Lebensideals", *Sitzungsberichte der Preussischen Akademie der Wissenschaften*, Phil.-Hist. Klasse., XXV (1928) 390 ff.

Roman wish for comprehending results at one glance, for making them conveniently accessible — as evidenced in the Roman encyclopaedias — helped in bringing about unity of science. Nor is the Roman practicality and gift for organizing without influence on the integration of science into society and on the later strength of empiricism as well as on the development of a scholastic method.[1] And surely the Greek achievement ought to be compared with Oriental knowledge. The ancients, being the first idolaters of Eastern peoples, made this comparison themselves. They sometimes complained that if the Greeks would only learn to collect data as did the Babylonians, or to persevere in the tradition, to cling to what they have and know as did the Egyptians — their efforts might well amount to something. The revolutionary temper of the Greek race, their willingness to try something new every day and to try everything they could possibly think of, was held to be destructive rather than constructive. One wonders whether, had the Greeks been different, they would have invented science. Whatever the answer to this question, the origins of science would be set in sharper relief by a confrontation of Western and Oriental learning.[2]

Here I have been able in the main merely to try to trace the outlines of the ideal image of the scientist and of science that emerges from the testimony. This ideal, inherited by the Western world, remained supreme until Bacon put into words a new ideal that had gradually taken shape since the beginning of the Renaissance. To Bacon the scientist of Antiquity had ventured on a task reserved to God and the angels. He wanted to understand everything. Bacon preached greater humility than the pagan had with regard to knowledge, more concern for human ends, more love of man and more interest in his welfare here.[3] Bacon's criticism in some respects is well founded. The ancients were not distinguished for their sense of practical philanthropy, of social justice, or for caring for the poor. But

[1] In my characterization of the Greek spirit I have in the main followed H. D. F. Kitto, *The Greeks* (Pelican Books, Harmondsworth, 1951) 179, 181 f. For the Romans and science see, e.g. R. H. Barrow, *The Romans* (Pelican Books, Harmondsworth, 1951) 137 ff.

[2] Such comparisons of Oriental and Greek learning, from Plato's time on, became more and more the fashion. I mention here only those given by Diodorus (II, 29) and by Pliny (VII, 56, 191 ff.).

[3] On Bacon cf. M. E. Prior, "Bacon's Man of Science", in *Roots of Scientific Thought*, ed. Philip P. Wiener and A. Nolan (New York, 1957) 382 ff.

if Bacon derided the ancients' pride, they would I think have charged him with *hubris* on account of his daring to change the world that is and to rebuild it. They would I believe also have denied that their wish for understanding is but pride. Speaking about the theoretical life and pondering its outcome, Seneca avers that men try to comprehend the riddle of the universe in order that "God be not without witness"[1] — God, that is, reason. Indeed, one may well say that motives and incentives for science in Antiquity, for natural science, are in the last analysis derived from human eagerness to testify to the existence of reason in the world of nature.

[1] *De otio,* IV, 4.

3

Basic Ideas and Methods of Babylonian and Greek Astronomy

B. L. VAN DER WAERDEN

I

In Babylonian astronomy, five periods may be distinguished.

First period: dynasty of Hammurabi

From this period we have very few texts bearing on astrology and astronomy. Only one astrological text is known. It contains very primitive predictions based on the aspect of the moon on the first day of the year. A few texts on star-worship are preserved, for example a beautiful "prayer to the gods of the night". There are three lists of so-called "month stars": each of the three lists contains 12 stars connected with the 12 months of the year. It is not certain, but probable, that these lists go back to the Hammurabi period.

The most interesting astronomical document of this period is contained in the great astrological series "Enuma Anu Enlil". It is a list of observed dates of appearance and disappearance of Venus, with astrological predictions. The observations were made during the twenty-one years of the reign of Ammizaduga (probably 1582–1562 B.C.).

Why were these phenomena observed and recorded? Maybe the observer was simply theoretically interested in the periodical return of Venus phenomena, maybe he made the observations because he believed in their astrological importance, maybe both motives were combined. In any case, we know why the records were copied and quoted many times during nine centuries. It was because they were connected with rules for astrological prediction, like this: "When on Arasẖamna 10th Venus disappeared in the east, and remained invisible 2 months 6 days, and reappeared on Tebētu 16th, the harvest in the country will be good."

Thus astrology was a very important stimulant for astronomical research and for the transmission of written observational records. But still, we have not yet explained everything.

The question remains: Why was it that the phenomena of Venus were considered important for human fate? In my opinion, the only satisfactory answer to this question is: because Venus was regarded as a mighty Goddess. Her name was Nīn·dar·an·na, the Splendid Mistress of Heaven, and she was identified with Ishtar, the Goddess of Love. In fact, many predictions from the phenomena of Venus are related to sexual love and fertility (and to war, for Ishtar was also a warrior goddess).

Astrology is sometimes called the mother of astronomy. It seems to me that astrology and astronomy are twin sisters, daughters of Cosmic Religion. Because the stars were regarded as mighty gods, it was important to watch the signs they send us, and to find out the significance of these signs for human fate.

Second period: Cassite and early Assyrian rule (*c.* 1400–900 *B.C.*)

In this period, astrology was highly developed. The great omen series "Enuma Anu Enlil" contains some 7,000 prediction rules. Most of them concern events of general interest such as harvests, wars, and the fate of kings. This kind of astrology is quite different from the horoscopic astrology we all know. In the old astrology, zodiacal signs do not occur, and knowledge of the moment of birth of an individual is not essential.

In one tablet of the great omen series we find very remarkable rules for computing the duration of day and night and the times of rising and setting of the moon. These rules are not based upon geometry, but are purely arithmetical. Use is made of sequences of numbers increasing or decreasing by constant differences. The rules are not very accurate, but the method of arithmetical progressions is very interesting. The same methods, much improved, were still used in the Seleucid period, when Babylonian mathematical astronomy was at its height.

Third period: late Assyrian rule

On this period we are rather well informed, because we have many texts from the library of Asurbanipal, which was destroyed in 612 B.C. Among these texts, we find:

(*a*) Numerous letters from astrologers to Assyrian kings, saying what was observed in the sky and what it signified astrologically;

(*b*) A list of differences of times of culmination of fixed stars (this list probably served for determining the time during the night);

(*c*) Detailed records of eclipses observed at Babylon, beginning 748 B.C. (note that Ptolemy reproduces Babylonian records of eclipses from the same period);

(*d*) A compendium of astronomy, called MUL APIN, consisting of two tablets, written in 700 B.C. or earlier. From this compendium we see that much was known about the fixed stars, their first and last appearance, their culmination, rising and setting, but very little about the planets and their periods. The zodiacal belt was called "path of the moon". It was known that the line in the middle of this belt is an oblique circle, and also that the sun and the five planets move in this belt. Some thirteen or fourteen "constellations in the path of the moon" are mentioned in the text, but not yet the division of the zodiac into twelve "zodiacal signs".

It is important to distinguish clearly between zodiacal signs and constellations. In late Babylonian texts, the zodiacal signs are named after the constellations they contain. Thus the cuneiform sign ab·sin may mean the sign Virgo, or the star Spica. We have to conclude from the context which is meant. If a planet is said to be at 3° 20′ ab·sin, it is clear that the sign Virgo is meant. If, on the other hand, a planet is reported to be standing just above ab·sin, at a cubit's distance, it is clear that ab·sin means the star Spica. Generally, in computational texts, we may expect the use of signs, and in observational texts the use of stars. However, there are exceptions to this rule, and quite a few cases of doubt remain.

In our texts, zodiacal signs do not appear before the

Fourth period: New-Babylonian and Persian Empire (*620–330 B.C.*)

In this period, the foundations of Babylonian mathematical astronomy were laid. Unfortunately, we have very few texts from this decisive period. Most of them are observational records, which were collected and copied for later use. Observations of eclipses started under Nabonassar (748 B.C.) and were continued during the entire New-Babylonian and Persian period. Other lunar and planetary observations were recorded from 590 B.C. onwards. In the course of time, the records became more and more detailed. They were written in a standardized telegram style. As an example, I shall quote a few lines from a text containing observations of Venus for the years 462–418 B.C. The text was published by A. Sachs in *Late Babylonian astronomical texts copied by Pinches and Strassmaier*[1] as Nr 1387. One of the sections of this text (Rev. Col. III, lower half) begins thus (transcription and interpretation are due to Mr. Peter Huber):

Text	*Meaning*
23 bar 30 15	In the year 23 on Nisannu 1st, which was the 30th day of the preceding month (i.e. the preceding month Addaru had 29 days), the crescent was visible 15 degrees of time (i.e. 60 minutes).
6 *ina* šú	On Nisannu 6th in the evening (Venus)
ina lu igi nim	appeared in Aries, high.
ina 3 ki 4 igi	First appearance on the 3rd or 4th.
gu 1 24	On Aiaru 1st (Nisannu had 30 days) the crescent was visible 24 degrees of time.
sig 30 16	On Simanu 1st, which was the 30th day of the preceding Aiaru, the crescent was visible 16 degrees of time.
22 *e* lugal	On Simanu 22nd (Venus) stood above Regulus
2/3 kùš lál	2/3 cubits just in conjunction.

This is the oldest extant text in which zodiacal signs appear. The text says that in 446 B.C. Venus disappeared "at the end of Pisces". Most probably this means "at the end of the sign Pisces".

From the observations lunar and planetary periods were derived, such as the famous "Saros": 223 months = 241 draconitic months, and even more accurate periods. Another period, 19 years = 235 months, was used in Babylon from 449 B.C. for regulating the calendar: every 19 years, 7 months were intercalated according to a fixed rule. The same period of 19 years was used by the Greek astronomers Meton and Euktemon (432 B.C.) in their astronomical calendar.

The text VAT 4924[2] contains statements of the following kind: Month Nisannu (419 B.C.) Jupiter and Venus at the beginning of Gemini, Mars in Leo, Saturn in Pisces.

These statements were not obtained by direct observation, for the "beginning of Gemini" is not marked at the sky. For astronomical purposes, such statements are worthless. The observed distance of a planet to a fixed star may be valuable to a later astronomer, but the information "Saturn in Pisces" has very little value.

[1] Brown University Press, Providence, R. I., 1955.

[2] Published by E. F. Weidner as Plate XVIII at the end of the *Archiv für Orientforschung*, XVI (1953).

Now, what was the purpose of this and similar texts? Information about the zodiacal signs in which the planets are is just what an astrologer needs to compose a birth horoscope. Thus I was led to conclude from this text, several years ago, that birth horoscopes were already being made in Babylonia at this early date.

At the time when I drew this conclusion, the oldest known horoscope was for the year 258 B.C. But in 1952 A. Sachs[1] published a Babylonian horoscope for the year 410 B.C. This horoscope proves that my conjecture was justified. It is always good to ask: for what purpose was this text written?

Let us ask a similar question. During many centuries, Babylonian scribes and priests observed the stars, calculated tables, wrote and copied thousands of clay tablets. Why did they do this, and why were they paid for it? The answer is quite obvious: first, because their activity was regarded as a service to the celestial gods, and secondly, because astronomy was necessary for horoscopic astrology. Cosmic religion and astrology always stimulated astronomical research.

Marxism teaches that economic conditions determine the thoughts in our brains. But, if we want to understand ancient astronomy and the existence of an influential class of priests, astronomers and astrologers, we have to turn the Marxist theory upside down. When in a clear winter's night we stand under the starry sky, we feel admiration and awe. This feeling seems to be the deepest root of cosmic religion. If you read Plato's *Phaedrus* and *Laws*, you will understand why Plato and his followers believed that the stars are gods, and that our souls participate in their divine nature. From this point of view, you will find it easier to understand why people believed in astrology, and why they paid their tribute to the temple of Anu. Thus, the economic existence of the priests, scribes and astronomers is explained by the religious feelings and needs of the people, not the other way round.

Among the accomplishments of this period, three are of fundamental importance, namely:

(1) the division of the zodiac into 12 signs of 30 degrees;
(2) the lunar and planetary observations accumulated during this period;
(3) the very accurate lunar and planetary periods derived from these observations.

[1] *Journal of Cuneiform Studies*, VI (1952) 49.

Fifth period: Seleucid era (311 B.C.–A.D. 75)

The temple archives of Uruk and Babylon have supplied us with a large number of astronomical and astrological texts dating from the last three centuries B.C. Since many of them are dated by the Seleucid era, the era of Seleucus I, they are usually called, in the jargon of science history, Seleucid texts. The latest Seleucid text is an almanac for the year 385 of the era, that is for A.D. 74–5.

Among these texts, we may distinguish, according to A. Sachs:

Astrological texts
Astronomical diaries
Almanacs
Goal-year texts
Astronomical tables
Procedure texts.

We shall restrict ourselves to mathematical astronomy, that is to tables and procedure texts. The tables are lunar and planetary tables, containing numerical values calculated beforehand for one year, or for a number of years. The procedure texts explain how the tables were computed. The rules of computation were recovered from the tables and procedure texts mainly by Father Kugler and Otto Neugebauer.

LUNAR THEORY. I shall show a small part of a lunar table concerning new moons for the years 208–210 Seleucid era. The tablet is in the British Museum; the old museum number is SH 272 and the number in Neugebauer's *Astronomical Cuneiform Texts* is 122. I shall show 10 lines of the first 4 columns of the reverse. The whole tablet contains 17 columns.

Month	*A*	*B*		*C*
VII	29; 30, 1, 22	11; 45, 59, 4	scorp	2,40
VIII	29; 48, 1, 22	11; 34, 0, 26	arci	2,29
IX	29; 57, 56, 38	11; 31, 57, 4	capri	2,25
X	29; 39, 56, 38	11; 11, 53, 42	aquar	2,31
XI	29; 21, 56, 38	10; 33, 50, 20	pisc	2,43
XII	29; 3, 56, 38	9; 37, 46, 58	aries	3, 1
210 I	28; 45, 56, 38	8; 23, 43, 36	taur	3,18
II	28; 27, 56, 38	6; 51, 40, 14	gemi	3,29
III	28; 11, 22, 42	5; 3, 2, 56	canc	3,35
IV	28; 29, 22, 42	3; 32, 25, 38	leo	3,31

All the numbers are in sexagesimal notation. Thus in columns A and B we find first the number of degrees, and next the numbers of minutes, seconds and thirds. Column A gives the motion of the sun in one month, from one new moon to the next. Column B gives the longitudes of the sun. By adding to any longitude B the motion A in the next line, the next longitude B is found. But how did the Babylonians calculate column A?

Between the maximum of column A in month IX and the minimum in month III, the numbers of column A form a decreasing arithmetical progression, the constant difference being $d=0; 18$ (this means $0° 18'$). Before maximum, the numbers form an increasing arithmetical progression with the same difference. The next term of the increasing series would be 30; 6, 1,22, but the 'ideal maximum' of the column, which can never be surpassed, is $M=30; 1, 59$. The excess of our calculated value 30; 6, 1,22 over M would be 0; 4, 2,22. Subtracting this excess from M, we obtain the correct value for month IX, namely 29; 57, 56, 38. In the same way, the 'ideal minimum' m of the column is $m=28; 10, 39, 40$.

Graphically, we may represent the values in column A by equi-distant points on a broken line with slope d on the ascending part and slope $-d$ on the descending part, thus:

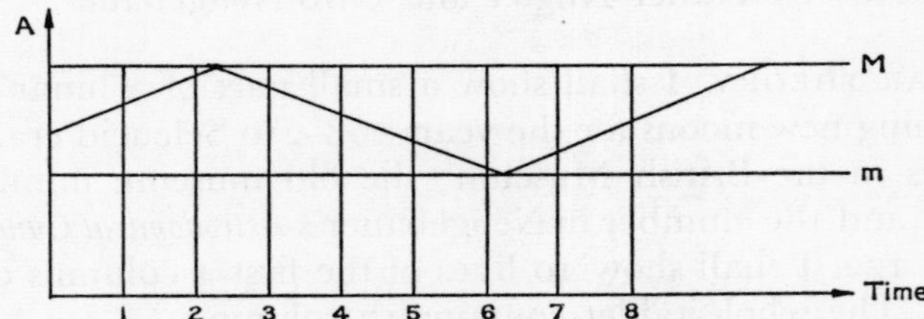

A function represented by such a broken line is called a *linear zigzag function*. Functions of this kind already occur in the calculation of the lengths of day and night in the Great Omen Series, as we have seen. The whole system of calculation of lunar and planetary tables is based upon linear zigzag functions.

The Babylonians knew that the motion of the sun in the zodiac is not uniform. The anomalous motion of the sun was represented by two different models. The two systems were called by Kugler System II and System I, by Neugebauer System A and System B. In System A, the zodiacal circle is divided into a fast and a slow arc. On the fast arc the sun's velocity is 30° per month, on the slow 28° 7′ 30″. Our text SH 272 belongs to System B. In this system, the monthly motion of the sun is given by a linear zigzag function. The resulting solar longitudes are given by arithmetical progressions of second order, which means that their differences form ordinary arithmetical progressions.

One planetary text is known, in which the positions of Jupiter are represented by an arithmetical progression of order 3, which means that their differences form an arithmetical progression of order 2.

Column C of our text SH 272 gives the duration of the day in large and small units of time, the large unit being 4 of our hours, and the small unit 4 minutes. The duration of the day depends on the longitude of the sun according to a modified linear zigzag function defined as follows:

Sun at 8° Aries: daylight 3,0;0 (i.e. 12 hours)
From 8° Aries to 8° Taurus: add 0;36 for every degree
From 8° Taurus to 8° Gemini: add 0;24 for every degree
From 8° Gemini to 8° Cancer: add 0;12 for every degree
From 8° Cancer to 8° Leo: subtract 0;12 for every degree
From 8° Leo to 8° Virgo: subtract 0;24 for every degree, etc.

The other columns give:

D: half the duration of night
E: a function of the moon's latitude, determining the magnitude of eclipses
F: lunar velocity
G: duration of the month (from one new moon to the next) in first approximation
H and J: correction to G
K=G+J: final duration of the month
L and M: date of the new moon

The five remaining columns concern the first and last visibility of the crescent.

Planetary Theory. To give an idea of Babylonian planetary theory, I shall describe the motion of Jupiter according to System A′. In this system, the zodiac is divided into 4 arcs: a slow arc from 9° cancer to 9° scorpio, a fast arc from 2° capricorn to 17° taurus, and two intermediate arcs in between. The motion of Jupiter in one synodic period is 30° on the slow arc, 36° on the fast arc, and 33° 45′ on the intermediate arc. The synodic period begins and ends with the heliacal rising, that is the first visibility of Jupiter. On the fast arc, the daily motion is

15′ during 30 days,
8′ during 3 months,
5′ retrograde during 4 months,
7′ 40″ during 3 months,
15′ during 30 days until heliacal setting,
15′ during 30 days until heliacal rising.

On the slow arc, these velocities are multiplied by $\frac{5}{6}$, on the middle arcs by $\frac{15}{16}$. The times (30 days, 3 months, etc.) are only approximate. The exact dates of the heliacal rising and setting and of the two stationary points, where the retrograde motion begins and ends, are determined by means of the *sun–distance principle*, which says that these four phenomena take place when the planet is at a fixed distance from the sun. The sun–distance principle implies that during one synodic period the sun moves the distance moved by the planet plus one complete revolution. For instance, on the slow arc the motion of Jupiter in a synodic period is 30°, hence the motion of the sun is 390°, and since the mean motion of the sun in one month is known, the time the sun needs to cover 390° can be calculated. The same principle is applied to all planets.

From this exposition it will be clear that the methods of the Babylonians are not geometrical, but purely arithmetical. The fundamental ideas of Babylonian astronomy are: the idea of periodic return of celestial phenomena, the artificial division of the zodiac into 12 signs of 30 degrees each, the use of longitude and latitude as co-ordinates of stars and planets, and the approximation of empirical functions by linear, quadratic and cubic functions, computed by means of arithmetical progressions of first, second and third order.

II

In Greek astronomy, the methods and ideas are completely different from the very beginning.

Thales and Anaximander

Not much is known of the astronomy of Thales, but we know that he was a geometer as well as an astronomer. He seems to be the author of a book on nautical astronomy.[1] He predicted a solar eclipse.[2] This prediction can only be explained if we

[1] Diels, *Fragmente der Vorsokratiker*, Thales B 1. [2] Ibid., Thales A 5.

assume that he had some knowledge of Babylonian methods.

More is known about Anaximander. Diogenes Laertius tells us: "He invented the gnomon" (i.e. the horizontal sundial with a vertical bar) "and he constructed a gnomon on a shadow-catcher [*skiotheron*] in Sparta, as Favorinus says in his *Miscellaneous Histories*. It showed the solstices and equinoxes. He also constructed *Horoskopeia*."

The last word is usually translated as "sundials". But the gnomon was already a sundial. Diogenes may have collected evidence from several sources: one said Anaximander made a gnomon, and another said he made sundials. Another possibility would be to suppose that by Horoskopeia, or hour-indicators, were meant the hour-lines on the horizontal plate or shadow-catcher of the gnomon.

In any case we may conclude that Anaximander constructed sundials with hour-lines. At the end of the first hour after sunrise, the shadow of the pointer is on the first hour-line, and so on. On his Spartan gnomon he must also have drawn transverse lines indicating the course of the shadow-point at the solstices and equinoxes.

Diogenes also informs us that Anaximander made a globe. So we see that Anaximander had a workshop, in which astronomical instruments were manufactured.

The cosmology of Anaximander is just the system of an engineer. The orbits of the sun and moon are said to be like chariot-wheels. "The rims of the wheels are hollow and full of fire, and each rim has an opening like the nozzle of a pair of bellows." Through these openings we can see the fire; the openings are the visible sun and moon. The inner and outer diameters of the sun's wheel are 27 and 28 times the size of the earth; for the moon's wheel the figures are 18 and 19. Eclipses occur when the orifice in one of the wheels is stopped up.[1] Anaximander constantly uses the language of the workshop.

GENERAL CHARACTER OF GREEK ASTRONOMY. Herodotus tells us that the Greeks had the gnomon from Babylonia.[2] This may well be true, for in the text MUL APIN we already find tables for the use of the gnomon. Yet, on the whole, Babylonian astronomy is mainly *arithmetical*, whereas Greek cosmology is *geometrical* and *mechanical* from the very beginning.

[1] Diels, *Fragmente der Vorsokratiker*, Anaximandros A 11, 21, 22.
[2] Herodotus, II, 109.

No matter whether we consider the oblique circular orbits of Anaximander, the concentric spheres of Eudoxus, or the eccentrics and epicycles of Apollonius and Ptolemy, the motions of the planets are always described by geometrical constructions in space. Mechanical analogies such as the chariot-wheels of Anaximander or the spindle of Plato occur in early and late Greek treatises (for example in Ptolemy's *Hypotheses of the Planets*).

Even in the latest phase of Greek astronomy, when tables were calculated for the use of astronomers and astrologers, all calculations were based upon geometrical constructions and proofs. In one or two exceptional cases, where computations were made by arithmetical progressions without geometrical justification, we clearly have Babylonian influence. For the *Anaphorikos* of Hypsicles, this influence was demonstrated by Neugebauer. Another case is found in the *Isagoge* of Geminus; here the author himself says that the method is due to the Chaldeans, and in fact the same method is found in cuneiform texts. Hence, these two exceptions actually prove the rule: *Greek astronomy always was geometrical and mechanical.*

Now what is the explanation of this remarkable fact? The only explanation I can find is that the Greeks were born geometers and engineers.

The Pythagoreans

I shall not try to distinguish between Pythagoras and his school, and I shall leave aside all uncertain speculations about Pythagorean metaphysics. We know for certain that the Pythagoreans taught:

(1) that the soul is immortal;
(2) that all living beings are akin;
(3) that the stars are divine, intelligent, living beings;
(4) that the souls are in eternal motion like the stars;
(5) that the motion of the stars and planets is circular and uniform;
(6) that "Heaven is harmony and number";
(7) that "all things exist by imitation of numbers".

These propositions are found in Aristotle.[1] "They formed the heaven out of numbers", says Aristotle.[2] This implies that they assumed the angular velocities of the planets and the radii of their orbits to be proportional to integers.

[1] Aristotle, *Metaphysics*, A, 5, 985b 32–986a 3; A, 6, 987b 11–12.
[2] Ibid. M, 6, 1080b 18–19.

(8) As a consequence of this assumption, there must be a least common multiple of the times of revolution of all planets and fixed stars. At the end of this time T, which is called the "Great Year" or "Perfect Year", all stars are in exactly the same positions as initially.

(9) The idea of the Perfect Year was adopted by Plato in the Timaeus. But the Pythagoreans went further: they assumed the *eternal return of all things*. Eudemus says:

> If we are to believe the Pythagoreans, that everything returns according to numbers, I shall once again stand here before you and tell you stories, bearing this little stick in my hand, and you will sit before me just so, and everything in the universe will be just as it is now, and hence the time will also be the same.[1]

Thus we see that the Pythagoreans were fatalists. In their opinion, no one can escape his fate, all souls and all bodies are in eternal cyclic motion. "There is nothing new, and everything repeats itself", said Pythagoras according to Dicæarchus.

By what reasoning did the Pythagoreans arrive at this conclusion? We have seen that the idea of a return of all stars to their initial positions is a necessary consequence of their ideas about heaven and number. But why should the fate of men follow the stars? The assumption that our fate depends on the stars is the basic idea of astrology. Hence we are bound to conclude that the Pythagoreans of which Eudemus speaks were *astrological fatalists*, and so was Pythagoras himself.

It is practically certain that astrology comes from Babylon. In a paper[2] on the Great Year, I have shown that the doctrine of Eternal Return and periodic cosmic catastrophes (Ecpyrosis and Deluge) came from Babylonia and Persia. I also believe that the ideas of the Pythagoreans concerning the importance of numbers were strongly influenced by Babylonian astronomy. The Babylonians, in their calculations of celestial motions, really "constructed the heaven out of numbers", whereas the Greeks usually constructed the heavens geometrically.

Greek tradition too calls Pythagoras a pupil of Zoroaster, or a pupil of the Magi of Babylon.

Religious character of Pythagorean astronomy. The ideas of the Pythagoreans concerning the cosmos were radically different from those of the leading physicists of the

[1] *Simplicii in Arist. Phys. comm.*, ed. Diels, p. 732.

[2] "Das grosse Jahr und die ewige Wiederkehr", *Hermes*, LXXX (1952) 129.

fifth century. Anaxagoras held that the sun, the moon and the stars are lifeless fiery stones, carried round by the whirling motion of the aether. The sun's solstices were explained by the repulsion of the cold air in the north. Democritus and Leucippus tried to explain all celestial phenomena by collisions of atoms.

By contrast, the Pythagoreans assumed the planets to be divine, living beings, who performed, because of their divine nature, perfect circular motions. They explained the solstices by assuming that the sun moves in the zodiacal circle, which is, in fact, the only reasonable astronomical explanation.

The question whether the stars are pushed about by pressure and collisions, or in eternal motion according to mathematical laws, is not only a scientific, but even more a religious issue. Anaxagoras was sentenced in Athens because he had taught that the sun and the moon are not gods, but only fiery stones. Plato complains, in the tenth book of the *Laws*, about the dangerous doctrines of the modern teachers of wisdom. He says: "When we try to give proofs for the existence of gods, and point to the sun, the moon, the stars, and the earth as gods and divine beings, they say that all this is only earth and stone."[1]

To meet this dangerous objection, Plato proceeds to explain that the ultimate cause of all motion is the soul, that all stars are in perfect circular motion and that therefore a most perfect, divine, reasonable soul (or several such souls) must be the cause of their motion.

This argument is developed at great length in the tenth and eleventh books of the *Laws*. It is quite clear why Plato considers mathematics and astronomy as most important parts of the education of future leaders of states. Formerly, he says, people thought that astronomy leads to atheism, but today astronomy teaches that reason reigns in the cosmos, and thus the mathematical sciences are indispensable for the strengthening of faith.

Plato's astronomy

In Plato's *Timaeus* and in the last book of the *Republic*, one and the same astronomical system is described. The spherical earth is at rest in the middle of the cosmos. The planetary spheres or circles and the sphere of the fixed stars all have a common daily motion about the axis of the universe. In

[1] *Laws*, X, 886D.

addition to this "Motion of the Same" the planets have their proper motions in oblique circles in the opposite direction, that is to the left (as seen from an observer on the earth, whose head is directed towards the north pole). The Motion of the Same rules over the proper motions, as Plato says. This means that the oblique circles of the proper motion are all subject to the daily motion of the whole cosmos.

Plato also describes the "Harmony of the Spheres". In the *Republic* he says that on each of the circles a siren stood, borne about in the revolution and singing one note, and that the eight sounds formed one harmony. The idea of the Harmony of the Spheres is certainly Pythagorean, and so are the other fundamental assumptions of Plato's astronomical system.

In the *Timaeus* the system is described as a scientific theory, a most probable hypothesis, but in the *Republic* the same doctrine is developed in the form of a mythical tale reported by Eros the Pamphylian, whose soul went forth while his body was lying on the battlefield. He comes to a daimonious meadow and sees how the unborn souls choose their fate, and then he comes upon a pillar of light, and sees a model of the world lying as a spindle on the knees of the goddess Ananké. Religious mysticism and scientific astronomy are interwoven in this myth.

EPICYCLES. The main features of Plato's astronomical system are quite clear, but there are details which Plato only vaguely indicates. In the *Republic* he describes the eight planetary spheres as whorls, fitting into each other like toy boxes. An ancient commentator, Dercyllides, tells us that each planetary sphere was supposed to have two surfaces, an outer and an inner one, and that the planets move on epicycles in the hollow space between the two spherical surfaces. In my treatise *Die Astronomie der Pythagoreer*[1] I have shown that this interpretation is quite reasonable and that it explains several passages in the *Republic* and *Timaeus* which would be incomprehensible otherwise. Thus, it appears that the epicycle hypothesis was proposed by the Pythagoreans and adopted by Plato, at least for Venus and Mercury.

The moving earth

There is another astronomical system, described by Aristotle and ascribed to "those in Italy, the so-called Pythagoreans",

[1] *Verhandelingen Kon. Ned. Akad., XX*, Amsterdam, 1951.

in which a fire is in the centre of the universe, whereas the earth moves in a circle about the centre. The side of the earth on which we are is always turned away from the central fire. By its rotation, the earth "causes day and night", says Aristotle. This implies that the time of revolution is just one day, and the daily rotation of the sun and the stars only apparent; in reality we rotate and they stand still, or nearly so.

This is a really great idea. Some sources ascribe this system to Philolaus, others to Hicetas.

From here to the idea of a rotation of the earth about its own axis it is not a great step. It is only necessary to make the earth larger, so that it includes the central fire. The central fire now warms the earth from the inside, and nourishes life on the earth. These ideas are ascribed by Simplicius to certain Pythagoreans. Doxographic tradition ascribes the idea of axial rotation of the earth to the Pythagorean Ecphantus and to Heraclides of Pontus.

THE SYSTEM OF HERACLIDES. About 350 B.C., Heraclides combined the ideas of circular motion and of axial rotation. He gave the earth two motions, just as we do nowadays: an axial rotation in one day, and a circular motion in one year. In his system, all planets and the earth move in circles about a common centre. The only difference with our heliocentric system is that Heraclides gave the sun a circular motion about the same centre. This system leads to a very good explanation of planetary phenomena. The usual geocentric interpretation of the system of Heraclides is unfounded, as I have shown in my Amsterdam treatise cited above.

THE HELIOCENTRIC SYSTEM. About 280 B.C., Aristarchus of Samos modified the system of Heraclides by assuming the sun to be at rest in the common centre of the planetary circles. He supposed the fixed stars to be so far away that they appear always in the same direction, as seen from the earth.

The only other Greek astronomer who accepted the heliocentric system seems to have been Seleucus of Seleucia near Babylon. All others assumed the earth to be at rest, and they had very good reasons for it. The reasons are clearly stated by Aristotle and Ptolemy.

(1) First, the circular motion of the earth cannot be reconciled with Aristotle's theory of natural motion. The natural

motion of earth particles is rectilinear: they fall in straight lines toward the centre until they are stopped. Therefore it is reasonable to assume that the natural motion of the whole earth is not circular, but rectilinear. If the earth were placed outside the centre of the universe, it would go straight towards the centre and remain there.

(2) Secondly, if the earth moved on a large circle about the sun, the apparent distances between fixed stars would change in the course of the year. This is a good scientific argument, although it can be met by assuming the fixed stars to be very far away.

(3) The third, decisive argument was expressed by Ptolemy as follows: if the earth rotated with enormous speed from west to east, everything that is not firmly attached to it, such as clouds and stones thrown up, would quickly fall back towards the west. As long as the law of inertia was not known, it was very difficult indeed to meet this argument.

In my opinion, the Greeks were quite right (from their point of view) to reject the hypothesis of the axial rotation of the earth.

Precision astronomy

From Anaximander to Aristarchus, many theories were invented, but they gave only a qualitative explanation of the observed phenomena. About 300 B.C., the period of precision astronomy began. Timocharis, Hipparchus and others made accurate observations and compared them with older Babylonian and Greek observations. The theories of Apollonius and Ptolemy aimed at an accurate calculation of planetary positions by means of epicycles and eccentres.

To achieve this, it was necessary to answer questions of the following kind. Given three observations of the longitude of the moon, how can we calculate the magnitude of the lunar epicycle, the position of the centre of the epicycle, and the positions of the moon on the epicycle? Or: given the radius of the epicycle and the initial positions and velocities, how can we calculate the apparent longitude of the moon at any given moment?

To answer questions of this kind, Ptolemy and his predecessors developed two kinds of geometrical methods:

GRAPHICAL AND TRIGONOMETRIC METHODS. For problems in the plane, the graphical method is quite simple and straightforward. The necessary circles and straight lines are drawn, and the important angles are measured. It is true that the method is not very accurate.

For spherical problems a projection of the sphere upon the plane is desirable. Two such methods were described by Ptolemy, in his short treatises *Analemma* and *Planispherium*. The first method is based upon orthogonal projection, the second upon 'stereographic projection', that is central projection from the north or south pole of the sphere on to the plane of the equator. The astrolabe, an instrument invented by the Greeks, is based on the same stereographic projection, and so is the astronomical water clock described by Vitruvius and reconstructed by Rehm.

Much more accurate than the graphical method is the method of trigonometry. Trigonometry was certainly known to Hipparchus (130 B.C.), but recent investigations by Otto Neugebauer show that Apollonius of Perga (200 B.C.) already knew plane trigonometry. Probably Apollonius invented the method, and it is quite possible that he also invented stereographic projection. He was a mathematical genius, equalled only by Archimedes and by no one else before Newton. Neugebauer rightly calls Apollonius "the father of Greek mathematical astronomy".

Now, two questions arise:

(i) Why were the Greeks interested in precision astronomy?

(ii) How can we explain that the Greeks, and no one else, developed the mathematical apparatus of precision astronomy?

THE MOTIVES. The answer to the first question is given by Ptolemy. The *Almagest* begins with an epigram:

> I know that I am mortal by nature, and ephemeral; but when I trace at my pleasure the windings to and fro of the heavenly bodies I no longer touch earth with my feet; I stand in the presence of Zeus himself and take my fill of ambrosia, food of the gods.

We do not know whether Ptolemy himself wrote this epigram, but in the foreword to the *Almagest* he says:

> Only mathematics, if one approach it with an inquiring mind, can offer its students knowledge that is secure and unchangeable, since its proofs are reached by paths that are beyond challenge, the paths of arithmetic and geometry. [By this consideration] we were led to apply ourselves, so far as possible, to all this kind of study,

but in particular to that part of it which considers the divine things that are in the heavens; for it is this study alone which makes inquiry into things which are eternal and unchanging.

In these words, we find two motives: first the great satisfaction which every mathematician feels when he ascertains the truth of a theorem by an indubitable proof, and secondly the veneration for the divine, eternal stars. In Ptolemy's mind, the two motives are interwoven: the eternal truth of mathematical theorems is closely related to the eternal nature of the divine stars. In the epigram, we find the motive of the pleasure of scientific investigation even more intimately connected with the delight of religious contemplation. These ideas are not specifically Ptolemaic; we find them in the writings of Plato as well as in Cicero's *Dream of Scipio*. Astronomy and astral religion were always closely connected in the mind of the Greek.

But Ptolemy not only presented a theoretical treatise. To the *Almagest*, he added tables, and several years later he computed a simplified set: the Handy Tables. These tables were copied and used by many generations of astrologers. Ptolemy himself wrote an astrological treatise. Hence, Ptolemy's astronomical investigations were not only meant for intellectual pleasure: they also had a very important practical application. Ptolemy's tables were more accurate than all Babylonian tables, because the Babylonians had no trigonometry.

WHAT ENABLED THE GREEKS TO INVENT TRIGONOMETRY? The need for accurate tables for astrological use was just as great in Rome, Asia Minor, Syria and Babylonia as in Hellenistic Egypt. Now, why did the Greeks invent the mathematical methods necessary for the computation of these tables, and why not the Romans or Syrians or Babylonians?

A tentative explanation would be: because the Greeks had geometrical methods at their disposal which were not known to the others. But this explanation does not work well. Apollonius did not find trigonometry or stereographic projection in the works of his predecessors: he just invented trigonometry and stereographic projection. He invented these methods, first because he needed them, and secondly because he was a genius. Of course, he needed a few theorems from Euclid, such as the theorem of Pythagoras, but the Babylonians also knew this theorem, and Euclid was available to anyone who could read Greek.

Quite generally, in the mathematical sciences, genius is much more important than learning. Newton needed a differential calculus; well, he invented it.

After Apollonius and Hipparchus, the mathematical tools and the observations needed for an improvement of lunar and planetary theory were available to Romans as well as to Egyptians and Syrians. Better tables were needed everywhere: astrology was international. But it was not a Roman, it was Ptolemy of Alexandria who improved on the theory and on the instruments of observation. Once again, the only explanation I can find is that the Greeks were born geometers and engineers.

Bibliography

SIR THOMAS HEATH, *Aristarchus of Samos* (Oxford, 1913)

F. X. KUGLER, *Babylonische Mondrechnung* (Freiburg, 1900)

F. X. KUGLER, *Sternkunde und Sterndienst in Babel* (Münster, 1907–10) I and II

O. NEUGEBAUER, *Astronomical Cuneiform Texts* (3 volumes, London, n.d.)

O. NEUGEBAUER, "On some astronomical papyri . . .", *Transactions of the American Philosophical Society*, XXXII (1942) 251

O. NEUGEBAUER, "Eccentric and epicyclic motion according to Apollonius", *Scripta Mathematica*, XXIV (1959) 5

A. REHM, "Zur Salzburger Bronzescheibe", *Jahreshefte österreichisches archäol. Inst. Wien*, VI (1903) 41

A. SACHS, "A classification of Babylonian astronomical tablets in the Seleucid period", *Journal of Cuneiform Studies*, II (1950) 271

A. SACHS, "Babylonian horoscopes", *J. of Cuneiform Studies*, VI (1952) 49

B. L. VAN DER WAERDEN, "Babylonian astronomy I", *Jaarbericht Ex Oriente Lux*, X (1948) 414; "Babylonian astronomy II", *Journal of Near Eastern Studies*, VIII (1949) 6; "Babylonian astronomy III", ibid. X (1951) 20

B. L. VAN DER WAERDEN, "Babylonische Planetenrechnung", *Vierteljahresschrift Natur. Ges. Zürich*, CII (1957) 39

B. L. VAN DER WAERDEN, "Das grosse Jahr und die ewige Wiederkehr", *Hermes*, LXXX (1952) 129

4

Conceptual Developments and Modes of Explanation in later Greek Scientific Thought

S. SAMBURSKY

Scientific change in Greek Antiquity can be fully appreciated only if Greek science is taken in its wider meaning, comprising specific achievements in various branches of mathematics and in the physical and biological sciences as well as scientific thought which aimed at the formation of comprehensive theories and of a philosophical foundation of a scientific world picture.

In Antiquity both these types of scientific activity did not merge into a single stream, as they have gradually in modern times, since Galileo and Newton, especially in the physical sciences to which I shall restrict myself here. From the seventeenth century, systematic experimentation and the mathematization of physics have been the two main factors which have led to the crystallization of a more or less consistent system of physical knowledge out of an ever-growing wealth of factual discoveries and of the various attempts at a theoretical foundation. In an increasing measure the leading scientists themselves have had their share in the synthesis of the picture of the physical world and have taken the lead from the philosophers in the epistemological investigation of scientific concepts.

In the 1,100 years of Greek Antiquity, from Thales until the closure of the Academy by Justinian, we witness the development of certain branches of the exact sciences gathering momentum in a relatively short period, reaching its apex in the third and second centuries B.C., and from then on slowly declining and fading out during the first two centuries A.D. The two greatest scientific contributions of the Greeks — geometry and astronomy — were accomplished before the end of the second century A.D., and the same can be said of their main achievements in acoustics, optics and mechanics.

Scientific thought, on the other hand, continued with uninterrupted vigour from the times of the Milesian philosophers until the latest neo-Platonists. Hypotheses about the creation and structure of the universe were produced, theories about the nature of space, time and matter discussed, scientific concepts analysed from an epistemological and purely logical point of view, and inquiries made into such problems as causality and determinism and the nature of physical action. But the main contributors to scientific thinking were not the great scientists like Euclid, Archimedes, Apollonius or Hipparchus, but rather the founders or representatives of philosophical systems of thought — men like Democritus, Plato, Aristotle, Epicurus and Chrysippus, and, in late Antiquity, the neo-Platonists. It is worth while remembering that of these people only Aristotle, who made the most important contribution to the picture of the physical cosmos, was also an outstanding scientist himself in the field of biology.

The main reason for this non-merging of scientific research and scientific thought in ancient Greece was lack of systematic experimentation and the consequent stagnation of technology, and the failure to develop algebraic notation and to introduce mathematical symbols and procedures in the description and explanation of physical phenomena. This prevented the axiomatic formulation of physical principles and the formation of a well-defined theoretical framework into which the results of observations or experiments could be fitted in an unambiguous way. In view of these serious drawbacks, it is astonishing to what extent arbitrariness was reduced to a minimum by the extraordinary flair of the Greeks for rational speculation in the right direction. Scientific thinking elaborated two main patterns in a qualitative non-mathematical way. These patterns became precursors of the basic trends of modern physical thought — continuum theory and atomism.

Aristotle's cosmos was the scientific world picture which became dominant in Greek and medieval thought. It was an all-embracing theory loosely related to experience and built on a few theoretical assumptions which partly were derived from pre-Aristotelian conceptions:

(1) the assumption that place (space) and matter form a strict continuum;
(2) the dichotomy between the unperishable, eternal and perfect heavens and the changing sublunar sphere;
(3) the assumption that matter is composed of the four sublunar elements, each of which results from the combination of two of the four basic qualities;
(4) the hypothesis of the fifth, celestial element;
(5) natural place and natural motion, the latter distinct from forced motion or motion against nature;

(6) the teleological principle, postulating a striving towards perfection;

(7) the explanation of physical action by the categories of potentiality and actuality closely related to the teleological principle.

Although the Aristotelian picture of the universe outlived rival systems, several of its conceptions and assumptions underwent notable modifications during the 800 years following Aristotle. These changes can be attributed to three main influences:

(a) The progress made in astronomy from Eudoxus to Ptolemy: the greater regard for observational evidence and an increasing demand for a more accurate description led to the unitary model of concentric spheres being discarded. It was replaced by the system of eccentric circles and epicycles, developing out of the principle of an harmonic analysis into circular motions. The increasingly complicated picture of the motions of the planets, the sun and the moon, and the failure to restore a unitary model for which no support was provided by the geocentric system, led to frustration and resignation at the end of Antiquity.

(b) Scientific and technical developments in optics, mechanics and other branches of physical sciences: geometrical optics, developed by Euclid, Archimedes, Hero and others led to conclusions which conflicted with Aristotelian conceptions about the nature of light. Aristotle's terminology had to be adapted to the observational evidence. Progress in mechanics, the construction of more complex machines and the introduction of cogged wheels and other mechanical devices brought about a mechanistic attitude, a greater awareness of the function of mechanisms. This had a considerable impact on scientific thought and was reflected in the modification of the meaning given to certain Aristotelian categories. In certain cases, as for instance in the case of weight and specific gravity, old concepts continued to co-exist together with new ones.

(c) The rise of new philosophical systems, such as Stoicism and neo-Platonism: the concept of the pneuma and its tension transformed the Aristotelian continuum theory into a field theory. The resulting conception of the interdependence of objects and events in space and time led to a strict determinism and to the beginning of functional thought. The pneuma also undermined the hypothesis of the fifth element. Neo-Platonism took over some of the Stoic ideas and led further to a revival and amplification of Plato's geometrical theory of matter and to a programmatic formulation of mathematical physics. The mystical trend of neo-Platonism originated the idea of action at a distance.

In addition to the impact of these factors, certain pre-Socratic ideas continued to prevail and to influence later scientific thought. The revival of Plato's theory of matter was in fact a revival of atomism in its non-mechanistic mathematical form. Democritean atomism, the mechanistic conception of matter, led an autonomous existence for several centuries in the Epicurean philosophy and further indirectly influenced scientific thought by establishing the concept of the vacuum. This was taken up in a more moderate form by Strato and Hero and also in Stoic cosmology which assumed the existence of a void outside the cosmos. In late Antiquity Plato and Democritus were often mentioned together as the authors of the explanation of matter by geometrical elements and conceptions, in contrast to Aristotle's qualitative theory of matter.

Creative scientific thought finally came to a standstill in the sixth century A.D., centuries after scientific research had ceased. The reasons for this are to be found not only in political circumstances. The struggle of the Church against paganism turned into a hostile attitude towards Greek civilization as a whole, including science and any attempt at a rational explanation of nature. On the other hand, pagan neo-Platonism itself, a strong rival of Christianity, contained elements which were incompatible with a scientific attitude. The doctrine of neo-Platonism was heavily tainted with irrational beliefs, and had strong leanings towards astrology and alchemy. The scientific component of Greek alchemy was extremely weak as compared with magic and the belief in the supernatural. Together with the revival of the Platonic idea of a rational explanation of phenomena by mathematics, there was an irrational or romantic tendency to regard nature as an indivisible unity which could not be decomposed or analysed into simpler elements. The combined effects of the irrational tendencies within neo-Platonism and of the anti-scientific attitude of the early Church, enhanced by the decline of the centres of learning in the sixth century, gave the final blow to scientific thought and brought to an end that continuous chain of rational thinking which linked the early Greek philosophers with some of the latest neo-Platonists.

In the following, some of the foregoing points will be elaborated and illustrated by quotations.

(1) *Mathematical astronomy*

Plato's celebrated challenge "to save the phenomena" (that is, to account for them) had a specific meaning: "By what assumed uniform and ordered motions can the phenomena in relation to the motions of the planets be saved?"[1] Thus the problem which Plato put to the scientists was to resolve the apparent planetary motions by some kind of 'harmonic analysis' into a sum of uniform circular movements which alone were assumed to represent the divine order of the celestial region, and which, especially for Plato, expressed the eternal system of the world-soul. Thus, Plato's disciples were confronted with a geometrical problem, and the solutions offered by Eudoxus and Callippus were obviously restricted to this purely geometrical aspect in a merely descriptive way. Aristotle, the realist, aimed at a more ambitious goal than a mere geometrical description. He conceived a physical model that differed from the pictures of Eudoxus in two essential features. The concentric spheres became material shells consisting of the fifth essence. Furthermore, by the addition of a large number of 'counteracting' spheres, the different sets of spheres belonging to each planet were replaced by a unified system representing one single and ordered geometrical entity.

The development that took place in the 400 years between 250 B.C. and A.D. 150 is associated with the names of Apollonius, Hipparchus and Ptolemy. It is characterized by a continuous and remarkably successful effort to "save the phenomena" by appropriate geometrical assumptions to which, however, the physical content, the unity of the picture was sacrificed. Very little was now said about spheres whose very name had suggested material structures, and circles were mentioned almost exclusively in the context of geometrical descriptions. The development began with the eccentric circle, which had already been introduced before the time of Apollonius, whose centres were assumed either as being fixed at a given distance from the earth, or as being movable — the planet moving along the circumference of the eccentric circle, while the centre of the eccentric itself described a circular motion. Then, the theory

[1] Simplicius, *In Aristotelis de caelo commentarium*, ed. J. L. Heiberg (Preussische Akademie der Wissenschaften, Berlin, 1894) 488, 23.

of the epicycles was conceived by Apollonius, and later re-established and developed by Hipparchus.

Ptolemy's *Syntaxis* (*Almagest*) shows amazing progress beyond the already remarkable achievements of Hipparchus. The increasing demand for more precise agreement between the observational data and the harmonic analysis into circular motions led to a still more complex description of the solar and lunar motions as well as of those of the planets. The phenomena could be saved only by an even bolder extension of the eccentric and epicyclic methods. An increasingly careful treatment of the orbits of each of the seven celestial bodies almost eliminated any prospect of a return to a unitary picture. Greater than ever was the gap between the success of the descriptive method of the astronomers and the failure of their efforts to explain the plurality of the intricate motions by a single physical hypothesis. Ptolemy himself, who was not only a great technician of science, but who had also a strong flair for its philosophical background, was painfully aware of this unsatisfactory situation. Here and there he allows himself to insert a comment on this problem and sometimes he can hardly disguise his disappointment over the lack of a unitary theory of the planetary system. His words have a curious apologetic air when, in the face of the complex geometrical description, he stresses that the concept of simplicity is relative and cannot be applied equally to terrestrial and celestial phenomena. Here are a few lines from the thirteenth book of his work:

> Nobody should regard these hypotheses as too difficult, considering the inadequacy of our devices. For no comparison of human things with divine ones can be fitting, nor can arguments be sufficient when they are adduced as evidence on such great matters from the most incongruous examples. Indeed, what can be more dissimilar than things that are eternal and unchanging and things that never remain the same, or things that can be obstructed by anything and things that are never obstructed, even by themselves? There is no other way than to try to adapt as far as possible the simplest hypotheses to the celestial motions and, if one does not succeed with these, to try others that are feasible. However, once every phenomenon is saved in consequence of these hypotheses, why should the complicated motions of the celestial bodies still appear so strange to us?[1]

Here we see Ptolemy resigned to an attitude which could be

[1] Ptolemaeus, *Syntaxis mathematica*, ed. J. L. Heiberg (Teubner, Leipzig. 1903) XIII, 2.

called that of a relativist or rather a positivist: we must do our best to give the simplest description possible of complex phenomena which in any case are outside that region where the usual notions of understanding or explanation are applicable. But this was not Ptolemy's entire view of the matter. In his later book, *Planetary Hypotheses*, he abandons the purely descriptive attitude and propounds some ideas about the possible physical structure and causes governing the planetary system. He may already have had these ideas when he wrote his *Syntaxis*, and if so, he possibly refrained from revealing them because of his own doubts as to their substantiality. Two souls dwell together in the breast of many a scientist, and Newton's lifelong speculations on the æther as the cause of gravitation, in spite of his very careful attitude in the *Principia*, is a famous example.

Ptolemy took up the ideas of Adrastus and of the Platonic writer Dercyllides and developed their hypothesis of the hollow and massive ætherial spheres whose combined rotations make the planets move in their apparent orbits. He believed in the reality of these spheres, but at the same time his considerations were guided by some principle of the economy of thought that sought to avoid redundant assumptions. He was equally convinced, however, that nature itself avoids redundancy: "It is not proper to suppose that there are in nature superfluous things which do not make sense, namely, complete spheres for motions for which a small part of these spheres would suffice."[1] Why suppose that there are massive spheres to which the planet is fixed when it is sufficient to assume a segment of these spheres produced by two parallel cuts on both sides of the circle along which the planet is carried around in its epicycle? One is thus left with a tambourine to whose rim the planet is attached. The tambourine is rotated in the hollow space between two concentric spherical surfaces which according to the requirements are supposed to be concentric or eccentric to the earth. But of these hollow spheres only the parts enclosing the tambourine need to be conceived as real; they are thus two rings or whorls, as Ptolemy characteristically calls them, reminding the reader of Plato's whorls in the *Republic*. This is all that is left of the system of concentric spheres in Ptolemy's final version, indeed a real 'economy edition'. He again stresses the absurdity of any attempt to combine all these systems of

[1] Ptolemaeus, *Hypotheses planetarum*, in *Opera omnia minora*, ed. J. L. Heiberg (Teubner, Leipzig, 1907) II, 6.

truncated spheres into one by some device similar to the counteracting spheres of Aristotle:

And senseless, too, are the counteracting spheres, not to mention the enormous increase in numbers which they bring about. For they occupy much space in the aether and are not necessary for the explanation of the planetary motions. They roll back together in one direction in order to produce a single unitary motion.[1]

What had Ptolemy to offer in place of Aristotle's unitary mechanism so forcefully discarded by him? There remained for him, in the age of the return to Pythagoras and Plato, the vitalistic hypothesis of a soul as the driving force of each planet, the soul residing in the planet and the system of bodies connected with the planet being kept in motion by the vital force emanating from it. Ptolemy illustrated his idea with a simile:

As an illustration of the motions of the celestial bodies, let us choose birds whose movements are well known to us — we are familiar with illustrations of this kind. The origin of their movements is in their vital force which produces an impulse that spreads into the muscles and from there into their feet or wings, where it ends. . . . There is no cogent reason whatsoever to assume that the motions of all these birds occur through their mutual contact. On the contrary, one has to postulate that they do not touch one another in order that they should not be a mutual hindrance to each other. Similarly, we have to suppose that among the celestial bodies each planet possesses for itself a vital force and moves itself and imparts motion to the bodies united with it by nature.[2]

Ptolemy thus appears here as a vitalist who attempts to transfer some basic concepts of vitalism to the dynamics of the heavens. He may possibly have been influenced by Galen who applied the concept of vital force (*psychiké dynamis*) to the dynamics of animal limbs. In his work on muscular motion, Galen described how the vital force regulates the concerted action of the muscles which are thus prevented from obstructing each other and the action of the whole limb by lack of coordination.

The last important comment made in Antiquity on the Ptolemaic system is Proclus's book *Outline of the Astronomical Hypotheses* (fifth century A.D.). Proclus writes in the spirit of what is said in the seventh book of the *Republic* about the limitations of the astronomers in the face of the true reality. True reality is the unseen reality that can never be grasped by

[1] Ibid.

[2] Ibid. II, 7.

material observation and the experimental procedure of science, but by the light of pure reason and intelligence alone. Proclus regards the Ptolemaic system as an ingenious device invented for practical purposes and rejects the idea that any reality can be attributed to the spheres or segments of spheres:

If some people have used epicycles or eccentric circles and assumed uniform motions in order to find numerical values of these motions by a combination of all of them — the epicycles, the eccentrics and the planetary motions on them — one may call this a beautiful invention suited to logical minds which, however, fail to grasp the nature of the whole which only Plato has understood.[1]

At the end of his *Outline* Proclus confesses his doubts and his longing for a "real" explanation of the celestial phenomena. This memorable passage is well worth quoting in full:

The astronomers who are eager to prove the uniformity of celestial motions are in danger of unconsciously proving that their nature is irregular and full of changes. What shall we say of the eccentrics and the epicycles of which they continually talk? Are these only inventions or have they a real existence in the spheres to which they are fixed? If they are only inventions, their authors have, all unaware, deviated from physical bodies into mathematical concepts and have derived the causes of physical motion from things that do not exist in nature. . . . But if the circles really exist, the astronomers destroy their connexion with the spheres to which the circles belong. For they attribute separate motions to the circles and to the spheres and, moreover, motions that, as regard the circles, are not at all equal but in the opposite direction. They confound their mutual distances and sometimes let them coincide in one plane, sometimes separate them and let them cross each other. Thus there will result all sorts of divisions, foldings-up, and separations of the celestial bodies. Further, the account given of these mechanical hypotheses seems to be haphazard. Why, in each hypothesis, is the eccentric in this particular state — either fixed or mobile — and the epicycle in that, and the planet moving either in a retrograde or in a direct sense? What are the reasons for those planes and their separations — I mean the *real* reasons that, once understood, will relieve the mind of all its anguish — this they never will tell us. In fact, they proceed in a reverse order: they do not draw conclusions from their hypotheses like the other sciences, but instead they attempt to construct hypotheses which fit these conclusions which should follow from them. . . . However, one should

[1] Proclus Diadochus, *In Platonis Timaeum commentarium*, ed. E. Diehl (Teubner, Leipzig, 1903) 272b.

bear in mind that these hypotheses are the most simple and most fitting ones for the divine bodies. They are invented in order to discover the mode of the planetary motions which in reality are as they appear to us, and in order to make the measure inherent in these motions apprehensible.[1]

Proclus's words reflect his feeling of frustration. The geocentric system had outlived its span of life and, as a purely descriptive theory, had ceased to be adequate to the advanced empirical state of affairs. Looking backward from our present vantage point we see that only the heliocentric system could offer the start for a new and more fruitful development. The purely descriptive phase of this system, associated with the names of Copernicus, Brahe and Kepler, was to give way in a relatively short time, with the rise of classical mechanics, to the explanatory phase, beginning with Newton. From then on, the mathematical theories of physics have undertaken not only to "save the phenomena" but also to explain them in the framework of systems based on the notion of a physical cause and expressed in well-defined mathematical language. The causal theories, if they do not quite "relieve the mind of all its anguish", at least satisfy to some extent the epistemological needs of those minds which expect more of a scientific theory than a mere material success.

(2) *Perturbation theory*

Conceptual difficulties were encountered in later discussions of the Aristotelian concepts "in accordance with nature" and "contrary to nature". Here, Stoic ideas as incorporated in neo-Platonism offered a solution of great significance for the general progress made in the approach to physical phenomena. As was so often the case in Greek scientific thought, the discussions began with an analysis of terminology. Aristotle almost casually uses the synonym — "natural" — for the first case: "It is natural as well as in accordance with nature".[2] Themistius (fourth century A.D.) takes exception to this: "What is in accordance with nature is also called natural, but this is a minority of cases. For there are natural things which are not in accordance with nature, such as animals deformed from birth. For these, too, are creations of nature which,

[1] Proclus Diadochus, *Hypotyposis astronomicarum positionum*, ed. C. Manitius (Teubner, Leipzig, 1909) VII, 50 ff.

[2] Aristotle, *Physica*, ed. and trans. P. Wickstead and F. M. Cornford (Loeb Classical Library, London, 1957) 193a 1.

however, failed and did not proceed in the usual way."[1] Simplicius (sixth century A.D.) is still more explicit:

We say that those natural things are in accordance with nature if they have the perfection proper to them. But there are some natural things which are not in accordance with nature, although they occur in accordance with the activity of nature, as is the case with animals deformed from birth, and generally with things suffering from some privation. . . . One could call 'natural' everything that accompanies or happens to the essence of nature as such, for instance infirmity or illness, but 'in accordance with nature' can be applied only to things that prove to be in accordance with the *purpose* of nature. Thus we say that to be healthy is in accordance with nature, but to be ill, though coming to pass as something natural, is contrary to nature.[2]

The question raised by these two commentators has a bearing on the teleological conception of nature. Nature behaves like an artist, with perfection as its aim. But by analogy with occasional failures in the arts, failures in nature may be assumed to be possible. "If in art [says Aristotle] attempts that have failed were aimed at a purpose which they did not attain, we may assume the same in nature, namely, that monstrosities are similar failures of purpose in nature."[3] Among such failures of purpose one has to count not only calves with two heads or a child with six fingers but also every possible deviation from the norm, including illness.

Philoponus (sixth century A.D.) takes issue with his colleagues over their view that a deviation from the normal pattern of nature could be called "natural". In his opinion only things in accordance with nature can be labelled natural, and such phenomena as illness or monstrosities have to be regarded in a wider framework as parts of a whole, in order to be considered natural. Philoponus's view is derived from the Stoic idea that if something goes wrong, the event or the object in question must be seen as a partial phenomenon embedded in a wider system. In the frame of this wider system, taken as a totality, the wrong is compensated in some way and the harmony of the whole is restored. In a qualitative way, this is reminiscent of the law of classical mechanics that, in a closed system, the sum of all internal forces vanishes.

[1] Themistius, *In Aristotelis physica commentarium*, ed. M. Wallies (Preuss Akad. d. Wissens., Berlin, 1900) 37, 7.

[2] Simplicius, *In Aristotelis physica commentarium*, ed. H. Diels (Preuss. Akad. d. Wissens., Berlin, 1882) 271, 11.

[3] *Physica*, 199b 2.

His train of thought leads Philoponus to a somewhat different aspect of the physical situation. When something "contrary to nature" happens to a physical object, one has to regard it as a perturbation caused by outside factors. The intervention of these factors, taken together with the resulting perturbation, restores the phenomenon as a "natural" one, as something happening in accordance with nature. The notion of the perturbation of a system is an eminently physical one, and in classical mechanics it has found its application and mathematical expression in the so-called perturbation theory. It is worthwhile to quote Philoponus's exposition:

Perhaps there are no things which are contrary to nature in an absolute sense, but one has to distinguish between things of a partial character which are not natural and are contrary to nature, and things which are a whole and are natural as well as in accordance with nature. . . . A deformity from birth is not natural for man nor is it according to nature. But taking nature as a *whole* in which nothing is contrary to nature (because there is no evil in the whole), a deformity from birth is natural and according to nature. . . . I will give you an illustration that will explain what happens with things contrary to nature: Suppose that a lyre player tunes his instrument according to one of the musical scales and is then ready to begin his music. Suppose, however, that someone else loosens the tension of some of the strings or all of them, or rather let us assume for the sake of this illustration that the strings are affected by the state of humidity of the environment and thus get out of tune. Now the player's fingers move the strings so that a perfect melody would result if the strings were still properly tuned; when the player strikes the lyre thus, the substance of the strings does not perform the melody that he had in mind, but instead an unmusical, distorted and indefinite sound is produced. . . . And just as we do not say that the sound of the untuned lyre is artistic or in accordance with art, although an artist produces it, neither do we say in the case of organic nature that it was a natural event, because it did not happen according to the well defined laws of nature. However, with regard to the nature of the whole we do say that it was a natural event, for it is in accordance with the nature of the whole that it destroys one thing when it creates another.[1]

Philoponus also criticizes Aristotle's teleological comparison of the ways of nature with those of art. For Aristotle this comparison works both ways; Philoponus's approach to the problem is based on the conception that an artist can inten-

[1] Joannes Philoponus, *In Aristotelis physica commentarium*, ed. H. Vitelli (Preuss. Akad. d. Wissens., Berlin, 1887) 201, 10.

tionally create monstrosities, conceived as works of art and "in accordance with art", whereas nature, whose purpose is always perfection, can only create them as freaks and never in accordance with its intentions.

(3) *Potentiality and fitness*

The increasing mechanical-mindedness of later Antiquity is thrown into relief by a consideration of the conceptual development of one of the central pillars of Aristotelian thought, the categories of potentiality and actuality. These concepts were of the utmost importance for the physical explanation of change. Water is potentially air, and it becomes actually so when the quality of cold is replaced by its opposite warmth. The situation is similar with changing colours and other accidental qualities. This explanation implies that the body that actualizes a certain state or property must possess a capacity for this actualization even when that state or that property is only a potentiality. In the later post-Aristotelian period an increasing need was felt to express the necessity for such a capacity within the frame of scientific terminology. Potentiality is only a necessary condition for actuality but it need not be a sufficient one. The technical term signifying the sufficient condition for actualization was *epitedeiotes*, meaning fitness, appropriateness or suitability, and it came into use as a definite scientific concept in the second century A.D. The use of *epitedeiotes* in this sense spread widely, especially in later neo-Platonism. Late neo-Platonists in an increasing measure made use of *epitedeiotes* as a physical or technical concept. A few instances may serve as an illustration. In the *De generatione et corruptione* Aristotle explains generation as a process towards the opposite whereby the object acted upon changes into the acting object by assimilation. Philoponus commenting on that passage remarks that these processes require the fitness of the active partner to accomplish this assimilation: "The density of matter can often prevent a change. Thus the black of the ink of a cuttle-fish will often overpower the white of milk, but never will this be done by the black of ebony. The change into the opposite requires matter to be fit to act and to be acted upon."[1]

Fitness played a further very important role in the discussions on the nature of the soul in the light of Plato's doctrine and

[1] Joannes Philoponus, *In Aristotelis de generatione et corruptione commentarium*, ed. H. Vitelli (Preuss. Akad. d. Wissens., Berlin, 1897) 149, 11.

Aristotle's criticism. In the *De anima* Aristotle refutes the notion of the soul as the mover of the body, by the following argument: If the locomotion of the soul were possible, it would also be possible for the soul that had left the body to enter it again; upon this would follow the possibility of the resurrection of dead animals. The gist of Philoponus's remarks is that Aristotle errs in assuming that, after death, the body is fit to be moved again by the re-entering soul. The soul is a source of energy that keeps the body moving as long as it is in the proper condition to be worked on, to wit — as long as it has the mechanical fitness which, however, it loses when death occurs:

> Some people say that the soul moves the body so to say by a mechanical device, as if the body were pushed by the motion of the soul, as, when children in their play make small, very thin hollow balls of wax and enclose in them some bluebottles or beetles so that, when these move, the ball is set in motion. Or like an animal which is enclosed in a cage moving the cage by its own pushing movements. . . . However, one can object to this and say that Aristotle was wrong when he maintained that if the soul moves the body by moving itself, it could re-enter and bring the dead to life. For instance, take a pillar whose action as a lever lifts up a wall or something similar. When the pillar slips the wall collapses and its joints break up and nobody is able to lift it again by applying the lever. One can find other similar examples. The argument is that in such cases mechanical devices alone are not enough, but there has to be a fitness of the object to be lifted. . . . Similarly a stick pushed against a door cannot move the door when it has not the fitness necessary to be moved but, having this fitness, it will move when pushed by the stick. But it will not do so when fastened by nails or when the hinges are loose. . . . When the shape or quality of the wax is lost, for instance when it becomes soft or undergoes some other change, the animal enclosed in it cannot move it any more.[1]

An interesting aspect of this passage is the way in which the hypothesis of the soul as a moving mechanism is treated here as a reasonable assumption anticipating in a way Descartes's doctrine by more than a thousand years.

(4) *The principle of least action*

It is a well known aspect of the Greek philosophy of nature that, since the time of the early pre-Socratics, philosophical principles were used in cosmology and in conjunction with very

[1] Joannes Philoponus, *In Aristotelis de anima commentarium*, ed. M. Hayduck (Preuss. Akad. d. Wissens., Berlin, 1897) 106, 8.

general physical statements. There was Anaximander and his invocation of the principle of sufficient reason to prove the state of rest of the earth in its symmetrical position in the centre of the universe. There was Democritus and his formulation of the principle of conservation of that which exists: "Nothing can come into being from that which is not nor pass away into that which is not."[1]

It is of some interest to examine a case in later Antiquity, in which a philosophical principle was applied to a physical phenomenon, after the great progress made in several branches of physics in the Hellenistic period. The example is taken from geometrical optics where men such as Euclid, Archimedes, Hero and Ptolemy had made considerable contributions. Hero in his book on *Catoptrics*, extant only in a Latin translation, gives a proof of the following proposition: Of all rays impinging on a mirror and reflected to the same point, those reflected according to the law of equal angles of incidence and reflection travel the shortest distance. Thus, if *MN* is the plane of the mirror and *A* and *C* are the object and the eye respectively, the actual path of the rays, namely *ABC*, such that *AB* and *BC* make equal angles with *MN*, is shorter than any other path *ADC* which does not satisfy the law of reflection. Hero adds that the reflection of the rays with equal angles is thus "in accordance with reason" (*rationabiliter* in the Latin translation). What he meant by this is difficult to decide.

Nearly five hundred years later his proof was repeated by

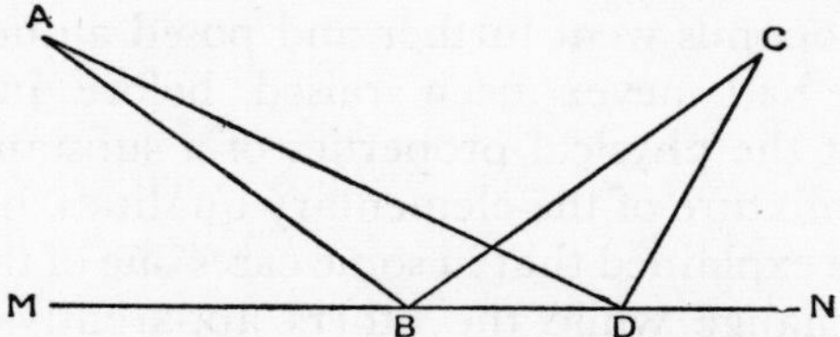

Olympiodorus, a contemporary of Philoponus, in his commentary on Aristotle's *Meteorologica*. Olympiodorus does not copy Hero verbatim as can be seen by slight variations which he introduces into the proof. What interests us here are his introductory remarks, which immediately precede the actual proof:

It is agreed by everyone that nature produces nothing in vain

[1] Diogenes Laertius, *Vitae Philosophorum*, ed. and trans. R. D. Hicks (Loeb Classical Library, London, 1950) IX, 44.

nor labours in vain. Thus, if we do not concede that reflection takes place with equal angles, it follows that nature does labour in vain with unequal angles, and that the visual rays, instead of reaching the object on a short road appear to arrive there on a longer roundabout way. For one finds that the straight lines which make unequal angles in going from the eyes to the mirror and from there to the object are longer than those which make equal angles.[1]

No matter whether this is Olympiodorus's original idea or whether it is his interpretation of Hero's "in accordance with reason", the passage quoted in the given context is the first version on record of the celebrated principle of least action, re-stated in modern times by Maupertuis in the middle of the eighteenth century, and constituting one of the basic tools of physics — today in the final version formulated by Hamilton. Maupertuis's philosophical argumentation has the same outspoken teleological tinge as that of Olympiodorus; so has the reasoning of Fermat who one hundred years before Maupertuis gave a proof of the same optical law, including it in his 'principle of least time' which he stated as "Nature always acts by the shortest course".

(5) *Functional dependence*

How can the physical properties of a body be described as resulting from a quantitatively defined mixture of the four Aristotelian qualities hot, cold, dry and moist? Galen made a rather primitive attempt to define 'standard' mixtures of these qualities. Philoponus went further and posed a question which in this form had never been raised before in Antiquity. Assuming that the physical properties of a substance all result from a given mixture of the elementary qualities, he asked how the fact can be explained that in some cases one of the properties may visibly change while the others apparently remain unchanged. Formulating this question was in itself a novelty, but the answer he gave implies for the first time the discussion of the functional dependence of one set of variable quantities on another, and the clear recognition of the course of a function, that is, in fact, of its first derivative. Philoponus asked why for instance the colour of honey may change from yellow to white while its taste is not affected at all. And similarly with wine: it can turn sour without changing its colour, whereas both

[1] Olympiodorus, *In Aristotelis meteorologica commentarium*, ed. W. Stueve (Preuss. Akad. d. Wissens., Berlin, 1900) 272, 5.

colour and taste should change as they depend on the mixture of the elementary qualities.

He then continues:

> Our explanation is as follows: each property is defined in a certain range, and is not given only at a single point. Whiteness is defined in a range (for when extreme whiteness is lost a body does not cease altogether to be white) and sweetness is defined in a range (there is a wide range of sweet substances) and so on. If the properties have ranges, it is obvious that the efficacies of the mixture from which these properties result must also have ranges. There must exist a certain extreme value for a mixture below which no property can come into existence, and for that given value the whole nature of the property will change at once. For instance, in order to exercise our minds on a paradigm, let ten parts of hot, cold, dry and moist be the amount which gives the full value of sweetness. If this amount is diminished by one for each of the primary qualities sweetness will slightly decrease but it will not vanish. But if the amount is reduced by five (assuming that up to this point sweetness can be preserved), the whole property of sweetness will disappear.

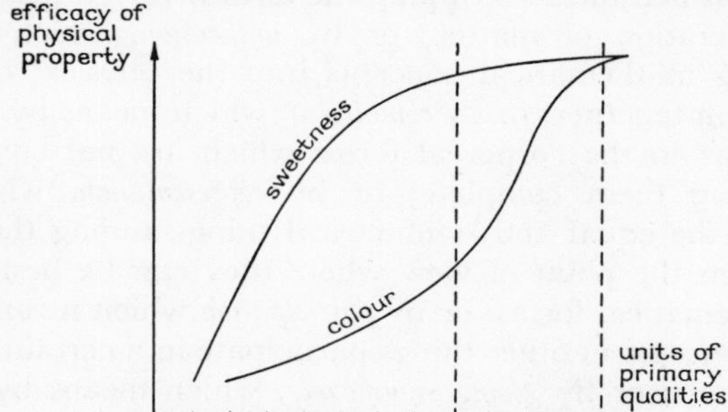

> If, now, the different properties of honey result from the same mixture, they will not originate according to the same law of change; but if, for instance, sweetness has reached its maximum value, colour and viscosity might not yet have reached their maximum but be much below it. Therefore, if the mixture is slightly varied, sweetness will not alter appreciably but colour may change completely, because it is near that particular and critical point of the mixture of primary qualities at which the colour in question can no more come into existence.[1]

Philoponus here gives a description of the dependence of two variables — sweetness and colour — on the independent variable 'primary quality'. This is the only case on record in Antiquity of the quantitative treatment of a functional relation-

[1] Philoponus, *De gen. et corr.* 170, 12.

ship, and it goes to show how the development of a concept of supreme importance for science was held up for lack of a suitable method of description — in this case graphical representation. Instances of functional thought of a qualitative nature occur in Stoic physics.

(6) *The mathematical approach to nature*

The neo-Platonic revival and the amplification of Plato's views on the role of mathematics as the language of science found its most eloquent expression in Iamblichus's (fourth century A.D.) definition of the method of mathematical physics in his *De communi mathematica scientia*:

> It is also the practice of mathematical science sometimes to attack perceptible things with mathematical methods, such as the problem of the four elements, with geometry or arithmetic or with the methods of harmony, and similarly other problems. And because mathematics is prior to nature, it constructs its laws as derived from prior causes. This it does in several ways: either by *abstraction*, which means stripping the form involved in matter from the consideration of matter; or by *unification*, which means by introducing mathematical concepts into the physical objects and joining them together; or by *completion*, which means by adding the missing part to the corporeal forms which are not complete and thus making them complete; or by *representation*, which means looking at the equal and symmetrical things among the changing objects from the point of view where they can be best compared with mathematical forms; or by *participation* which means considering how concepts in other things participate in a certain way in the pure concepts; or by *giving significance*, which means by becoming aware of a faint trace of a mathematical form taking shape in the realm of perceptible objects; or by *division*, which means considering the one and indivisible mathematical form as divided and plurified among individual things; or by *comparison*, which means looking at the pure forms of mathematics and those of perceptible objects and comparing them; or by *causal approach* from prior things, which means positing mathematical things as causes and examining together how the objects of the perceptible world arise from them. In this manner, I believe, we can attack mathematically everything in nature and in the world of change.[1]

This is a clear formulation of a programme for mathematical physics which had to wait for about 1,400 years to see the beginning of its realization.

[1] Iamblichus, *De communi mathematica scientia*, ed. N. Festa (Teubner, Leipzig, 1891) XXXII.

Commentaries

Commentary by G. E. M. de Ste. Croix

My function is supposed to be mainly that of commenting upon Mr. Edelstein's paper, but in fact I propose to deal mainly with matters outside it, some of them raised by other contributors to this Symposium. Mr. Edelstein's paper is of a very general nature, and much of it expresses ideas already familiar to many of us from his well-known article in the *Journal of the History of Ideas* for 1952, referred to on p. 20, n. 1. It is not that I have no disagreements with Mr. Edelstein. In particular, I would criticize his lack of interest (see p. 23, n. 3) in the basic characteristics of the Greek and Roman economic and social systems, of which slavery was an essential part — but perhaps that is because, unlike most of those who are interested in ancient science, I am primarily what I might call a straight political and economic historian and have only recently become interested in the history of science. But I would prefer not to indulge in criticisms of Mr. Edelstein's work which he cannot be here to answer.*

I can divide up what I have to say under four heads.

First, developing a point made by Mr. Edelstein, I want to make a plea that except when we are contrasting modern scientific thought in its more general aspects with its ancient counterpart we should try as far as possible to avoid using such expressions as "the Greeks" or "Greek science" or "Greek thought". These are not simple, homogeneous categories. Only a small fragment of ancient scientific thought has survived to our time, and this reflects mainly the prevailing interests and preferences of the educated classes of the Graeco-Roman world; let us not forget that. Even within this attenuated body of evidence there are points of view far more radically opposed to each other than the rival trends of thought surviving in the natural sciences today — the modern comparison, as Mr. Edelstein remarks, would rather be with modern schools of

* Mr. Edelstein was prevented by illness from being present at the Symposium.

philosophy, now (I suppose) as far apart as ever they were. And, of course, a great deal of ancient science *is* primarily — or is inextricably mixed up with — philosophy, and sometimes even theology; and even if one believes, as I do, that science has progressed in the degree to which it has extruded philosophy and theology and confined them to their own proper spheres, these philosophical and theological elements in ancient science often form an integral part of the whole, and one must not try to play them down, although one may perhaps be forgiven for taking a special interest in those fields where they are least important.

This brings me to my second point. Where, for us in this room today, are the limits of ancient science to be drawn? Taking courage from the paper prepared for the Symposium by Mr. Guerlac, to which I feel very sympathetic, I am going to express the hope that history, in the sense of historiography in general, will not be excluded, because history (in my sense) is part of man's attempt to understand the world in which he lives, above all the workings of human society itself. It is significant that the earliest Greek word for what we should call scientific research is ἱστορίη: this is the word which Mr. Edelstein translates "science" in that splendid fragment of Euripides which he quotes on p. 16. No doubt Euripides was thinking mainly of cosmology, but ἱστορίη might be used of any kind of research, and it is applied by Herodotus, for example, to his own activities — geographical and anthropological as well as strictly historical. It is well known to Greek historians that there is a very striking similarity in method, thought and even vocabulary between Thucydides and the best of the contemporary Hippocratic writings: I refer particularly to *Epidemics* I and III, the *Prognostic*, and (above all, perhaps) that great work, *On Ancient Medicine* (Περὶ ἀρχαίης ἰητρικῆς), beginning as it does with an explicit rebuke to those who approach medicine *a priori*, ὑπόθεσιν αὐτοὶ αὑτοῖς ὑποθέμενοι.[1] I believe that of all ancient scientific works, outside mathematics, these late fifth century B.C. Hippocratic writings, and even more Thucydides, come nearest in spirit and method to their modern counterparts. I would go so far as to say that the gulf between Thucydides and the modern historian, great as

[1] The use of the word ὑπόθεσις here reminds one strongly of the famous passage just before the end of the *Principia*, where Newton says, "Hypotheses non fingo. Quicquid enim ex phaenomenis non deducitur, hypothesis vocanda est."

it is (above all in that Thucydides virtually never identifies his sources of information), is probably a good deal smaller than that between any other Greek or Roman scientific writer and his modern counterpart. To my mind, it is a sad reflection on the piecemeal and fragmented way in which we tend to approach Greek and Roman civilization that most of those who write about ancient scientific thought should pay almost no attention to Herodotus and Thucydides and their successors, although they are prepared to devote a great deal of time to thinkers who were thoroughly hostile to almost everything we should recognize as empirical science. (More of this presently.)

As a political historian, again, (and here I come to my third point) I can only deplore the fact that most historians of ancient science should make no attempt, or only the most perfunctory attempts, to relate the evolution of ancient scientific thought to the development of political institutions. I believe there are close connexions. Greek political institutions evolved in the most remarkable manner from the seventh century to the end of the fifth, in the direction of increased democracy: increasing participation in public affairs and government on the part of broader and broader sections of the citizen population, and ultimately (at Athens and in some other cities) of the whole citizen population. After the fifth century this development was arrested, and eventually reversed, although Greek democracy was not entirely stamped out until well into the Roman period. Is it entirely fortuitous that the first great development of proto-scientific thought in so many fields, which culminated in Anaxagoras, Democritus, Herodotus, Thucydides and the early Hippocratics, should be arrested at the very time the political progress ceases, and that in the fourth century this kind of thinking should appear mainly in a significantly different form, with much greater emphasis on the purely philosophical side, with a stronger infusion of specifically religious ideas, and with a very influential current of thought within it which was consciously anti-scientific, openly hostile to all empirical science?

I come now to my fourth subject, on which I want to spend the rest of my time. Discussion about whether Greek science is entitled to be called 'scientific' in anything like the modern sense of the word has too often centred on the question whether it made use of experiments. Although I myself believe that the experimental side of Greek science was a good deal more developed at some periods and in some fields than is generally realized (a reading of Ptolemy's *Optics* might surprise many people), I would of course admit that the use of the experimental method remained rudimentary, in that experiments were rarely made the starting point for a modified theory, and fresh experiments designed to confirm or contradict the theory. Only successful experiments are recorded, and many of them might more appropriately be called appeals to analogy.

But I believe that arguing about experiments gets us nowhere. Instead, I propose that we concentrate on something much simpler and more fundamental: observation. Systematic observation was practised very extensively by some Greek scientists, though sometimes a man who made admirable use of empirical methods in one field might employ entirely *a priori* ones in another. One thinks particularly of Aristotle, who was a wonderfully acute and accurate observer in the biological sphere, but when he came to deal with physics was content to take for granted a fallacious law of falling bodies which he might easily have disproved by dropping weights from a height — as was realized, incidentally, long before the time of Galileo, not least by Philoponus in the sixth century A.D.

Now if practitioners of any empirical science decry and deliberately turn away from observation, that science will become sterile, and even if it preserves internal coherence it will decline into at best no more than a branch of philosophy. What I want to emphasize is that observational methods were not merely insufficiently used by most Greek scientists: they were subjected to a tremendous intellectual onslaught, first by the Eleatics, Parmenides and Zeno, and then by Plato and all good Platonists and neo-Platonists (and many others) after him — a good example, from Proclus in the fifth century A.D., is given by Mr. Sambursky on p. 69.

I have time to illustrate from one field only: astronomy, often described as the greatest of all Greek scientific achievements. Greek mathematical astronomy, and indeed the whole axiomatic method in geometry, proceeding by a strict series of proofs, were, I believe, something quite new in the second quarter of the fourth century B.C.[1] (This, I realize, is very different from the view expressed by Mr. van der Waerden.) The greatest name is Eudoxus of Cnidus, who was active precisely in the second quarter of the fourth century. Now it is said again and again in the books (and it appears from

[1] It will be sufficient to refer to O. Neugebauer, *The Exact Sciences in Antiquity* (2nd ed., Providence, R.I., 1957) especially pp. 147–8.

p. 65 that Mr. Sambursky accepts it) that the first mathematical systematization of the movements of the heavenly bodies, that of Eudoxus (the system of homocentric or concentric spheres), was inspired by Plato, who set the following problem for astronomers: By the assumption of what uniform and ordered movements can the apparent motions of the planets be accounted for? As far as I know, there is no valid historical evidence for this — nothing better than the statement of a writer who lived no less than five hundred years after Eudoxus, namely Sosigenes, preserved by Simplicius in his Commentary on Aristotle's *De Caelo*.[1] (It seems clear to me that this particular statement is not attributed by Simplicius to Aristotle's pupil, Eudemus, who is mentioned earlier in the same sentence.)

But it is not only that there is no good evidence in favour of bringing in Plato: in fact, it is perfectly clear from Plato's own writings that he was quite uninterested in the details of the actual movements of the heavenly bodies (as in physical phenomena generally) and indeed specifically urged that they be ignored. By the time Plato came to write the *Laws*,[2] towards the end of his life, Eudoxus's theory was available to him, and he rejoices in the fact (which he speaks of as something recently learnt) that the sun, moon and planets never stray from perfect circular paths. Of course the Greek words *πλανῆται, πλάνετες*, actually mean "wanderers", but Plato now explicitly denies that they can be said to "wander". This was most gratifying to Plato, because he was very anxious to regard all the heavenly bodies as divine (he actually wanted prayers and sacrifices to be addressed to them), and their divinity would become much more acceptable in his eyes if they could be conceived as moving in perfect circles. Eudoxus had, so to speak, made astronomy respectable by explaining away (or so it seemed) the worst celestial irregularities. But earlier, when he wrote the *Republic* and the *Timaeus*, the system of Eudoxus was not yet known to Plato. The heavenly bodies, he says in the *Republic*,[3] are interesting solely as illustrations, *παραδείγματα*; in astronomy, as in geometry, we must proceed by abstractions, *προβλήμασι χρώμενοι*, and "we shall leave the things in the heavens alone" (*τὰ δ' ἐν τῷ οὐρανῷ ἐάσομεν*). Plato intends all this quite seriously, and he goes on at length about it, beginning

[1] P. 488, lines 21–4.

[2] See *Laws*, VII, 817E, 820E–822C; cf. X, 898C–899B; XII, 966E–967E.

[3] VII, 527DE (cf. AB), 528E–530C; cf. X, 616B–617B.

with a passage in which Socrates rebukes poor Glaucon for saying that astronomy is actually of use to the farmer, the seaman and the general.

To give more point to this, may I quote a short passage from Neugebauer's book, *The Exact Sciences in Antiquity* (p. 152):

> The often adopted notion that Plato "directed" research fortunately is not borne out by the facts. His advice to the astronomers to replace observations by speculation would have destroyed one of the most important contributions of the Greeks to the exact sciences. But if modern scholars had devoted as much attention to Galen or Ptolemy as they did to Plato and his followers, they would have come to quite different results and they would not have invented the myth about the remarkable quality of the so-called Greek mind to develop scientific theories without resorting to experiments or empirical tests.

From the time of Parmenides, early in the fifth century, and above all in the person of Plato and his numerous followers, a sustained attack was carried on against empirical science, as something unworthy of the real intellectual, as something immensely inferior to abstract thought. Sometimes of course you might, regrettably, be obliged to start with everyday phenomena, and even Plato recommends, in the *Symposium* (211B–212A), that the ultimate conception of beauty be reached by a series of stages, like the rungs of a ladder (ἐπαναβαθμοί), beginning with beautiful human bodies; but when you get to the end of the process, by which time you will have recognized that physical beauty is a trivial affair (σμικρόν τι, 210 C), you kick the ladder away.

Greek mathematical astronomy, however, could never have arisen except upon the basis of prolonged and detailed observation. Far too little work has been done on the observational side of Greek astronomy: I believe this neglected subject would greatly repay study. Mr. van der Waerden has said in his paper that the period of "precision astronomy" began after 300 B.C. It is true that the earliest *specifically recorded* observations *of the fixed stars* by Greek astronomers seem to be those of Aristyllus and Timocharis in the early third century B.C. But we have scarcely any sources of information about individual observations apart from Ptolemy's *Almagest*. Detailed observations of the apparent movements of the sun must have been carried on well before the end of the fifth century, and the work of Eudoxus and Callippus in the fourth century shows that a vast amount of observational data about sun, moon and planets was already available by the mid-fourth century. Mr. de Santillana, in his paper for this Symposium[1] (below, pp. 813 ff.), maintains that the tradition of Eudoxus's stay in Egypt and even of his learning the Egyptian language is to be accepted. If so, I think we may assume that Eudoxus's purpose was to avail himself of some of the empirical knowledge he needed. Mr. de Santillana says he was warned by a high authority (could it have been Mr. Neugebauer, I wonder) that the Egyptians "had no astronomy that could be worth anything" to Eudoxus. As far as our knowledge goes, it is certainly true that Egyptian astronomy was not at all a mathematical science. But Eudoxus could supply the mathematics himself: what he may have needed was the observational data. Did he perhaps go to Egypt because he believed that the records he wanted were available there? (And did he supplement this information from Babylonian sources?) It is true that apart from the cuneiform evidence we have very little specific information about pre-Greek astronomical observation. But equally we have no details of individual observations made or taken over by Eudoxus. Yet the solar, lunar and planetary theories of Eudoxus and his successors, as their otherwise unnecessary complexity shows, were specifically designed to *σώζειν τὰ φαινόμενα*, to "save the phenomena" — that is, to produce theories which would square with the observed facts. Ever since the fundamental work of Schiaparelli,[2] nearly a century ago, it has been realized that Eudoxus and his successors must have been calculating on the basis of a large body of empirical data, observed and noted down as accurately as the primitive instruments and recording methods of their day permitted. And this fact, so often kept out of sight, is every bit as important in the history of science as the fact that the homocentric spheres were complex and brilliant mathematical constructions, which receives all the attention nowadays.

So Greek scientific astronomy was born: a combination of applied mathematics and plain observation. It grew and flourished, although as far as I can see not very much more

[1] Utilizing the conclusions of his article, "Eudoxus and Plato. A study in chronology", *Isis*, XXXII (1947) 248–62.

[2] Well summarized by J. L. E. Dreyer, *A History of Astronomy from Thales to Kepler* (2nd ed., New York, 1953) Ch. 4. Copernicus, a mathematician first and foremost, realized very well that the Greek astronomers had to make observations of the planetary movements before producing the theories which accounted for them: see the *Letter against Werner*, trans. E. Rosen, *Three Copernican Treatises* (2nd ed., New York, 1959) 99.

independent observation was carried on after the time of Hipparchus (the third quarter of the second century B.C.), except for Ptolemy in the second quarter of the second century of the Christian era. As I have said, many people would regard this astronomy as the supreme Greek achievement in the scientific field. But the system of the *Almagest*, mathematically brilliant as it was, had fatal — not merely serious — defects: it did not calculate (or even provide a basis for calculating)[1] the actual distances of any of the heavenly bodies except the sun and moon; it treated each member of the solar system separately from all the others, without attempting to give an integrated picture; and above all it provided no foundation on which a Newton could construct a unified description of the universe in *physical* terms, for it was purely *geometrical* in character.[2] In only one important way, indeed, had it any real contact with physical fact: it provided a series of *bearings from the earth* for each celestial body separately, and nothing more.[3] As Mr. Needham has reminded us, on p. 143, the resulting geocentric synthesis "was in fact objectively wrong". This is often denied, with the addition that the modern system is only "very much simpler"; but this is true, if at all,[4] only if the Ptolemaic system is regarded as nothing but a series of geometrical hypotheses — which is exactly what it was intended to be, but its greatest deficiency is precisely that it was no more than that.

In conclusion, I would reiterate that we should not overlook the forces I have described in the classical world which were

[1] See, e.g. Dreyer, op. cit., pp. 188, 338.

[2] Nor was it part of the purpose of Ptolemy or any other ancient astronomer to give *reasons* for the introduction of epicycles and eccentrics — or of the equants which were the one thoroughly objectionable feature of the system, in pure theory, from the point of view of Copernicus: see the opening of his *Commentariolus* (Rosen, op. cit. p. 57). The one major part of the Ptolemaic system which could be shown to be seriously erroneous before Kepler and Galileo was the lunar theory: its defects are well described by Copernicus in the same work (Rosen, op. cit. pp. 71–2).

[3] It also gave, of course, the possibility of calculating the sizes and distances of sun and moon. (The moon's size and distance were worked out by Hipparchus and Ptolemy with a considerable degree of accuracy, in terms of the radius of the earth but the figures for the sun were vastly underestimated.)

[4] If we merely insert into the Ptolemaic system the known distances from the earth to the nearest stars, it becomes evident at once that since the "fixed stars" taken as a whole are required to rotate daily around the earth, many stars, especially those nearest the celestial equator, would have to move at a speed enormously faster than that of light, a concept which is irreconcilable with the principles of contemporary physics.

actively hostile to empirical science. If we do, we shall be making much the same mistake as the political historians who speak of the decay and disappearance of Greek democracy without ever asking the vital question: who wanted democracy and who wanted to destroy it?

The anti-scientific attitude of so many pagan thinkers was taken over in an intensified form by early Christianity. In later times it may be, as Mr. Lynn White maintains in his fascinating paper, that Christianity contributed factors making for technological advance which had been lacking in the pagan world. But in the first five Christian centuries at any rate (after that my own knowledge of the literature fails) I have found in the Fathers of the Church attitudes to Greek science ranging only from indifference to hatred, with sometimes a note of fear. At the best, the believer may know just so much of geometry and astronomy, for example, as may be useful for the understanding of the Scriptures: that is Origen; most of the other Fathers are much less accommodating.

From our own selfish point of view today, one of the worst consequences of all this is the total disappearance of a vast quantity of Greek and Roman scientific literature, much of it before the Empire became Christian. Only a fraction remains, and of that fraction a high proportion consists of the "standard works" described by Mr. Edelstein on p. 30, mostly saturated with teleology and the syncretistic religious outlook which had become widespread by the Antonine period. But enough survives of the more vigorous products of classical thought to give us a glimpse of a very real flowering of the scientific spirit.

Commentary by William D. Stahlman

The following comments are restricted to the paper by Mr. van der Waerden and to a portion of Mr. Sambursky's paper which deals with Greek astronomy.

I

We are indebted to Mr. van der Waerden for having summarized the basic ideas and methods of Babylonian and Greek astronomy in a compass almost unbelievably short. I am certain that Mr. van der Waerden has accomplished the impossible; for where others have required volumes, he has managed to set forth the essential and defining characteristics of these differing astronomies in a very few pages.

It is only natural in these circumstances that a commentator might easily forget the severe space limitations under which the paper was conceived and then proceed to base his comments on details which, of necessity, were omitted from the original paper. I hope that I shall not fall prey to this obvious error.

The 'arithmetical' nature of the textual evidence upon which we assess the Babylonian accomplishment in scientific — or, more precisely, mathematical — astronomy is by now so completely unquestioned that it in fact serves as the major defining characteristic of that effort. This cannot be overemphasized, and Mr. van der Waerden has clearly indicated that this is the principal procedural difference between Babylonian and Greek mathematical astronomies. Whereas the Greek approach was at once *geometrical* and *mechanical*, the Babylonian was *arithmetical* and, we may add, *non-mechanistic* in so far as present textual evidence allows of cosmological conclusions. This difference is, of course, all the more striking to a twentieth-century reader since we are immersed in a scientific matrix which judges the Greek approach to have been much more 'reasonable'. Yet it must be clear that this reaction is a bias based upon the obvious success of modern scientific method, and the historian's first regard must be to avoid confusing that which is merely 'understandable' with that which is truly 'reasonable'.

The problem, then, is to attempt an 'understanding' of the Babylonian proclivity for purely numerical relationships in astronomical phenomena, seemingly in the absence of causal explanations of a physical nature. One such attempt might consist in differentiating our desire for ascribing a *causal linkage* to natural events from a second, characteristically human, desire to *predict* future events. Both, clearly, are aims of modern scientific method. Science proceeds on the assumption that predictability and causal explanation are mutual products of any successful scientific explanation. Thus, one might argue, what we witness in Babylonian astronomy is the clear desire to predict certain natural phenomena, without our concomitant requirement for causal explanations. It appears to me that the difficulty in such an analysis lies not so much in what I have stated, but rather in the usual next step, which is to attempt to reconstruct the motivation for predicting celestial phenomena in the first place. That is, we might conclude that whereas the Greeks (at least by Hellenistic times) clearly associated these two desiderata, the Babylonians simply never arrived at a formulation of scientific method which extended beyond the prediction of future events based upon careful arithmetical analysis of sequences of preceding similar events. Such an explanation assumes, of course, that it is possible to predict certain events without having adequate causal explanations for them, and we know that this occurs regularly, even in modern times (e.g. in weather prediction).

We are on much less certain grounds when we next ask why the Babylonians directed their energies toward such predictions over literally centuries of time. While it is undeniable that astrology — first of a more general nature, then of the horoscopic variety prevalent in Hellenistic times — and astral or cosmic religion represent meaningful dimensions of Babylonian thought, their use as *the* major device in motivating mathematical astronomy remains unsatisfying. I submit for discussion that we need look only to the Babylonian accomplishment in pure mathematics to find a more plausible explanation. Mr. van der Waerden rightly calls attention to the mathematical genius of Apollonius and to the well-supported relation between his mathematical inventions and their later application to astronomical problems. Why may we not understand the development of Babylonian astronomy in a parallel manner? What is the textual evidence which would deny to the Babylonians the mathematical inventiveness and curiosity of an Apollonius? Indeed, the evidence appears to point in the opposite direction. One need only recall well-known texts of a purely number-theoretic nature (e.g. Plimpton 322) in order to demonstrate amply Babylonian mathematical curiosity and, presumably, the "great satisfaction" which the Babylonian mathematician felt upon solving interesting new arithmetical problems. It is surely not too rash to assume that the connexions between mathematicians and the development of mathematical astronomy as we know them from Greece applied with equal force in other cultures. The facts that (1) there are clear parallels between Greek geometrical thinking and Greek mathematical astronomy on the one hand, and Babylonian arithmetical thought and their subsequent mathematical astronomy on the other hand, and (2) that the mathematical techniques involved in Babylonian astronomy were developed and in general use long before their application to astronomy add important support to this interpretation. (Example: Venus tablets of Ammizaduga.)

The major difficulty in extending this inquiry is the lack of textual evidence of the type which could shed unambiguous light on the problem. Mr. van der Waerden points out the unfortunate paucity of texts from the period of approximately the sixth to the fourth centuries B.C. In view of the relative abundance of Seleucid era texts, which contain, as is well known, Babylonian mathematical astronomy *full-blown*, it is only reasonable to assume that the application of sophisticated mathematical techniques to astronomical problems began during the late New-Babylonian and Persian Empire periods in Babylonian political history. The fact is that the known texts from these immediately pre-Seleucid periods are of such a nature that they do not really help in deciphering the prehistory of Seleucid mathematical astronomy, and this is simply one datum which must be squarely faced.

Therefore, it appears to me that we are forced to admit our inability to go further into the motivation of Babylonian mathematical astronomy, until or unless new data from pre-Seleucid periods are uncovered.

II

Turning now to Mr. Sambursky's study of late Greek science, I should like to comment only on a part of his analysis of Ptolemy's astronomy.

In an as yet unpublished paper which I read to the American History of Science Society during their annual meeting in 1954, I analysed Ptolemy's *Planetary Hypotheses* with results which accord quite well with Mr. Sambursky's conclusions. Ever so briefly, these indicate that in later life Ptolemy advanced certain hypotheses concerning the physical nature of the cosmos-in-the-large which supplement and are logically consistent with his earlier *Almagest*, but which, on the surface, appear to differ radically from the *Almagest*. First, recall the character of the *Almagest*. There are many indications that the system of epicycles and deferent circles elaborated there was not intended by Ptolemy to be his description of celestial reality. On the contrary, everything points to the interpretation that Ptolemy used these geometrical devices simply to "save the phenomena" — simply as mathematical tools necessary in the prediction of celestial phenomena. To be sure, the Introduction to the *Almagest* makes it clear that Ptolemy agreed with some important Pythagorean and Aristotelian cosmological principles, as, for example, the fittingness of uniform circular motion for celestial bodies, and the central and stationary position of the earth. But beyond this, I would say that the system of the *Almagest* is that of a mathematician who saw his primary problem to be the construction of a mathematical model which would lend itself to the computation of accurate astronomical tables. Thus phrases like "let us assume" and "if we imagine" recur repeatedly in reference to the epicyclic models in the *Almagest*. As another example, after having proven the equivalence of eccentric motion and one type of epicyclic motion, Ptolemy makes it clear that he had the choice of selecting for certain purposes *either* a double epicycle *or* one epicycle combined with an eccentric deferent circle. The decision in favour of the latter was for mathematical simplicity, and considerations of physical reality are not mentioned. Again we might recall the glaring defect of the lunar theory of the *Almagest*, where, in order to make the epicycles accurately fit the moon's motion in longitude, the parallax and hence the apparent diameter of the moon in extreme values is far from the reality. This fact must have been known by Ptolemy, and it means that he must have known that his mathematical model was such that in this case one phenomenon was saved at the expense of another.

These examples could be multiplied, and with this in mind it is perhaps not surprising that he should devote another work to the problem of celestial reality. This is precisely the object of Book II of the *Planetary Hypotheses*. Ptolemy begins by saying that what he has given in Book I are the relationships between the motions of the heavenly bodies in terms of the circles they describe, and that now it remains to analyse the shapes of the bodies or spheres within which these orbits are traced. Here again the dicta of Aristotle are very apparent: the bodies which are associated with each of the celestial motions are not influenced from without; they are external and unchanging, as befits wonderful nature; they are such that the *rays* from the heavenly bodies penetrate them unhindered and unchanged — the nearest Ptolemy gets to calling them crystalline. The heavenly bodies are each round in shape (which both Plato and Aristotle had legislated), and each has a particular motion which *in some way reflects and indeed arises from a unique essence or power within it.*

It is this later emphasis to which I wish to direct attention, for it appears to me that, if I interpret it correctly, we must modify one of Mr. Sambursky's points. Ptolemy writes as follows:

> Physical considerations lead us to the assertion that the ethereal bodies allow no influence [to act upon them] and do not change — *even though, for all time, they differ from one another* — in accordance with that which befits their wonderful nature. . . .[1]

Thus, Ptolemy clearly states that it is his opinion that each heavenly body is quite *unique* — "for all time, they differ from one another" — and hence it should not be surprising that the astronomer cannot construct a "unitary picture". The sun, the moon, and the planets, *by their physical nature*, require separate treatments.

Because of the very clear and unambiguous statement of this view in his *Planetary Hypotheses*, it seems to me incorrect to force an interpretation upon the brief passage which Mr. Sambursky cites from Book XIII of the *Almagest* such that Ptolemy is "painfully aware of this unsatisfactory situation"; that is, that "sometimes he can barely disguise his disappointment over the lack of a unitary theory of the planetary system" (above, p. 66). Indeed, the passage cited from the *Almagest* makes the best sense when we admit (1) that Ptolemy was first and foremost a mathematician who was following the dictum of Plato to the effect that the very first thing which must be done is to "save the appearances" mathematically; (2) that Ptolemy was also deeply convinced of an actual, physically complete, dichotomy between terrestrial and celestial reality; and (3) that he was aware that the epistemological implications stemming from this dichotomy, plus the further assumption of the uniqueness of each heavenly body, would necessarily deprive his system of any unitary appearance. It is in this sense that it is incorrect to refer to the diverse schema of the *Almagest* as a "system". But this is quite different from, and I fail to find any indication of, a resultant "disappointment" on the part of Ptolemy. Indeed, I would go one step further and suggest that, on the basis of my reading of the texts, a much more plausible source of potential disappointment for Ptolemy would have been some negation of *parsimony* in his mathematical model. Time and again he suggests, as Mr. Sambursky points out, that *simplicity*,

[1] Cl. Ptolemaeus, *Opera astronomica minora* (ed. Heiberg, Leipzig, 1907, 111–12.

in the sense of parsimony, is the true architectural key to the cosmos.[1] The fact that Ptolemy does not complain of any lack of parsimony in the mathematical models of the *Almagest*, and that he explicitly constructs the most parsimonious cosmos of which he can conceive in his *Planetary Hypotheses* — the "economy edition" to which Mr. Sambursky refers — would suggest that he was not disappointed after all.

Commentary by G. E. L. Owen

The professed aim of this Symposium is to determine the intellectual, social and technical conditions under which scientific advances have been made. But such a programme assumes that we can identify a scientific advance when it has occurred, and that is a risky assumption. The papers of Mr. van der Waerden and Mr. Sambursky bring out two of the risks in it. But the risks, so far as I can see, are not of equal weight.

Mr. van der Waerden's paper compels us to ask: when the evidence for an early stage of science is late and scanty and confused — as it certainly is for the earliest Greek theories he discusses — what safe grounds can we have for hailing any scientific achievement? What, for example, can justify van der Waerden's flat claim to "*know* that Thales was a geometer as well as an astronomer" or "that he predicted a solar eclipse"? What we know, if we know anything, is that part at least of Thales's prowess in geometry is a piece of pious interpretation by Aristotle's pupil Eudemus.[2] And since Eudemus's *History of Geometry* is pretty certainly the source of all that is recorded about Thales's skill in this field, we had better talk warily about the rest too.[3] As for Thales the "astronomer", van der

[1] References to Ptolemy's plea for parsimony are numerous. One which Professor Sambursky does not mention occurs in Book II of the *Planetary Hypotheses* where Ptolemy explains his rejection of Aristotle's counteracting spheres. Such spheres, Ptolemy argues, would waste nature's substance, and, we are reminded, Mercury and Venus occupy the space between the moon and the sun, ". . . in order that this space, which is so large according to appearances and proofs from the distances, should not remain empty, as if nature had forgotten and deserted it". Nature is parsimonious, *physically speaking*, and thus by the time he wrote this Ptolemy has extended his notion from mathematical models to physical reality.

[2] Proclus *in Euclid* (ed. Friedlein) I, p. 352, 14–17; cf. D. R. Dicks, *Classical Quarterly*, N.S. IX (1959) 301–4.

[3] *Fragmente der Vorsokratiker*, ed. Diels-Kranz (8th ed.) 11A 20.

Waerden's argument that "he seems to be the author of a book on Nautical Astronomy" goes blandly beyond our earliest authority, the patchwork history of Diogenes Laertius. Diogenes knew a more plausible rumour which ascribed the book to an obscure Samian — the man's very obscurity makes him the likelier candidate.[1] Then the notorious prediction of the eclipse: surely this has been the focus of enough controversy to be left out of our pretensions to knowledge?[2] Greek science, with the exception of prognostic medicine and post-Eudoxan astronomy, was not concerned with establishing methods of prediction. A theory which yields predictions is likely to have two virtues: it makes experimental checks possible and it increases our control of the environment; and neither of these concerns lay close to the heart of the Greek scientist. So tales of prediction belong to the magical rather than to the scientific tradition — as when Anaxagoras, who lived over a century later, was credited with predicting the fall of a meteorite in which he expressed interest.[3] As to the claim that Thales's prediction "can only be explained if we assume that he had some knowledge of Babylonian methods" — alas, it cannot be explained on that assumption either.[4]

Nor is van der Waerden more cautious with Thales's successors. Diogenes Laertius's statement that Anaximander invented the gnomon falls foul of a far earlier and better authority, Herodotus[5]; and even if the report that Anaximander "constructed a sphere" had better grounds than the unsupported word of that same Diogenes, it would still be wishful thinking to conclude from this that "Anaximander had a workshop in which astronomical instruments were manufactured". Indeed, when we have less than thirty words left of Anaximander's book how can we know that "Anaximander constantly [*constantly!*] used the language of the workshop"? I shall not consider the argument that Pythagoras himself was an "astrological fatalist" or dissect the evidence by which we "know for certain that . . . the Pythagoreans taught that the stars are divine, intelligent, living beings [and] that the souls are in eternal motion like the stars". Mr. van der Waerden's approach to late and suspect evidence is a model indeed to other workers in the field — a model of charity, scarcely of historical scholarship.

[1] Op. cit. 11A 1.

[2] See e.g. Otto Neugebauer, *Exact Sciences in Antiquity* (2nd ed.), pp. 142–3.

[3] *Vorsokratiker*, ed. Diels-Kranz, 59A 1 and 11.

[4] Neugebauer, loc. cit.

[5] Herodotus, II, 109.

Mr. Sambursky's rich paper forces a different question upon us. When there is plenty of contemporary evidence, as there is for Hellenistic science and philosophy, how cautious should we be in acclaiming some scientific achievement when — so far as we can tell, at least — neither the author nor his contemporaries recognized it as any such thing? Both the speakers I am discussing want to date certain important discoveries very much earlier than is usual. Van der Waerden, as appears from his paper and more explicitly from his book *Science Awakening*,[1] believes that Thales launched Greek geometry with a fairly clear (innate?) idea of what would count as an Euclidean proof. Sambursky, with more and better evidence available to him, holds (more plausibly, as I think) that we were on the brink of the scientific renaissance in the sixth century A.D. He maintains that the discoveries characteristic of Hellenistic science failed to find due recognition because of political upheavals and the repressive attitude of Christians and neo-Platonists. It is chiefly to Sambursky's paper that I am asked to address myself. So let me recall the advances that he detects in late Greek science, that is to say, the areas in which he thinks science had by then begun to free itself from Aristotle.

He says that Aristotle's picture of the physical world came to be challenged or modified as the result of three main influences. One of these influences was the development of astronomy whereby astronomers turned their efforts to saving the phenomena by "appropriate geometrical assumptions to which the physical content, the unity of the picture, was sacrificed". A second influence was the progress of mechanics and a growing "mechanical-mindedness" which led to the modification of certain Aristotelian concepts and in particular of Aristotle's analysis of potentiality. A third was the rise of new philosophical systems, especially those of the Stoics and neo-Platonists, which threw up fresh ideas about causal connexion and incidentally originated the notion of action at a distance. I shall discuss some questions arising under these three heads of Sambursky's argument.

Mathematical astronomy

On this head Mr. Stahlman has anticipated some of my questions, and I shall accordingly confine myself to one point. In Sambursky's analysis the Ptolemy of the *Almagest* is grouped with Eudoxus, not with Aristotle. His problems and methods

[1] Especially p. 89.

are geometrical rather than physical, and he is "resigned to an attitude which could be called that of a relativist or rather a positivist: we must do our best to give the simplest description possible of complex phenomena which in any case are outside that region where the usual notions of understanding or explanation are applicable". Now it is notorious that in the opening chapters of the first book of the *Almagest* Ptolemy defends certain hypotheses of Aristotelian physics, to the effect that the sky and fixed stars rotate about a central stationary earth. And he defends these propositions even while admitting that, *so far as saving the stellar phenomena is concerned*, there may be nothing to choose between his hypotheses and those of the heliocentrists.[1] So here, some would say, he shows the cloven hoof, and Sambursky's general account of the *Almagest* must be modified accordingly.

But it is worth noticing the form of Ptolemy's reply to the heliocentrists. Of his two opening arguments, one is strongly *a priori* and depends on the Aristotelian theory of natural places. The other, which contends that to an observer on a moving earth the intervals between the stars would seem to vary, is equally unsatisfactory. It denies his opponents an option that he subsequently takes up himself; for it can be met by supposing that the distance of the earth from the fixed stars is sufficiently large in comparison with the size of its orbit, and this is the kind of proportion that Ptolemy himself postulates as holding between that distance and the diameter of the earth. So far, indeed, Ptolemy shows small signs of Sambursky's "positivist, working to save the phenomena". But in the seventh chapter of the book he concedes that these arguments may carry no conviction and produces a third; and here I think Sambursky's Ptolemy shows his hand. For this last argument, though it does not profess to save the celestial phenomena better than a heliocentric hypothesis, does claim to save certain sublunary phenomena with which that hypothesis could not be squared. The argument is simply that if the earth were moving at great speed all the loose furniture on its surface would be swept backwards.[2] I am not concerned with the adequacy of this rejoinder. I suggest merely that the method to which Ptolemy turns for the clinching refutation of his opponents is, *mutatis mutandis*, the method which Sambursky takes to be characteristic of the *Almagest*. *Mutatis mutandis*; for the observations that are saved here are not the "complex phenomena which are

[1] *Syntaxis*, ed. Heiberg, p. 24, 14–16. [2] Op. cit. pp. 24, 14 – 26, 3.

outside that region where the usual notions of understanding or explanation are applicable". Ptolemy is generalizing from our everyday knowledge of the behaviour of bricks and clods. But the impulse to find the simplest description that will save the phenomena is clear enough.

Potentiality and fitness

Sambursky maintains that "the increasing mechanical-mindedness of later Antiquity" made scientists dissatisfied with Aristotle's account of potentiality. It was improved by importing a "physical or technical concept", *epitedeiotes* or fitness. The analysis of "fitness", as Philoponus explains the notion, seems to be as follows.[1] Although it is true that doors *can* be opened by pushing them with a stick, it does not follow of any door that it *will* be opened by such pushing, *unless* it is not jammed, not nailed up, etc. These further conditions which are introduced in the "unless"-clause are summed up by saying: unless the door is *fit* or suitable to be so opened. Wax balls *can* be moved by the motion of an insect inside; it does not follow of any wax ball that it *will* be so moved, unless it is not soft, etc. Now Aristotle's conception of potentiality, we are told, serves merely to explain the "can" which occurs in the first clause of such sentences. It does not cover those further conditions of actualization which are specified in the "unless"-clauses at the end. So the notion of fitness, which does profess to cover such conditions, is a valuable addition to the arsenal of scientific concepts.

One may wonder, in general, whether it is illuminating to import a concept which suggests a positive condition, but which turns out to do duty for an indefinite range of conditions which are largely negative and which vary from case to case. But we can make the difficulty more precise. In what sense, after all, is this concept an improvement on Aristotle's careful explanation of different types of potentiality?

It will be recalled how Aristotle takes care to point out that, while it is true that men *can* do long division, it does not follow of a given man that he will produce a long division sum however much he wants to, *unless* he has been trained. But if he has been trained then it is true of him, in a *stronger* sense of "can", that he can do long division.[2] "Unless the man is

[1] Philoponus *in De generatione et corruptione*, ed. Vitelli, p. 149, 10–14; *in De anima*, ed. Hayduck, pp. 107, 26–109, 6.

[2] E.g. *De anima*, 417a 21–b 2, 429b 5–10, *Physics* 255a 33–b 5.

trained", or "unless the door is not jammed": the parallel with the account of "fitness" does not need pointing, But Aristotle's account does not stop here. He turns his attention, in effect, to the different kinds of "unless"-clause that may appear in such contexts. Such clauses indicate conditions (lack of training in a man, jamming in a door, etc.) under which a thing can not, in the stronger sense of "can", do something that it might reasonably be expected to do. They indicate *adunamiæ*, disabilities. But, Aristotle remarks, the disabilities are very various in kind. Men as a species can procreate. But a boy cannot procreate yet, a man cannot procreate at a certain time, a eunuch cannot procreate at any time. To say that even in the most favourable circumstances a man will not procreate if he is under age, or momentarily disabled, or permanently sterilized, is to mention three different types of disability.[1] Such distinctions are simply masked if we replace the conditional clauses by the single requirement "unless he is *fit*". So how is this requirement an improvement on Aristotle's analysis?

(Sambursky says that "fitness" was designed to provide a "sufficient condition for actuality" whereas Aristotle's "potentiality" provided only a "necessary condition". But I doubt whether he is right to say this. It certainly does not follow, if a door is fit to be moved, that it will be moved. The fitness, like the potentiality, is one of a set of conditions which are *jointly* sufficient for the door to open.[2])

Moreover, whether or not this is an improvement on Aristotle's analysis, how closely is it connected with an increasing interest in mechanics? One of the illustrations which Sambursky quotes from Philoponus is indeed that of a pillar supporting a wall. But another is a children's game and a third is a stock example of the use of a liquid dye.[3] Can we be sure, in brief, that the concept of fitness is some kind of conceptual advance? Can we be sure, in particular, that it is a scientific advance?

Causality and action at a distance

Sambursky maintains that, when Stoic physics had led to a "strict determinism", "the mystical trend of neo-Platonism originated the idea of action at a distance". I shall end by discussing this latter claim.

[1] *Metaphysics*, 1019b 15–19.

[2] For Aristotle see further *Metaphysics*, Θ, 7, especially 1049a 5–8.

[3] For Aristotle's own use of "mechanical" illustrations cf. Bouitz, *Index Aristotelicus*, 124a 61–102.

Sambursky tells me that the evidence on which he stands here is a passage of Iamblichus quoted in Simplicius' commentary on the *Categories*.[1] The question under discussion is whether, when A acts on B, A's acting and B's being acted on are one and the same thing. Porphyry had replied that even in the case in which A pushes and B is pushed the two must be sharply distinguished. Iamblichus objected that this reply gave too much away:

> It does not follow that what is true of one sort of action is true of every sort. It was wrong to start from these *end*-actions, hitting and pushing. We must not give the Stoics the very point on which we constantly differ from them, namely that what acts acts in virtue of some proximity and contact.
>
> [*A: contact is not a necessary condition of action.*] It is better to say that not everything acts by proximity and contact, that action depends rather on the appropriateness [fitness, *epitedeiotes*] of the agent to the patient. Many things with which we are all familiar operate without making contact. Even in those cases in which we see that the agent needs to be juxtaposed with its object we must say that the contact is not essential but merely a consequence of the fact that the things which have the power of acting or being acted on have spatial positions (for this is characteristic of bodies and of things having such powers). On the other hand, in cases where the presence of an interval between two bodies does not prevent the one from acting and the other from being acted on, in these cases the activity can take place with neither break nor hindrance. Thus the strings of the lyre are in sympathy though they are at a distance from each other, and a man within range of the fire receives its form even at a distance.
>
> [*B: nor is contact a sufficient condition of action.*] On the other hand, many things do not act even when they are brought into contact: a plaster or any other medical application, for example, if it is applied to a stone.
>
> Consequently, given that in many cases what is in contact does not act, and that in many other cases what acts is not in contact, acting in the strictest sense of the word cannot be just pushing and hitting. Even when we see things hitting other things it cannot be the contact that is responsible. Even in these cases it is the affinity in the agent that furnishes the power to act.

This is an impressive passage, to be sure, and uncommonly clear-headed for Iamblichus; but it is also a very puzzling one. How can he have been content to quote instances of action at a distance which his Stoic opponents would flatly refuse to

[1] *In Cat.*, ed. Kalbfleisch, pp. 302, 28–303, 9.

recognize? Iamblichus knew as well as we do that for the Stoics the heat of a fire was transmitted by physical intermediaries which filled the whole intervening space. Why was he not more careful in defending his original contribution to science?

Because, I submit, it was not, and was not seen as, any such thing. Iamblichus was not building for the future but arguing for some converted contemporaries. He was not pioneering, but taking a fairly perfunctory hand in a debate as old as Aristotle.

This was the course of the debate. Aristotle's *Physics* ends with a proof that all movements in the physical world depend ultimately on one source of motion. There is one First Mover, who keeps the sky and fixed stars turning. The problem is how the First Mover can be supposed to move anything at all; for Aristotle argues that such a Mover must be wholly without parts or extension in space, yet the whole analysis of motion that has been carried out in the preceding seventh book of the *Physics* has gone to show that motion can occur only when there is contact between the thing moved and that which imparts the motion. And the definition of "contact" given earlier in the same work restricts this relation to material bodies having extension in space.[1]

In the *Physics* the problem is left unsolved. We are told that the First Mover is somehow located at the edge of the universe,[2] but we are not told how it can have contact with what it moves. But elsewhere Aristotle offers a solution. It turns partly on an ambiguity in the Greek verb *haptesthai*, "to be in contact" or "to touch". Contact, he now suggests, may sometimes be asymmetrical, a one-way relation; for there is a sense of "touch" in which something may touch me not by coming into physical contact with me but by touching my emotions; and in this way too it can cause me to act.[3] In the twelfth book of the *Metaphysics* the First Mover is said to act in this way on the outer heaven. The heaven, Aristotle concludes, loves what moves it; and thus it is moved without having spatial contact with its mover.

This suggestion sparked off a brisk controversy that began with Aristotle's friends and pupils. Theophrastus left the broader use of "contact" unchallenged but thought the particular explanation of the sky's motion unhelpful: why should love of a non-physical non-moving thing like the First Mover induce the sky to spin rather than stay still?[4] Another

[1] 226b 21–23. [2] 267b 6–9. [3] *De generatione et corruptione*, 323a 12–33.
[4] *Metaphysics*, 7b 23–8a 2.

pupil, Eudemus, kept the First Mover but discarded the wider use of "contact". Contact, he maintained, is always physical contact, and when one moving body moves another they must always be in contact either directly or via physical intermediaries that are moved.[1] And then in their turn the Stoics took up the debate. They embraced Eudemus's restricted use of "contact"[2]; and they generalized his account of interaction between moving bodies so as to make it cover all causal connexions. On the way they had to deal with Aristotle's example of action which does not depend on physical contact. That example was a case of *psychological* reaction, and all such cases were now firmly assimilated or reduced to simple physical interaction. Chrysippus argued that the mind just as much as the body is corporeal and capable of physical contact.[3] A man whose emotions are touched is no doubt exhibiting some psychological disposition, just as a moving cylinder exhibits a disposition to roll if pushed. But such dispositions must be brought into play at the given time by some causal interaction that involves contact between bodies. The cylinder must be pushed, the man must be at the end of a causal chain that terminates spatially and temporally in a physical state of the man himself.[4] It was arguments like these that provoked the neo-Platonists and set off that old quarrel with the Stoics to which Iamblichus refers.

Aristotle had derived much of his own theory of the First Mover from Plato's *Timaeus*, and the neo-Platonists borrowed largely from both of them. For neo-Platonism, only things on the lowest level of existence stand in spatial relationships with each other. All the higher forms of causal connexion, those forms for which the texts of Plato and Aristotle had supplied so much of the model, are quite independent of any spatial contact. And just as Aristotle, in defence of his own transcendent first cause, had tried to break down the requirement of physical contact between mover and moved by citing everyday cases of psychological reaction, so Plotinus, in defence of his own views of psychological causation, tried to break down the same requirement by discovering action at a distance in everyday

[1] Fragments, ed. Wehrli, 123a–b.

[2] Plutarch, *De comm. not.*, 1080e. That the Stoics did not discard the notion of contact as Sambursky supposes (*Physics of the Stoics*, p. 96), is further proved by the passage quoted above from Iamblichus; cf. the following footnote and Stobæus *Ecl.* I, 154, 8–14.

[3] *Stoicorum veterum fragmenta*, ed. von Arnim, II, 790.

[4] Op. cit. II, 974.

states of affairs familiar to the Stoics. The universe is said by the Stoics to be a living creature: but in any living creature there can be interaction between distant parts. Hair, nails, horns can affect and be affected by what occurs in a remote part of the creature *without any intervening part being affected.*[1] Whether Plotinus meant by this that nails grow without any detectable change in the surrounding flesh, or that we can feel a pain in our nails without any communicating part of the body feeling the pain, is not clear. But his motives and interests are clear, and they are those of his follower Iamblichus. Iamblichus's instances of action at a distance are put forward in the same cause and can be matched by others in Plotinus. None of them would begin to look like evidence to a Stoic.

In short I find it hard to see Iamblichus's argument as anything but a conventional contribution to an old debate, a debate which had certainly taken fresh shape with the emergence of fresh schools but whose motivation was at no stage scientific. The reasonings of Aristotle and Plotinus on this head belong rather to theology than to physics; and when we recall the context of exact science in which the concept of action at a distance was canvassed in the seventeenth and again in the nineteenth century, it comes near to an act of heroic faith to see any prefiguring of that idea in the religious confusions of the Roman Empire.

Though, for my part, I should think a ration of heroic faith essential to our inquiries. There are risks in it, but (unlike those we run in failing to assess the worth of the evidence) they seem worth the taking.

Commentary by J. P. Vernant

My remarks will take as their point of departure some of Mr. van der Waerden's conclusions. Mr. van der Waerden underlines the fact that, from the beginning, Greek astronomy showed trends which opposed it to that of the Babylonians. This phenomenon seems all the more surprising since, in this sphere, the Greeks were offshoots of the East: they owed to it the observations and methods which, following a more or less legendary tradition, enabled Thales to predict an eclipse, and the instruments, like the gnomon, which Anaximander brought to Sparta. But the first Ionian natural philosophers transformed the knowledge which they had thus borrowed very profoundly,

[1] Plotinus, *Enneads*, IV, 4, 32.

to build up a new type of astronomy. In the first place, it was an astronomy based on geometry, no longer on arithmetic. The Ionians saw the world-order in a spatial framework; they were able to represent the positions, sizes, distances and movements of the stars by geometrical constructions; they sometimes made mechanical models. In the second place, while Babylonian astronomy remained integrated with an astral religion and aimed at astrological predictions, that of the Greeks was presented at once as a *theoria*, a body of knowledge having as its aim the systematization of the universe, and with no end other than itself. Perhaps I would be prepared, on this point, to go beyond Mr. van der Waerden's conclusions. It seems to me that one cannot say that the Pythagoreans, any more than the Ionians, had an astrology in the normal sense.

The introduction of geometry to, and secularization of, astronomical thought, such were the two aspects which essentially characterized the Greek phenomenon. That these two aspects are interdependent is demonstrated, in a striking manner, by Anaximander's example. By placing the earth in the centre of the universe, by affirming that it thus remained motionless, not needing any support because, being at an equal distance from all points of the celestial circumference, it had no reason to move in one direction rather than in another, Anaximander made cosmology geometrical; he situated the physical world in a purely mathematical space, consisting of reversible and symmetrical relationships. But, at the same time, he separated himself from all the ancient cosmogonies which distinguished between cosmic 'levels' devoted to different divine powers, which attributed religious virtues to the various directions of space, and which represented the earth as emerging from the primordial waters (as again did Thales) or as founded in the subterranean depths of Erebos (as did Hesiod). With Anaximander, this mythical imagery, now useless, disappears: to understand the position and the stability of the earth, it is sufficient to know that all the radii of a circle are equal.

How can this intellectual mutation be explained? Mr. van der Waerden's reply seems not so much to bring a solution as to pose a problem. One will readily agree that the Greeks were geometers (one could, however, dispute the contention that they were, during the period considered, "mechanics"). But why? It cannot be a mere question of ethnic characteristics: the other Indo-Europeans do not manifest analogous gifts; besides, the Ionian Greeks, who founded the first cosmology, were precisely the most hybrid: Herodotus attributed to Thales a "Phoenician" origin. The phenomenon is a cultural, not a racial, one. It arises out of a psycho-social analysis putting astronomy, and more generally Ionian physics of which it is a part, into its context of civilization, into the spiritual framework proper to the seventh-century Greek.

From this point of view, a primary factor is to be noted. In the system of the Greek *Polis*, writing, as an intellectual tool, assumed a social function and took on a psychological character quite different from that in the kingdoms of the Middle East. The Greek case was here a privileged one because it presented successively the two forms of writing; the Mycenean world used, indeed, a form of writing — the linear B — reserved for professionals, for a class of specialist scribes, whose role was to establish as accurate a computation as possible of the various aspects of social life, rigorously controlled and regulated by the palace: not only economic production and the exchange, but also the organization of the religious calendar, the celebration of prescribed dates with the requisite rites. With the downfall of Mycenean power, about the twelfth century, this writing disappeared at the same time as the class of scribes involved in the system of palace economy. When the Greeks re-introduced writing, between the ninth and eighth centuries, by borrowing it from the Phoenicians, it was not only a different type of writing, phonetic and no longer syllabic, but a radically different cultural fact: no longer the speciality of a class of scribes, but the instrument of a communal culture, the intellectual link between all those who constituted the human community of the city. The social and psychological significance of writing was thus, in some way, inverted: writing no longer had as its object the production of archives for the king, enclosed in the secrecy of the palace; it fulfilled henceforward the function of an agent of publicity; it revealed, exposed to all the citizens, knowledge formerly forbidden or reserved for certain religious 'orders' (*gene*). To use Greek expressions again, writing allowed the making communal, *es koinon*, of privileges which, until then, had rightfully belonged to certain individuals like the *basileus*. The need to draw up laws, manifested from the beginning of the *Polis*, was very significant in this respect. Drawn up, written on a *pinax* exposed to the view of everyone, the laws escaped from the private authority of the *basileis*, whose function was to 'speak' the law, to become public property, truly communal, a general rule superior to each individual and applicable to all equally. Because of the publicity conferred by writing, *diké*, without ceasing to appear as an ideal value, was in a position to act on a properly human level, to be realized in a legal system, *nomos*, submitted to discussion and revision, modifiable by the decision of the assembly. When in their turn individuals decided to make public their learning by means of writing: either in the form of books like those that Pherecydes and Anaximander were the first to write; or in the form of *parapegma*, of monumental inscription on stone, analogous to those which the city erected in the names of its magistrates and its priests (certain citizens had astronomical abjurations or chronological tables inscribed); or in the form of a *pinax*, of a chart or annotated map of the world; their ambition was not to share with others a personal opinion, but, in giving their message *es to koinon*, to make it the common property of the whole city, a standard, like the law, to be recognized by all. Divulged, their wisdom acquired objectivity; it became 'truth'. It was no longer a question of a religious secret, reserved for a few members of the elite, favoured by divine grace. It is certainly true that the truth of the sage, like the religious secret, was a revelation of the essential, the unveiling of a superior reality which was beyond by far the greater part of mankind: but by delivering it up to writing it was torn away from a closed circle of secrets and exposed in the full light of day to the eyes of the whole city; it showed a recognition that it was by right accessible to all men, an agreement to submit it, like political matters, to the judgement of all, with the hope that it would be definitively accepted and recognized by all.

Thus, within the framework of a city where the *logos*, the word (understood in the sense of discussion, of controversial debate), became the political instrument par excellence, writing, which reproduced the spoken word and ceased to be a trade secret of scribes to become the common property of all the citizens, imposed on the creations of the mind the very standards of public life.

Henceforward argument, controversy, even polemics, were to become the rule of the intellectual game as of the political one. Just as the whole magistracy, whatever might be the prestige of its head, was subjected to *euthunai*, to a 'rendering of account' before the whole of the city, in the same manner the 'knowledge' given to the community by writing 'rendered account' and demonstrated its veracity by dialectic procedures.

But perhaps one can go even further. To this secularization, to this rationalization of social life, seems aptly to correspond the advancement of a new conception of space. It will be observed that the expression *es koinon* applied to that which, being of common interest to the city, must be the object of a public debate, is duplicated by another which has the same meaning: *es meson*. The Greeks maintained that certain deliberations, or certain privileges of the king, or the power (the *arché*, the *kratos*, the *dunasteia*) could not belong to any particular person, but must be deposited "in the centre", "in the middle". The recourse to a spatial image to express the consciousness which the city has of itself, the sentiment of its existence as a political community, has no simple value of comparison. It reflects the birth of an entirely new social space. The urban constructions are no longer, in fact, grouped as formerly around a royal fortress, surrounded by walls. The town is now centred on the *agora*, common land, seat of the *Hestia Koiné* — a public place where problems of general interest were debated. It is the town itself which is surrounded by walls, protecting and circumscribing in its totality the human group which constitutes it. There, where the royal citadel used to stand, a private and privileged residence, it erected temples which were opened for a public cult. On the ruins of the palaces, on the Acropolis which it henceforward consecrated to the gods, it is still itself that the city projects on to the plane of the sacred as it realizes itself, on the profane level, in the space of the Agora. This urban framework, which men like Hippodamos of Miletus — town-planner and politician — still attempted to rationalize, defined in fact a mental space, discovered a new spiritual horizon, which we must define in a more precise manner. In the centre of the city, the agora constitutes a public and common area: all those who go there show themselves, inasmuch as they are citizens, to be equals: *homoioi*, *isoi*. However different they may be in the concrete terms of social life, they find themselves, by their very presence in that socialized and 'political' space, in relationships of symmetry, equality, and reciprocity. It is what is implied, in particular, by the institution of the *Hestia Koiné*, of the Common Hearth. Installed in the *Prytaneion*, on the *agora*, the public hearth is a symbol of the community: as the centre, it is, in some measure, at an equal distance from the domestic hearths of the divers families, which it had to represent equally without identifying itself with one rather than another. A central, public, egalitarian, and symmetrical area, but also a secularized one; made so by confrontation and argument, and which was in opposition to the religious space of the acropolis as the realm of the *hosia*, of the profane affairs of the human city, was to that of the *hiera*, of the sacred interests which concern the divine.

Thus was projected and expressed in space the new conception of the social order which characterized the city. Society was no longer formed of a hierarchical pyramid having the king at its summit, an exceptional personage, intermediary between the gods and men. All the citizens were situated on the same level, and the level was subject to a regular order, to a law of symmetry and reciprocity, as is fitting for equals.

To mark the relationship between this 'geometrization' of social thought in the Greek cities and the geometrical orientation of nascent astronomy, it would be necessary to compare, for sense and vocabulary, the fragments of Anaximander on the position of the earth — which, he says, remains *mese*, *en meso*, central, in the middle, by reason of its *homoiotes*, its similitude or symmetry, such that it does not suffer the domination, *kratos*, of anything — with a political tale such as that of Herodotus (III, 142, 14–15). At the death of Polycrates, Mæandrius, designated by the tyrant as his successor, called all the citizens to an assembly; he recalled that he had not been able to approve Polycrates reigning despotically over men who were his *homoioi*; he decided then to depose the *arché* (he could say, the *Kratos*) *es meson*, and to proclaim the *isonomia*: the equal participation of everyone in the power. That this preoccupation with the centre should have had, with the first Ionian philosophers, a political significance, can be seen again in Herodotus (I, 170). Thales proposed to all the Ionians, after the disasters they had undergone, that they have a single council *en bouleuterion*, which was to be held at Teos, since this isle is situated at the centre of the Ionian channel, *meson ionies*. The Greeks were conscious enough of this analogy between social and astronomical space to call the earth *Hestia*, precisely by virtue of its central position, and to apply the term *cosmos* to the harmonious ordering of a city, even before using it to designate the physical universe.

Discussion

J. Millás-Vallicrosa

In his excellent paper, Mr. van der Waerden has pointed out the dichotomy of ancient astronomy: the arithmetical approach of the Babylonians and the geometrical approach of the Greeks. The author does not explain the cause of this difference of outlook, but I do not think that it can be explained, in the way attempted by Mr. Vernant, by referring to the esoteric, non-public character of ideographic writing, as opposed to the open character of phonetic writing. There were cultures like the Ugaratic, otherwise similar to the Babylonian culture, which made use of phonetic writing; also bilingual inscriptions have been discovered in ideographic and phonetic scripts. I believe that, rather than the two approaches mentioned being in opposition, one might speak of a true and progressive evolution. At first astronomical observations were interpreted in a magical, religious or imaginative manner; later, especially in the case of the Babylonians, over a period of many centuries, astronomical observations and measurements were made in order to obtain tables and ephemerides, often to serve the purposes of astrology. With these measurements and observed quantities the Greeks were able to attempt the construction of diagrams and figures to represent the movements. The arithmetical data were antecedent to geometrical representation.

W. Hartner

On p. 50 Mr. van der Waerden says that Thales predicted a solar eclipse and that this can only be explained if we assume that he had some knowledge of Babylonian methods. He obviously refers to Herodotus's rather dubious and confused account which I believe it would be wise to reject as a fairy-tale devoid of historical interest. Without devoting too much time to the matter, I found out years ago that the arguments supporting such an assumption are utterly weak: since systematic observation of eclipses in Babylon did not start before the time of Nabonassar, the statistical material collected until the time of Thales (about 150 years) cannot possibly have sufficed to yield the knowledge of the exeligonos cycle, according to which solar eclipses recur in approximately the same place after 57 years and 1 month. To the best of my knowledge, there is no evidence of the exeligonos cycle in Babylonian astronomy at such an early date. But even if we assume that Thales knew the cycle, he could not have used it for his prediction because, on account of the very considerable variation in latitude of the curves of centrality, the eclipses preceding the "Thales eclipse" in the exeligonos were not visible in the region of Ionian Asia Minor. For further details I refer to the study of the subject to be published by my collaborator and friend Mr. Schramm.

W. Artelt

Mr. van der Waerden argues from Diogenes's statement that Anaximander made a globe: "Thus, we see that Anaximander had a workshop . . ." (above, p. 51). That may have been so, but it need not have been so. If we are told that someone made something that does not always mean he made it with his own hands and his own tools or in his own workshop. For example, if we hear that a prince erected a monument that does not mean that he had his own workshop.

J. W. Herivel

Mr. Sambursky has suggested that the Greek failure to achieve any axiomatic formulation of physical principles contributed towards the ultimate stagnation of their physics. I suggest that the existence of Archimedes's works *On the Equilibrium of Planes* and *On Floating Bodies* provides examples of just such a formulation of two physical subjects. Moreover, the spirit of these writings of Archimedes had a decisive influence on the development of Galileo's, and then Newton's, thought in dynamics. It seems, therefore, that the correct *method* of mathematical physics was available to the Greeks from 212 B.C. onwards. That they made no use, or extension, of it was then most likely due to their failure to supply the proper postulatory basis for a correct theory of motion to replace that of Aristotle. This is especially surprising in the case of Archimedes himself, who of all the Greeks would seem to have been the most likely to supply such a theory, considering his genius both in mathematics and mechanics. That he did not do so may then have been due to his lack of a certain philosophical caste of mind which we find in Galileo, Newton, Maxwell and Einstein in company with mathematical genius and physical intuition. In any case, I suggest that the fact that Archimedes either did not, or could not, supply a correct theory of motion must be regarded as one of the most important factors leading to the ultimate stagnation of Greek physics, and through it Greek science as a whole.

A. P. Yushkevich

I will make a few comments on Mr. van der Waerden's paper. His exposition of the ideas and methods of ancient astronomy is excellent, although I think that the relationship between rational astronomy and Greek religious thought was more exactly presented in Mr. Vernant's commentary.

But the explanation of the progress of Greek astronomy (it would be better to say Hellenistic) given by Mr. van der Waerden seems to me to be insufficient. Mr. van der Waerden poses the following question: why was it the Greeks rather than the Romans, the Egyptians or the Syrians who perfected graphic and analytic methods, as well as the instruments indispensable to the development of ancient astronomy? And he replies: "The only explanation I can find is, that the Greeks were born geometers and engineers." I will leave aside the fact that the Greeks were also arithmeticians and sometimes even admirable calculators (Archimedes). The essential point is that if one explains the progress of the sciences by the specific national faculties of the scientists who practise them, one loses oneself in a labyrinth of insoluble questions. It is well known that the hub of science moved, from the third and second centuries before our era, from Greece properly speaking to the Hellenistic countries, Alexandria in particular. Was it that the Alexandrian Greeks suddenly became more endowed with talent than their compatriots in other countries? And why did the Greeks of the third and fourth centuries of our era cease to make new scientific and technical inventions?

The same question might be asked of other nations, countries and periods. Many scientific and technical inventions were made in the countries of Islam until the end of the Middle Ages; then followed a long period of scientific stagnation which is only now ending. No great physico-mathematical discoveries were found in Russia before the eighteenth century, yet, at the beginning of the nineteenth century, there appeared in Russia men of genius like Lobachevsky, Chebyshev, Liapunov, Markov, etc., etc. The people remained the same, but its gift for science grew very rapidly.

It is my opinion that the percentage of talented men or

geniuses is almost constant among different races, and that it is in the conditions of social and cultural life (including those at each moment progress already made) that one must seek the causes of progress in science in general and of its particular branches.

As for the astronomy of Hipparchus and Ptolemy, I believe that its flourishing was directly connected with the synthesis of the geometrical and arithmetical methods of Greek deductive science with previous observations as well as oriental methods of calculation — a synthesis produced by the favourable social conditions of the new Hellenistic states (and which was pursued for some time in the corresponding provinces of Rome). The progress of Alexandrian techniques played its part in this. The explanation of these phenomena of the history of astronomy given by Professor Neugebauer in *The Exact Sciences in Antiquity* seems to me to be near the truth.

I will add that the nationality of Ptolemy as well as for example that of Diophantus is unknown to us. And finally, the 'purity' of Greek blood is more than doubtful; in fact, the Greeks were a mixed race as Mr. Vernant has just told us.

V. P. Zubov

The difference between the passage in Philoponus, quoted by Mr. Sambursky (*Phys.* 201, 10) and the texts of Aristotle himself become less noticeable if one recalls that the same seminal idea was to be found in the *De generatione animalium* (IV, 4, 771b): τὸ παρὰ φύσιν εἶναι τρόπον τινὰ κατὰ φύσιν. It would seem also necessary to seek the sources of the ideas expounded by Philoponus in *De generatione et corruptione* (170, 12), among the medico-pharmacological writings dedicated to the problem *de gradibus medicinarum* from Galen onwards. Finally, one ought to consider Iamblichus's text, quoted by Mr. Sambursky (*De comm. math. scientia*, XXXII), as a programme or rather a schedule of what the Greeks did in the field of optics and acoustics (the theory of music), that is to say in the most mathematical field of ancient physics.

B. L. van der Waerden

Mr. Stahlman feels that we ought to connect early Babylonian algebra with late Babylonian astrology. He conjectures that Babylonians were interested in astronomy from the mathematicians' point of view. It is possible, but we cannot prove it. Between Babylonian algebra, which flourished (say) between 1800 and 1600 B.C., and Babylonian astronomy, which was at its height in the Persian time, more than ten centuries elapsed. As Mr. Stahlman himself says, we have to wait for new data before we can decide this question. However, there is another question which we can answer at once, namely: why did the scribes make elaborate calculations during many centuries for which they were paid? The answer is: because people believed in cosmic religion and in astrology.

Mr. Owen asks: how can we know that Anaximander had a workshop, and how can we claim that he uses the language of the workshop? We have only late reports of what he actually wrote. My answer is: doxographers may misrepresent mathematical theories, but they usually do not invent characteristic technical expressions like "the nozzle of a pair of bellows". These expressions must go back to Anaximander himself. Moreover, Anaximander is reported to have made a globe. Now it is not easy to make a spherical globe out of wood, and without a workshop it is impossible. He may not have made a globe with his own hand, but he must have had a workshop at his disposal. He also erected a gnomon at Sparta, which implies the construction of hour-lines.

I am very glad to hear Mr. de Ste. Croix's statement that we have no valid evidence for Plato's having asked the astronomers to find out what combinations of uniform circular motions would "save the phenomena". Geminus, who certainly knew Eudemus's *History of Astronomy*, asserts that the Pythagoreans were the first to postulate uniform circular motions to "save the phenomena". This version seems much the more probable.

S. Sambursky

I should like to reply to two of the points made by my commentators:

(1) Ptolemy: Greek mathematical astronomy must be understood as an expression of the structural, morphological approach of the Greeks to nature. Uniform and circular motion in the closed world of antiquity corresponded to our inertial motion, and thus the harmonic analysis of the planetary movements into uniform and circular ones showed that there was a stationary structure behind the apparent irregularities in heaven. In a similar way Kepler in modern times was mainly concerned with structure and harmony although he tried to replace the structural approach by a dynamical one — a step which was successfully taken only by Newton. There seems to

be little doubt that Ptolemy, too, frustrated by the increasing complexity of the 'harmonic analysis', looked for some dynamical explanation which could restore the unitary picture still prevailing at the time of Aristotle. It is evident that such an explanation could never be given in the framework of the geocentric hypothesis.

(2) Iamblichus: There may have possibly been some allusions to action at a distance in the classical Greek period. But Iamblichus was the first to make a deliberate attempt in that direction in his endeavour to replace the Stoic concept of contiguous action. It is perhaps worth quoting the relevant passage, taken from Simplicius's commentary on the *Categories*:

> One need not share the view of the Stoics, with whom we will continue to differ, that action takes place by contact and touch. It is much more correct to say that not everything acts by contact and touch, but that action happens according to the fitness of the active part with regard to the passive one, and further, that many things are active without any perceptible contact, as we all certainly know. On the other hand, many things which are in contact do not act at all, such as plaster or some medical drug when put on a stone. [Simpl. *In Categ.* 302, 29]

The significance of this idea of Iamblichus is that it is often much more helpful in a scientific investigation to discover that there is no connexion between two phenomena than it is to discover a new dependence.

PART TWO

Chinese Science

5

Poverties and Triumphs of the Chinese Scientific Tradition

JOSEPH NEEDHAM

I

Introduction

Herein the attempt will be made to delineate some of the advantages and disadvantages which attended the growth and development of the Chinese tradition of science and technology in contrast with that of Europe.* The inspiration of the title comes from certain famous phrases chosen by French authors of the last century. I refer of course to the "Servitudes et Grandeurs" of the military life about which Alfred de Vigny wrote, and later on the "Splendeurs et Misères" of courtesans immortalized by Honoré de Balzac. It is surely quite clear by now that in the history of science and technology the Old World must be thought of as a whole. But when this is done, a great paradox presents itself. Why did modern science, the mathematization of hypotheses about nature, with all its implications for contemporary technology, take its meteoric rise only in the West at the time of Galileo? This is the most obvious question which many have asked but few have answered. Yet there is another of quite equal importance. Why was it that between the second century B.C. and the fifteenth century A.D. East Asian culture was much more efficient than the European West in applying human knowledge of nature to useful purposes? Only an analysis of the social and economic structures of Eastern and Western cultures, not forgetting the great role of systems of ideas, will in the end suggest an explanation of both these things.

* The system of romanization for Chinese words and phrases adopted in this paper is that of Wade-Giles, with the substitution of the letter *h* for the aspirate apostrophe.

Full documentation and bibliographical material, together with the Chinese characters of proper names and technical terms, will be found in *Science and Civilization in China*, the successive volumes of which are in course of publication by the Cambridge University Press.

In what follows I cannot, of course, attempt to go very far in exploring such great subjects. I would only like first of all to describe some of the outstanding contrasts between the Chinese scientific and technological traditions and those of Europe, then to say something about the social position of scientists and engineers in classical Chinese society, and lastly to take up certain of the questions inscribed upon our order-paper (see p. 10) and to give some interim answers to them from the point of view of one who is a student of Chinese civilization. But before proceeding further it is necessary to define modern and medieval science. I make an important distinction between the two. The sciences of the medieval world were all tied closely to their ethnic environments, and it was very difficult, if not impossible, for people of those different environments to find any common basis of discourse. That did not mean that it was not possible for inventions of great sociological importance to pass from one civilization to another; this they undoubtedly did throughout the Middle Ages. But the mutual incomprehensibility of the ethnically-bound concept systems severely restricted contacts and transmissions in the field of scientific ideas. When we say that modern science developed only in Western Europe in the time of Galileo at the Renaissance, we mean, I suppose, that there alone there developed the fundamental bases of the structure of modern science such as the application of mathematized hypotheses to nature, the full understanding and use of the experimental method, the distinction between primary and secondary qualities, and the systematic accumulation of openly published scientific data. At the end of this paper I propose to examine more closely the position of the Galilean break-through with regard to natural science considered as a whole, and to its development both in East and West.

II

The face of science and technology in traditional China

Before the river of Chinese science flowed, like all other such rivers, into this sea of modern science there had been remarkable achievements in mathematics. Decimal place-value and a blank space for the zero had begun in the land of the Yellow River earlier than anywhere else, and decimal metrology had gone along with it. By the first century B.C. Chinese artisans were checking their work with sliding calipers decimally graduated. Chinese mathematical thought was always profoundly algebraic, not geometrical, and in the Sung and the Yuan (twelfth to fourteenth centuries A.D.) the Chinese school led the world in the solution of equations, so that the triangle called by Pascal's name was already old in China in A.D. 1300. We often find examples of this sort; the system of linked and pivoted rings which we know as the Cardan suspension was commonly used in China a thousand years before Cardan's time. As for astronomy, I need only say that the Chinese were the most persistent and accurate observers of celestial phenomena anywhere before the Renaissance. Although geometrical planetary theory did not develop among them they conceived an enlightened cosmology, mapped the heavens using our modern co-ordinates, and kept records of eclipses, comets, novae and meteors still useful, for example to the radio-astronomers, today. A brilliant development of astronomical instruments also occurred, including the invention of the equatorial mounting and the clock-drive; and this development was in close dependence upon the contemporary capabilities of the Chinese engineers. Their skill affected also other sciences such as seismology, for it was a Chinese man of science, Chang Hêng, who built the first practical seismograph about A.D. 130.

Three branches of physics were particularly well developed in ancient and medieval China — optics, acoustics and magnetism. This was in striking contrast with the West where mechanics and dynamics were relatively advanced but magnetic phenomena almost unknown. Yet China and Europe differed most profoundly perhaps in the great debate between continuity and discontinuity, for just as Chinese mathematics was always algebraic rather than geometrical, so Chinese physics was faithful to a prototypic wave theory and perennially averse to atoms. One can even trace such contrasts in preferences in the field of engineering, for whenever an engineer in classical China could mount a wheel horizontally he would do so, while our forefathers preferred vertical mountings — water-mills and wind-mills are typical examples.

A pattern which we very often find in comparing China's achievements with those of Europe is that while the Chinese of the Chou, Chhin and Han, contemporary with the Greeks, did not rise to such heights as they, nevertheless in later centuries there was nothing in China which corresponded to the period of the Dark Ages in Europe. This shows itself rather markedly in the sciences of geography and cartography. Although the Chinese knew of discoidal cosmographic world-maps, they were never dominated by them. Quantitative cartography began in China with Chang Hêng and Phei Hsiu about the time when Ptolemy's work was falling into oblivion, indeed soon after his death, but it continued steadily with a consistent use of the rectangular grid right down to the coming of the Jesuits in the seventeenth century A.D. The Chinese were also very early in the field with advanced survey methods and the making of relief maps. In the geological sciences and in meteorology the same pattern presents itself.

Mechanical engineering and indeed engineering in general was a field in which classical Chinese culture scored special triumphs. Both the forms of efficient harness for equine animals — a problem of linkwork — originated in the Chinese culture-area, and there also water-power was first used for industry about the same time as in the West (first century A.D.), not, however, so much for grinding cereals as for the operation of metallurgical bellows. The development of iron and steel technology in China constitutes a veritable epic, with the mastery of iron-casting some fifteen centuries before its achievement in Europe. Contrary to the usual ideas, mechanical clockwork began not in early Renaissance Europe but in Thang China, in spite of the highly agrarian character of East Asian civilization. Civil engineering also shows many extraordinary achievements, notably iron-chain suspension-bridges and the first of all segmental arch structures, the magnificent bridge built by Li Chhun in A.D. 610. Hydraulic engineering was always prominent in China on account of the necessity of control of waterways for river conservation (defence against flood and drought), irrigation, and the transport of tax grain.

In martial technology the Chinese also showed notable inventiveness. The first appearance of gunpowder occurs among them in the ninth century A.D., and from A.D. 1000 onwards there was a vigorous development of explosive weapons some three centuries before they appeared in Europe. Probably the key-invention was that of the fire-lance at the beginning of the twelfth century A.D., in which a rocket composition enclosed in a bamboo tube was used as a close-combat weapon. From this derived, I have little doubt, all subsequent barrel guns and cannon of whatever material constructed. Other aspects of technology also have their importance, especially that of silk in which the Chinese excelled so early. Here the mastery of a textile fibre of extremely long staple appears to have led to the first development of technical devices so important as the driving-belt and the chain-drive. It is also possible to show that the first appearance of the standard method of converting rotary to longitudinal motion is found in connexion with later forms of the metallurgical blowing-engine referred to above. I must pass over other well-known inventions such as the development of paper, block-printing and movable-type printing, or the astonishing story of porcelain.

There was no backwardness in the biological fields either, and here we find many agricultural inventions arising from an early time. As in other subjects, we have texts which parallel those of the Romans such as Varro and Columella from a similar period. If space permitted one could take examples from plant protection which would include the earliest known use of the biological control of insect pests. Medicine is a field which aroused the interests of the Chinese in all ages, and which was developed by their special genius along lines perhaps more different from those of Europe than in any other case. I think that I can do no more here than refer simply to one remarkable fact, namely that the Chinese were free from the prejudice against mineral remedies which was so striking in the West; they needed no Paracelsus to awaken them from their Galenical slumbers for in these they had never participated. They were also the greatest pioneers of the techniques of inoculation.

III

Contrasts between China and the West

Let us come now to the further examination of some of the great contrasts to which I have already referred. In the first place it can be shown in great detail that the *philosophia perennis* of China was an organic materialism. This can be illustrated from the pronouncements of philosophers and scientific thinkers of every epoch. The mechanical view of the world simply did not develop in Chinese thought, and the organicist view in which every phenomenon was connected with every other according to hierarchical order was universal among Chinese thinkers. Nevertheless this did not prevent the appearance of great scientific inventions such as the seismograph, to which we have already referred. In some respects this philosophy of nature may even have helped. It was not so strange or surprising that the lodestone should point to the pole if one was already convinced that there was an organic pattern in the cosmos. If, as is truly the case, the Chinese were worrying about the magnetic declination before Europeans even knew of the polarity, that was perhaps because they were untroubled by the idea that for action to occur it was necessary for one discrete object to have an impact upon another; in other words, they were inclined *a priori* to field theories, and this predilection may very well also account for the fact that they arrived so early at a correct conception of the cause of sea tides. One may find remarkable statements, as early as the San Kuo period, of action at a distance taking place without any physical contact across vast distances of space.

Again, as we have said, Chinese mathematical thought and practice was invariably algebraic, not geometrical. No Euclidean geometry spontaneously developed among them and this was doubtless inhibitory for the advances they were able to make in optics, where, however, incidentally, they were never handicapped by the rather absurd Greek idea that rays were sent forth by the eye. Euclidean geometry was probably brought to China in the Yuan (Mongol) period but did not take root until the arrival of the Jesuits. Nevertheless all this did not prevent the successful realization of great engineering inventions — we have mentioned two already, the most useful method of interconversion of rotary and rectilinear motion by means of eccentric, connecting-rod and piston-rod; and the successful achievement of the oldest form of mechanical clock. What this involved was the invention of an escapement, namely a mechanical means of slowing down the revolution of a set of wheels so that it would keep time with humanity's primary clock, the apparent diurnal revolution of the heavens. In this connexion it is interesting to find that Chinese practice was not, as might at first sight be supposed, purely empirical. The successful erection of the great clock-tower of Su Sung at Khaifêng* in A.D. 1088 was preceded by the elaboration of a special theoretical treatise by his assistant Han Kung-Lien, which worked out the trains of gears and general mechanism from first principles. Something of the same kind had been done on the occasion of the first invention of this kind of clock

* A working model of this water-wheel link-work escapement system constructed by Mr. John Combridge was demonstrated at the Symposium.

by I-Hsing and Liang Ling-Tsan early in the eighth century A.D., six centuries before the first European mechanical clocks with their verge-and-foliot escapements. Moreover, though China had no Euclid, that did not prevent the Chinese from developing and consistently employing the astronomical co-ordinates which have completely conquered modern astronomy and are universally used today, nor did it prevent their consequent elaboration of the equatorial mounting, although there was nothing but a sighting-tube, and as yet no telescope, to put in it.

Thirdly, there is the wave-particle antithesis. The prototypic wave theory with which the Chinese concerned themselves from the Chhin and Han onwards was connected with the eternal rise and fall of the two basic natural principles, the Yang and Yin. From the second century A.D. onwards atomistic theories were introduced to China time after time, especially by means of the Buddhist contacts with India, but they never took any root in Chinese scientific culture. All the same this lack of particulate theory did not prevent the Chinese from curious achievements such as the recognition of the hexagonal system of snowflake crystals many centuries before this was noticed in the West. Nor did it hinder them from helping to lay the foundation of knowledge of chemical affinity, as was done in some of the alchemical tractates of the Thang, Sung and Yuan. There the absence of particulate conceptions was probably less inhibitory than it otherwise might have been, because it was only after all in the post-Renaissance period in Europe that these theories became so fundamental for the rise of modern chemistry.

I should not want to disagree altogether with the idea that the Chinese were a fundamentally practical people, inclined to distrust all theories. One must beware, however, of carrying this too far, because the neo-Confucian school in the eleventh, twelfth and thirteenth centuries A.D. achieved a wonderful philosophical synthesis strangely parallel in time with the scholastic synthesis of Europe. One might also say that the disinclination of the Chinese to engage in theory, especially geometrical theory, brought advantages with it. For example, Chinese astronomers did not reason about the heavens like Eudoxus or Ptolemy but they did avoid the conception of crystalline celestial spheres which dominated medieval Europe. By a strange paradox, when Matteo Ricci came to China at the end of the sixteenth century A.D. he mentioned in one of his letters a number of the foolish ideas entertained by the Chinese, among which prominently figured the fact that "they do not believe in crystalline celestial spheres"; it was not long before the Europeans did not either. Moreover, this fundamental practicality did not imply an easily satisfied mind. Very careful experimentation was practised in classical Chinese culture. For example the discovery of magnetic declination would not have occurred unless the geomancers had been attending most carefully to the positions of their needles, and the triumphs of the ceramics industry could never have been achieved without fairly accurate temperature measurement and the means of repetition at will of oxidizing or reducing conditions within the kilns. The fact that relatively little written material concerning these technical details has come down to us springs from social factors which prevented the publication of the records which the higher artisans certainly kept. Enough remains, either by title, like the *Mu Ching* (*Timberwork Manual*) which we shall speak of again, or in MS form, like the Fukien shipwrights' manual, to show that this literature existed.

IV

The social position of scientists and engineers in traditional China

Something must now be said of the social position of scientists, engineers and artisans in Chinese feudal-bureaucratic society. The first factor which springs to mind is the relatively 'official' character of science, pure and applied. The astronomer, as has been well said, was not a citizen on the outskirts of the conventions of his society, as perhaps in the Greek city-states, but a civil servant lodged at times in part of the imperial palace, and belonging to a bureau that was an integral part of the civil service. On a lower intellectual plane, no doubt, the artisans and engineers also participated in this bureaucratic character, partly because in nearly all dynasties there were elaborate imperial workshops and arsenals, and partly because during certain periods at least those trades which possessed the most advanced techniques were 'nationalized', as in the Salt and Iron Authority under the Former Han. One finds also a strong tendency for technicians to gather round the figure of one or another prominent official who encouraged them and supported them as his personal followers. At the same time there is no possible doubt that throughout the ages there was always a large realm of handicraft production independently undertaken by and for the common people. No doubt when any large, new or unusually complex piece of machinery was constructed (such as the early water-mills and the early mechanical clocks), or any outstandingly large civil engineering project undertaken, all this was done either in the imperial workshops or under the close supervision of important officials. The imperial workshops went by many names of which Shang-Fang was one of the most usual. Occasionally the names of some of the artisans working in these factories have come down to us. We have, for example, an inscription on the lid of a black lacquer box dated 4 B.C. which is remarkably interesting because it bears the names of no less than five administrators for seven technicians. We may conclude that something like 'Parkinson's Law' was already manifesting itself in ancient China.

The imperial workshops were situated not only at the capitals of successive dynasties but also in the most important provincial cities, the nodes in the administrative network. In the relatively private sector, particular localities derived fame from skills which tended to concentrate at sites of natural resources; one thinks of the lacquer-makers of Fuchow, the potters of Ching-tê-chen or the well-drillers (for brine and natural gas) of Tzu-liu-ching in Szechuan. However, Chinese technical skill tended to wander far and wide; there were Chinese metallurgists and well-drillers in second-century A.D. Parthia and Ferghana, while eighth-century A.D. Samarkand knew Chinese weavers and paper-makers. People were always asking for Chinese technicians; for example in A.D. 1126 when the Chin Tartars besieged the Sung capital at Khaifêng, all kinds of craftsmen were asked for as hostages, and as late as A.D. 1675 a Russian diplomatic mission officially requested that Chinese bridge-builders should be sent to Russia.

As regards the question of status, it is a very difficult one and still under investigation. The technical workers we have been mentioning were for the most part free plebeians (*shu-jen* or *liang-jen*). Only in very few cases do we hear of slaves or semi-servile people mentioned as producers of wealth; certain classical passages indeed specify free workers, as in the salt factories of the Han. Of course whatever the extent of government-organized production from time to time, the State relied upon an inexhaustible supply of obligatory unpaid labour in the form of the *corvée* (*yao* or *kung-yu*). In the Han period every male commoner between the ages of twenty and fifty-six was liable for one month's labour service a year; technical workers performed these obligations in the imperial workshops or at the nationalized factories, which were never primarily staffed by slaves. Eventually there grew up the practice of paying dues in lieu of personal service, so that a large body of artisans 'permanently on the job' (*chhang-shang*) resulted. Among the slave or semi-servile portion of the population there were no doubt a certain number of artisans, but it is highly doubtful whether it ever exceeded 10 per cent. in any period of Chinese history. The problem of servile and semi-servile status in Chinese civilization is still very much under discussion, but most Western scholars believe that it was always primarily domestic in character and that the class was recruited by penal process; to become a convict meant to be 'enslaved to the State' for a term of years or for life, after which the prisoner could be allocated either to houses of great officials or to the imperial workshops or State factories.

Research now under way will throw much light upon the forms of slavery, semi-servility, free labour and the *corvée* system in classical Chinese society. Whatever the details of the conclusions which will be reached, we are constrained already to notice that ancient and medieval Chinese labour conditions proved no bar to a long series of 'labour-saving' inventions altogether prior to those arising in Europe and Islam. I shall return to this point a little later on. I want first to glance over some of the chief categories into which the lives of eminent scientists and engineers of ancient and medieval Chinese society seem to fall. One may divide such life-histories into five groups: first, high officials, the scholars who had successful and fruitful careers; secondly, commoners; third, members of the semi-servile groups; fourth, those who were actually enslaved; and fifth, a very significant group of minor officials, that is to say, scholars who were not able to make their way upwards in the ranks of the bureaucracy. The numbers of examples which we have found in our work varies very considerably among these different groups.

In the first place, among the high officials, we have already mentioned Chang Hêng. Chang Hêng was not only the inventor of the first seismograph in any civilization but the first to apply motive power to the rotation of astronomical instruments, one of the outstanding mathematicians of his time, and the father-figure in the design of armillary spheres. He became the President of the Imperial Chancellery. High provincial officials are often credited with important technical developments. Thus the introduction of the water-powered metallurgical blowing-engine is attributed to Tu Shih, who was Prefect of Nanyang in 31 B.C. Occasionally we find also a eunuch prominent in technical advance; the most obvious case is that of Tshai Lun, who began as a confidential secretary to the Emperor, was made Director of the Imperial Workshops in A.D. 97, and announced the invention of paper in A.D. 105.

On the contributions to science of Chinese princes and the remoter relatives of the imperial house an interesting monograph could be written. They were favoured with leisure, since though generally well educated they were in most dynasties ineligible for the civil service and yet disposed of considerable wealth. Though most of them did nothing for posterity, there were a memorable few who devoted time and riches to scientific pursuits. Liu An, the Prince of Huainan (fl. 130 B.C.), with his entourage of naturalists, alchemists and astronomers, is one of the most famous figures in Chinese history. Another Han prince, Liu Chhung (fl. A.D. 173), is relevant also since he was the inventor of grid sights for cross-bows and a famous shot with them into the bargain. In the Thang we meet with Li Kao, Prince of Tshao (fl. A.D. 784), interested in acoustics and physics but prominent here because of his successful development of treadmill-operated paddle-wheel warships.

Curiously enough, it seems exceptional to find an important engineer who attained high office in the Ministry of Works, at any rate before the Ming. This was probably because the real work was always done by illiterate or semi-illiterate artisans and master-craftsmen who could never rise across that sharp gap which separated them from the 'white-collar' literati in the offices of the Ministry above. Still there were exceptions. There was Yuwên Khai (fl. A.D. 600), chief engineer of the Sui dynasty for 30 years. He carried out irrigation and conservation works, superintending the construction of what afterwards became part of the Grand Canal; he built large sailing carriages, and with Kêng Hsün devised the standard steelyard clepsydra of the Thang and Sung. One word more here about the tendency for technicians to cluster in the entourages of distinguished civil officials, who acted as their patrons. It is more than probable that the first water-mills and metallurgical blowing-engines were the work of technicians in the service of Tu Shih. Here an outstanding example is Shen Kua (fl. A.D. 1080), one of the greatest scientific minds in Chinese history, an ambassador, too, and an elder statesman. In his interesting and many-sided scientific book, the *Mêng Chhi Pi Than* (*Dream Pool Essays*), he describes the invention of movable-type printing by Pi Shêng about A.D. 1045, and says that after this commoner died, his fount of type "passed into the possession of my followers, among whom it has been kept as a precious possession until now". This gives a striking glimpse of the technicians gathered round important official patrons.

No doubt the greatest group of inventors is represented by commoners, master-craftsmen, artisans who were neither officials, even minor ones, nor of the semi-servile classes. Besides Pi Shêng, just mentioned, we have the great builder of pagodas, Yü Hao, who assuredly had to dictate his celebrated *Mu Ching* (*Timberwork Manual*) to a scribe. Yü Hao was a man of the tenth century A.D. but we may find his like in every dynasty. The second century A.D. saw the life of Ting Huan, renowned for his pioneer development of the Cardan suspension, the seventh century A.D. was the time of Li Chhun, the constructor of segmental arch bridges already mentioned, and the twelfth century A.D. the time of the greatest naval architect in Chinese history, Kao Hsüan, who specialized in the making of warships with multiple paddle-wheels. Sometimes we do not even have the surname — an omission which makes one wonder whether such men were not living on the borders of one of the semi-servile groups where surnames were not customary; for example there was the old craftsman (*lao kung*) who made astronomical apparatus in the first century B.C., or again that "artisan from Haichow" who presented to the Empress in A.D. 692 what was in all probability a complicated anaphoric clock. In the category of regular commoners we should probably also place minor military officers. Here I should like to mention Chhiwu Huai-Wên, a Taoist swordsmith who served in the army of Kao Huan the 'king-maker', founder of the Northern Chhi dynasty, and took charge of his arsenals (*c.* A.D. 545). Chhiwu Huai-Wên was one of the earliest protagonists, if not the inventor, of the co-fusion process of steel-making, a process ancestral to the Siemens–Martin open-hearth furnace, and he was also a celebrated practitioner of the pattern-welding of swords.

And now we come to the exceptional cases, those who came down in history as brilliant scientific or technical men and yet whose social standing in their own time was very low indeed. The only one of clearly semi-servile rank in our registers is Hsintu Fang (fl. A.D. 525). In his youth he entered the household of a prince of the Northern Wei, Thopa Yen-Ming, as a 'dependent' or 'retainer'. This prince had collected many pieces of scientific apparatus — armillary spheres, celestial globes, trick hydrostatic vessels, seismographs, clepsydras, wind-gauges, etc., and had also inherited a very large library. As a client or pensioner of known scientific skill Hsintu Fang's position with relation to Thopa Yen-Ming must have been something like that of Thomas Hariot's to the 9th Earl of Northumberland in our own country (*c.* A.D. 1610). It seems that the prince intended to write certain scientific books with the aid of Hsintu, but owing to political and military events felt obliged to flee to the Liang emperor in the south in A.D. 528, so that Hsintu Fang had to write the books himself. After this he remained in seclusion, probably in poverty, until he was called to the court of another potentate, Mujung Pao-Lo, Governor of Tung-shan, whose younger brother recommended him to Kao Huan (the 'king-maker' just mentioned). This great lord he served as estate agent, a post which exercised his talents in surveying and architecture. He never rose higher than the position of dependent in one or other of the great semi-aristocratic houses but nevertheless left behind him a very high reputation in Chinese scientific history. Such an ingenious man of lowly origins could thus find shelter in a troublous time, if not official recognition or any considerable status, in the homes of unusual patricians.

Examples of technologists who were positively slaves are very rare indeed, but we have already mentioned Kêng Hsün (fl. A.D. 590). He began as a client of a Governor of Ling-nan, but when this patron died, Kêng Hsün, instead of going home, joined some tribal people in the south, and eventually led them in an uprising. When this was defeated and Kêng Hsün captured, a general, Wang Shih-Chi, realizing his technical ability, saved him from death and admitted him among his family slaves. Here his position was yet not so low that he could not receive instruction from an old friend, Kao Chih-Pao, who had in the meantime become Astronomer-Royal, and it was as a result of this that Kêng Hsün built an armillary sphere or celestial globe rotated continuously by water-power. The Emperor rewarded him for this by making him a government slave and attaching him to the Bureau of Astronomy and

Calendar. The following Emperor freed him altogether, and he eventually rose to the position of Acting Executive Assistant in the Astronomical Bureau. His case shows that a long period of slavery was no bar to official, if not very exalted, position.

We now reach the last of our group of technicians and one of the most numerous, namely that of the minor officials — men who were sufficiently well educated, even if of lowly origin, to enter the ranks of the bureaucracy, but whose particular talents or personalities frustrated all hopes of a brilliant career. Among these men we should include Li Chieh (fl. A.D. 1100), the man who, building on the earlier works of Yü Hao and others, produced the greatest definitive treatise of any age on the millennial tradition of Chinese architecture and building technology, the *Ying Tsao Fa Shih.* Li Chieh never rose above the rank of Director of Buildings and Construction and ended his official career as a magistrate in a provincial town. Yen Su (fl. A.D. 1030) was a Leonardo-like figure — scholar, painter, technologist and engineer under the Sung Emperor Jen Tsung. He designed the type of clepsydra with an overflow tank which remained standard for long afterwards, invented special locks and keys, and left specifications for hydrostatic vessels, hodometers and south-pointing carriages. His writings included treatises on time-keeping and on the tides, but most of his life was spent in provincial administrative posts, and although he did become an Academician-in-waiting of the Lung-Thu Pavilion, he never rose above the position of Chief Executive Officer of the Ministry of Rites, and had no connexion with the Ministry of Works or other technical directorates. It was just the same with the two men of greatest practical importance in the pre-European history of the mechanical clock. Liang Ling-Tsan, the assistant of I-Hsing in the eighth century A.D., was a minor official in the War Office; and Han Kung-Lien, the principal collaborator of Su Sung 350 years later, was only an acting secretary in the Ministry of Personnel. It was this group of minor officials which provided one of the most striking texts on the life of technologists and scientists in medieval China which have come down to us. The engineer Ma Chün (fl. A.D. 260) was a man of outstanding ingenuity; he improved the drawloom, constructed a puppet theatre operated by water-power, invented the square-pallet chain-pump used so widely throughout the Chinese culture-area afterwards, designed (like Leonardo later on) a rotary arcuballista, and successfully constructed a south-pointing carriage, almost certainly making use of a simple form of differential gear. His friend Fu Hsüan devoted to his memory a remarkable essay — the text to which we have alluded. Fu Hsüan describes how Ma Chün was quite incapable of arguing with the sophisticated scholars nursed in the classical literary traditions, and in spite of all the efforts of his admirers, could never attain any position of importance in the service of the State, or even the means to prove by practical test the value of the inventions which he made. No document throws more light than this upon the inhibitory factors affecting science and technology which arose from the feudal-bureaucratic tradition of the scholar-gentry.

V

Feudal-bureaucratic society

I now turn to address myself to some of the questions arising from our order-paper (see p. 10). First, one may ask what the long-term effects of the feudal-bureaucratic system, the mandarinate in fact, really were. In classical Chinese society certain sciences were orthodox and others the opposite. The institution of the calendar and its importance for a primarily agrarian society, and also to a lesser extent the belief in State astrology, made astronomy always one of the orthodox sciences. Mathematics was considered suitable as a pursuit for the educated scholar, and similarly physics, up to a point, especially as they contributed to the engineering works so characteristic of the centralized bureaucracy. The need of Chinese bureaucratic society for great works of irrigation and water-conservation (flood protection and tax-grain transport) meant not only that hydraulic engineering was regarded favourably among the traditional scholars but also that it helped in its turn to stabilize and support the form of society of which they were an essential part. Many students believe that the origin and development of feudal-bureaucratic society in China was at least partly dependent on the fact that from very early times the undertaking of great hydraulic engineering works tended to cut across the boundaries of the lands of individual feudal lords, and thus had the effect of concentrating all power in the centralized bureaucratic imperial State. By contrast with these forms of applied science, alchemy was distinctly unorthodox, the characteristic pursuit of disinterested Taoists and other recluses. Medicine was in this respect rather neutral; on the one hand the demands of traditional filial piety made it a respectable study for the scholars, while on the other its necessary association with pharmacy connected it with the Taoist alchemists and herbalists.

In the end I believe we shall find that the centralized feudal-bureaucratic style of social order was in the earlier stages favourable to the growth of applied science. Take the case of the seismograph which we have already mentioned more than once. It is paralleled by the existence of rain-gauges and even snow-gauges at a remarkably early time, and it is highly probable that the stimulus for such inventions came from the very reasonable desire of the centralized bureaucracy to be able to foresee coming events. Thus, for example, if a particular region was hit by a severe earthquake, it would be advisable to know this as soon as possible in order that help might be sent and reinforcements supplied to the local authorities in case of popular uprising. Similarly the rain-gauges set up on the edge of the Tibetan massif would have played a most useful part in determining the measures to be taken for the protection of hydraulic engineering works. Moreover Chinese society in the Middle Ages was able to mount much greater expeditions and pieces of organized scientific field work than was the case in any other medieval society. A good example of this would be the meridian arc surveyed early in the eighth century A.D. under the auspices of I-Hsing and the Astronomer-Royal, Nankung Yüeh. This geodetic survey covered a line no less than 2500 kms long reaching from Indo-China to the borders of Mongolia. About the same time an expedition was sent down to the East Indies for the purpose of surveying the constellations of the Southern Hemisphere within 20° of the south celestial pole. It is doubtful whether any other State in the world at that time could have engaged successfully in such activities.

From early times Chinese astronomy had benefited from State support but the semi-secrecy which it involved was to some extent a disadvantage. Chinese historians sometimes themselves realized this, for example in the dynastic history of the Chin dynasty (A.D. 265–A.D. 420) there is a passage which says:

> Astronomical instruments have been in use from very ancient days, handed down from one dynasty to another and closely guarded by official astronomers. Scholars therefore have had little opportunity to examine them, and this is the reason why unorthodox

cosmological theories have been able to spread and flourish.

However, one must not push this too far. It is quite clear that in the Sung period at any rate the study of astronomy was quite possible and even usual in scholarly families connected with the bureaucracy. Thus we know that in his earlier years Su Sung had model armillary spheres of small size in his home and so came gradually to understand astronomical principles. About a century later the great philosopher Chu Hsi also had an armillary sphere in his house and tried hard to reconstruct the water-power drive of Su Sung, although unsuccessfully. Besides, there were periods, for example in the eleventh century A.D., when mathematics and astronomy played quite a prominent part in the celebrated official examinations for the civil service.

VI

Invention and labour power

We can now return to the question raised before, the relation of invention to labour power. Chinese labour conditions were no bar to a long series of 'labour-saving' inventions. Whether one thinks of the efficient trace-harness for horses (from the fourth century B.C. onwards) or the appearance of the still better collar-harness in the fifth century A.D., or of the simple wheelbarrow in the third century A.D. (though not in Europe till a thousand years later), one constantly finds that in spite of the seemingly inexhaustible masses of man-power in China, lugging and hauling was avoided whenever possible. How striking it is that in all Chinese history there is no parallel for the slave-manned oared war galley of the Mediterranean — land-locked though most of the Chinese waters were, sail was the characteristic motive power throughout the ages; and the arrival of great junks at Zanzibar or Kamchatka was only an extension of the techniques of the Yangtze and the Tung-thing Lake. When the water-mill appeared in the first century A.D. for blowing metallurgical bellows the records concerning Tu Shih distinctly say that he considered it important as being both more humane and cheaper than man-power or animal-power, and it gives food for thought to find around A.D. 1300, four centuries before similar developments in Europe, water-power widely applied to textile machinery, especially silk-throwing and hemp-spinning.

All this is in considerable contrast to the position in Europe, where we do know of classical examples of refusal of innovation for fear of technological unemployment. I suppose that the best known example is the Roman one of the imperial refusal to make use of a machine for moving temple columns on the ground that it would put the porters out of work, and another case equally well established is that of the frame knitting machine in the seventeenth century A.D. It looks as if the Chinese example shows that shortage of labour may not in every culture be the sole stimulus for labour-saving inventions. Of course the problems here are very complicated and much further investigation is necessary.

VII

Philosophical and theological factors

It is clear that a full-dress comparison will eventually have to be made between the effects upon science and technology of the Confucian–Taoist view of the world as compared with those of Christendom and Islam. Now the Confucian school which dominated the minds of the literati for more than 2000 years was primarily, as is generally known, this-worldly in character, occupied with a form of social ethics which purported to show the way whereby human beings could live in happiness and harmony together within society. The Confucians were concerned with human society and with what the West called natural law, that way of behaviour which it consorted with the actual nature of man that man should pursue. In Confucianism ethical behaviour partook of the nature of the holy, but it was not divine and had nothing to do with divinity since the conception of a creator God was unnecessary in the system. The Taoists, on the other hand, walked outside society; their Tao was the Order of Nature, not merely the order of human life, and it worked in a profoundly organic way in all its operations. Unfortunately, while the Taoists were extremely interested in nature, they tended to distrust reason and logic, so that the workings of the Tao tended to remain somewhat inscrutable. Thus on the one hand interest was concentrated purely in human relations and social order, while on the other hand interest in nature existed very strongly but tended to be mystical-experimental rather than rational-systematic.

No doubt one of the central features here is the contrast between conceptions of the laws of nature in China and in the West. In one of those preliminary surveys which had to be undertaken before the main work of our group could be carried through, my collaborators and I engaged in a rather thorough investigation of the concepts of laws of nature in East Asian and West European culture. In Western civilization the ideas of natural law in the juristic sense and of the laws of nature in the sense of the natural sciences can easily be shown to go back to a common root. Without doubt one of the oldest notions of Western civilization was that just as earthly imperial law-givers enacted codes of positive law to be obeyed by men, so also the celestial and supreme rational Creator Deity had laid down a series of laws which must be obeyed by minerals, crystals, plants, animals and the stars in their courses. There can be little doubt that this idea was intimately bound up with the development of modern science at the Renaissance in the West. If it was absent elsewhere, could that not have been one of the reasons why modern science arose only in Europe; in other words, were medievally conceived laws of nature in their naïve form necessary for the birth of modern science?

There can be little doubt that the conception of a celestial law-giver 'legislating' for non-human natural phenomena had its first origins among the Babylonians. The sun-god Marduk is pictured as the law-giver to the stars. This conception found continuation not so much among the pre-Socratics or the Peripatetics in Greece as with the Stoics whose conception of universal law immanent in the world included non-human nature as much as man. In the Christian centuries the conception of the legislating Godhead was greatly increased by the stream of Hebrew influence. Throughout the Middle Ages the conception of divine legislation over non-human nature remained more or less a commonplace, but at the Renaissance the metaphor began to be taken very seriously indeed. The turning point occurred between Copernicus, who never used the expression 'law' and Kepler who did, though strangely enough not for any of his three great laws of planetary motion. It is curious to find that one of the very first applications of the expression 'law' to natural phenomena occurs not in astronomy or any of the biological sciences but in a geological-mineralogical context in one of the works of Agricola.

The Chinese world-view depended upon an entirely different line of thought. The harmonious co-operation of all beings arose, not from the orders of a superior authority external to themselves, but from the fact that they were all parts in a hierarchy of wholes forming a cosmic and organic pattern, and what they obeyed were the internal dictates of their own natures. Our investigations led to the conclusion that Chinese conceptions of law did not develop the idea of laws of nature for several different reasons. First, the Chinese early acquired a great distaste for precisely formulated abstract codified law from the abortive tyranny of the politicians belonging to the School of Legalists during the period of transition from feudalism to bureaucratism. Then when the bureaucratic system was finally set up, the old conceptions of natural law in the form of accepted customs and good *mores* proved more suitable than any others for Chinese society in its typical form, so that in fact the elements of natural law were much more important relatively in Chinese than in European society. But most of it was never put into formal legal terms, and since it was overwhelmingly human and ethical in content it was not easy to extend its sphere of influence to any form of non-human nature. Finally, and perhaps most important of all, the available ideas of a Supreme Being, though certainly present from the earliest times, became depersonalized so soon, and so severely lacked the idea of creativity, that they prevented the development of the conception of laws ordained from the beginning by a celestial law-giver for non-human nature. Hence the conclusion did not follow that other lesser rational beings could decipher or reformulate the laws of a great rational Super-Being if they used the methods of observation, experiment, hypothesis and mathematical reasoning. Of course this did not prevent the great development of science and technology in ancient and medieval China, many aspects of which we have already discussed, but it may have had a deep influence at the time of the Renaissance.

In the outlook of modern science there is, I presume, no residue of the notions of command and duty in the laws of nature; they are now thought of as statistical regularities valid only in given times and places or for specified dimensions of size, descriptions not prescriptions. We dare not trespass here upon the great debate concerning subjectivity in formulations of scientific law, but the question does arise whether the recognition of statistical regularities and their mathematical expression could have been reached by any other road than that which Western science actually travelled. We might ask perhaps whether the state of mind in which an egg-laying cock could be prosecuted at law was necessary in a culture which should later on have the property of producing a Kepler.

VIII

The linguistic factor

Further study of the social relations of science and technology in China will of course also have to concern itself with the role of language. There is a commonly received idea that the ideographic language was a powerful inhibitory factor to the development of modern science in China. We believe, however, that this influence is generally grossly over-rated. It has proved possible in the course of our work to draw up large glossaries of definable technical terms used in ancient and medieval times for all kinds of things and ideas in science and its applications. Furthermore the Chinese language at the present day is found to be no impediment by the scientists of the contemporary culture. The National Academy at Peking (Academia Sinica) publishes today a wide range of scientific journals covering nearly all branches of research, and this language used today takes benefit from fifty years of work by the National Institute of Compilation and Translation which has defined technical terms for modern usage. We are strongly inclined to believe that if the social and economic factors in Chinese society had permitted or facilitated the rise of modern science there as well as in Europe, then already 300 years ago the language would have been made suitable for scientific expression.

At the same time also it is wise not to underestimate the capacities of the classical language. We do not recollect any instance where (after adequate consideration) we have been seriously in doubt as to what was intended by a classical or medieval Chinese author dealing with a scientific or technical subject, provided always that the text was not too corrupt, and that the description was sufficiently full. The general tendency was, of course, to make the descriptions too laconic. We often lack details because the literary scholars of later times abbreviated the records, not being themselves interested in scientific and technological matters. Similarly, the technical illustrations sometimes offer difficulties probably because the Confucian artists felt impatience at being asked to limn such inelegant and banausic objects. But where we do have sufficient details, as in the case of Su Sung's own description of his astronomical clock-tower in A.D. 1090, the *Hsin I Hsiang Fa Yao*, then it becomes possible to reconstruct down to the smallest detail what exactly was done.

Moreover the classical language is capable of a magnificently crystalline epigrammatic formulation which is not at all unsuitable for the best kind of philosophical thinking. Of this I may give an example from the works of Chu Hsi. In the twelfth century A.D., writing of his theory of organic development, a kind of emergent evolutionism or organic materialism recognizing a series of integrative levels, he said, "Cognition or apprehension is the essential pattern of the mind's existence, but that there is something in the world which can do this is what we may call the spirituality inherent in matter." To say all this took him only 14 words: *So chio chê hsin chihli yeh; nêng chio chê, chhi chih ling yeh.* In other words, the mind's function is perfectly natural, something which matter has the potentiality of producing when it has formed itself into collocations with a sufficiently high degree of pattern and organization. The fact that Ma Chün could not talk like this, and explain his ideas to the supercilious scholars of the Chin court, only meant that he was neither a philosopher nor an orator, it did not mean that he could not explain to his own artisans exactly what he wanted made in the world of gear-wheels and link-work.

IX

The role of the merchants

The last point which I must make here concerns the position of merchants in classical Chinese society. This brings us back to what I said before concerning the nature of feudal-bureaucratism. The institution of the mandarinate had the effect of creaming off the best brains of the nation for more than 2000 years into the civil service. Merchants might acquire great wealth yet they were never secure, they were subjected to sumptuary laws, and they could be mulcted of their wealth by inordinate taxation and every other kind of governmental interference. Moreover they never achieved a mystique of their own. In every age the sole ambition of the sons of even wealthy merchants was to get into the official bureaucracy; such was the prestige value of the world-outlook of the scholar-gentry that every channel of advancement led through it and every young man of whatever origin wanted to get into it. This situation prevailing, it was evidently impossible for the mercantile classes of Chinese culture to acquire anything like the positions of power and influence in the State which they attained during the Renaissance in Europe. In other words, not to put too fine a point upon the matter, whoever would explain the failure of Chinese society to develop modern science had better begin by explaining the failure of Chinese society to develop mercantile and then industrial capitalism. Whatever the individual prepossessions of Western historians of science, all are necessitated to admit that from the fifteenth century A.D. onwards a complex of changes occurred; the Renaissance cannot be thought of without the Reformation, the Reformation cannot be thought of without the rise of modern science, and none of them can be thought of without the rise of capitalism, capitalist society and the decline and the disappearance of feudalism. We seem to be in the presence of a kind of organic whole, a packet of change, the analysis of which has hardly yet begun. In the end it will probably be found that all the schools, whether the Weberians, or the Marxists, or the believers in intellectual factors alone, will have their contribution to make.

The fact is that in the spontaneous autochthonous development of Chinese society no drastic change parallel to the Renaissance and the 'scientific revolution' in the West occurred at all. I often like to sketch the Chinese evolution as represented by a relatively slowly rising curve, noticeably running at a higher level, sometimes a much higher level, than European parallels between, say, the second and the fifteenth centuries A.D. But then after the scientific renaissance had begun in the West with the Galilean revolution, with what one might almost call the discovery of the basic technique of scientific discovery itself, then the curve of science and technology in Europe begins to rise in a violent, almost exponential, manner, overtaking the levels of the Asian societies and bringing about the state of affairs which we have seen during the past two or three hundred years. This violent disturbance of the balance is now beginning to right itself. No doubt in true historical thinking the 'ifs' so attractive to popular thought are out of place, but I would be prepared to say that if parallel social and economic changes had been possible in Chinese society then some form of modern science would have arisen there. If so, it would have been, I think, organic rather than mechanical from the first, and it might well have gone a long way before receiving the great stimulus which a knowledge of Greek science and mathematics would no doubt have provided, and turning into something like the science which we know today. This is of course a question of the same character as "If Caesar had not crossed the Rubicon", etc., and I only state it in this categorical form in order to convey some idea of the general conclusions which a prolonged study of Chinese scientific and technological contributions has induced in the minds of my collaborators and myself.

X

The Old World origins of the new science

In conclusion I should like to return to the question raised at the beginning, and to go a little further into the distinction between modern science on the one hand, and ancient and medieval science on the other. I shall thus have to deal somewhat more fully with certain points that have already been touched upon. As the contributions of the Asian civilizations are progressively uncovered by research, an opposing tendency seeks to preserve European uniqueness by exalting unduly the role of the Greeks and claiming that not only modern science, but science as such, was characteristic of Europe, and of Europe only, from the very beginning. For these thinkers the application of Euclidean deductive geometry to the explanation of planetary motion in the Ptolemaic system constituted already the marrow of science, which the Renaissance did no more than propagate. The counterpart of this is a determined effort to show that all scientific developments in non-European civilizations were really nothing but technology.

For example, our most learned medievalist has recently written:

> Impressive as are the technological achievements of ancient Babylonia, Assyria, and Egypt, of ancient China and India, as scholars have presented them to us they lack the essential elements of science, the generalized conceptions of scientific explanation and of mathematical proof. It seems to me that it was the Greeks who invented natural science as we know it, by their assumption of a permanent, uniform, abstract order and laws by means of which the regular changes observed in the world could be explained by deduction, and by their brilliant idea of the generalized use of

scientific theory tailored according to the principles of non-contradiction and the empirical test. It is this essential Greek idea of scientific explanation, 'Euclidean' in logical form, that has introduced the main problems of scientific method and philosophy of science with which the Western scientific tradition has been concerned.

Again in a recent interesting and stimulating survey entitled *Science since Babylon* we read:

What is the origin of the peculiarly scientific basis of our own high civilization? . . . Of all limited areas, by far the most highly developed, most recognizably modern, yet most continuous province of scientific learning, was mathematical astronomy. This is the mainstream that leads through the work of Galileo and Kepler, through the gravitation theory of Newton, directly to the labours of Einstein and all mathematical physicists past and present. In comparison, all other parts of modern science appear derivative or subsequent; either they drew their inspiration directly from the successful sufficiency of mathematical and logical explanation for astronomy, or they developed later, probably as a result of such inspiration in adjacent subjects. . . . Our civilization has produced not merely a high intellectual grasp of science but also a high scientific technology. By this is meant something distinct from the background noise of the low technology that all civilizations and societies have evolved as part of their daily life. The various crafts of the primitive industrial chemists, of the metallurgists, of the medical men, of the agriculturists — all these might become highly developed without presaging a scientific or industrial revolution such as we have experienced in the past three or four centuries.

Even the distinguished and enlightened author of *Science in History* writes (in correspondence):

The chief weakness of Chinese science lay precisely in the field which most interested them, namely astronomy, because they never developed the Greek geometry, and perhaps even more important, the Greek geometrical way of seeing things which provided the Renaissance with its main intellectual weapon for the break-through. Instead they had only the extremely precise recurrence methods deriving from Babylonian astronomy, and these, on account of their exactitude, gave them a fictitious feeling of understanding astronomical phenomena.

Finally the author of a noted book, *The Edge of Objectivity*, says:

Albert Einstein once remarked that there is no difficulty in understanding why China or India did not create science. The problem is rather why Europe did, for science is a most arduous and unlikely undertaking. The answer lies in Greece. Ultimately science derives from the legacy of Greek philosophy. The Egyptians, it is true, developed surveying techniques and conducted certain surgical operations with notable finesse. The Babylonians disposed of numerical devices of great ingenuity for predicting the patterns of the planets. But no Oriental civilization graduated beyond technique or thaumaturgy to curiosity about things in general. Of all the triumphs of the speculative genius of Greece, the most unexpected, the most truly novel, was precisely its rational conception of the cosmos as an orderly whole working by laws discoverable in thought. . . .

The statement of Einstein here referred to is contained in a now famous letter which he sent to J. E. Switzer of San Mateo, California, in 1953. It runs:

Dear Sir,

The development of Western science has been based on two great achievements, the invention of the formal logical system (in Euclidean geometry) by the Greek philosophers, and the discovery of the possibility of finding out causal relationships by systematic experiment (at the Renaissance). In my opinion one need not be astonished that the Chinese sages did not make these steps. The astonishing thing is that these discoveries were made at all.

Sincerely yours,

Albert Einstein.

It is very regrettable that this Shavian epistle with all its lightness of touch is now being pressed into service to belittle the scientific achievements of the non-European civilizations. Einstein himself would have been the first to admit that he knew almost nothing concrete about the development of the sciences in the Chinese, Sanskrit and Arabic cultures except that *modern* science did not develop in them, and his great reputation should not be brought forward as a witness in this court. I find myself in complete disagreement with all these valuations and it is necessary to explain briefly why.

First, these definitions of mathematics are far too narrow. It would of course be impossible to deny that one of the most fundamental elements in Galileo's thinking was the geometrical study of kinematic problems. Again and again he praises the power of geometry as opposed to "logic". And geometry remained the primary tool for studying the problems of physical motion down to the early nineteenth century. But vast though the significance of deductive geometry was, its proofs never exhausted the power of the mathematical art. Although we speak of the Hindu–Arabic numerals, the Chinese were in fact the first, as early as the fourteenth century B.C., to be able to express any desired number, however large, with no more than nine signs. Chinese mathematics, developing the earlier Babylonian tradition, was always, as I have already said, overwhelmingly arithmetical and algebraical, generating such concepts and devices as those of decimal place-value, decimal fractions and decimal metrology, negative numbers, indeterminate analysis, the method of finite differences, and the solution of higher numerical equations. Very accurate values of π were early computed. The Han mathematicians anticipated Horner's method for obtaining the roots of higher powers. The triangle of binomial coefficients, as we have seen, was already considered old in the *Ssu Yüan Yü Chien* of A.D. 1303. Indeed in the thirteenth and fourteenth centuries A.D. the Chinese algebraists were in the forefront of advance as their Arabic counterparts had been in previous centuries, and so also the Indian mathematicians when they originated trigonometry (as we know it) nearly a thousand years earlier. To say that whatever algebra was needed by Vieta and by Newton they could easily have invented themselves may be uncritical genius-worship, but it is worse, it is unhistorical, for the influence of Asian ways of computation on European mathematicians of the later Middle Ages and the Renaissance is well established. And when the transmissions are examined the balance shows that between 250 B.C. and A.D. 1250, in spite of all China's isolations and inhibitions, a great deal more mathematical influence came out of that culture than went in.

Moreover the astronomical application of Euclidean geometry in the Ptolemaic system was not all pure gain. Apart from the fact (which some of these writers unaccountably seem to forget) that the resulting synthesis was in fact objectively wrong, it ushered the Western medieval world into the prison of the solid crystalline celestial spheres — a cosmology incomparably more naïve and *borné* than the infinite empty spaces of the Chinese *hun-thien* school or the relativistic Buddhist philosophers. It is in fact important to realize that Chinese thought on the world and its history was over and over again more boldly imaginative than that of Europe. The basic principles of Huttonian geology were stated by Shen Kua in the late eleventh century A.D., but this was only a counterpart of a Plutonian theme recurring since the fourth century A.D., that of the *sang thien* or mountains which had once been at the bottom of the sea. Indeed the idea of an evolutionary process, involving social as well as biological change, was commonly entertained by Chinese philosophers and scientifically interested scholars, even though sometimes thought of in terms of a succession of world renewals following the catastrophes and dissolutions assumed in the recurrent *mahākalpas* of Indian speculation. One can see a striking echo of this open-mindedness in the calculations made by I-Hsing about A.D. 710 concerning the date of the last general conjunction. He made it come out to 96,961,740 years ago — rather a different scale from "4004 B.C. at 9 o'clock in the morning".

Thirdly, the implied definitions of science are also much too narrow. It is true that mechanics was the pioneer among the modern sciences, the 'mechanistic' paradigm which all the other sciences sought to imitate, and emphasis on Greek deductive geometry as its base is so far justifiable. But that is not the same thing as saying that geometrical kinematics is all that science is. Modern science itself has not remained within these Cartesian bounds, for field theory in physics and organic conceptions in biology have deeply modified the earlier mechanistic world-picture. Here knowledge of magnetic phenomena was all-important, and this was a typically Chinese gift to Europe. Although we do not know the way-stations through which it came, its priority of time is such as to place the burden of proof on those who would wish to believe in an independent discovery. The fact is that science has many aspects other than geometrical theorizing. To begin with, it is nonsense to say that the assumption of a permanent, uniform, abstract order and laws by means of which the regular changes in the world could be explained, was a purely Greek invention. The order of nature was for the ancient Chinese the *Tao*, and as a *chhang Tao* it was an "unvarying Way". "Every natural phenomenon," says the fourth century B.C. *Chi Ni Tzu* book, "the product of Yin and Yang, has its fixed compositions and motions with regard to other things in the network of nature's relationships." "Look at things," wrote Shao Yung in the eleventh century A.D., "from the point of view of things, and you will see their true nature; look at things from your own point of view, and you will see only your own feelings; for nature is neutral and clear, while feelings are prejudiced and dark." The organic pattern in nature was for the medieval

Chinese the *Li*, and it was mirrored in every subordinate whole as one or another *wu li* of particular things and processes. Since the thought of the Chinese was in all ages profoundly organic and impersonal they did not envisage laws of a celestial law-giver — but nor did the Greeks, for it is easily possible to show that the full conception of laws of nature attained definitive status only at the Renaissance.

What the Chinese did do was to classify natural phenomena, to develop scientific instruments of great refinement for their respective ages, to observe and record with a persistence hardly paralleled elsewhere, and if they failed (like all medieval men, Europeans included) to apply hypotheses of modern type, they experimented century after century obtaining results which they could repeat at will. When one recites this list of the forms of scientific activity it becomes difficult to see how anyone could deny them their status as essential components of fully developed world science, biological and chemical as well as astronomical and physical, if it was not in the interest of some instinctive *parti pris*.

Elaborating, *kho hsüeh*, the traditional and current Chinese term for science, means "classification knowledge". The first star catalogues, probably pre-Hipparchan, open its story in China. It is then exemplified in the long series of rational pharmacopœias which begin with the second-century B.C. *Shen Nung Pên Tshao*. It helped to lay the basis of our knowledge of chemical affinity in the theories of polarities (*i*) and categories (*lei*) found in treatises such as the fifth-century A.D. *Tshan Thung Chhi Wu Hsiang Lei Pi Yao*. If systematic classifications of parhelic phenomena in the heavens (*Chin Shu*), and of the diseases of men and animals on earth (*Chu Shih Ping Yuan*), were worked out a full thousand years before Scheiner and Sydenham, this was only the expression of the firm hold which the Chinese had on this basic form of scientific activity. Perhaps the view of science which I am criticizing rests partially on too great a preoccupation with astronomy, and too little with biology, mineralogy and chemistry.

Then as to apparatus. That the Hellenistic Greeks were capable of producing highly complicated scientific instruments is shown by the anti-Kythera computing machine, but this is a very rare, indeed a unique example. It would be fairer to admit that throughout the first fifteen centuries of our era Chinese instrument-making was generally ahead, and (as in such instances as the seismograph and the mechanical clock) often much ahead, of anything that Europe could show. Actually the invention of clockwork was directly connected with the very absence of planetary models in Chinese thinking, for while on ecliptic co-ordinates no real body ever moves, declination circles are tracks of true motion, and the equatorial-polar system was a direct invitation to construct planetaria mechanically rotated. So, too, modern positional astronomy employs not the ecliptic co-ordinates of the Greeks but the equatorial ones of the Chinese. Nor need we confine ourselves to the astronomical sciences here, for a wealth of advanced techniques is to be found in those alchemical treatises of which the *Tao Tsang* is full.

Surely, again, observation, accurate and untiring, is one of the foundation-stones of science. What records from an antique culture are of vital interest to radio-astronomers today? Nothing from Greece, only the nova, comet and meteor lists of China's star-clerks. They it was who first established (by the seventh century A.D. at least) the constant rule (*chhang tsê*) that the tails of comets point away from the sun. Renaissance astronomers who quarrelled so much among themselves about the priority of the study of sun-spots might have been somewhat abashed if they had known that these had been observed since the first century B.C. in China, and not only observed but recorded in documents reliably handed down. When Kepler penned his New Year letter on the hexagonal form of snowflake crystals in A.D. 1611 he did not know that his contemporary Hsieh Tsai-Hang was puzzling over just the same thing, not, however, as a new idea but as a fact which had been known and discussed since the original discovery reported by Han Ying in the second century B.C. When we look for the original root of the cloud-seeding process in the comparison of snow-flake crystals with those of various salts and minerals, we find it not in the eighteenth-century A.D. experiments of Wilcke but in the acute observation of Chu Hsi in the twelfth century A.D. Thus it will surely be apparent that if God could geometrize so could the Tao, and the Europeans were not the only men who could trace its operations in forms both living and non-living. Finally if an example is needed from the biological sciences, let us remember the brilliant empirical discovery of deficiency diseases clearly stated by the physician Hu Ssu-Hui in the fourteenth century A.D.

Degree of accuracy in observation is also relevant. Indeed it is a vital feature, for it springs from that preoccupation with quantitative measurement which is one of the most essential hallmarks of true science. The old astronomical lists gave stellar positions in measured degrees, of course, the hydraulic engineers were recording precisely the silt-content of rivers in the first century B.C., and the pharmacists early developed their systems of dosages, but another example, less known, is more striking. Of the dial-and-pointer readings which make up so much of modern science, a search throughout the medieval world between the eighth and the fourteenth centuries A.D. would reveal instruments capable of giving them only in China. I refer to the needles of the magnetic compasses used first by geomancers, then (at least a century before Europe) by the sea-captains. Now it is a remarkable fact (as we have seen) that the Chinese were worrying about the cause of magnetic declination for a considerable time before Europeans knew even of magnetic directivity. Indeed the geomantic compass in its final form embodies two additional rings of points, one staggered $7\frac{1}{2}°$ east and the other $7\frac{1}{2}°$ west — these represent the remains of observations of declination, eastwards before about A.D. 1000 and westwards thereafter. We have reason to believe that this disturbing discovery was first made some time in the ninth or tenth centuries A.D., and it could never have been made if the observers had not been marking with extraordinary accuracy — and honesty — the 'true path' of the needle. It is even legitimate to compare this feat in principle with the discovery of the inert or noble gases so long afterwards by Rayleigh and Ramsay, residual bubbles which others had put down to experimental error or simply neglected. The honesty deserves emphasis also, for it was not shown so clearly when Europeans came up against the same phenomenon four or five centuries later. Or one might say that they had a greater tolerance of error, being content with 'there or thereabouts'. The history of magnetic declination in the West has been obscured by the fact that the compass-makers 'fiddled' the instrument by fixing a card askew to make it read right, and little or nothing was written about the matter till the sixteenth century A.D. Similarly, Robert Norman used to 'fiddle' his compasses to make the needles lie horizontally, until one day he lost his temper and really looked into the trouble, so rediscovering 'dip' or inclination.

Perhaps the greatest objection to the attempt of the Hellenizers to save European superiority is the fact that the Greeks were not really experimenters. Controlled experimentation is surely the greatest methodological discovery of the scientific revolution of the Renaissance, and it has never been convincingly shown that any earlier group of Westerners fully understood it. I do not propose to claim this honour for the medieval Chinese either, but they came just as near it theoretically, and in practice often went beyond European achievements. Although the ceramics technologists of China undoubtedly paid great attention to their temperatures and to the oxidizing-reducing atmospheres of their kilns, I shall not return to this here, for the Hellenizers would no doubt include the immortal products of the Sung potters in that "background noise of low technology" which was all that non-European cultures could attain. I prefer, then, to take other examples: Tu Wan's labelling of fossil brachiopods ("stone-swallows") to demonstrate that if they ever flew through the air it was only to drop down by process of weathering, or the long succession of pharmaceutical experiments on animals carried out by the alchemists from Ko Hung to Chhen Chih-Hsü, or the many trials made by the acoustics experts on the resonance phenomena of bells and strings, or the systematic strength-of-material tests which internal evidence shows must have been undertaken before the long beam bridges across the Fukienese estuaries could have been constructed. Is it possible to believe that apparatus so complex as that of the water-wheel linkwork escapement clocks, or indeed much of the textile machinery, could ever have been devised without long periods of workshop experimentation? The fact that written records of it have not come down to us is only what we should expect in a medieval literary culture. The fact that none of it was carried out on isolated and simplified objects, such as balls rolling down inclined planes, is again only what was characteristic of pre-Renaissance practice everywhere.

The erroneous perspective which I am criticizing can be seen particularly well in the use of the possessive plural personal pronoun. Some Western historians of science constantly speak of "*our* modern culture" and "*our* high civilization" (I italicize). *The Edge of Objectivity* reveals even more clearly the mood in which they approach the comparative study of men's efforts to understand and control the natural world.

> Anxious though our moments are, today is not the final test of wisdom among statesmen or virtue among peoples. The hard trial will begin when the instruments of power created by the West come fully into the hands of men not of the West, formed in cultures and

religions which leave them quite devoid of the Western sense of some ultimate responsibility to man in history. The secular legacy of Christianity still restrains our world in some slight measure, however self-righteous it may have become on one side and however vestigial on the other. Men of other traditions can and do appropriate *our* science and technology, but not our history or values. And what will the day hold when China wields the bomb? And Egypt? Will Aurora light a rosy-fingered dawn out of the East? Or Nemesis?

This is certainly very near the edge. It would induce in the reader a lamentable and unworthy attitude of mind in which fear would jostle its counterpart, possessiveness. Surely it would be better to admit that men of the Asian cultures also helped to lay the foundations of mathematics and all the sciences in their medieval forms, and hence to set the stage for the decisive break-through which came about in the favourable social and economic milieu of the Renaissance. Surely it would be better to give more attention to the history and values of these non-European civilizations, in actual fact no less exalted and inspiring than our own. Then let us give up that intellectual pride which boasts that "we are the people, and wisdom was born with us". Let us take pride enough in the undeniable historical fact that *modern* science was born in Europe and only in Europe, but let us not claim thereby a perpetual patent thereon. For what was born in the time of Galileo was a universal palladium, the salutary enlightenment of all men without distinction of race, colour, faith or homeland, wherein all can qualify and all participate. Modern universal science, yes; Western science, no!

Chronology of China

	HSIA kingdom (legendary ?)	*c.* 2000 B.C./*c.* 1500 B.C.
	SHANG (YIN) kingdom	*c.* 1500 B.C./*c.* 1030 B.C.
CHOU dyn. (Feudal Age)	Early Chou period	*c.* 1030 B.C./722 B.C.
	Chhun Chhiu period	722 B.C./480 B.C.
	Warring States period	480 B.C./221 B.C.
First Unification	CHHIN dyn.	221 B.C./207 B.C.
	HAN dyn.	
	Earlier or Western Han	202 B.C./A.D. 9
	Hsin interregnum	A.D. 9/A.D. 23
	Later or Eastern Han	A.D. 25/A.D. 220
First Partition	Three Kingdoms Period (San Kuo)	A.D. 221/A.D. 265
	Shu (west)	A.D. 221/A.D. 264
	Wei (north)	A.D. 220/A.D. 265
	Wu (south-east)	A.D. 222/A.D 277

Second Unification	Chin dyn.: Western	A.D. 265/A.D. 317
	Eastern	A.D. 317/A.D. 420
	Former (or Liu) Sung dyn.	A.D. 420/A.D. 479
	Northern Wei dyn. (Tho-Pa Tartar) later split into Eastern and Western	A.D. 386/A.D. 554
Second Partition	Northern and Southern Empires (Nan Pei Chhao)	A.D. 479/A.D. 581
	Chhi (southern)	A.D. 479/A.D. 502
	Liang	A.D. 502/A.D. 557
	Chhen	A.D. 557/A.D. 581
	Chhi (northern)	A.D. 550/A.D. 581
	Chou (northern)	A.D. 557/A.D. 581
Third Unification	Sui dyn.	A.D. 581/A.D. 618
	Thang dyn.	A.D. 618/A.D. 906
Third Partition	Five Dynasty period (Wu Tai)	A.D. 907/A.D. 960
	Later Liang	A.D. 907/A.D. 923
	Later Thang	A.D. 923/A.D. 936
	Later Chin	A.D. 936/A.D. 946
	Later Han	A.D. 947/A.D. 950
	Later Chou	A.D. 951/A.D. 960
	Liao dyn. (Chhi-Tan Mongol)	A.D. 907/A.D. 1125
	Hsi-Hsia State	A.D. 990/A.D. 1227
Fourth Unification	Northern Sung dyn.	A.D. 960/A.D. 1126
Fourth Partition	Southern Sung dyn.	A.D. 1127/A.D. 1279
	Chin (Ju-Chen Tartar) dyn.	A.D. 1115/A.D. 1234
Fifth Unification	Yuan (Mongol) dyn.	A.D. 1260/A.D. 1368
	Ming dyn.	A.D. 1368/A.D. 1644
	Chhing (Manchu) dyn.	A.D. 1644/A.D. 1911
	Republic	A.D. 1912 on

Bibliography

A. Beer, Ho Ping-Yü, Lu Gwei-Djen, J. Needham, E. Pulleyblank, and G. I. Thompson, "An 8th-century meridian line; I-Hsing's chain of gnomons and pre-history of the metric system", *Vistas in Astronomy*, IV (1961) 3

J. D. Bernal, *Science in History* (London, 1954) and private correspondence with the writer

G. Bonmarchand, "Le commerce de la Chine", art. in *Histoire du commerce*, III, *Le Commerce extra-Européen jusqu'aux temps modernes*, ed. J. Lacour-Gayet (Paris, 1953)

T. F. Carter, *The Invention of [Paper and] Printing in China, and its Spread Westwards*, 2nd edn. ed. by L. Carrington Goodrich (New York, 1955)

Chang Chun-Ming, "The genesis and meaning of Huan Khuan's *Discourses on Salt and Iron*", *Chinese Social and Political Review*, XVIII (1934) 1

A. C. CROMBIE, "The significance of medieval discussions of scientific method for the scientific revolution", art. in *Critical Problems in the History of Science*, ed. Marshall Clagett (Madison, Wisc., 1959) 79

FÊNG YU-LAN, *A History of Chinese Philosophy*, trans. D. Bodde (2 vols., Princeton, N.J., 1952–3)

A. FORKE, *The World Conception of the Chinese* (London, 1925)

E. M. GALE, *The* Discourses on Salt and Iron, *a Debate on State Control of Commerce and Industry in Ancient China* (Leiden, 1931) Chs. 1–19 (trans.)

E. M. GALE, P. A. BOODBERG and T. C. LIN, "The Discourses on Salt and Iron" Chs. 20–8 (trans.), *Journal of the Royal Asiatic Society* (*North China Branch*), LXV (1934) 5

C. C. GILLISPIE, *The Edge of Objectivity; an Essay in the History of Scientific Ideas* (Princeton, N.J., 1960)

A. GRAHAM, *Two* [11*th-century* A.D.] *Chinese Philosophers, Chhêng Ming-Tao and Chhêng Yi-Chhuan* (London, 1958)

M. GRANET, *La pensée chinoise* (Paris, 1934)

M. GRANET, *La civilisation chinoise* (Paris, 1948)

W. HARTNER, "Some notes on Chinese musical art", *Isis*, XXIX (1938) 72

W. HARTNER, "Chinesisches Kalendarwissenschaft", *Sinica*, V (1930) 237

HO PING YÜ and J. NEEDHAM, "Theories of categories in early medieval Chinese alchemy", *Journal of the Warburg and Courtauld Institutes*, XXII (1959) 173

HO PING YÜ and J. NEEDHAM, "The laboratory equipment of the early medieval Chinese alchemists", *Ambix*, VII (1959) 58

HO PING YÜ and J. NEEDHAM, "Elixir poisoning in medieval China", *Janus*, XLVIII (1959) 221

HO PING YÜ and J. NEEDHAM, "Ancient Chinese observations of solar haloes and parhelia", *Weather*, XIV (1959) 124

HOU WAI-LU, assisted by CHANG CHI-CHIH, LI HSÜEH-CHIN, YANG CHAO and LIN YANG, *A Short History of Chinese Philosophy* (Peking, 1959)

HU SHIH, *The Development of the Logical Method in Ancient China* (Shanghai, 1922)

HU SHIH, *The Chinese Renaissance* (Chicago, Ill., 1934)

P. HUARD and MING WONG [Huang Kuang-Ming], *La Médecine chinoise au cours des siècles* (Paris, 1959)

E. R. HUGHES, *Chinese Philosophy in Classical Times* (London, 1942)

E. R. HUGHES, *The* Great Learning *and the* Mean-in-Action (London, 1942)

E. H. HUME, *The Chinese Way in Medicine* (Baltimore, 1940)

ST. JULIEN, *Histoire et fabrication de la porcelaine chinoise* (Paris, 1856)

ST. JULIEN and P. CHAMPION, *Industries anciennes et modernes de l'empire chinois* (Paris, 1869)

LI THAO, many excellent papers on the history of medical sciences in China, in *Chinese Medical Journal* (1940–60)

LU GWEI-DJEN and J. NEEDHAM, "A contribution to the history of Chinese dietetics", *Isis*, XLII (1951) 13

LU GWEI-DJEN and J. NEEDHAM, "Hygiene and preventive medicine in ancient and medieval China", *Journal of the History of Medicine* (1962);

H. MASPERO, *Le Taoïsme* (Paris, 1950)

H. MASPERO, "L'Astronomie chinoise avant les Han", *T'oung Pao*, XXVI (1929) 267

H. MASPERO, "Les instruments astronomiques des chinois au temps des Han", *Mélanges chinois et bouddhiques*, VI (1939) 183

J. NEEDHAM, assisted by WANG LING, KENNETH ROBINSON, HO PING-YÜ and LU GWEI-DJEN, *Science and Civilization in China* (Cambridge, 1954–)

Vol. I *Introductory Orientations* (1954)
Vol. II *History of Scientific Thought* (1956)
Vol. III *Mathematics, Astronomy, Meteorology, Geography and Cartography, Geology, Palaeontology, Seismology and Mineralogy* (1959)
Vol. IV, pt. 1 *Physics (incl. Optics, Acoustics and Magnetism)* (1962)
Vol. IV, pt. 2 *Mechanical Engineering* (in the press)
Vol. IV, pt. 3 *Civil Engineering and Nautics* (in the press)

J. NEEDHAM, "Natural law and laws of nature in China and the West", *Journal of the History of Ideas*, XII (1951) 3 and 194; (also Hobhouse Lecture, Bedford College, London, 1951)

J. NEEDHAM, "The missing link in horological history; a Chinese contribution" (Wilkins Lecture, Royal Society), *Proceedings of the Royal Society A*, CCL (1959) 147

J. NEEDHAM, *The Development of Iron and Steel Technology in China* (Dickinson Lecture, Newcomen Society) (London, 1958)

J. NEEDHAM, *Chinese Astronomy and the Jesuit Mission: an Encounter of Cultures* (London, 1958)

J. NEEDHAM, "Les mathématiques et les sciences en Chine et dans l'Occident", *Pensée* (1957) no. 75, 1; also in *Science and Society*, XX (1956) 320

J. NEEDHAM, *Classical Chinese Contributions to Mechanical Engineering*, Grey Lecture, King's College, Newcastle-upon-Tyne (1961)

J. NEEDHAM and D. LESLIE, "Ancient and medieval Chinese thought on evolution", *Bulletin of the National Institute of Science, India*, VII (1952) 1

J. NEEDHAM, and LU GWEI-DJEN "The earliest snow crystal observations", *Weather* XVI (1961)

J. NEEDHAM and K. ROBINSON, "Ondes et particules dans la pensée scientifique Chinoise", *Sciences*, I (1960) no. 4, 65

J. NEEDHAM, WANG LING and D. J. DE SOLLA PRICE, *Heavenly Clockwork: the Great Astronomical Clocks of Medieval China* (Cambridge, 1960)

F. Y. NESTERUK, N. A. FIGUROVSKY, A. P. YUSHKEVITCH, I. D. STRASHUN and V. N. FELDCHINA, *Iz Istoria Nauki i Tekhniki Kitaya* (*Essays in the History of Science and Technology in China*) (Moscow, 1955)

D. J. DE SOLLA PRICE, *Science since Babylon* (New Haven, Conn., 1961)

E. PULLEYBLANK, "The origins and nature of chattel slavery in China", *Journal of Economic and Social History of the Orient*, I (1958) 185

N. G. SWANN, *Food and Money in Ancient China* (Princeton, N.J., 1950)

E. G. R. TAYLOR, *The Haven-Finding Art* (London, 1956); and private correspondence with the writer

THAN PO-FU, WÊN KUNG-WÊN, HSIAO KUNG-CHÜAN and L. MAVERICK, *Economic Dialogues in Ancient China: selections from the* Kuan Tzu *Book* (New Haven, 1954)

WANG LING, "On the invention and use of gunpowder and firearms in China", *Isis*, XXXVII (1947) 160

WANG LING and J. NEEDHAM, "Horner's method in Chinese mathematics; its origins in the root-extraction procedures of the Han dynasty", *T'oung Pao*, XLIII (1955) 345

W. WILLETTS, *Chinese Art* (2 vols., London, 1958)

K. C. WONG [Wang Chi-Min] and WU LIEN-TÊ, *A History of Chinese Medicine* (2nd ed., Shanghai, 1936)

YANG LIEN-SHÊNG, *Money and Credit in China* (Cambridge, Mass., 1952)

A. P. YUSHKEVITCH, *Istoria Matematike v Srednie Veka* (*Comparative History of Medieval Mathematics in East and West*) (Moscow, 1961)

Commentaries

Commentary by Willy Hartner

The limit imposed on the length of commentaries compels me to select, from the wealth of facts and arguments contained in Mr. Needham's paper, a few of those topics which are of particular interest to me, and to leave it to others to comment on those in which I feel ignorant or at least incompetent. Owing to my lack of sociological training, I will have to disregard above all those statements and conclusions which bear on the social conditions and their interrelation with, or impact on, the evolution of scientific thought and of technological progress. I am aware that I will thus not be able to do full justice to Mr. Needham's intentions.

May I start with a general remark. Mr. Needham is annoyed by that well-known supercilious attitude evidenced by the average European when facing problems of non-European civilizations. I wholeheartedly subscribe to the last passage of his paper, and venture to say that it has been also one of my own main concerns to point out the ridiculousness — and no less the dangers — of such an attitude. But it seems to me that enumerating priorities of scientific or technical achievements is not the best way to prove the superiority of one civilization to another. As long as two civilizations, *A* and *B*, live in an almost complete isolation from one another, it seems of little use to apply a time-scale common to both, stating for example that this or that was found in *B* a thousand years before it became known for the first time in *A*. Only in the case of civilizations that have been in constant touch, such as the Aztec and the Maya, or which have sprung from the same roots, such as the Islamic and that of the Christian Middle Ages, does it make real sense to proceed in this way.

It needs no proof, because it cannot possibly be seriously contested, that the Chinese civilization as a whole, and Chinese science in particular, is one of the most impressive testimonies of the greatness of human spirit, second to none of the other great civilizations. But this does not mean that it was superior to them: each one of them has its intrinsic value, its "poverties" and its "triumphs", and all our efforts to define their relative greatness will necessarily fail because we will always be at a loss to work out standards by which organisms having such a complex structure can be measured and compared.

Mr. Needham claims that "decimal place-value and a blank space for the zero had begun in the land of the Yellow River earlier than anywhere else" (p. 118); in another place he says (p. 143): "Although we speak of Hindu–Arabic numerals, the Chinese were in fact the first, as early as the fourteenth century B.C., to be able to express any desired number, however large, with no more than nine signs." These assertions, I am afraid, are untenable and, moreover, apt to create a confusion in a field pretty well cleared up thanks to the common efforts of sinologists, Assyriologists, and historians of mathematics. The nine signs for the numerals 1–9 used in the fourteenth century B.C. were the same in principle as the ones used in modern Chinese; the next three, by the way, for 10, 100, 1000, can also be traced back to the beginnings of Chinese script (only that for 10,000 does not seem to appear before the Chou) and the same of course is true of the symbols used for the cyclical count.

Now I am not quite sure whether I interpret Mr. Needham correctly: if the horizontal stroke indicating unity (which is found repeated, on the oracle-bones, up to four times) is counted as one symbol only, there remain as other distinct symbols the ones indicating 5, 6, 7, 8, 9, 10, 100, and 1000, which makes indeed 9 *in toto*. Judging from Table 23 of the third volume of his *Science and Civilisation in China* (p. 15), the highest number recorded on oracle-bones seems to be 5,000. By extrapolation we can easily construct all numbers up to 9,999, but nothing can be said about numbers exceeding that limit, for the simple reason that we just do not know whether there existed any convention to render them in an unambiguous way. The much later pre-classical and classical texts, to my knowledge, never employ any method other than the one in use until recently, and even the astronomical texts make no exception, despite the fact that the clumsiness of a number like the following: *san-pai liu-shih-wu ssu-fen tu chih i* ("three hundreds six tens five [and] one out of four parts of a degree") for $365\frac{1}{4}°$, must have been felt as a pretty heavy burden to a man dealing with astronomical problems. The ideogram for zero (*ling* 零), which is definitely late, was only used to indicate one or more omitted positions (e.g. *san-pai ling san*, "three hundreds, no tens, three"

=303, or *san-ch'ien ling san,* "three thousands, no hundreds or tens, three"=3003).

I am afraid that what Mr. Needham understands by place-value (see also op. cit. pp. 12 ff.) differs essentially from what is commonly accepted as such: when he says (ibid. p. 13) that in the compound $\overset{\times}{⊚}$ =500, the symbol ⊚ (which occurs only in combination with the digits for 1–9) indicates place-value, he will find himself at variance with the mathematicians, to whom the occurrence of numerals having a fixed and invariable value (such as 500) is the very criterion for the fact that there is no question of place-value. Actually, I see no reason whatsoever to make a distinction, as Mr. Needham does, between the above sign for 500 and its Herodianic Greek equivalent, 𐅅, only because Greek H standing alone means 100, while the Chinese symbol occurs only in combination with the digits 1–9, so that 100 is written $\overline{⊚}$, and not just ⊚. The only characteristic difference between the two is, that the Greek system employs addition *and* multiplication: H, HH, HHH, HHHH, 𐅅, 𐅅H, . . . as against the old Chinese which, anticipating the later classical use, operates with multiplication alone. Furthermore (ibid. p. 13 below), Mr. Derek Price's theory that the peoples having an alphabet, contrary to those employing an ideographic script, necessarily felt tempted to run through all the letters, not stopping at 9, applies neither to the Phoenicians nor to the Romans. The Greek, Hebrew, and Arabic alphabetical numerals of course have a common source.

Place-value, either decimal or not, thus has to be strictly excluded for the period preceding the invention of the so-called rod-numerals. These, undoubtedly, have to be counted among the forerunners of the later commercial numerals (*Su-chou-tzŭ* attested since the late Ming; but the lying cross, x, for 4 (occurring also, according to Needham's Table 22, among the late counting-rod forms, in the thirteenth century), appears to have been borrowed from India, where it is found already in the Kharoṣṭhī inscriptions. But it was only after the introduction of a symbol for zero that the Chinese rod-numerals as well as the Hindu numerals were transformed into a perfect place-value system. I admit the possibility that this happened a little (maybe a century or two) earlier in the Far East than in India, but the evidence available so far still appears to be so scanty that no convincing conclusion can be drawn from it.

Against all this it will be well to remember that the Babylonian place-value system was in use already by the beginning of the second millenium B.C. (the fact that its basis was 60 instead of 10 is no disadvantage!). When, about or shortly before the middle of the first millenium B.C., a separation mark indicating omitted places was introduced, the Babylonian system had become pretty nearly perfect, except that there was no way to indicate the 'absolute' value of a number (1,20 thus could mean $60+20=80$ as well as $1\frac{20}{60}=1\frac{1}{3}$). But at the latest in Ptolemy's *Almagest*, the Greek equivalent of the Babylonian system had attained perfection: it consistently employed a symbol for zero (incidentally identical with ours: 0) and was capable of expressing unambiguously any desired number, either integer or fraction. The circumstance that it operated with the traditional letter-numbers — one or at the most two letters to a sexagesimal place — was not considered, nor was it in fact, a drawback; until the very latest times the Arabs followed the same usage in spite of the fact that the Hindu numerals had been in use in the Islamic world for about 1,000 years and had been continuously employed there, side by side with the alphabetical (*abjad*) numbers. In continuation of the Babylonian-Greek tradition, astronomical tables exclusively employed the latter; for all other purposes, already in al-Bīrūnī's time, extensive use was made of the Hindu place-value numerals. Thus it has to be recognized as an incontestable fact that if the Chinese did contribute to the formation of the Hindu–Arabic place-value system, their impact was felt only at a late stage of the evolution. The earliest phase of Chinese script shows no trace whatever of a place-value count.

As it will not be of interest to enter upon a discussion of the many of Mr. Needham's statements to which I subscribe without reserve, I will restrict my remarks to some more of those which I consider less convincing. Mr. Needham, in his *magnum opus* as well as in many of his papers, has furnished a multitude of proofs to refute the widespread belief that the Chinese were theoreticians rather than a practical people. But I am afraid that he now goes too far in stating (p. 123) that they were a "fundamentally practical people, inclined to distrust all theories". There can be no doubt that the attitude of the average philosopher, scientist, or physician was characterized, all through the ages, by a strong traditionalism capable of hampering the free evolution of scientific thought. In medicine, for example, the theory of *yin* and *yang* combined with that of the five elements plays such a predominant role that there is hardly one single phenomenon that does not find itself adapted to, or forced into, this scheme (which itself is based on rather scanty empirical facts). Thus, to me, Chinese natural philosophy, no less than that of Christian scholasticism, appears as one of the real prototypes of deductive thought. It is true there was an astounding number of great men who succeeded in freeing themselves from the fetters of tradition and of preconceived theory and indulged in unbiased research (there were indeed perhaps more such men in the Chinese than in the European Middle Ages), but the circumstance that the old theory survived till the last of the twenty-four dynasties demonstrates with sufficient clarity that traditionalism eventually proved stronger than empiricism. In fact it would be against all the available evidence to affirm (and Mr. Needham would be the last to do so) that serious attempts to overthrow tradition were ever made.

To give an example of the strength of the traditional view, may I refer to the fictitious organ called the "three burning-spaces" (*san-chiao*) invented at a very early stage of the *yin-yang* theory and still maintained, in spite of contrary evidence, in the textbooks of the later half of the *Ch'ing* dynasty. Moreover, this was applied to the immunization against smallpox (A.D. 1000 or later), obviously derived from observation and experiment, but then adapted to the *yin-yang* theory, so that, depending on the sex of the child to be immunized, the cotton soaked with the pustule secretion had to be put either into the left or the right nostril.

As to the world systems devised in China, I dare say that their inferiority to the highly ingenious geometrical models due to Eudoxus, Apollonius, Hipparchus, Ptolemy, the Arab astronomers, Copernicus, and Tycho Brahe, simply cannot be questioned. It never occurred to me that the crystalline spheres should have impeded the development of astronomy. No, they certainly proved very useful during the course of two millennia until, after Tycho had shown them to be non-existent, Kepler devised his new theory, in which they were no longer needed.

Coming back to the *yin-yang* theory, I find it difficult to follow Mr. Needham — who, unless I am mistaken, is thinking of it — when he writes: "Chinese physics was faithful to a prototypic wave theory (and perennially averse to atoms)" (p. 119), or: "they were *a priori* inclined to field theories". I am afraid that such statements do not serve to clear up the historical situation, but rather are apt to cause confusion.

We are looking forward with great interest to a detailed account of the surveying method employed in the early part of the eighth century by I-Hsing and Nan-kung Yüeh to measure a meridian arc (p. 132; cf. *Science and Civilisation in China*, III, 292 f.) because, judging from what Mr. Needham has told me privately, the results obtained seem to bear witness to extraordinary mathematical skill, implying even the existence of a developed trigonometry of which nothing is so far known. But looking back at what had been achieved in that field during earlier centuries, we are bound to state that the results were disastrous. In the *Chou-pei suan-ching*, which was considered a classic by all later generations, it appears that two shadow-lengths, namely those of the solstices, had been actually observed and measured. They safely exclude any date prior to the Han. The remaining twenty-two solar terms were found — *horribile dictu!* — by way of *linear* interpolation. It will be difficult to account for the fact that the star positions and planetary periods observed about the same time, or even known earlier, prove to be extremely good and testify to considerable skill and mathematical insight. On the other hand, in view of the circumstance that not even the shadows corresponding to the sun's position in the equator (equinoxes) were actually observed, it cannot surprise us that the inequality of the lengths of the seasons was discovered at such a late date (fifth century or later).

As a last critical observation on a special topic picked out from Mr. Needham's tremendously interesting paper, I venture to say a word about the translation of a passage from a work by Chu Hsi, consisting of fourteen words, which he gives in the following transliteration: *so chio chê, hsin chih li yeh; nêng chio chê, chhi chih ling yeh*. He translates this as follows: "Cognition or apprehension is the essential pattern of the mind's existence, but that there is something in the world which can do this is what we may call the spirituality inherent in matter". In trying to reconstruct the original Chinese text, I found that it reads in all probability as follows:

所 覺 者 心 之 理 也。

能 覺 者 氣 之 靈 也。

If this be true, I find Mr. Needham's translation too paraphrastic for, literally, the text evidently means: "Cognition [i.e. that which is apprehended] is the *li* [characteristic or essential pattern] of the mind; the faculty of apprehending [*facultas percipiendi*] is the *ling* [spiritual force] of the *ch'i*". It is true that, in the neo-Confucian terminology, this last term, *ch'i*, has assumed a definite material aspect — more so than it had in earlier times; still it must not be overlooked that it is essentially different from *chih* 質, which remains the common word for macroscopic, solid, matter. Hence, I cannot approve of rendering it in the above passage just by "matter"; what is meant, evidently, is a material pneuma or kind of extremely rarified fluid, the "subtle matter" *par excellence* (this term, coined by Needham himself, hits the point), and it is because of the spiritual power (*ling*) of this *ch'i* that cognition becomes possible.

Commentary by Pierre Huard

I will begin by saying that, on the whole, I am in agreement with Mr. Needham on what he calls, in Balzacian terms, the triumphs and poverties of Chinese science. I will base my comments on his communication mainly on biological and medical evidence.

Let us begin with the period of triumph. Chinese Antiquity can appropriately be compared with Mediterranean Antiquity so far as the keenness of social struggle, the diversity of thought, political organization, and the development of techniques are concerned. The Han dynasty (206 B.C.–A.D. 220), during which the Chinese first extended their rule and legislation on the large scale, can readily be compared with the Sassanid and Roman empires.

In a recent and very remarkable work, Mr. Bridgman[1] has shown that the evolutionary curve of medicine was peculiarly similar to that of Greece and Rome.

The shamans and the medicine men of the Hsia, Shang, Yin and Chou dynasties, like those of the present-day Altai or Kamchatka, were essentially magicians but were also capable of pre-scientific research, establishing a sketchy nosology and

[1] Dr. R. F. Bridgman, "La Médecine dans la Chine antique", extract from *Mélanges chinois et bouddhiques*, pub. by the Institut belge des Hautes Études chinoises, X (1955) 213.

therapeutic structure. About the fourth and third centuries B.C., at the time when the foundations of the Book of Rites (*Li-Ki*) and the administrative *Chou-li*, or Rites of the Chou dynasty were being laid, a class of true physicians, known as *Pien ts'io* (*c.* third century), was constituted, who refused to be confused with the wizards. They adapted to medicine the system of the world based on the correspondence of the microcosm with the macrocosm, and founded a physiology, followed by a pathology, centred on the *yin-yang* doctrine.

In a rationalist climate, the study of the pulse, of the circulation of the blood, and of breathing were codified. Adequate therapeutics, including acupuncture, was conceived of: Shun-yu Yi (*c.* 176 B.C.) foresaw imperfectly the value of clinical observation and, in a less formalist society, could have become another Hippocrates. These developments suggest parallels with Greek medicine, seen in the abandonment of magic and the introduction of the interrogation of the patient, the search for antecedents, clinical examination, and the classification of symptoms. Medicine was becoming a real scientific discipline, constituting a valid antecedent of the modern clinic (see Bridgman). If the attitude found in this first century B.C. had continued, great progress would have been possible. But, at the end of the Han period, the same interruption of development came about in the Far East as in the West, and allowed the development of dogmatism and classificatory mania. Yet despite the crumbling of the Ancient Empire, we find Chih Fa-tsun giving the earliest description of measles (*c.* A.D. 307), and Ko Hung (*c.* A.D. 281–380) that of smallpox (A.D. 326), five hundred years before Rhazes. Ko Hung also described the symptoms of leprosy, including the principle one, hypaesthesia.

During the Middle Empire (the Sui and T'ang dynasties, A.D. 581–907), the great Buddhist pilgrims Hsüan-tsang and Y-Tsing, the merchants of Canton, and the missions brought about the penetration, within the empire, of astronomical, mathematical and medical data and of techniques of Indian, Iranian, Arabian and Byzantine origin, which stimulated scientific progress. Surgical therapeutics included the stripping of cataract, the orthopaedic treatment of fractures and the extraction of bone. Medical therapeutics made use of Byzantine theriac, of ephedra in respiratory diseases, of oil of Croton as a purgative, and, for the first time in the world, of calomel in the treatment of venereal disease. Deficiency diseases were known as well as their rational dietetic treatment. The dry and wet forms of beri-beri were well distinguished. An ethics of noble character surrounded certain doctors, like Sun Szu-miao (A.D. 318–82), with the halo of the good Samaritan. The T'ang civilization appears, in its entirety, as an extremely brilliant culture, far superior to other contemporary civilizations, whether Irano–Arabic or Carolingian.

After the fall of the Middle Empire, the Sung dynasty (A.D. 960–1127) was never able to re-unify the empire. But political and military defeats become unimportant when compared with the progress in technology (for example in the invention of printing, the compass, gunpowder) and in science (in mathematics and medicine). Paediatrics was far advanced. Measles, scarlet fever and smallpox were distinguished. Materia medica became enriched by exotic drugs. Legal medicine was created. The great classics were printed xylographically and illustrated with diagrams, sometimes in colour.

The Yuan dynasty (A.D. 1260–1367) mongolized China politically but put her in close relationship with the Islamic, Jewish and Christian world. With foreign practitioners, Chinese medicine adopted Arab lapidaries, Indian chaulmoogra (an Indian plant), opium and mandrake. In this period algebra reached its height, and Chinese algebraists were the greatest of the Eurasian Middle Ages.

A popular revolution brought to power the Ming dynasty (A.D. 1368–1644). A mercantile bourgeoisie was born which promoted great maritime voyages (A.D. 1405–1424), which alas failed to bear fruit. Chinese science produced its last masterpieces with Chu Tsai yü (A.D. 1584), who calculated a musical scale, and Li Shih-chen (A.D. 1518–93), author of the celebrated *Pen-ts'ao kang-mu*, translated into numerous foreign languages. He mentioned syphilis, which had appeared in Canton about A.D. 1505–6, at roughly the same time as its existence was remarked by European, Arab and Indian doctors; it was treated throughout Eurasia, by mercury and China root (squine, a Chinese plant).

Despite all this, there did not appear in the Far East a movement comparable with the European Renaissance. Calculation on paper was abandoned in favour of calculation on the abacus, and the great algebraists of the preceding period became incomprehensible. The period of the triumphs of Chinese science was at an end.

The period of poverty, however, was far from being an uninteresting one. During the last imperial dynasty, that of the Manchu (A.D. 1644–1911), the great emperors K'ang-hsi and Ch'ien-lung ordered the compilation of great encyclopaedias. They asked Jesuits to make Chinese translations of numerous European scientific books, much more for their own personal instruction than to spread knowledge of them throughout the empire. Indeed, they thought such knowledge politically dangerous, and there was, from this point of view, an undeniable resemblance between the imperial despotism and the enlightened despotism of Europe. It was thus that the Manchu *Anatomy* composed by Father Parennin[1] was kept in privacy when it could have played a part analogous to that played in Japan by the *Kaitai Shinsho*.

Nevertheless, one must realize that large-scale inquiries concerning the natural and medical sciences and techniques were undertaken by the Jesuits under the patronage of the Chinese court. They have left us some very interesting documents of which I will mention a few examples. There is first of all a series of diagrams in colour showing the manufacture of tea and of porcelain, preserved in the Musée des Beaux-Arts of Rennes (the Robien collection).[2] There is the herbarium of the Father d'Incarville,[3] also preserved in the Musée, and an album of plants, handpainted under his direction.[4] There is also the celebrated roll of the goldfish of China, with illustrations of

[1] R. P. Parennin, *Treatise on human anatomy etc.* Written in Manchu at Peking and finished 1 May 1723. Several copies of this MS are known, one at the Royal Copenhagen Library, another at the Museum National d'Histoire Naturelle de Paris, MS 2009, a third at the Bibliothèque Nationale, Paris. This treatise comprises 8 volumes (*pen*), four of which are devoted to anatomy, three to pathology, and the last to medical physics and gynaecology. It is copiously illustrated.

[2] The albums concerning the manufacture of porcelain and tea were brought back from China by the chevalier Pierre Louis Achille de Robien (1736–92), who stayed at Canton from 1766 to 1777. They became part of the collection of his relative, the Marquis Paul Christophe de Robien (1731–95), president of the Parliament of Brittany, who died at Hamburg. These collections are now at the Musée de Rennes. There is another album on the manufacture of porcelain practically the same as that at Rennes, comprising, like that one, 26 plates; this is in the Bibliothèque Nationale, Cabinet des Estampes. There are only a few variations in the tone of the colours and in the subjects dealt with; these reproduce the process of making porcelain in the celebrated manufacture of Ching-te-chen.

[3] The herbarium of Fr. d'Incarville is kept at the Laboratorie de Phanérogamie of the Museum d'Histoire Naturelle.

[4] The *Pen ts'ao* of the Asiatic Society, and MSS Museum d'Histoire Naturelle 5018–5019.

birds, mammals and insects, coming from the same source: Chinese artists guided by European missionaries.[1] Finally, there are the 500 diagrams of the treatise on ethnology by Fu Heng, devoted to non-Chinese peoples.[2]

Western science contributed to a mathematical renaissance which was to bear fruit only in the nineteenth century. With Wang Ch'ing-jen we see a refutation of classical anatomical errors, based on dissections done in person (A.D. 1790). Japan welcomed vaccination and Chinese materia medica as marking important progress. Another very remarkable intellectual movement (and authentically national) was the reaction against the official doctrine of the literary civil service, which had become a state religion, elaborated by Chu Hsi during the Sung period, in the form of neo-Confucianism. The *Han-hsüeh* school was represented successively by Ku Yen-wu (b. 1613), a sort of Chinese Luther or Erasmus, one of the rare reformers that imperial China knew, by Wang Mang (of the Han period), and by Wang An-shih (of the Sung period). It was continued by Yen Yüan, by the feminist Yüan Mei, and by Tai Chen, the most powerful mind of this school, which aimed at a return to the sources of Chinese culture, rid of the glosses of commentators and rejuvenated by concrete studies in history, philology, geography, and the sciences, leaving also a place for sport. The new China was already germinating in the minds of those thinkers who despised literary competitions and (Tai Chen at least) felt the necessity of studying nature to understand its laws, and admitted the importance of the exact sciences, making the study of texts a weapon against an obsolete tradition.

Despite the already very wide gulf which existed, at this period, between Chinese pre-Galilean and pre-Cartesian science and European science, there was much in common to the medicine (e.g. venereology, study of the pulse, legal medicine, vaccination, materia medica) and to the technology (e.g. manufacture of porcelain, architecture, laquerwork, metallurgy) of the two ends of Eurasia. The literary and artistic patrimony of China was becoming known, and sinophiles were becoming greatly interested in the material and scientific aspects of the Far Eastern civilization. The greatest empire of

[1] MS Museum National d'Histoire Naturelle 5066; reproduced by George Hervey in *The Goldfish in China in the Eighteenth Century* (London, 1950).

[2] Fu Heng, *Houang-Tsing Tche-Kong-t'ou*, 1751; Bibliothèque Nationale, Cabinet des Estampes.

the world passed also for the most civilized, and the French government hastened to have its victories portrayed by official artists.[1]

Thirty years later, in the nineteenth century, China was for Europeans but a pagan and barbarous state which the allied forces were going to put right. Yet there was still occasional Chinese scientific thought, especially noteworthy in mathematics. On the technical side, it was a Confucian-type scholar, Lin Tse-hsü (1785–1850; it was he who, by ordering the destruction of foreign opium, precipitated a war), who was also the patron of the Chinese steam navy. He was followed by forward-looking viceroys like Ting Pao-chen, Chang Chih-tung and Li Hung-chang, who encouraged the efforts of technologists (like Hsü Shou, a former scholar, and his son Hsü Chien-yin) and the construction of arsenals.

At the end of this discussion, we must consider the question of the intrinsic value of Chinese science. It is a question which raises and will continue to raise numerous problems. The fruitful comparative approach has so far been used only on a airly small scale. Nothing valuable will be achieved, in any case, without the collaboration of Chinese and Japanese teams, working on the spot, in liaison with Western teams. From this point of view much remains to be done.

In his conclusion, Mr. Needham says that he would like Westerners to stop talking of "our science", speaking of the discoveries made since the Renaissance, for which he proposes the name of modern universal science. May I say that on this point he is in agreement with the great Manchu emperors, who invited missionaries not to call their science *hsi* (i.e. Western) but *hsin* (i.e. modern, new).

Finally, I would like to pay homage to the monumental work of Mr. Needham, who has extracted Chinese science from the obscure retirement where the greater number of sinologists had left it, in order to put it at the disposal of researchers throughout the world. He has thus encouraged the dissemination of a new humanism, already half foreseen by George Sarton, in which a better and reciprocal comprehension of Western and Far Eastern science will no longer allow one to doubt the "roundness of the earth".

[1] Cf. Louis Reau, *L'Europe française au siècle des lumières* (Paris, 1938).

Commentary by Wong Chu-Ming

The causes of Chinese science's lagging behind that of the West are:

(1) The rigidity of the social structure, making the class of literate functionaries the ruling class. It is a classical factor and a very important one. But there has always been an element of nonconformism, Taoist in Antiquity, Buddhist in the Middle Ages, *Han-hsüeh* in modern times, which, at all times and under divers names, has been interested in science, and could have furthered its development. We may recall the scientists Shen Kua (A.D. 1031–95), author of the *Essays Written at the Villa Torrent of the Dream*; Sung Ying-hsing, partisan of *The Exploitation of the Works of Nature* (A.D. 1637); and Li Shih-chen (A.D. 1518–93), author of the *Pen-ts'ao kang-mu* (general compendium of medical matters).

(2) The fact that the written language was essentially literary and metaphorical in nature. It was very different from vulgar parlance and technical language, and thus inventors were able to make their discoveries known only with difficulty. For example, we may consider the case of Sung Ying-hsing, who wrote in a detailed manner on the procedures of industrial manufacture, and that of Li Shih-chen, who produced a systematic mineralogical, botanical and zoological classification. It is impossible, without a technical glossary, to understand the works of the hydraulic engineer Li Ping (*c.* 300 B.C.). In fact the diversion works on the Min-chiang are called "Fish's Mouth" because they have the same shape as a fish's head; "The Neck of the Precious Bottle" is simply an opening in a rocky mountain to allow the regulation of flow.

(3) The contempt for manual labour symbolized by the long finger nails of the scholar; the contempt for mercantile activity which made the merchants one of the lowest social classes.

(4) The logic, product of the essentially concrete and non-analytic language, which did not make possible the elaboration of axiomatic and deductive reasoning necessary for the development of science. The practical applications of a problem were more important than theoretical exposition.

(5) The immensity of the empire, the wars and the revolutions, which explain why scientific liaison was difficult, and why certain important advances were lost or ill transmitted. As far as Li Ping is concerned, we have no texts. The first text

on hydraulics dates from A.D. 1360 and is attributed to Ouyang Hsüan.

(6) That in the West man is the measure of all things, whereas in China every problem presented itself in a different light. This factor was cumulative. It was necessary to wait for a new scientific attitude, corresponding to a new stream of Chinese culture and to a modification of Chinese economics, to allow the East–West gap to be bridged. Chinese scientists like Hsü Kuang-ch'i (A.D. 1562–1633), Li Chih-tsao (d. A.D. 1630), and Hsü Shou (nineteenth century) began to spread knowledge of Western science, and from that time there were no longer any notable differences between modern science in the West and modern science in the Far East.

Discussion

B. L. van der Waerden

Mr. Needham has written a very valuable paper on Chinese science. But he also gives some consideration to the importance of Greek science for our modern science, and since this is the main theme of our present session I should like to say a few words on this subject. Newtonian mechanics is admittedly the basis of most of our modern science. In it three threads come together and each of the threads comes from Greece. The first thread is that of Greek astronomy, of planetary astronomy, of which, as I learned from Mr. Needham, the Chinese had nothing. It goes to Copernicus and Kepler, and it was only by means of Kepler's laws that it was possible for Newton to construct his mechanics. Without Kepler's laws he would have been totally lost. The second thread is the conics of Apollonius which Newton used, but it was not only the conics of Apollonius, it was the whole structure of Greek axiomatic geometry, which forms the model of Newton's axiomatic mechanics. The third thread comes from Greek mechanics. Archimedes discovered some essentials; Philoponus and Themistius had some consideration of the notion of impetus which probably influenced Galileo, who found the law of inertia. This was the third essential thing for Newton. Everybody knows that Greek science was absolutely essential for our science, and I am astonished that Mr. Needham writes that he disagrees with this opinion. I am willing to admit that the third thread need not necessarily have come from the Greeks, and let us say for the sake of argument that Galileo might have found his law of inertia without the Greeks; but it seems to me quite clear that without Greek science the other two would have been quite impossible. Mr. Needham objects to statements by a number of authors quoted on pp. 140–42 on the grounds that the definitions of mathematics they give are too narrow and that our science does not consist only of Newtonian mechanics. Of course it does not consist only of this, but this is one of its essential parts and without it modern science is largely unintelligible. I should be grateful if Mr. Needham would explain his position further.

S. E. Toulmin

Let me make a distinction and then ask some questions arising from it. The distinction is this: when we ask, why was Babylonian science like *this*?, or why was Chinese science like *that*?, we may be asking two rather different sorts of question. On the one hand, there are questions about the arguments and motives relevant to the work of an individual scientist in some society or other; on the other, about the reasons which led that society to lend or withold its support and encouragement to particular inquiries — by state subsidies, or otherwise — and to accept or be indifferent to their results. The latter type of question is the one to which (as I understood it) the title of this Symposium primarily refers — "The Structure of Scientific Change": the former is the one to which the *Observer* (9 July 1961) referred in describing the subject of this meeting as "The Springs of Scientific Discovery".

The distinction is important because any intellectual or technical step has not only to be made once; it must become part of a tradition. Like a variant in organic evolution, it must not only occur — it must become established. And the distinction is necessary here, because we have already seen strong cross-purposes arising through neglect of it. In one earlier discussion, for instance, Stahlman and van der Waerden agreed about the character of Babylonian science. Stahlman said: why should not mathematicians in Babylon have been interested in their subject for its own sake as an intellectual inquiry? Van der Waerden answered: the Babylonian state only paid them because of their services as astrologers — to which I would add (following Neugebauer) — and as calendarists. And now van der Waerden takes issue with Needham about the arguments and intellectual filiations between individual scientists, when Needham himself is talking about the way in which social and economic factors influenced the character and pace of development of Chinese science.

Now, as to my second group of questions, Needham has touched on some important and interesting points, and I would like to ask some questions. For instance, he mentions the factor of *publication*, which clearly affects the rate at which ideas become accepted in a society; and he discusses the influence of a bureaucratic structure of society on the growth of scientific skills and knowledge. As to the first of these points, let me take up his statement that social factors "prevented the publication of the records which the higher artisans certainly kept" (above, p. 124). Why does he say *certainly kept*? Surely in other comparable cases, craft skills have usually been passed down by example, from master to apprentice, without the use of written records: from Mesopotamia, for instance, we have the odd recipe for glass-making or perfumery, but the bulk of the artisan tradition was presumably communicated through a system of apprenticeship — often from father to son. The skills of the astronomical computers are the obvious exceptions; but there the skills themselves were essentially those of a literate, not a manual guild. So let me ask Needham: is it so certain that there must have been these records in the case of the Chinese artisanate?

Again, about the role of bureaucracy: Needham makes out an excellent case for believing that the Chinese state organization greatly hastened the development — for instance — of rain-gauges, snow-gauges and the like. Yet how far does he think that this same system was capable of encouraging original speculative thought in science? Does a bureaucratic organization allow, or encourage, full freedom of discussion? For surely it is this full freedom of discussion which, like a harsh environment, imposes the strong selective pressure necessary if novel and unorthodox ideas are to make good their claims to attention and acceptance. Needham quotes only one passage bearing on this, in which secrecy is deplored, on the grounds that it has permitted "unorthodox cosmological theories . . . to spread and flourish" (above, p. 132).

So let me put two final questions to Needham. First, do we have the evidence — autobiographical, biographical or circumstantial — with the help of which we can reconstruct the arguments and motives involved in any major intellectual step followed by an individual scientist in China? (The sort of thing we are always able to discuss in the case of Western scientists from Copernicus on.) Secondly, does one find in China the active recognition that heterodox ideas may actually be *a good thing* — that unless novel intellectual variants are given a fair chance to measure up against *idées reçues*, there can be no improvement in our ideas? Like Hartner, I feel that this second question lies close to the heart of the question, did the Chinese have a true *science*?; that one necessary feature of a full science is the possibility of rejecting authority and establishing the superiority of a modified system of ideas.

B. L. van der Waerden

I never meant to say that Babylonian scribes did scientific work only because they were paid for it. Of course, the inventors of Babylonian astronomy were highly interested in science. As for the scribes who collected observations and made extensive calculations during many centuries, I do not know what their personal attitude was towards science. The question was: why was their work considered important and why were they paid for it? My answer was: because people believed in cosmic religion and thought they needed horoscopes.

J. Needham

What I have to say can be divided into comments on a number of specific points that have been raised, and an effort to formulate better a fundamental general point. I agree with Mr. Huard that the Ming period was somewhat "Byzantine", but I no longer feel that it was so wholly a decadent period in the history of Chinese science as has often been maintained. For, as he will doubtless agree, although mathematics and astronomy did then suffer a decline, in the field of medicine it was an exceptionally prosperous time which saw the appearance of many great treatises; and contemporaneously geography, agronomy and animal husbandry also flourished. I was interested in the reference of Mr. Wong Chu-Ming to the "fish-head" or "fish-snout" at Kuanhsien, for it happens that I know that great hydraulic engineering system going back to the third century well, and studied it thoroughly once again in 1958. The "snout" is in fact the technical term for the iron-shod division head set where the waters part. This shows us once again that Chinese texts on technical matters can best be understood when one knows the terrain as well as the technological product. With most of what Mr. Huard and Mr. Wong said I am of course in full agreement, as also with Mr. Hartner's strictures on some of the aberrations which scientific men of the medieval age manifested in China as well as elsewhere. He will be interested to know, in connexion with interpolated values, that in a study which I have in the press (collaborating with Mr. Arthur Beer, Mr. Pulleyblank and Miss Lu Gwei-Djen) on the eighth-century A.D. meridian line of I-Hsing and Nankung Yüeh, we found that the table of polar altitudes and sun shadow figures as given in the dynastic history was wholly computed, but at the same time every evidence exists that the survey parties did actually make their observations. What we think happened was that I-Hsing having, in his time, no method of 'producing a smooth curve' from the data, presented to the throne a set of figures calculated with the aid of trigonometrical methods, then very new. Next, regarding Mr. Hartner's physiological example of the *san chiao*, I should like to point out that the Chinese medical literature constitutes a veritable ocean, and that the doctrine of a "fictitious organ" cited by him was only one, and not at all the most reasonable, of the opinions held by Ming physicians. In the *Lei Ching* of Chang Chieh-Pin, for example, we find these "three coctions" interpreted as something more like Galenic faculties, absorptive, transformative, and excretive, physiological functions rather than anatomical entities; and in much of what Chang Chieh-Pin says we might be listening to his contemporary J. B. van Helmont, though no mutual influence could have existed between them. Lastly, some of the Ming inoculators may well have held baseless views about the left and right nostrils, but others developed empirical techniques of remarkable interest for attenuating the toxicity of the virus, such as incubation at body temperature for prolonged periods.

Modern science was born, Mr. Hartner says, because it broke loose from dependence upon authority, whether philosophical or theological, and dared to judge according to observed fact and experiment. If this was all that was required, Chinese society could have developed modern science too, for I could quote many examples of statements derogatory of "the opinions of former scholars" in Chinese texts — for instance the *Chiu Thang Shu* itself, reporting I-Hsing's new results on the meridian arc, or a Ming student of snowflake forms complaining that some of his predecessors had seen pentagonal ones. Of course, the sceptical tradition of Chinese scholarship reached its height in the philological revaluations and textual criticism which started in the Sung and never looked back, a movement which long anticipated the parallel humanism of the European eighteenth century A.D. Another important point was raised by Mr. Toulmin when he wondered whether the feudal-bureaucratic structure of Chinese society did not discourage original scientific speculation. I think it was in fact somewhat inhibitory, but one must remember that the Confucians were not always in power, and the Taoists, on the contrary, had no objections to heterodoxy, being "always ready to hear or see some new thing". It can be no coincidence that their influence is felt so often in the developments of Chinese science and technology. Buddhist influence too was very much on the side of open-mindedness in proto-scientific speculation, and they were also very influential from time to time. As for Mr. Toulmin's question about the records of the artisans, my firm belief is that they did actually exist; I mentioned the *Mu Ching* and the Fukien shipbuilding manual; I might add another case, namely the statement about A.D. 1400 that "the information on the guiding stars [used by the navigators in their voyages, as far as East Africa and Kamchatka] was all collected and written down"; this was a prelude to the great achievements of the Ming navy in long-distance navigation under Chêng Ho.

Let us now turn to the point of greatest substance raised by Mr. van der Waerden in his Homeric defence of the Greeks. I fear that he has not taken in any of the points I was trying to make in the last section of my paper. I did not say that the Greek *praeparatio evangelica* was not an essential part of the background of modern science. What I did want to say was that modern exact and natural science is something much greater and wider than Euclidean geometry and Ptolemaic mathematical astronomy; more rivers than those have emptied into its sea. I presume that Mr. van der Waerden is a mathematician and a physicist, perhaps a Cartesian; but I myself am professionally a biologist and a chemist, more than half a Baconian, and I therefore do *not* think that what constituted the spearhead of the Galilean break-through constitutes the whole of science. What happened to crystallize the mathematization of experimental hypotheses when the social conditions were favourable does not exhaust the essence. If mechanics was the primary science, it was *primus inter pares*. If physics celestial and terrestrial has the battle-honours of the Renaissance, it is not to be confused with the whole army of science, which has many brave regiments besides.

"The spearhead, but not the whole, of science." In pondering over a better way of representing the situation, it occurred to me that we ought perhaps to make a clearer distinction between factors which were concerned in the direct historical genesis of modern science, and factors which fell into place later after the Galilean break-through. We shall also have to distinguish more clearly between science and technology. Suppose we erect a classification of four pigeon-holes, science vertically on the left and technology vertically on the right, and let the upper boxes represent direct historical genesis while the lower ones represent subsequent reinforcement. Then taking the upper left-hand compartment first, the contribution of the Greeks will have the greatest share, for Euclidean deductive geometry and Ptolemaic astronomy, with all that they imply, were undoubtedly the largest factor in the birth of the "new, or experimental, science" — in so far as any antecedents played a part at all, for we must not undervalue its basic originality. In spite of Ptolemy and Archimedes, the occidental ancients did not, as a whole, experiment. But Asian contributions will not be absent from this compartment, for not only must we leave a place for algebra and the basic numerational and computational techniques, we must not forget the significance of magnetism, and knowledge of this realm of phenomena had been built up exclusively in the Chinese culture-area, which thus powerfully influenced Europe through Gilbert and Kepler. Here one remembers also the adoption of the Chinese equatorial coordinates by Tycho. But the Greeks predominate. In the upper right-hand compartment the situation is entirely different, for in technology Asian influences in and before the Renaissance (especially Chinese) were legion — I need mention only the efficient horse-harnesses, the technology of iron and steel, the inventions of gunpowder and paper, the escapement of the mechanical clock, and basic engineering devices such as the driving-belt, the chain-drive, and the standard method of converting rotary to rectilinear motion, together with nautical techniques such as the leeboard and the stern-post rudder. Alexandria also ran.

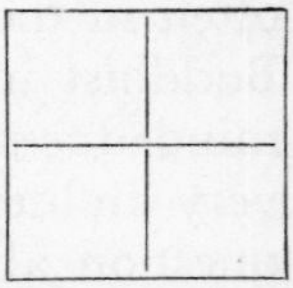

The lower compartments will now be available to take achievements of the Asian cultures which, though not genetically connected with the first rise of modern science yet deserve all praise; they may or may not be directly genetically related to their corresponding developments in post-Renaissance modern science. A case of direct influence could be found in the Chinese doctrine of infinite empty space instead of solid crystalline celestial spheres, but it did not operate until after Galileo's time. Cases of later incorporation would be the development of undulatory theory in eighteenth-century A.D. physics, which immensely elaborated characteristically Chinese ideas without directly building on them, or the use of ancient and medieval Chinese records by radio-astronomers. So also, if atomism, not mathematics, proved to be the soul of chemistry, which found itself so much later than physics, this elaborated Indian and Arabic ideas of great subtlety without knowingly basing itself thereon. A good case of the absence of any influence would be the seismograph as used in China from the second to the seventh centuries A.D.; though an outstanding achievement, it was almost certainly unknown to any of the scientific men who developed seismographs in post-Renaissance Europe. Chinese biological and pathological classification systems occupy the same position; they were clearly unknown to Linnaeus and Sydenham, but none the less worthy of study, for only by drawing up the balance-sheet in full shall we ever ascertain what each civilization contributed to human advancement. It is not legitimate to require of every scientific or technological activity that it should have contributed to the advancement of the European culture-area. What happened in other civilizations is entirely worth studying for its own sake. Must the history of science be written solely in terms of one continuous thread of linked influences? Is there not an ideal history of human thought and knowledge of nature, in which every effort can find its place, irrespective of what influences it received or handed on? Modern universal science and the history and philosophy of universal science will embrace all in the end.

It only remains to consider the contents of the right-hand lower compartment. Here we have to think of technical inventions which only became incorporated, whether or not by re-invention, into the corpus of modern technology after the Renaissance period. A case in point might be the paddle-wheel boat, but it is uncertain, for we do not know whether the first European successes were based on a Byzantine idea never executed, or on a vast fund of practical Chinese achievement during the preceding millennium. A better case would be the differential gear, for though present in the south-pointing carriage of ancient China, it must almost certainly have arisen again independently in Europe. So also the Chinese methods of steel-making by the co-fusion process and by the direct oxygenation of cast iron, though of great seniority to the siderurgy of Europe, were not able to exert any influence upon it, if indeed they did, which is still uncertain, until long after the Renaissance. Similarly it might be unwise to connect too closely the crucible steel of Huntsman with that of the age-old Indian wootz process.

In all this I have tried to offer an *opinio conciliatrix* in friendly fashion to those who may have been shocked by the objective attitude which I always seek to adopt in weighing European claims. If we think out the matter as I suggest, we may feel greater need for recognizing several kinds of values; the value of that which helped directly to effect the Galilean break-through, the value of that which became incorporated in modern science later on, and last but not least, the value of that residue which yet renders other civilizations no less worthy of study and admiration than Europe.

Supplementary Note

No reference was made in my reply, as written at Oxford, to the points on mathematical notation raised by Mr. Hartner in his commentary, because he did not raise them at the time. If he had done so, discussion might perhaps have been more satisfying than it can now be.

I feel that Mr. Hartner does not clearly distinguish between Shang bone forms, rod-numerals (as used on counting-boards), cursive script numerals, mercantile script, etc. Our references to "nine signs" were of course never intended to include symbols for 10, 100 and 1000 used as numerals, but the basic figures for 1 to 9. I fear that Mr. Hartner has misunderstood the significance of the systematically-used place-value components *which were not themselves functional numerals*. These assured that there were no symbols which did not manifestly indicate their decimal place-value position. Hence no doubt the development of the late Chou and Han counting-boards (from the time of Confucius in the sixth century B.C. onwards), where the zero was invariably indicated by a blank space (*khung wei*). We disagree altogether with Mr. Hartner's view that place-value did not exist in China until the coming of an actual symbol for the zero from India or Indo-China early in the eighth century A.D. It is true that we do not yet know the 10,000 place-value component in Shang script, but the Shang people would have had no difficulty in expressing numbers higher than that according to their system if they had desired to do so. Nor as yet can any firm date be fixed for the first beginnings of the Han counting-board system; all one can say is that the Shang numerals carried within themselves the homing mechanism which infallibly guided them to their correct decimal place-value locations on the counting-board. One cannot draw adequate conclusions only from the letter of the 'rhetorical' mathematical texts as they have come down to us; one must always have in mind the zero-blank chequer-pattern or matrix counting-board technique which is clearly implied by all of them from the *Chou Pei Suan Ching* to the *Ssu Yuan Yü Chien*. The zero-blank spaces preceded the introduction of the 'rhetorical' term *ling* by about a couple of millennia. But this is not the place to embark on further explanations; the reader is simply requested to read carefully the relevant parts of Section 19 in Vol. 3 of *Science and Civilisation in China*, and to form his own conclusions.

On Mr. Hartner's other points not covered in my reply written at Oxford (for example his remarks on neo-Confucianism), I can only record friendly dissent, since further discussion would strain too much the patience of the readers of this volume.

PART THREE

Science and Technology in the Middle Ages

6

What was Original in Arabic Science?

S. PINES

Because of limitations of time and space, the subject, "What was original in Arabic science?", cannot be discussed here in full. The present paper will deal first and foremost with various Arabic physical theories and methods. It will also try to point out the similarities and the differences between the evolution of Arabic physics and that of Western European physics.

One glaring omission is the absence of any attempt to indicate or discuss appropriately the importance and the unprecedented character of contact between Arabic and Hindu science. Since, so far as we know, the Arabs were the first people belonging to a Western civilization[1] to have assimilated to some extent Indian medicine, astronomy and mathematics, some historical and sociological observations would seem to be germane to our main theme.

It is pretty certain that at least at the beginning of the period of translations from Greek into Arabic, which extended from the end of the eighth until the tenth or eleventh century, one of the principal reasons for the Arab eagerness to master Greek learning was of a utilitarian nature: such sciences as medicine, astrology and alchemy appeared to be of great practical use. We find accordingly that these three sciences were sometimes considered as 'the fruit', that is, the goal of knowledge. This view is mentioned, for example, by Abu'l-Barakāt al-Baghdādī[2], who rejects it. He disbelieves in alchemy (p. 232) and, because of the insufficiency of our knowledge (p. 236), in astrology, and considers that, though medicine derives for the greater part from experiments and inferences based on the principles of physics, and though knowledge of, and training in, the natural sciences increases the physician's capacity for medical reasoning, a physician as such need not be versed in such subjects as the problem of the eternity or

[1] Al-Bīrūnī opposes the Hindu to the Western, i.e., Moslem and perhaps also Greek scientists; see S. Pines, " 'La Philosophie Orientale' d'Avicenne", *Archives d'histoire doctrinale et littéraire du Moyen Age*, XIX (1953) 16, n.2.

[2] *Kitāb al-Mu'tabar*, ed. Serefettin Altkaya, (Hyderabad, 1358H.) II, 231 ff.

temporal creation of the world, the finite and the infinite, time and space, motion and repose. Some knowledge of the (four) elements, a little information about forces and their effects, about the less subtle points of the science of generation and corruption and of qualitative change, and about the properties of animals and plants, is relevant to medicine. A physician knows these things by means of his senses and by experience, as he knows anatomy and the faculties of medicines (p. 232).

This utilitarian approach was doubtless furthered by the fact that many of the greatest Arabic scientists and astronomers were also practising physicians, a combination which was much rarer in the ancient world and in medieval Latin Europe. The contrast in this respect between Christendom and Islam may at least in part be explained by the fact that the Arabic intellectuals versed in Greek learning had as a rule no opportunity of teaching it at universities; the corresponding Moslem institution generally did not dispense instruction in the Greek sciences.[1] The recognition of the practical usefulness of scientific knowledge was sometimes, at least when alchemists and astrologers were concerned, connected also with the notion that this knowledge meant political and military power. It is true that this anticipation of Roger Bacon's fancies and of modern experience is generally encountered in wildly improbable legends, such as the story that the alchemical art of Jābīr b. Ḥayyān was the primary cause of the fortune of the Abbasids and the Barmecids and of the rise of the Fatimid dynasty.[2] Greek and Roman Antiquity offers, as far as I can see, no counterpart to these tales. Of possibly greater significance is the notion that the spread of popularized scientific knowledge constitutes a powerful revolutionary factor. With regard to their political purpose there is a certain resemblance between the *Encyclopédie* of the eighteenth-century *philosophes* and that of the Brethren of Purity written in the tenth century with a view to furthering the subversive Fatimid propaganda. I ought to add that, at least from the time of Al-Fārābī, the Aristotelian Arabic philosophers were sharply opposed to the utilitarian approach to science, though not, as far as Al-Fārābī and some of his successors are concerned, to philosophers exercising the kingly art of politics.

[1] Asad Talas, *La Madrasa Nizamiya et son histoire* (Paris, 1939) 38, 50, 53 ff.

[2] See P. Kraus, *Jābīr Ibn Ḥayyān* (Cairo, 1943) I, p. xlii, n.6 and MS Paris Bibl. Nat., ar. 1688, f. 177r.

But in the context of this paper this a side-issue. The main subject, namely a consideration of various approaches and attitudes to physical theory, shall now be discussed. It seems convenient to concentrate on three fundamental attitudes:

(1) The attitude of the Peripatetic philosophers, among whom Avicenna will be included, though his claim to the appellation is questionable. Admittedly there are fundamental differences of opinion between Al-Fārābī, Avicenna, Averroës and other Aristotelian philosophers with regard to physical theory. To mention but one example, the fact that Avicenna believed in absolute determinism, whereas Averroës apparently did not, cannot be indifferent in this connexion. Nevertheless, the philosophers and scientists of this school, which was the most influential though perhaps not the most original of Islam, may be bracketed together because of the essential similarity of their outlook.

(2) The attitude which I shall call aprioristic. Abū Bakr al-Rāzī, the Rhazes of the Latins, will serve as a representative of this attitude, which will be defined with reference to him. The doctrines of Abu'l-Barakāt al-Baghdādī and, to a certain extent, those of Fakhr al-Dīn al-Rāzī also exemplify this approach.

(3) The attitude of the mathematicians, illustrated by reference to Ibn al-Haitham (the Alhazen of the Latins), al-Bīrūnī and Al-Khāzinī.

The characteristics of the Arabic Peripatetics with whom I shall begin can, as I believe, be best brought out by indicating, with regard to certain selected points, which of the multiform and sometimes opposed tendencies of the Aristotelian physics they chose to emphasize and then develop. In other words, no claim that they have initiated an absolutely new departure (if there is such a thing in the history of ideas) will be made on their behalf. In spite of this restriction, they could, of course, manifest very considerable originality of thought.

For obvious reasons, their interpretation of the Aristotelian doctrine depended to a great extent on that of the Greek commentators. In some cases, the fact that they had at their disposal Greek texts whose originals are no longer extant, and which are only now becoming known to us in their Arabic version, explains the unfamiliar aspect of the Peripateticism of these philosophers. For instance, Alexander of Aphrodisias's treatise *On the Principles of the All*, of which the Arab version (the Greek original is lost) has been recently edited by A.

Badawi,[1] was a seminal work of this kind and accounts (especially if it is augmented with texts from Alexander's lost commentary on Aristotle's *Physics*, of which the Arabs had a fuller knowledge than we have) for much of the Arabic and Jewish Aristotelianism (for instance, for many aspects of Maimonides's thought). The world of this Alexandrian physical doctrine was up to a certain point materialistic and monistic; the last in view of the fact that in it no sharp demarcation line separated the animate from the inanimate, or the heavenly from the terrestrial bodies.

According to Alexander, the world of nature is conceived of as that of moved bodies which have an intrinsic principle of motion. These principles of motion were apparently conceived of as efficient or instrumental, at all events not final, causes. For they, or the bodies which they set in motion, were moved by desire. This being so, the objects of their desire obviously constituted the final causes.

The realm of nature could be divided into three categories: (*a*) that of the inanimate bodies of the sublunar world; (*b*) that of the animate bodies of the sublunar world; (*c*) that of the celestial animate bodies. Within the last two categories the principles of motion of the bodies concerned were constituted by their souls, which were identical with the natures of these bodies. Within the first category, however, the principles of motion were intimately bound up with the natural inclinations of the bodies and perhaps derived from these inclinations or were identical with them.

Within the second and the third categories the souls were the forms of their bodies. In the case of the animate bodies of the sublunar world, the souls resulted from the particular corporeal mixture that constituted their bodies. This was not true of the soul or souls of the celestial bodies, for the latter bodies were simple and not compound. However, the definition of this soul as the form of the celestial body makes it clear that within this category there existed likewise an analogous inseparable connexion between the body and the soul — though the latter cannot be said to result from the former, for the reason just given and also because the celestial body always had been, and always would be, animated by its soul; both of them were eternal. For evident reasons it cannot be doubted that the natural inclinations were as dependent as the souls upon the bodies in which they inhered.

[1] In *Arisṭū 'inda'l-'Arab* (Cairo, 1947) 253–77.

Another interpretation (or perhaps a variation on Alexander's interpretation) of Peripatetic physical theory is also possible. It shows in addition a predilection for mechanistic explanations. This interpretation is found in a number of treatises by Ya'qūb al-Kindī (ninth century) dealing with various physical problems. Al-Kindī, who was usually and perhaps justifiably reputed to have been the earliest Arab philosopher — a claim going back to his Moslem biographers — seems to have been first and foremost a compiler and occasionally a plagiarist, who could draw upon a rich and curious stock of erudition. It is virtually certain that the theories which will now be discussed derived from Greek sources; the use in the treatises in question of such Greek geographical terms as the Pillars of Hercules[1] can serve as a sufficient proof of this origin. But the question has also another aspect. For the theories in question also form a part of the general history of ideas in Islam. They are principally concerned with the four sublunar elements.

According to the prevalent Peripatetic doctrine each of these elements had two sets of fundamental characteristics, namely:

(i) two of the fundamental qualities, i.e.,
  (*a*) either cold or heat
  (*b*) either dryness or humidity;

(ii) gravity or levity, i.e., a tendency, manifested in a displaced portion of an element, to go down or to go up. For instance the element earth had (*a*) cold and dryness and (*b*) gravity.

By a triumph of what Emile Meyerson might have called the impulse towards identification, these two independent sets of characteristics became unified in Al-Kindī's theory,[2] heat and cold, the two active qualities,[3] becoming, respectively, the cause of natural upward motion and the cause of natural downward motion. Of the two passive qualities, dryness and humidity, the first was held to cause in the element to which it belongs the rapidity of either the downward or the upward natural motion, and the second the slowness of these motions.

In Al-Kindī's opinion, though he might have stated it more clearly,[4] this theory seems also to account for the natural places

[1] Or rather the Signs of Hercules; see *Rasā'il al-Kindī al-falsafiyya*, ed. M. A. Abu Ridah (Cairo, 1953) II, 132.

[2] Op. cit. II, 93 ff. This theory seems to be an amplification of Aristotle's remark in *Meteor.*, 342a 15 ff.

[3] Cf. *Al-Kindī,* op. cit. I (Cairo, 1950) 224.

[4] Ibid. II, 93.

of the elements. Given his premises, this appears to be a logical consequence of the Peripatetic doctrine attributing to each of the four elements two fundamental qualities. The laws governing the natural motions, according to Al-Kindī, could clearly account in a plausible way for the fact that the natural place of air, which was supposed to have as its qualities heat and dryness, was higher than that of any other sublunar element, and a similar correlation obtained between the fundamental qualities and the natural places of the other elements.

Al-Kindī went even further in his attempt to unify the Peripatetic physical theory. He took as his starting-point a statement of Aristotle's,[1] according to which motion causes heat. Aristotle had sought to prove this assertion by the empirical fact that lead sometimes melts in rapidly moving projectiles; and Al-Kindī tells us[2] that he tried to verify this statement. For, as he says: "Information about a datum of sensation can only be disproved or proved true by [another piece of] information about a datum of sensation." The theory that motion causes heat was used to account for the sun's heating the earth. According to this explanation, the heat given off by the sun is due to the latter's motion. Al-Kindī accepted this view and in certain passages appears to have considered that this is the sole cause of solar heat (he is not always consistent on this point). In addition, he believed that, in the final analysis, the tides are brought about by the heat produced by the revolutions of the sun and the moon. He held that the latter, because of its nearness to the earth, exerts a considerable action upon it, especially upon the elements water and earth; whereas the sun influences in particular the two other elements.

The immediate causes of the solar, but not of the lunar, tides are also stated:[3] these are the winds due to the unequal distribution of the heat produced by the motion of the sun.

These explanations obviously indicate an ambition to work out a comprehensive unified physical theory.

A similar ambition is in some degree also in evidence in the views on the phenomena in question which are ascribed by Maimonides to Aristotle[4] and have a certain affinity with Al-Kindī's theory. According to these views, the differences between the four sublunar elements are, at least in part, a function of the distances of their natural places from the heavenly sphere. For matter situated near the sphere acquires,

[1] *Meteor.*, 341a, 17 ff. [2] Op. cit. II, 118. [3] Op. cit. II, 123.
[4] *Guide for the Perplexed*, II, 13; ed. Munk (Paris, 1861) II, 149.

because of this proximity, the dispositions required for receiving the form of fire. And the same applies *mutatis mutandis* to the three other elements. The interest presented by this rather jejune explanation is, in the context of the *Guide for the Perplexed*, of a methodological nature. Because of the internal unity shown by its recourse to a single cause, Maimonides seems to regard it as a typical example of a satisfactory physical theory, and so uses it in order to expose the profoundly unsatisfactory character of Aristotle's celestial physics, according to which, for no explicable physical reason, the direction and the velocity of the motions of the various spheres differed.

It is true that, because of the progress of mathematics since Aristotle's time, the philosopher's astronomy was held to be outdated. But this did not make the problem posed by the science of astronomy any less troublesome, but rather more so. For the usually accepted astronomical theory, namely the Ptolemaic system, was a *skandalon* and a stumbling-block for the Arabic Peripatetics. In this domain mathematical theory, reduced by Aristotle to the status of a mere abstration from reality, took, as it were, its revenge. For the separation advocated, for instance, by Al-Fārābī between mathematical theory designed to save the appearance (*sōzein ta phainomena*) on the one hand, and celestial physics supposed to study the real nature of the heavenly bodies on the other, did not work, or at least not to the satisfaction of the Arabic Aristotelians of the stricter kind. They had worked out the concept of laws of nature (though they generally did not use the term) and physical theories corresponding to this concept and could not stomach the idea that such devices as the eccentrics and the epicycles should, under the pretext of *sōzein ta phainomena*, flout these laws. Hence the following exhortation and personal confession of Averroës in his *Great Commentary* on Aristotle's *Metaphysics*:[1] "This old astronomy [he means the one accepted by Aristotle and his contemporaries] should be investigated from the beginning. For it is the true astronomy, validated by the principles of physics." Several details, omitted here, follow. They concern Averroës's conception of this correct astronomical theory, which, according to him, can explain the motions of the heavenly bodies whereas the Ptolemaic system is incapable of doing so. He proceeds:

In my youth I hoped that I should be able to complete such an

[1] Ed. Bouyges (Beirut, 1948) III, 1663 f.

investigation. But now in my old age, having been formerly hindered from doing this by various obstacles, I have lost the hope of accomplishing it. But these words may perhaps incite some investigator to inquire into these things. For in our times the science of astronomy is non-existent. For astronomy as it is found in our time conforms to [mere] opinion rather than to that which exists [literally "rather than to existence"].

The term "existence" with which this passage ends is a key-word for the Arabic and perhaps particularly for the Spanish Arabic Aristotelians.

In opposition to the Mutakallimūn they held that existence — that is, physical existence — had an order of its own which it followed invariably, or as near as made no difference. In modern parlance, it was considered to be subject to natural laws even though this term was not used, perhaps because it suggested something superimposed from outside. In spite of Aristotle's having pointed out some essential differences between the nature of the heavens formed out of the fifth essence and that of the terrestrial world constituted by the four elements, the Arabic Peripatetics, who in this respect followed certain Greek philosophers, preferred the physical theories embodying this order (or these laws) to be as unified as possible; more unified than Aristotle's plain text warranted.

In addition, the theories mentioned above suggest that occasionally they had a certain predilection for mechanistic explanations. The fact that, but for a large exception, they almost extruded the final causes from the Aristotelian scheme of physics clearly fits in with the last point.

The exception referred to is evidently constituted by the separate intelligences and the Prime Mover, regarded in the Aristotelian system as the final cause *kat'exochēn*. But some interpretations, for instance those inspired by the views of Alexander of Aphrodisias alluded to above, could considerably circumscribe the function of these intelligences, so that their role in physical theory is in a way reminiscent of that of the Cartesian God as described by Pascal.[1] They were needed — in some case perhaps chiefly because of the authority of Aristotle — in order to account for the fact of circular motion. But apart from this fact, physical theory had no use for them; and even circular motion could, if one were so minded, be explained, with some warrant from Aristotle's text, as being caused by a natural characteristic of the Fifth Body.

[1] *Pensées*, in *Œuvres complètes*, ed. J. Chevalier (Paris, 1954) no. 194.

Aristotle's dictum, "Nature does not do anything in vain", was often invoked by the Arabs, especially when some biological problem was being discussed. But it generally served as a heuristic principle[1] which did not necessarily have anthropomorphic or theological overtones. In other words, it did not by any means imply that a hypostatized nature pursues certain ends and avoids everything that is not conducive to them. An illustration of the tendency to account for the state of the world by referring to efficient rather than to final causes may be found in Avicenna's *Kitāb al-Shifā'* (the *Sufficientia* of the Latins) at the end of the section corresponding to Aristotle's *Meteorologica* (I, 276 in the Teheran lithograph). Avicenna makes the point that the permanence of the species, which was one of the main articles of Aristotle's natural science, cannot be absolutely assured by natural generation, as "copulation is a voluntary thing and not a necessity". According to him, their permanence is due to the fact that certain positions of the heavenly spheres bring about at recurring intervals mixtures of the elements that occasion a spontaneous generation of individuals of the various species. This may seem a fanciful explanation, but it does away with the need to have recourse to final causes. It also provides an illustration of a fundamental postulate of the physical theory of the Arabic Aristotelians, namely the postulate of the permanence and stability of the universe and of all the living species and the varieties of inanimate substances it contains, and of the recurrent cyclic character of all the main processes that take place in it. It was this postulate which the Arabic Aristotelians had first and foremost in mind when they spoke about the order prevailing in all that exists. In modern terms, they believed in the uniformity of the laws of nature, but interpreted this thesis as implying the essential immutability of the universe. It is a point which is also made by Leibniz in his polemical correspondence with Samuel Clarke. According to these Arabic philosophers, human science depended on the acceptance of this postulate and their main quarrel with the Mutakallimūn was due to its rejection by these theologians.

The comprehensive Peripatetic physical theory was most vulnerable to epistemological arguments because of its many loose ends and because of its being a singular compound of inferences from observation and experience, of semantic analysis, of common-sense views and of the personal opinions

[1] A rather similar conception may be found in Kant's *Kritik der Urteilskraft*, para. 67.

of Aristotle and Alexander and various other commentators sometimes accepted out of mere reliance on authority; and yet the wholesale claim was made that it was entirely based upon the conclusions of Aristotelian reason. This was not due to a lack of interest in epistemological criteria. Though methodical doubt was never, to my knowledge, as radically employed by any Arab thinker in pursuit of absolutely certain knowledge as it was by Descartes — Al-Ghazālī's universal scepticism marks a temporary psychological crisis (Ghazālī recounts its various phases and his final deliverance from doubt in his autobiographical work, *Al-Munqidh min al-Ḍalāl*) and is not a necessary stage on the way to certainty — yet some of the philosophers, Avicenna among others, knew of the possibility of a universal test by doubt.[1]

But the Peripatetic philosophers considered themselves as the inheritors of a coherent body of scientific thought, and, in contradiction to the philosophers whom I call aprioristic, were not minded to jettison some of its main conclusions, for instance those concerning time and place, in pursuance of a certitude which seemed to them fallacious, being, as they believed, based on the inferior faculty of imagination. This traditionalist attitude did not mean that they were afraid to tinker with, and have independent views upon, subsidiary points of the dominant scientific theory. It did not even prevent them from formulating working rules for scientific discovery by induction which may have been more precise than those of their Greek model. But in practice these rules seem to have been intended to be followed only in very circumscribed fields of scientific research. Mr. Crombie[2] has called attention to the rules, set forth in Avicenna's great medical work *Al-Qānūn fi'l-Ṭibb*, which propound a method for discovering whether a particular drug has curative properties. A similar method is formulated in a more generalized and more abstract form in some of Avicenna's philosophical treatises.[3] Certain crucial points are stated even more clearly in the following passage[4] by Abu'l-Barakāt al-Baghdādī, who may on the whole be fairly described as an aprioristic philosopher, but in this question obviously follows Avicenna's lead:

[1] See S. Pines, "La conception de la conscience de soi chez Avicenne et chez Abu'l-Barakāt al-Baghdādī", *Archives d'histoire doctrinale et littéraire du Moyen Age*, XXI (1955) 22 ff.

[2] In *Avicenna, Scientist and Philosopher, A Millenary Symposium*, ed. by G. M. Wickens (London, 1952) 89 ff.

[3] See S. Pines, op. cit., pp. 95 ff.

[4] See ibid., pp. 97 ff.

As for experience, an example is provided by the following judgment: scammony purges human bodies of yellow bile. In this [example] the frequency of the phenomenon puts out of court [the notion] that it might be due to chance. Because of the frequency of the experience these judgments may be regarded as certain, even without our knowing the reason [for the phenomenon]. For there is certain knowledge that the effect in question is not due to chance. It must accordingly be supposed that it is due to nature or to some modality thereof. Thus the cause qua cause, though not its species or mode of operation, is known. For experimental science is also constituted by a knowledge of the cause and by an induction based on all the data of sensation; whereby a general science is reached. . . . But in the cases in which the experiment has not been completed, because of its not having been repeated in such a way that the persons, the time and the circumstances varied in everything that did not concern the determining cause, whereas this cause [remained invariable], the experiment does not prove certain knowledge, but only probable opinion.

In this text the words "experience" and "experiment" have been used to translate one and the same Arabic term. This seems to be justified, because in the latter part of the passage Abu'l-Barakāt adumbrates a theory of the experimental method or comes close to doing so. He appears to think that if one wishes to verify a hypothesis according to which a certain factor is the cause of a physical occurrence, the other factors involved should be analysed and shown to be subject to variation, whereas the presumed cause should remain invariable. Experiment has been described as a question addressed to nature. Abu'l-Barakāt's method, which doubtless was equally Avicenna's, appears to answer to this description.

But, as the example of scammony used by both philosophers suggests, they probably tended to believe that this method should be mainly or exclusively used in medicine. There is no warrant for thinking that, at least as conceived by the Peripatetic philosophers, this programme of research constituted an appreciable danger to Aristotelian physics. As has already been indicated, this science seemed intellectually satisfying mainly because of its presupposing an eternal immutable cosmic order. Viewed from this angle it may even appear as more coherent than Newtonian science, which by destroying the ordered cosmos engendered a spate of theistic and non-theistic cosmogonies beset with various antinomies.

In a way this new sixteenth- and seventeenth-century science may be called to mind by the multiform ideas of Abū Bakr al-Rāzī (d. either A.D. 923 or 925 or 932), except only — it is a large exception — for the fact that he not only did not mathematize physics, but was actively opposed to mathematics and blamed Galen for taking an excessive interest in geometry.[1] Because of these views he himself was taken to task by Al-Bīrūnī.[2]

It has already been suggested that Rāzī exemplifies an intellectual attitude, which is also represented by Abu'l-Barakāt al-Baghdādī (d. A.D. 1152) and, in certain of his writings, by Fakhr al-Dīn al-Rāzī (d. A.D. 1209), who was deeply influenced by Abu'l-Barakāt. The relation between the ideas of the last and those of Abū Bakr al-Rāzī is less clear; it is not proven that this is a case of historic filiation. On the other hand, there is an undeniable intellectual affinity between these two philosophers. The 'Platonism' of the two should also be taken into account. For Rāzī considered himself a disciple of Plato, and Abu'l-Barakāt was certainly influenced by this Greek thinker. Moreover many of the physical doctrines characterizing the representatives of the philosophical tendency with which we are dealing were sometimes ascribed in the Arabic doxographic tradition, inaccurately, to Plato. It is, at least in the case of Rāzī, in a way a genuine, but circumscribed Platonism. For the only dialogue used to any considerable extent by this writer seems to have been the *Timaeus*; and its doctrines, taken over by him, sometimes suffered a sea-change in the transition.

The intellectual tendency with which we are concerned may be characterized by a special kind of anti-Aristotelianism much better than by the rather peculiar brand of Platonism of these writers. Perhaps the most significant element in this anti-Aristotelianism was generated by Aristotle's epistemological presuppositions. These become manifest in the critique of Aristotle's notions of place (that is, of his negation of space) and of time. According to these notions both the existence of place as the limit of the containing body, and that of time, defined as "the number of motion according to prior and posterior", were bound up with the existence of bodies. In the last analysis, they were functions of the eternal and orderly cosmos. Against this view, Rāzī and Abu'l-Barakāt (who, however, considerably differs from his predecessor in his notion

[1] See S. Pines, "Rāzī critique de Galien", *Actes du VIIe Congrès International d'Histoire des Sciences* (Jerusalem, 1953) 486.

[2] See Al-Bīrūnī, *Risāla fī Istikhrāj al-Awtār min al-Dā'ira* (Hyderabad, 1948) 3.

of time) took their stand upon *a priori* self-evident human certitudes — a position which, though much less radical, resembles in its epistemological implications those of Descartes and of Kant, and the opposition between these two throws light upon the medieval discussions.

In the view of Rāzī[1] the reality of the existence of an infinite three-dimensional space independent of bodies is proven by the fact that men whose judgment has not been corrupted by scholarly quibbles are certain of its existence. The same applies to the concept of time, considered as a flowing substance existing independently of motion. Thus, in a way which *mutatis mutandis* may remind us of Descartes's method of philosophizing, the certitude which attached in the human mind to these concepts was a proof of their external reality.

Rāzī differentiated between absolute and relative space, the latter being the extension of bodies, and between absolute and limited time. The former was not subject to number (or measure), whereas the latter was measured by means of the revolutions of the heavenly spheres. These distinctions are reminiscent of the neo-Platonic antitheses of separate and non-separate time and space. There is in addition an obvious analogy, which, as I believe, goes beyond mere nomenclature, between the terms used by Rāzī and those used in Newtonian physics. Certain aspects of the problem involved will be discussed below.

The epistemological priority of absolute time and space in Rāzī's doctrine carried with it ontological implications.

In Rāzī's view the cosmos was by no means a primary datum, whose order ought to be understood, but whose existence need not be accounted for. Absolute space and time were more fundamental than the cosmos; and this held also for matter, which was eternal, had an atomic structure, and subsisted before bodies were formed in a state of dispersion. The cosmos characterized by the order prevailing in it was thus something derivative and not self-sufficient. We find accordingly that Rāzī believed that it was created and would in the fullness of time be dissolved. At least the first of these events presupposes a divine intervention, accounted for by Rāzī, perhaps late in life, by a gnostic myth adapted to his purpose, in which God, the Soul and Matter play a part; absolute space and time making up the number of the five pre-eternal entities, in whose existence the universe was a mere interlude.

[1] On Rāzī's physical doctrine, see S. Pines, *Beiträge zur islamischen Atomenlehre* (Berlin, 1936) 34 ff.

The recourse to a myth does not, however, mean that Rāzī wholly dispensed with a natural explanation of the structure of the universe. Any inconsistency of which he may have been guilty may have been due — though this is by no means certain — to his having passed in the course of his intellectual evolution through several different phases.

In fact his explanation is more mechanistic than the Aristotelian one. It is even simpler and more unified than the likewise atomistic theories of Democritus and Epicurus. For, contrary to these philosophers, Rāzī does not seem to have supposed that the diversity of the various substances was due to their atoms having different forms. He considered that this diversity, all the different qualities of the substances, such as heaviness and lightness, hardness and softness and so forth, derived from the different proportions in which the atoms of matter were combined in them with intervals of empty space. The position of the elements, and their "natural" movements could also be explained in this way: the denser elements, earth and water, having a downward and the others an upward motion. In the heavenly spheres, there existed an equilibrium of matter and empty space. Hence their circular motion.

It was a comprehensive theory and might have been used to explain many, perhaps most, natural phenomena. It seems to me to be characteristic not only of Rāzī, but also of the whole scientific tendency which he represents, that this was not done. To a certain extent the respect shown by the philosophers in question for the irreducible character of certain empirical facts may be due to their connexion with medicine. Rāzī is supposed to have been the earliest physician known to us who has left records of case-histories.

Whatever the reason, we find that Rāzī does not seem to have seen fit to explain alchemical phenomena by means of his general theory of matter, though, contrary to the Aristotelian philosophers of this and later periods, he believed in and practised alchemy. His preoccupation with this despised science was paralleled by, and probably connected with, his interest in the kindred science concerned with the properties of various minerals and stones. This latter domain of knowledge was generally not rejected outright by the Aristotelain philosophers, but was held by them in scant esteem, probably because it consisted of a jumble of miscellaneous information concerning bizarre phenomena, some of them of magical nature, whose causes were unknown. Rāzī, on the other hand, keenly appreciated the mere accumulation of empirical data. His attitude in this matter is stated in the introduction to his *Book of Properties*. What follows is based on a copy of the work found in the papers of P. Kraus.

At the beginning of this introduction he voices his conviction that he will be blamed for composing the treatise, the critics referred to being people who hasten to deny statements whose falseness they cannot prove. In fact they are constantly observing phenomena similar to those the truth of which they deny. For instance, to quote but one example of many mentioned by Rāzī, they often see a magnet attracting iron. Yet, if someone claimed that there exists a stone attracting copper or gold or glass, they would be quick to give him the lie and to consider him an ignoramus. In fact they disbelieve all phenomena the causes of which are unknown to men, but on the other hand, on the basis of all kinds of imaginings, incorrectly pretend that the efficient causes of certain phenomena belonging to this category have been discovered. Brushing aside this claim, Rāzī maintains that "up to this very day" no explanation has been given of numerous phenomena which he enumerates, one of them being the attraction exercised by scammony upon yellow bile, and another the fact that a magnet rubbed with garlic loses its power, but recovers it when washed in vinegar.

Rāzī does not claim that all the information he compiled could *prima facie* be regarded as trustworthy. According to him, none of the statements he reports should be considered as reliable unless they have been put to the test of experience. But they should be recorded, even if they have not been tested and even if the causes of the phenomena which are supposed to take place are unknown. For neglect might lead to the loss of great benefits. There is a certain similarity between this point of view and the Peripatetic doctrine of experience already mentioned (though Rāzī does not, at least in this context, establish the rules of the experimental method): both of them are interested in phenomena or in their sequence rather than in knowing their causes. It is not impossible that this doctrine may have been influenced by the medical attitude of which Rāzī was one of the representatives. But he lays much greater emphasis than the Aristotelians usually did on practical utility. And his feeling of satisfaction at the accumulation of uncorrelated and unexplained phenomena seems to have been foreign to them. His sense of the value of the discovery of more and more facts may partly account for the belief in the indefinite progress of the science which he expressed in his *Book of Doubts concerning Galen*[1]; a work in which he claimed to have been justified in criticizing that great man for whom he professes the deepest veneration, because "the art of medicine is a philosophy" and philosophy brooks no blind acquiescence in the opinions of the masters. A reason for believing that latter-day philosophers and scientists may be right in their criticism of eminent predecessors lies, he says, in the fact that the sciences "continually develop as time passes and approach more and more to perfection". For this reason it takes a man living at a later period a short time to make discoveries "for which an earlier [scientist] who had also made them required a [very] long time. [The later scientist] can accordingly clarify these discoveries and, for this reason, proceed more easily to making new discoveries." Hence the later scientists may, according to Rāzī, be considered as superior to the earlier, but only if they have a perfect knowledge of the work of their predecessors.

The Arabic scientific and philosophical doctrines of which Rāzī provides perhaps the earliest example appear to be made up of disparate elements, yet they possess a certain internal logic of their own.

The Aristotelian cosmic order having been destroyed by a recourse to the spontaneous certainties of the human mind, and the cosmic order being no longer a primary datum, the philosopher had to construct his universe out of the primordial entities: infinite space (parts of which are empty of matter) infinite time, matter in its simplest atomic form, the soul and God. A mechanistic explanation deriving the properties and the natural motions of the elements from the proportion of their material atoms to the vacua likewise existing in them went some way, but not far enough, towards reconstructing the cosmos. In fact, Rāzī was a Platonist of sorts and not a Democritan. He required divine intervention, a myth. One has, in addition, the impression that he was averse to having his world mapped out and all the strangeness of the phenomena explained away, and rejoiced in the prospect of an indefinite process of discovering and testing new facts and data.

Certain parallels to Rāzī's attitude may be found in Europe in the fifteenth, sixteenth and seventeenth centuries, that is, in the period of transition from medieval to Newtonian physics. But obviously the analogy is by no means complete. For the

[1] See "Rāzī critique de Galien", pp. 481 ff.

Arabic scientific tendency of which Rāzī is a representative shows, when confronted with modern physical theory, a lack of one of the latter's most essential features, namely, the effort towards mathematization. Whatever one may think of the ultimate truth of Kant's ideas on natural science, he correctly stated certain particularities of Newtonian physics when he said in the preface to *Metaphysische Anfangsgründe der Naturwissenschaften*[1] that every natural science contains only as much true science as it contains mathematics, and justified this assertion by pointing out that every natural science must have a "pure" section based upon an *a priori* knowledge of the natural objects; the empirical section of these sciences being founded upon the "pure" section. In the case of natural objects, *a priori* knowledge did not for Kant mean only knowledge of their concepts; a corresponding intuition of the object was also required, in other words the concept must be "constructed". The argument is clinched by Kant's statement that intellectual cognition proceeding by a "construction" of concepts is of a mathematical nature.

Rāzī's physics consisted, as far as its principles were concerned, of fundamental ideas which, given the different level of scientific knowledge, were similar to a surprising extent to those of Newton's system. But they wholly lacked the latter's mathematical basis, that is, in Kant's language, the "construction" of the *a priori* concepts.

Such a basis might have been provided by Arabic mathematicians. But there is no indication of such an endeavour on the part of any of them. In fact, no outstanding mathematician is known to have wholeheartedly adopted the physical doctrines of Rāzī or any other aprioristic system. This does not mean that they were steadfast Aristotelians; some of the greatest among them were not. Outside of pure mathematics their task, as certain among them saw it, was merely to save the appearances (*sōzein ta phainomena*). Hence (but this was not always the sole reason) the suspicion, sometimes mingled with exasperation, with which some of them looked upon the claims of astronomical or Aristotelian physical theories to be the only adequate representation of reality. Duhem was wrong in speaking[2] about the realism of the Arabic astronomers. This can be proved by the following passage of Ibn al-Haitham:[3]

[1] See Cassirer's edition of Kant's works, IV, p. 372.

[2] *Le Système du monde* (Paris, 1914) II, 117 ff, 130.

[3] Quoted by Baihaqī in *Tatimmat Ṣiwān al-Ḥikma*, ed. M. Shafi (Lahore,

We have imagined positions that are in accord with the celestial motions. If we wanted to imagine other positions also in accord with these motions, there would be nothing to hinder us from doing so. For it has not been demonstrated that it is impossible that there are other positions than those (imagined by us) which would yet be in accord with the motions in question.

This was probably also the point of view of Al-Bīrūnī (d. A.D. 1048). It may be one of the reasons for the dissatisfaction (or impatience) with the ruling astronomical system of his time. This sentiment is plainly expressed in the following passage from *al-Qānūn al-Mas'ūdī*[1] which follows upon a statement concerning a detailed theory of the moon's motion: "How difficult it is to represent this, especially for one who only represents these numerous spheres in order that the motions in the ether should be uniform and that, [at least as far] as they are concerned, differences [of motion] should be avoided." In another passage of *al-Qānūn al-Mas'ūdī* (III, 1314), he appears to describe the circles of the atronomers as mere lines: hence, according to him, it is not impossible for them to intersect.

The irritation betrayed by these passages should not be interpreted as an attack upon astronomy, of which Al-Bīrūnī thought highly. With regard to geometry his ideas were those of a Platonist:[2]

It is the science of reciprocal relations of the genera falling under quantity. Through it one attains what knowledge is required of the measure of everything that [exists] between the centre of the earth and the most remote [things] perceptible to the senses, and can be measured, gauged or weighed. By this [science] forms are known separately from matter. One grasps them by means of a true demonstration and receives their imprints so that a man grounded in this science does not lose hold of them, [a mishap] which often befalls many of those versed in logic with regard to whatever conclusions one arrives at through following that art. After that one ascends through training in geometry from physical to metaphysical knowledge.

1935) fasc. I, 79, from Ibn al-Haitham's last work. While there is no reason to doubt that Ibn al-Haitham meant to indicate in this passage that astronomy was concerned only with saving the appearances, the formulation of this thesis is puzzling: one would have expected him to state that it is possible to imagine several different theories of the celestial motions that would be in accord with the positions of the heavenly bodies. Bayaqī may have misquoted.

[1] (Hyderabad, 1954) II, 838.

[2] See *Risāla fī Istikhrāj al-Awtār fi'l-Dā'ira* (Hyderabad, 1948) 3 ff.

In the passing reference to the superiority of mathematics over logic Al-Bīrūnī perhaps reveals his antagonism to Aristotelianism. This hostility often came to the fore when he dealt with what he called the natural sciences, which in his use of the term were apt to exclude kinematics. His questions to Avicenna, which were published together with the latter's answers, appear to have been motivated by a profound scepticism about Peripatetic physics. They were certainly not formulated in mere innocence and ignorance, because Al-Bīrūnī hoped to receive a satisfactory answer. They were a challenge, and Avicenna may well have been aware of this.

In these questions Al-Bīrūnī expresses *inter alia* his doubts about Aristotle's proof of the existence of only one world; he rejects the Greek philosopher's argument[1] against the idea that the heavenly sphere may have the shape of an egg or a lentil (but mentions in this context his own efforts to disprove this idea)[2]; he states that he does not know whether the partisans of the view that all the four elements gravitate towards the centre of the earth are right or those who hold (with Aristotle) that air and fire tend to move away from the centre; he mentions some experimental evidence favouring the idea that empty space may exist.

His disbelief in the Aristotelian physical doctrine went even further. Several statements made by him in various works show that he rejected the cornerstone of that doctrine on which, according to its partisans, their assurance of the existence of a cosmic law and order was based: it is pretty certain that Al-Bīrūnī, probably under the influence of John Philoponus, refused to consider the world as eternal.

This scepticism cannot, of course, of itself found a science of physics. Al-Bīrūnī had apparently no such ambition. His sense of the dubiousness of physics is shown also in his opposition to what he calls physical proofs in astronomy, which he criticized Ptolemy for employing. Thus he commented unfavourably on the Greek astronomer's making the point that the people who believed in the diurnal rotation of the earth's attributed motion to something heavy and gross (that is, the earth) rather than to something light and subtle (that is, the heavens). This argument is described by Al-Bīrūnī as a physical rather than a mathematical one, and as being merely persuasive.[3] His own objection to the theory of the rotation of the earth, about which

[1] *De Caelo*, 287a 19 ff. [2] Cf. *al-Qānūn al-Mas'ūdī*, I, 30.
[3] Cf. op. cit., I, 49 f.

for a time he kept an open mind, was drawn from the behaviour of objects separated from the main body of the earth such as projectiles, and was supported by his own calculation of the great size of the earth and of the speed which, because of that size, its hypothetical diurnal rotation would have. This objection he described as mathematical, obviously because he considered it valid. In Aristotelian terminology it could be called physical.

In certain restricted fields conscious attempts were made to mathematize Aristotelian physics. According to Khāzinī (end of the eleventh and beginning of the twelfth centuries A.D.), for instance, physics and geometry are combined in the science of weight, which has to do with quality as well as quantity.[1] This assertion was made good in his exposition of this science, which included the relevant laws of Aristotelian physics as well as the discoveries of Archimedes and his successors. The former seems to have been meant to provide the theoretical framework for the mathematical statements.

Another example of the mathematization of a physical notion may be found in Ibn al-Haitham's treatise *On Light.*[2] In this work the term *forma substantialis* is described (p. 2) as something which subsists in a natural body and is one of the constituents of its quiddity. Light is described as a *forma substantialis* of bodies which are naturally luminous and a *forma accidentalis* of gross bodies irradiated from outside. Transparency (p. 6), which is the faculty receptive of light, is another *forma substantialis*, being one of the constituents of the quiddities of transparent bodies. The intensity of this faculty varies in different bodies; but it is found in all of them. In other words, even bodies considered opaque possess to some extent this faculty. Quoting in this connexion Ptolemy (p. 16), Ibn al-Haitham establishes a law of refraction (pp. 13 ff.), according to which the difference in the intensity of transparency between the body whence the light proceeds and the refrangent body determines the angle of refraction. If the first of these bodies is more transparent than the second, this angle is proportionally more obtuse; in the opposite case, it is proportionally more acute. In the same context (pp. 17 ff.) Ibn al-Haitham remarks that according to the natural scientists (he means the physicists

[1] Extracts from his work have been published by N. Khanikoff in *The Journal of the American Oriental Society*, VI (1859); see p. 11.

[2] The following quotations refer to the Hyderabad edition, 1357 H. The Arabic name of the work is *Risālat al-Ḍaw'*.

who accept Aristotle's doctrine) water can be divided into particles that are so small that with further division they lose the form of water and become air, the form of which is more subtle and transparent than water. When the same process is applied to air, the latter becomes fire, which in its turn can theoretically become (the substance of) the heavenly spheres, if this substance is conceived as more subtle than fire. In fact, it is in the opinion of the physicists in question the subtlest form in existence. But clarifying, as he writes (p. 13), the geometrical demonstration of another Arabic mathematician named Abu Sa'd al-'Alā' Ibn Suhayl, he maintains that from the mathematical point of view transparency can have no absolute maximum; in other words there can always be a body more transparent than any given body.

Speaking of the scholastic physics of the fourteenth century, Anneliese Maier treats at length of the calculations of the intensities of various forms, but points out that these calculations were as a rule wholly arbitrary, as there existed no possibility whatever of measuring the intensities discussed.[1] The remarks of Ibn al-Haitham should be considered in this context, if their full significance is to be appreciated. For, in contradistinction to the Latins, he indicated a way of describing the intensity of a *forma substantialis*, namely the form of transparency. According to him, this intensity is a function of the angle of refraction. In other words, his theory involved the use of a continuous geometrical function. A *forma substantialis* was thus fully mathematized.

But other Aristotelian forms were not treated in this way and Ibn al-Haitham's methods were not applicable to them, especially outside the field of optics. The Aristotelian real world was refractory to mathematization. Ibn al-Haitham himself indicated this when speaking of the mathematical theory according to which transparency could be indefinitely intensified; he pointed out that this theory had no relevance for physics. The position was obviously unsatisfactory from the point of view of the mathematicians, who were debarred from making valid statements about physical reality and were reduced to saving the appearances.

They might have adopted an alternative to the Aristotelian physics. Rāzī's and Abu'l-Barakāt's aprioristic conceptions of time and space and their doctrines of matter provided one.

[1] See *Die Vorläufer Galileis im 14. Jahrhundert* (Rome, 1949) 114 ff. and 124.

And, as Newtonian physics proved, theories of this kind were capable of being mathematized (if, of course, the mathematical techniques were available). As a matter of fact, Al-Bīrūnī seems to have been fascinated — both attracted and repelled — by Rāzī and his ideas. As I have indicated, he did not by any means take Aristotle's physics for granted. But neither did he accept Rāzī's. Sometimes he seems to have put them on a par. But he was certainly not convinced that Rāzī's concepts of time and space were *a priori* indubitable truths.

Ibn al-Haitham took up a more positive attitude with regard to space (or place).[1] He rejected Aristotle's definition of place as the surface of the surrounding body (this being his formulation of the definition) and favoured the conception which regarded space (or place) as constituted by the imaginary matter between the opposite points of a surface surrounding an imaginary vacuum, which in actual fact is occupied by a body. In other words a three-dimensional space exists. In certain essential points this doctrine position resembles those of Rāzī and of Abu'l-Bārākāt. But there are crucial differences. In contrast to these two philosophers, Ibn al-Haitham does not refer in his argumentation to *a priori* certitudes concerning space.

It may, I believe, be reasonably argued that the co-ordination of certain mathematical methods with *a priori* conceptions of time and space had a great deal to do with the birth of Newtonian physics. Kant's views as set forth in the *Anfangsgründe* seem to corroborate this statement. In the Moslem world this combination of the mathematical and the aprioristic scientific method failed to materialize.

In the second half of the twelfth and the first of the thirteenth centuries philosophical thought showed perhaps most vitality in Spain and the Eastern lands, Iraq, Persia and Central Asia. In Spain a rigorous Aristotelianism prevailed in physics, one of its main tasks being to substitute an acceptable astronomy for Ptolemy's mathematical devices. In the East on the other hand scientific trends and opinions show a significant resemblance with the tendencies and ideas of Latin scholasticism in the fourteenth and fifteenth century. A doctrine identical with, or at least very similar to the scholastic theory of impetus had been worked out, in the last analysis under the influence of John Philoponus's famous text, by Avicenna and after him by Abu'l-Barakāt, and carried to a considerable degree of elabora-

[1] See his *Risālat al-Makān* (Hyderabad, 1357 H).

tion.[1] The first of these philosophers maintained *inter alia* that in the absence of an obstacle the *virtus impressa* and the motion engendered by it would persist indefinitely, while the second in the course of an exposition concerning falling bodies came to a conclusion which, put into modern language, means that a constant force produces not a constant velocity, but acceleration.

Anti-Aristotelian aprioristic conceptions of space and time had wide currency; and the Aristotelian notion of matter also came under fire. Suhrawardī, founder of the Ishrāqā school of philosophy, was refining, but without mathematization, upon a theory which reminds one of certain scholastic views on the *intensio formarum*. He rejected the Peripatetic concept of matter.

A protracted debate on a high level about essential Peripatetic doctrines was initiated in this period by Fakhr al-Dīn's largely anti-Aristotelian, outspokenly critical commentary on Avicenna's *Kitāb al-Ishārāt wa'l-Tanbīhāt*. A generation later his attacks were countered in another commentary on this same work composed by a faithful Avicennian, the well-known mathematician and astronomer Naṣīr al-Dīn al-Ṭūsī. In consequence, the writing of treatises of arbitration between the two became a recognized literary genre.

In the second half of the thirteenth century a change may be discerned in the intellectual climate of Islam. The philosophical tradition was and remained for many centuries, perhaps down to the nineteenth century, a living force in the Moslem East. As late as the seventeenth century one encounters in Persia Ṣadr al-Dīn al-Shīrāzī, an outstanding representative of this tradition, who incorporated in his "Four Books" a considerable portion of traditional philosophical lore and obviously understood and was fully aware of the significance of the various topics. Yet one has the impression that in the intellectual domain no radically new departure occurred during all these long centuries. It is true that both Ibn Khaldūn and Ibn Taimiyya, a not altogether unoriginal critic of philosophical logic, are included in this period, but they are outside the scope of the present paper.

External historical factors can easily be made responsible for this slackening of intellectual effort. In Spain the Moslems were suffering one setback after another, tended to consider themselves as effete and doomed, and finally were irretrievably defeated. And the Eastern countries were laid waste by the

[1] See S. Pines, "Études sur Awhad al-Zamân Abu'l Barakât al-Baghdâdî", *Revue des études juives,* New Series, III (1938) 3–64, IV (1938) 1–33.

Mongol invasions. The evolution of the sciences is not autonomous, and political, sociological and military factors have an evident bearing upon it.

But relations of cause and effect of this kind can be most uncertain. To cite a relevant example, Persian literature flourished under Mongol rule. It will be safer to stick to the history of science *stricto sensu*. It will not, it is true, provide us with an answer as to the whys and the wherefores of the historical development under discussion, but it will at least help us to put the question in a more precise manner.

The history of science, in contradistinction for instance to many approaches to the history of philosophy, has, as it were, a built-in principle of valuation. In assessing scientific achievements of the past, it tends to judge their value by their similarity or opposition to the conceptions of modern science, which means for the purpose of this paper Newtonian physics, and in certain cases by the fact that they have furthered or hindered the process through which Newtonian physics was constituted.

It is a solidly established, though sometimes over-emphasized, conclusion of historical research that Galilean and Newtonian physics derive to some extent from the anti-Aristotelian scholastic doctrines of the fourteenth and fifteenth centuries. As has been suggested above, these doctrines are very similar to certain likewise anti-Peripatetic conceptions of the Arabs. Nevertheless, in spite of the Moslems' having had a much earlier start, it seems, in view of the fact that the relevant texts were not translated into Latin, very improbable that the conceptions referred to (with, in my opinion, the single exception of the Arabic version of the theory of impetus) have influenced the parallel Latin theories. The alternative and more likely supposition is that the kind of Aristotelianism which existed both in the Moslem lands and in Latin Christendom, in conjunction with the knowledge of Greek, Hindu and Arabic mathematics, astronomy and medicine, possessed both by the Moslem and the Latin scientists, led as it were dialectically to an aprioristic critique of Aristotelain doctrine. This was the phase in Islam and in Western Europe in which — to use Mr. Popper's term, giving it a somewhat more extended connotation — Aristotelianism was ripe for "falsification". In Western Europe this consummation was achieved through the mathematization of certain *a priori* concepts, the development of the appropriate experimental method, a vast accumulation of new knowledge.

All this appeared to bring about a clean break with the past and was accompanied by a sense of immense superiority over the inferior period called the Middle or Dark Ages; the scientific doctrines of that period were held to be monuments of human folly.

In the early Arabic attacks on Aristotelian physics, such as those of Rāzī and Abu'l-Barakāt, and in Al-Bīrūnī's "doubts", there is an unmistakable and urgent wish to "falsify" that doctrine. Moreover, these challenges were taken seriously by the champions of Peripateticism. There were grounds for believing that in the ensuing discussions the dominance of Aristotelian physics was at stake. But no final conclusion could be reached without the mathematization referred to above, and (except in certain restricted fields) this was never attempted. Any reasons which may be given in order to account for this fact can only be purely hypothetical.

By A.D. 1300 or even earlier, and throughout the following centuries, these debates, expounded again and again in philosophical treatises, had lost their urgency and had been transformed into a mere topic of scholarly tradition. The awareness that the issues had to be decided by a reference to physical reality or to *a priori* reasoning became blurred. Ṣadr al-Dīn al-Shīrazī, to quote but one very distinguished example out of many, was, as already indicated, capable of grasping all the implications of the arguments and counter-arguments he set forth in the section of his *magnum opus* dealing with physics; he did not hesitate to state which views he favoured and in fact took up on several issues an anti-Peripatetic position. And yet, for the reasons given, his *Natural Science* is in a sense, first and foremost, a mere exposition of the various conflicting doctrines. It is a closed world of strictly bookish scholarship. As far as only physical doctrine is concerned, that is, if we leave aside mathematics, astronomy in the medieval sense of the term, and several other disciplines, it is this development and the consequent loss of the impulse towards, and the capacity for, a radical refutation of Aristotelian physics which constitute the decline of Arabic science.

7

Al-Bīrūnī and the Theory of the Solar Apogee: an example of originality in Arabic Science

WILLY HARTNER and MATTHIAS SCHRAMM

The wording of the theme which we have been invited to discuss seems simple enough at first sight. But when looking at it more closely doubt starts arising as in the heart of Doctor Faustus trying to translate the first words of St. John's Gospel into his beloved German.

At the risk of furnishing a new proof of the so-called German thoroughness, we turn to the *Concise Oxford Dictionary* to scrutinize the various meanings of the word "original". *Existing from the first*, as illustrated by "original sin", may be safely excluded; the same, probably, is true of the second definition: *that has served as a pattern*. On the contrary, *not derived or dependent, not imitative, novel in character and style*, will have to be taken into consideration, and equally what follows: *inventive, creative, thinking or acting for oneself*.

Islamic science at its very outset appears to be purely receptive and derived from earlier models, hence not original according to whichever of the above definitions it may be. But already at a very early stage, there is observable a tendency to attain as comprehensive as possible a survey of the whole of Greek scientific activity and reasoning. As concerns the motives underlying this phenomenon, it may be true that practical aims prevail, and this has been emphasized time and again. But, to those who prefer reading manuscripts to re-reading what others have said about the matter, it becomes evident that the true stimulus or incentive, already in early 'Abbāsid times, perhaps even in the late Ummayad period, has been a genuine desire for factual knowledge and understanding. In fact, this desire, and the circumstance that Islamic scientists never got tired of quenching their thirst for knowledge, is an essential characteristic of medieval Islam.

Of the examples pertinent to our subject — their name is legion — we limit ourselves to quoting here the translations of Ḥunain b. Isḥāq (*c.* A.D. 850) and the various members of his family. They certainly do not comprise only those works which could be considered of practical interest; on the contrary, we find among them the whole Galenic opus including its purely theoretical and logical writings, works by Aristotle and Plato, Euclid, Archimedes, Menelaos, and others.

By the end of the fourth century of the Hegira, about A.D. 1000, we may say without exaggeration that there was no important scientific work preserved from Greek Antiquity that was not translated into Arabic, and that Indian writings had met with due interest as well. The influence of the latter on the development of scientific thinking, though definitely lesser than the one exercised by Greek literature, can be perceived above all in mathematics; but it should not be underrated in astronomy and astrology either. In fact, never before in history has there been an activity comparable to the one displayed by the early translators.

Instead of trying to enumerate the most prominent achievements (such a list would be very long), we deem it preferable to present an analysis of one special problem, one which we believe illustrates better than anything else the perfect mastery and the extreme care with which one of the greatest Islamic scholars — at the same time one of the truly great figures in the whole history of science — treated a subject that was no less important than complex and difficult to deal with. We do not hesitate to count it among those achievements which bear witness to true originality, the word *original* having to be taken here in the sense of "not imitative" and "novel in character", but certainly not in that of "not derived or dependent"; for there can be no doubt that any great accomplishment is necessarily derived from and thus dependent on the work done by preceding generations.

As is well known, Hipparchus had been the first to account for the unequal lengths of the four seasons by devising a model in which the earth no longer occupies the centre of the sun's circular orbit.[1] He introduced for the first time the conception of uniform circular motion round a point eccentric to the earth, which automatically yields two extreme points diametrically opposite to one another: the apogee and the perigee, and the straight line connecting them, which evidently goes through the centre of motion as well as through the centre of the earth. Without a developed trigonometrical method he arrived at the

[1] We refrain from mentioning Apollonius in this context on account of the scarcity of the information available.

conclusion that the apogee is situated in the point $5\frac{1}{2}°$ of Gemini and that the centre of motion is distant from the centre of the earth by approximately two-and-a-half sixtieths of the radius. His method as well as his results are discussed *in extenso* in Ptolemy's *Almagest* (IV, 3). Ptolemy claimed to have re-observed and checked the data given by Hipparchus and found his own results to be identical with the ones obtained 300 years before by his admired predecessor.

In the Islamic period, we find that from the very beginning special attention was paid to this part of the theory of the sun. To give an idea of the errors of observation susceptible of falsifying the results, it will suffice to mention the fact that, while the transit of the sun through the points of the spring and the autumn equinoxes is relatively easily observable, a reliable observation of the moment at which the sun passes through the points of the summer and winter solstices meets with the very greatest difficulties. The reasons are obvious: evidently the speed of variation of the sun's declination reaches its maximum (*c.* 24′ in one day) near and at the equinoxes, and its minimum (*c.* 12″ in one day) at the solstices.[1] A direct observation of the latter quantity was out of the question; even when observing with a telescope only an experienced and skilled observer will be able to attain good results.

According to al-Bīrūnī's historical survey as offered in Book 6, Chs. 7 and 8, of his *Masᶜūdic Canon* (*al-Qānūn al-Masᶜūdī*), the first observations were carried out in the Shammāsīya Quarter of Baghdad, or perhaps rather near the gate carrying the same name, in the year 199 Yazdajird (A.D. 830–1). Our author states that he has drawn his information from Abū Jaᶜfar al-Khāzin's commentary to the *Almagest*. What appears striking is that these early astronomers were independent enough to discard the method employed and described by Ptolemy, and to replace it by a method of their own (at least we do not know what other source they could have drawn from) which proves far superior to the Greek one. Instead of observing the sun's passage through the four cardinal points of its annual course, they measured its passage through the points 15° Taurus, 15° Leo, 15° Scorpio, and 15° Aquarius. This small but significant modification enabled them to obtain more reliable measurements without, on the other hand, requiring a modification of the method of computation as well. Obviously, the drawbacks

[1] In the last 12 hours before and in the first 12 hours after the solstices, the variation amounts to no more than 3·5″.

of the new method are by far outweighed by its advantages. But in spite of this methodological improvement, the practical result obtained proved completely erroneous, because it yielded a value for the longitude of the apogee which was about 20° too small.

Only one year later, Thābit b. Qurra or the Banū Mūsā, or both, re-observed two of the quarters, and obtained a far better result: $82\frac{3}{4}$° (according to the *Kitāb fī sanat al-shams bi 'l-arṣād*).[1] As this comes pretty close to the effect produced by the precession of the equinoxes (rejecting Ptolemy's obviously erroneous confirmation of Hipparchus's value and counting nearly one-thousand years corresponding to *c.* 15° when using Thābit's new value of one degree in 66 years), Thābit, taking recourse to the principle which later became known under the name of *Occam's razor*, concluded that the two motions must necessarily be equal.

During the next two centuries, the phenomena in question were re-observed repeatedly; as for the methods employed, both the original Ptolemaic and the new "method of the four fuṣūl" were made use of. The following list will give an idea of the strong interest that Islamic astronomers took in the subject.

Thābit b. Qurra or the Banū Mūsā or both, 201 Yazdajird (A.D. 832), at Baghdad (Ptolemaic method)

Khālid al-Marwarrūdhī, ᶜAlī b. ᶜĪsā al-Ḥarrānī and Sanad (Sind) b. ᶜAlī, 212 A.Y. (A.D. 843), at Baghdad (Ptolemaic method)

al-Battānī, 251 A.Y. (A.D. 882), at Raqqa (Ptolemaic method)

Sulaimān b. ᶜIṣma al-Samarkandī, 257 A.Y. (A.D. 888), at Balkh (Ptolemaic method)

Abu 'l-Wafā', 343 A.Y. (A.D. 974), at Baghdad (Ptolemaic method); 345 A.Y. (A.D. 976), at Baghdad (method of the four fuṣūl)

Abū Ḥāmid al-Ṣaghānī, 355 A.Y. (A.D. 985), at Baghdad (method of the four fuṣūl).

This and a series of his own observations of the seasons and of the fuṣūl (carried out in the Jurjāniyya, the Western part of Khwārizm, 385 A.Y.=A.D. 1016), the accuracy of which ranks astonishingly high, is the material serving as a basis for al-Bīrūnī's learned dissertation. He starts his investigation by re-telling Ptolemy's account of the course of his own work. According to his habit, he presents the method in a not strictly historical way; thus he introduces sines instead of chords, he discusses variations resulting from the equation of time and he

[1] MS London India Office 734, f. 6r, l. 13 ff.

studies the effect produced by introducing an improved value of the mean solar motion gained from his own determination of the tropical year. In order to avoid errors otherwise inevitable, he defines the latter as the period contained between two subsequent passages of the sun through the autumnal point; as becomes evident in the later course of his dissertation, he is clearly aware that an arbitrarily chosen starting-point will not serve to yield a correct value of the period in question. After having dealt with everything worth knowing of Ptolemy's procedure, he discusses and analyses with the same thoroughness the results of his Islamic predecessors.

He then presents and evaluates the results of his own observations, whereby he finds the solar apogee to be situated at 84° 59′ 51″ 9‴. In doing so he surprises his readers by developing and applying a method of his own, consisting of three essentially different variants, all three of which he shows to lead to the same numerical result. He bases himself on a theorem set forth for the first time by Archimedes and discussed by himself in a special *risāla*, which is of methodological interest because he describes in it more than twenty different proofs. The theorem, in short, reads as follows: if a broken line is inscribed in a circular arc, and if the perpendicular is drawn from the point bisecting the arc on the (major part of the) broken line, then the broken line too is bisected by the perpendicular. It is significant to state in the present context that al-Bīrūnī was interested not only in the purely mathematical (methodological) aspects of the subject, but also recognized the applicability of new theorems to practical problems. No doubt, others before him had introduced new concepts and methods into astronomy, as for instance tangents and co-tangents as well as the spherical sine theorem; but a systematic consideration of the criteria according to which preference is to be given to one method or another obviously appears for the first time in al-Bīrūnī's writings.

From the whole of the material providing the basis for his investigation, al-Bīrūnī infers that there undoubtedly exists a continual motion of the apogee in the direction of increasing longitudes. But at this stage of his analysis he expressly refrains from making any statement as to whether such motion is regular or irregular.

To illustrate the course of the discussion from this point, we give in the following a literal translation of a passage in which al-Bīrūnī describes and analyses the introductory part of

Ptolemy's account (*Almagest*, III, 1) of the length of the solar year:[1]

Hipparchus, investigating the motion of the apogee, in a way similar to the one followed by ourselves, recognized that the revolutions in the sphere of the zodiac, which are the years belonging to the sun, are not equal[2] and that the mean motion, when occurring in the sphere of the apogee, is uniform in respect of the revolutions. He therefore tried to find it [i.e. the mean motion] without having recourse to the years because of their irregularity. And he appears to have become aware that the motion which is common to the apogees is identical with the one proper to the sphere of the fixed stars. He then went in quest of the uniform revolutions referring to the sun's conjunctions with the fixed stars and its return to each one of them. Ptolemy, believing that in doing so he had been looking for the length of the solar year, tried to show as a necessary consequence that, if the solar year were defined by the sun's return to the fixed stars [i.e. one particular fixed star], anyone else beside Hipparchus would be at liberty to define it [i.e. the year] as its return to any given planet, so that there would result many [different] years to the sun [i.e. many different definitions of the solar year]. His [i.e. Ptolemy's] answer is that the year is much too obvious in its characteristics to leave concealed from the awareness of plants and animals and, it is unnecessary to say, of man the fact that it is the period comprising the four seasons, which are bound to the sun's return to its place in the sphere of the Zodiac. To this, somebody taking the place of Hipparchus would have to say: "First and foremost, leave the year aside, for the reason that its limitation [definition] is based on a datum [position] that depends on the moon. Then know that I have not been looking for it because it does not remain fixed to one and the same measure [length], in such a way that it could yield the mean way [motion] of the sun and its uniform revolutions, by which the motion of the sphere of the apogee falls short of that of the Zodiac. I am not in the possession of any observations that might yield the value of the motion of the apogee in regard to its position within them [i.e. the signs of the Zodiac]. Therefore I am inclined to share your opinion concerning the motion of the planetary apogees, namely, that it is identical with that of the fixed stars, although you may disagree with me on the question of the solar apogee. As to this, I by no means agree with you because, to me, its motion is beyond doubt. And because that motion comprises the apogees altogether, in my opinion the sun's revolution in the sphere of the apogee is equal to its return to a fixed star. But I do not wish to call it [the named period] a

[1] *Qānūn* (Hyderabad, 1954–61) II, 662, l. 1–663, l. 6.

[2] The negation contained in MS orient. 1613 of the Preussische Staatsbibliothek is erroneously omitted in the printed edition.

year, so that you do not scold me and convict me of inconsistency. If I could find the duration [revolution] of its uniform motion from its returns to the planets, why then should I avoid doing so [literally, refrain from trying to derive it from it].

In discussing the question of the variation in the length of the year because of the motion of the apogee, al-Bīrūnī deals first with a theorem stating that the equation of solar motion reaches its maximum when, if seen from the centre of the universe, the sun stands at right angles to the line of apsides. The two subsequent theorems treat of the relation connecting the apparent motion (as observed from the centre of the universe) with the corresponding equation. The conclusion is that the sun's passage through two arcs appearing equal to the observer will be fastest in the one whose distance from the apogee is greatest.

These theorems would have sufficed to demonstrate the dependency of the length of the year on the choice of the point of departure. But al-Bīrūnī, instead of contenting himself with such a general statement, now makes this question the starting-point of a thorough investigation on the kinematic conditions of uniform circular motion observed from an eccentric point. He crowns and concludes his demonstrations with the theorem that the apogee and the perigree are the points at which the apparent velocity reaches its extreme values (minimum and maximum) and that, in passing from one to the other, a continual increase or decrease of velocity will be observed. To the best of our knowledge, this is the first time that the concept of accelerated motion was made the subject of a mathematical analysis, which fact alone would be sufficient to count al-Bīrūnī among the greatest mathematical geniuses.[1]

[1] Contrary to what might be believed at first sight, Ptolemy's determination of the stationary points of the planets as based on "Apollonius and other mathematicians" (*Almagest* XII, 1, cf. O. Neugebauer's article on Apollonius's planetary theory in *Communications on Pure and Applied Math.*, VIII, 1955, pp. 641–8) cannot be regarded as an anticipation of al-Bīrūnī's conclusions. For, evidently, Ptolemy and his predecessors operate with the conception of two given and constant angular velocities. The variable velocity, which results from these, if applied to the epicyclic or eccentric model, is not taken into consideration, but only the singular case of a change from positive to negative direction. No attempt whatever is made to introduce the idea of velocity passing through zero. The lack of a general definition of velocity becomes evident as soon as we try to generalize Ptolemy's method in order to determine the point in which the resulting velocity assumes a given value. On the contrary, al-Bīrūnī's true concern is to furnish a mathematical definition and analysis of the variable velocity of an object in each point of its orbit.

In view of the uniqueness of his investigations, which vie in importance with the ones that led 600 years later to the discovery of the infinitesimal calculus, we give here one characteristic passage in transliteration, followed by a literal translation:[1]

wa idhā kāna 'l-amr ᶜalā hādhā istabāna anna 'l-buṭ' ᶜan djanbatay al-awdj wa annahu ghāyat al-buṭ' ᶜindahu thumma yatanāḳaṣu wa yadhhabu naḥwa 'l-surᶜa wa anna ghāyatuhā ᶜinda 'l-ḥaḍīḍ thumma yatanāḳaṣu wa yadhhabu naḥwa 'l-buṭ' ᶜan djanbatayhi *li-anna 'l-tabāṭu' wa 'l-isrāᶜ yakūnāni biḥasab tazāyud al-tafāḍul fi 'l-taᶜdīlāt wa tanāḳuṣihi.* [In English]: This being the case, it is obvious that slowness occurs on both sides of the apogee, and the maximum of slowness *in* it. Then it [i.e. slowness] diminishes and passes over towards rapidity, the maximum of which is [reached] in the perigee. Then it [i.e. rapidity] diminishes and passes over towards slowness to both sides of it, *because retardation and acceleration occur according to the increase and the diminution of the differences in the equations.*

The phenomenon of accelerated motion, so far demonstrable and put in evidence only by way of geometrical considerations of a rather general character, thus becomes accessible to a strictly mathematical treatment. Using modern terminology for the sake of brevity and clarity, we summarize al-Bīrūnī's method as follows.

The apparent motion, σ, is composed of the mean motion, $M=\omega t$, having the constant angular velocity ω, and of an additional term $\chi(t)$, the 'equation' dependent on the time t, or we may say as well, on the mean motion, to be added to or subtracted from the latter: $\sigma=\omega t\pm\chi(t)$. In forming, for the arbitrarily chosen time intervals $\Delta_0 t=\Delta_1 t=\Delta_2 t=\ldots$, the differences $\Delta_0\sigma$, $\Delta_1\sigma$, $\Delta_2\sigma\ldots$, we have to take into account only the $\Delta_0\chi$, $\Delta_1\chi$, $\Delta_2\chi\ldots$. A geometrical demonstration then serves to show that the differences of the latter ($\Delta^2\chi$), in passing from the apogee to the perigee (where the equation is to be deducted), are always negative, and that for symmetrical reasons the opposite is true of the other half of the deferent.

The proof runs as follows: To each equation χ corresponds a triangle having two sides of constant length, namely the radius of the deferent and the distance of its centre from the observer, while the length of the third side (distance sun-observer) is variable. These triangles can be arranged (by turning them round the centre of motion by the amount $180°-\omega t$) in such

[1] *Qānūn* II, 666, ll. 9–12.

a way that the sides represented by the radius vector as well as the corners representing the equations coincide with each other. Then the free corners will again lie on a circle concentric with the deferent, whose radius is equal to the distance of the observer from the centre of the deferent; because $\Delta_0 t = \Delta_1 t = \Delta_2 t \ldots$, the arcs contained between two neighbouring corners will be equal, corresponding to the angle $\omega \Delta t$. According to Euclid (*Elements*, III, 8), it is evident that $\Delta_0 \chi > \Delta_1 \chi > \Delta_2 \chi \ldots$, in the case of equations to be deducted from the mean motion, and that $\Delta_0 \chi < \Delta_1 \chi < \Delta_2 \chi \ldots$, in the opposite case.

To illustrate the perfect mastery with which al-Bīrūnī handles these wholly novel concepts, we refer to the following conclusion, which he presents at the end of his demonstration: in passing from the smallest to the greatest velocity, the moved object's motion must coincide with the mean motion, ωt, at one particular point. It will be the point at which the equation reaches a maximum, because it is there (and only there) that $\Delta \chi$ vanishes, whence we will have $\sigma = \omega t$.

From these kinematic considerations it results that the values obtained for the length of the tropical year will necessarily vary according to the choice of the point on the zodiac from which the measurements begin, as al-Bīrūnī had claimed before. For the sake of simplicity, it is first assumed that two such measurements are carried out simultaneously, one starting at the apogee, and the other at the perigee. During the subsequent year, the lengths of the apogee and of the perigee will be increased by a small amount. Hence, by the time the sun again stands in the apogee or in the perigee, it will have passed its starting-point, in respect of the zodiac, by a certain amount δ, which appears identical in both cases to the observer placed eccentrically to the motion of the sun, but centrally with regard to that of the apogee. But considering the fact that near the perigee the sun passes faster through that angle δ than it does near the perigee, a greater value for the length of the tropical year must result in the first case than in the second.

Al-Bīrūnī points out that, as a consequence of his demonstration, in order to obtain a reliable value for the tropical year, only two places in the circle of the zodiac can serve as starting-points, namely two places near the points at which the equation becomes a maximum (i.e. the intersecting points of the ecliptic with the perpendicular to the apse-line through the earth), because only there will the angle δ be traversed with a mean velocity that is equal to ω.

Here we may insert a remark about the history of one of the most important and fertile concepts in the whole of mathematics: the concept of mathematical functions. The question of its origin and development is usually treated with striking onesidedness: it is considered almost exclusively in relation to Cartesian analysis, which in turn is claimed (erroneously, we believe) to be a late offspring of the scholastic *latitudines formarum*. But the specific development of the concept during the course of the last two centuries clearly shows that such an interpretation is much too narrow. Because of the methods employed in astronomical computation, operating with functions had already reached a high degree of perfection by the time the first attempts were made to form a general conception of functions. In fact we find that Ptolemy had already succeeded in adapting the methods of Greek geometry to the discussion of functional relations.

Al-Bīrūnī's demonstrations, as found in the subsequent part of ch. 7 of his work, may be regarded as a model investigation of such functional relations. In treating the question of the influence of the motion of the apogee on the lengths of the four seasons, he discusses the characteristic positions of the apogee, and then proceeds to define the conditions under which the length of a season becomes a maximum or a minimum, and to investigate in which of the sections it increases or decreases. Going one step farther, he enters upon an analogous discussion of the sum of two successive seasons.

Already in the preceding chapter (ch. 6, "On the mean solar motion according to the method employed by Ptolemy"), al-Bīrūnī had tried to obtain a reliable result by choosing a particular point of the zodiac as his point of departure and by then comparing the earliest observations at his disposal with his own. Obviously the long time involved considerably reduced the probable error. On this basis, al-Bīrūnī pointed out the very great errors occurring in the observation of the solstices, even when such observations were carried out with great skill and care and with the really gigantic instruments which he describes as having been used by his predecessors. Thus we learn that, in A.D. 988, Abū Sahl al-Qūhī, observing in Baghdad, employed a special room of which the floor was given the shape of a spherical shell 15 cubits in diameter, the centre coinciding with an opening in the roof of the building. Six years later, at Raiy, Abū Maḥmūd al-Khujandī used a sextant with a radius of 40 cubits. Even then, al-Bīrūnī states, there were considerable differences in the results. But even in observing the equinoxes, he adds, the errors occurring should not be under-rated. Thus the latitude of the place of observation is not always known with sufficient accuracy. For instance, the values for the latitude of Baghdad, as indicated by two of his immediate predecessors, Abū Ḥāmid al-Ṣaghānī and Abu 'l-Wafā', vary by $1\frac{1}{6}'$ (here al-Bīrūnī mentions the exact situation of the places of observation within the city of Baghdad; their actual distance evidently excluded discrepancies of this magnitude). He finally shows that the consequences of such small errors can be considerable, and that in particular a difference of only a few minutes of the day (1 day=60 minutes of a day) may lead to a difference of one or several degrees in determining the longitude of the apogee.

After a short excursus on al-Nairīzī's view of the motion of the apogee, which he refutes with sarcastic remarks, he concludes as follows: there can be no doubt that its value comes very close to that of precession. But because of the circumstance that the observations at his disposal are not accurate enough, he is unable to make any definite statement as to its exact value: "Truly, we despair of the possibility of finding the value of that motion in this way, having at hand no other observations than those to which we have referred."

Thus there remained for al-Bīrūnī only one possibility, to assume as a hypothesis, which for the time being can neither be proved nor refuted, that the motion of the apogee is identical with that of precession. If we remember that Thābit b. Qurra had postulated the same identity on the basis of a purely formal teleological principle, the difference of approach becomes particularly striking.

No less significant is what follows. Al-Bīrūnī, not contenting himself with an approximate determination, now tries to establish a value as accurate as possible for the motion of precession. Because of his extraordinary skill, he goes far beyond the rough estimate of 1° in 100 years found by Ptolemy. In this context it will be well to note that al-Bīrūnī refrained from using any of Ptolemy's own observations but preferred to have recourse to the earliest observations made by Timocharis. We may safely conclude from this that he was perfectly aware of the deficiency of Ptolemy's observations. Al-Bīrūnī derives his own value from a comparison of one observation of Spica made by himself with a corresponding one made by Timocharis, then checks his value by comparing the observations of Regulus made by Hipparchus with those carried out by earlier Islamic astronomers.

By comparing the printed text of the *Canon* with a manuscript formerly preserved in the Preussische Staatsbibliothek (MS orient. 1613), we gain a remarkable insight into al-Bīrūnī's working technique. We thereby obtain two series of independent values, which is due to the circumstance that al-Bīrūnī operates with two different initial data: one series is based on Timocharis's observation of Spica as related by Ptolemy, namely the longitude of Virgo 22° 20′, the other, on the value 20° 36′ 55″ 43.‴ The reason of this discrepancy becomes obvious when we remember that the former value represents a reconstruction, because what Timocharis had actually observed in 294 B.C. was an occultation of Spica by the moon. Evidently, al-Bīrūnī started operating with the longitude as calculated by Ptolemy, but then replaced it by the value obtained from his own lunar theory.

As for the latter value, he says in the introduction to his catalogue of fixed stars (Bk. IX, ch. 3, sect. 3) that he has taken into account the parallax as well as the difference of longitude between Alexandria and his own place of observation, Ghazna. For his own observation of A.D. 1009, we find in both series a similar discrepancy: in the first, he makes it Libra 9° 24′, in the second, 9° 30′. Undoubtedly, this too was due to a later correction, the reason of which, however, remains unknown.

From these considerations al-Bīrūnī obtained a value for the motion of precession far superior to the Ptolemaic value: he states that the longitudes increase by one degree in 68 years and 11 months (the modern value is *c.* $71^{a}7\frac{1}{2}^{m}$). In accordance with his hypothesis, al-Bīrūnī then deducts the value of the daily motion of the apogee from the sun's daily motion as derived from his own value for the length of the tropical year. He thus obtains a value for the sun's mean daily motion that is to be regarded as well founded.

Considering the fact that all his calculations so far had been based on the provisional mean motion resulting from the inaccurate length of the tropical year, he then once again re-calculates, with the improved value, the position of the apogee and the amount of eccentricity. It need hardly be said that in doing so he again employs new methods specially devised for the purpose. We point out in particular that he proceeds to a gradual generalization of his method, thus far applicable only to one-quarter of the zodiac, which finally furnishes a no less perfect than elegant method for computing the values in question from three arbitrarily chosen successive observations. By a final correction, al-Bīrūnī takes account (ch. 9) of the circumstance that it is strictly speaking illicit to deduct the daily motion of the apogee from the sun's daily motion in the ecliptic, because they move around different centres. His new model of solar motion furnishes the position of the sun in the sphere of the apogee for the very same two autumnal equinoxes which he had used as starting-points for his determination of the tropical year, and from those positions he then derives the mean daily motion in the sphere of the apogee.

A particularly good opportunity to check all these investigations would offer itself at the moment the sun, when passing through the autumn equinox, has a mean anomaly of 90° ("a mean motion of 90° in the sphere of the apogee"). Already in ch. 8 al-Bīrūnī had shown how the moment can be computed (it will have been reached, according to modern astronomy, about the year 1250). Apart from the new methods mentioned for finding the necessary parameters, al-Bīrūnī proposes to observe the altitude of the culminating sun on consecutive days about the probable time of its passage through the apogee, and to determine *ex post facto* the situation of the latter from the increase and decrease of corresponding intervals of longitude.

Al-Bīrūnī's investigations concerned above all the future course of events. Is the centre of the sphere of the apogee really carried around in the circumference of a circle whose centre coincides with the centre of the universe? Al-Bīrūnī employs this as an hypothesis, which, however, "is valid only as long as nothing else becomes so evident that we must accept it, be it in our life-time, or be it in a later epoch, in which others will be living than ourselves".

8

Motives and Opportunities for Science in the Medieval Universities

GUY BEAUJOUAN

I
The intellectual revolution and the foundation of the universities[1]

"A common belief", writes Paetow,[2]

> is that liberal arts were taught in the universities in very much the same way as they had been in the lesser medieval schools. Such a conception is dangerously erroneous because it helps to obscure one of the greatest intellectual and educational revolutions in history, that which occurred in the 12th and 13th centuries and was the direct cause of the rise of universities. Its chief features were interest in logic or dialectic and philosophy, the systematization of theology, the rise of canon law and Roman civil law and of medicine.

Two aspects of this revolution deserve attention, the re-writing of text-books and the broadening of the place given to what we nowadays call science. Whatever the merits of Sicilian and Iberian translations might have been in the twelfth century, Islamic science would have remained the monopoly of a very small élite if the universities had not made it accessible to the majority of their students. Between the abacus and the algorism, between the collections of excerpts from the Roman *agrimensors* and the *Elements* of Euclid, between the text-books of the cathedral and monastic schools of the early Middle Ages and those of the universities, there is more than a difference of form or a change in fashion, there is a considerable progress.

One must also take into account the enormous capital in intellectual enthusiasm represented by the gathering of

[1] H. Rashdall, *The Universities of Europe in the Middle Ages*, new ed. by F. M. Powicke and A. B. Emden (Oxford, 1936); excellent bibliography of the works published since in S. Stelling Michaud, "L'histoire des universités au Moyen-âge et à la Renaissance au cours des 25 dernières années", extract from *XIe Congrès international des sciences historiques, Rapports* (Stockholm, 1960) I, 97–143.

[2] L. J. Paetow, *The Arts Course at Medieval Universities* (Urbana, 1910) 7.

'scholars' and masters in the large university centres. The whole of medieval science was indeed dedicated to the service of God, but whilst the monastic teaching of the *quadrivium* (arithmetic, music, geometry and astronomy) was, in the preceding centuries, chiefly directed towards the computation of the ecclesiastical calendar, the practice of plainsong and the interpretation of the Holy Scriptures, the science of the universities was the servant, albeit at times unruly, of a theology itself constituting a science. The attempt made by Albertus Magnus and Thomas Aquinas to assimilate Aristotelian science and to adapt it to theology cannot be fully understood apart from the context of the university world.

The twelfth century had, moreover, brought to the Christian West a markedly broadened conception of science, thanks especially to Hugh of Saint Victor and to Dominicus Gundisalvi of Toledo. In the writings of the latter, for instance, the *scientia doctrinalis* includes arithmetic, geometry, optics (*scientia de aspectibus*), astronomy, music, the science of weights (*scientia de ponderibus*, i.e. statics and metrology), and finally mechanics (*scientia de ingeniis*). Though reconsidered and filled out on many occasions during the thirteenth century, this conception of a science receptive to technology was not, unfortunately, taken over as such into the curricula of the newly founded universities.[1]

II
The place of the exact sciences in the universities[2]

One would naturally expect the statutes of the great universities to indicate with some precision what subjects were taught. At Oxford, the faculty of arts in fact gave properly organized scientific teaching. One finds there, as well as the writings of Aristotle, the algorism, the *computus* and the sphere (usually in the writings of Sacrobosco), the arithmetic of Boethius and the first books of Euclid's *Elements*. According to the statutes of 1431, candidates for the degree of bachelor of arts had to study

Arithmeticam per terminum anni, videlicet Boecii; Geometriam

[1] G. Beaujouan, *L'interdépendance entre la science scolastique et les techniques utilitaires (XIIe, XIIIe et XIVe siècles)* (Paris, 1957). See also A. C. Crombie, "Quantification in medieval physics", *Isis,* LII (1961) 143–60.

[2] The references are to be found in G. Beaujouan, "L'enseignement de l'arithmétique élémentaire à l'Université de Paris aux XIIIe et XIVe siècles", in *Homenaje a J. M. Millás Vallicrosa* (Barcelona, 1954) I, 93–124.

per duos anni terminos, videlicet librum Geometrie Euclidis, seu Alicen Vitulonemve[1] in perspectivam; Astronomiam per duos terminos anni, videlicet *Theoricam planetarum*, vel Tholomeum in *Almagesti;* Philosophiam naturalem per tres terminos, videlicet libros *Phisicorum*, vel *Celi et Mundi*, vel *de proprietatibus elementorum* aut *Metheororum*, seu *de Vegetabilibus et plantis*, sive *de Anima*, vel *de Animalibus* aut aliquem de minutis libris, et hoc de textu Aristotelis.[2]

But well organized scientific teaching occupying a relatively important place in the curriculum was not the rule in all medieval universities. Whatever the cause (whether English participation in the translations of the twelfth century, the inheritance of the Platonism of Chartres, the personal role of Grossteste, the preponderance of the Franciscans, or less subjection to the popes), we must indeed acknowledge the preeminence of Oxford in the field of mathematics, optics and logic applied to the exact sciences. The contrast with Paris, the seat of theology and dialectic, is in this respect characteristic. In spite of the extraordinary wealth of documentation collected together by Denifle and Chatelain in the *Chartularium universitatis parisiensis*, one finds only an isolated reference, in the middle of the fourteenth century, to an obligation for candidates for the bachelor's degree to swear that they had attended at least a hundred classes in mathematics (this rule moreover being interpreted in a strictly limited manner). Mathematics appear also in the curriculum for the *licentia docendi* in the statutes of 1366, but in a somewhat vague fashion. The contrast between the silence of the rules and actual teaching makes one think that, in Paris, mathematics was not the subject of regular and compulsory teaching as at Oxford. Very early, young masters developed the habit of gathering together a few pupils in their homes on feast days in order to give them lessons outside the official curricula. Such a habit was not without a certain danger to orthodoxy. In 1276, a rule was made in an attempt to control these secret meetings which were suspected, with good reason, of making students too interested in the forbidden fruit of prohibited Averroïst doctrines. But the permission then prescribed was hardly ever asked for, except in cases where the applicant had some interest in doing so. For this reason one finds only scattered evidence, here and there in the archives, of

[1] Alhazen or Witelo.

[2] S. Gibson, *Statuta antiqua Universitatis Oxoniensis* (Oxford, 1931) 234–5; A. B. Emden, *A Biographical Register of the University of Oxford* (3 vols., Oxford, 1957–9).

some masters taking classes in mathematics at home on feast days: for example, Sunon of Sweden in 1340 on the *Sphere* of Sacrobosco; Robert the Norman in 1358 on the *Centiloquium* and the *Quadripartitum* of Ptolemy; John of Austria called Mullechner in 1382 on Euclid; James Peter Roodh of Abo in 1427 on the *Theory of the Planets*.

Thus the University of Paris appears to have tolerated, although not really encouraged, the private teaching of the exact sciences without including it in the *cursus studiorium*. Its opinion and influence on this matter is clearly discernible in the statutes of the University of Vienna, dated 1 April 1389:

> We think it better for our students to spend their holidays in frequenting the schools rather than the taverns, and to argue with their tongues rather than to fight with their daggers; we are therefore willing that on holidays, after dinner, bachelors of our university should discuss and should read "gratuitously", for the love of God, the *computus* and other branches of mathematics, stressing, however, those useful to the service of the Catholic Church.

At Heidelberg also, in 1443, algorism, the "de proportionibus", "perspective", and the theory of the planets are to be found amongst the books "quos non oportet scolares formaliter in scolis ratione alicuius gradus audivisse".

The doctor entrusted with the teaching of astrology at Bologna was also obliged "legere secundum puncta, ea servando, solum diebus festivis et vacationum".[1]

In primo anno.

Algorismi de minutis et integris.
Primus [liber] Geometrie Euclidis cum commento Campani.
Tabule Alfonsi cum canonibus.
Theorica planetarum [Gerardi].

In secundo anno.

Tractatus de sphera [Johannis de Sacrobosco].
Secundus [liber] Geometrie Euclidis.
Canones super tabulis [Johannis] de Lineriis.
Tractatus astrolabii Messahale.

In tertio anno.

Alkabitius [Liber introductorius].
Centiloquium Ptolemei cum commento Haly.
Tertius [liber] Geometrie [Euclidis].
Tractatus quadrantis.

[1] L. Thorndike, *University Records and Life in the Middle Ages* (New York, 1944) 279–82.

In quarto anno.

Quadripartitus totus [Ptolemei].
De urina non visa [Guillelmi Anglici].
Dictio tertia Almagesti [Ptolemei].

The system of private scientific teaching on feast days was greatly favoured by an increasing number of new colleges: it is enough to mention the two scholarships founded in 1378 by Charles V, at the college of Master Gervase in Paris, to encourage the study of astrology. The place occupied by Merton College at Oxford in the history of medieval science is too obviously important for there to be need to mention it here. The colleges had the immense advantage of being able to provide in their libraries rather specialized works for their students to read. I have especially in mind Salamanca and its *Colegio viejo de San Bartolomé*, whose manuscripts the professor of astrology, Diego Ortiz de Calzadilla, was able to use, before being appointed technical advisor to John II of Portugal. He was to be one of the examiners of Christopher Columbus's plan, which he helped to reject in 1484 (not without a semblance of good reason).[1]

From the thirteenth century to the fifteenth the idea of the *quadrivium* gradually became unbalanced in the universities, to the advantage of astronomy. At Bologna, Salamanca, Cracow and elsewhere, mathematics became an auxiliary to the study of judicial astrology. Scientific texts are very often listed in manuscripts in the following order: algorism, the sphere and the *computus* (all three by Sacrobosco), the quadrant attributed to Robertus Anglicus, the astrolabe of Messahalla, *Theorica planetarum Gerardi*. This corpus occurs so often that one is forced to recognize in it the frame-work of the teaching of the exact sciences in the fourteenth century. Such classes were given to a limited number of pupils who were supposed to have some practical knowledge of calculation and of using the astrolabe, an instrument of great pedagogical value. The drawing up of horoscopes had, at least, the merit of compelling one to do practical exercises. However poor an opinion we may have of judicial astrology, we must admit that the care given to the use and to the improvement of astronomical tables is one of the most interesting manifestations of the medieval scientific mind. Astronomy, like optics, works with angles, and so its

[1] G. Beaujouan, *Manuscrits scientifiques médiévaux de l'Université de Salamanque et de ses "Colegios mayores"* (Bordeaux, 1962).

calculations and observations could claim precision and universality because they avoided that uncertainty regarding the value of measurements which weighed so heavily upon the progress of science.

III
Controversies about natural philosophy[1]

In the thirteenth century the statutes of Oxford contrasted the *quadrivium* with the three philosophies (natural, metaphysical and moral). In the fifteenth century (at Salamanca for instance) the chairs of astrology and of natural philosophy were also very clearly differentiated. The study of Aristotle's *De Caelo* is obviously dependent on natural philosophy, for, whereas astronomy *gives an account of the appearances*, physics is concerned with *the very principles of nature*. Here, then, we have a distinction that can never be sufficiently stressed making its appearance both in the organization of the universities and in the very conception of science.

Once the hard battle for its introduction into the universities had been won, the philosophy of Aristotle became, everywhere, the basis of teaching, even appearing to identify itself with science and rational knowledge as against faith. Aristotle's system is so universal in its scope that the scholastics were dazzled by it; hence the respect for authority for which they have been reproached. But this criticism is largely unjust, for it misrepresents the essentially controversial character of university disputes and the fact that frequent disagreements among authorities obliged scholars to make up their minds for themselves.

Teaching consisted largely in reading the texts of Aristotle and adding some appropriate explanations. In time, commentaries as such were gradually discontinued, and were replaced by a series of questions connected with another university exercise, that of the *questiones disputatae*. This, in Gilson's phrase, was "a kind of dialectic joust". A question would be asked and a thesis chosen by the master, objections would be raised by him and by members of the audience (*opponentes*), then a bachelor defended the thesis (*respondens*), replying with suitable arguments. After intervening when necessary in the course of the discussion, the master drew the conclusions.

[1] An admirable synthesis of medieval philosophy with a very good bibliography is E. Gilson, *History of Christian Philosophy in the Middle Ages* (London, 1955).

Much more spectacular than these exercises done in class on a subject chosen previously were the great biannual public debates in the course of which the most eminent masters allowed anyone to ask them questions, at times tricky ones, on any subject whatsoever.[1] Later, the master would re-examine the debate at his leisure and put the arguments in order, omitting any imprudent words likely to give rise to denunciations.

It would be a mistake to despise the scholastic habit of raising difficulties, whatever the cost, in order to have the pleasure of overcoming them afterwards; objections that could appear most unusual or scandalous ended thus by being taken into consideration and widening the horizons of science. A typical attitude is that of Buridan.[2] As a master of arts he had to take the oath that "if he happened to argue or to have to decide on some question of faith and of theology, he would conclude according to faith, and would refute any arguments contrary to it. This is why", he adds, "if I wish to dispute it, I must say what I believe must be said according to theology, or else fail to keep my oath; I must then get rid of the reasons contrary to it, but I cannot refute them if I have not raised them." By virtue of such principles he could maintain that "one must be aware of the fact that many men have held it probable that it is not contrary to appearances that the earth should move in a circle and that it should complete, daily, one rotation from west to east." Certainly, he adds, those who declare themselves for this theory do so "for the mere joy of arguing", but their reasons deserved to be examined. Nicole Oresme took up this discussion and developed with some warmth the arguments in favour of a diurnal motion of the earth, but he unexpectedly concluded that, after all, he did not believe in it.

The technique of scholastic dialectic was not the only antidote for the dangers of conformity. The disagreement between authorities forced the masters to take sides, whether they liked it or not. From the second quarter of the thirteenth century, Aristotle's cosmology and Ptolemy's astronomy were in conflict with each other. The only celestial motion allowed

[1] P. Glorieux, *La littérature quodlibétique de 1260 à 1320* (Le Saulchoir, 1925): a panorama of curiosities of the university public. The quodlibet was not the exclusive property of theologians: at Bologna, for example, the professor of astrology was required to take part in at least one quodlibetal disputation each year.

[2] E. Faral, "Jean Buridan", in *Histoire littéraire de la France* (Paris, 1950) XXVIII, 2e partie.

by Aristotelian physics was the uniform rotation of the concentric spheres, but astronomers could account for the appearances only by using eccentrics and epicycles. Duhem has depicted in a masterly manner the ups and downs of this battle[1] and has shown how it ended, about 1280, with Bernard of Verdun and Richard of Mediavilla (Middleton?). Aristotle was henceforth driven out of the heavens, and his authority was confined to the sublunary world.

Moreover, the philosophy of the Stagirite was not assimilated everywhere with the same enthusiasm. Robert Grosseteste, for instance, did not break with the Platonic and Augustinian tradition: his cosmology of light led him to give first place among the natural sciences to geometrical optics and to the mathematical concepts connected with it. His conception of experimental science owed much to Aristotle, but retained its independence. He was thus in the forefront of a scientific revival[2] of which the most illustrious exponent was Roger Bacon and of which the most brilliant success was the more or less accurate explanation of the rainbow by Dietrich (Theodoric) of Freiberg.[3] Thus, more than by his own work, Grosseteste contributed to the progress of science by the influence he exercised on the very distinctive trend of thought at the University of Oxford and, at the same time, on a great many Franciscan thinkers. It was indeed precisely amongst the Grey Friars that a certain disrespect towards Aristotle was most easily manifested as Roger Bacon and Petrus Johannis Olivi[4] clearly show.

The chief obstacle to a possible philosophical and scientific conformity was the obvious disagreement between the teaching of Aristotle and some fundamental dogmas of the Church. Here are some of the doctrines professed by the masters of the faculty of arts at Paris when they interpreted the philosophy of Aristotle according to the commentaries of Averroës: the

[1] P. Duhem, *Système du monde* (Paris, 1915–16) III, IV.

[2] See the very scholarly work of A. C. Crombie, *Robert Grosseteste and the Origins of Experimental Science, 1100–1700* (Oxford, 1953).

[3] W. A. Wallace, *The Scientific Methodology of Theodoric of Freiberg* (Fribourg, 1959). For somewhat different scientific judgements see C. B. Boyer, "The theory of the rainbow: medieval triumph and failure", *Isis*, XLIX (1958) 378–90. Dietrich was a Dominican, but he seems to have been receptive to renascent neo-Platonic influences.

[4] In his question on the movement of projectiles, he writes: "Mihi autem qui de dictis Aristotelis parum curo et efficaciam demonstrationum non capio magis videtur quod. . . ." This important text has been published by A. Maier, *Zwischen Philosophie und Mechanik* (Rome, 1958) 290–323.

insignificance of the role of a God on whom a cosmic order is imposed and who has not the power to alter it; the eternity of matter leading to a denial both of creation *ex nihilo* and of an end of the world; the unity of the 'active intellect', therefore the impossibility of the survival of the individual soul; an astrological fatalism carrying with it the negation of free will. They evidently expected to escape the disapprobation of the theologians by saying that there could easily be two contradictory answers to a problem, one according to faith, the other according to reason, and both true. It is not surprising that such opinions should have been anathemized by the Bishop of Paris, Etienne Tempier.

By proclaiming that God cannot be denied the power of creating several worlds or of subjecting the celestial spheres to a rectilinear movement, the condemnations of 1277 constituted for Pierre Duhem "l'acte de naissance de la science moderne".[1] Indeed, according to him, they made easier, if they did not provoke, the breaking up of the Greek cosmos, the 'infinitization' of the universe, and the geometrization of space. But for Mr. Koyré they were only "une intrusion maladroite d'un retardataire impénitent et ignorant dans une domaine où il n'avait que faire".[2] If the condemnations of 1277 deserve an important place in this story, it is not because of their questionable intervention in the realm of physics, but because they are a kind of indicator marking the moment when Aristotelian science and the Christian faith gave up the Thomistic dream of a close union. While the Averroïsts shut themselves up in an Aristotelian shell, theology moved away from Aristotle and the masters of the faculty of arts regained, henceforth, a greater freedom of thought, in relation both to theologians and to Aristotle himself.

Thus, if we can believe Duhem, modern science was born in 1277. "No," replies Miss Anneliese Maier,[3] "1277–1377 is not

[1] The theories first outlined by Duhem in his *Études sur Léonard de Vinci* were taken up again and developed in *Le système du monde* (Paris, 1954–9) VI–X: these volumes were left unpublished.

[2] A. Koyré, "Le vide et l'espace infini au XIVe siècle", *Archives d'histoire doctrinale et littéraire du Moyen-âge*, XXIV (1949) 45–91.

[3] A. Maier, *Studien zur Naturphilosophie der Spätscholastik* (5 vols., Rome, 1949–58): I, *Die Vorläufer Galileis im 14. Jahrhundert* (1949); II, *Zwei Grundprobleme der scholastischen Naturphilosophie* (1951); III, *An der Grenze von Scholastik und Naturwissenschaft* (1952); IV, *Metaphysische Hintergründe der spätscholastischen Naturphilosophie* (1955); V, *Zwischen Philosophie und Mechanik* (1958).

the first classical century as far as physics are concerned, but it is certainly the classical century for natural philosophy." It would be mistaken to suppose that, in order to return the scientific revolution once more to the seventeenth century, Miss Maier has seriously contradicted Duhem. The merit of this great German historian seems to be above all else the resolute manner in which she has penetrated, like a man of the fourteenth century, into the very heart of medieval natural philosophy, instead of adopting the inevitably artificial and anachronistic point of view of the history of science as seen in present-day terms.

Where does the difference lie? It has been said that science is satisfied with 'functional intelligibility', that it answers the question 'how?' Philosophy, on the contrary, seeks a 'causal and essential' explanation, and answers the question 'why?', or better still '*propter quid?*' As heir to Aristotle, and to the extent that it endeavours to free itself from him, medieval physics can be defined as "the explanation of natural phenomena with the help of some general principles, uncontradicted by experience". Mr. Koyré has described it as "l'union d'une métaphysique finaliste avec l'expérience du sens commun". It should be pointed out in passing that the search for final causes is less noxious than is supposed; its fecundity in biology need no longer be doubted. As regards the world of inanimate bodies, it reduced to defining a kind of "natural appetite". By this means, the so much criticized notion of final causes led, for example, Buridan to the fundamental concept of natural law. 'Scholastic science' is also reproached for allowing too much use of *a priori* notions and for believing too readily in the demonstrative value of deductive reasoning and of logical argument. There are so many references to "Nihil contra naturam potest esse perpetuum", to the idea that "an elementary body can only have a single simple motion", or "that a power cannot be eternally inefficacious and never pass into activity"! But *a priori* principles are not all harmful; an example is the 'principle of economy' as Mr. Crombie has so rightly stressed.

One of the great merits of the scholastics is to have attempted to quantify qualities, but in so doing they adopted an attitude totally different from that of modern science: for, as Anneliese Maier has pointed out profoundly, they took into consideration "*intensive magnitude* and not *extensive magnitude reduced to terms of time and space*". In the case of local motion, for example, speed was studied as a property capable of a given degree of intensity, but was not reduced to the actual measurement of the space covered during a unit of time. For this reason the physics of *calculationes* remained a deductive science; it envisaged movements of every possible kind without stopping to consider whether they existed in nature or not. Calculating with numbers and not with measurements, it buried itself in the mathematics of proportions. It even developed a mania for breaking up magnitudes into "proportional parts" and was thus caught up by the summation of a mathematical series. The thinkers of the fourteenth century generally believed that it was impossible to reconcile mathematical accuracy with common-sense experience. Buridan certainly affirmed that one must be satisfied with approximate measurements, but he did not put into practice this excellent principle. Miss Maier believes that this was because he considered induction starting from inaccurate measurement to be contrary to the dignity of philosophy.

To put medieval physics back into its logical context and its ontological perspective is *ipso facto* to understand why certain results were obtained and why certain obstacles could not be cleared away.[1] We know how much the scholastics contributed to the refining and defining of some of the fundamental concepts of modern science.[2] What a harvest of profound observations was garnered concerning causality and physical law, necessity, contingency, chance (hence probability), mass or *quantitas materiae*, the infinite, the continuous, space and time! We may also mention the distinction between force and energy, temperature and quantity of heat, and so on. And we may recall the medieval subtleties on the notion of functions and the manner in which Nicole Oresme arrived at the threshold of analytical geometry and the integral calculus. But all this must not conceal the essential facts. Encouraged by the theologians and by the very teaching organization, the masters of the faculty of arts beat on every side against the walls of Aristotelian physics; but starting out as they did from the works of Aristotle, they almost all remained imprisoned inside

[1] I do not wish here to draw up a balance-sheet of medieval science. For this see G. Beaujouan, "La Science dans l'Occident médiéval chrétien", in *Histoire génerale des sciences*, ed. R. Taton (Paris, 1957) I, 517–82; and especially A. C. Crombie, *Augustine to Galileo* (2nd ed., 2 vols., London, 1961; published as *Medieval and Early Modern Science*, New York, 1959).

[2] C. Wilson, *William Heytesbury: Medieval Logic and the Rise of Mathematical Physics* (Madison, 1956).

the fortress which they were beginning to demolish. We need not repeat what Mr. Koyré has already so neatly said about the void and space. And we need not insist upon the distinction made by Nicolas Bonet between natural time and that of the mathematicians, nor upon the speculations concerning the infinite: this indicates a very timorous appreciation of the connexion between physical reality and the abstract concepts of mathematics.[1]

The manner in which Thomas Bradwardine attempted to amend the fundamental law of Aristotelian dynamics is typical.[2] According to him the ratio of force to resistance must not be multiplied by *n*, but must be raised to the power *n*, in order to produce a speed *n* times greater. Even if it does not correspond to any concrete reality and even if it was foreshadowed by Alkindi, Bradwardine's 'prelogarithmic' function was a revolutionary novelty. But its author compressed it into a formula so acceptable to a strict Aristotelian that Pierre Duhem himself was deluded by it: "proportio velocitatum in motibus sequitur proportionem potentie motoris ad potentiam rei mote". Playing on the fact that $2 \times 2 = 2^2$, a numerical example immediately presented itself to maintain the equivocation, as if to prove Aristotle right. A force 8 over a resistance 2 results in a speed twice as great as that of a force 6 over a resistance 3.

Another case of that characteristic attitude which aimed at improving Aristotle's system, rather than eliminating it, is the following. When, in order to account for the motion of a projectile, the scholastic thinkers appealed to a *vis derelicta* (as did Franciscus de Marchia) or to an *impetus* (as did Buridan), they certainly contradicted the explanation put forward by Aristotle (by means of air pressure); but they did not really contradict the fundamental principle "omne quod movetur ab aliquo movetur". They only put an intrinsic cause of motion

[1] See V. P. Zoubov, "Walter Catton, Gerard d'Odon et Nicolas Bonet", *Physis* (Firenze, 1959) I, 261–78, on the supporters of the theory according to which the continuous is composed of a finite number of indivisibles: "Leurs paradoxes géometriques n'étaient qu'une échappatoire pour *sauver* les principes d'une ontologie finitiste au-delà du domaine proprement géométrique." Miss Maier similarly emphasizes that the thinkers of the thirteenth and fourteenth centuries had not envisaged a purely mathematical infinity, but rather tangible infinities in the physical world.

[2] See the collected texts, with an excellent commentary, by M. Clagett, *The Science of Mechanics in the Middle Ages* (Madison, 1959); H. L. Crosby, *Thomas of Bradwardine, his "Tractatus de proportionibus"* (Madison, 1955).

in place of a mistaken extrinsic cause. Except for William of Ockham, Marsilius of Inghen and some isolated eccentrics, most thinkers accepted the view of motion as a *process* and did not consider it as *a state requiring no cause to maintain it*. Hence Mr. Koyré and Miss Maier deny them the honour of having discovered the principle of inertia. And when Buridan attempted to explain the rotation of the heavens by impetus, he did not succeed in freeing himself from the Aristotelian principle according to which celestial mechanics and terrestrial phenomena are governed by different laws. In the absence of any resistance, he thought that the movement of the heavens would be perpetual, whereas under similar conditions motion in the sublunary regions would be instantaneous.

If, therefore, the 'scientific revolution' did not take place in the fourteenth century, this was not the fault of the Church, but quite simply because the philosophy of Aristotle resisted attack thanks to its close-knit logical texture and above all to its impressive cohesion.

The attitude of William of Ockham[1] is distinctive in this respect. He wished, so Gilson tells us, "to rid the field of philosophy of the imaginary causes and essences that encumbered it". He proceeded to outline some extremely modern concepts such as those of "equivalent place" and of motion as a state. But, preoccupied as he was with the evidence of the particular, he largely gave up the search for general scientific principles. One realizes why the Parisian nominalists who studied physics did not go the whole way with him. For them, to give up Aristotle was practically to abandon natural philosophy. One might argue that the scientific revolution of the seventeenth century did not strike at the roots of philosophy: quite true, but Miss Maier might reply that the classical age was a period of great interest in synthesis and no longer cared for detailed ontology as the scholastics did.[2]

Without going outside the thirteenth and fourteenth centuries, one can see that if Aristotle's natural philosophy more or less successfully warded off attacks from the inside, it showed itself much weaker when it came up against sciences whose autonomy the universities respected, for example optics and astronomy.

[1] H. Shapiro, *Motion, Time and Place according to William Ockham* (New York, 1957).

[2] A. Maier, "Die Stellung der scholastischen Naturphilosophie in der Geschichte der Physik", in *Aus der deutschen Forschung . . . E. Telschow gewidmet* (Stuttgart, 1956) 33–40.

IV
The teaching of medicine and its influence

However distinctive in their object and in the manner in which they were taught, the quadrivium sciences and natural philosophy were governed entirely by the faculty of arts, which seemed a kind of anteroom to the three other faculties: those of theology, law, medicine. The faculty of medicine was the only one that offered scientific teaching at an advanced level. But there, more than anywhere else, ontological perspectives, bookish pedantry and logical subtleties could run up against an unavoidable reality: that of human suffering.

A. Birkenmajer has laid stress on "le rôle joué par les médicins et les naturalistes dans la réception d'Aristote aux XIIe et XIIIe siècles". Mr. Crombie has argued that Grosseteste may have studied medicine and that Graeco–Arabic medical literature inspired his famous "theory of experimental verification and falsification".[1] We also know now that one must look in the treatises of the graduation of compound medicines not only for the source of scholastic theories on the quantification of qualities but even for the origins of the famous law expounded by Thomas Bradwardine (the logarithmic speed function for the ratio force/resistance).[2] As for the influence of medicine on late medieval thought, it is enough to recall the *Summulae logicales* of Petrus Hispanus (who became Pope under the name of John XXI), the universal animism of Arnald de Villanova and, above all, the notoriety that Italian medical Averroïsm was to enjoy throughout the sixteenth century.

The universities of Bologna and Padua occupy a special place in the intellectual history of the Middle Ages for three reasons: they had a lay and democratic organization, they brought the liberal arts and medicine under the protection of a single community (opposed to that of the jurists), and they provided teaching leading to lucrative positions.[3] Having thus

[1] A. C. Crombie, *Robert Grosseteste*, pp. 74–81.

[2] Clagett, *The Science of Mechanics*, p. 439, n.35.

[3] *Studi e memorie per la storia dell' Università di Bologna* (Bologna, 1956) nuova serie, I. One should read in particular the articles by A. Maier on the Bolognese philosophers of the fourteenth century (pp. 299–312), by A. Pazzini on medicine (pp. 391–415) and by M. Villa on mathematics (pp. 479–85). See also B. Nardi, *Saggi sull' aristotelismo padovano dal secolo XIV al XVI* (Firenze, 1958), and J. H. Randall, *The School of Padua and the Emergence of Modern Science* (Padova, 1961).

escaped the domination of the theologians, philosophical thought appealed strongly to doctors of medicine and was soon identified with a materialist and rather anti-clerical Averroïsm (against which Etienne Tempier, and the learned Franciscan John Pecham, Archbishop of Canterbury, had fought). Bound to the authority of the "Philosopher" and of the "Commentator", this anti-clerical Averroïsm exemplifies, more than any other philosophical trend, the dry conformity for which the scholastics and the Church itself have usually been blamed.[1]

One ought to write a series of volumes named "on the borders of medicine and scholastic philosophy" in the manner of Miss Maier: here there is a vast field to explore for the history of science.

At Bologna and Padua, medicine was taught in the same faculty as the liberal arts and tended to make much use of astrology. This was certainly consistent with Averroïst doctrines, but such a symbiosis also existed almost everywhere else, even under different philosophical influences (among Jews as well as Christians). Whatever else the importance of this tradition of the astronomically-minded *medicus* (from Pietro d'Abano to Copernicus), the chief merit of the Italian professors of medicine was not that they favoured astrology but that they wished to open their pupils' eyes. The great novelty in this field was undoubtedly the introduction in Italy, at the very beginning of the fourteenth century, of the practice of anatomical dissection of the human body. The method of approach was prescribed as early as 1316 in Mondino dei Luzzi's little masterpiece on anatomy. But every time they had to choose between what they saw and what Galen and Avicenna had taught them, Mondino and his followers bowed before the authority of books. They lacked confidence in themselves. North of the Alps the first dissections came later: about 1340 at Montpellier and in 1407 in Paris. The most interesting part of medieval medical literature is the surgical treatises. Here we must distinguish between the universities which, like Bologna, opened their doors to surgeons and those like Paris which scorned them. But all medical students were brought into some contact with reality before they left the university by having to spend a period of time with a qualified practitioner in order to complete their theoretical training.

We have to admit, however, that even in Italy physicians

[1] It was not until 1363 that there was a faculty of theology at Padua, and 1364 at Bologna.

did not make much progress in the science of biology. Why?[1] The reason is above all that in the two fields where they were the most likely to keep their eyes open, namely in anatomy and botany, they were unable to translate their observations into diagrams. They did not succeed in creating, perfecting and diffusing among their students, a scientifically adequate system of illustration. If the copyist sometimes deliberately corrected the text he was reproducing, or set out to improve on a purely geometrical figure in the original, he usually only succeeded in debasing the illustrations from the point of view of natural history. Because of this lack of "graphical accuracy" of which Sarton speaks,[2] observations could not improve upon one another and it was virtually impossible to disseminate them. Without printing and engraving the work of Vesalius himself might have had little influence.

A connexion could be made with the origin of naturalistic art, although this would take us outside the universities. Guido da Vigevano, who in 1345 drew the most famous anatomical figures of the Middle Ages, had ten years before composed a very interestingly illustrated treatise on military art.[3] He thus started the association between medicine and military engineering, such as we find again about 1420 in the *Bellicorum instrumentarum liber* of Giovanni Fontana. Moreover surgeons used better and better instruments like the one invented by Henri de Mondeville for removing arrows from wounds, or the system of pulleys or counterweights by means of which Guy de Chauliac prevented a broken rib from impeding respiration. Oculists invented spectacles. The alliance of medicine with technology can also be found among several makers of clocks and of astronomical instruments, for example Giacomo de Dondi, Giovanni de Dondi, and Jean Fusoris.[4]

[1] For a good general account see A. Castiglioni, *History of Medicine* (New York, 1949) and B. L. Gordon, *Medieval and Renaissance Medicine* (London, 1960). For the fourteenth century see G. Sarton, *Introduction to the History of Science* (Baltimore, 1947–8) III. On university teaching see V. L. Bullough, "The development of the medical University of Montpellier", *Bulletin of the History of Medicine,* XXX (1956) 508–23; "The medieval medical university at Paris", ibid. XXXI (1957) 197–211; "Medieval Bologna and the development of medical education", ibid. XXXII (1958) 201–15.

[2] G. Sarton, *The Appreciation of Ancient and Medieval Science during the Renaissance* (Philadelphia, 1955) 91.

[3] Mr. A. R. Hall has referred to a forthcoming critical edition of this, cf. *Actes du VIIIe congrès international d'histoire des sciences* (Florence–Milan, 1956) III.

[4] E. Poulle, *Un constructeur d'instruments astronomiques au XVe siecle: Jean Fusoris* (in the press).

V
Conclusions

The intellectual life of Europe over three centuries cannot be explained in a few words, like a magical formula. Another paper could have been written on "motives and opportunities for science at royal and princely courts" within the same chronological limits, from about 1150 to 1450. We would see there Frederick II of Hohenstaufen writing a carefully illustrated treatise on falconry, keeping up a truly international correspondence, and organizing mathematical competitions which redounded to the fame of Leonardo Fibonacci of Pisa. Frederick was also accused of practising horrible experiments, such as shutting prisoners in a barrel in order to see their souls come out when they died, or bringing up newly-born babies in complete silence to discover what language they would speak.

A century later, the archives of the kingdom of Aragon bear witness to an interesting scientific policy: a decree of 1352 provided every ship with two nautical maps; there were experiments in the transmutation of metals; studies were made on methods of begetting at will male or female offspring; and so on. In the same way, according to the point of view chosen, Italy would be seen in the lively colours of the Renaissance instead of in the dull tradition of Averroïsm.

It almost seems as if there were two co-existing worlds divided by invisible iron curtains. But we must beware of arbitrary classifications, and examine, in each particular case, the pulse and the hazards of actual life. Albertus Magnus was a biologist by temperament rather than as a result of his university training; Raymond Lull was interested in the navy because he came from Majorca; John Fusoris made brass astronomical instruments because his father made pewter pots. An aggravating uncertainty still hangs over the biographies of three of the greatest scientists of the thirteenth century: Jordanus Nemorarius, Gerard of Brussels and Petrus Peregrinus de Maricourt. It is difficult to say whether we must thank the universities for their remarkable works on statics, kinematics and magnetism. Algebra, commercial arithmetic, the last books of Euclid's *Elements*, alchemy, veterinary art, and geography generally remained outside the curricula of medieval universities. But these sciences attracted the attention of men trained in the universities. At times they were even taught in those private classes where one could learn anything it pleased the master to expound.

Medieval science did not suffer from a lack of freedom. One must not bring the Church of the counter-Reformation or the trial of Galileo into a discussion of the Middle Ages. It would be difficult to find in the thirteenth and fourteenth centuries a Christian thinker persecuted for scientific ideas still regarded as having any scientific value. Moreover, constraint was unnecessary because, as Mr. Hartner has said, medieval scientists hardly ever left "the natural limits of intellectual life as defined by religious faith".[1]

Aristotle's philosophy also set, in the thirteenth and fourteenth centuries, the limits of the university mind. Even when encouraged by the Church, the medieval scientist still did not stray. At least this has been the accepted view since Miss Maier began to publish her magnificent studies. But such a judgment depends to some extent on the historical perspective adopted *a priori*. Once a scholar succeeds in acquiring the mentality of a scholastic in order to comprehend the work of a contemporary of Nicole Oresme in its setting, he develops *ipso facto* a tendency to irritation when he sees anyone looking in the fourteenth century for forerunners of classical science. But if that same scholar is invited to present a history of dynamics to readers in 1961, he is obliged willingly or unwillingly to select and put together the texts of major interest to a twentieth-century physicist. In his fine history of medieval mechanics, which he has dedicated to Miss Maier and to Mr. Koyré, Marshall Clagett[2] comes in this way to conclusions to which Duhem would not have objected.

The vast field of the medieval philosophy of nature cannot without artificiality be made simply part of the straightforward history of the exact sciences. If in spite of this we find ourselves obliged to form a summary judgement, we are bound to recognize that medieval science was not revolutionary. But it believed in progress, and indeed progressed.

[1] W. Hartner, "Remarques sur l'historiographie et l'histoire de la science du Moyen-âge en particulier au 14e et au 15e siècle", in *Actes du IXe congrès international d'histoire des sciences* (Barcelona, 1959) 69–87.

[2] *The Science of Mechanics in the Middle Ages,* cf. above, p. 230, n. 2.

9

The Medieval Language of Proportions: Elements of the Interaction with Greek Foundations and the Development of New Mathematical Techniques *

JOHN E. MURDOCH

Bolstered by a strain of twentieth-century hindsight, it has become fashionable, and rather incisively expressive, for historians to refer to the *Grundlagenkrisis* of Greek mathematics.[1] The sufferers in this particular 'time of troubles' in ancient intellectual history are usually singled out as the Pythagorean advocates of 'universal arithmetic'. But, we are told, the attack was double-flanked; it was a *Krisis* with two edges. On the one hand, Zeno is supposed to have prodded them with the horrors of the infinite, and to have laid bare the early (pre-Eleatic) Pythagorean confusion of arithmetic and geometry. This half of the account of the struggle, historically ill-founded in the author's opinion, will not form part of the prelude to the story in medieval mathematics I wish to tell. It is the other side of the historian's analysis of this period in Greek mathematics which will be pertinent. This other side — mathematically a sharper weapon in the battle, and on firmer historical ground — was the discovery of the irrational or incommensurable. This revelation was a frustration which the Pythagoreans perpetrated upon themselves; the magnitude of its importance is reflected in the pointed, if apocryphal, stories of the fate suffered by that member of the sect who disclosed the secret of what they had unearthed.

* Much of the source material for this paper is at present unedited. I have tried to indicate something of at least the whereabouts of this literature in the footnotes and hope later to publish several sections of the paper in an expanded form with full textual documentation. I should like to thank the American Philosophical Society for their assistance in obtaining microfilm and photostat material pertinent to the primary sources utilized in the present paper.

[1] The by now classic example is H. Hasse and H. Scholz, "Die Grundlagenkrisis der griechischen Mathematik", *Kant Studien*, XXXIII (1928) 4–34. But the moving force of the idea goes back at least to the writings of Paul Tannery.

Simply put, the corner into which this discovery backed the Pythagoreans was that, within their system of 'universal arithmetic', no way could be found to measure two magnitudes which were incommensurable to one another. Or, to say the same thing in terms more congenial to the core of the present paper, their theory of proportionality could account only for commensurable magnitudes.[1] In this light, it was the new theory of proportionality developed by Eudoxus which formed the most successful, certainly the most lasting, resolution of the *Grundlagenkrisis*. For, unlike its Pythagorean predecessor, it was able to include incommensurables in its domain. Specifically, this greater scope was guaranteed by Eudoxus's formulation of a new criterion for determining the equality of proportions, one which would allow, as the Pythagorean criterion would not, of equal standing, so to speak, for all magnitudes of the member proportions, be these magnitudes commensurable to one another or not. At least one form of the Pythagorean clause which rendered their club of proportionality so exclusive has been preserved for us by Euclid as a definition of proportional numbers (*Elements*, VII, Def. 20): "Numbers are proportional when the first is the same multiple, or the same part, or the same parts, of the second that the third is of the fourth."[2]

It is clear that the relations of "integral multiple", and "aliquot part or parts" — and Euclid so specifies them — can only obtain either between magnitudes which, for each proportion, are commensurable, or, as Euclid has it, between numbers. Thus, this whole definition of equality of proportions must suffer a similar limitation.

Eudoxus, still using the arithmetical technique of integral multiples (but in a different, and most ingenious fashion), bursts the sphere of commensurables with the following (once again Euclid, V, Def. 5):

Magnitudes are said to be in the same ratio [in the same *proportion*,

[1] *Terminological note:* It is customary to refer to the theory of *proportion*, and the *ratios* treated in it ('translating', respectively, the Greek ἀναλογία and λόγος). But the medieval Latin tradition of Euclid's *Elements*, and the mathematics surrounding it, translated these Greek terms, respectively, by *proportionalitas* and *proportio* (via the Arabic *tanāsub* and *nisba*). In keeping with the emphasis of the present paper, I have thus anglicized the *Latin* terms, and have employed them consistently throughout to refer to the mathematical entities and doctrines in question.

[2] This, and all following passages from the Greek of Euclid's *Elements*, are from the translation of Sir Thomas Heath (3 vols., Cambridge, 1926; reprinted New York, 1956).

in medieval terms], the first to the second and the third to the fourth, when, if any equimultiples whatever be taken of the first and third, and any equimultiples whatever of the second and the fourth, the former equimultiples alike exceed, are alike equal to, or alike fall short of, the latter equimultiples respectively taken in corresponding order.

Or, symbolically: $A/B = C/D$ if, and only if, for all positive integers m, n when $nA \gtreqless mB$ then, correspondingly $nC \gtreqless mD$.

Such is the simplicity and the mathematical magnificence of Eudoxus's achievement. Yet, as the following pages will at least partly show, for more than 2000 years almost all mathematicians were totally unimpressed with its simplicity, often plagued by what it meant, and frequently had words for it that suggested anything but magnificence. It goes without saying that they harboured comparable sympathies for the mate to this definition (*Elements*, V, Def. 7) which, in a similar fashion, is the criterion for determining the greater of two proportions — once again, no matter what the magnitudes.[1]

This much may tell, howsoever briefly, the tale of Eudoxus's rescue — and there appear to have been others — of Greek mathematics from the impasse of the incommensurable. Yet it reveals but one of the keystones of his theory of proportionality, and if one is properly to trace the fortunes of Eudoxus (to be sure in the guise of Euclid) through the Middle Ages, the second facet needs introducing. It legislates the conditions that magnitudes must satisfy in order that a proportion obtain between them (V, Def. 4): "Magnitudes are said to have a ratio [a *proportion*, in medieval terms] to one another which are capable, when multiplied, of exceeding one another."

That is, any two magnitudes A and B (where $A < B$) can be said to have a proportion to one another, if, and only if, there is a positive integer n such that $nA > B$.

With this, Eudoxus asserted the required homogeneity of the mathematically comparable and barred the infinitely large and the infinitesimally small from the magnitudes entering into proportion. In so doing, one feels, he rendered explicit an assumption tacit in Greek geometry at least since the time of Hippocrates of Chios: an assumption, moreover, which was crucial for so much of later Greek mathematical development.

[1] Though this definition, as well as that of the equality of proportions (V, Def. 5), is crucial to Eudoxus's theory, we can, as most medieval remarks and reactions to it are similar to those to V, Def. 5, conveniently ignore it in what follows.

For this "part of the regular machinery of geometry" (as Heath has called it) lay at the basis of all proofs by the so-called method of exhaustion, and so furnished the fundamental tool for the investigation of quadrature problems throughout Antiquity and for some time to come. It was, so to say, the most widely heralded 'continuity postulate' in Greek mathematics.

This postulate, together with the definition of equal proportions, formed Eudoxus' masterful contribution to Greek systems of proportionality. Both these accomplishments were preserved in the legacy of Greek mathematics, but only as two definitions of the fifth book of Euclid's *Elements*; proper credit to Eudoxus was neglected for centuries.

Whitehead once claimed that the whole history of philosophy was but a series of footnotes to Plato. With greater reserve, I should like to begin what follows with a case history in mathematics drawn from the medieval footnotes to these two definitions, and hence, unknowingly, to Eudoxus. Approached optimistically, this case history might be taken to reflect some of the features, virtuous or not, of the tenor of medieval mathematics in general.

Book V, Definition 4: a principle of continuity

The as yet unedited, and still somewhat tangled, corpus of the medieval *Euclides latinus* is our logical point of departure. Of the numerous versions of *Elements* current, or at least existent, in the Middle Ages we need, at least at the outset, to distinguish but five.[1] These five are: (1) the Boethian–Agrimensores compilation (hereafter = 'Boethius'), (2) Gerard of Cremona's translation of al-Nairīzī's (d. *c.* 922/3) commentary on the *Elements*, which is accompanied by the text of Euclid itself (= al-Nairīzī), (3) Gerard of Cremona's translation from, apparently, the so-called Isḥāq ibn Ḥunain-Thābit ibn Qurra Arabic text (= Gerard), (4) what I shall call the 'Adelard of Bath enunciation tradition' (= Adelard tradition), and, finally, (5) what appears to be a *mélange* of the Boethian and Adelardian traditions as preserved in MS Paris Bibliothèque

[1] The most recent, and most accurate, information on the corpus of translations can be found in Marshall Clagett, "The Medieval Latin Translations from the Arabic of the *Elements* of Euclid with Special Emphasis on the Versions of Adelard of Bath", *Isis*, XLIV (1953) 16–42. All of the translations from the Arabic that I shall cite date from the twelfth century. As the points I wish to make do not, for the most part, bear upon dating problems, more detailed information will be here excluded.

Nationale, fonds latins 10257 (= BN 10257).[1] Looking for the moment just at V, Def. 4, the Eudoxean continuity principle, our corpus yields the following results:

'Boethius': Proportionem vero ad se invicem magnitudines habere dicuntur, quae possunt sese invicem multiplicatae transcendere.

al-Nairīzī: Quantitates, inter quas dicitur esse proportio, sunt quarum possibile, cum multiplicantur, alias addere.

Gerard: Quantitates quarum quedam ad alias proportionales esse dicuntur, sunt quarum quasdam cum multiplicantur super alias addere possibile est.

Adelard tradition: Quantitates que dicuntur continuam proportionalitatem habere, sunt quarum eque multiplicia aut equa sunt aut eque sibi sine interruptione addunt aut minuunt.

BN 10257: Illa continue proportionalitatis esse dicuntur, quorum uno modo multiplicia aut equalia sibi sunt aut equaliter sese continue superant et a se continue superantur.

Thus, only three of the five translations have preserved the definition in its proper Euclidean or Eudoxean form.[2] Two, those representing what was the most popular tradition, have substituted an entirely new assertion in its place, an assertion defining continuous proportionality and one which, as far as I have been able to discover, is nowhere to be found in earlier

[1] For the present texts, and in all of what follows, I have used the following editions and MSS: (1) 'Boethius': as in Cassiodorus, *Institutiones*, ed. R. A. B. Mynors (Oxford, 1937) 169–72; (2) al-Nairīzī: Euclides, *Opera omnia, Supplementum*, ed. M. Curtze (Leipzig, 1899); (3) Gerard: Paris, Bibliothèque Nationale, fonds latin (hereafter = BN) 7216, 1r–108r; (4) Adelard I: BN 16201, 35r–82r; (5) Adelard II: British Museum, Additional MS 34018, 1r–78v and BN 11245, 1r–57v; (6) Adelard III: Oxford, Balliol College 257, 1r–98v; (7) Hermannus Secundus or Herman of Carinthia: BN 16646, 1r–108r; (8) Campanus of Novara: ed. publ. by Hervagius (Basel, 1558), corrected by MS BN 16197, 1r–134v; (9) BN 10257 (*mélanges*) 1r–88r. (4)–(8) constitute the core of what I have above called the 'Adelard tradition' (the distinction of the various Adelard versions I–III is due to Clagett, op. cit.). Because of the axiomatic ordering of the *Elements*, subsequent references to these texts will not specify foliation or pagination.

[2] Since writing the present paper, I have discovered a unique Latin translation of the whole (save Book XIV) of Euclid's *Elements* directly from the Greek in BN 7373, 2r–175v. It contains a correct — indeed most accurate — rendering of V, Def. 4: "Proportionem ad se invicem habere quantitates dicuntur que possunt multiplicate se invicem superare." I am preparing an article analysing this new translation which will appear in the near future.

Euclidean (or other) texts, no matter what the language. Moreover, none of the texts carrying the addition betrays the slightest hint of its origin. The most that can be concluded is that it is very likely not a product of Adelard's own imagination. For, as is clear above, the *mélanges* of BN 10257 present the same invented notion, but in a translation essentially different from that of Adelard, and thus strongly suggestive of a prior source. The Arabic tradition is the logical candidate for such a source, but, in the manuscripts and editions extant, the addition is nowhere to be found, at least to my knowledge.[1]

Though the medieval substitution for Eudoxus's principle of continuity is but a faded excuse for what it has replaced, and though, as we shall see, this newcomer to Book V occasioned no small amount of confusion, we must not infer that scholastic toilers in this branch of the quadrivium were completely dull to commitments to continuity. In a sense, just the opposite is the case. For, though they may have had the principle preserved as Definition 4 in only the least used, 'non-Adelardian' translations, they were keenly alive to the idea it expresses. They applied it in the *Elements* where it should be applied (V, 8 and X, 1), and not infrequently displayed their understanding of its implications. The Latin al-Nairīzī had already pointed out to them the connexions of Eudoxus's postulate with requirements of homogeneity and the exclusion of the infinitely large and small, and they were quick to elaborate, or, perhaps, to observe much the same on their own.

Among the most interesting and significant reflections on the postulate are those of the thirteenth-century mathematician Campanus of Novara: they occur as an *additio* to his version of Book X, Proposition 1 (in which, V, Def. 4 is applied, and which is itself another form of the continuity principle). The proposition, as Campanus has it, asserts:

> If two unequal quantities be given, and if from the greater, greater than half be subtracted, and again from the remainder greater than half be taken, and we continue successively in the same

[1] Thus (1) not in the Ishāq-Thābit text (MSS Arab. Bodl. Or 448 and Thurston 11), (2) not in the al-Ḥajjāj text accompanying the Arabic version of al-Nairīzī's commentary (ed. Heiberg, Besthorn, Thomson et al., Copenhagen, 1893–1932), (3) not in the longer recension of al-Ṭūsī (ed Rome, 1597), and finally (4) to judge from MSS in the Princeton University Library, not in al-Tūsī's shorter version. But it must be remembered that we appear to possess but the second recensions of (1) and (2). Information from the Oxford Arabic MSS, here and elsewhere, has been kindly furnished me by Mr. Marshall Clagett.

way, then it is at last necessary that there remain a quantity less than the lesser of those given.

In his proof, Campanus explicity applies the property of the Eudoxean principle, and then, at the conclusion of his labours, submits the following:

> However, it is necessary to observe that III, 15 [=III, 16 of the Greek], which asserts that an angle of contingence is less than any angle contained by two straight lines, seems to contradict this proposition. For [following the dictates of X, 1], given any rectilinear angle, if more than half be subtracted from it, and again from the remainder more than half, it seems necessary that this can be repeated a sufficient number of times so that there remains a rectilinear angle less than an angle of contingence — the opposite of which is concluded by III, 15. But these are not angles univocally, for the curved and the straight are, taken absolutely, not of the same genus. Nor is it true that an angle of contingence can be taken so many times that it may exceed any rectilinear angle. . . . Therefore, it is clear that any rectilinear angle is greater than an infinite number of angles of contingence.

And Campanus's cautions are well-founded. For his angle of contingence — in current English vernacular a 'horn-angle', signifying the angle contained between the circumference of a circle and a tangent to it — is a non-Archimedean or (historically more correctly) non-Eudoxean magnitude. This is so precisely because it cannot, relative to rectilinear angles, obey the continuity principle set down in Book V. Campanus is perfectly right; he has succeeded in pointing out that one of the magnitudes considered by Euclid must run afoul the requirements demanded of others. What is more, his reflections on these horn-angles in Book III raise the question of other assumptions about the geometrical continuum. But before we follow him here, it will be well to unravel some of the further features and forms of the medieval X, 1. The continuity principle it contains — Eudoxus in disguise — has an interesting history.

The first step in revealing this history is to note that Euclid adds a corollary to the proposition to the effect that "the theorem can be similarly proved even if the parts subtracted be halves." Campanus, in his own fashion, has it too. But only Campanus. As far as I have been able to discover, no medieval version of the *Elements*, Latin or Arabic, contains it as well.[1] This — the mere omission of a corollary — may seem to be of

[1] Once again, this must be qualified by the newly discovered translation in BN 7373; it does contain the corollary.

antiquarian insignificance; but this is not so, its effects in Arabic mathematics were far-reaching. Here, the best place to begin is a bit of history by the thirteenth century Naṣīr al-Dīn al-Ṭūsī. It occurs in his longer version of Euclid, a comment to X, 1:[1]

Sheikh Abū 'Ali ibn al-Haitham al-Baṣrī . . . has come to the conclusion that this proposition is but a special one. Thus, he has written a work on it in which he maintains that the proposition really is generally valid — no matter what kind of part be subtracted from the whole — but that, in the form in which Euclid has expressed it, it is only a special case. But Sheikh Aḥmed ibn al-Surrī contradicted him in an essay in which he showed that the proposition as stated by Euclid is general; and he was right.

Though al-Ṭūsī is not explicit about precisely what it was in Euclid's way of putting X, 1 that so excited his predecessors (at least, indeed, until al-Surrī (twelfth–thirteenth century) set them straight), the matter becomes clear if we turn to other, earlier Arabic efforts. Thus, al-Kūhī (tenth century) claimed, wrongly, that X, 1 was not effective if parts less than half be subtracted.[2] His remark reflects the fact that there was concern that this bit of Euclid should work when something less than continual halving was the case; so when Thābit ibn Qurra takes but thirds in determining the volume of a paraboloid.[3] What is more, Ibn al-Haitham (in a work other than that referred to by al-Ṭūsī) struggled to show that by taking just halves one ends up, in effect, by taking more than half (and so, presumably, doing what Euclid said could be done).[4] But why should he have played this game had Euclid's corollary been present? That it was not is pointed out not only by its absence in our (admittedly late and often incomplete) texts of the Arabic Euclid, but quite explicitly by Omar Khayyam:[5]

[1] Heinrich Suter, "Die Abhandlungen Thābit b. Kurras und al-Kūhīs über die Ausmessung der Paraboloide", *Sitzungsberichte der Physikalisch-Medizinischen Sozietät zu Erlangen*, XLVIII (1918) 224–5.

[2] Suter, op. cit. p. 221.

[3] Suter, op. cit. pp. 208–10.

[4] H. Suter, "Abhandlung über die Ausmessung des Paraboloides von Ibn al-Haitham", *Bibliotheca Mathematica*, ser. 3, XII (1912) 303–4. To judge from al-Ṭūsī's report of al-Surrī's criticism, apparently al-Haitham did not realize that something very much like his proof could be 'reversed' to establish the generality of Euclid's formulation.

[5] I am indebted to Mr. A. I. Sabra for a suggested translation of this passage based upon his recent edition, hitherto unavailable to me, of the Arabic text: Omar Khayyam, *Explanation of the Difficulties in Euclid's Postulates* (Alexandria, 1961). The recent Omar Khayyam, "Discussion of

This is Theorem 1 of Book X of the *Elements*. Its demonstration was based solely on Book V, and thus we have transferred it to this place since we need it in these [i.e. Khayyam's own] demonstrations. But Euclid said, 'subtract from the greater [magnitude] *more than its half*', and he did not say, 'subtract from it [a magnitude] *equal to its half or more than its half*', so that the assertion would be more general. It is remarkable that he used this Theorem in Theorem 13 of Book XII [=XII, 16 of the Greek original], and said, 'if from the greater there be subtracted an *equal* to its half and from the remainder an *equal* to its half'. Had his assertion here [i.e., in X, 1] been thus [i.e., in terms of subtracting either an *equal to, or more than, the half*], it would have been more useful to him in that place [i.e. in XII, 13=XII, 16]. So heed this.

Hence, I think we can conclude that no small stir was created by the limited form of X, 1 in the Arabic tradition. Though certainly some of the puzzles were also caused by an incomplete appreciation of the force of what they did have of Euclid at this point, I think it fair to say that these troubles were aided and abetted by the loss of the corollary. But the Arabs would not have been temporarily run aground on these occasions, had they not sought to extend and revise the methods of quadrature and cubature they had absorbed from the Greek legacy. It was thus also partly a result of asking more deeply and more exactly of the commitments their procedures were forcing them to accept, that led them to question this piece of their Euclidean raw material.

On the other hand, the problems caused, and most often resolved, in Arabic mathematics by this omission in Euclid do not seem to have recurred in the Latin West. Here, the reaction to X, 1 (again mostly without its corollary) was a rather passive one. Throughout the *Elements*, and in various opuscula of medieval Latin mathematics the fashion was almost always to accept (rightly to be sure) the 'take *more than half*' form of X, 1 itself. Perhaps one of the most interesting occurrences of this habit is to be found in the medieval versions of the quadrature in Archimedes's *De mensura circuli*, Proposition 1. Here, the continuity contention of X, 1 appears in the 'compression' of the circle between the inscribed and circumscribed polygons multiplying their sides *ad placitum*. In the most exact medieval

Difficulties in Euclid", trans. by Ali R. Amir-Moez, *Scripta Mathematica*, XXIV (1959) 292–293 is unreliable at this point; the earlier Russian translation by B. Rozenfeld and A. P. Yushkevich (*Istoriko-matematicheskiie Issledovaniia*, VI, 1953, pp. 91–2) is more accurate. Note that XII, 16 is, to my knowledge, the only place Euclid applies X, 1 in its corollary form.

rendering of this bit of Archimedes, William of Moerbeke reproduced the Greek with rigorous fidelity. In reaching a magnitude less than that by which the circle, by contrary hypothesis, exceeds the triangle to which it is claimed equal, Moerbeke renders Archimedes's razor-like brevity word for word:[1] "Et secentur periferie [sc. polygonii] in duo equa et sint portiones iam minores excessu quo excedit circulus trigonum."

There is no talk of 'how much' is taken by the multiplication of sides of the inscribed polygon; one even jumps directly from an inscribed square to the sought-for result. In the versions from the Arabic, things are not so rapid and brief. At each step of the successive subtraction more than half not only *is* taken, but we are *told* that this is so. Even the opening move is so specified: the first inscribed polygon, a square, takes *more than half* of the circle itself.[2] It is quite true, of course, that a proper description of Archimedes's procedure does involve 'taking more than half' at each step, the first included. Thus, X, 1 (and not its corollary) fills the bill to perfection. Indeed, later re-workings of the version of Gerard of Cremona of the *De mensura* explicitly point their finger at this proposition of the *Elements*.[3] What is more, the circle quadrature contained in the *Elements* (XII, 2) was glossed in an equally, if not more, specific fashion. Here, a marginal note to Gerard of Cremona's translation of Euclid (later incorporated into the text itself) tells us that, in a quadrature proof such as this, one must note "that when an equilateral square falls in a circle it is more than half of it, and if an octagon fall in it then the triangular sectors which occur in it are more than half of [the remainder], and similarly if there fall [in the circle] a figure having sixteen sides, and so on ad infinitum". Both here and in the expansions of Archimedes, the medieval mathematician had successfully filled in the pertinent assumption of continuity for the particular procedures presented in his text. But he had not delved further into the generality of this assumption, or these procedures. No intellect was piqued to ask whether the desired result (in Archimedes, an excess of the circle over some inscribed polygon less than its excess over the triangle) could be reached if one

[1] M. Clagett, "Archimedes in the Middle Ages: the *De mensura circuli*", *Osiris*, X (1952) 617.

[2] Ibid., p. 600. The two versions from the Arabic there reproduced are by Gerard of Cremona and, apparently, Plato of Tivoli.

[3] Ibid., pp. 607, 610, 611, 615.

did *not* always subtract more than half. Thus, for example, the gambit of inscribing an equilateral triangle (where, for the first step, *less* than half is taken) was not entertained. A plausible reason for this lack of concern for the form and generality of X, 1 in the Latin West is not difficult to discover. It seems fair to find it in the absence of that extensive exploration into advanced areas of quadrature which characterized some of the efforts of their Arabic predecessors.

But it would be wrong to imagine that this limited form of X, 1 was the sole, or even the most used postulate of continuity in medieval Latin geometry. Other principles are employed, sometimes in place of X, 1, sometimes in roles in which X, 1 would not suffice. Perhaps the most important group of these variant assumptions of continuity is that which might be labelled 'postulates of betweenness'. In all of their various medieval Latin forms these postulates entail the following: for all magnitudes a and b, when $a > b$, then there is a third magnitude, c, such that $a > c > b$. So, for example, we find such a postulate consistently, but tacitly, appealed to in the quadrature and cubature problems of the *De curvis superficiebus* of John of Tinemue.[1] Somewhat later, Albert of Saxony applies an assumption of betweenness in his *De quadratura circuli*; it functions in a proof of the same first proposition of Archimedes's *De mensura circuli* which we have already seen to be a frequent customer of the 'Euclidean' principle of continuity, X, 1. With Albert, its role is made explicit:[2] "Thirdly I suppose that if two [unequal] continuous quantities be given, [a quantity] greater than the lesser can be cut off from the greater. This is clear from the fact that any excess, by which one quantity exceeds another, is divisible."

This may be an odd way to state the property of betweenness but Albert is tailoring it to fit the Archimedean quadrature procedure of the *De mensura*. By appeal to this, rather than to the traditional X, 1, he has avoided the successive construction of inscribed and circumscribed polygons with increasing numbers of sides. This circumvention is effected because Albert has indeed packed a generalized X, 1 (together with various

[1] M. Clagett, "The *De curvis superficiebus Archimenidis*: a medieval commentary of Johannes de Tinemue on Book I of the *De Sphaera et Cylindro*", *Osiris*, XI (1954) 295–358. See Propositions 1–3, 6, 8.

[2] H. Suter, "Der Tractatus 'De quadratura circuli,' des Albertus de Saxonia", *Zeitschrift für Mathematik und Physik*, Historisch-literarisch Abteilung, XXIX (1884) 92.

assumptions validating the existence of additional magnitudes from consideration of the sums and differences of given magnitudes) into his postulate of continuity. Also notable is his grounding of his assumption upon the properties of divisibility of the geometric continuum; a move characteristic of the later medieval philosopher-mathematician. Thus, we find similar support brought forth for the property of betweenness by Nicolaus of Cusa.[1] This all seems to be evidence for a meeting between, on the one hand, concern about the assumptions of mathematical procedure and, on the other hand, the traditional philosophical discussions of continua found in treatments of Book VI of Aristotle's *Physics*. The former was becoming more philosophical, the latter more mathematical.[2] It seems that earlier attempts to ground postulates of betweenness did not, at least, appeal to this type of bridge.[3]

Yet another form of this type of assumption of continuity is found throughout other treatises on quadrature. Perhaps its most interesting and significant occurrence is its application in Campanus's discussion of the horn-angle and the angle of a semicircle (i.e., the angle between the circumference of a circle and its diameter). Can one move from a right angle through all values of acute angles without at any time arriving at a value equal to that of an angle of a semicircle? It is claimed, Campanus argues, that such a value will be reached on the basis of the postulate of continuity which asserts: "Contingit reperire maius hoc [i.e., the right angle greater than the angle

[1] Nikolaus von Cues, *Die mathematischen Schriften*, trans. J. Hofmann (Hamburg, 1952) 76.

[2] A particularly good example of both tendencies, especially the latter, is to be found in Thomas Bradwardine's *Tractatus de continuo*. I have prepared an edition, translation and analysis of this treatise for publication in the near future.

[3] Thus, for example, the Banū Mūsā (in a work translated for the Latin West by Gerard of Cremona) attempt a geometrical proof of a betweenness assertion, one which tacitly uses other, more general, betweenness properties in its argument. In fact, the betweenness properties employed by the Banū Mūsā rest directly upon XII, 16 of Euclid (though, as is their custom, they do not trouble to cite it). But XII, 16 in turn utilizes the continuity claims of X, 1 (interestingly enough, in its corollary form); hence, the Arab geometers have silently based their proof on the central continuity principle of Greek mathematics itself. They could have used it instead. (For this bit of the Banū Mūsā see Clagett, "Archimedes", p. 592; I am also indebted to Mr. Clagett for the privilege of examining the manuscript of his forthcoming volume on the Arabic *Archimedes latinus*, which contains a new critical text of the Banū Mūsā treatise.)

of a semicircle] et minus eodem [any acute rectilinear angle], ergo contingit reperire equale." But, Campanus counters, this claim is erroneous: angles of semicircles and horn-angles do not obey this principle of continuity. And he was right; for, as we noted above, their non-Archimedean, non-Eudoxean, character frees them from compliance. It is worth adding that these remarks of Campanus soon became of basic authority for almost all later scholastic discussions of these unusual angles, discussions which, under the increasing favour given to mathematical treatments of the continuum, are found everywhere in fourteenth- and fifteenth-century philosophical literature (almost invariably, for example, in questions on Aristotle's *Physics*).[1] Once again the philosophical meets the mathematical.

The particular form in which Campanus expressed the "from greater to lesser, therefore through an equal" assumption of continuity was naturally suited to kinematic procedures in geometry. But another, so to say, "static" form of the same assumption became equally popular in investigations on quadrature; it merely claimed that when there *was* a greater, and *was* a lesser, so then there also *exists* an equal.[2] It is curious to note that just such a principle was hotly debated in late Greek Antiquity; and, moreover, also with respect to the problem of the quadrature of the circle.[3] The apparent link between these Greek discussions and their medieval counterparts was, in addition to the pertinent remarks of Aristotle himself, most probably the Latin translation of Themistius's *Commentary on the Posterior Analytics*.[4] The deliberations of ancient philosophers over mathematical principles and methods were bearing fruit in the philosophical-mathematical minds of the Middle Ages.

In face of the danger of multiplying entities beyond necessity,

[1] Bradwardine was to repeat Campanus's observations in his *Geometria speculativa* (ed. Paris, 1503; Tract. 2, Ch. 3, Concl. 6) and so to become a second standard source for this authoritative position, particularly in fifteenth–sixteenth-century works.

[2] Thus, for example, once again Albert of Saxony — who also reports the 'kinematic' form (Suter, "Der Tractatus", p. 87) — and Nicolaus of Cusa (op. cit. pp. xx, 37). Incidentally, Albert, following Campanus, denies the applicability of both forms of the axiom to horn-angles.

[3] Cf. Oskar Becker, "Eudoxos-Studien II & III", *Quellen und Studien zur Geschichte der Mathematik*, etc., B. Studien, II (1933) 369–87; III (1936) 236–44.

[4] Cf. Themistius, "Paraphrasis of the Posterior Analytics in Gerard of Cremona's translation", ed. J. R. O'Donnell, *Mediaeval Studies*, XX (1958) 265.

I should like to conclude this footnote to the Eudoxean postulate by drawing attention to one final feature of the medieval 'continuity kit'. It is of unusual importance: the express assertion of a postulate for the existence of a fourth proportional. Such a postulate is employed in XII, 2 of the *Elements* (Euclid's quadrature of the circle). In the Middle Ages it received proper application in this proposition, but was also specified as a required axiom and added to the list in Book I.[1] It reads: "By as much as some one quantity is to another quantity of the same genus, so much is any third [quantity] to some fourth of the same genus."

This is immediately followed by an observation concerning its generality:

> This is to be obeyed in continuous quantities, be the antecedents [i.e. the first and third quantities] greater than or equal to the consequents [the second and fourth quantities]. For magnitude decreases in infinitum. In numbers, if the first be a submultiple of the second, so any third will be an equal submultiple of some fourth. Multitude, indeed, increases in infinitum.

As numbers were limited, for the most part, to positive integers for the scholastics, this rationale for the applicability of their principle is understandable and correct. When compared with the other assumptions of continuity we have discussed which were, in a certain sense, medieval creations, the present postulate strikes one as more elegant and powerful, more subtle and, perhaps, more useful. At least it could function — and this was frequently seen — where the expressly Greek X, 1 could not. One may add to its medieval role in the quadrature of XII, 2 that Albert of Saxony invoked an instance of it to secure the division of a quantity into incommensurable parts and that it became one of Nicolaus of Cusa's standard geometrical tools.[2] But we must not take it that the fourth proportional postulate was always used with genius, or even correctly. A case in point: an elaborated version of the *Quad-*

[1] The assumption occurs in most versions of the Adelard tradition, but within this tradition Campanus appears to be alone in specifying it in Proposition XII, 2. In the translation of this assumption, in which I have tried to represent the consensus of the whole Adelard tradition, note that (1) "of the same genus" appears to be a later addition, (2) in some MSS the relation of "less than" is substituted for that of "equal to" as obtaining between the "antecedents" and "consequents". Other variants are here not noted.

[2] Suter, "Der Tractatus", p. 50; Nicolaus of Cusa, op. cit. p. 17.

ratura per lunulas (which is a Latin fragment of Simplicius's commentary on the *Physics*) appeals to it, and cites chapter and verse from Campanus, in order to justify what is an erroneous generalization of lune squaring.[1] Curiously, it is just that generalization which historians argue is, or is not, to be assigned, by Aristotle's charge, to Hippocrates of Chios.

Taken in sum these medieval vicissitudes of principles of continuity are but a part, yet I hope a characteristic one, of the more involved topical history the mathematical continuum has in the Middle Ages. On the one hand, their push towards new developments in higher mathematics led the Arabic mathematicians to question one of the bases of such mathematics as found in their Greek heritage. But we have seen that their questioning was not without a catalyst from the state of their translations themselves. What was transmitted substantially affected the nature, if not the scope, of their mathematical worries. In contrast, medieval Latin scholars were docile when faced with much the same text. Mathematical reasons do not seem to have goaded them to revise the assumptions of continuity in their new-found learning. Elaboration sets the tone; not revision. And at least a segment of this penchant for supplementing and expanding found common cause in the borderland area between mathematics and philosophy; for the latter, too, involved a deep interest in striking new ground for the problems of the continuum.

Book V, Definition 5: the equality of proportions

The case history that can be developed from the medieval sequence of footnotes to our second definition is more complex and extensive; accordingly, we shall have to be more selective. Moreover, not only is the story here more involved than that which we have just treated, but its features are significantly different. Unlike the medieval status of Definition 4 it is not a matter of frequently not having the definition in its proper place; on the contrary, it is ever-present and translated, in essence, correctly. It is not a question of doubting generality. It is not a case in which short cuts are devised expressing the

[1] M. Clagett, "The *Quadratura per lunulas*. A thirteenth-century fragment of Simplicius's Commentary on the *Physics* of Aristotle", *Essays in Medieval Life and Thought Presented in Honor of Austin Patterson Evans* (New York, 1955) 107. This version omits the statement of Simplicius announcing the invalidity of the argument.

same notion. It is not an instance of the elaboration of an understood core. Rather, it is, as I have mentioned above, a problem in misunderstanding.

This failure of comprehension was not a peculiarly Latin malaise; it has roots in the Arabic tradition, and we shall consequently begin to follow its trail there. In this regard, one of the earliest works which we possess that reveals this perplexity about Definition 5 is that of the ninth-century Aḥmed ibn Yūsuf (Ametus filius Josephi) translated into Latin by Gerard of Cremona under the title of *Epistola de proportione et de proportionalitate.*[1] Ametus's main aim was to investigate the "cause and essence" of proportion[2] and proportionality, and further to inquire of Euclid's meaning when he speaks of the "multiples" which are assumed for them. This was, and continued to be, the crux of the problem; the technique of taking *equimultiples* which Eudoxus had invented (and Euclid had reported) for framing a thoroughly general definition of equal proportions was simply not comprehended. One of the primary creations of Greek mathematics was proceeding to go to waste. Ametus's struggles are an instructive example of this lack of appreciation. In Socratic fashion he offers a battery of alternative definitions of proportionality, upon criticism occasionally withdrawing one of those submitted. Thus, he sets forth a reputed "Pythagorean" definition specifying those proportions as equal between whose members there occur, respectively, equal "augmenta". He follows with a suggestion more recognizably Pythagorean: equality of proportions obtains when "ut sit in primo de partibus secundi quantum in tertio de partibus quarti".[3] Rightly he sees that this is no general definition, but one limited to cases involving commensurable magnitudes. Two further non-Euclidean/non-Eudoxean definitions are also submitted: one a question-begging affair (and admitted to be so), the other a variant of the spurious Euclidean stipulation of

[1] A critical edition, with translation, introduction and commentary of the Latin text of this work has recently been prepared by Sister Walter Reginald Schrader in her doctoral dissertation (University of Wisconsin, 1960). I am most grateful to her for the privilege of examining this text for its bearing upon the problems under discussion.

[2] Ametus devotes considerable space to puzzles about the meaning of proportion (or, as the Greeks have it, ratio) as well, but our attention will be limited to his remarks about proportionality or the equality of proportions.

[3] The text offers this as a definition of "proportio", but the sense of the definiens demands it be of "proportionalitas".

proportionality as the "similitude" of proportions.[1] Yet among this plethora of alternative Ametus does come up with the genuine thing: a reasonable replica of Eudoxus's criterion of equimultiples. Once brought up, it is immediately scorned for bringing in things that have nothing to do with that defined and for ignoring the proper road of definition *per genus et differentiam*! However, this does not mean that Eudoxus's definition need be totally rejected; it finds its place instead as a fundamental property of proportions which is later *demonstrated* to hold.[2] Generally put, Ametus's objections to V, Def. 5 were that it was not basic enough to be regarded as a "first principle". His understanding of it seems clear enough; it was rather a disagreement over its position of priority within the system. Other Arabs followed this lead and attempted similar, or sometimes new, demonstrations of the Eudoxean definition. But there were dissenters; so al-Nairīzī (whose interpretation of what Euclid means differs widely from his true intentions) holds such proofs futile.

If Ametus successfully represents Arabic dissatisfaction with this part of Book V, his therapy is not the most frequent. The more popular custom was rather to give an 'anthyphairetic' definition of the equality of proportions, one which expanded them as continued fractions. Thus, if the expansion of the two proportions in question yielded two series of terms which were, one by one, correspondingly equal, then the proportions were equal. Further, when the series of terms was finite, the proportions involved were between commensurables; when the series was infinite, the proportions were between incommensurables. Hence, this criterion of proportionality is, as Eudoxus's, general. Though the employment of this notion to determine the equality of proportions bristles throughout various Arabic texts, its origin, or at least earliest occurrence, is Greek. Historians have shown, through the comments of Alexander of Aphrodisias,

[1] In the medieval Arabic and Latin translations this occurs as the fourth definition of Book V. Thus, the two definitions (following the Greek numbering) which form the basis of this paper are numbered 5 and 6 in medieval tradition.

[2] Ametus's proof rests upon the application of a previously proved proposition; but the latter, as Campanus later objected, involves moves and principles which already assume knowledge of the equality of proportions. Presumably, Ametus might have replied that one of his earlier (in our eyes unsatisfactory) definitions of proportionality would suffice for this knowledge. For this role he might well have selected that definition equivalent to the spurious Euclid "similitudo proportionum".

that Aristotle's reference (*Topics*, 158b 29 ff.) to equal proportions in terms of having the same ἀνταναίρεσις (=ἀνθυφαίρεσις) is to be interpreted as the continued fraction criterion we have given above (and, as a creation, conjecturally assigned to Theaetetus).[1] Consequently, this manner of supplying conditions for equal proportions has come to be known as 'anthyphairetic'. It appears in explicit form (as it does in no extant Greek text) in, for example, the comments of al-Māhānī (ninth century) and al-Nairīzī to Book V. But as has been appropriately observed, these two mathematicians do not, as some of their successors, attempt to construct a bridge, as it were, between their anthyphairetic conception of proportionality and the "equimultiple" definition of Eudoxus.[2] Those who did indulge in such bridge-building — be it between anthyphairetic procedures and Eudoxus or between considerations pertinent to numeral proportions and Eudoxus — were all working within the pattern exemplified by Ametus of explaining the Greek technique of equimultiples in terms of more basic, better known, conceptions and methods.[3] These conceptions and methods were invariably arithmetic, drawn from considerations primarily applicable to number. Perhaps the most successful effort in so explaining Eudoxus (one sympathetic to, indeed defending, his definition) was that of al-Jayyānī (eleventh century). He works from an analysis of proportions in terms of "parts" (the 'Pythagorean' manner of Book VII of the *Elements*) to the 'multiple analysis' of Eudoxus, revealing, as his concluding blow, their essential equivalence.[4] Thus, if the 'part analysis' approach of the arithmetical books was acceptable to the mathematical palates of his contemporaries, so they must drop their guard against the atrocious equimultiples and adopt Eudoxus as well. The understanding al-Jayyānī reveals

[1] Cf. O. Becker, "Eudoxos-Studien I", *Quellen und Studien zur Geschichte der Mathematik*, etc., B. Studien, II (1933) 311–33. This interpretation was also reached independently by Dijksterhuis and Zeuthen.

[2] E. B. Ploiij, *Euclid's Conception of Ratio and His Definition of Proportional Magnitudes as Criticized by Arabian Commentators* (Rotterdam, n. d.) 50–3, 61.

[3] So, for example, Ibn al-Haitham, Omar Khayyam and al-Ṭūsī; cf. Ploiij, op. cit., pp. 53–66 and Omar Khayyam, op. cit.

[4] Ploiij (op. cit., pp. 15–47) has translated, and given the text in facsimile, of this work. The key notion in his argument is the observation (offered as obvious) that although part analysis is not *sufficient* to account for proportionality among incommensurables, nonetheless, certain negative information about part relations is pertinent; thus it *cannot* be the case that $nA > B$ and $nC < D$ while yet $A/B = C/D$.

in his explanation of the troublesome Definition 5 leaves little to be desired; it matches, one can claim, that of Isaac Barrow (who is customarily mentioned as the first thoroughly to penetrate the Eudoxean mysteries).

Viewing the Arabic efforts to explain or supplant the fifth definition more broadly, the general characteristics are not difficult to perceive. The most notable of them is certainly the priority accorded arithmetical manners of analysis. It is from this that their interpretations and deductions of the Eudoxean view for the most part proceed. Apparently they did not (save al-Jayyānī) adequately appreciate the arithmetical basis of Eudoxus's method itself; their arithmetical procedures not only differed markedly from those of Eudoxus, but they almost always failed to see the connexion between their ways and his. Secondly, particularly in their emphasis upon the anthyphairetic definition, but also less markedly in their other approaches to the problem, they relied upon procedures of approximation. And lastly, they often felt the need to place the equimultiple properties of Definition 5 in a subordinate and, as it were, demonstrated position.

When one turns to the reaction of the Latin West to the equimultiple criterion, these three Islamic features all but vanish. Demonstration of the definition is remote from their minds; approximative procedures are nowhere to be found; the employment of arithmetical ideas may remain, but in a form rather crude and jejune; the understanding of Eudoxus reaches a new low ebb. Complaints about the substance of this definition in Book V succinctly reflect the fact, if not the measure, of incomprehension. Roger Bacon castigates Euclid for using "exceedingly obscure words" in his definition, words which are employed in "no part of mathematics, philosophy or theology"; further, he claims, it would require a long and useless treatise to explain what he is up to, and it would be idle to follow his lead.[1] When the struggles with what Euclid did mean are recorded, it is easy to see the cause of Roger's impatient railing. These troubles lurk not only in the comments (and in the margins) of the Latin Euclid, but seem to infect reflections in independent mathematical opuscula whenever Euclid's view of the equality of proportions is mentioned.[2]

As one might expect the problems begin with the "ex-

[1] Roger Bacon *Communia mathematica*, ed. R. Steele (Oxford, 1940) 86, 94.

[2] Thus, the translations above (p. 241, n. 1) designated as Adelard III, Campanus, Adelard II (marginally) and an Anonymous translation of Books V and VI in MS Vaticana, regin. lat. 1268, 72r–91v all contain one form or

positio" of the spurious definition stating the conditions of continuous proportionality (which we have above noted took the place of the genuine V, Def. 4 in the most current of the medieval translations). Equimultiples are invoked in this unauthentic definition as the *modus explicandi*; one might even take it as a statement of the Eudoxean criterion for the special case of continuous proportionality. But one word prevents this, and forces misinterpretation: the equimultiples are said, as a condition, *equally* (*eque*) to exceed or fall short of one another. Nothing could be further from Eudoxus's true intentions; only *that* there be a corresponding excess or defect is required; that the excesses or defects be equivalent in amount is not only not specified, but makes no sense. A reinterpretation, a non-Eudoxean one, is demanded to account for this equivalence. This 'new look' can be best expressed by quoting Campanus's view of what the real sense of the definition is: "Continuous proportionals are those [quantities] of which all equimultiples are continuous proportionals" (i.e., $A/B=B/C$ if, and only if, $nA/nB=nB/nC$). True, but certainly not the Greek meaning. Indeed, in order to fit this circular elucidation to the "excess" and "defect" indicated in the definition, it must be added, Campanus and his adherents claim, that this excess (or defect) be taken "quantum ad proportionem" and not (as Eudoxus had actually contended) "quantum ad quantitatem".[1]

This was, they held, the significance of their added definition. Almost as a matter of course a similar interpretation[2] was fostered upon the genuine Eudoxean definition of equal proportions which immediately followed; in deference to its spurious predecessor, it became looked to as a definition of discontinuous proportionality.

another of the sort of difficulties specified below. As to 'opuscula' one might cite the *Communia mathematica* of Bacon and the late fourteenth-century *Geometria* of Wigandus Durnheimer. In what follows, I have drawn the common pattern of these difficulties from the version of Campanus; it appears to have set the tone for almost all others.

[1] That is, for example, 4 exceeds 2 and 8 exceeds 4 with equal excesses *quantum ad proportionem* (since $4/2=8/4$), but not *quantum ad quantitatem* (as in the case, for instance, for the excesses obtaining between 4 and 2, 8 and 6). It is, of course, the former type of excess that agrees with the equimultiples nA, nB and nC when $A/B=B/C$.

[2] That is: $A/B=C/D$ if, and only if, $nA/mB=nC/mD$. I do not wish to suggest that the spurious definition necessarily caused them to misunderstand the genuine V, Def. 5 (there was already too much a tradition in misinterpretation for this to be likely), but rather that it did give this particular, in effect circular, form to their misunderstanding.

The question naturally arises as to what the scholastics did with their interpretation of Eudoxus. What use can one make of the useless? The applications of the definition within the body of the *Elements* are of no help; they are either such as to render the proper relation of equimultiples unapparent, or, when they do bring the proper meaning to the fore, it passes unnoticed. About the most our medieval mathematicians accomplish in this regard is to drop an appropriate reference to the definition, with no indication of really knowing why. Alternatively, within the larger fabric of late medieval mathematics, and within the later versions of the *Elements* themselves, thinking bound to another definition of equal proportions takes hold: "Equal proportions are those whose *denominations* are equal."[1] The meaning is clear: the denomination of a proportion is the number (whole or fractional) expressing it in its lowest terms. Logically, this notion goes back to the Greek πυθμήν, the "root number" of a proportion.[2] Historically, however, the manner in which the denomination idea became connected with the theory of proportionality, indeed even insinuated itself into Book V,[3] is somewhat more involved. I suggest that the path may well have been something like the following.

If anything, the denomination interpretation of proportions and their equality bespeaks the application of a notion originally arithmetical, yet not arithmetical in the sense of the "parts

[1] The definition explicitly occurs, for example, in Roger Bacon (op. cit. p. 91) and Bradwardine (*Geometria speculativa*, Tract. III, Ch. 3, Regula 3 and *Tractatus de proportionibus*, Ch. I, Pars. 3, Supp. 1). It seems to have become standard in the scholastic treatises on proportion in the fifteenth-sixteenth centuries (e.g. those of Alvarus Thomas and George Lokert).

[2] Thus, in Nicomachus I, 19, 6–7; 20, 1; 21, 1; II, 19, 3. (For other related uses of πυθμήν — especially its application in Apollonius's doctrine of multiplication — cf. Heath, *Greek Mathematics*, I, 55–7, 115–17.) However, Boethius does not translate or express this Nicomachean notion by "denominatio", but rather by "radix proportionum" (*Inst. arith.*, I, 28) and other, more expanded, phrases. In the *early* medieval mathematical tradition "denominatio" usually signifies a partial quotient (the Abacists) or the denominator of a fraction. It seems probable, though I have not been able to discover incontrovertible evidence, that the present idea of "denominatio" may have come from the Greek πυθμήν notion via the Arabic *'ass* or *uqūd*.

[3] An anonymous addition to the *Questio de proportione dyametri* ascribed by Suter to Albert of Saxony even claims that the 'denomination axiom' is asserted and proved by Euclid in Book V (Suter, "Die Quaestio 'De proportione dyametri ad costam ejusdem' des Albertus de Saxonia", *Zeitschrift für Mathematik und Physik*, Hist.-Liter. Abt., XXXII, 1887, 52).

analysis" of Book VII of the *Elements*. It was not a case of "arithmeticization" through superposing the techniques of one book upon another; at least not simply that. If we look at Campanus's list of definitions to Book VII we find something unique among medieval versions. There occur definitions not in the text of Euclid itself; his source for these additions is not hard to find, it is Jordanus de Nemore's *Arithmetica*.[1] Among these added definitions is found one which *replaces* the Euclidean definition of equal proportion for numbers (VII, Def. 20). It is a form of the criterion of "equality of denominations" we have been discussing. This may not mark the initial occurrence of the denomination concept into the *Elements*, but I believe it gives the most influential case of such penetration. It seems that once thus firmly established in Book VII, "denominationes" seeped back into the more general theory of proportionality of Book V; in fact, in his comments to several of the definitions of the latter book, Campanus himself assisted the process. So much for a plausible account of how medieval thinking about proportion became "denomination dominated".

It remains to ask of the effectiveness of the denomination definition of equal proportions, and of the generality the medievals intended it, and the denomination idea itself, to have. To the latter first: Thomas Bradwardine in his *Tractatus de proportionibus*, employs the notion of denomination as one of the criteria which distinguish rational from irrational proportions. A rational proportion, he tells us, is one which "is immediately denominated by a given number" (so 2/1 is immediately denominated by the number 2, 6/2 by the number 3, etc.). This much, save for the addition of the adverb *immediate*, was standard procedure, and traditionally admissible. But he goes on to apply "denomination" to proportions between incommensurables: these irrational proportions, he claims, "are not immediately but only mediately (*mediate*) denominated by a given number, for they are immediately denominated by a given proportion, which is, in turn, immediately denominated

[1] Campanus sprinkles the usual definitions of Book VII over this book and the two following. His additions in all three of these books are almost totally drawn from Jordanus's *Arithmetica*; so are the postulates and axioms he sets down in Book VII. These moves do a good deal to explain the later medieval simultaneous citation of Euclid and Jordanus in treating points relative to proportions and proportionality. I hope to prepare an article treating more fully of Campanus's relation to Jordanus at this juncture.

by a number".[1] This extension of the role of denomination would certainly not have satisfied all medieval mathematicians. Thus, Campanus, in a general comment to the definitions of Book V of the *Elements*, denies its application to that infinity of irrational proportions, for, he asserts, their denominations are not knowable. Moreover, he adds, Book V does include irrationals in its domain, and hence Euclid was forced to abandon — unlike the arithmetician — the definition of equal proportions by equal denominations.[2] Nevertheless, Albert of Saxony and other later scholastics follow Bradwardine's generalization, and not Campanus's restriction.[3] Subscribers to the extension are not difficult to find; what it all means is harder to unravel. At least three interpretations suggest themselves:[4] if we express an irrational proportion as $(A/B)^{x/y}$, then either (1) the whole irrational proportion is immediately denominated by the rational *proportion* A/B and is mediately denominated by the number n (which may be an integer, proper or improper fraction) and which, in turn, immediately denominates the rational proportion A/B (thus, $(4/2)^{3/2}$ is immediately denominated by 4/2 and mediately by 2, while 2, in turn, immediately denominates 4/2); or (2) the whole irrational proportion is immediately denominated by the rational proportion x/y and mediately denominated by the number n, which, in turn, immediately denominates the rational proportion x/y (thus, $(4/2)^{3/2}$ is immediately denominated by the proportion 3/2 and mediately by the number $1\frac{1}{2}$, which, in turn immediately denominates 3/2); or finally (3)

[1] Bradwardine, *Tractatus de proportionibus*, ed. and trans. H. Lamar Crosby (Madison, 1955) 67. This whole idea may well be older than Bradwardine.

[2] Campanus even claims that the lack of amenability of irrational proportions toward receiving denominations forced Euclid to take refuge in the terminology of multiples which we have seen both Campanus himself and other medievals so unable to penetrate. In point of fact, it was the unsuitability of an arithmetic definition for equality of proportions which did cause Eudoxus to seek 'refuge' in his multiples, but not the denomination definition Campanus imagined.

[3] Cf. Suter, "Die Quaestio", pp. 44–5 and Albertus de Saxonia, *Tractatus proportionum* (ed. Venice, 1496) fol. 43r. Nicole Oresme adopts a related, but significantly different, generalization. He seems not to be caught in the difficulties one finds in Bradwardine, Albert of Saxony and others. For Oresme see Edward Grant, "Nicole Oresme and his *De proportionibus proportionum*", *Isis* LI (1960) 301.

[4] Recent correspondence with Mr. Edward Grant has been helpful concerning this point. I shall not present all the pros and cons here.

the whole irrational proportion is immediately denominated by the rational proportion A/B and mediately denominated by the number x/y which, in turn, immediately denominates the rational proportion A/B (thus, $(4/2)^{3/2}$ is immediately denominated by the proportion 4/2 and mediately by the number $1\frac{1}{2}$ which, in turn, immediately denominates 4/2). However, none of these possible interpretations of the Bradwardinian extension of denomination are without problems; problems connected with an inconsistency in the meaning of denomination and, secondly, with the equality criterion for proportions we have been examining. For, if we attempt to fit this extended application of denomination back into the equality criterion based upon this notion, it is clear that the criterion proves unsatisfactory.[1] The first interpretation has the advantage that the denomination involved serves a function consonant with the traditional meaning of the term — and consonant, incidentally, with Bradwardine's own use of the term when dealing merely with rational proportions. On the other hand, its suitability for the equality criterion is distinctly null; for there would be no way to discriminate irrational proportions with equal bases but differing exponents; clearly, equal (immediate and mediate) denominations for the bases would not entail equal irrational proportions. The second interpretation suffers a similar, if inverse, difficulty: there would be no discrimination of irrational proportions with equal exponents but differing bases. Moreover, this interpretation possesses a second disadvantage: the idea of the exponent's denominating the whole irrational proportion is at variance with the meaning "denomination" receives a few lines earlier, when Bradwardine is treating of rational proportions (and when, in the application to irrational proportions itself, Bradwardine speaks of the number, in turn, immediately denominating the rational exponent involved). In this way of looking at the matter, his extension covering proportions between incommensurables involves an ambiguity of the pivotal term itself. Another, related change in the

[1] As far as I have been able to discover, precisely this attempt has not been, understandably, hazarded by any medieval writer. However, Bradwardine and his followers *do* extend the notion of denomination to irrational proportions, and he himself heads the crucial section of his *Tractatus de proportionibus*, which does not exclude irrational proportions from its domain, with the equality criterion in question. He gives, in short, no indication that his assertion of the equality criterion is not to apply to all proportions, both rational and irrational; all, by his extension, have denominations.

meaning of "immediate denomination" is occasioned by the third interpretation; but it fits somewhat better, if only half way, with the equality axiom. One can infer the equality of proportions from the equality of the *two* denominations A/B and x/y; but the converse by no means follows. And the scholastics were perfectly well aware of this requirement of convertibility for definitions, and even scolded inherited mathematical works for not expressing it verbatim. In sum, we must conclude that this generalization of the conception of denomination to irrational proportions miscarried. They did not succeed in repeating Eudoxus's victory, if that were at all their aim, with new found tactics. It seems that Campanus's successors paid little heed to his caveat against treading upon the ground of the irrational under the banner of denomination. Their error rendered their substitute definition for the equality of proportions ineffective (though one must admit that even without their ill-fitting extension the definition is trivial and of little use).

The conclusion must be that, with the failure to comprehend the Eudoxean key to Book V, the Latin West lost one of the two thoroughly general criteria for equal proportions that they possessed. Their efforts to enthrone another were mathematically futile. Though the effective anthyphairetic definition was available to them in the Latin translation of al-Nairīzī, this too they ignored, so losing their second chance. Still, one resemblance with the Arabic attitude to V, Def. 5 remained. In their abortive attempt to reconstitute proportionality on the basis of denominations, like their predecessors they rested upon an arithmetical base. But the techniques and conceptions they drew from this foundation did not, like those of the Arabs, successfully serve a field for proportionality larger than that of numbers or commensurables. In this, their 'arithmeticization' for the equality of proportions fell bankrupt.

The medieval role of proportions and proportionality

Thus far, I have tried to indicate something of the medieval response to the two cornerstones of the general theory of proportionality that were bequeathed to the Middle Ages by Greek Antiquity. I do not think that it would be historically immodest to see in this reaction some factors at play which were tvpical of medieval mathematical activity. I could conclude at this point by re-emphasizing these factors in a more general way, but before attempting this it will be well to mention, however briefly, a few of the more dominant functions that the whole language of proportion and proportionality exercised during this period. This will take us beyond the two 'primitive propositions' of this language we have been discussing; and rightly so, for the difficulties and puzzles which the foundations of the theory of proportionality may have caused in the Middle Ages cannot be taken as a measure of the conscious application of the theory — and its appendages — itself. Rather than a history of diminished enthusiasm, one finds an increased interest in this segment of mathematics, and a growing courage in extending the bounds of its applications. Of course, the sustained role that proportionality played during this period was in a certain sense a natural one for a tradition following the outlines of the Greek mathematical past. For the theory of proportionality furnished the Greeks with what was, in effect, their theory of measure: compare, for example, the modern 'πr^2' with the Euclidean–Eudoxean "Circles are to one another as the squares on the diameters" (XII, 2). This manner of measure remained with science well into the early modern era; the language of proportions is still the *modus operandi* of Galileo. It obviated the choice of standard units and the determination of constants. But to trace this expected use of proportions through the science and mathematics of the Middle Ages would be almost endless and, in a way, a declaration of the obvious. I should instead like to recount several illustrations of the medieval awareness of the importance of proportions and proportionality in cases in which their role loomed even larger than one might normally expect for inheritors of the Greek tradition. Yet even this account will remain incomplete and selective. I have, for example, made no attempt to treat the extent to which Pythagorean tendencies in philosophy urged the utility of proportions in the interpretation of the universe.

A general idea of the medieval sensitivity to the significance of proportions can be gleaned from some of the reflections upon the import of the mathematics of Book V of the *Elements*: al-Nairīzī declares that its principles pertain to all Books, and Ametus extols the utility of proportionality for finance, statics, optics and music. In the Latin West the remarks to Book V often emphasized its role for all quantity, reserving treatment of its various "species" for the other books of Euclid;[1] Roger

[1] Thus, for example, in the anonymous translation of Book V in MS Vat. reg. lat. 1268, and in that of Adelard III.

Bacon declares that "those propositions which are in the fifth [book] of Euclid, and those similar to them, are prior to all, since they are appropriate to figures and numbers and all things mathematical, and, through the medium of mathematics, to yet other things and sciences".[1] The extent to which Bacon's judgment was to be borne out can be sensed from the intrusion of proportionality into philosophy and even theology: often in philosophy, to be sure, where the question itself was mathematical (for example, the problem of the incommensurability of the diagonal of a square with its side), but also often where, at least originally, the substance was not mathematical (so the relation of movers to their mobiles and the variations of intensible and remissible forms — of which more will be said later). In theology, the trend appears, for instance, in John Peckham's attempt to confirm the oneness of the Trinity by means of a proportionality at once arithmetic, geometric and harmonic.[2] As important as such fortunes of proportionality may be for medieval intellectual history, what follows will limit itself to its role in the areas of mathematics and the exact sciences, or at least to a part thereof.

Even at the very basic level of arithmetic, proportions began to extend their mark in the later Middle Ages.[3] The more 'advanced' algorisms like those of the Jordanus corpus became, relative to earlier medieval efforts, predominantly concerned with proportions; even Jordanus's *Arithmetica* devoted an increased attention to their machinations. A more specialized and important part of the medieval interest in this sphere of mathematics is reflected in the quite considerable preoccupation with the doctrine of the composition of proportions (e.g., A/C is "composed of" $A/B \cdot B/C$, etc.). Interest in the doctrine was naturally catalyzed by its importance for the 'transversal theorem' of the mathematics of astronomy;[4] yet independent treatises concerned with it are found throughout the Middle

[1] Bacon, op. cit. p. 125.

[2] Guy Beaujouan, "Recherches sur l'histoire de l'arithmétique au moyen âge", *École Nationale de Chartes, Positions des Thèses*, etc. (Paris, 1947) 18. Peckham is an example of "medieval Pythagoreanism".

[3] Beaujouan, op. cit. p. 19.

[4] That is, the relations established by a spherical triangle and an intersecting great circle (the transversal) were calculated by the technique of composing proportions. For a summary view of antique developments (Menelaus, Ptolemy, Pappus) in this regard see Sir Thomas Heath, *History of Greek Mathematics* (Oxford, 1921) II, 266–70, 284–6, 419–21.

Ages, both Arabic and Latin.[1] Through the translation of Ptolemy, Thābit, Ametus and others — and perhaps directly — the Arabic concern with the composition of proportions was transferred to the Latin West. The eighteen cases of composed proportion (for six quantities) enumerated in the works of the two Arabs are conspicuous in Jordanus' *Arithmetica* (Book V) and Leonardo Fibonacci's *Liber abbaci* (where its Greek–Arabic origin is confessed in an application to an arithmetical problem).[2] Another short, separate work, variously ascribed to Thābit, Campanus or even al-Kindī, combines an exposition of the eighteen cases with a brief, axiomatized introduction; an epitome of it, usually ascribed to Jordanus, caps the 'composition' tradition.[3] This little corpus of specialized proportion treatises not only reflects what was a corner of mathematical activity in Islam and the West, but formed, as we shall partly see, a cache of mathematical doctrine which contained elements important for later, fourteenth-century developments in the calculus of proportions and its application to the problems of motion.

Naturally, proportionality filled roles in medieval mathematics more general than that in the specialized opuscula of the 'composition' tradition. A case in point would be its function in algebra, where once again credit for the groundwork must be principally assigned to Arabic sources. For example, the Rule of Three and the Rules of Single and Double False Position all appealed to a proportionality base. Nor was it merely a matter of applying such rules when in search of the unknown; the Arabs soon began to specify the involvement of proportions and to classify their methods of solution in terms of their employment.[4] These techniques, if

[1] Thus, the special tracts of Thābit ibn Qurra: *De figura sectore* (Latin trans. ed. A. Björnbo; Erlangen, 1924); Ametus: *Epistola* (see above); al-Tūsī: *Traité du quadrilatère* (ed. and trans. Caratheodory; Constantinople, 1891); etc. The idea of proportion composition was also of appreciable weight in more general works. Thus, Avicenna re-established the spurious Euclidean definition (VI, Def. 5) of a composed proportion within the context of the general theory of Book V — mathematical convictions playing a role in the transmitted text of the *Elements* (cf. K. Lokotsch, *Avicenna als Mathematiker*, Erfurt, 1912, p. 22).

[2] M. Cantor, *Vorlesungen über Geschichte der Mathematik*, 2nd ed. (Leipzig, 1899) II, 15, 67.

[3] For the Thābit-Campanus: MS BN Lat 7377B, ff. 94v–98r; for the Jordanus: MS Erfurt Amplon. 4° 376, ff. 117v–119v.

[4] Cf. Al-Karkhī (=al-Karajī) Al-Kāfī fī'l Ḥisāb (*Genügendes über Arithmetik*), trans. A. Hochheim, II (Halle, 1879) 15–17, III (Halle, 1880)

largely without the Arabic methodological reflections, are later found flourishing in the Latin West where, one might claim, a characteristic trait of thirteenth- and early fourteenth-century algebra was a concern with proportionality operations. Similar roles, if at times mathematically less respectable ones, are also to be found in medieval Latin geometry.[1]

But it was not the extended medieval Latin use of proportions in mathematics proper — be it arithmetic, algebra or geometry — that is most worthy of note. The signal development was rather in their application to the physical sciences, and particularly to questions of mechanics. The classic work in this vein was the early fourteenth-century *Tractatus de proportionibus velocitatum in motibus* of Thomas Bradwardine. The core of this treatise concerned itself with the problem of relating variations in forces and resistances to variations in velocities. Bradwardine's resolution — naturally phrased within the context of Aristotelian physics — was his so-called 'dynamical law'; in modern terms it amounts to: $F_2/R_2=(F_1/R_1)^n$ where $n=V_2/V_1$ (or, with even greater sophistication: $V=\log_a F/R$ where $a=F_1/R_1$). The advantages which Bradwardine's 'function' exhibited over previous resolutions of the question (as well as the disadvantages it did not overcome) have often been pointed out;[2] for present purposes the groping towards a new 'calculus' of proportions which assisted him in the formulation of his law is more pertinent. The key to this new calculus lay in the relating of proportions by exponents, or, more medievally, in the consideration of the "proportions of proportions".[3] And the matrix to this key was the technique of inserting or finding means between the terms of a given proportion, a technique

4–5; Ibn al-Bannā, "Le Talkhys", trans. A. Marre, *Atti dell' Accademia pontificia de' nuovi Lincei*, XVII (1865), 314; al-Qalasādi, "Traité de l'arithmétique", trans. F. Woepcke, *Atti d. Accad. pont. d. nuovi Lincei*, XII (1859) 414–15; al-Akfānī as in E. Wiedemann, "Beiträge zur Geschichte der Naturwissenschaften XIV", *Sitzungsber. d. Phys.-Med. Sozietät zu Erlangen*, XXXIX (1907) 31–5.

[1] Examples, from two extremes, can be seen in the last tract of Oresme's *Algorismus proportionum* and the more popular *Geometria speculativa* of Bradwardine (Tract. III, Ch. 6, where proportions are — rather trivially — invoked as the basis for quadrature problems).

[2] Cf. M. Clagett, *The Science of Mechanics in the Middle Ages* (Madison, 1959), Ch. 7; Anneliese Maier, "Der Funktionsbegriff in der Physik des 14, Jahrhunderts", *Die Vorläufer Galileis im 14. Jahrhundert* (Rome, 1949) 81–110.

[3] The term is not Bradwardine's, but a later invention. Thus, for Oresme, it appears that $F_2/R_2=(F_1/R_1)^n$ constitutes a "proportio proportionum"; cf. E. Grant, op. cit. p. 295, n. 13.

very much a part of mathematical precedent. In the ninth and tenth definitions of Book V Euclid had already stated as basic principles (a status which not a few medievals felt to be in error) that, given $A/B=B/C=C/D$, then $A/C=(A/B)^2$ and $A/D=(A/B)^3$. But of greater force in the formulation of Bradwardine's calculus, was the generalization that these Euclidean principles received at the hands of the composed proportion theorists. The elaborations of the possible cases of composed proportion were themselves not relevant, but the introductory theorems that medieval Latin composition opuscula (Thābit–Campanus and Jordanus) had prefaced to the deduction of these cases were indeed crucial. Bradwardine even appropriates two of these theorems as "suppositions";[1] the composition tradition, originally an adjunct to spherical trigonometry, was bearing fruit in a novel manner. Still, this new calculus rooted in the doctrine of the insertion of means was in no sense fully developed by Bradwardine; it looks more like work in progress. It seems that one of the major difficulties can be located in Bradwardine's failure to fit his new 'exponential' way of thinking about proportions with the hard facts of the *Elements*. His success here was, if anything, but partial. He often limits and twists Euclid to match his purposes, but without consistency and in an *ad hoc* fashion. Bradwardine had, in effect, stipulated a new meaning for "greater than" and "excess", for "less than" and "defect". To say, for example, that A/B was "greater than" C/D, was to claim the existence of an n such that $A/B=(C/D)^n$.[2] Though this was ingenious enough, Bradwardine was still not consistent in distinguishing exponential and arithmetic relations, and frequently took principles of the existent proportionality tradition to be, without emendation, amenable to both. Oresme, in his fascinating *De proportionibus proportionum*, was more careful and astute. Even if he did not expressly remark upon the unconventional senses the new calculus of proportions required of older, Euclidean propositions, he nonetheless applied the necessary innovations with consistency; *pars*, *partes*, *multiplex* and *commensurabilis* are regularly given exponential, rather than arithmetic interpreta-

[1] Bradwardine, *Tractatus de proportionibus*, p. 76; cf. Thābit-Campanus *De proportionibus*, MS BN 7377B, 94v–95r and Jordanus, *De proportionibus* MS Erfurt. Amplon. 4° 376, 117v–118r.

[2] So, for instance we must interpret the (rather startling) central theorem "Proportione aequalitatis nulla proportio est maior vel minor" (Bradwardine, op. cit. p. 80) with these new meanings in mind.

tions.[1] But even Oresme was not to succeed in gaining complete mathematical generality for the new view of proportions; he hesitated to apply the exponential part analysis, and the idea of composing proportions, to cases of "minor inequality", i.e., to proportions A/B where $A < B$. To do so would apparently run counter to the Euclidean part-whole axiom and would *potius abusio vocabulorum videtur.*[2] It seems, therefore, that at least one of the conventions of the mathematical tradition was not clearly distinguished from the relations pertinent to the new calculus of proportions; with this, the proper generality for the calculus fell abruptly short of realization.

This limitation of domain may have been mathematically unfortunate, but it in no way prevented a most fertile applying of the calculus in the realm of mechanics (where, to be sure, the relevant proportions of forces and resistances were, by Aristotelian assumption, always of *major* inequality). Among the many applications none is more interesting, or better deserves mention as an illustration of the extent to which proportionality considerations had penetrated late medieval science, than Oresme's treatment of the incommensurability of celestial motions.

Proportions and proportionality had long been regarded as crucial implements for astronomical investigations.[3] The so-called 'middle books' of the Arabs included their study as an essential part of astronomy's mathematical propaedeutic, and, in the Latin West, a recommended preparation for competence in astrology similarly legislated acquaintance with their major features.[4] On the other hand, it had often been realized that the possible incommensurability of the heavenly motions could constitute an objection to the accuracy and confidence of astrological prediction.[5] Oresme brings the full force of his

[1] E. Grant, op. cit. pp. 297–302: for example, A/B is *pars* of C/D when $A/B = (C/D)^{1/n}$; A/B is *commensurabilis* to C/D when $A/B = (C/D)^{m/n}$ (m and n being positive integers).

[2] Thus, 2/1 may be a third part of 8/1, and 4/1 = 4/2 · 2/1; but 1/2 may not be held to be part of 1/8 nor 1/4 = 1/2 · 2/4. Cf. E. Grant, op. cit. p. 298 and A. Maier, *An der Grenze von Scholastik und Naturwissenschaft*, 2nd ed. (Rome, 1952) 263.

[3] Cf. e.g., Abraham ibn Ezra, *Sefer ha-mispar: Das Buch der Zahl*, ed. and trans. Moritz Siberberg (Frankfurt, 1895) 4, 47; his astronomical works are pertinent to the other half of the background of Oresme's accomplishment, see below.

[4] A. Björnbo, "Ein Lehrgang der Mathematik und Astrologie im Mittelalter", *Bibliotheca Mathematica*, ser. 3, IV (1903) 288–90.

[5] So, for example, Ibn Ezra and John Duns Scotus; Duhem has briefly discussed the relevant role of these two authors in his *Système du monde*, VIII,

calculus of proportions to bear upon the question.[1] Still speaking 'pure' mathematics, Oresme had pointed out that for any given unknown, and hence random, set of proportions it is more probable that any two of the set would be incommensurable to one another (or constitute an "irrational proportion of proportions") than they would be commensurable (i.e., if A/B and C/D are two proportions randomly chosen from the given set, then it is probable (*verisimile*) that $A/B \neq (C/D)^{m/n}$ — where m and n are positive integers). This is carried yet a step further: the more numerous the set of proportions, the greater the probability that the two picked will be incommensurable. So much for the mathematics of it all; the next move rests upon the applicability of the calculus of proportions to velocities, forces, resistances, distances traversed and times of traversal, in particular to these elements in the motions of heavenly bodies. If at this point we relieve ourselves of the specific stages of the argument, it is nonetheless clear that Oresme's propositions concerning the probable incommensurability of randomly selected proportions afford him ground for concluding that "it is probable that any two proposed motions of celestial bodies are incommensurable, and it is most probable that some motion of the heavens is incommensurable to some motion of another sphere".[2] Oresme had thus mathematically established the likelihoods of astronomical fact; another mathematical point was to make his conclusion militate against the feasibility of astrological prediction. For, given the conjunction of any two heavenly bodies, it follows, upon the probability of the incommensurability of their motions, that they shall never come to just such a conjunction again: it is mathematically impossible that they do so even though they continue wandering the skies to eternity.[3] The traditional

443–8. Cf. Averroës (elaborating on Alexander of Aphrodisias) *Epitome* on the *De generatione et corruptione*, trans. S. Kurland (Cambridge, Mass., 1958) 137–8.

[1] For this, and the details of what follows, see the excellent brief account in E. Grant, op. cit. 306–13.

[2] E. Grant, op. cit. p. 311. We must here keep in mind, however, not only the new sense Oresme had assigned to 'incommensurable', but also that he followed Bradwardine's 'function' in determining relations between variant velocities. Thus, V_2 would be *incommensurable* to V_1 where $F_2/R_2 = (F_1/R_1)^n$ and $V_2/V_1 = n$ but n is an *irrational* exponent.

[3] V. P. Zoubov, "Quelques observations sur l'auteur de traité anonyme 'Utrum dyameter alicuius quadrati sit commensurabilis costae ejusdem' ", *Isis*, L (1959) 130–4. The anonymous treatise, which has resemblances with the present argument from Oresme, has earlier been ascribed to Albert of Saxony by H. Suter.

objection against astrology based on incommensurable heavenly motions had become hardened by the mathematical precision of the new calculus of proportions. And thus, one might add, by a kind of evidence than which no greater can be had; at least, that is, for us *viatores mundi*.

Even these few examples should make it apparent that the medieval lack of comprehension of crucial parts of the Eudoxean theory of proportionality did not stifle mathematical imagination in this section of exact thought, nor blemish the products of this imagination with logical inelegance. On the other hand, the creative ingenuity of the fourteenth-century calculus of proportions should not blind us to the futility of the attempts to penetrate the even greater ingenuity of the Greeks. Rather, both the misunderstanding and the brilliant originality are parts, and significant ones, of the fortunes of proportion and proportionality in the Middle Ages. Such duplicity can, I think, be found in other areas of mathematics and science of the time; one feels it almost characteristic of medieval mathematical history.

In our case, the misinterpretation was at least partially occasioned by the status of one text in the medieval corpus of Latin translations. A textual addition appears to have dictated the form, if not the fact, of the misunderstanding. In a similar way, Campanus's additions, or importations as it were, to the seventh book of the *Elements* may well have been an influential nexus between this lack of comprehension and the substituted definition of equal proportions which formed, so to say, the standard therapy of the deficiency. Another effect of textual variation was revealed in the omission of a corollary to the crucial X, 1; it produced among the Arabs, not so much misunderstanding, but mathematical controversy. Within the confines of our case history it should be evident that textual factors have exercised no mean formative role in moulding features of medieval mathematical history; should one look more broadly at medieval science, substantially the same effect can be observed. The historian must face the fact that it is not merely the medieval presence of the Greek tradition, in all its inestimable importance, that he must consider in tracing the development of Arabic and Latin science; account must also be taken of the precise form of this tradition — step by step, axiom by axiom and proposition by proposition. An accurate history of all the features of transmission is a necessary condition to a fully understood history of medieval science.

Our case history has secondly illustrated the give and take of medieval Latin philosophy and mathematics. Common concern here, and often elsewhere, had waked philosophical imaginations to the task of meta-mathematical reflection. If, in discussions of the continuum and the problems of motion, scholastic natural philosophy came to benefit from the advantages of *rationes mathematice*, reciprocally, the mathematical treatises of the later Middle Ages often suffered the intrusion of philosophical conceptions and methods. Though mathematics may not have gained in rigor by this *rapprochement*, it most certainly gained adherents and a wider sphere of application. With logic — which also gave new vitality and ideas to investigations like those of the continuum and motion — mathematics became a major force in supporting and forming new avenues of analysis for traditional, often previously more sheerly philosophical problems.

The final, and I think in many ways the most important, distinguishing mark which the medieval history of proportions exhibits is its consistent tendency to read arithmetical conceptions into the geometrical, and into theories dealing with general magnitude. In effect, number was being considered an element of geometry;[1] the Greek distinction between the continuous and the discrete was beginning to undergo erosion. We have seen this ascendancy of the arithmetical displayed in a variety of circumstances: in successful, anthyphairetic substitutions for the Euclidean definition of equal proportions, as well as in the unsuccessful, "denomination" substitution offered for the same; in explanations or demonstrations of this Euclidean criterion; and finally, though we have not emphasized it, in the new calculus of proportions of the late medieval Latin West. That this last development continued the arithmetic bias so strikingly apparent in the footnotes to the Euclidean–Eudoxean criterion is evident both on reflection, and on the express admission of its adherents. Euclid himself had (illicitly it is often claimed) already bridged the hiatus between the continuous and the discrete by showing that commensurable, magnitudes were related to one another as number to number (X, 5). Bradwardine, probably unwittingly, and Oresme, in full cognizance of his moves, parallel Euclid's procedure by relating proportions — including those between incommensurable magnitudes — by the numbers which were their 'exponents'. What is more, Oresme expressly admits that such

[1] Cf. the explicit statement of al-Jayyānī, Ploiij, op. cit. p. 16.

a relation, or proportion, of proportions, "will be as the proportion of these numbers; surely", he adds, "a proportion of numbers *per arismeticam investiges*".[1]

It must not be thought that the medieval accommodation of the geometrical to the arithmetical was a one-way process. Though numerical examples and arithmetic analyses were frequently applied to problems involving continuous magnitudes, so too geometrical demonstrations were given of arithmetical properties and procedures. Still, if the relation was reciprocal, priority and a greater scope for the arithmetical was predominant. This seems particularly true in the medieval history of Euclid's Book V. It may even be just to maintain that the Middle Ages, both Arabic and Latin, were something of a halfway-house between the guarded Greek separation of general magnitudes from the discrete multitudes which were number and, on the other hand, the confident declaration of John Wallis that "the whole fifth book of Euclid's *Elements* is Arithmetic". If the medievals were historically no stimulus for Wallis's determined position, still their speculations pointed in his direction.

[1] E. Grant, op. cit. p. 305, n. 40.

10

What Accelerated Technological Progress in the Western Middle Ages?

LYNN WHITE, JR.

In *The Cambridge Historical Journal* for 1955,[1] A. G. Keller called attention to a letter of Bessarion which poses a major problem in the history of technical innovation. About 1444, the Cardinal wrote to Constantine Palaeologus, despot of the Morea and the best hope of Greek resurgence against the Turks, urging him to send young men to Italy to learn the practical arts. Bessarion had been impressed not only by Western textiles, glass and metallurgy, and by improved arms and ships: he was particularly struck by the use of water-power to eliminate hand labour, for example in sawing timbers and for working the bellows of furnaces. Evidently he had seen nothing of the sort in the Byzantine realm, and I know of no firm evidence that water or wind power was applied at that time to any industry other than milling grain either in Byzantium or in Islam. Yet by 1444 such machinery had long been used and was common in the West. To be specific, the first water-powered saw-mill appears about 1235 in Villard de Honnecourt's sketchbook,[2] while the earliest evidence of powered bellows for a furnace comes in 1214 from the Trentino.[3]

We are only beginning to understand that the Europe which has hitherto been envisaged as chiefly occupied with scholastic debates and building Gothic cathedrals was likewise plunging headlong into the age of power technology. By about 1322 a chronicler of St. Mary's of Pipewell in Northamptonshire could record that one of the chief reasons for deforestation was the

[1] A. G. Keller, "A Byzantine admirer of 'Western' progress: Cardinal Bessarion", *Cambridge Historical Journal*, XI (1955) 343–8.

[2] *The Sketchbook of Villard de Honnecourt*, ed. T. Bowie (Bloomington, 1959) plate 58. On the problem of the powered marble saws in *Mosella*, cf. below p. 282.

[3] W. Kuhn, "Das Spätmittelalter als technisches Zeitalter", *Ostdeutsche Wissenschaft*, I (1954) 73: "laborare ad unam rotam . . . cum uno furno."

search for timbers for the vanes of windmills.[1] The conclusion is inescapable that, whatever the fecundity of the medieval East in other realms of culture, modern technology was born of the Western Middle Ages.

I

The contrast between the technological mood and movement in the medieval West and those in its sister cultures of the Greek and Muslim East is the more curious because communications were generally good and parallel developments frequent even in technology. For example, the first Christian to fly mechanically was the Anglo-Saxon monk Eilmer of Malmesbury who, some time between 1000 and 1010, built wings with which he flew some six hundred yards before crashing, as he said, because he had forgotten to add a tail. Yet in either 1003 or 1008 the famous Iranian student of Arabic philology al-Jauharī met his death attempting flight in some apparatus from the roof of the old mosque of Nishapur in Khorasan. Since, to judge by finds of coins in Scandinavia, by about 985 nomadic activity had temporarily severed the old trade route from the Northern Seas down the Volga to the Caspian and on to Persia, it is unlikely that Eilmer had heard of al-Jauharī, or the latter of Eilmer. But it is entirely possible, in terms of roads and sea lanes then open and frequented, that both had heard of the successful glider flight of Abu'l-Qāsim 'Abbās b. Firnās in Cordoba about A.D. 875.[2]

As Ibn Firnās and al-Jauharī illustrate, technical impulses were by no means lacking in the Near East, and the West's eventual superiority is the more surprising because both Byzantium and Islam, together with the West, had inherited the full equipment of the Roman–Hellenistic world. There is no evidence that any significant techniques were lost during the transition from Antiquity to the Middle Ages. In the Levant there was complete continuity and vitality of culture. In the more turbulent Occident, political disintegration and economic decay made engineering on the old Roman scale

[1] "Et quot virgae molendinorum venticorum dabantur in temporibus diversorum abbatum nemo novit nisi Deus cui omnia patent"; W. Dugdale, *Monasticon anglicanum* (2nd ed., London, 1682) I, 816.

[2] L. White, jr., "Eilmer of Malmesbury, an eleventh-century aviator. A case study of technological innovation, its context and tradition", *Technology and Culture,* II (1961) 97–111.

infrequent. Yet even there the full technology of Antiquity was available when required: the 276-ton monolith which crowns the tomb of Theodoric the Ostrogoth was brought to Ravenna from Istria and was lowered with fantastic accuracy on to a high drum of masonry.[1] More than two centuries later Charlemagne transported not only sizeable columns but also a great equestrian statue of Zeno across the Alps from Ravenna to Aachen.[2] As for the Roman method of building roads: it appears that neither Islam nor Byzantium chose to retain it any more than the West. The cost of maintenance was out of all proportion to benefits derived, and once the surface of a Roman road began to disintegrate, an unsurfaced road was preferable.[3] Similarly, the hypocaust would seem to have been wasteful of fuel. It remained in use only until Europe invented the more economical and efficient fireplace with chimney-mantel, and then the hot-air stove.[4]

When a seemingly desirable technique vanished, the reason was generally technological advance rather than regression. For example, the Gallo–Roman toothed grain harvester powered by an animal was ingenious, yet was unknown during the Middle Ages. Its defect in medieval eyes was that it wasted the straw, and was therefore appropriate only to a regime of cereals little related to animal husbandry.[5] As we shall see, one of the great agrarian advances in Northern Europe during the early Middle Ages was the development of a much more intensive and productive agricultural system combining grain with stock raising. In such a complex, straw had great value, and the Gallo–Roman harvester was worthless.

Again, historians of numismatics have habitually lamented a post-classical decay of the art of minting, virtue being represented, in their opinion, by the magnificent sculptural relief of

[1] A. Gotsmich, "Das Grabmal Theoderichs in Ravenna", *Universitas*, XII (1957) 1183–94.

[2] Agnellus, *Liber pontificalis ecclesiae ravennatis*, C. 94, ed. O. Holder-Egger in *Monumenta Germaniae historica, Scriptores rerum langobardicarum et italicarum, saec. VI–IX* (Hanover, 1878) 338; Einhard, *Vita Karoli Magni*, C. 26, ed. G. H. Pertz in ibid., *Scriptores*, II (1829) 457.

[3] P. Fustier, "Notes sur la constitution des voies romaines en Italie", *Revue des études anciennes*, LX (1958) 85.

[4] R. J. Forbes, *Studies in Ancient Technology*, VI (Leiden, 1958) 36–57; for the medieval developments, A. Dachler, "Die Ausbildung der Beheizung bis ins Mittelalter", *Berichte und Mitteilungen des Altertums-Vereins zu Wien*, XL (1906) 141–62, remains useful.

[5] J. Kolendo, "La moissonneuse antique en Gaule romaine", *Annales: economies, sociétés, civilisations*, XV (1960) 1102–3.

the best Greek and Roman coins. Not only Western medieval but also Byzantine and Islamic currencies are much flatter. But for bankers, money-changers and merchants, these later coins had a new convenience: they would stack.

We are learning to view the early Middle Ages in new ways. What our grandfathers regarded as decay may indicate merely a shift of interest. In judging our own time we recognize that Picasso's purposes are not those of Ingres; so in contrasting a Roman carved gem with the Sutton Hoo enamels we are today less prone to detect evidence of decline. Changing tastes and conditions may lead to the degeneration of a few techniques or skills in a period when technology as a whole is advancing. The technology of torture,[1] for example, reached new perfection during the Renaissance; its decline in the Age of Reason did not mean that eighteenth-century technology as a whole was degenerating.

But in trying to understand Western medieval technology, it is not enough to probe into the classical inheritance and into the technologies of the medieval Greeks and Muslims. Below the level of the written records, in the subhistory where most of mankind, including the lower classes of Europe, have dwelled until very recently, there was a vast technical osmosis extending over the entire Old World. Joseph Needham[2] is in process of demonstrating in detail such relations between the West and the Far East, while in a brief article[3] I have indicated similar diffusions from Central and South Asian areas to which our medieval ancestors are usually thought to have had no debt.

Exchanges of technological ideas between the Mediterranean-European peoples and those south of the Ethiopian highlands and the Sahara have scarcely been examined. My colleague in Los Angeles, the geographer Joseph E. Spencer, who has been tracing the very curious global distribution of the agricultural invention of terracing, believes that terraces reached the Niger region from Western North Africa, but that they never penetrated to the zone of heavy rainfall along the Guinea Coast, although terraces have elsewhere proved very useful in similar

[1] While there is a large literature on the legal aspects of torture, there is little on its changing mechanics. One aspect is handled by W. Treue, *Kulturgeschichte der Schraube* (Munich, 1955).

[2] *Science and Civilization in China* (3 volumes to date, Cambridge, 1954–9).

[3] L. White, jr., "Tibet, India and Malaya as sources of Western medieval technology", *American Historical Review*, LXV (1960) 515–26.

terrains and climates.[1] The trigger of Benin crossbows is so similar to that used quite recently by Norwegian whalers, that it is assumed to have been introduced by Danish, Dutch or English sailors in the early sixteenth century.[2] But an analogous possible transmission in archery, this time through Arab traders along the East Coast of Africa, warns us that the connexion may be earlier. In the National Gallery, Hieronymus Bosch's *The Crowning with Thorns* (of the very late fifteenth century) shows one of Christ's tormentors wearing, thrust in the folds of his Infidel turban, an arrow with a chisel-shaped head[3] almost identical with one excavated in Uganda from a site thought to date likewise from the fifteenth century.[4]

Even the New World was not entirely removed from medieval technology. It is now clear that by the thirteenth century the Greenland Eskimos had borrowed the art of cooperage from the Norse settlements.[5] Claims that they also adopted the holding screw from the Vikings as a means of attaching bone points to shafts have been doubted. The discussion is not, however, closed: an arrowhead with a holding screw was excavated in north-western Greenland in a stratum of the sixteenth century, or earlier than any Eskimo contact with Europeans other than the Norse.[6]

Clearly, in a world teeming with ideas and far more open to their transmission than we have been accustomed to think, technological originality must be understood not only as capacity to generate new concepts and skills but also as the penchant for seizing imported techniques and developing them to new levels of efficiency and types of application.

Such, then, is the context within which we must discuss technological acceleration during the Western Middle Ages. It is a problem which naturally divides into two questions. First, how early and in what ways did the West begin to show

[1] J. E. Spencer and G. A. Hale, "The origin, nature and distribution of agricultural terracing", *Pacific Viewpoint* (Wellington), II (1961) 34.

[2] H. Balfour, "The origin of West African crossbows", *Annual Report of the Smithsonian Institution* (1910) 635–50.

[3] L. Baldass, *Hieronimus Bosch* (2nd ed., Vienna, 1959), plate 110.

[4] P. L. Shinnie, "Excavations at Bigo, Uganda", *Antiquity*, XXXIII (1959) 57, fig. 3b.

[5] E. Holtved, "Archaeological investigations of the Thule district," *Meddelelser om Grønland*, CXLI (1944), Part 2, pp. 14–15, 18, 26, 54; T. Mathiassen, "Inugsuk, a medieval Eskimo settlement in Upernivik district, West Greenland", ibid., LXXVII (1930) 237–9, 295–6.

[6] Holtved, op. cit. Part 1, p. 214, Plate 11.30; Part 2, pp. 46, 74, 78.

its distinctive originality in technological matters and its velocity of technical change? Second, for what reasons did this happen and continue to happen?

II[1]

(1) Between the first half of the sixth century and the end of the ninth century Northern Europe created or received a series of inventions which quickly coalesced into an entirely novel system of agriculture. In terms of a peasant's labour, this was by far the most productive which the world had seen. The earliest new item, the heavy plough, was derived from some Northern peasant society as yet unidentified. The three-field system of rotation, appearing in the later eighth century, was a hybridization of the Mediterranean autumn planting with the ancient Baltic spring planting. The development of open fields aided cattle raising in conjunction with agriculture. Modern harness, arriving probably from Central Asia and first appearing *c.* 800 in the Trier *Apocalypse* (f. 58r), made the horse commonly available in Northern Europe for farm labour. Finally, the nailed horseshoe, emerging simultaneously in Siberia, Byzantium and the West at the end of the ninth century, greatly confirmed the horse's economic uses.

As the various elements in this new system were perfected and diffused, more food became available, and population rose. New supplies of proteins were made available by the stress on dairy products, and by the large part which legumes played in the spring planting of the three-field rotation of crops. Moreover the surplus of oats and barley from the spring planting gradually enabled most northern peasants to shift from the ox to the more efficient horse for ploughing and hauling. Mediterranean peasants, in a climate which did not permit extensive spring plantings, continued to plod behind the ox. In the north the greater speed of the horse enabled peasants to live further from their fields, and this led to the decay of small hamlets and the growth of large agricultural villages with a type of life which was almost urban. And the new productivity of each northern peasant enabled more of them to leave the land for the cities, industry and commerce.

More than any other single factor, this agricultural revolution of the early Middle Ages helps us to understand the shift of

[1] The documentation for this section will be found in my *Medieval Technology and Social Change* (Oxford, Clarendon Press, 1962).

Europe's focus from the Mediterranean to the Northern plains. In general, the lands of ancient civilization continued to prosper using the Roman methods of agricultural production. But the surge forward of the new agrarian technology of Northern Europe provided the basis for late medieval and early modern civilization.

(2) Moreover in the early eighth century Western Europe seized the initiative in improving methods of warfare, and created a novel military technology so superior that its foes had no alternative but to adopt it.

The stirrup was the most important military invention prior to the cannon. Before the stirrup, a horseman's spear was held at the end of his arm, and the blow was struck with the strength of his biceps. When the saddle with a high pommel and cantle was supplemented with stirrups, a warrior could lay his spear at rest, held between his upper arm and body. Now the blow was delivered not by his arm but by the weight of a charging stallion and rider. The increase of impact altered warfare fundamentally.

The stirrup emerged in India in the late second century B.C. as the big-toe stirrup. By the fifth century A.D. the boot-wearing Chinese had expanded it into the foot stirrup. In the sixth century it is found among the rider peoples of the Altai. In A.D. 694 the Muslim armies fighting in Northern Iran received it from Turkistan. About A.D. 730 it reached Gaul. The Franks were, then, almost the last nation using horses to learn of the stirrup, yet they were the first fully to realize its implications for warfare. In 732, the year before he fought off the Arabs at Poitiers (a battle which, since 1955, has been redated 733), Charles Martel decided drastically to renovate the Frankish host in terms of the new mode of fighting. He began seizing Church lands and distributing them to retainers, and from this military revolution the feudal system developed, as well as the chivalric stratum of European society.

The new violence of the lance at rest called for heavier armour, which in turn produced the crossbow as an 'anti-tank gun'. The shield became pointed at the bottom to offer better protection to the knight's left leg. Heraldic devices grew up to permit identification of the warrior under his carapace. With a lag of about a century, most of the features of Frankish warfare were taken over by both Byzantines and Saracens. It is significant that by 1087, before the First Crusade, the pointed shield is found in Cairo. The Muslims of Andalusia particularly complained that, whereas in Morocco one could fight with light equipment, in Spain they were compelled to assume the heavy armour, the long lances held at rest, the bucklers, the pennons and surcoats of their Frankish adversaries. Moreover they armed their Muslim infantry with the crossbow. Thus, having seized the leadership in agrarian methods in the sixth century, the medieval West did the same in military technology two hundred years later, and thereafter radiated to surrounding cultures much more than it absorbed in matters of warfare.

(3) Finally, by the year 1000, the West had begun that process of saving human labour by applying natural power to industry which so captured Bessarion's imagination over four centuries later. By 983 there may have been a fulling mill on the banks of the Serchio in Tuscany, while a document of 1008 almost certainly indicates others along a stream in Milan. The appearance of the place-name Schmidmülen in the Oberpfalz in 1010 can only mean that water-driven trip-hammers were then sounding in the forges of Germany. Before the end of the eleventh century we have evidence of the use of water-power in the metal and textile trades from the Pyrenees to Britain.

In 1185 the first horizontal-axle windmill appears. Within seven years this new device is found from Yorkshire to Syria, whither it was taken by German Crusaders. In the thirteenth century, one hundred and twenty windmills were built in the vicinity of Ypres alone. In the same period the application of water-power to fulling became so general that, as E. M. Carus-Wilson has shown, the centre of English textile manufacturing shifted from the south-east to the north-west where mill sites were more plentiful. And in general the Continent seems to have anticipated England in such matters. By the early fourteenth century, mills for tanning and laundering, mills for sawing, for crushing anything from olives to ore, mills for operating the bellows of blastfurnaces, the hammers of forges or the grindstones to finish and polish tools, weapons and armour, mills for reducing pigments for paint, or pulp for paper, or the mash for beer, were in ever vaster numbers to be found all over Europe. This medieval industrial revolution powered by water and wind reached its ultimate refinement ninety years after Bessarion's letter when, in 1534, the Italian Matteo del Nassaro set up a mill on the Seine at Paris to polish diamonds, emeralds and the like — a mill taken over by the royal mint in 1552 for the production of the first 'milled' coins. The Europe which followed Columbus and Vasco da Gama into the oceanic routes had had five centuries of growing experience with power technology in industry. No other civilization, not even the Chinese, was nearly so well equipped. The world hegemony of the West during the subsequent five hundred years — now terminating — may partly be understood in this context.

But if the West seized the initiative in agricultural systems in the sixth century, in military methods in the eighth, and in industrial production in the eleventh, how are we to account for this distinctive talent of the European Middle Ages for technological progress? And why did Europe differ so markedly in this respect from its two sister cultures of Byzantium and Islam?

III

No historian in our time dares use the word *cause*. Historical understanding is arrived at, these days, less in terms of causes, in the vernacular sense, than through the isolation of various elements in an historical situation which seem to exert a "gravitational" influence upon each other and to move in a cluster in the direction of the movement which we are trying to comprehend.

(1) The transition from Antiquity to the Middle Ages is best seen as the reassertion of dominance by the native elements in each of the three chief parts of the Roman Empire. The bland cosmopolitan culture of Imperial times — itself a blend of Latin, Greek and Levantine ingredients — began to differentiate once more into vigorous localisms. A distinctive feature of the Islamic world, or of Byzantium, or of the West, may therefore be partly intelligible as the re-emergence of an indigenous trait.

The heart of the Western Middle Ages lay between the Loire and the Rhine. In a remarkable study of Gallo-Roman tombs, J. J. Hatt, the Director of the Archaeological Museum at Strassburg, has shown that from *c.* A.D. 100–275 the sepulchral art of the region of Trier and the Rhineland, the valleys of the Saône and Seine, and Aquitaine, illustrates craftsmen at work with their distinctive tools (of which he gives an inventory) in a way which far exceeds the incidence and elaboration of such scenes in any other province of the Empire.[1] The men who lay

[1] J. J. Hatt, *La tombe gallo-romaine* (Paris, 1951) 192–4, 246, 293–5.

beneath these stones had had no sense of inferiority because they laboured with their hands. They wanted posterity to remember them as good workers.

And who were these craftsmen? They were Celts, and thought of themselves as Celts. Hatt has tabulated the occurrence of Celtic names in funerary inscriptions both by period and by region. Our traditional notion that the civilizing of Gaul was identical with its Latinizing must be revised: the Romans planted the cities, but thereby created a Celtic urbanism. Hatt shows that there is a consistent and very marked increase in the percentage of Celtic names in the second and third centuries as compared with the first century. Clearly, Celtic peasants were migrating to the cities and becoming the artisan class; but they continued to prize their Celtic identity, as their names show. Moreover, the highest proportion of Celtic names appear in the parts of Gaul where depictions of craftsmen with their tools are most common.[1]

This is not coincidence. Northern Gaul was a centre of marked technical innovation in Roman times. Any etymological dictionary will show that an astonishing number of Latin terms for carts and wagons (e.g. *cisium*, *reda*, *carrus*, *carruca*) are of Celtic derivation. Presumably the Germans got the heavy horse from the Celts since in the eighth century their laws call it *marach*,[2] a Celtic word. The marvellous technique of forging 'damascened' swords from faggots or rods of iron and steel of different qualities was perhaps invented by Celts under Roman rule.[3] Not only the powered grain-harvester mentioned above, but also the scythe, the hinged flail and the most advanced form of vineyardist's pruning knife seem to be Gallo-Roman.[4] The barrel, a most ingenious application in wood of the principle of the masonry vault, is quite clearly Celtic in origin.[5] Finally, the most puzzling and spectacular item credited to Roman technology appears in the heart of the Celtic area: the water-powered marble saws mentioned in Ausonius's *Mosella*. An unpenetrated jungle of difficulties surrounds this

[1] Ibid. pp. 26–31.

[2] *Monumenta Germaniae historica*, *Leges*, III, 69, 317; cf. A. Holder, *Alt-celtischer Sprachschatz* (Leipzig, 1904) II, 417.

[3] É. Salin, *La civilisation mérovingienne*, III (Paris, 1957) 109.

[4] C. Parain, "Das Problem der tatsächlichen Verbreitung der technischen Fortschritte in der römische Landwirtschaft", *Zeitschrift für Geschichtswissenschaft*, VIII (1960) 364–5.

[5] F. M. Feldhaus, *Die Technik der Vorzeit, der geschichtlichen Zeit und der Naturvolker* (Leipzig, 1914) 285.

poem.[1] The *Mosella* — a work so much superior to anything else from Ausonius's stylus as to arouse immediate suspicion — is not found in the oldest MSS of his works, or in any MS earlier than the tenth century. There is no marble in the Moselle region: the only marketable stone is slate, which cannot be sawed. There is no other known powered saw until that of Villard already mentioned. I personally incline to regard the *Mosella* as a tenth-century forgery. But if it is authentic and of the late fourth century, its saws are prime evidence of a powerful technological impulse in the area which was to become the centre of Western medieval vitality.

(2) In 1952 the Californian sociologist Margaret Hodgen published *Change and History: a study of dated distributions of technological innovations in England, A.D. 1000–1899*, an investigation of what she calls "the crucial phenomenon of the acceptance of the new". With incredible labour she had studied the history of over twelve thousand English parishes, and concluded that even neighbouring parishes have had surprisingly different histories of technical change. The chief factor making for innovation in a community is prior innovation.

Applying this hypothesis to the Middle Ages as a whole, it would appear that to some extent the greater originality of the West is related to the fact that Latin Christendom was far more profoundly shaken than the East ever was by wave after wave of barbarian invasion, extending, with interruptions, from the third century into the tenth. The Orient indeed experienced turmoil, but was spared the degree and prolongation of chaos so characteristic of Europe during the Early Middle Ages. And Byzantium in particular retained a sense of Roman majesty, and an Hellenic contempt for things outlandish, which made it psychologically a bit hostile to innovation. The West, in contrast, was a molten society, ready to flow into new moulds. It was singularly open to change, and agreeable to it.

(3) A third major reason for the technical dynamism of the Western Middle Ages is a fundamental change in the attitude towards nature which occurred with the spread of the new religion. Sambursky is correct in declaring that "the last traces of the old Greek mythological subservience to the cosmos were eliminated by the influence of Christianity",[2] as is Forbes in holding that "Christianity, by its opposition to animism,

[1] Cf. *Isis*, XLVI (1955) 291–2.

[2] S. Sambursky, *The Physical World of the Greeks* (New York, 1956) 241.

opened the door to a rational use of the forces of nature".[1] Nevertheless, exactly how the high dogmas of the new faith affected the ordinary peasant and artisan remains obscure: we know strangely little of the history of popular piety. It has long been said that small change occurred: the local *genii* were renamed after local saints, and paganism continued in Christian garb.

Quite the contrary, the shift from animism to the cult of saints was seismic. The spirit of a tree or waterfall or lake was in the natural object, part of it, guarding it, and only partly anthropomorphic. Such a spirit was not like ourselves. A saint, on the other hand, was entirely a human being, on our side as against the phenomena of nature. When saint replaced animistic sprite as the most frequent and intimate object of popular religious concern, our race's earthly monopoly on "spirit" was confirmed, and man was liberated to exploit nature as he wished. The cult of saints smashed animism and provided the cornerstone for the naturalistic (but not necessarily irreligious) view of the world which is essential to a highly developed technology.

The cult of saints was common to all Christendom. It helps us to understand the medieval West, but not in contrast to the medieval East. However, the change in man's attitude towards nature which was inherent in adoption of the cult of saints was greatly reinforced by a distinctive development in Northern Europe about the time of Charlemagne.

From the earliest times land had been distributed among peasants in allotments sufficient to support a family: the assumption was subsistence farming, plus enough to pay rent or taxes. Then, as I have said, in Northern Europe and there alone, a great change occurred in methods of farming. Beginning in the early sixth century, the new heavy plough began to spread, equipped with a mouldboard to turn the sod. Friction with the soil was so much greater than in the case of the older two-ox scratch-plough that normally eight oxen were needed. But no peasant had eight oxen of his own. So the peasants began to combine their ox-teams to work a single plough, each taking strips of ploughed land in proportion to his contribution. Thus the standard of land distribution in much of the north ceased to be the needs of a family and became the ability of a new power-engine to till the earth. No

[1] R. J. Forbes, "Power", in C. Singer et al., *A History of Technology* (Oxford, 1956) II, 606.

more fundamental change in the idea of man's relation to the soil can be imagined: once man had been part of nature; now he became her exploiter.

This new attitude was reflected in Charlemagne's effort to replace the old 'passive' names of the months with new names describing human assaults upon nature: June was to be "Ploughing Month"; July, "Haying Month"; August, "Harvest Month".[1] But also the new orientation emerges in the change in illustrated calendars which begins shortly before 830.[2] The old Roman calendars had occasionally shown genre scenes of human activity, but the dominant tradition (which continued in Byzantium) was to depict the months as static personifications bearing symbolic attributes. The new Carolingian calendars, which set the pattern for the Western Middle Ages, are very different: they show a coercive attitude towards natural resources. The pictures change to scenes of ploughing, harvesting, wood-chopping, people knocking down acorns for the pigs, pig-slaughtering. Man and nature are two things, and man is master. Now, with the old underbrush of animism cleared away, the new attitude provided a soil far more favourable than the old for the sprouting of technological innovations.

(4) Our problem, then, seems partly to be explained by Celtic cultural genes in the West, partly by the fluid attitudes induced by centuries of turmoil, and partly by the emergence of a novel psychological relationship with the physical environment — a relationship produced to some extent by a new attitude towards the supernatural and to some extent by an improvement in agrarian methods in Northern Europe. But I believe that a fourth factor is to be found in the distinctive temper of Latin monasticism.

While Graeco–Roman society had by no means entirely rested on the backs of slaves, and while the effect of slavery in retarding technological advance has certainly been exaggerated, nevertheless manual labour was so associated with slavery in late Antiquity that any free man who dirtied his hands with it, even in the most casual way, demeaned himself.[3] Socrates

[1] Einhard, op. cit. C. 29, ed. cit. II, 458.

[2] H. Stern, *Le calendrier de 354* (Paris, 1953) 356–7; also his masterly "Poésies et représentations carolingiens et byzantins des mois", *Revue archéologique*, XLVI (1955) 164–6.

[3] M. J. Finley, "Was Greek civilisation based on slave labour?", *Historia*, VIII (1959) 145–64, provides a thoughtful introduction to a vast literature

was a stone-cutter and unabashed about it; but his disciple Plato was more typical in his time.[1] Plato once sharply rebuked two Greeks who had constructed apparatus to help solve geometrical problems: they were comtaminating thought.[2] Plutarch tells us that Archimedes was ashamed of the machines he built.[3] Whatever may have been the Syracusan's sentiments, Plutarch's are clear. In the later classical tradition there is scarcely a hint of the dignity and potential for serenity inherent in labour.

The seeds of a very different view of work were to be found in the Jewish community. The fourth Commandment from Sinai said, "Six days shalt thou labour" and this was as religiously binding as the injunction to rest on the seventh day. Rabbi Nathan II taught that "Like the Sabbath, work is commanded. . . . Like the Torah, so work is given as a covenant".[4] Many great rabbis worked habitually as woodcutters, shoemakers, tailors, carpenters, and the like.[5] One recalls that the highly educated St. Paul, who had sat at the feet of Gamaliel and who boasted Roman citizenship, not only was a tentmaker but at times supported himself by his trade during his evangelistic missions (Acts, xviii: 3). Moreover, until the fourth century, the Jewish heresy called Christianity remained largely a proletarian faith. By proclaiming that (as St. Peter put it) "God is no respecter of persons" (Acts x: 34) the new religion gave dignity to the humble, and, by implication, to their banausic activities.

But once the persecutions were ended, once the Emperor Constantine himself had been converted and the *labarum* had

of controversy on the nature and effects of ancient slavery. On the social and intellectual context of classical technology, see especially L. Edelstein, "Recent interpretations of ancient science", *Journal of the History of Ideas*, XIII (1952) 579–85, R. Mondolfo, "The Greek attitude to manual labour", *Past and Present*, VI (1954) 1–5, and K. D. White, "Technology and industry in the Roman Empire", *Acta classica: Proceedings of the South African Classical Association*, II (1959) 78–89.

[1] P. M. Schuhl, "Remarques sur Platon et la technologie", *Revue des études grecques*, LXVI (1953) 465–72, shows that Plato was well informed about certain technical matters, but does not deny his basic attitude towards manual labour.

[2] Plutarch, *Marcellus*, XIV.

[3] Ibid. XVII.

[4] S. Kalischer, "Die Wertschätzung der Arbeit in Bibel und Talmud", in *Judaica: Festschrift zu Hermann Cohens siebzigstem Geburtstage* (Berlin, 1912) 583.

[5] *Authorized Daily Prayer Book*, ed. Joseph H. Hertz (New York, 1954) 630, note; Kalischer, op. cit. p. 605.

displaced the eagle as the symbol of Roman might, the Church was flooded by conformists trying to make the best of the new religious situation with minimal inconvenience to themselves. It seemed to many that Constantine had merely managed to paganize Christianity.

The result was monasticism: the effort to retrieve the supposed purity and simplicity of the apostolic church. Integral to monasticism, in both East and West, was the Jewish idea that labour with the hands is not merely a mortification of the flesh, or a practical economic necessity, or even a means of providing charity to one's neighbour: it is a service to God himself, a form of prayer, a joyful oblation.[1] Surprisingly, a concept of work as pure penance for sin, unconnected with prayer and praise, seems to have appeared only once in Christian monasticism: in St. Columba's Irish rule of the seventh century.[2] Otherwise, with amazing consistency in theory, and only slightly less in practice, the monks of the first millennium both in the Greek East and in the Latin West worked as a form of worship. In doing so they defied the classical attitude towards manual labour which continued to be sustained by the aristocratic society which was their context. So great was the general respect for the labouring monk that we can scarcely escape the conclusion that the attitudes of peasants and artisans towards their own labours, and towards the moral value of labour, were improved. Here we can identify another post-Roman psychic innovation favourable to the vigorous expansion of technology.

But since both Greek and Latin monks shared an identical *mystique* of labour,[3] this does not help us to account for the

[1] J. Leroi, "La reforme studite", in *Il monachesimo orientale* (*Orientalia christiana analecta*, CLIII, Rome, 1958) 194, correctly points to the lack of an adequate history of manual labour in monasticism, which is more deplorable because "aucune observance ne peut mieux servir à définer l'orientation profonde d'un type de vie monastique, ou d'une école spirituelle dans l'histoire du monachisme". Much material, but embedded in a matrix of rhetoric, is to be found in L. Redonet y López Dóriga, *El trabajo manual en las reglas monásticas* (Madrid, 1919). More satisfactory are H. B. de Warren, "Le travail manuel chez les moines à travers les siècles", *La vie spirituelle*, LII (1937) 80–123, A. T. Geoghegan, *The Attitudes towards Labor in Early Christianity and Ancient Culture* (Washington, 1945) and E. Delaruelle, "Le travail dans les règles monastiques occidentales du IVe au IXe siècle", *Journal de psychologie normale et pathologique*, XLI (1948) 51–64.

[2] Delaruelle, op. cit. p. 61.

[3] Indeed, one might argue that Eastern ascetics were even more convinced than Western of the spiritual value of work with the hands, since the

greater technical acceleration in the West as compared with Byzantium. We must look for significant regional modulations of the common melody.

Monks, both Eastern and Western, held that, in addition to manual labour, the reading of pious books was an essential part of the spiritual life. In theory at least, all monks were literate, and in every generation no small number of them were good scholars. In late Antiquity, with rare exceptions, learned men did not work, and workers were not learned. The monks were the first large group of intellectuals to get dirt under their fingernails: surely a fact related to the growth of technology.

Yet very early a contrast began to develop between the types of erudition fostered in Benedictine abbeys and in those following the tradition of St. Basil. St. Benedict of Nursia had not thought of his disciples as extending their studies beyond the precincts of divinity,[1] but men like his younger contemporary Cassiodorus saw that if anything not only of sacred but of secular learning was to survive in the turbulent West, it would be in the monasteries. In the Greek realm, a literate laity made it unnecessary for monks to devote much attention to worldly writings. Even on such a frontier of Byzantine culture as Calabria, where the Hellenic tradition had long been under Latin attack, by 1457 the sixteen hundred MSS of its Greek abbeys included only six secular items: two Homers — one a fragment — a part of Aristophanes, the *Hecuba* of Euripedes, Galen's treatise on medicaments, and the Greek *Physiologus*. Moreover all five of the literary MSS (excluding Galen) are listed in only two of the seventy-eight monasteries, Seminara and Mesiano, and these were located no more than twenty

Greek abbeys never developed lay brothers, *conversi*, especially designated for manual labour and distinguished from choir monks whose prime duty was *opus Dei*; cf. P. de Meester, *De monachico statu iuxta disciplinam byzantinam* (Vatican City, 1942) 93–5. The elaboration of Benedictine liturgies from the ninth century onward made such a division of function inevitable; cf. P. Schmitz, "L'influence de saint Benoît d'Aniane dans l'histoire de l'Ordre de saint Benoît", *Settimane di studio del Centro Italiano di Studi sull' Alto Medioevo: V, Il monachesimo* (Spoleto, 1957) 401–15. According to K. Hallinger, "Woher kammen die Laienbruder?", *Analecta sacri Ordinis cisterciensis*, XII (1956) 38, *conversi* are found in many places in the eleventh century, but not at Cluny before 1100.

[1] "Certis temporibus occupari debent fratres in labore manuum, certis iterum horis in lectione divina": *Sancti Benedicti Regula monachorum: textus critico-practicus secundum Cod. sangall. 914*, ed. P. Schmitz (Maredsous, 1955), § XLVIII, p. 109.

miles apart.[1] Throughout the Western Middle Ages, monastic libraries and monastic learning had a much higher secular component.[2] While religious studies, quite naturally, were dominant, the pagan Latin authors were sedulously copied and perused. Benedictines were no less devout than 'Basilians', but the cultural environment of their labours had sunk to so low a level that it became part of their religious duty to cultivate all learning, sacred and secular alike. The catastrophes which overwhelmed the West prevented the working intellectuals in the abbeys from withdrawing themselves from worldly concerns as completely as was possible for the Oriental monks. Thus the high valuation of manual labour which was common to both Greek and Latin monasticism was able to permeate Western medieval society more freely than the society of the Byzantine Empire. The viability and continuing economic importance of the idea that *laborare est orare* is nowhere better seen than in the latest and most distinctive form of Occidental ascetism, Puritanism, in which to work not only *in* but *through* one's 'calling' became both the prime moral necessity and the chief means of serving and praising God.[3]

(5) There is another contrast between the Greek and the Latin Middle Ages which helps to illuminate the different practical effects in these two regions of an identical monkish doctrine of labour. Historians of theology and philosophy have long pointed to two very different moods which seem to pervade the thought of the two great segments of Christendom: emphasis on *theoria*, contemplation, intellectual or mystical understanding in the East; emphasis on *praxis*, activity, the disciplining of the will by good works in the West. In the past such contrasts between Latin voluntarism and Greek intellectualism have been based on what authors have said. The historian must ask not only what they said, but the extent to which they really meant what they said.

Fortunately a new school of historians of exegesis, by using methods somewhat like those of art historians, is penetrating not only the convictions but also the religious tastes of the past:

[1] *Le "Liber visitationis" d'Athanase Chalkéopoulos* (1457–1458), ed. M. H. Laurent and A. Guillon (*Studi e testi*, CCVI, Vatican City, 1960) 47, 107, 111. There is no indication that these libraries had yet been looted by the neo-Hellenic enthusiasts then emerging in Northern Italy.

[2] Cf. M. L. W. Laistner, *Thought and Letters in Western Europe, A.D. 500 to 900* (Ithaca, 1957) 228–35.

[3] E. Troeltsch, *Social Teaching of the Christian Churches* (New York, 1931) 609–12.

they are exposing the subliminal mind. For our purposes the exegesis of the Martha-Mary pericope (Luke x: 38–42) is of particular significance. Since the first great crisis in the history of the Church was the Petrine-Pauline confrontation, inevitably Martha was identified with the synagogue and observance of the Mosaic law, whereas Mary represented the Church and the freedom of the New Covenant. But as soon as Christianity had definitely seceded from Judaism this exegesis vanished, and, in keeping with the Hellenizing of Christian thought, Origen took Martha to represent the active and Mary the contemplative life.[1] Thenceforth in the Greek Church it became customary to regard this episode as giving Christ's sanction to the contemplative rather than the practical life, to the monastic rather than the secular.

One discovers, however, a quite different style of exegesis in the West. St. Ambrose, himself formerly a high Roman official, looks at the sisters of Bethany and feels that they represent *actio* and *intentio*: they are both essential, and the one cannot rightly be called superior to the other.[2] Then Augustine, with his devastating originality, inverts the Greek exegesis and the structure of values which pervades it. His constant preoccupation is the contrast between time and timelessness, between Church Militant and Church Triumphant: a contrast which makes each of his writings, almost each of his sentences, an antiphon of praise. To him, Mary and Martha are symbols of two stages in the perfect life: Martha the life of the soul in the context of time and space; Mary, in the context of eternity. To be sure, by grace the elect soul may catch occasional glimpses, foretastes, of timeless blessedness, but for practical purposes we must be Marthas troubled about many things: "In Martha erat imago praesentium, in Maria futurorum. Quod agebat Martha, ibi sumus; quod agebat Maria, hoc speramus."[3] Whereas in the Greek Orthodox world activity was something

[1] T. Camelot, "Action et contemplation dans la tradition chrétienne", *La vie spirituelle*, LXXVIII (1948) 275. It is notable that St. Ephraem Syrus, writing in Syriac and almost uninfluenced by Platonic tendencies, adopts elaborate stratagems to avoid ranking Martha's activism below Mary's contemplative bent; cf. I. Hausherr, "Utrum sanctus Ephraem Mariam Marthae plus aequo anteposuerit", *Orientalia christiana*, XXX (1933) 153–63.

[2] D. A. Csányi, "Optima pars", *Studia monastica*, II (1960) 56–7.

[3] *Sermo* 104: 4, cited by A. M. de la Bonnardière, "Marthe et Marie, figures de l'église d'après saint Augustin", *La vie spirituelle*, LXXXVI (1952) 425.

to be transcended, in the Latin Catholic world it was a spiritual obligation. In this Western atmosphere, technology could thrive.

Until after 1100 at least, the activity and attitudes of the monastic orders so permeated every tissue of the medieval organism that one would not expect the technological adventure of that era to be confined to the abbeys, or perhaps even centred there. Nevertheless, the monks maintained interest and at times leadership in the field. In the twelfth century, for example, the Cistercians set the pace in applying water-power to a variety of industrial processes: in St. Bernard's own abbey of Clairvaux there were three waterwheels powering different shops devoted to grinding grain and sifting the flour mechanically, to fulling and to tanning, all of which is recounted with great satisfaction in a contemporary life of the Saint.[1]

(6) A sixth and final aid to our understanding of the acceleration of Western medieval technology is found in Christian theology as enunciated with a Latin intonation. Christianity, both Eastern and Western, in theory at least ascribes infinite worth to even the lowliest of human beings as potentially "children of God; and if children then heirs . . . and joint-heirs with Christ" (Romans viii: 16–17). Despite the rigidity of class structures, spiritual egalitarianism continued to resound in the churches with every chanting of the *Magnificat*, while through the centuries preachers and commentators like Isidore of Seville noted with interest that God's foster-father, St. Joseph, was a blacksmith, while the Prince of the Apostles was a fisherman.[2] But the Greek East, with its more contemplative bent, its tendency to abstraction, has felt less impulse than the West to make faith concrete in works.[3] Only in the West does one find a religious urge to substitute a power machine for a man where

[1] Cited in Singer et alii, op. cit. II (1956) 650.

[2] "Joseph justus, cui virgo Maria desponsata exstitit, faber ferrarius fuit . . . et Petrus princeps apostolorum piscatoris officium gessit"; Isidore, *Regula monachorum*, V, 2, in J. P. Migne, *Patrologia latina*, LXXXIII (Paris, 1862) 873.

[3] R. E. Sullivan, "Early medieval missionary activity: a comparative study of Eastern and Western methods", *Church History*, XXII (1954) 17–35, shows that while the Greek evangelists in the Slavic north were very theological in their emphasis and seldom supported themselves economically, the Western missionary was not only a preacher but a "farmer, builder and technician" who introduced not only a new religion but new crops and skills. Moreover, Western preaching was less concerned with doctrine than with ethics.

the required motion is so severe and monotonous that it seems unworthy of a child of God. As early as the sixth century an abbot in Gaul, troubled by the sight of his monks grinding grain in hand mills, built a water-driven mill, "hoc opere laborem monachorum relevans".[1]

Human history is not mathematical. Valid results are at times achieved on the basis of wrong assumptions. The New World is not abolished by the fact that Columbus sailed westward to find the East Indies and died thinking that he had succeeded. To deny or minimize the culturally desirable products of Christianity because one may consider Christianity to be a fabric of illusions, is as subjective as to argue that Christianity is true because some of its effects seem salutary.

The nineteenth-century revulsion against abuses symbolized in Blake's "dark Satanic mills" has blinded historians to the fact that Western labour-saving power technology is profoundly humane in intent, and is largely rooted in religious attitudes. Its ideology is the Christian doctrine of man as developed not in the context of Greek contemplative intellectualism but rather in the framework of Latin voluntarism.[2] The power machines of the Western Middle Ages which amazed Bessarion were produced in part by a spiritual repugnance towards subjecting anyone to drudgery which seems less than human in that it requires the exercise neither of intelligence nor of choice. The Western Middle Ages, believing that the Heavenly Jerusalem contains no temple (Rev., xxi: 22), began to explore the practical implications of this profoundly Christian paradox. Although to labour is to pray, the goal of labour is to end labour.

[1] Gregory of Tours, *Vitae patrum*, C. 18:2, ed. B. Krusch in *Monumenta Germaniae historia, Scriptores rerum merovingicarum*, I (Hanover, 1885) 735.

[2] Lynn White, jr., "Dynamo and Virgin Reconsidered", *American Scholar*, XVII (1958) 183–94.

Commentaries

Commentary by A. P. Yushkevich

The original contributions of medieval mathematicians

I would like to add to the accounts given by Mr. Hartner and Mr. Schramm, and by Mr. Pines, of medieval science by discussing the contributions of the mathematicians of this period. First, it would be useful to say a few words about the mathematics of preceding periods.

Without considering the individual peculiarities of different countries and the relatively small deviations in the chronological order, one can distinguish a few broad periods in the development of mathematics. They are as follows:

(1) The period of the introduction of practical mathematical calculations, corresponding essentially to the beginning of slavery. This was the mathematics of the countries of the ancient east: Egypt, Babylon, China and India. It was in Babylon that these sciences underwent their greatest development. In this period, problems were closely linked to practical needs, but there were already abstract problems. Mathematics and mathematical texts consist of problems solved by means of rules generally lacking in scientific foundation. Only a beginning was made with the systematization of problems, and for the most part this was based on superficial peculiarities rather than fundamental mathematical features. Mathematics was not yet divided into different branches such as arithmetic and geometry. Neugebauer emphasizes that the central feature was the numerical determination of solutions satisfying certain arithmetical or geometrical conditions. At the same time, there appeared the first discursive deductions of new truths from those already known, in the form of some algebraic and geometrical transformations. Deductive connexions were rare, and chains of reasoning short and detached.

The principal results of this were: a sexagesimal place-value system, sexagesimal fractions, approximate extraction of square roots, algebraic solutions of equations of the first and second degree, Pythagoras's theorem, and triplets of Pythagorean numbers. We may include also the use, towards the middle of the first millennium before our era, of arithmetical series in theories of the motion of the moon and planets.

(2) The period of the creation of theoretical mathematics at the time when slavery was practised, in Greece and in the Hellenistic and Roman states. Under relatively democratic conditions of political life, and of intense ideological struggles between factions, new forms of rational scientific knowledge arose. After the partial assimilation of knowledge accumulated in the east and some initial development of it, there began the process of differentiation of the sciences and in particular of mathematics. For the first time mathematics was conceived of as a science (as by Aristotle). Arithmetic and geometry were transformed into great deductive systems. Logical deduction became the motivating force in the development of mathematics. The structure of deduction was subjected to a special logical examination, the science of logic made its appearance. The axiomatic method of the ancients came into being. Mathematical concepts and methods became more and more numerous. Side by side with the elementary branches of mathematics there appeared (in connexion with the needs not only of mathematics itself but also of mechanics, mathematical astronomy, probably the theory of sundials, etc.) the first integral and differential methods and certain techniques of higher synthetic geometry as well as analytical geometry. Ancient mathematics contained the germs of numerous ideas of the fourth period — the period of the mathematics of variable quantities — and even of modern times.

In Greece, the mathematical natural sciences were developing: statics, hydrostatics, acoustics, and theoretical astronomy, where geometrical and kinematic models were employed. From that time astronomy became one of the most important sources of complex problems and of the most elegant mathematical methods, and this it remained for many centuries.

The progress of mathematics begun in the Greek city-states was continued in the Hellenistic kingdoms and under Rome. But the classical developments mentioned above ceased. Infinitesimal methods were used only very rarely in natural science and technology. The branches of mathematics considered the most important were those directly linked to astronomy and geography: spherical geometry, some graphical procedures like that of descriptive geometry, the trigonometry of chords, methods of approximate calculation, as well as theory of numbers and algebra. One notices here the influence of the synthesis of Eastern traditions and true Greek science.

This new and important orientation of research came to an end with the decline of the Roman Empire and of ancient civilization.

(3) The third period, corresponding to the feudal era. This was the period of elementary mathematics. Constant quantities and invariable geometrical figures were studied almost exclusively. The third period began, in the first place, in China and India, then in the Islamic countries and in Europe. The mathematics of this period had many characteristics in common with the mathematics of the ancient east. It is probable that the initial liaisons between China and India on the one hand, and Babylonian civilization on the other, were here of great importance. But the mathematics of the Middle Ages was much more advanced in content, methods and results.

The mathematics of the Middle Ages in the various regions of Asia and Europe had common characteristics and distinctive features. First, I will draw attention to what there was in common.

Medieval mathematics was primarily a mathematics of calculation, an assembly of numerous algorithms for the numerical solution of algebraic, geometrical and trigonometrical problems. These problems, as well as the algorithms for solving them, became more and more complex. Gradually, these algorithms, at first unconnected, came together to form the different branches of mathematics.

The common direction of the development of mathematics is ultimately explained by the similarity of the practical problems in Asia and Europe at the time considered. The needs of building, trade, transport, commerce, of the financial institutions of the state, legal needs and so on, all provided everywhere a similar impetus for the separation of the groups of problems concerning proportion, equations of the first and second degree, similar figures, Pythagoras's theorem, the calculation of volumes, etc. The practical bias of medieval mathematics, taken as a whole, is shown in the Chinese work, *Mathematics in Nine Books*, dating from the second or first century B.C., in the Arabic *Résumé of Calculus of Al-Ǧabr and Al-Muqābala* by Al-Khwārizmī (ninth century A.D.), in the Indian *Patiganita* by Srīdhara (eleventh century), in the *Liber abaci* by Leonardo of Pisa (thirteenth century), and in many other writings.

But mathematical problems did not only reflect the direct needs of everyday life. The success of mathematics was indispensable to the development of other sciences of the time, such as optics, geography, statics and astronomy, linked to some extent with astrology. Thus, with the problems of the calendar was closely connected, in China and in India, the solution in integers of indeterminate equations of the first degree; in China the interpolation by polynomials up to the third degree; in India, in the Arabic countries and in Europe the plane and spherical trigonometry as well as certain methods of approximate calculation. In the Arabic countries and in Europe the development of optics stimulated the study of conic sections. And these are only some examples.

Eventually there was an internal development of the more abstract branches of mathematics which is observed everywhere where mathematical knowledge extended beyond the limits of calculation in small numbers and the measurement of the simplest figures. This internal development is indispensable to mathematical progress because of the close correlation between the different branches of mathematics and their deductive character. This development, the generalization or the inversion of problems and methods born of practical experience, is shown even in the works written for practical purposes which I have just cited. Examples are the general solution of a system of linear equations, invented in China, and the cyclic method for the solution of indeterminate equations, now known as Pell's, invented in India.

The parallel development of mathematics in different regions during the Middle Ages was greatly favoured by commercial, cultural, and political relations between the countries of Asia and Europe. It is true that communications were sporadic even within the limits of one country, but over sufficiently long periods scientific ideas travelled long distances and were assimilated under analogous conditions. The exchange of ideas between the Islamic countries and Europe has been fairly well studied; the study of relations between India and the Islamic countries is not complete, and we have very little information about China. Nevertheless I will mention some examples. Consider Sun-tzu's problem (third or fourth century A.D.): to find a positive integer from the remainders after its division into given numbers. This is to be found with the same numbers in Leonardo of Pisa and a little later in a Byzantine manuscript. One meets algebraic problems involving Pythagoras's theorem taken from *Mathematics in Nine Books* in the works of the Indians Brahmagupta (seventh century A.D.) and Bhaskara II (twelfth century A.D.). It is almost indisputable that Arab mathematicians learned the rule of two false positions directly from China, as well as the method now known as Horner's for the extraction of roots. It is certain that from the thirteenth to the fifteenth centuries Chinese astronomy and mathematics were well known in Persia and in central Asia, and vice versa. Moreover, we know that in the seventh century Indian scientists collaborated with the Chinese astronomers.

I have said that there are fairly clear differences in the development of mathematics in the different regions of Europe and Asia. The causes of these differences are numerous and far from being entirely known. I would like to emphasize here that Greek civilization exercised a minimal influence on Chinese science. In India Greek influence was a little stronger. By contrast, the scientists of the Islamic countries pursued their researches in the territories where Greek traditions were alive, and at the same time they profited from ideas coming from the east. Finally, Europeans from the eleventh and twelfth centuries were able to draw more and more on both the Greek and the Arabic heritages. We should remember that social conditions in these four regions were not identical. Mr. Needham has described very clearly the difference between the social structures of China and Europe in the Middle Ages. I will offer a mathematical analogy. A differential equation of the first order has as its general solution a set of functions, each of which depends upon an arbitrary constant. If an initial condition is given, the constant is determined and the equation has a unique solution. If the initial condition is changed, the solution is different. Thus, the initial social and cultural conditions were different in different countries, but the differential laws of social development were fairly analogous, if not identical.

Chinese mathematics was, in its outlook, the farthest removed from that of the Greeks. There were no great mathematical systems. Compared with arithmetic and algebra, geometry played a minor role. But in the province of arithmetic and related fields, great progress was made. I will mention a few of the results:

Decimal place-value system (but without the symbol for zero);

Decimal metrology and then decimal fractions;

The rule of two false positions;

An algorithm for the solution of systems of n linear equations with n unknowns similar to the method of determinants, and, in close connexion with it, the introduction of negative numbers;

The method of numerical solution of algebraic equations now known by the names of Horner and of Ruffini;
Linear transformations of roots (to facilitate the computation of fractional roots);
Interpolation using polynomials of the second and third degrees;
Algebraic symbolism;
The solution of indeterminate equations.

I will now mention the best-known achievements of the Indian mathematicians and astronomers, stimulated to a certain extent by the works of the Hellenistic scientists:
The scale of notation together with the use of zero;
The solution of equations of the first and second degree, using a fairly well-developed symbolism and negative numbers (perhaps under the influence of Chinese mathematics);
The first elements of trigonometry;
The summation of fairly complicated arithmetical series (this was studied also in China);
The rule for calculating the combinations of m elements n at a time (also known in China);
The methods of diophantine analysis.

The most brilliant accomplishment of Indian mathematics was the expansion in power series of $\tan^{-1} x$, sine and cosine. Here, starting from the desire to calculate more exactly the value of π, the Indians of the fifteenth and sixteenth centuries came close to certain infinitesimal methods invented in Europe in the seventeenth century. But they did not do much to develop their ideas further in this direction.

Let us turn to the Islamic countries. As I have already indicated, the peculiarity of these countries was the rapid assimilation of Indian and Greek and later the partial assimilation of Chinese mathematics. This made it possible for the Islamic scientists to study computing algorithms whilst relying on more powerful methods and to pursue their researches to a higher scientific level. In the cases where Chinese and Indian scientists gave only a few rules for calculation, the Islamic mathematicians completed scientific theories. Compared with the works of Indian and Chinese scientists, Arabic mathematical works were more systematic, more complete, and distinguished by the greater use of proofs, even in books of a purely practical character. At the same time one often finds in the theoretical works numerical examples and procedures of an applied character. This was the first return to the outlook peculiar to Hellenistic times.

The contribution of the mathematicians of the Islamic countries is important. In the realm of computing arithmetic, they completed and perfected approximate methods for the extraction of roots, the procedures for the verification of calculations, their most favourable arrangement, and so on. Al-Kāshi's (fifteenth-century) calculation of π to seventeen decimal places was a brilliant example of this. In connexion with the extraction of roots of a given degree, we meet for the first time in al-Kāshi the binomial theorem for any positive integer exponent. The time and place of origin of this rule are unknown, but probably it was proposed by Omar Khayyām (eleventh century). The technique of operations on whole numbers and sexagesimal fractions had been perfected. Al-Kāshi introduced decimal fractions and stressed their advantages.

For the first time, algebra became an independent science having its own field of study and methods of research. This is well shown in the algebraic treatise of Khayyām. Knowing the importance of cubic equations for the calculation of the sine of 1° (i.e., for the construction of trigonometrical tables) and for the solution of geometrical problems, the detailed geometrical theory of cubic equations was constructed and used to determine upper and lower limits for their roots. Later an analogous study was made of quartic equations (by al-Kāshi), but the results of these researches are now unknown. Together with the geometrical theory was invented a number of approximate methods (by al-Bīrūnī in the eleventh century, al-Kāshi, and others).

Trigonometry also became an independent mathematical science. This is most noticeable in the specialized treatise by Nasīr al-dīn al-Ṭūsī (thirteenth century). In particular, all six cases of the spherical triangle were solved for the first time. As I have already mentioned, in order to calculate more exact trigonometrical tables, approximate methods had to be perfected, together with the iterative method of numerical solution of the equation now known as Kepler's equation. An extensive use of proportions in trigonometry, acoustics and practical arithmetic necessitated the perfection of the ancient theory of composed ratios. This theory was used to derive the rule of three. Such theoretical justifications of the methods of the mathematics of computing were peculiar to the Islamic countries. Another example is the geometrical proof of the Chinese rule of two false positions.

A wide application of approximate calculations involving operations on irrational quantities resulted in a series of researches into the general theory of proportions, which culminated in the perfection of the theory based on the representation of each ratio in the form of a continued fraction. Mr. Murdoch has discussed this subject in part in his interesting paper. I would like to emphasize here a point which he left aside. In the theory of proportions developed by the Islamic scientists, positive irrational numbers were for the first time thought of abstractly as true numbers (by Khayyām and al-Ṭūsī).

In geometry, attention may be drawn to the birth of the theory of construction using a compass with only one opening (Abū 'l-Wafā, tenth century). In Europe, the study of this problem was begun again at the time of the Renaissance. Another series of remarkable studies concerning the theory of parallels was undertaken by al-Ğauharī (ninth century), and followed up by Thābit ibn Qurra, ibn al-Haitham, Omar Khayyām, al-Ṭūsī and others. Some ideas were put forward which were later developed by Saccheri and Lambert, and in fact the first propositions of non-Euclidean geometry date from this time. The original contribution in the field of infinitesimal analysis was less important. Nevertheless we should note the determination by ibn al-Haitham of the volume of a solid of revolution, containing for the first time the equivalent of the evaluation of the integral $\int_a^b x^4 dx$. Some valuable ideas were expressed on the properties of continuous magnitudes, above all in the theory of proportions. Hartner and Schramm have shown us in their penetrating paper that it was al-Bīrūnī who first submitted to mathematical analysis the phenomenon of accelerated motion and the progress of a function in the neighbourhood of a maximum or a minimum.

After this brief, and far from complete, summary of the original contributions of the mathematicians of the Islamic countries, it remains for me to say a few words about Europe. From the eleventh and twelfth centuries, we find in Europe an increasing familiarity with the scientific and philosophical works of the Arabic peoples and — through them, as well as directly — with the writings of Antiquity. The ideas and methods elaborated or perfected in the Islamic countries took root and led to new results in the most advanced European countries. This is to be seen, for example, in the books of Leonardo of Pisa, who emphasized the significance of Arabic science for the Latin peoples. All the discoveries of Arabic mathematicians did not become known to Europeans, but those that did considerably enriched mathematical knowledge. It would be a mistake to underestimate the role of Arabic algebra and trigonometry in the progress of the sciences in Europe, particularly in connexion with the invention of the infinitesimal calculus. I have in mind the point made in the preceding section by Mr. van der Waerden. But the essential feature of the development of European mathematics in the Middle Ages did not consist in the direct continuation of the Greek or the Arabic traditions. Together with the assimilation of oriental arithmetic and algebra, the principles of ancient geometry, the astronomy of the Ptolemaic school and the optics of ibn al-Haitham, and with the first attempts to become familiar with the works of Archimedes and Apollonius (so rich in fruitful ideas), in the Europe of the Middle Ages were born the ideas that were to play a decisive role in the sixteenth and seventeenth centuries.

A new scientific and philosophical outlook appeared, and among the leading representatives of this outlook I include Robert Grosseteste and Roger Bacon (thirteenth century). Starting from the natural philosophy of Aristotle, but at the same time expressing the aspirations of their age and anticipating the future, these thinkers proclaimed new principles for the natural sciences. Later these principles were formulated more profoundly by Galileo and Francis Bacon. In the development of the natural sciences, in principle the greatest importance was accorded to mathematics. Grosseteste wrote: "All the causes of natural actions must be expressed by lines, angles and figures." Bacon underlined the fact that mathematics was the door and the key to the other sciences. This idea widened the actual attempts at mathematical analysis of mechanical, optical, thermal and other phenomena, and stimulated research in this direction.

As Mr. Beaujouan pointed out in his paper, one of the principal scientific merits of the scholastics was their aspiration to make quantitative the study of qualities; thus was born the theory *de latitudinibus formarum* completed by Richard Swineshead, Nicole Oresme and others in the fourteenth century.

This theory was developed in isolation from observation of nature, and that was its weakness. But here the abstract study of the possible laws of movement, including purely mechanical movement, was begun. This resulted in the clarification of concepts and the perfection of graphical representation containing some of the germs of the ideas of the new dynamics, of the concept of function, and of the method of coordinates, as well as in the first use of summation of infinite series other than geometrical progressions. If we add the reflections of Thomas Bradwardine (fourteenth century) on the nature of the infinite and the continuous, anticipating to a certain extent the modern theory of sets, as well as the attempt by Jordanus Nemorarius (thirteenth century) to construct a symbolic algebra, we shall see in thirteenth- and fourteenth-century European mathematics and mechanics an assemblage of ideas that were called upon to play, three centuries later and under other conditions, the principal role in the development of the exact sciences. I leave aside the question of the influence of these works. If it was not decisive, it existed all the same. To be certain of it, one has only to compare the deduction of the law of accelerated motion by Galileo and by Oresme.

I have just mentioned the names of Grosseteste, Bacon, Swineshead and Bradwardine. All these scientists represented the Oxford scientific school. Mr. Beaujouan has pointed out that in the thirteenth and fourteenth centuries the University of Oxford played a special part as a centre of *avant-garde* mathematical research. I should like to emphasize again the role of this university in the clarification of the ideas which, in a different guise, directed the development of the mathematics of the ensuing period, that of the mathematics of variable quantities, of Galileo and Descartes, Newton and Leibniz.

Commentary by R. W. Southern

Mr. Beaujouan has written a paper on the motives and opportunities for science in medieval universities, and it may be convenient if I try to arrange my remarks for the purposes of directing the discussion under three headings: the motives, the opportunities, and then lastly the conception of science which we can find in the Middle Ages. The points I want to make are in some ways very obvious but I think for that very reason they are apt to be overlooked in the enthusiasm for the history of science.

If we turn to the motives for scientific study in the Middle Ages I have little doubt that the most important of these motives was practical. Of course there are always people who are interested in odd subjects, but if there is to be a considerable impetus in any field of study there must be a motive which makes its appeal to a considerable body of people and, as I say, I think the practical motive was the one which drew most people to scientific study. The earliest travellers who went to Spain to study scientific doctrines were attracted mainly I believe by astrology, and this, of course, is very practical. As long as it was believed that the stars had an influence over human behaviour, astrology offered the finest field for human thought that could be found. It was an immensely difficult field of study, accessible only to a few, but to those few it offered a magnificent opportunity for power and influence. The collapse of this view of the planetary system and its influence on human life is perhaps the biggest set-back which has ever been suffered by European thought, in the sense, I mean, of making necessary a quite new start; but this set-back was not experienced during the Middle Ages.

I have mentioned astrology, but that was only one — though possibly the most important — field in which the practical motive in scientific study can be observed. All natural objects, plants, animals, stones, were thought to have secret natural properties which it was the purpose of scientific thought to discover and utilize for the purpose of human life. Mr. Beaujouan says, "The whole of medieval science was indeed dedicated to the service of God." I confess that I am not completely sure about that, although it was, of course, a motive which was very often expressed both by medieval and modern writers. We should be much more conscious of the practical motive, if it had not been doomed to final frustration by aiming at too lofty results. The contempt for mechanical arts in which some results might have been achieved by observation and experiment, and the guidance of a noble but false view of the hidden forces of nature, combined to make the practical motive in medieval scientific work a long history of useless endeavour. It was none the less real on that account.

The second motive for scientific study on which I think one must insist is the Biblical one. The ancient view, that the deepest meanings of the Bible lay in allegorical interpretation, and that the key to this allegorical interpretation in its turn lay in the knowledge of the virtues and secret nature of created things, died a slow death. It is not yet dead. And it provided an obvious motive for scientific study. It is probably true to say that no great advances in the allegorical interpretation of the Bible were made after the age of the Fathers, though one might have to qualify this judgment in some respects with regard to authors like St. Bernard and Richard of St. Victor. But it is perfectly obvious that if any real advance was to be made in Biblical interpretation, it could only be made by new discoveries as to the nature and constitution of the natural world. I must leave it to others to decide how far this aim was in fact a practical motive in scientific work. I think it is certainly true that it profoundly influenced the work of the thirteenth-century Franciscan school, and was to have an important place in the ideas of Roger Bacon. But here once more the effort was, in fact, doomed to disappointment. No major scientific discoveries were made which added to the knowledge of the allegories lying behind the Biblical text.

In retrospect I think we must say that the first motive — the practical one — might have led to scientific progress if the preconceptions about the natural world had been more favourable, but that the second motive — the allegorical one — was an enemy of scientific progress because it provided no coherent framework within which new discoveries could be made.

Thirdly there is the philosophical motive, perhaps the most respectable of all motives for scientific study. Mr. Beaujouan says, "the science of the universities was the servant, albeit at times unruly, of a theology itself constituting a science", and this no doubt is in a large sense a perfectly true remark. But it is important to remember that it was not so much science, as certain ancient doctrines of a semi-scientific kind about the universe, which constituted the challenge to medieval theologians, and medieval scholars were not so much concerned with the scientific basis of these doctrines as with their philosophical and theological implications. How far, for instance, could they be fitted into any possible scheme of Christian theology? With what modifications could they be entertained by a Christian? What modifications in traditional Christian thought did they necessitate? These were the questions which stimulated the study of these ancient doctrines. Now the whole process of adaptation brought, of course, a great enlargement in the scope of European thought, but it was not an enlargement of a strictly scientific kind. What took place was not, I think we must recognize, a confrontation of science and theology, but a confrontation of ancient dogmas, ancient doctrines about the universe and Christian thought. In all these three motives then, the practical, the Biblical, and the philosophical we must recognize limitations of a special kind which imposed a very strict limit to the possibilities of scientific development in the Middle Ages and even down to the seventeenth century.

Now secondly what opportunities were there for scientific thought in medieval universities? I shall only say this: once more it is important to remember that all the opportunities arose from the commenting on ancient texts and the discussions which these comments gave rise to. This limiting factor was not nearly so crippling in practice as it might have been, but it was nevertheless a most serious limitation to scientific thought and continued to be so down to our day. The bookish bias in education, which Europe inherited from the ancient world, has been the most serious of all obstacles to the development of science, and in the interesting remarks of Mr. Minio-Paluello I think we could see to what extent medieval scientific thought was directed towards the explanation of texts. We seemed in what he said to hear more about obscure variant readings and misreadings and misunderstandings of ancient texts than we ever heard about triangles and their properties. Even a man like Grosseteste was only a scientist in the sense that Sir David Ross is a scientist, and I mean that as a compliment, of course. He was a man of clear mind and profound sagacity who was primarily concerned to understand ancient texts. His original contributions to scientific thought arise either in the course of his comments of Aristotle's works or in very brief treatises which may be looked on as an appendix to these comments. The independent works are very short, like those on the rainbow, on colour, on sound, on the comets; they are just the sort of thing that a conscientious modern editor of Aristotle might feel obliged to put in an appendix to his commentary on the *Parva naturalia* or some other work of Aristotle. That is the context of the scientific work of even the most advanced and important of medieval scientists.

Now this brings us to the third point: 'science'. To what extent, and in what sense, is it appropriate to talk about medieval science at all? This was the question which kept obtruding itself on my mind as I read Mr. Beaujouan's paper. There is after all a great difference between the study of natural phenomena by methods appropriate to that study — measurement, classification, systematic experiment and so on — and a study which is basically a study of ancient doctrines contained in difficult, and often obscure texts. This dichotomy seems to me to be the very centre of our problem in considering medieval science, and the problem of Grosseteste is perhaps the central problem in that wide area of medieval thought. Mr. Crombie has made great claims for Grosseteste. Grosseteste did, he said, what neither the Greeks nor the Arabs succeeded in doing. I quote from him: he "consciously formulated a conception of the roles of induction and experiment in scientific inquiry. To do so was the achievement of Grosseteste and the Oxford school" — a real advance therefore on anything achieved by Greece or the Arabs. Now I am not competent to say whether Mr. Crombie is right or wrong on this point. My own impression, for what it is worth, is that Grosseteste was a very cautious man, who wanted to insist that experiment was only valuable when a man had got a firm grasp of the doctrines of the ancients. I will quote only one passage from Grosseteste on comets in support of this. "I say", he says, "that those who consider an experiment in natural science and form their own opinions from their experiments without a foundation of doctrine [*absque fundatione rationum*] necessarily fall into false opinions . . . according to the diversity of their experiments."

This suggests to me a very considerable limitation on the area within which experiment is useful. But altogether I want to know a great deal more about the role of experiment, not only in Grosseteste but also in his followers, before I can feel at all confident that when we talk about medieval science we are talking about something which is intelligible to us today. It is puzzling; and never more puzzling than when we come to read about experiments in Roger Bacon, that great exponent of the beauties and necessity for experimentation. But what did he mean by this? Not, I believe, at all what we mean. I take only one example. In one of the most striking passages in which he writes about the need for experiment he describes the role of the faithful experimenter and the nature of his *experientia perfecta* which is opposed in his mind to the *debiles et imperfectae experientiae*, and he says that the faithful experimenter considers the nature of the eagle, and other long-lived creatures, and then he *excogitat vias nobiles* for the prolongation of life. He then tells the practical alchemist to prepare a body of similar complexion so that the experimenter may use it. It is very clear from this that Bacon's faithful experimenter was a very superior person, who did not soil his fingers in finding out how the devil to do it. He left that to the practical alchemist. He looked at the raw material, the eagle, the elephant, and other creatures of long life, then he looked at the desired end, longevity, and he told his assistant: "go ahead, make something like that (pointing to the eagle, elephant, etc.), so that I can use it on that" (pointing to the debilitated human frame). The genius of the faithful experimenter lay therefore in identifying the likely sources of the necessary virtue, but he left to a mere mechanic the job which we should consider the real crux of the problem: how to bring the two things together.

Medieval science, then (I speak as a fool), could not develop far because in its motives, in its opportunities, and in its whole conception of the method of science, it was condemned to avoiding that field of systematic observation and limited objectives which alone would lead to any substantial advance beyond the science of the ancient world.

Commentary by L. Minio-Paluello

I ought probably to start with an apology for appearing as the commentator on a paper for which I am perhaps the least competent person in this Symposium. It was the first part of its title that made me accept this role; it is, in fact, the second — unknown to me at the time — that summarizes the substance of Mr. Murdoch's painstaking, accurate, wide, imaginative inquiries into a complicated group of problems of which I know next to nothing.

By way of trying to make things clearer to myself I may, perhaps, be allowed to set out in my own words what seem to me to be the more important points of this paper. They include, in the first instance, the documentation of the almost complete failure, on the part of Arabic- and Latin-speaking mathematicians of the Middle Ages, to grasp the significance of Eudoxus's revolutionary statements on ratios between magnitudes, in relation to continuity and incommensurability. There is then an account of medieval attempts at shaping new conceptual or algorithmical instruments in order to meet some of the needs which Eudoxus had already met. The paper then contains a survey of the wide provinces in which scholastic scientists, philosophers, theologians thought the theory of proportions to be either indispensable or illuminating. It offers, finally, some general remarks on the historical development and interaction of arithmetic and geometry. On the whole, it seems that Mr. Murdoch's interest lies mainly with the problem of continuity and the long-drawn attrition between numbers and continuous magnitudes.

The two Eudoxean statements which most frequently failed to be understood are those which appear as Definitions 4 and 5 in Euclid's *Elements* V.

Definition 4, presented by Murdoch as a 'principle of continuity' is this: "Magnitudes are said to have a ratio to one another, which are capable, when multiplied, of exceeding one another." The medieval failure, in this case, is not very serious. It consists mainly in the fact that, for some unaccountable reason, this definition was ousted by another, non-Euclidean, definition in the most popular Latin Euclid, namely Adelard of Bath's translation from the Arabic and its adaptations.

Definition 5 sets out the condition or conditions under which two magnitudes can be said to have the same ratio as two other magnitudes:

> Magnitudes are said to be in the same ratio, the first to the second and the third to the fourth when, if any equimultiples whatever be taken of the first and third, and any equimultiples whatever of the second and fourth, the former equimultiples alike exceed, are alike equal to, or alike fall short of, the latter equimultiples, respectively taken in corresponding order.

By this definition Eudoxus transformed the Pythagorean integer-numerical concept of ratio — which could only apply to commensurable quantities — into a concept which also applies to incommensurable magnitudes. This definition was accessible, in Arabic and in Latin, in accurate renderings: what was at fault, in Murdoch's view, was the understanding of Eudoxus's basic doctrine of continuity. Arabic mathematicians, in varying degrees, tried to explain or supplant, with *arithmetical* procedures, Eudoxus's definition. They also relied on methods of approximation, or tried to turn the definition into a theorem. Latin mathematicians, on the other hand, went completely wrong, being misled by the spurious Definition 4 which had supplanted the 'principle of continuity'. In the spurious text, a definition is given of 'continuous proportion' (*A* is to *B* as *B* is to *C*) in terms resembling those of the genuine Definition 5. But whereas Definition 5 stipulates that, between the first two terms and the second two, there must be a correspondence either in equality or in excess or in defect *simpliciter*, the spurious Definition 4 stipulates that there must be either equality or *equal* excess or *equal* defect. Thus, the possibility of applying the concept of ratio to incommensurables disappears. Latin commentators, passing from spurious 4 to genuine 5, applied the criterion of *equal* excess and defect to the Eudoxean definition of proportionality: in this way they missed its distinctive characteristic.

The positive contribution of medievals, mentioned by Murdoch, consisted mainly in the following developments:

(*a*) Campanus's elaboration of Euclid X, 1, where Campanus qualifies Euclid's view that, if two unequal quantities be given, the greater can be successively reduced by more than half to a lower value than the smaller. Campanus's qualifications are based on a consideration of horn-angles.

(*b*) The Arabic attempts to cater for continuity, in connexion with X, 1. This is particularly interesting in view of the fact that a corollary to X, 1, was missing in the Arabic translations.

(*c*) The Arabic use of the 'antanairesis' method of continued fractions for the interpretation of V, 5, and other Arabic attempts to by-pass its difficulties.

(*d*) The Latin use of the concept of 'denomination' as a substitute for 'ratio', keeping this a little less committed to the integer-numerical value; above all, Bradwardine's attempt at applying this concept to ratios between incommensurables.

(*e*) The application of the theory of proportions to wider fields, the most important being again Bradwardine's use of the concepts and methods of proportions in his 'discovery' of the logarithmic formula of velocities. It is of a very special interest to see how the doctrine of proportions and incommensurability affected astronomy and astrology and led Oresme to suggest the impossibility of astrological predictions.

Mr. Murdoch concludes his paper with remarks, well founded on his inquiry, that during the centuries under consideration priority and greater scope was allowed to arithmetical as against geometrical methods.

This paper is an exceptionally good example of the fruitfulness of and need for detailed, meticulous investigations into texts and their wording; particularly so when one has to deal with translations where misunderstandings by the interpreter or implicit obscurities leading to misinterpretations by the reader may affect, for evil and for good, developments of new concepts.

May I now add a few points, perhaps of a less precise nature, and suggest one or two queries in connexion with Murdoch's contribution?

(1) One is a little astonished that in a paper on the language and scope of proportionality no mention has been made of Boethius. Boethius was certainly a powerful influence for the arithmetical bias in the treatment of proportions and for upholding the 'Pythagorean' definition, although he speaks also of proportions of quantities in a wider field. In this connexion, Murdoch's mention of the varied interests shown by medievals in connexion with proportionality might well have been an echo of Boethius, *Arithmetica*, II, 40:

> Nunc res admonet quaedam de proportionibus disputantes, quae nobis vel ad musicas speculationes, vel ad astronomicas subtilitates, vel ad geometricae considerationis vim, vel etiam ad veterum lectionum intelligentiam prodesse possint, arithmetica introductione commodissime terminare.

It is also probable that the medieval technical use of 'proportio' (for ratio) and 'proportionalitas' (for proportion between three or more magnitudes) is due to Boethius. The Latin 'ratio' would have been the normal rendering of λόγος, and 'proportio' was the normal rendering of ἀνὰ λόγον, ἀναλογία. But 'proportio — proportionalitas' took their place through the impact, I should suggest, of Boethius's *Arithmetica* and *Musica* and through his adaptation of Euclid.

(2) 'Proportio' as a rendering of ἀνὰ λόγον, ἀναλογία has a quite wide application in the theory of language, as one of the most important ways in which one and the same word may have different uses. Partly along this line, partly in other ways, different, sometimes contrasting, uses of 'proportio, analogia' developed in the field, for example, of theology. 'Analogy of being' and other predicates between created things and God is one way of accounting for some kind of comparison between the incomparables, the incommensurables, the 'improportionata'!

(3) Was it at all possible to gather the value of the Eudoxean doctrine of proportion and incommensurables from the Latin texts of Euclid? (I do not dare to talk of the Arabic texts, but I suggest that what I say of the Latin ones applies to them too.) The Latin texts are these:

Euclid, V, 4: Proportionem vero ad se invicem magnitudines habere dicuntur que possunt sese invicem multiplicate transcendere.

Euclid, V, 5: Quantitates que dicuntur secundum proportionem unam . . . sunt quarum prime et tertie multiplicationes equales multiplicationibus secunde et quarte equalibus fuerint . . . *similes* vel *additione* vel *diminutione* vel equalitate. . . .

The first of the two definitions may well sound a rather imprecise statement. In the second, misinterpretation was almost inevitable. How can one discover that 'similes additione vel diminutione' means 'at the same time greater or at the same time smaller'? If the words are to be construed in a meaningful way, would not the interpretation of 'additio' as 'amount added' or 'amount of increase', and of 'diminutio' as 'amount of decrease' be a sensible way of making sense of a difficult passage?

(4) Can one really call Euclid V, Definition 4 a 'principle of continuity'? It is true that its wording allows for the terms 'ratio, proportio' to be applied to incommensurables. But, for people whose knowledge of 'continuous' quantities was very limited, the realization that Definition 4 was meant to cater for them was not easy. And everybody might expect something more explicit for a 'principle of continuity' even in the frame of Euclidean definitions.

(5) The spurious Definition 4 in Book V in Latin texts is very unlikely to be attributable to Adelard. Should it come from an Arabic text? Or even from a Greek text in which an apparently incomplete set of definitions had been supplemented with a definition of 'continuous proportion'? That proposition is included in the literal translation of the complete text by Adelard, a very careful rendering of an Arabic text. It may also be noticed that this text also includes another Definition 4 in Book V (of *ἀναλογία*), and this extra definition is also found in extant Greek MSS.

(6) Murdoch says that the new definition "equal proportions are those whose denominations are equal", used by scholastics of the thirteenth and fourteenth centuries, insinuated itself in an involved manner. Can it not be that 'denominatio' is in fact another word for *λόγος* (ratio), and that the definition is a rendering of Euclid V, 6: *τὰ τὸν αὐτὸν λόγον ἔχοντα μεγέθη ἀνάλογον καλείσθω*?

(7) Murdoch points out that Bradwardine's attempt to apply the theory of denomination to equality of ratios between incommensurables is not successful because, although it is true that one can infer the equality of ratios from the equality of the ratios of the two couples of terms and the equality of ratios

of the two couples of exponents, the converse is not possible. One may agree on this possibility and impossibility. But was this really Bradwardine's aim? Was he not, in fact, just using, and successfully using, an algorithm in which ratios between incommensurables were possible, without wanting to define or use equality between such ratios in proportions?

Commentary by Bertrand Gille

It need hardly be said that all our interest has been aroused by Mr. Lynn White's paper. So we are even more impatient than ever to see the book that he has promised us this year. Mr. White has presented the problem very clearly, drawing attention to the technical advances of the medieval West as compared with those of Antiquity and the Byzantine and Moslem East, and delineating the progress in the realms of agriculture, armaments, and industry. Five causes or groups of causes, three of them intellectual, are put forward as having provoked this movement.

The very brief commentary given here is centred around two important aspects of this problem: Mr. White's thesis itself and the methodological questions which it raises.

(1) On the actual facts everyone is more or less in agreement; it is only on the broad outlines that discussion still continues. We will now consider a few specific facts relating to origins and dates: an example in point being the horse-shoe.

The chronological arrangement of the facts is of special importance for their interpretation. Besides the date and origin of any invention, we must with equal force consider the moment when this technical advance comes into general use. The two conditions of progress, invention and innovation (in the sense of the use of inventions) must both be taken into account, and if the first is important in the history of ideas, the second is crucial for general history.

Now, if one excepts military art, whose influence, at least during the period with which we are concerned, is less significant, it would appear that medieval 'invention' was at its height during the twelfth and thirteenth centuries: this is true in the case of the water-mill and its derivatives, of the modern harness, and of triennial rotation of crops. Here we have one of those great technical break-throughs which were later misnamed the 'Industrial Revolution'. If the chronology of invention is continuous, that of the use of inventions is discontinuous.

There we have a phenomenon on which greater stress must be laid.

The reasons underlying these advances are not easy to grasp. One must be cautious in assessing them. But Mr. Lynn White's analysis seems to be rather incomplete.

(*a*) We cannot ignore elementary and obvious facts. The centre of civilization was in the north. In these northern regions were to be found heavy, deep and rich soils, abundant luxuriant forests, permanent water-courses, and fertile meadows. This explains the use of techniques which would have been of little value to the countries bordering the Mediterranean: the water-mill, the heavy plough, the triennial rotation of crops, the open fireplace. Had other conditions prevailed, there too, without doubt, there would have been similar innovations and a rapid development from primitive techniques.

(*b*) From the middle of the twelfth century, the population of Western Europe seems to have grown considerably. It is for this reason that agriculture was transformed (e.g. the clearing of land, triennial rotation), despite the fact that winter feeding was still insufficient and ill-balanced. The countryside was peopled, the towns overflowed their Gallo–Roman walls. Growth of population and technical progress were closely linked.

(*c*) Growth of population was linked also with social evolution. Between the years 1150 and 1250 there was a great extension of the franchise in favour of urban expansion and the creation of a merchant and industrial middle class based upon technical progress.

(*d*) This growth of population and social evolution were accompanied by a substantial revival of commerce consolidated during the twelfth century. New routes were opened for the export of Flemish cloth, and the trade in metals or agricultural products in their turn stimulated technical progress. This effort was to lead to the re-establishment of a balance of payments with the East and to the minting, in the second half of the thirteenth century, of gold coins.

(*e*) Changing intellectual attitudes certainly played a part. A young French historian, M. le Goff, is in the course of writing a thesis on the medieval conception of labour. The monastic way of life did more perhaps to further the cause of technical innovation than of invention. The role of the Cistercians seems to have been important in this respect.

Thus we might say that a first industrial revolution was

discernible during the twelfth and thirteenth centuries. It was naturally accompanied by a number of structural, economic, political and social changes. At the end of the thirteenth century a setback occurred, the repercussions of which were felt throughout the course of the fourteenth century. The Hundred Years War, the epidemics culminating in the Black Death, and the insolvency of the Italian banks in the middle of the fourteenth century, mark a period of crisis which led to a long-term fall in prices. Technical progress, taken as a whole, stopped. If certain minor innovations took place, it was not until the second third of the fifteenth century that real forward movement began once more. When prices began to rise again, the demands of the contractors led to further innovations. Progress was very marked in the third quarter of the fifteenth century. Financial stability continued through the Renaissance and down to the time of the great geographical discoveries.

(2) This is largely hypothetical. There are still significant gaps in our knowledge. Technical history is lacking in method, and technical evidence is difficult to obtain. Here we shall only consider a few points for study.

(*a*) It is difficult to assemble the evidence. Let us arrange such evidence as we have very summarily in growing order of objectivity:

Indirect sources, simply alluding to facts (judicial acts, literary works);

Semi-direct sources such as corporation rules or acts drawn up by notaries;

Direct sources, that is, technical treatises;

Diagrammatic representations, often misleading, but always useful and valuable;

Technical objects themselves brought to light by research. Russian, Polish and Czech scholars have shown us what riches can be discovered by this method.

A first step in this research is the assembly of all this documentation. Miss Carus-Wilson has attempted this for fulling-mills, the Centre d'Histoire de la Sidérurgie de Nancy has done the same for iron, and Mr. Millás-Vallicrosa has done it for agricultural documents — thus proving that it is not an impossible task.

(*b*) Criticism is indispensable. Correct analyses can solve the problems of dating. Semantic problems must be correctly expressed: the origins of borrowed words and of objects are not necessarily indiscoverable. One would need lexicons of the appropriate terms, with a history of terms parallel to the history of things. For these actual objects methods of analysis and dating have slowly been perfected (e.g. the work of Salin and France-Lanord on Merovingian iron, the work of German historians on the analysis of ancient lava-flows).

(*c*) Finally, the interpretation poses particular problems in each case:

The most difficult problems are those of inventions. Of these the solutions will always be more or less uncertain. There are two stages. The first, which is practical, empirical, and concrete, will always be the more difficult to appreciate. The second, the stage of ideas rather than of theory, was going on from the days of Alexandria, and continuing in the Byzantine encyclopaedias down to the tenth century. The problems, broken down and simplified, are to be found in engineering manuscripts, in Bacon's text, in the letter of Leonardo da Vinci to Sforza. Here too can be included the unfeasible flight of Eilmer of Malmesbury. Between the two we have the rational technical movement which gave us the great treatises.

Now for the problem of dissemination, we must seek the paths of the diffusion of knowledge and discover the reasons for it. We have quoted the Cistercians as an example: another factor was the movement of labour. We are faced with the major problem of the connexion between Eastern and Western techniques, of whose intermediary stages we are ignorant. From the middle of the fifteenth century, politics played their part.

Then there is the problem of technical equilibrium. All the techniques are more or less interlinked. Even their errors led to progress. These technical systems must be taken into account.

Lastly we have the problem of a technical society. Because technical structures and social and economic structures must be related, there are periods of technical adaptation just as there are periods of stagnation which are also of interest.

The task is an enormous one. It has hardly been outlined. This discipline does more than any other to further international collaboration. Valid results will only be obtained so long as the inquiries are well-defined and specific. It is easy to speculate as to what these might be. If we succeed we shall owe it in great part to Mr. Lynn White's brilliant essay.

Discussion

O. Temkin

Mr. Pines discusses the "working rules for scientific discovery by induction" (p. 190), and in this connexion he cites al-Baghdādī as following Avicenna. The quotation begins: "As for experience, an example is provided by the following judgement: scammony purges human bodies of yellow bile . . .". The rules, as Mr. Crombie has indicated in his work on Grosseteste, go back to Galen. They then spread to the East and West. It is not by chance that these rules for scientific discovery by induction originated in Galen's pharmacological work. Pharmacology was a subject open to experimentation by any practitioner, and many medieval practitioners (especially 'empirics') did experiment, often to the detriment of their patients.

Scammony, the example chosen, is of interest too, because it is *the* example occurring again and again in medieval texts down to the Renaissance. As far back as Antiquity, scammony was credited with a specific action (purging of yellow bile) which could not be explained, but had to be accepted as proved by experience. Thus it came close to occult remedies where nature revealed its power through experience only. Does it actually have the effect ascribed to it? It is not clear by what criterion the ancient and medieval doctors judged a bilious purge. As to modern doctors of pharmacology, they have little to tell about scammony, and that little may be copied from older texts. Thus we are in a bad position for judging the effectiveness of the prime example of medieval rules for discovery by induction.

J. Millás-Vallicrosa

Regarding Mr. Pines's paper, I would like to draw attention to the sharply critical discussions that went on between some Arabic scientific authors not only about general and philosophical problems, but also about many particular and specific questions. There were periods of particularly scientific criticism. In Moslem Spain, during the eleventh century, a great critical and polemical literature developed round very particular questions of astronomy, for instance the movements of precision or trepidation, of the apogees, etc. We also find in discussions among the agronomic authors of Moslem Spain in the eleventh and twelfth centuries a strong critical sense, controlled by observation and experience of the facts.

A. C. Crombie

Mr. Southern has rightly reminded us that we run the risk of entirely misunderstanding medieval conceptions of the natural world and methods of dealing with it, if we abstract what may look to us like 'science' from the actual world of men, thought and institutions in which these conceptions and methods existed. The same is true of the scientific interests and activities of any period, but especially of a period like the Middle Ages in which these had only a minor place among the whole variety of concerns that moved men to thought and action. Because of its particular position in European history, a time when education and in a large sense society in general were dominated by Christian theological and ecclesiastical preoccupations, coming before a time of dramatic progress in science and more generally in the secular use of reason in the West, the medievil period perhaps provides motives as well as opportunities for misunderstanding more than most periods. In any case it has been notorious as a field of scholarship in which claims for the historical importance of medieval science, both as an activity of the period and as a preparation for the subsequent explosion of science in the West, have been matched by counter-claims that no such thing as medieval science ever existed or could have existed. I shall not hesitate to acknowledge that I have been responsible for claims that now seem to me exaggerated, but it is nearly a decade since my book on Grosseteste was published and it must be admitted that the tone of that book was provoked at least in part by counter-claims that seemed and still seem to me wholly unhistorical. Since then much further work has appeared throwing light on this whole question.

In a broad sense I agree with much of what Mr. Southern has said, and I certainly agree with what he has attempted to do: to see medieval science in its historical context. But as I thought about his remarks I could not help wondering whether he and historians of medieval science were in fact discussing the same texts or at times even the same people, or at least the *whole* of such texts and people. The historical exploration of any field has nearly always begun with the study of obviously important events (whether so considered by contemporaries or afterwards by historians), with important political actions or important works of art, and the history of science is no exception. Mr. Southern has rightly drawn attention to the need to take into our view influential opinions and attitudes of mind found outside the field of successful science, and often standing in opposition to it. Yet in restoring the balance upset by over-enthusiastic estimations of the scientific attitude of medieval thinkers and of the scientific content of their writings, he has chosen a set of examples that are equally unbalanced in the opposite direction. The texts and critical studies that have been published show, I think, that the well-known examples of successful science produced in the medieval world were recognized then as the products of a rational intellectual tradition inherited from Greek Antiquity and may be recognized now as belonging to the intellectual tradition that continues in modern science. This is not of course to say that there have been no changes in motives and opportunities, and in intellectual and practical objectives and methods, in the course of this long tradition, or that there have not been periods of virtual stagnation in contrast with periods of explosive progress such as the seventeenth century or the last hundred years. The scientific tradition was virtually lost in the West between the sixth and the twelfth centuries; the 'medieval science' we are discussing belongs essentially to the thirteenth and fourteenth centuries, after it had been recovered.

I should like to consider some of Mr. Southern's points in turn, beginning with the practical motives for science. It is of course true that astrology provided an important practical motive for astronomy in the Middle Ages, as it had in Antiquity for some time before Ptolemy wrote and as it continued to do down to the time of Kepler. But it was during this long period when astrology was taken seriously, especially of course in Antiquity and in the sixteenth and seventeenth centuries, that classical geometrical astronomy was most flourishing. Astrology can scarcely be said to have doomed astronomy to failure. Nor, in the Middle Ages, as in earlier and later times, was it the only important practical motive for astronomy. Roger Bacon himself, after an intelligent discussion in the *Opus maius* (IV, Section on Mathematicae in divinis utilitas) of what, in accordance with accepted doctrine, *judicia astronomiae* might be expected to foretell,[1] goes on immediately to discuss the *correctio calendarii*. Of this scandal of the time he wrote: "Nam quilibet potest videre ad oculum, si aspiciat coelum, quod luna est prima secundum veritatem per tres dies vel quatuor antequam signetur in calendario . . . et quilibet rusticus potest in coelo hunc errorem contemplari."[2] Treatises on the *computus* and the *Sphere* figured widely in medieval mathematical teaching, as Mr. Beaujouan has pointed out, largely because of the practical importance of the determination of the date of Easter in the Christian year. The reform of the Julian calendar was a limited and quantitative problem which medieval writers set out to solve and in fact solved. The systematic attack on it began with Grosseteste, who wrote four treatises on the calendar, as well as one on the *Sphere*.[3] The problem was dealt with by first identifying the reasons for the error in the Julian calendar, and then proposing specific remedies for it involving, among other things, accurate determinations of the length of the solar year and of the ratio of the mean lunar month to this, so that an accurate relationship between the solar and lunar calendars as well as between the lengths of the day and the solar year could be established. Methods of reckoning were admittedly taken largely from previous writers; modern scientists do the same. By the end of the thirteenth century mathematical and observational astronomy, stimulated by these practical motives, had become sufficiently accurate for astronomers to recognize, for example, the superiority of Ptolemy's system to Aristotle's on grounds of measurement. Modest progress in comparison with that of the Arabic astronomers whose work Mr. Hartner and Mr. Schramm

[1] It is worth noticing Bacon's empirical approach to this: "One can examine history in past times, and study the effects of the heavens from the beginning of the world, as in floods, earthquakes, pestilences, famines, comets, prodigies, and other things without number, which have occurred both in human affairs and in nature. After one has collected these facts, one should consult the tables and canons of astronomy, and one will find that there are appropriate constellations corresponding to each particular effect. One should then study with the help of tables similar constellations in the future, either near or remote as one wishes; and one will then be able to make predictions of effects, which will be similar to those in the past, since if a cause be posited, so is the effect." (*Opus Majus*, ed. J. H. Bridges, Oxford, 1897, I, 389.)

[2] Ibid. I, 275–6.

[3] Cf. D. A. Callus (ed.), *Robert Grosseteste, Scholar and Bishop* (Oxford, 1955) 112–15; Roger Bacon, *Opera hactenus inedita*, ed. R. Steele (Oxford, 1926) VI, 213 ff.

have described, but progress nevertheless. It was followed in the fourteenth century by more revolutionary developments in cosmology, notably Oresme's discussion of the possibility that the earth rotated. And if the blocking of reform of the calendar until 1582 reflects a striking institutional reluctance to apply scientific results, we should remember that the Gregorian calendar was not accepted in England until 1752 and in Russia until 1918.

At the end of his paper Mr. Beaujouan pointed out that if we look outside the universities we find a world of scientific and technological activity different from that inside. The opportunities for academic science arose largely, as Mr. Southern has said, from the established procedures of the commentary and subsequent discussion; I shall say something about this later. But outside the universities the problems arose largely out of practical activities and requirements such as those of surveying, navigation, cartography and later of gunnery, of telling the time of day at different times of year and different latitudes, of assaying ores and precious metals, of surgery, the prescribing of drugs of known properties, and the diagnosis and control of disease. The technological writings of the Middle Ages are still relatively unexplored, and yet it seems to me that it is there that one must chiefly look for those habits developed by the demands made by the problems themselves for accurate, repeatable results.[1] These are of the essence in practical life where it matters if you are given short measure or the wrong product, are subjected to incompetent surgery, or arrive at an unintended destination. They are also of the essence in experimental science. For the history of science in the whole medieval and early modern period, the relations between the intellectual habits and methods of theoretical science and of practical technology present a vast field of research that has scarcely been investigated. The history of 'practical mathematics' in the Middle Ages would especially repay systematic study. There is a world of difference between the limited objectives of medieval practical science and the lofty fancies of Roger Bacon's grandiose programme for getting control over nature and for tapping hidden sources of natural power. Such programmes have always been doomed to frustration, at least in their details. Yet I think that a programme such

[1] Cf. A. C. Crombie, "Quantification in medieval physics", *Isis*, LII (1961) 143–60; Lynn White, jr., *Medieval Technology and Social Change* (Oxford, 1962).

as that of Roger Bacon, put forward in the thirteenth century by a product of the universities who was by no means incapable of accurate scientific work (as shown especially in his optics), is, like the Cartesian programme of the seventeenth century or the evolutionary programme of the nineteenth, in itself an historical phenomenon of which we must take account if we are to admit vision as well as problem-solving as part of the history of science.

In fact in no period has science ever been regarded by its leading exponents simply as problem-solving. It has been seen, in Antiquity and in the Middle Ages as well as more recently, as a view into the rationality of nature; a view of a special kind, of course, that enables particular problems to be solved. The great rational illumination in the medieval Latin West was provided, after all, not by astrology or magic but in the twelfth century by Euclid's geometry and Aristotle's logic, and in the thirteenth by Aristotle's natural philosophy and the scientific writings of Ptolemy, Galen and other Greek authors, with various Arabic commentaries. This was the science of the period. Grosseteste may have been like Sir David Ross as an editor and translator, but in addition he had also to be his own Einstein as well as something of an Astronomer Royal. His independent treatises were not simply aimed at elucidating the meaning of Aristotle's text, but were original attempts to investigate the world, at the frontiers of research as then known to him. Moreover the medieval commentary was not merely bookish, but was the means of publishing original results, including results of observations, as Albertus Magnus's *De animalibus* shows most authentically; not that all commentaries were original. Grosseteste, Roger Bacon and their contemporaries thus inherited the rational view of nature of some of the best Greek authors, and they attempted, with modest results certainly, to extend its frontiers. For them nature was a world of discoverable causal connexions, even though not all the same kind of causal connexions as were accepted in the seventeenth century or are accepted now. If Grosseteste envisaged the use of experiment only within a system of established principles,[1] this, after all, is how it is in fact most frequently used in any established science, although, of course, it would by a considerable limitation if experiment could not be used to explore the consequences of new principles.

[1] A good example is his tract *De calore solis*; see Callus (ed.), *Robert Grosseteste*, pp. 116–20.

But, as is obvious and as I have indeed said myself, the medieval theory and use of experiment was only a beginning, and not the only beginning, of the experimental science that developed more fully and adequately later; and it lacked many of the most important procedures of the experimental method as used since the sixteenth century. All that I am concerned to show now is that medieval science, in its content of thought and its procedures in research, belongs recognizably to the tradition that began in Greece and continues still. Mr. Southern is right to remind us of arguments used by Roger Bacon that seem to us bizarre. But we should remember also that for Bacon the *dominus experimentorum* was Pierre de Maricourt, a pioneer in the experimental investigation of magnetism to be acknowledged by Gilbert, who incorporated his results into his own *De magnete*. The modern editions of Pierre de Maricourt's text and, to mention another obvious example, of Theodoric of Freiberg's *De iride*, with its wealth of optical experiments and use of models, should be enough to establish the existence of experimental science in the Middle Ages as an historical phenomenon and an historical problem, although, of course, these examples of successful science by no means define the limits of the phenomenon or the problem. To recognize this historical fact does not commit us to asserting that the methods and theoretical aims of science did not change, over large areas of thought radically, between the fourteenth and seventeenth centuries, but neither has scientific thought since the seventeenth century been monolithic, although most of the changes have been much less radical.

The existence of experimental science at the heart of medieval intellectual culture constitutes one of the most interesting of historical problems, in part for the reasons indicated by Mr. Southern. To find even a few systematic experimental inquiries actually carried out, within the context of an academic system based on making commentaries on standard texts and aiming primarily to train servants of Church and State, may indeed seem unexpected. Yet to some extent this is a surprise which we may prepare for ourselves by not taking seriously the demand voiced by such a man as Roger Bacon for experiment and for scientific means of obtaining power over nature, and the growth of a coercive attitude to nature and of actual technology to which Mr. Lynn White has drawn attention. These, and the discussions of the logic of experimental argument in writings belonging to the centre of the academic world, provide a context in which some actual experimental investigations may seem natural.

Yet it must be admitted that it was not these experimental treatises that constituted the most characteristic part of the medieval scientific tradition, but rather the theoretical discussions of how science proceeds. A study of these allows us to see, I think, both the nature of the real contribution made by medieval academic writers to the historical development of scientific thinking in the West, and the nature of their failure in so far as they failed. Without stressing the influence of theoretical methodology on the solving of actual problems, I do not think that there is any doubt that the discussion, especially from Grosseteste to Ockham and later in fifteenth- and sixteenth-century Padua, of the forms of argument used in establishing causal connexions between events and in finding explanations of them, provided an important part of the logical framework in which experimental science developed. These discussions, in commentaries of the *Posterior analytics* and similar writings, were concerned with logical and epistemological theory associated with science and not with solving scientific problems: they were applied to examples that were usually not original and they yielded virtually no original scientific results (as Mr. Pines and Mr. Temkin have illustrated). But they were part of the vigorous logical culture of the medieval universities and they established a large part of the terms in which the same problems were discussed by scientists down into the seventeenth century if not later.

A second theoretical question to which medieval academic science made a genuine contribution was that of quantification. The work of Anneliese Maier and of Marshall Clagett, building on that of Duhem, has shown how the academic natural philosophers and mathematicians of the thirteenth and fourteenth centuries, working from within Aristotelian physics, developed quantified concepts of space, time, speed, instantaneous velocity, acceleration, specific weight and so on, and mathematical procedures for manipulating these concepts in various kinematical, dynamical and statical problems. Mr. Murdoch's paper provides further examples connected with the theory of proportions. These theoretical investigations yielded mathematical concepts and theorems that were taken over into the scientific context of seventeenth-century physics. But, here again, an excessive concern with logical foundations as distinct from solving scientific problems left most of the medieval treatment of these questions as a series of dead-ends from the scientific point of view. For example, it was not the medievals, but Galileo, who applied what has been called the Merton Mean Speed Theorem to falling bodies. The medievals were speculating about possible mathematical worlds; Galileo was concerned to discover the mathematical structure of the one actual world.

To the extent that theoretical methodology was dissociated from attempts to solve scientific problems, theoretical quantification from actual measurement, I agree, then, with Mr. Southern that, when viewed from any point of time after 1600, medieval academic science, considered as an intellectual movement, must appear with a built-in formula for frustration. The concentration of attention on philosophical foundations in preference to scientific problems left the main scientific framework of cosmology, physics and physiology inherited from the Greeks and Arabs still intact until the seventeenth century. Methodology, even when meant to be applicable to scientific problems as distinct from being concerned with questions of explanation, was rarely tested by technical success or failure in accurately delimited fields. Moreover, sheer lack of mathematical knowledge in many cases imposed restrictions of its own. Hence a large part of the reason for the return to Antiquity for its science from the end of the fifteenth century. But, as we look at medieval science through the refracting glass of these later motives, opportunities and scientific methods and their obvious successes, we need to remember both that it is in the thirteenth century that the appearance in the West of a new rational technology may be recognized in such examples as the magnetic compass, spectacles, and the mechanical clock, and that it was in this period that Greek scientific thinking first established its ascendancy over the Western intellect as a stimulus to rational research.

R. W. Southern

I entirely agree with a great many of Mr. Crombie's remarks, and of course he knows much more about medieval science than I do. Nevertheless I think that here and there he is scarcely fair to the scope of our discussion. For example, he makes a great deal of the "practical" science outside the universities, and very instructive his remarks are. But since the subject of our discussion is "the motives and opportunities for science *in the medieval universities*", I do not think it really helps, in proving that I have chosen a set of unbalanced examples tending to an underestimate of their motives and opportunities, to show that things were quite different and apparently, in some respects at least, much better *outside* the universities. The same remark applies to some extent to his points about astronomy. I did not of course mean to assert that the *only* important practical motive for studying astronomy in the Middle Ages was astrological, and I have not forgotten that the requirements of the Church calendar made some study of astronomy essential. But the main work of this kind had, I think, been done by monastic scholars of the early Middle Ages before the days of the universities. I may be mistaken, but I should be surprised if this was an important motive in scientific studies in the universities. The only real issue between Mr. Crombie and myself is the question of balance, and it is difficult to strike the right one. I may well have erred in this in emphasizing my points, and I think Mr. Crombie sometimes does the same. For instance it seems misleading to speak of Euclid's geometry and Aristotle's logic (in *this* order) as the source of rational illumination in the twelfth century, or to place the scientific writings of Ptolemy beside Aristotle's natural philosophy as the source of this illumination in the thirteenth century. This is surely to get the balance quite wrong.

H. L. Crosby, jr.

In his paper Mr. Murdoch makes two complaints against the mathematics of Thomas Bradwardine's *De proportionibus* to which I should like to reply.

The first of these complaints he directs against the general obscurity of Bradwardine's mathematical utterances and most specifically against what he takes to be the ambiguity with which Bradwardine expresses his conception of the way in which a proportion between incommensurables may be said to be denominated by proportions between commensurables. To this complaint it should be replied that the obscurity of Bradwardine's language is well known and the justice of criticisms made against it granted. On the other hand, not only does it appear that those of Bradwardine's contemporaries and immediate successors, both at Oxford and elsewhere, who were familiar with his *De proportionibus* were agreed in their understanding of it, but it may also be shown that the meaning of his statements concerning the nature of what we would now call 'exponential functions', or 'logarithmic functions', and what he himself called "second order proportions" is made quite unambiguously clear upon the grounds of internal evidence alone.

Among the simplest instances of this internal evidence there is, for example, Bradwardine's use of the irrational proportion between the diagonal and side of a square as an illustration of what he understands to be the equivalence between irrational proportions and two rational proportions related to each other as base and exponent. The irrational proportion between the diagonal and side of a square is, he says, equivalent to "*medietas duplae proportionis*". Considering the universal familiarity of all mathematicians since Antiquity with the relationship referred to, *medietas duplae proportionis* cannot possibly mean anything else than 'the square root of the proportion of two to one'. Bradwardine's employment of this example is only one item of internal evidence among many others which, taken together, make unambiguously clear what it was that he meant in saying that "an irrational proportion is not immediately but only mediately denominated by a given number, being immediately denominated by a given proportion which is, in turn, immediately denominated by a number". He meant simply that a proportion between incommensurables, while it cannot be directly specified by means of a number (or by a ratio between integers), can be so specified by a ratio between integers which is raised to some root or power.

The second and more serious of Mr. Murdoch's complaints is one which is central to the principal aim of his paper: namely, that of tracing the fortunes of Western mathematics in its attempt either to understand Eudoxus's criterion of proportional equivalence or else to substitute some other criterion in its stead. Not only Bradwardine but also all other Latin mathematicians of the Middle Ages had, as he shows us, substituted for Eudoxus's criterion of equivalence a criterion of 'denominational' equivalence, and what Mr. Murdoch contends is that this substitution made it impossible for scholastic mathematics to deal satisfactorily with the problems posed by proportions between incommensurables. That this was the case is, he believes, made clear by the fact that Bradwardine's attempt to formulate an equivalence between irrational proportions and exponential functions fails — fails because this equivalence cannot be 'fitted back' into the equidenominational criterion of proportional equivalence which Bradwardine, together with all the other scholastics, had adopted.

What Mr. Murdoch appears to have in mind is this: since Bradwardine has said that proportions are equal whose denominations are equal and has also said that an irrational proportion may be denominated by an exponential function, it should then follow that the denomination of the irrational proportion is equal to that of the exponential function. But, says Mr. Murdoch, although equivalent pairs of integral ratios which serve as the bases and exponents of exponential functions are sufficient to determine (i.e., 'denominate') equivalent irrational proportions, equivalent irrational proportions are not sufficient to determine the equivalent pairs of integral ratios which serve as the bases and exponents of equivalent exponential functions.

This is quite true. But it should be noted that two integral ratios related to each other as base and exponent do not, after all, constitute a proportion in the usual sense of that term, and Bradwardine never speaks of them as being such. He nowhere speaks of an irrational proportion being denominated by some other (rational) proportion; he says merely that a proportion between irrationals may be denominated by a function composed of *two* proportions. The equivalence which he thus establishes between an irrational proportion and the exponential function which determines it cannot therefore be legitimately interpreted as equivalent to the equidenominational equivalence in terms of which he characterizes the equality of proportions proper. In the proper and mathematical sense, a proportion is, as Bradwardine explains, the relation existing between *two* quantities of the same kind: *Proportio est duarum quantitatum eiusdem generis unius ad alteram habitudo*. Since the relation between the two integral proportions constituting the base and exponent of an exponential function is *not* one which is confined to two quantities of the same kind, it is not to be considered a proportion.

It is therefore improper (and, indeed, quite meaningless) to ask that Bradwardine's definition of such a function be 'fitted back' into his equidenominational criterion of proportional equivalence, and this seems to me the quite obvious reason why (as he remarks on p. 260, n. 1) Mr. Murdoch should never have been able to discover any medieval mathematician who attempted to do so. It is simply not the case that Bradwardine's formulation of his exponential function represents (as Mr. Murdoch maintains it does) an abortive attempt to arrive at "a thoroughly general criterion for equal proportions". Medieval mathematics may, indeed, have been greatly the poorer for not having possessed or not having understood Eudoxus's criterion of equivalence, but it should at least be clear not only that Bradwardine was not, in his *De proportionibus*, attempting to develop such a criterion but that its possession would have been of no great value to him in solving the problem to which his treatise *is* devoted: namely, the problem of developing a mathematical equation which would permit a consistent quantitative generalization of Aristotle's axioms concerning motion.

Merely as a footnote, it being clearly understood that this lies outside the bounds of Bradwardine's own ideas and purposes, it may perhaps be of interest to note that, *if* Bradwardine had been concerned to extend, via his concept of an exponential or logarithmic function, the range of applicability of his denominational criterion of equivalence, a possible course would have been open. As has already been noted, equivalent pairs of ratios serving as bases and exponents are sufficient to determine equivalent irrational proportions. On the other hand, equivalent irrational proportions are sufficient to delimit that *class* of exponential functions each member of which is equivalent to the equivalent irrational proportions and each of which is therefore also equivalent to the others. In medieval language, such irrational proportions might be said to 'denominate' a class of rational functions.

J. R. Ravetz

I would like to address a question to Mr. Murdoch. The detailed comparative study of the Latin and Islamic mathematical texts has shown, in this case, the clear superiority of the Islamic. The same pattern is seen in the use of 'Archimedean' mathematical techniques in the study of the rainbow, and in mathematical astronomy. From this one gets the impression that scholastic science at its best was inferior to that of the Islamic culture-area. Were there any fields of study in which the Latins excelled?

J. Needham

We have all listened to Mr. Lynn White's brilliant paper with great enjoyment and appreciation. I would like to say, however, that I am not convinced that Europe was technologically and industrially ahead of China until about A.D. 1450; I think Mr. White's date is rather too early. All the evidence of the travellers, notably Marco Polo himself, is that the standard of life in Cathay and Manzi, especially in the great cities such as Hangchow (on which see the admirable recent book of Jacques Gernet) was markedly above anything known at the time in Europe. Agricultural productivity (always in terms of land area, not manpower yield) was surely higher than Europe until the fifteenth century A.D.

Next, regarding labour-saving machinery, I should like to emphasize once again what was said in my own communication, namely that my collaborators and I have never come across any case of refusal of labour-saving invention for fear of technological unemployment in ancient and medieval China. This is quite surprising, but we are perhaps dazzled by the great population increase there since the eighteenth century and forget that the vast regions of China were not always so heavily peopled. Moreover, the humane sparing of human labour is specifically mentioned in the accounts of fundamental inventions, such as the water-powered furnace bellows of Tu Shih in the eighteenth century. We get the same theme in accounts of sailing rather than rowing, and it recurs in art motifs, such as the carved boat in my possession where the fishermen are taking their ease while the cormorants are doing all the work.

Mr. White made a very interesting remark about the substitution of pro-human saints for anti-human nature spirits; I believe we can match this in China where so often the *genius loci* was a deified historical character, not only a legendary culture-hero. An obvious case is Li Ping throned to this day in the temple beside the great hydraulic works at Kuan-hsien in Szechuan, but there are plenty of others — incense burns before the shrine of Tshai Lun in every paper-mill, the pearl-divers bow in the temple of Meng Chhang far in the south, who was once a benevolent Governor there, and Kungshu Phan guards every carpenter's shop and engine-room.

I was glad indeed that Mr. White acknowledges so many technological influences on Europe from Asia in the medieval centuries. We can get trace-harness back to the Former Han and even the Warring States periods (fourth century B.C. onwards) and collar-harness back to the Northern Wei (fifth century A.D. onwards). As for his military revolution, I would like to footnote it by saying that the crossbow, which was the standard weapon of the Han armies, seems to have been introduced to Europe twice, and that, when catapult artillery came back after its disappearance in the ninth century A.D., it was no longer the torsion ballistae of the Romans but the trebuchets or mangonels of the Chinese which worked on the swape principle. I do not believe that pattern-welding of swords was essentially Celtic, since China had it at least as early, and I am more inclined to suppose that it spread in both directions from some Central Asian focus — as indeed so much later did the windmill from Seistan. Lastly I would like to mention the remarkable case of the water-powered blowing-engines of the thirteenth century A.D. in China, which exemplify, for the first time (so far as I can find) in any culture, the standard method of conversion of rotary to rectilinear motion, with eccentric, connexion-rod and piston-rod. Does it not seem inevitable that this was carried back to Europe by one of the friars or merchant-travellers who passed the length of the Old World at that time?

F. Greenaway

I should like to make some remarks based on Mr. Lynn White's question, "How early and in what ways did the West begin to show its distinctive originality in technological matters and its velocity of technical change?" He gives many examples himself, but they mostly refer to techniques for the conversion of one substance to another, or for changing the shape or location of objects and to the subsequent utilization of the objects or materials so converted. This is what we usually mean when we talk of technology. I want to say something about a different aspect, a technique which provides a service by eliciting useful technical information, namely the amount of silver or gold in a specimen. This is a technique which has a longer history of continuous application than any other I know, the assaying of silver and gold. The determination of the amount of gold in a specimen by heating it in an absorbent crucible was practised in Babylonian times. The use of lead in this process to absorb dross was clearly known not much later. One could discuss at length the means by which the technique of assaying reached the West. For example, did it come via the Arabs or independently or both? There is only time to point to one step, from the twelfth century to the fourteenth century, and to draw attention to the kind of evidence which exists.

In the *Dialogus de Scaccario* of about 1182 Robert Fitznigel describes how taxes were gathered by the Count of Exchequer.[1] The work is mainly administrative in significance, but a long passage describes the way in which specimens of coin are cupelled, i.e. heated in a crucible with lead to determine the silver content of the coin submitted as tax. The weighing was not against calibrated weights but the yield of silver in the cupellation indicated a correction to be applied to the number of coin demanded. This might well have been no advance on a practice carried out traditionally for centuries before. But when we look at another assaying text of 1343 the technique has elements which are not technically new but, I suggest, conceptually new. In an edict of Philip de Valois of 1343,[2] the methods of assaying laid down are qualified with two interesting remarks. One is advice to make a balance which will be faithful and true leaning neither to right nor to left. The other, and this is the important one in the present context, is advice to the assayer to carry out a test beforehand on a specimen of the lead which is to be used in testing the silver. The object of the test is to determine whether the lead contains any silver itself and if so how much.

This blank run on one's reagent is good analytical practice, but it is startling to find it as early as this. I said this was conceptually new. By this I mean that the older description of assaying was that of a rule of thumb procedure, which gave information about a material object for administrative purposes. It cannot be said to imply any theory of method any more than it implies a theory of constancy of composition. The later procedure does, I think, imply a belief that the methods used for eliciting information by test were based on a process which could itself be quantitatively examined, to supplement and perfect the information obtained.

It would be too much to infer from this one comparison a general forward movement of ideas about the quantitative examination of the composition of substances with a view to their control, but it can be supported.

Nicolas Oresme's *De Moneta* of the fourteenth century discusses the role of money in the economy and there are frequent

[1] *Dialogus de Scaccario* (*The Course of the Exchequer*) *by Richard, Son of Nigel, Treasurer of England and Bishop of London.* Translated from the Latin with Introduction and Notes by Charles Johnson (London 1950). For description and discussion of assaying see pp. 36–43.

[2] Philippe de Valois, quoted in J. Boizard (or Boisard), *Traité des Monnoyes* (Paris, 1692) 166, 173, 182.

references to the coinage which do entail an acceptance of methods of determining the assay of silver at the high level of understanding of the 1343 edict rather than the low level of the *Dialogus de Scaccario*. In particular the discussion of the morality of the debasement of the coinage by the ruler is only intelligible if we suppose that the assay of the coinage could be carried out absolutely and independently.

There are other supports for my contention that there was this forward movement in quantitative understanding. A reference in the *Red Book of the Exchequer* to a range of assays says that if in a series of tests, one is different from the others, it is to be regarded as being probably due to gross experimental errors.[1]

One technique does not make a technology, but it does suggest that this particular technique, which was of vital importance for the silver-based economy of the Middle Ages, was an important field in which the West began to show its distinctive originality. So far as velocity of change is concerned, I suggest that the generalization of Nicolas Oresme on the one hand, and the incorporation of an analytical technique in a statute, indicate a widespread acceptance of the possibility of quantitative uniformity in the eliciting of technical information.

I should like to think that this idea of the controlled eliciting of socially useful technical information about substances, as distinct from the more familiar idea of socially useful material production, deserves further study.

M. Daumas

I suspect that Mr. Lynn White is according too much influence to Christianity in the technical progress of the period of Western European history that we are considering. One must beware of intellectual over-simplification. If Christianity changed the attitude to manual labour, it changed only that of a small minority of individuals who had hitherto taken no part in the development of techniques and who did not participate in it for a long time, not perhaps until the end of the sixteenth century. Until then technical development was primarily in the hands of the manual workers with no theoretical knowledge. Transmission was by word of mouth and by the

[1] *The De Moneta of Nicholas Oresme and English Mint Documents*. Translated from the Latin with Introduction and Notes by Charles Johnson (London, 1956). The *Red Book of the Exchequer*, f. 264, quoted and translated at p. 81, refers to selection of good results from several assays. Other references to assaying *passim*.

direct apprenticeship of one man to another. The curve of progress was essentially dependent on the needs of consumers and on the number of workers. Thus, economic and above all demographic factors are what determined this progress. Until a very late period, the role of the engineers was simply to collate the new techniques they came across: the sawmill cited by Mr. White was badly designed by Villard de Honnecourt, In such a form, it could not work; and since the workers themselves were unable to read or follow a design, one may ask oneself just what influence the encyclopaedic collections quoted by Mr. Gille exercised on progress.

E. Olszewski

Mr. Lynn White's highly interesting paper dealing with the elements that promoted the development of technology in Middle Ages has raised some doubts in my mind.

It seems in the first place that it is impossible to appraise correctly the causes why it is specifically in Western Europe and not in the Islamic countries that we see a rapid development of technology, without first making a thorough analysis of the economic situation and of the social systems in these areas. An analysis of these elements would show that in many cases it was these factors as well as social ideology, religious beliefs and the organization of religious life, that accelerated the development of technology, while Mr. White has seen only the last-named factors as effective.

There is undoubtedly a direct connexion between the technical progress and the forms of monastic life in Middle Ages. This matter was thoroughly analysed thirty years ago by Louis Mumford in his *Technics and Civilization*. But it cannot be said that the *cause* here was the monastic organization, and the effect the development of technology. I think that just the opposite would be more true. To put it in a few words, it was not the Christian saints who did away with the nymphs who had under their care the rivers and streams and made them free for the water-wheels, but just the contrary — it was the water-wheels that drove away the water nymphs and made place for the Christian saints.

S. Pines

I am grateful to Mr. Temkin for pointing out the fact that the adumbration of experimental method which is found in Arabic philosophical texts derives from Galen. It was not my intention to contend that the Arabic philosophers were original in this respect. I wished merely to indicate that this approach to science was not wholly foreign to their very way of thinking. Quite apart from this, Galen had a considerable influence on the Arabic anti-Peripatetic philosophers. Many of the anti-Aristotelian conceptions and arguments set forth in Arabic philosophical works go back to him. Mr. Millás-Vallicrosa's remarks point to a fruitful field of inquiry.

W. Hartner

Mr. Yushkevich, instead of commenting on the paper presented by Mr. Schramm and myself, has given a short survey of the history of mathematics and astronomy in Antiquity and during the Middle Ages up to recent times, as seen from his very specific point of view, which I confess is not in every respect the same as my own. However that may be, it is this development of mathematical thought which forms the background of our study. So I would like to thank him for his contribution.

G. Beaujouan

I will reply to Mr. Southern's observations by recalling that my paper was not concerned with the whole of medieval science, but only with science as taught in medieval universities. It is for this reason that I excluded from my discussion the whole tradition that stemmed from Isidore of Seville and from Rhabanus Maurus, a tradition which introduced a certain amount of elementary scientific knowledge into literal commentaries on the Bible. The pragmatic character of medieval science is more evident at the courts of princes than in the universities; one only has to look at the court of Frederick II of Hohenstaufen, for example, or again at the influence of the Aragonese kings of the fourteenth century. But it cannot be too strongly stressed how artificial it is to talk in general terms of 'medieval science' as if it were a single activity. It is of little value to look at second-hand compilations or even more or less philosophical speculations on the theory of knowledge: the only thing that counts in reality is the works of the masters who effectively furthered the progress of science by discovering or *re*-discovering truths, re-formulations or new ideas (men like Jordanus Nemorarius, Pierre de Maricourt, Theodoric of Freiberg, Thomas Bradwardine, Jean Buridan, Nicole Oresme, etc.).

J. E. Murdoch

Mr. Minio-Paluello has succinctly summarized the burden of my paper, helpfully suggested some of the features of the larger context in which its subject falls, and has offered observations concerning some of its finer points which acutely expand, and urge reconsideration of, various of the partial conclusions I have drawn. Though I believe that several of the comments he has made call for qualification, or rejection, others form, I feel, substantial additions to what I have said, particularly those which mark out important medieval intellectual currents which, though germane to my subject, I have neglected, and those which supplement my claims regarding the influence of textual characteristics and variants within medieval mathematical history.

(1) To begin with, he has correctly drawn attention to the omission of Boethius from what I have written of the history of proportion and proportionality in the Latin Middle Ages. This omission was a conscious one on my part, occasioned partly by the impossibility of treating all facets of this history within a single paper, but also by the relative lack of stimulation which Boethius's utterances seemed to have held for that particular portion of this history with which I have been concerned. Often, like Scripture in philosophical discussions, Boethius is cited as an authority without substantially contributing to the nucleus of the point under investigation. It is of course true that his contentions were frequently in the background of the arithmetical bias exhibited by medieval comments to the theory of proportion, but this part of the Boethian influence seems to have been more effectively expressed through the intermediary of Jordanus's *Arithmetica* rather than through a direct reaction to Boethius's works themselves. Thus, for example, it is in Jordanus that the denomination notion appears to have had its most significant, if not original, source; *denominatio* in Boethius has quite another sense and, as I have indicated (see p. 257, n. 2), he uses another term, and even circumlocutions, to express the notion so popular in later medieval mathematics. Furthermore, the medieval philosopher-mathematician seems more frequently to name Jordanus — when he names anyone at all — as the cache of his arithmetical glosses on the general theory of proportionality in Book V of Euclid (so, for example, Benedetto Vittorio in his *Commentaria in tractatum proportionum Alberti de*

Saxonia (ed. Bologna, 1506) consistently explains Campanus on Book V in terms of Jordanus, and vice versa). Yet, even in face of Jordanus, and more remotely Boethius, as influences in the rising arithmeticism of the Latin West, I believe that the medieval inability to see Book V of the *Elements* in thoroughly general terms was equally, if not more, effective in continuing and extending this arithmetical bias. Though the fifth book was often said to be the most fundamental of the *Elements*, this in no way should be taken as genuine appreciation of its proper generality.

Boethius did play a direct role in one of the points of the reaction to Greek mathematics I have been treating: he formed, as it were, one of the ultimate sources for the *explanation* of the fourth proportional axiom I have mentioned above as a medieval addition to the *Elements*, though his remarks were not related to the axiom itself (cf. *De institutione musica*, I, 6 and II, 3).

Finally, it is certainly possible that *proportio* and *proportionalitas* derived their place in medieval mathematical vocabulary through their occurrence in Boethius. But the consistent use of these terms in translating the similarly related Arabic words *nisba* and *tanāsub* may well have formed another factor, perhaps a confirming one, in the history of their medieval mathematical applications.

(2) The use of proportion and related notions in theology and theories of languages mentioned by Mr. Minio-Paluello is another area I have omitted from consideration here. Although these applications of the idea of proportion are undoubtedly of greater importance to the whole fabric of medieval intellectual history than the developments I have stressed, they were only occasionally something more than tangential to the mathematics of it all. On such occasions the connexion between the theological and the mathematical became less casual and more causal; so, for example, when the question of the mathematical possibility of proportion or proportionality between infinite and finite quantities was raised in purely theological contexts.

(3) Mr. Minio-Paluello suggests that one might conceivably carry the significance of the Latin text of Euclid one step further than I have done in my paper: namely, that the defective nature of the text relative to the Greek original occasioned not only, as I have maintained, the form of the particular misinterpretation given to Eudoxus's technique of equimultiples, but that it made any correct interpretation

virtually impossible. The text Mr. Minio-Paluello quotes does indeed make such an hypothesis plausible. He has, I feel, correctly emphasized another instance of the substantial effect the precise form of translated texts had upon medieval mathematics; yet I do not think that we can go so far as to maintain that the effect was, in this instance, such as to *prevent* a proper interpretation of the text in question. In an attempt to clarify the situation, I should like to offer further evidence relevant to his conjecture, evidence which qualifies, I believe, the extent to which the text of Eudoxus's definition might possibly have affected medieval misunderstanding.

The crucial point brought forward in the passage cited is that the equimultiples of Eudoxus's criterion are said to be *similes vel additione vel diminutione vel equalitate*. Given this, it is claimed, "misinterpretation was almost inevitable", for such terms certainly did not adequately represent the required meaning, namely, that the equimultiples *at the same time* either exceed, fall short of, or are equal to one another. *Similes* suggests rather that the equimultiples should undergo *an equal amount* of excess or defect. Did not the presence of this misleading *similes* contribute appreciably to the medieval misinterpretation of Eudoxus? Can it not, perhaps, even excuse it? Here several considerations are, I believe, most pertinent.

First, with just the quoted erroneous text, the medieval geometer might well have felt urged to remove the disjunct *equalitate* from the scope of *similes*; for what sense within the context at hand, could he have made of *similes . . . equalitate*? Yet, he could scarcely have effected this limitation and remained faithful to the letter of the text. Indeed, such a consideration may have caused him to correct the text, corrections which did exist, as I shall presently show. Secondly, Minio-Paluello cites the text in question as it appears in the dominant Adelard tradition. But a more correct translation employing *simul* in place of *similes* (a substitution which properly rendered the Greek ἅμα) was available to the medieval mathematician in the apparently less popular versions of Gerard of Cremona and Hermann of Carinthia. So also could the proper notion be had from the older Boethian version or the translation of Al-Nairīzī's commentary. Thus, the misunderstanding cannot be excused on grounds that no correct text was at hand. What is even more important in this regard is that correct texts are also to be found in Adelard versions themselves. Hence, within the enunciations of this definition found in various manuscripts of what Marshall Clagett has termed the Adelard II tradition — by far the most frequently used version — one finds *simul* occurring almost as many times as *similes*. Moreover, in at least three cases of which I know, an original *similes* has been corrected to *simul*, clearly indicating an awareness of the proper meaning of 'at the same time'. Similar remarks can be made about manuscripts in the Adelard I and Adelard III traditions. As a consequence, the medieval mathematician could easily have been familiar with an essentially correct version of Eudoxus's definition, even in the most popular of his versions of Euclid. Once again, no excuse for misunderstanding.

We need now to look at the comments — when they exist — accompanying the correct enunciations employing *simul*. Since writing the main body of this paper, I have been able to examine two manuscripts carrying the appropriate *simul* which also give glosses expressing Eudoxus's meaning correctly (MSS Bibliothèque Nationale, lat. 7374 and Oxford, Savile 19). Hence, at least two medieval writers were on the right track; examination of further copies of the medieval Euclid may reveal others, if only in the margins or, literally, between the lines. These two cases should not be construed as an appreciation of Eudoxus's wisdom similar to that exhibited earlier by Al-Jayyānī, or later by Isaac Barrow. (Furthermore, curiously enough, both of these manuscripts also have glosses interpreting the spurious fourth definition of continuous proportionality in Book V in strictly Eudoxean terms. Thus, they are consistent, but at the price of ignoring the explicit claim for equal excess and defect in this spurious definition.)

As I know of no instances of a correct idea of what Eudoxus was up to when the *similes* variant of the definition occurs, we might, in terms of present evidence, say that the *simul* form was a necessary condition for a glimmer of proper understanding. But it was certainly not sufficient. For there are cases of correct enunciations with *simul* glossed as if the 'same amount' and not 'at the same time' were involved, cases in which the misinterpretation seems to have been due to carrying over the mistaken idea of *equal* excess and defect from the spurious fourth definition. Consequently, one can conclude that there were two points in the text of the *Elements* itself which contributed to the medieval lack of understanding of Eudoxus. The problem is to gauge the probable weight of their respective effects. In the case of the erroneous '*similes* version' of the Definition 5, ample opportunity was available to know a correct '*simul* version'. And, given such a correct version, misinterpretation need not follow. But there were no versions, as far as I have discovered, of the spurious definition without the equal excess and defect specification. Thus, with respect to this text, save for appeal to the more rarely used medieval versions like that of Gerard of Cremona, which lacked the spurious definition itself, consequent misinterpretation appears, as I have held above, to have been foisted on the medieval mathematician as a matter of course. Moreover, by far the most frequent unwitting explanation of Eudoxus in the Middle Ages was that based on Campanus's dodge of excess or defect *secundum proportionem*. And this was clearly brought about by the text of the spurious definition.

Finally, there are several other factors which make it erroneous to claim that Eudoxus was impossible to grasp given the state of the medieval Euclid. Thus, the seventh definition giving the criterion for *unequal* proportions, should have made it quite clear that excess or defect at the same time, and not in equal amount, was in question. This, particularly if only a 'similes version' of the fifth definition were at hand. Further, some of the applications of the puzzling fifth definition (for example that in VI, 1) also made the substance of Eudoxus's technique apparent. So one must conclude, I believe, that possibilities for an appropriate understanding of the equimultiple technique were available, possibilities, one feels, far more numerous and fertile than the two brief realizations of Eudoxus's method I have thus far found.

(4) The labelling of V, Definition 4 as a "principle of continuity" is, I think, most appropriate. In fact, it is the most important one — in all of its various forms — in Greek mathematics. It is not its providing for the application of 'ratio' or 'proportio' to incommensurables that renders it a continuity principle, for it is not principally concerned with this question at all — as is Definition 5. It is, rather, properly so called because it excludes infinitesimals from the domain of magnitudes capable of having proportion to one another. Further, it is possibly true, as Minio-Paluello suggests, that in medieval mathematics — though not in Greek — one might expect something more explicit as a continuity principle. I would suggest that the medieval reworkings and explanations of the "principle" in V, Definition 4 (as it was found in X, 1) provided precisely that.

(5) The additional definition of ἀναλογία or *proportionalitas* to which Minio-Paluello refers — one employing the idea of *similitudo* or *identitas proportionum* in the definiens — seems to have had little effect on the history of Eudoxus in the Middle Ages. The only case of its discussion which I have seen thus far is that of Ametus filius Josephi referred to above.

(6) The fact that the original of the denomination idea within medieval versions of the *Elements* occurs firstly within the text of Book VII, and secondly only in the comments to Book V, while the sixth definition of V remains untouched in its own, appropriate medieval translation, makes me think the derivation of the denomination criterion from this latter definition highly unlikely. Moreover, not only would such a source create a unique case of rendering λόγος by *denominatio*, but the appearance of the latter term in the required sense in arithmetical works prior to its occurrence in the equality criterion seem to point to an origin outside the context of the *Elements*.

(7) As Mr. Minio-Paluello's final comment is directly related to the more detailed criticisms of Mr. Crosby, I shall key my reply more specifically to the latter in hope of answering both. I am charged, it appears, with unjustly maligning Bradwardine's achievements in his *De proportionibus*. In answering, it is best to begin with an indication of the limits which I intended my criticism of this medieval work to have. Certainly, Bradwardine's main purpose was not to extend the denomination idea to irrational proportions, nor to expand the equality of denomination criterion to include the same. Nor again was his aim to derive and use "an algorithm in which ratios between incommensurables were possible" as Minio-Paluello suggests. Denominations, incommensurables and irrational proportions are considerations tangential to the principal burden of Bradwardine's treatise. Rather, it is unquestionably the case that Bradwardine's central purpose was, as Crosby points out, to evolve a "function" (or better "relation") between changing velocities, forces and resistances which more adequately fit the physical postulates of Aristotelian natural philosophy, than did the suggestions of his predecessors. I have tried to say just this above (p. 365). My criticism was not of this, but of a *part* of the mathematics Bradwardine uses to introduce this central, physical section of his treatise. It is also true, as Crosby asserts, that Bradwardine's success or failure in this part of his mathematics was of "no great value to him" in solving the main

problem of his work. But this is not to deny that confusion does reign in the mathematical passages of the *De proportionibus* I have cited. I believe that Bradwardine's efforts are here obscure and confused; this is the extent of my criticism.

But Mr. Crosby also opposes this belief. Our disagreement rests, or at least should rest, on making sense of the assertion about mediate and immediate denominations for irrational proportions which Crosby repeats above. I feel that this sentence of the *De proportionibus* is puzzling. Yet, whatever one's interpretation, it must at least satisfy the following: there are three "entities" involved, the first is *immediately* denominated by the second, the second is *immediately* denominated by the third, therefore the first is only *mediately* denominated by the third. The problem is, basing oneself on Bradwardine's words, to discover precisely what three "entities" are intended. The most one can gain with any degree of assurance from the text in question, is that the first is the *irrational* proportion itself, the second a *rational* proportion, and the third a number; but precisely *which* rational proportion and number are the second and third designed to signify? Once again, if $(A/B)^{x/y}$ is the irrational proportion involved, it is not "unambiguously clear", as Crosby maintains, what the remaining two elements of Bradwardine's assertion should be taken to be. It is this puzzle that the three interpretations I have given above were intended to offer alternative answers to. Crosby concludes that Bradwardine simply means in this curious passage that an irrational proportion is to be "specified by a ratio between integers which is raised to some root or power". He does not tell us exactly which elements are to fill slots two and three of Bradwardine's utterance. Yet I think what he says implies that he would opt for the third alternative interpretation given above: A/B is the *rational* proportion, x/y is the *number*. But, if this is so, then his resolution is guilty of overlooking the flagrant inconsistency in the use of *denominatur* that this third interpretation entails: how can Bradwardine, in the very sentence before, maintain that a rational proportion is immediately denominated by what is, in effect, that proportion in its lowest terms expressed as an integer, proper or improper fraction (e.g., $\frac{6}{2}$ is immediately denominated by 3, $\frac{6}{4}$ by $1\frac{1}{2}$, etc.), and now maintain that the *exponent* is serving the function of immediate denomination for the rational base proportion? Clearly, he can do so only by taking *immediate denominatur* to mean two different things in the two succeeding passages. And this does not even broach the question of fitting his extension of denominations back into the equality criterion utilizing this conception. I would think that this abrupt change in the meaning of the crucial term would render this interpretation of the passage something less than evident.

Furthermore, this is in no way inconsistent with thoroughly agreeing with Crosby that there is no question at all that Bradwardine meant "the square root of the proportion of two to one" when he uses the expression *medietas duplae proportionis*. For this phrase, in and of itself, does not raise the problem of immediate and mediate denomination. It is only when we begin to interpret it in terms of Bradwardine's puzzling use of "denomination" that difficulties appear.

Secondly, Crosby agrees that the third interpretation I have given will not, if "fitted back into" the equality axiom based on denomination, give the desired convertibility for cases involving irrational proportions. However, he counters, Bradwardine is not to be charged with this failure, as he does not take irrational proportions to be proportions "in the usual sense of that term". That they are not so, he claims, follows from the fact that they are not "confined to two quantities of the same kind", a condition specified by Bradwardine's proper and mathematical definition of proportion. But nothing could be further from the case; Bradwardine's own words oppose it. For, directly after the definition Crosby cites, we find the words *Et haec est duplex*, and the dichotomy is filled out by two *gradus* of proportions: rational and irrational. Moreover, should we take $(\frac{2}{1})^{1/2}$ — Bradwardine's *medietas duplae proportionis* — as a sample irrational proportion, it most certainly *is* one confined to two quantities of the same kind. For it can express, as Crosby himself says, the proportion of the diagonal of a square to its side; and these are two homogeneous quantities, for both are straight lines. Bradwardine's inclusion of *eiusdem generis* in his definition of proportion was intended, following the Euclidean tradition, merely to exclude proportions between, for example, a line and a surface, and not to banish irrational proportions from its realm.

Thirdly, I believe that Crosby has interpreted my critical remarks about Bradwardine's, and the general medieval, use of the denomination test for equal proportions in a manner which, taken to the letter, they do not have. He claims that I have erroneously maintained that Bradwardine's "exponential function represents an abortive attempt to arrive at a thoroughly general criterion of equal proportions". I must reply that I have not. Instead, I have held, and still hold, that Bradwardine's extension of the denomination notion to incommensurables, coupled with his express assertion of the denomination equality criterion, constituted the abortive attempt. This is not at all the same thing as his formulation of his "exponential function". Further, Crosby states that I have contended that the medieval substitution of the denomination rule for the misunderstood Eudoxean criterion "made it impossible for scholastic mathematics to deal satisfactorily with the problems posed by proportions between incommensurables". Once again I must demur. Certainly, the work of Nicole Oresme and others successfully, and brilliantly, did resolve questions involving proportions between incommensurables. What I have said, for example, of Oresme's application of the new calculus of proportions to the possible incommensurability of heavenly motions speaks for this. I have only claimed, rather, that the substitution of the denomination criterion for Eudoxus made it impossible for medieval mathematicians to solve *one* problem involving proportions between incommensurables, to wit, that of constructing a truly general definition or test for equal proportions.

Finally, Crosby suggests that if we grant Bradwardine a mathematical sophistication he did not possess, he could have given his denomination criterion the required convertibility and generality. Yet, even bestowing this modernization upon Bradwardine, the technique of discriminating among irrational proportions by considering the bases and exponents involved would still not have the generality of Eudoxus's technique of equimultiples. For how could one determine the appropriate exponents for transcendental irrational proportions? They would themselves be irrational. (Oresme well realized the difficulties here, if not in these terms.) And how then build up a criterion of equality to satisfy all cases? The denomination technique was bound to fall short and founder.

(8) In answer to Mr. Ravetz's query about fields of scientific endeavour in which the Latins surpassed (and not merely equalled) the efforts of their Islamic forerunners, one can surely bring forth the thirteenth- and fourteenth-century developments in mathematically treating kinematics and dynamics: the accomplishments begun at Merton College, for example, and continued on the Continent are most notable. But an even greater contrast is to be found in the area of logic.

Here the Latin West formulated, as Islam had not, significant additions to the Aristotelian base common to both. These developments in logic should in themselves be considered as an important part of the history of science in the Middle Ages. Moreover, they constitute an important entry within this history in another way: the application of logical conceptions and techniques to the problems of natural philosophy. Here, one can claim, I believe, the existence of an avenue of approach as fertile and significant as that of the medieval mathematical treatment of such problems. The fact that it has heretofore received less attention by historians misrepresents, in a way, the measure of its importance.

PART FOUR

Problems in the Sociology of Science

11

The Function of Dogma in Scientific Research[1]

THOMAS S. KUHN

At some point in his or her career every member of this Symposium has, I feel sure, been exposed to the image of the scientist as the uncommitted searcher after truth. He is the explorer of nature — the man who rejects prejudice at the threshold of his laboratory, who collects and examines the bare and objective facts, and whose allegiance is to such facts and to them alone. These are the characteristics which make the testimony of scientists so valuable when advertising proprietary products in the United States. Even for an international audience, they should require no further elaboration. To be scientific is, among other things, to be objective and open-minded.

Probably none of us believes that in practice the real-life scientist quite succeeds in fulfilling this ideal. Personal acquaintance, the novels of Sir Charles Snow, or a cursory reading of the history of science provides too much counter-evidence. Though the scientific enterprise may be open-minded, whatever this application of that phrase may mean, the individual

[1] The ideas developed in this paper have been abstracted, in a drastically condensed form, from the first third of my forthcoming monograph, *The Structure of Scientific Revolutions*, which will be published during 1962 by the University of Chicago Press. Some of them were also partially developed in an earlier essay, "The essential tension: tradition and innovation in scientific research", which appeared in Calvin W. Taylor (ed.), *The Third (1959) University of Utah Research Conference on the Identification of Creative Scientific Talent* (Salt Lake City, 1959).

On this whole subject see also I. B. Cohen, "Orthodoxy and scientific progress", *Proceedings of the American Philosophical Society*, XCVI (1952) 505–12, and Bernard Barber, "Resistance by scientists to scientific discovery", *Science*, CXXXIV (1961) 596-602. I am indebted to Mr. Barber for an advance copy of that helpful paper. Above all, those concerned with the importance of quasi-dogmatic commitments as a requisite for productive scientific research should see the works of Michael Polanyi, particularly his *Personal Knowledge* (Chicago, 1958) and *The Logic of Liberty* (London, 1951). The discussion which follows this paper will indicate that Mr. Polanyi and I differ somewhat about what scientists are committed to, but that should not disguise the very great extent of our agreement about the issues discussed explicitly below.

scientist is very often not. Whether his work is predominantly theoretical or experimental, he usually seems to know, before his research project is even well under way, all but the most intimate details of the result which that project will achieve. If the result is quickly forthcoming, well and good. If not, he will struggle with his apparatus and with his equations until, if at all possible, they yield results which conform to the sort of pattern which he has foreseen from the start. Nor is it only through his own research that the scientist displays his firm convictions about the phenomena which nature can yield and about the ways in which these may be fitted to theory. Often the same convictions show even more clearly in his response to the work produced by others. From Galileo's reception of Kepler's research to Nägeli's reception of Mendel's, from Dalton's rejection of Gay Lussac's results to Kelvin's rejection of Maxwell's, unexpected novelties of fact and theory have characteristically been resisted and have often been rejected by many of the most creative members of the professional scientific community. The historian, at least, scarcely needs Planck to remind him that: "A new scientific truth is not usually presented in a way that convinces its opponents . . .; rather they gradually die off, and a rising generation is familiarized with the truth from the start."[1]

Familiar facts like these — and they could easily be multiplied — do not seem to bespeak an enterprise whose practitioners are notably open-minded. Can they at all be reconciled with our usual image of productive scientific research? If such a reconciliation has not seemed to present fundamental problems in the past, that is probably because resistance and preconception have usually been viewed as extraneous to science. They are, we have often been told, no more than the product of inevitable *human* limitations; a proper scientific method has no place for them; and that method is powerful enough so that no mere human idiosyncrasy can impede its success for very long. On this view, examples of a scientific *parti pris* are reduced to the status of anecdotes, and it is that evaluation of their significance that this essay aims to challenge. Verisimilitude, alone, suggests that such a challenge is required. Preconception and resistance seem the rule rather than the exception in mature scientific development. Furthermore, under normal circumstances they characterize the very best and most creative research as well as the more routine. Nor can

[1] *Wissenschaftliche Selbstbiographie* (Leipzig, 1948) 22, my translation.

there be much question where they come from. Rather than being characteristics of the aberrant individual, they are community characteristics with deep roots in the procedures through which scientists are trained for work in their profession. Strongly held convictions that are prior to research often seem to be a precondition for success in the sciences.

Obviously I am already ahead of my story, but in getting there I have perhaps indicated its principal theme. Though preconception and resistance to innovation could very easily choke off scientific progress, their omnipresence is nonetheless symptomatic of characteristics upon which the continuing vitality of research depends. Those characteristics I shall collectively call the dogmatism of mature science, and in the pages to come I shall try to make the following points about them. Scientific education inculcates what the scientific community had previously with difficulty gained — a deep commitment to a particular way of viewing the world and of practising science in it. That commitment can be, and from time to time is, replaced by another, but it cannot be merely given up. And, while it continues to characterize the community of professional practitioners, it proves in two respects fundamental to productive research. By defining for the individual scientist both the problems available for pursuit and the nature of acceptable solutions to them, the commitment is actually constitutive of research. Normally the scientist is a puzzle-solver like the chess player, and the commitment induced by education is what provides him with the rules of the game being played in his time. In its absence he would not be a physicist, chemist, or whatever he has been trained to be.

In addition, commitment has a second and largely incompatible research role. Its very strength and the unanimity with which the professional group subscribes to it provides the individual scientist with an immensely sensitive detector of the trouble spots from which significant innovations of fact and theory are almost inevitably educed. In the sciences most discoveries of unexpected fact and all fundamental innovations of theory are responses to a prior breakdown in the rules of the previously established game. Therefore, though a quasi-dogmatic commitment is, on the one hand, a source of resistance and controversy, it is also instrumental in making the sciences the most consistently revolutionary of all human activities. One need make neither resistance nor dogma a virtue to recognize that no mature science could exist without them.

Before examining further the nature and effects of scientific dogma, consider the pattern of education through which it is transmitted from one generation of practitioners to the next. Scientists are not, of course, the only professional community that acquires from education a set of standards, tools, and techniques which they later deploy in their own creative work. Yet even a cursory inspection of scientific pedagogy suggests that it is far more likely to induce professional rigidity than education in other fields, excepting, perhaps, systematic theology. Admittedly the following epitome is biased toward the American pattern, which I know best. The contrasts at which it aims must, however, be visible, if muted, in European and British education as well.

Perhaps the most striking feature of scientific education is that, to an extent quite unknown in other creative fields, it is conducted through textbooks, works written especially for students. Until he is ready, or very nearly ready, to begin his own dissertation, the student of chemistry, physics, astronomy, geology, or biology is seldom either asked to attempt trial research projects or exposed to the immediate products of research done by others — to, that is, the professional communications that scientists write for their peers. Collections of 'source readings' play a negligible role in *scientific* education. Nor is the science student encouraged to read the historical classics of his field — works in which he might encounter other ways of regarding the questions discussed in his text, but in which he would also meet problems, concepts, and standards of solution that his future profession had long-since discarded and replaced.[1] Whitehead somewhere caught this quite special feature of the sciences when he wrote, "A science that hesitates to forget its founders is lost."

An almost exclusive reliance on textbooks is not all that distinguishes scientific education. Students in other fields are, after all, also exposed to such books, though seldom beyond the second year of college and even in those early years not exclusively. But in the sciences different textbooks display different subject matters rather than, as in the humanities and many social sciences, exemplifying different approaches to a

[1] The individual sciences display some variation in these respects. Students in the newer and also in the less theoretical sciences — e.g. parts of biology, geology, and medical science — are more likely to encounter both contemporary and historical source materials than those in, say, astronomy, mathematics, or physics.

single problem field. Even books that compete for adoption in a single science course differ mainly in level and pedagogic detail, not in substance or conceptual structure. One can scarcely imagine a physicist's or chemist's saying that he had been forced to begin the education of his third-year class almost from first principles because its previous exposure to the field had been through books that consistently violated his conception of the discipline. Remarks of that sort are not by any means unprecedented in several of the social sciences. Apparently scientists agree about what it is that every student of the field must know. That is why, in the design of a pre-professional curriculum, they can use textbooks instead of eclectic samples of research.

Nor is the characteristic technique of textbook presentation altogether the same in the sciences as elsewhere. Except in the occasional introductions that students seldom read, science texts make little attempt to describe the *sorts* of problems that the professional may be asked to solve or to discuss the *variety* of techniques that experience has made available for their solution. Instead, these books exhibit, from the very start, concrete problem-solutions that the profession has come to accept as paradigms, and they then ask the student, either with a pencil and paper or in the laboratory, to solve for himself problems closely modelled in method and substance upon those through which the text has led him. Only in elementary language instruction or in training a musical instrumentalist is so large or essential a use made of 'finger exercises'. And those are just the fields in which the object of instruction is to produce with maximum rapidity strong 'mental sets' or *Einstellungen*. In the sciences, I suggest, the effect of these techniques is much the same. Though scientific development is particularly productive of consequential novelties, scientific education remains a relatively dogmatic initiation into a pre-established problem-solving tradition that the student is neither invited nor equipped to evaluate.

The pattern of systematic textbook education just described existed in no place and in no science (except perhaps elementary mathematics) until the early nineteenth century. But before that date a number of the more developed sciences clearly displayed the special characteristics indicated above, and in a few cases had done so for a very long time. Where there were no textbooks there had often been universally received paradigms for the practice of individual sciences. These were scientific achievements reported in books that all the practitioners of a given field knew intimately and admired, achievements upon which they modelled their own research and which provided them with a measure of their own accomplishment. Aristotle's *Physica*, Ptolemy's *Almagest*, Newton's *Principia* and *Opticks*, Franklin's *Electricity*, Lavoisier's *Chemistry*, and Lyell's *Geology* — these works and many others all served for a time implicitly to define the legitimate problems and methods of a research field for succeeding generations of practitioners. In their day each of these books, together with others modelled closely upon them, did for its field much of what textbooks now do for these same fields and for others besides.

All of the works named above are, of course, classics of science. As such their role may be thought to resemble that of the main classics in other creative fields, for example the works of a Shakespeare, a Rembrandt, or an Adam Smith. But by calling these works, or the achievements which lie behind them, paradigms rather than classics, I mean to suggest that there is something else special about them, something which sets them apart both from some other classics of science and from all the classics of other creative fields.

Part of this "something else" is what I shall call the exclusiveness of paradigms. At any time the practitioners of a given specialty may recognize numerous classics, some of them — like the works of Ptolemy and Copernicus or Newton and Descartes — quite incompatible one with the other. But that same group, if it has a paradigm at all, can have only one. Unlike the community of artists — which can draw simultaneous inspiration from the works of, say, Rembrandt *and* Cézanne and which therefore studies both — the community of astronomers had no alternative to choosing *between* the competing models of scientific activity supplied by Copernicus and Ptolemy. Furthermore, having made their choice, astronomers could thereafter neglect the work which they had rejected. Since the sixteenth century there have been only two full editions of the *Almagest*, both produced in the nineteenth century and directed exclusively to scholars. In the mature sciences there is no apparent function for the equivalent of an art museum or a library of classics. Scientists know when books, and even journals, are out of date. Though they do not then destroy them, they do, as any historian of science can testify, transfer them from the active departmental library to desuetude in the general university depository. Up-to-date works have taken their place, and they are all that the further progress of science requires.

This characteristic of paradigms is closely related to another, and one that has a particular relevance to my selection of the term. In receiving a paradigm the scientific community commits itself, consciously or not, to the view that the fundamental problems there resolved have, in fact, been solved once and for all. That is what Lagrange meant when he said of Newton: "There is but one universe, and it can happen to but one man in the world's history to be the interpreter of its laws."[1] The example of either Aristotle or Einstein proves Lagrange wrong, but that does not make the fact of his commitment less consequential to scientific development. Believing that what Newton had done need not be done again, Lagrange was not tempted to fundamental reinterpretations of nature. Instead, he could take up where the men who shared his Newtonian paradigm had left off, striving both for neater formulations of that paradigm and for an articulation that would bring it into closer and closer agreement with observations of nature. That sort of work is undertaken only by those who feel that the model they have chosen is entirely secure. There is nothing quite like it in the arts, and the parallels in the social sciences are at best partial. Paradigms determine a developmental pattern for the mature sciences that is unlike the one familiar in other fields.

That difference could be illustrated by comparing the development of a paradigm-based science with that of, say, philosophy or literature. But the same effect can be achieved more economically by contrasting the early developmental pattern of almost any science with the pattern characteristic of the same field in its maturity. I cannot here avoid putting the point too starkly, but what I have in mind is this. Excepting in those fields which, like biochemistry, originated in the combination of existing specialties, paradigms are a relatively late acquisition in the course of scientific development. During its early years a science proceeds without them, or at least without any so unequivocal and so binding as those named illustratively above. Physical optics before Newton or the study

[1] Quoted in this form by S. F. Mason, *Main Currents of Scientific Thought* (New York, 1956) 254. The original, which is identical in spirit but not in words, seems to derive from Delambre's contemporary éloge, *Memoires de . . . l'Institut . . ., année 1812*, 2nd part (Paris, 1816) p. xlvi.

of heat before Black and Lavoisier exemplifies the pre-paradigm developmental pattern that I shall immediately examine in the history of electricity. While it continues, until, that is, a first paradigm is reached, the development of a science resembles that of the arts and of most social sciences more closely than it resembles the pattern which astronomy, say, had already acquired in Antiquity and which all the natural sciences make familiar today.

To catch the difference between pre- and post-paradigm scientific development consider a single example. In the early eighteenth century, as in the seventeenth and earlier, there were almost as many views about the nature of electricity as there were important electrical experimenters, men like Hauksbee, Gray, Desaguliers, Du Fay, Nollet, Watson, and Franklin. All their numerous concepts of electricity had something in common — they were partially derived from experiment and observation and partially from one or another version of the mechanico-corpuscular philosophy that guided all scientific research of the day. Yet these common elements gave their work no more than a family resemblance. We are forced to recognize the existence of several competing schools and sub-schools, each deriving strength from its relation to a particular version (Cartesian or Newtonian) of the corpuscular metaphysics, and each emphasizing the particular cluster of electrical phenomena which its own theory could do most to explain. Other observations were dealt with by *ad hoc* elaborations or remained as outstanding problems for further research.[1]

One early group of electricians followed seventeenth-century practice, and thus took attraction and frictional generation as the fundamental electrical phenomena. They tended to treat repulsion as a secondary effect (in the seventeenth century it had been attributed to some sort of mechanical rebounding) and also to postpone for as long as possible both discussion and systematic research on Gray's newly discovered effect, electrical conduction. Another closely related group regarded repulsion

[1] Much documentation for this account of electrical development can be retrieved from Duane Roller and Duane H. D. Roller, *The Development of the Concept of Electric Charge: Electricity from the Greeks to Coulomb* (Harvard Case Histories in Experimental Science, VIII, Cambridge, Mass., 1954) and from I. B. Cohen, *Franklin and Newton: An Inquiry into Speculative Newtonian Experimental Science and Franklin's Work in Electricity as an Example Thereof* (Philadelphia, 1956). For analytic detail I am, however, very much indebted to a still unpublished paper by my student, John L. Heilbron, who has also assisted in the preparation of the three notes that follow.

as the fundamental effect, while still another took attraction and repulsion together to be equally elementary manifestations of electricity. Each of these groups modified its theory and research accordingly, but they then had as much difficulty as the first in accounting for any but the simplest conduction effects. Those effects provided the starting point for still a third group, one which tended to speak of electricity as a "fluid" that ran through conductors rather than as an "effluvium" that emanated from non-conductors. This group, in its turn, had difficulty reconciling its theory with a number of attractive and repulsive effects.[1]

At various times all these schools made significant contributions to the body of concepts, phenomena, and techniques from which Franklin drew the first paradigm for electrical science. Any definition of the scientist that excludes the members of these schools will exclude their modern successors as well. Yet anyone surveying the development of electricity before Franklin may well conclude that, though the field's practitioners were scientists, the immediate result of their activity was something less than science. Because the body of belief he could take for granted was very small, each electrical experimenter felt forced to begin by building his field anew from its foundations. In doing so his choice of supporting observation and experiment was relatively free, for the set of standard methods and phenomena that every electrician must employ and explain was extraordinarily small. As a result, throughout the first half of the century, electrical investigations tended to circle back over the same ground again and again. New effects were repeatedly discovered, but many of them were rapidly lost again. Among those lost were many effects due to what we should now describe as inductive charging and also Du Fay's famous discovery of the two sorts of electrification. Franklin and Kinnersley were surprised when, some fifteen years later, the latter discovered that a charged ball which was repelled

[1] This division into schools is still somewhat too simplistic. After 1720 the basic division is between the French school (Du Fay, Nollet, etc.) who base their theories on attraction–repulsion effects and the English school (Desaguliers, Watson, etc.) who concentrate on conduction effects. Each group had immense difficulty in explaining the phenomena that the other took to be basic. (See, for example, Needham's report of Lemonier's investigations, in *Philosophical Transactions*, XLIV, 1746, p. 247). Within each of these groups, and particularly the English, one can trace further subdivision depending upon whether attraction or repulsion is considered the more fundamental electrical effect.

by rubbed glass would be attracted by rubbed sealing-wax or amber.[1] In the absence of a well-articulated and widely received theory (a desideratum which no science possesses from its very beginning and which few if any of the social sciences have achieved today), the situation could hardly have been otherwise. During the first half of the eighteenth century there was no way for electricians to distinguish consistently between electrical and non-electrical effects, between laboratory accidents and essential novelties, or between striking demonstration and experiments which revealed the essential nature of electricity.

This is the state of affairs which Franklin changed.[2] His theory explained so many — though not all — of the electrical effects recognized by the various earlier schools that within a generation all electricians had been converted to some view very like it. Though it did not resolve quite all disagreements, Franklin's theory was electricity's first paradigm, and its existence gives a new tone and flavour to the electrical researches of the last decades of the eighteenth century. The end of inter-school debate ended the constant reiteration of fundamentals; confidence that they were on the right track

[1] Du Fay's discovery that there are two sorts of electricity and that these are mutually attractive but self-repulsive is reported and documented in great experimental detail in the fourth of his famous memoirs on electricity: "De l'Attraction & Répulsion des Corps Electriques", *Memoires de . . . l'Académie . . . de l'année 1733* (Paris, 1735) 457–76. These memoirs were well known and widely cited, but Desaguliers seems to be the only electrician who, for almost two decades, even mentions that some charged bodies will attract each other (*Philosophical Transactions . . .*, XLII, 1741–2, pp. 140–3). For Franklin's and Kinnersley's "surprise" see I. B. Cohen (ed.), *Benjamin Franklin's Experiments: A New Edition of Franklin's Experiments and Observations on Electricity* (Cambridge, Mass., 1941) 250–5. Note also that, though Kinnersley had *produced* the effect, neither he nor Franklin seems ever to have *recognized* that two resinously charged bodies would repel each other, a phenomenon directly contrary to Franklin's theory.

[2] The change is not, of course, due to Franklin alone nor did it occur overnight. Other electricians, most notably William Watson, anticipated parts of Franklin's theory. More important, it was only after essential modifications, due principally to Aepinus, that Franklin's theory gained the general currency requisite for a paradigm. And even then there continued to be two formulations of the theory: the Franklin–Aepinus one-fluid form and a two-fluid form due principally to Symmer. Electricians soon reached the conclusion that no electrical test could possibly discriminate between the two theories. Until the discovery of the battery, when the choice between a one-fluid and two-fluid theory began to make an occasional difference in the design and analysis of experiments, the two were equivalent.

encouraged electricians to undertake more precise, esoteric, and consuming sorts of work. Freed from concern with any and all electrical phenomena, the newly united group could pursue selected phenomena in far more detail, designing much special equipment for the task and employing it more stubbornly and systematically than electricians had ever done before. In the hands of a Cavendish, a Coulomb, or a Volta the collection of electrical facts and the articulation of electrical theory were, for the first time, highly directed activities. As a result the efficiency and effectiveness of electrical research increased immensely, providing evidence for a societal version of Francis Bacon's acute methodological dictum: "Truth emerges more readily from error than from confusion."

Obviously I exaggerate both the speed and the completeness with which the transition to a paradigm occurs. But that does not make the phenomenon itself less real. The maturation of electricity as a science is not coextensive with the entire development of the field. Writers on electricity during the first four decades of the eighteenth century possessed far more information about electrical phenomena than had their sixteenth- and seventeenth-century predecessors. During the half-century after 1745 very few new sorts of electrical phenomena were added to their lists. Nevertheless, in important respects the electrical writings of the last two decades of the century seemed further removed from those of Gray, Du Fay, and even Franklin than are the writings of these early eighteenth-century electricians from those of their predecessors a hundred years before. Some time between 1740 and 1780 electricians, as a group, gained what astronomers had achieved in Antiquity, students of motion in the Middle Ages, of physical optics in the late seventeenth century, and of historical geology in the early nineteenth. They had, that is, achieved a paradigm, possession of which enabled them to take the foundation of their field for granted and to push on to more concrete and recondite problems.[1] Except with the advantage of hindsight, it is hard to find another criterion that so clearly proclaims a field of science.

[1] Note that this first electrical paradigm was fully effective only until 1800, when the discovery of the battery and the multiplication of electrochemical effects initiated a revolution in electrical theory. Until a new paradigm emerged from that revolution, the literature of electricity, particularly in England, reverted in many respects to the tone characteristic of the first half of the eighteenth century.

These remarks should begin to clarify what I take a paradigm to be. It is, in the first place, a fundamental scientific achievement and one which includes both a theory and some exemplary applications to the results of experiment and observation. More important, it is an open-ended achievement, one which leaves all sorts of research still to be done. And, finally, it is an accepted achievement in the sense that it is received by a group whose members no longer try to rival it or to create alternates for it. Instead, they attempt to extend and exploit it in a variety of ways to which I shall shortly turn. That discussion of the work that paradigms leave to be done will make both their role and the reasons for their special efficacy clearer still. But first there is one rather different point to be made about them. Though the reception of a paradigm seems historically prerequisite to the most effective sorts of scientific research, the paradigms which enhance research effectiveness need not be and usually are not permanent. On the contrary, the developmental pattern of mature science is usually from paradigm to paradigm. It differs from the pattern characteristic of the early or pre-paradigm period not by the total elimination of debate over fundamentals, but by the drastic restriction of such debate to occasional periods of paradigm change.

Ptolemy's *Almagest* was not, for example, any less a paradigm because the research tradition that descended from it had ultimately to be replaced by an incompatible one derived from the work of Copernicus and Kepler. Nor was Newton's *Opticks* less a paradigm for eighteenth-century students of light because it was later replaced by the ether-wave theory of Young and Fresnel, a paradigm which in its turn gave way to the electromagnetic displacement theory that descends from Maxwell. Undoubtedly the research work that any given paradigm permits results in lasting contributions to the body of scientific knowledge and technique, but paradigms themselves are very often swept aside and replaced by others that are quite incompatible with them. We can have no recourse to notions like the 'truth' or 'validity' of paradigms in our attempt to understand the special efficacy of the research which their reception permits.

On the contrary, the historian can often recognize that in declaring an older paradigm out of date or in rejecting the approach of some one of the pre-paradigm schools a scientific community has rejected the embryo of an important scientific perception to which it would later be forced to return. But it is very far from clear that the profession delayed scientific development by doing so. Would quantum mechanics have been born sooner if nineteenth-century scientists had been more willing to admit that Newton's corpuscular view of light might still have something significant to teach them about nature? I think not, although in the arts, the humanities, and many social sciences that less doctrinaire view is very often adopted toward classic achievements of the past. Or would astronomy and dynamics have advanced more rapidly if scientists had recognized that Ptolemy and Copernicus had chosen equally legitimate means to describe the earth's position? That view was, in fact, suggested during the seventeenth century, and it has since been confirmed by relativity theory. But in the interim it was firmly rejected together with Ptolemaic astronomy, emerging again only in the very late nineteenth century when, for the first time, it had concrete relevance to unsolved problems generated by the continuing practice of non-relativistic physics. One could argue, as indeed by implication I shall, that close eighteenth- and nineteenth-century attention either to the work of Ptolemy or to the relativistic views of Descartes, Huygens, and Leibniz would have delayed rather than accelerated the revolution in physics with which the twentieth century began. Advance from paradigm to paradigm rather than through the continuing competition between recognized classics may be a functional as well as a factual characteristic of mature scientific development.

Much that has been said so far is intended to indicate that — except during occasional extraordinary periods to be discussed in the last section of this paper — the practitioners of a mature scientific specialty are deeply committed to some one paradigm-based way of regarding and investigating nature. Their paradigm tells them about the sorts of entities with which the universe is populated and about the way the members of that population behave; in addition, it informs them of the questions that may legitimately be asked about nature and of the techniques that can properly be used in the search for answers to them. In fact, a paradigm tells scientists so much that the questions it leaves for research seldom have great intrinsic interest to those outside the profession. Though educated men as a group may be fascinated to hear about the spectrum of fundamental particles or about the processes of molecular replication, their interest is usually quickly exhausted by an account of the beliefs that already underlie research on these problems. The outcome of the individual research project is indifferent to them, and their interest is unlikely to awaken again until, as with parity nonconservation, research unexpectedly leads to paradigm-change and to a consequent alteration in the beliefs which guide research. That, no doubt, is why both historians and popularizers have devoted so much of their attention to the revolutionary episodes which result in change of paradigm and have so largely neglected the sort of work that even the greatest scientists necessarily do most of the time.

My point will become clearer if I now ask what it is that the existence of a paradigm leaves for the scientific community to do. The answer — as obvious as the related existence of resistance to innovation and as often brushed under the carpet — is that scientists, given a paradigm, strive with all their might and skill to bring it into closer and closer agreement with nature. Much of their effort, particularly in the early stages of a paradigm's development, is directed to articulating the paradigm, rendering it more precise in areas where the original formulation has inevitably been vague. For example, knowing that electricity was a fluid whose individual particles act upon one another at a distance, electricians after Franklin could attempt to determine the quantitative law of force between particles of electricity. Others could seek the mutual interdependence of spark length, electroscope deflection, quantity of electricity, and conductor-configuration. These were the sorts of problems upon which Coulomb, Cavendish, and Volta worked in the last decades of the eighteenth century, and they have many parallels in the development of every other mature science. Contemporary attempts to determine the quantum mechanical forces governing the interactions of nucleons fall precisely in this same category, paradigm-articulation.

That sort of problem is not the only challenge which a paradigm sets for the community that embraces it. There are always many areas in which a paradigm is assumed to work but to which it has not, in fact, yet been applied. Matching the paradigm to nature in these areas often engages much of the best scientific talent in any generation. The eighteenth-century attempts to develop a Newtonian theory of vibrating strings provide one significant example, and the current work on a quantum mechanical theory of solids provides another. In addition, there is always much fascinating work to be done in improving the match between a paradigm and nature in an area where at least limited agreement has already been demonstrated. Theoretical work on problems like these is illustrated by eighteenth-century research on the perturbations that cause planets to deviate from their Keplerian orbits as well as by the elaborate twentieth-century theory of the spectra of complex atoms and molecules. And accompanying all these problems and still others besides is a recurring series of instrumental hurdles. Special apparatus had to be invented and built to permit Coulomb's determination of the electrical force law. New sorts of telescopes were required for the observations that, when completed, demanded an improved Newtonian perturbation theory. The design and construction of more flexible and more powerful accelerators is a continuing desideratum in the attempt to articulate more powerful theories of nuclear forces. These are the sorts of work on which almost all scientists spend almost all of their time.[1]

Probably this epitome of normal scientific research requires no elaboration in this place, but there are two points that must now be made about it. First, all of the problems mentioned above were paradigm-dependent, often in several ways. Some — for example the derivation of perturbation terms in Newtonian planetary theory — could not even have been stated in the absence of an appropriate paradigm. With the transition from Newtonian to relativity theory a few of them became different problems and not all of these have yet been solved. Other problems — for example the attempt to determine a law of electric forces — could be and were at least vaguely stated before the emergence of the paradigm with which they were ultimately solved. But in that older form they proved intractable. The men who described electrical attractions and repulsions in terms of effluvia attempted to measure the resulting forces by placing a charged disc at a measured distance beneath one pan of a balance. Under those circumstances no consistent or interpretable results were obtained. The prerequisite for success proved to be a paradigm that reduced electrical action to a gravity-like action between point particles at a distance. After Franklin electricians thought of electrical action in those terms; both Coulomb and Cavendish designed their apparatus

[1] The discussion in this paragraph and the next is considerably elaborated in my paper, "The function of measurement in modern physical science", *Isis*, LII (1961) 161–93.

accordingly. Finally, in both these cases and in all the others as well a commitment to the paradigm was needed simply to provide adequate motivation. Who would design and build elaborate special-purpose apparatus, or who would spend months trying to solve a particular differential equation, without a quite firm guarantee that his effort, if successful, would yield the anticipated fruit?

This reference to the anticipated outcome of a research project points to the second striking characteristic of what I am now calling normal, or paradigm-based, research. The scientist engaged in it does not at all fit the prevalent image of the scientist as explorer or as inventor of brand new theories which permit striking and unexpected predictions. On the contrary, in all the problems discussed above everything but the detail of the outcome was known in advance. No scientist who accepted Franklin's paradigm could doubt that there was a law of attraction between small particles of electricity, and they could reasonably suppose that it would take a simple algebraic form. Some of them had even guessed that it would prove to be an inverse square law. Nor did Newtonian astronomers and physicists doubt that Newton's law of motion and of gravitation could ultimately be made to yield the observed motions of the moon and planets even though, for over a century, the complexity of the requisite mathematics prevented good agreement's being uniformly obtained. In all these problems, as in most others that scientists undertake, the challenge is not to uncover the unknown but to obtain the known. Their fascination lies not in what success may be expected to disclose but in the difficulty of obtaining success at all. Rather than resembling exploration, normal research seems like the effort to assemble a Chinese cube whose finished outline is known from the start.

Those are the characteristics of normal research that I had in mind when, at the start of this essay, I described the man engaged in it as a puzzle-solver, like the chess player. The paradigm he has acquired through prior training provides him with the rules of the game, describes the pieces with which it must be played, and indicates the nature of the required outcome. His task is to manipulate those pieces within the rules in such a way that the required outcome is produced. If he fails, as most scientists do in at least their first attacks upon any given problem, that failure speaks only to his lack of skill. It cannot call into question the rules which his paradigm has supplied, for without those rules there would have been no puzzle with which to wrestle in the first place. No wonder, then, that the problems (or puzzles) which the practitioner of a mature science normally undertakes presuppose a deep commitment to a paradigm. And how fortunate it is that that commitment is not lightly given up. Experience shows that, in almost all cases, the reiterated efforts, either of the individual or of the professional group, do at last succeed in producing within the paradigm a solution to even the most stubborn problems. That is one of the ways in which science advances. Under those circumstances can we be surprised that scientists resist paradigm-change? What they are defending is, after all, neither more nor less than the basis of their professional way of life.

By now one principal advantage of what I began by calling scientific dogmatism should be apparent. As a glance at any Baconian natural history or a survey of the pre-paradigm development of any science will show, nature is vastly too complex to be explored even approximately at random. Something must tell the scientist where to look and what to look for, and that something, though it may not last beyond his generation, is the paradigm with which his education as a scientist has supplied him. Given that paradigm and the requisite confidence in it, the scientist largely ceases to be an explorer at all, or at least to be an explorer of the unknown. Instead, he struggles to articulate and concretize the known, designing much special-purpose apparatus and many special-purpose adaptations of theory for that task. From those puzzles of design and adaptation he gets his pleasure. Unless he is extraordinarily lucky, it is upon his success with them that his reputation will depend. Inevitably the enterprise which engages him is characterized, at any one time, by drastically restricted vision. But within the region upon which vision is focused the continuing attempt to match paradigms to nature results in a knowledge and understanding of esoteric detail that could not have been achieved in any other way. From Copernicus and the problem of precession to Einstein and the photo-electric effect, the progress of science has again and again depended upon just such esoterica. One great virtue of commitment to paradigms is that it frees scientists to engage themselves with tiny puzzles.

Nevertheless, this image of scientific research as puzzle-solving or paradigm-matching must be, at the very least, thoroughly incomplete. Though the scientist may not be an explorer, scientists do again and again discover new and unexpected sorts of phenomena. Or again, though the scientist does not normally strive to invent new sorts of basic theories, such theories have repeatedly emerged from the continuing practice of research. But neither of these types of innovation would arise if the enterprise I have been calling normal science were always successful. In fact, the man engaged in puzzle-solving very often resists substantive novelty, and he does so for good reason. To him it is a change in the rules of the game and any change of rules is intrinsically subversive. That subversive element is, of course, most apparent in major theoretical innovations like those associated with the names of Copernicus, Lavoisier, or Einstein. But the discovery of an unanticipated phenomenon can have the same destructive effects although usually on a smaller group and for a far shorter time. Once he had performed his first follow-up experiments, Röntgen's glowing screen demonstrated that previously standard cathode ray equipment was behaving in ways for which no one had made allowance. There was an unanticipated variable to be controlled; earlier researches, already on their way to becoming paradigms, would require re-evaluation; old puzzles would have to be solved again under a somewhat different set of rules. Even so readily assimilable a discovery as that of X-rays can violate a paradigm that has previously guided research. It follows that, if the normal puzzle-solving activity were altogether successful, the development of science could lead to no fundamental innovations at all.

But of course normal science is not always successful, and in recognizing that fact we encounter what I take to be the second great advantage of paradigm-based research. Unlike many of the early electricians, the practitioner of a mature science knows with considerable precision what sort of result he should gain from his research. As a consequence he is in a particularly favourable position to recognize when a research problem has gone astray. Perhaps, like Galvani or Röntgen, he encounters an effect that he knows ought not to occur. Or perhaps, like Copernicus, Planck, or Einstein, he concludes that the reiterated failures of his predecessors in matching a paradigm to nature is presumptive evidence of the need to change the rules under which a match is to be sought. Or perhaps, like Franklin or Lavoisier, he decides after repeated attempts that no existing theory can be articulated to account for some newly discovered effect. In all of these ways and in others besides the practice of normal puzzle-solving science can and inevitably does lead to the isolation and recognition of anomaly. That recognition proves, I think, prerequisite for almost all discoveries of new sorts of phenomena and for all fundamental innovations in scientific theory. After a first paradigm has been achieved, a breakdown in the rules of the pre-established game is the usual prelude to significant scientific innovation.

Examine the case of discoveries first. Many of them, like Coulomb's law or a new element to fill an empty spot in the periodic table, present no problem. They were not 'new sorts of phenomena' but discoveries anticipated through a paradigm and achieved by expert puzzle-solvers: that sort of discovery is a natural product of what I have been calling normal science. But not all discoveries are of that sort: many could not have been anticipated by any extrapolation from the known; in a sense they had to be made 'by accident'. On the other hand the accident through which they emerged could not ordinarily have occurred to a man just looking around. In the mature sciences discovery demands much special equipment, both conceptual and instrumental, and that special equipment has invariably been developed and deployed for the pursuit of the puzzles of normal research. Discovery results when that equipment fails to function as it should. Furthermore, since some sort of at least temporary failure occurs during almost every research project, discovery results only when the failure is particularly stubborn or striking and only when it seems to raise questions about accepted beliefs and procedures. Established paradigms are thus often doubly prerequisite to discoveries. Without them the project that goes astray would not have been undertaken. And even when the project has gone astray, as most do for a while, the paradigm can help to determine whether the failure is worth pursuing. The usual and proper response to a failure in puzzle-solving is to blame one's talents or one's tools and to turn next to another problem. If he is not to waste time, the scientist must be able to discriminate essential anomaly from mere failure.

That pattern — discovery through an anomaly that calls established techniques and beliefs in doubt — has been repeated again and again in the course of scientific development. Newton discovered the composition of white light when he was unable to reconcile measured dispersion with that predicted by Snell's recently discovered law of refraction.[1] The electric battery was discovered when existing detectors of static charges failed to behave as Franklin's paradigm said they should.[2] The planet Neptune was discovered through an effort to account for recognized anomalies in the orbit of Uranus.[3] The element chlorine and the compound carbon monoxide emerged during attempts to reconcile Lavoisier's new chemistry with laboratory observations.[4] The so-called noble gases were the products of a long series of investigations initiated by a small but persistent anomaly in the measured density of atmospheric nitrogen.[5] The electron was posited to explain some anomalous properties of electrical conduction through gases, and its spin was suggested to account for other sorts of anomalies observed in atomic spectra.[6] Both the neutron and the neutrino provide other examples, and the list could be extended almost indefinitely.[7] In the mature sciences unexpected novelties are discovered principally after something has gone wrong.

If, however, anomaly is significant in preparing the way for new discoveries, it plays a still larger role in the invention of new theories. Contrary to a prevalent, though by no means universal, belief, new theories are not invented to account for observations that have not previously been ordered by theory at all. Rather, at almost all times in the development of any advanced science, all the facts whose relevance is admitted seem either to fit existing theory well or to be in the process of

[1] See my "Newton's optical papers" in I. B. Cohen (ed.), *Isaac Newton's Papers & Letters on Natural Philosophy* (Cambridge, Mass., 1958) 27–45.

[2] Luigi Galvani, *Commentary on the Effects of Electricity on Muscular Motion*, trans. by M. G. Foley with notes and an introduction by I. B. Cohen (Norwalk, Conn., 1954) 27–9.

[3] Angus Armitage, *A Century of Astronomy* (London, 1950) 111–15.

[4] For chlorine see Ernst von Meyer, *A History of Chemistry from the Earliest Times to the Present Day*, trans. G. M'Gowan (London, 1891) 224–7. For carbon monoxide see Hermann Kopp, *Geschichte der Chemie* (Braunschweig, 1845) III, 294–6.

[5] William Ramsay, *The Gases of the Atmosphere: the History of their Discovery* London, 1896) Chs. 4 and 5.

[6] J. J. Thomson, *Recollections and Reflections* (New York, 1937) 325–71; T. W. Chalmers, *Historic Researches: Chapters in the History of Physical and Chemical Discovery* (London, 1949) 187–217; and F. K. Richtmeyer, E. H. Kennard and T. Lauritsen, *Introduction to Modern Physics* (5th ed., New York, 1955) 212.

[7] Ibid. pp. 466–470; and Rogers D. Rusk, *Introduction to Atomic and Nuclear Physics* (New York, 1958) 328–30.

conforming. Making them conform better provides many of the standard problems of normal science. And almost always committed scientists succeed in solving them. But they do not always succeed, and, when they fail repeatedly and in increasing numbers, then their sector of the scientific community encounters what I am elsewhere calling 'crisis'. Recognizing that something is fundamentally wrong with the theory upon which their work is based, scientists will attempt more fundamental articulations of theory than those which were admissible before. (Characteristically, at times of crisis, one encounters numerous different versions of the paradigm theory.[1]) Simultaneously they will often begin more nearly random experimentation within the area of difficulty hoping to discover some effect that will suggest a way to set the situation right. Only under circumstances like these, I suggest, is a fundamental innovation in scientific theory both invented and accepted.

The state of Ptolemaic astronomy was, for example, a recognized scandal before Copernicus proposed a basic change in astronomical theory, and the preface in which Copernicus described his reasons for innovation provides a classic description of the crisis state.[2] Galileo's contributions to the study of motion took their point of departure from recognized difficulties with medieval theory, and Newton reconciled Galileo's mechanics with Copernicanism.[3] Lavoisier's new chemistry was a product of the anomalies created jointly by the proliferation

[1] One classic example, for which see the reference cited below in the next note, is the proliferation of geocentric astronomical systems in the years before Copernicus's heliocentric reform. Another, for which see J. R. Partington and D. McKie, "Historical studies of the phlogiston theory", *Annals of Science*, II (1937) 361–404, III (1938) 1–58, 337–71, and IV (1939) 113–49, is the multiplicity of 'phlogiston theories' produced in response to the general recognition that weight is always gained on combustion and to the experimental discovery of many new gases after 1760. The same proliferation of versions of accepted theories occurred in mechanics and electromagnetism in the two decades preceding Einstein's special relativity theory. (E. T. Whittaker, *History of the Theories of Aether and Electricity*, 2nd ed., 2 vols., London, 1951–53, I, Ch. 12, and II, Ch. 2. I concur in the widespread judgment that this is a very biased account of the genesis of relativity theory, but it contains just the detail necessary to make the point here at issue.)

[2] T. S. Kuhn, *The Copernican Revolution: Planetary Astronomy in the Development of Western Thought* (Cambridge, Mass., 1957) 133–40.

[3] For Galileo see Alexandre Koyré, *Études Galiléennes* (3 vols., Paris, 1939); for Newton see Kuhn, op. cit. pp. 228–60 and 289–91.

of new gases and the first systematic studies of weight relations.[1] The wave theory of light was developed amid growing concern about anomalies in the relation of diffraction and polarization effects to Newton's corpuscular theory.[2] Thermodynamics, which later came to seem a superstructure for existing sciences, was established only at the price of rejecting the previously paradigmatic caloric theory.[3] Quantum mechanics was born from a variety of difficulties surrounding black-body radiation, specific heat, and the photo-electric effect.[4] Again the list could be extended, but the point should already be clear. New theories arise from work conducted under old ones, and they do so only when something is observed to have gone wrong. Their prelude is widely recognized anomaly, and that recognition can come only to a group that knows very well what it would mean to have things go right.

Because limitations of space and time force me to stop at this point, my case for dogmatism must remain schematic. I shall not here even attempt to deal with the fine-structure that scientific development exhibits at all times. But there is another more positive qualification of my thesis, and it requires one closing comment. Though successful research demands a deep commitment to the *status quo*, innovation remains at the heart of the enterprise. Scientists are *trained* to operate as puzzle-solvers from established rules, but they are also *taught* to regard themselves as explorers and inventors who know no rules except those dictated by nature itself. The result is an acquired tension, partly within the individual and partly within the

[1] For the proliferation of gases see Partington, *A Short History of Chemistry* (2nd ed., London, 1948) Ch. 6; for the role of weight relations see Henry Guerlac, "The origin of Lavoisier's work on combustion", *Archives internationales d'histoire des sciences*, XII (1959) 113–35.

[2] Whittaker, *Aether and Electricity*, II, 94–109; William Whewell, *History of the Inductive Sciences* (revised ed., 3 vols., London, 1847) II, 213–71; and Kuhn, "Function of measurement", p. 181 n.

[3] For a general account of the beginnings of thermodynamics (including much relevant bibliography) see my "Energy conservation as an example of simultaneous discovery" in Marshall Clagett (ed.), *Critical Problems in the History of Science* (Madison, Wisc., 1959) 321–56. For the special problems presented to caloric theorists by energy conservation see the Carnot papers, there cited in n. 2, and also S. P. Thompson, *The Life of William Thomson, Baron Kelvin of Largs* (2 vols., London, 1910) Ch. 6.

[4] Richtmeyer et al., *Modern Physics*, pp. 89–94, 124–32, and 409–14; Gerald Holton, *Introduction to Concepts and Theories in Physical Science* (Cambridge, Mass., 1953) 528–45.

community, between professional skills on the one hand and professional ideology on the other. Almost certainly that tension and the ability to sustain it are important to science's success. In so far as I have dealt exclusively with the dependence of research upon tradition, my discussion is inevitably one-sided. On this whole subject there is a great deal more to be said.

But to be one-sided is not necessarily to be wrong, and it may be an essential preliminary to a more penetrating examination of the requisites for successful scientific life. Almost no one, perhaps no one at all, needs to be told that the vitality of science depends upon the continuation of occasional tradition-shattering innovations. But the apparently contrary dependence of research upon a deep commitment to established tools and beliefs receives the very minimum of attention. I urge that it be given more. Until that is done, some of the most striking characteristics of scientific education and development will remain extraordinarily difficult to understand.

Commentaries

Commentary by A. Rupert Hall

Allow me first to summarize my sense of Mr. Kuhn's paper. In the first place, he is concerned to establish the concept of what he calls a "paradigm" in science. This, he writes (p. 358), is "a fundamental scientific achievement and one which includes both a theory and some exemplary applications to the results of experiments and observation. More important, however," he goes on, "it is an open-ended achievement, one which leaves all sorts of research still to be done. And finally it is an accepted achievement in the sense that it is received by a group whose members no longer try to rival it or to create alternates for it." The paradigm, then, includes besides the theoretical structure of some part of science the experimental or observational technique which the scientist employs, and the whole body of connexions between the experimental or observational level, and the theoretical or explanatory level, which in turn is conditioned by certain fixed postulates. Perhaps Mr. Kuhn will accept a certain translation of his term paradigm into somewhat simpler language if I say he is concerned with the intellectual framework within which most scientists, at any given time, think and work. Now Mr. Kuhn's point is that his framework is, in most sciences at most times, essentially stable and unchanging. In fact he argues that any generation of scientists tends to resist a change within it. Not, of course, because they are opposed to discovery or even to innovation so long as the innovation is a mild one — a mere internal displacement. So we see Joseph Priestley, to add an example to those given by Mr. Kuhn, a discoverer if ever there was one, nevertheless resisting reconstruction of the intellectual framework of the phlogiston theory, and seeking (by means which seemed to some in his own time mere expedients) so to modify but not destroy a familiar framework that it would accommodate the new chemical discoveries to which he had himself contributed so greatly.

This last point seems to me to be particularly important. Mr. Kuhn is quite right to point to the general historical reluctance to exploit, initially, the breakdown of a prevailing theory. The first move is to attempt to patch it up, to redraft definitions or modify constants. An established theory, whether it be Aristotle's, or Ptolemy's, or Newton's, is never rejected at the first appearance of a contrary instance, even one that it is so well verified as to constitute a true crux. I think we might go even further than Mr. Kuhn and point out that at the stage where the old framework is already bursting at the seams, when almost everyone recognizes that the paradigm hardly fits the facts any longer, there is still very often a tendency to reassemble its parts with the very minimum of changes, so that a new paradigm is still something of a compromise with the old. The conspicuous example, on which I need not elaborate, is that of the Copernican universe, so revolutionary in its basic premise, so conservative in almost everything else. For the same reason certain reconstructions of the theoretical framework of a science have been incomplete, as again was Copernicus's in relation to mechanics, or Harvey's in relation to physiology. For while Harvey assures us of the circulation of the blood, he says not a word to confirm or deny all else concerning the role of the blood in physiological function that was so essential to the traditional Galenic scheme of things.

I do not mean to suggest — and I presume that in spite of the title of his paper Mr. Kuhn does not mean to suggest — that the limitation to innovation that I have just mentioned springs merely from innate conservatism. On the contrary, it is produced in some cases, like Harvey's, by sheer lack of information; Harvey could not clear up every problem of vascular physiology, nor Lavoisier every question concerning oxidation, at one stroke. And innovation is restricted again by the inability of the imagination to go beyond the necessary — to foresee *all* the consequences of what has been begun. Hence a new paradigm is not merely open-ended, as Mr. Kuhn says, it may also contain elements — as Copernicus's did and Galileo's and Lavoisier's — that are simply false — false because they are carry-overs from an earlier framework of thought.

With this argument of Mr. Kuhn's it seems to me, we can have little quarrel. Nor can we object to his contention that the establishment of paradigms is a feature of a developed science, that lack of common ground and absence of common principles are tokens of immaturity. Speaking of Greek science Mr. Edelstein in his paper has made exactly the same point:

"Rival systems of science were competing with one another, rival systems which were in fact rival sciences. For there was nothing one could call science in the modern sense of the term, a body of knowledge valid everywhere, a system of principles, of rules of procedure and of theories, well defined and generally accepted." (p. 29).

Everyone will readily concede that without agreement on some fundamentals, above all agreements on (*a*) the form of a scientific argument and (*b*) the tests of its validity, no cumulative progress of science is possible at all. And as Mr. Kuhn points out, such contributions to that progress as most individual scientists ever make do not disturb those fundamentals; they merely confirm them, or reveal fresh entailments from them.

That this is so sets out in another shape the paradox, involved in the fact that science is both dogmatic and devoted to discovery, that Mr. Kuhn points out at the beginning of his paper and in his remarks on the education of scientists. (Here, parenthetically, I must reject Mr. Kuhn's statement (p. 351) that scientific education has been dogmatic only since about 1800. What of the medieval "authorities"? If, later, it appears less so it is rather because science was rarely taught systematically. Jacques Rohault was dogmatic enough.) How is the intellectual freedom which is essential to originality in science to be reconciled with the necessity of adhering to a certain code, to established themes and recognized practices?

Mr. Kuhn himself resolves this paradox in two ways. In the first place, there is scientific progress within the terms of the existing accepted framework; it is perfected and extended in its application to the facts of experiment and observation. In the second place, when sufficiently significant "anomalies" or "discoveries" have accumulated which the framework cannot accommodate, and when — a crucial condition — a scientist has appeared with sufficient ability to offer a more adequate alternative — the framework itself is replaced.

Here, it seems to me, certain things must be said against Mr. Kuhn's thesis, or at least in modification of it. Subjected to close examination, his concept of a rigid, textbook authenticated paradigm or intellectual framework, to which all scientists are firmly dedicated, as set out in the first part of his paper, begins to dissolve somewhat in the second. Mr. Kuhn now recognizes that it is rarely or never perfect; that acceptance of it is never complete. This is a very important concession: since it is difficult to conceive, historically, of any theoretical model in science that has not been subjected to constant tinkering throughout its history. This was true of the dogmatically-taught systems of Aristotle and Galen and Ptolemy. It was true of the phlogiston theory and of Newtonian mechanics. No scientific concept or system of scientific reasoning has ever been regarded as *absolutely* sacrosanct.

The most obvious theoretical reason for this restriction of dogmatism in science is, I suppose, the fact that no natural science constitutes a purely formal system. There is always a measure of doubt to be exploited or repressed about what the facts of nature are; a measure of doubt handled with crudity, for instance, in medieval science; with high refinement and sophistication in modern science. But there is another reason for it no less significant, in that (as Mr. Needham hinted in his reply to Mr. van der Waerden in the second session) there has never yet been a single unified intellectual framework for the whole of science. We find rather — in the science of the past as well as in that of the present — a whole series of paradigms (to use Mr. Kuhn's word once more) that are often overlapping and interpenetrating. Consequently there exist areas of inconsistency, not to say lacunae. It is as though a house consisted of many floors, on different levels, connected by rather ramshackle, *ad hoc* ladders and staircases. Borrowing examples from Mr. Kuhn, I could point out that the Ptolemaic paradigm never completely fitted with the Aristotelian, and that both were already disturbed, in the Middle Ages, by the nascence of a new one, concerning the science of motion.

Once we admit that the paradigm or intellectual framework is somewhat less than monolithic, and allow that in most periods it has been a somewhat crazy, rambling structure, then we may begin to wonder whether reluctance to change it, beyond narrow limits, is not as much due to lack of human capacity as to the weight, or inertia, of scientific dogma. For hardly anyone writing on a scientific subject, now or in the past, has been able to avoid making *some* decisions, some critical evaluations. Even a modern textbook on inorganic chemistry is not completely dictated by the nature of the subject even though all textbooks on inorganic chemistry must be very closely alike. The more we depart from textbooks to the "open end" of the framework, or to the intersection of one group of scientific theories with another, the more the limit upon change and originality is set not by anything in the nature of science, but by our own capacities. Dogma becomes less a necessity than an apology for weakness.

Therefore I find myself less of a friend to dogma in science — or at least to the dogmas that have prevailed in science — than Mr. Kuhn appears to be. I agree that routine science suffices for the routine work of, say, an analytical chemist or a botanical taxonomist. It suffices for describing what has not been described before, and even for explaining *within the existing terms of explanation* what has not been explained before. All this is important. One can do a good deal with any reasonably good theory once one has it. But all this is the small change of science. The structure of scientific change, surely, is conditioned by the really big shifts of ideas effected from time to time by rather few individuals. The scope of Mr. Kuhn's paper left him little opportunity to discuss this. Clearly it is true that most scientists are doing rather dull jobs most of the time; the same might be said of most historians and most painters. The vast majority of the human race is intellectually parasitic: the really interesting and important people are those who are not. History singles out the people who create dogmas, willy-nilly, rather than those who merely observe them.

Since Mr. Kuhn has not said very much on these larger shifts or earthquakes, the changes from one paradigm to another, perhaps I may be allowed one observation. That is, he does not seem to me to have distinguished adequately between his paradigms — appropriate to Ptolemaic astronomy or Newtonian mechanics, or to corpuscular and undulatory theories of light, or what have you — and the larger envelope of science. Obviously a corpuscularian theorist will regard all optical phenomena in a different way from that in which they are regarded by a wave-theorist. So also a Copernican astronomer will regard the celestial bodies otherwise than a Ptolemaic astronomer regards them. But the two cases, it seems to me, are not the same. The differences of aspect are not identical. In the former case the same tests of validity apply to either theory; in the latter they do not. At least, so it seems to me, though I have no space to go into that question now, and therefore it also seems to me that we cannot consider all problems of changes of paradigm, or scientific perspective, on the same footing. I should not imagine, to take another example, that one can proceed very far in equating as examples of scientific change, the Darwinian revolution with the Mendelian revolution: though I do not mean by that the former has, somehow, a greater ultimate significance.

Before I finish, I should like to thank Mr. Kuhn for a stimulating paper, and to express the hope that he will go on to consider the wider changes in scientific thought that he has obviously contemplated carefully, even though here he seems to be concerned rather with the minor tactics than with the grand strategy of scientific change.

Commentary by Michael Polanyi

The paper by Mr. Thomas Kuhn may arouse opposition from various quarters, but not from me. At the end of it he says that the dependence of research upon a deep commitment to established beliefs receives the very minimum of attention today. I could not agree more; I have tried in vain to call attention to this commitment for many years. I hope that if I join forces with Mr. Kuhn we may both do better. His mastery of the history of science should help to establish this fact so firmly that its vast implications will have to be faced by all.

Mr. Kuhn's paper introduces two new terms into the analysis of science; one is "dogma", the other "paradigm". He calls dogma the substance of what scientists are taught by textbooks in preparation for their career and says that this dogma is derived at any particular period from a major discovery which serves as a paradigm to that period. Thus dogma is merely a way of transmitting to succeeding generations a paradigm-based way of regarding and investigating nature to which scientific opinion is deeply committed at the time. The function of the paradigm is, in the words of Mr. Kuhn, to tell scientists

> about the sorts of entities with which the universe is populated and about the way the members of that population behave. And in addition it informs them of the questions that may legitimately be asked about nature and of the techniques that can properly be used in the search for answers to them.

A commitment to a paradigm has thus a function hardly distinguishable from that which I have ascribed to a heuristic vision, to a scientific belief, or a scientific conviction. Of such commitments I have said that they indicate to scientists

> the kinds of questions which seem reasonable and interesting to explore . . . the kind of conceptions and relations that should be upheld as plausible even when some evidence seemed to contradict

them; or which on the contrary should be rejected as unlikely even though there was evidence which seemed to favour them and which could not be readily explained on other grounds.[1]

I have also identified these commitments with the holding of the premises of science.

Mr. Kuhn gives historical examples extending from the time of Galileo to Maxwell of the way the current commitment of scientists to a paradigm has caused them to resist new discoveries which later proved valid. Such cases could be multiplied, but they are not quite to the point for they show the dangers rather than the advantage of scientists being committed to a particular view of nature; so I will mention some illustrations of my own to illustrate this advantage.

I once selected for this purpose a table of figures printed in *Nature* (CXLVI, 1940, p. 620) showing that the time of gestation, measured in days, of animals ranging from rabbits to cows, is a multiple of the number π.[2] Scientists have rightly refused to pay any attention to this evidence, and indeed no amount of confirmatory evidence could convince them that such a relationship exists. We might say in general, that if scientists did not suppress the offerings of cranks, science would be swamped by trash.

But the *prima facie* rejection of unsound claims is indispensable also *between* scientists. In June 1947 Lord Raleigh, F.R.S., published in the *Proceedings of the Royal Society* a simple experiment purporting to show that a hydrogen atom impinging on a metal wire could transmit to it energies ranging up to 100 electron volts. This fact, if true, would be of immense importance. Yet various physicists I asked about Lord Raleigh's paper only shrugged their shoulders. They could find no fault with the experiment, yet not one believed in its results, nor thought it even worth repeating. The whole matter was soon forgotten.[3] More than ten years later I came across a paper which seemed to show that Raleigh's observations had been due to a chemical reaction induced by the impact of hydrogen atoms on substances absorbed into the surface of the metal. The physicists had been right in disregarding Raleigh's claims.[4]

I may add that inexplicable things frequently happen in every laboratory. For example, traces of helium or traces of gold may unaccountably turn up in sealed vessels and this

[1] *Personal Knowledge* (London, 1958) 161.

[2] *The Logic of Liberty* (London, 1951) 17.

[3] Ibid. p. 12.

[4] *Personal Knowledge*, p. 276.

result may prove reproducible. At a time when the artificial transmutation of elements first appeared possible a number of scientists accepted such observations as evidence that transmutation had taken place. But once the true conditions of transmutation had been elucidated observations of this kind, though just as frequent as before, were no longer heeded, let alone published, by scientists.[1]

These examples confirm Mr. Kuhn's view that the usual and proper response to our failure to explain some odd piece of experience "in terms of the prevailing beliefs concerning the nature of things" is "to blame one's talents or one's tools and to turn next to another problem" and that "if he is not to waste time, the scientist must be able to discriminate essential anomaly from mere failure". But I would remark that Mr. Kuhn does not ask how the scientist can discriminate between the two; and to this point I must yet return.

Mr. Kuhn gives a long list of essential anomalies which have in various cases led to important reconsiderations of prevailing scientific beliefs. This illustrates an essential fact; but one should also mention that anomalies might be recognized for years on end without inducing any scientist to reconsider the current theories with which they conflict. The theory of electrolytic dissociation proposed by Arrhenius in 1887 was contradicted from the start by a prominent group of strong electrolytes like common salt and sulphuric acid. These were carefully tabulated as 'the anomalies of strong electrolytes' for more than 30 years, without any scientist doubting that their behaviour was yet governed by the law that they failed to obey.[2] There are a number of anomalies in physics which continue to persist without causing much desire to reconsider the theories which lead to them. Indeed, a most important contradiction, namely that between the wave and particle nature of matter, has been accepted as representing a fundamental paradox enshrined in the principle of complementarity. Niels Bohr has suggested that the conflict between determinism and statistical irreversability should also be accepted as an instance of complementarity.

According to Mr. Kuhn the pursuit of science by the collective commitment of all research workers to the same paradigmatic discoveries is characteristic only of the "mature sciences", for which he quotes the example of physics. He shows

[1] See my *Science, Faith and Society* (Oxford, 1946) 75–6; Appendix.

[2] *Personal Knowledge*, pp. 292–3.

that during the time preceding the discoveries which laid the foundation for any particular branch of physics, inquiries into the same subject matters tended to be confused. At this stage individual contributions by-passed rather than supplemented each other, and substantial observations were forgotten for lack of collateral support. He says that this early stage is "less than scientific" by contrast to the later, mature condition of science. I think we might rather call the earlier stage an unsystematic and the later a systematic pursuit of science. For this allows us to observe that science may remain unsystematic, and indeed may *become* unsystematic, at any time in countries where the authority of scientific opinion has either not yet been established or, having once been established, has subsequently been weakened or destroyed. In these conditions, not only will scientific education tend to degenerate but all the higher forms of scientific life will also be corrupted by extraneous influences, be it by politics, business or nepotism. This should remind us that collectively established scientific beliefs and — I should add also — commonly held standards of scientific value, form the constitution of the republic of science, under which it administers all the wealth and authority at its command. The collective commitment of scientists to a set of beliefs and values must be safeguarded through institutional channels controlled by scientific opinion. In fact, the very holding of common beliefs inevitably creates an authority which in its turn assures the continued holding of these beliefs. This is an important social implication of Mr. Kuhn's views which he leaves unmentioned.

Mr. Kuhn's analysis necessarily leads him to classify scientific discoveries into two kinds — those which merely articulate accepted scientific beliefs by extending their application (or else merely sustain them by solving in their light a variety of hitherto puzzling experiences), and others which change our very beliefs about the nature of things, thus establishing a new paradigm to guide further discoveries.

I am sure Mr. Kuhn would agree that the distinction is a matter of degree and I will not labour this point. Yet it is worth recalling a previous examination of this distinction which has led me to reject the view implied in Mr. Kuhn's analysis that it corresponds to two different levels of discovery.[1] One of the greatest and more surprising discoveries of our own age, von Laue's discovery of the diffraction of X-rays by crystals, was

[1] Ibid. pp. 276–7.

made by the sheer power of believing more concretely than anyone else in current theories of crystals and X-rays. Likewise, the theory of Brownian motion which Einstein produced in 1905 was but an amazingly literal articulation of the hitherto current kinetic theory of gases. Discoveries made by the surprising confirmation of existing theories might in fact be likened to the feat of a Columbus whose genius lay in taking literally and as a guide to action that the earth was round, which his contemporaries held vaguely and as a mere matter for speculation. Such advances are no less bold and revolutionary than the innovations of a Copernicus or Planck, or of Einstein himself, as the discoverer of relativity.

Admittedly a discovery which involves considerable conceptual reform requires a different kind of originality from that which enlarges an existing intellectual track into a broad avenue. But both are equally free creations of the mind, and at the same time the scope of both is equally circumscribed by the range of hidden possibilities that are accessible from the intellectual position already reached. We find proof of this predetermination when we see how two or three scientists of the highest originality, working in different places and very different circumstances, make the same discoveries at the same time, and indeed produce it sometimes in such different forms that they believe they have arrived at contradictory positions. We must acknowledge here that the most important case of this kind was the discovery of quantum mechanics which involved a particularly far-reaching change of conceptual framework.

I have so far only reported, supplemented and amended the account given by Mr. Kuhn of the process of scientific discovery, looking at it in the same way as he did. I must now say briefly why I believe that this tears open and leaves open the main questions concerning the nature of scientific method and the foundations of scientific knowledge.

The affirmation that commitment to a framework of accepted beliefs is indispensable to the pursuit of science contradicts the current view which the founders of the Royal Society expressed 300 years ago by their motto *nullius in verba* — we accept no authority — a phrase that was but an echo to Descartes's principles of universal doubt, which had guided the preceding century of rebellious minds in preparing the way for the rise of modern science. It is clear that this doctrine of universal doubt makes no sense within the context of modern science. A scientist who would query and try to test all the information transmitted to him by scientific journals and textbooks would be condemning himself to total sterility. But on the other hand scientific originality includes a capacity to doubt accepted beliefs. The original mind holds beliefs which nobody else shares for the time being, beliefs which, even when fully proved in the view of their originator, may appear highly questionable, and perhaps altogether incomprehensible, to most scientists. We have to face then both rejections of authority that are futile and other rejections of authority to which science owes its greatest advances. Is there any rule for distinguishing between the two? Or for that matter, any rule by which scientists can distinguish their own failure to apply the current framework of scientific beliefs from the presence of an essential anomaly incompatible with these beliefs — or any rule by which scientists can ascertain whether an anomaly, once established, is to be regarded as a challenging problem, or rather as a basic paradox intrinsic to a new framework of science?

There are of course no such rules. We have some useful maxims to guide us, but the choice of the maxim to be applied and the discretion left open in applying it still leaves responsibility for his own conclusion to the individual worker engaged in research. But who is he to bear such responsibility? And on what grounds should we trust his judgment?

These questions point beyond my task here. I want only to say that I can accept the excellent paper by Mr. Kuhn only as a fragment of an intended revision of the theory of scientific knowledge. Otherwise it would not only fail to answer the questions it raises, but appear altogether to ignore them.

Discussion

B. Glass

I ought first to identify myself as a practising scientist — a geneticist — rather than a historian or philosopher of science. As a consequence Mr. Kuhn's presentation of the method of scientific advance and its dependence upon paradigms has put me in the position of seeing myself in a mirror and wondering whether what I see there is a true image or a distorted one. First I have had to understand what is meant by a "paradigm" — a new word for me. I now recognize that the paradigm looks backwards while moving forwards, whereas the dogma, a related creature with which I am more familiar, also looks backwards but stands its ground.

Although I agree in the main with Mr. Kuhn's thesis — in fact, to such an extent that my own paper in this conference may be said to be little more than an elaboration and exemplification of it — nevertheless I feel that his emphasis needs modification in some respects.

First, it seems that the relationship of the paradigm to the scientist's *basic assumptions* and to his use of *hypothesis* and *theory* should be clarified. For while scientists do indeed often work on the basis of accepted and even unquestioned assumptions, within my own knowledge they are careful to distinguish their observations from their hypotheses and theories and even rather often discuss the validity of their basic assumptions — I think more often today than when I was a younger scientist.

Secondly, I believe emphasis should be placed on the effect of the rapid growth of science on the frequency of the periods of crisis or overturn of the older bodies of concepts, and on the consequent shortening of the periods during which particular paradigms hold sway. Ninety-five per cent of all the scientists who have ever lived are living and working now, according to one estimate I have heard; and scientific knowledge is approximately doubling in every decade. Within my own working life as a geneticist I have already seen two very fundamental overturns of prevailing conceptual models, or to use Mr. Kuhn's term, paradigms. The young scientist of today, therefore, must be trained to expect relatively frequent overturns of his basic ideas within his own field. In fact, the logarithmic growth of scientific knowledge may soon relegate the use and importance of paradigms to a minor role.

This consideration brings me to a third and final point, wherein I fear I disagree more sharply with Mr. Kuhn's analysis. On p. 350 he discusses the relation of his thesis to scientific education. As chairman of one of the science curriculum studies into which the National Science Foundation of the United States has poured some ten millions of dollars already I can at least speak for my fellow biologists of this generation in America. I have found complete unanimity among them in the belief that science must be taught — I do not say *has* been taught — as a variety of methods of investigation and inquiry rather than as a body of authoritative facts and principles. They also agree emphatically that students must be taught that scientific laws and principles are approximations derived from the data of experience and that they remain forever subject to alteration and correction or replacement in the light of new evidence. I am appalled to think that, if Mr. Kuhn is right, we should go back to teaching paradigms and dogmas, not as merely temporary expedients to aid us more clearly to visualize the nature of our scientific problems, but rather as part of the regular, approved method of scientific advance.

S. E. Toulmin

Mr. Kuhn has given us a highly suggestive paper on an important topic, but he has (in my opinion) presented his central position in a needlessly paradoxical form. If the air of paradox is removed, the nature of the points at issue can be seen more clearly; but this involves *both* giving up the suggestion that science necessarily involves dogmatism, *and* going in more detail into the precise *mode d'emploi* of the "paradigms" of which he speaks.

He begins by referring to our ideal of the scientist or an "objective and open-minded" investigator who "rejects prejudice at the threshold of his laboratory"; and (throwing out an allusion to the novels of Sir Charles Snow) he asks: "Can it really be like that in practice?" And of course we know very well, both from Snow's novels and from our own experience, that 'scientists are human too' — that they sometimes allow their personal emotions to distort their approach both to their colleagues and to their subject-matter. After this beginning,

Kuhn goes on to argue that scientists are necessarily like that — on account of the nature of their traditions — that in their work they necessarily rely, in some sense which justifies his use of the word "dogma", on *preconceived ideas*. Yet this is (I am convinced) a mistaken conclusion: the points to which Mr. Kuhn draws our attention do nothing to imply a lack of objectivity and open-mindedness on the part of scientists — they are simply points of logic.

There lies in such phrases as "preconceived ideas" a crucial ambiguity, and I am now obliged (such is the philosopher's trade) to draw a distinction. One may have preconceived ideas in the sense of holding prejudged (prejudiced) beliefs; or alternatively in the sense of employing preformed concepts. Now the objectivity and open-mindedness we demand of the scientist is this — that he should not be influenced in the laboratory or the field by prejudices about the answers he will find to the questions he asks there — he must leave nature to answer his questions for herself, without prompting. If we are too sure before an empirical study what answers we shall get, we may seriously misinterpret the results, or fail even to see clearly what is happening.

On the other hand, though we must, as scientists, leave nature to answer our questions for herself, it is *we* who frame the questions. Our questions are formulated in terms of certain concepts antecedent to the investigation in question. And this cannot but be the case. However objective and open-minded a scientist may be, his questions necessarily involve the use of preformed concepts. In this sense, he relies on preconceived ideas; but it is a sense which emphatically does not involve any suggestion of dogmatism. For these concepts are the common coin of scientific discussion in a given period, the basis of common understanding between scientists, and of their language: they are essential if there is to be any agreement between scientists about what questions are relevant, sensible, even intelligible. The "collective commitment" of scientists to such preformed concepts or paradigms (if we accept the word) accordingly implies in no way attachment to a dogma or anything of the sort. The point is, rather, a logical one.

Having got so far, we must make a further distinction. Mr. Kuhn uses the word paradigm in a narrower and a wider sense: to refer *either* more narrowly to the particular set of basic concepts (e.g. the Newtonian concepts of mass, force and momentum) which are determined by an influential theory, and in terms of which questions arising in the subsequent application and extension of the theory have to be framed; *or alternatively*, and more widely, to a whole masterpiece of science — a book, not a set of principles — by which a great man (e.g. Newton again) imposes on his followers a certain mode and style of expression and exposition. This is unfortunate, for though reliance on paradigms in the narrower sense may be proper and necessary, the example set by paradigms in the wider sense may indeed lead to prejudice: the story of the corpuscular theory of light in the eighteenth century is an illustration — for this had little weighty evidence in its favour and rested mainly on Newton's supposed authority. And for our studies of the history of science it is essential not to confuse the proper role of new theories, in fixing and clarifying our notions, with the inadvertent effect that they may have, of prejudicing our beliefs. If we are to allow the term "paradigms" to get into circulation, we must surely restrict it to the narrower signification — to refer to the basic forms of concept introduced by a new framework of fundamental theory, i.e. to the scientists "preconceived ideas", in the innocent and indispensable sense of that phrase.

If we do so restrict it, there arises one further question — Mr. Kuhn talks of sciences as having a "pre-paradigm" stage. If he *does* mean by his "paradigms", even in part, what I have called "preformed concepts", then one must ask: Is there any such thing as a pre-paradigm stage? In the beginnings of science, men approached nature with prior notions and preformed ideas as much as in later ages: their paradigms may have been greater in number and less consistent than they became later on, when some unifying theory transformed them. But they are there all the same, and the idea of a naïve pre-pre-conception stage in science is surely just a myth.

E. F. Caldin

As a practising physical chemist, doing experimental research of the normal kind, I recognize up to a point the picture painted by Mr. Kuhn in his very interesting paper. As he says, research is normally done within a stable theoretical framework. The entities envisaged are molecules, atoms, and subatomic particles, and the rules are (for instance) those of quantum theory. These are our most general hypotheses, and we tend to stick to them; this is characteristic of the normal progress of a developed science. A crisis can arise only within such a stable framework. Mr. Kuhn's examination of normal research is very welcome. Beyond this point, however, I have several reservations about his argument:

(1) I do not think scientists' procedure can be called dogmatic (assuming that we are using the word "dogma" in the common debased sense of an unquestioned irrational belief). Our beliefs are held on evidence, and we know that they are technically hypotheses. Scientists are not committed even to conservatism, in the objectionable sense. Rather, they are concerned with a tradition, which develops and can be corrected. I return to this in a moment.

(2) I think we must take into account the *structure* of the scientific theory implicit in what Mr. Kuhn calls a paradigm. The tradition of a developed science is not a single hypothesis; it is a combination of hypotheses, with a hierarchical structure. Below the most general hypotheses (molecules, atoms, electrons, quanta) are subsidiary hypotheses, concerning for example the arrangement of atoms in the molecules of a particular material; below these again are more specific hypotheses about the positions and dimensions of those atoms, the distribution of energy, and so on. The task of science, outside times of crisis, is to find a self-consistent set of subsidiary hypotheses, to account for a mass of observations.[1] When Mr. Kuhn suggests that scientists usually seem to know "all but the most intimate details of the result" before they start, I should like to refer to these different levels of hypothesis, and distinguish their functions somewhat as follows. Broadly speaking, our fundamental assumptions delimit the possibilities that can be entertained; our subsidiary hypotheses about the structures of molecules give us a picture of the probable outcome, which sets the programme of the research; and the actual observations enable us to fill in the lowest-level hypotheses. Mr. Kuhn suggests that scientific research is like assembling a Chinese cube whose outline is known from the start. I agree that it consists in solving puzzles, but not that sort of puzzle. It is perhaps more like making a working model of a machine out of pre-constructed parts; but this too is a dangerous analogy, and better avoided.

(3) The reason that scientists tend to hold on to their most general assumptions is simply that their understanding of phenomena normally comes about by combining these funda-

[1] This is done partly by theoreticians, but also by experimentalists, as I argued elsewhere: *British Journal for the Philosophy of Science,* x (1959) 209.

mental hypotheses with adjustable subsidiary ones. This is obviously the most economical way to make progress. There is a vast mass of observations to be understood, and no one wants to adopt new basic hypotheses before they are seen to be improvements on the old. When anomalies arise, one tries first to adjust the subsidiary hypotheses. For instance, when the specific heat of hydrogen calculated from the quantum theory was found to disagree with experiment, the quantum hypothesis was not scrapped; a new subsidiary hypothesis about two different states of the hydrogen molecule was tried, and found to give agreement. This situation continually recurs in research. The tradition is developed and corrected.

(4) Finally may I add a word on the teaching of science. Many undergraduates suppose, when they arrive at the university, that science *ought* to be taught dogmatically, to save them thinking. A large part of our task is to persuade them to change their minds and to see that science involves puzzle-solving. To help bring this about, we (at Leeds) expect them to read original papers, as distinct from textbooks, at least in the second and later years. Perhaps the state of scientific education, at least in universities, is less gloomy than Mr. Kuhn has painted it.

T. S. Kuhn

I am grateful to those who have commented on my paper, both formally and informally. They provide cause as well as occasion for clarification, extension, and perhaps also modification of the thesis that I have had to compress so much in meeting the space limitations of the Symposium. Since clarification is the appropriate preclude to substantive addition or change, I respond first to the stimulating commentary of Mr. A. R. Hall.

The support for my overall thesis derived by Mr. Hall from his own wide and profound researches in the history of science is gratifying. But that support would reassure me more if so many of the concrete criticisms to which Hall next turns did not seem to depend on misunderstanding. At no point, to take an extreme example, did my paper suggest "that scientific education has been dogmatic only since about 1800". It did say that the modern pattern of textbook instruction begins to appear only around that time. But it immediately insists that before systematic textbook instruction there had been paradigms and that these gave the sciences which possessed them the same dogmatic character subsequently derived from texts. Compare Hall's reference to "medieval 'authorities' " with my use of Aristotle's *Physica* to exemplify a paradigm. In rejecting a statement I never made Hall provides evidence for what I thought I had said. That the fault in cases like this may be due to my lack of clarity only makes the need for rejoinder more urgent.

A similar failure of communication makes it difficult for me to comment on a more central series of criticisms that are scattered through Hall's commentary. When he insists that resistance to innovation cannot derive "merely from innate conservatism" and that "sheer lack of information" must also play a role, Hall makes points which I think of as my own. But if that is so, then I cannot understand the further set of criticisms which he constructs upon them. For example, the view of science to which my paper objects holds that the true scientist, in the absence of sufficient information, draws no conclusions at all. I have maintained, and Hall seems to agree, that there is no such option. Unless he is to abandon research entirely, the practitioner of a mature science must commit himself to a set of concepts that additional information may cause him to replace. They are as much a part of his professional tool kit as are his laboratory instruments. How can recognizing the inevitability of such commitments make Hall "less a friend of dogma" or allow him to view it as "less a necessity than an apology for weakness"? Does he have in mind a type of science whose practitioners need not be human beings? *Ipso facto*, they might not even need instruments. Or again, a point made explicitly in my paper, is it helpful to point out in this connexion that paradigms (or "elements" of a paradigm) may be "simply false"? That could be true of all scientific theory at this or any earlier time, but it does not prevent current theory from providing a generally successful and always essential guide to research.

Undoubtedly the brevity of my text is to blame for Mr. Hall's impression that I take science to be a "monolithic" enterprise dominated by a single paradigm. Let me therefore gratefully accept his synoptic characterization of the science of any age as "a somewhat crazy, rambling structure" none of whose many specialties are ever governed by quite the same, or even by quite compatible, paradigms. But wholehearted endorsement of that position need not undermine my thesis about the essential role played by individual paradigms in the research effort of the various scientific specialties. The incompatibility between Aristotle's cosmology and Ptolemy's astronomy, to use Hall's example, plays a significant role in the development of both fields. But that does not disguise the fact that from Hellenistic times until the sixteenth century cosmology and mathematical astronomy were usually quasi-independent specialties, each guided by its own paradigms and pursuing its own problems. Nor do I see the force of the other argument by which Hall seeks to "dissolve" my thesis. To say that reception of a paradigm leaves work to be done is not to say that adherence to the paradigm is therefore incomplete. Neither Newton nor his most dedicated and literal-minded followers supposed that the *Principia* contained complete solutions to all the problems to which Newton's Laws and techniques were applicable. They only supposed, with Lagrange, that Newton had completed certain fundamental tasks to which no physicist need return again.

Mr. Hall closes with two criticisms of my failure to distinguish large-scale from small-scale scientific change. One of them — exemplified by an apparent logical distinction between the Copernican Revolution and the transition from the corpuscular to the wave theory of light — I do not understand sufficiently to rebut. Let me therefore only make clear my conviction that, though the first of these paradigm-changes had vastly greater and more far-reaching effects than the second, the two are very close both in logical structure and in psychological impact upon those scientists most involved.

Earlier Hall makes a similar point by reverting to a great-man theory of history. On that interpretation, I presume, Lagrange and his contemporaries failed to invent, say, special relativity because none had Einstein's creative power (which may be so) rather than because they lacked, among other things, Maxwell's electromagnetic theory. Does that attitude still make sense? Historians of science, including Mr. Hall, have recently been particularly successful in showing how the way to a paradigm-change is prepared by weaknesses disclosed and concepts prepared within the prior tradition. Would we, for example, still suggest that Lavoisier, by the power of his intellect, could have 'straightened out' chemistry if he had lived before the work of the pneumatic chemist? Besides, there is nothing easy or, to those concerned, uninteresting about the best of the problems which adherence to a paradigm leaves to be solved. Examine the dynamical writings of Euler, Lagrange, Laplace, or Gauss. Or consider the two examples contributed by Mr. Polanyi: Einstein's work on Brownian motion and von Laue's on X-ray diffraction. In no derogatory sense are these examples of, to use Hall's phrase, the "intellectually parasitic".

Mr. Toulmin's attempt to remove the "air of paradox" from my paper is more developed than Mr. Hall's and may lead to correspondingly more useful clarification. But I doubt that the paradox, if it is that, depends upon the sorts of elementary analytical mistakes Toulmin points to. Dismiss individual idiosyncrasy from consideration entirely as I tried to do in the third paragraph of my prepared text. The scientist will still require, as Mr. Toulmin himself insists, "preformed concepts" in order to undertake research. But *with respect to future research* those concepts — ones which the individual acquires principally through education — are necessarily "prejudged" as well as "preformed". They are, that is, the still operant results of a past selection made by the profession from a number of competing alternative bases for research.

Perhaps Mr. Toulmin will go this far with me. But he seems also to feel that because the need for *some* set of preformed concepts is "logical" — does he mean 'merely logical' and thus inconsequential as tautologies are sometimes said to be? — it can make no difference which *particular* set of concepts the profession in fact chooses to embrace. Neither history nor logic supports that conclusion. Nature, to use Toulmin's own metaphor, will only answer or refuse to answer questions that are put to it. Those questions necessarily vary with the conceptual base in whose terms they are framed. That is why the most significant episodes in scientific development so often prove to be the occasions when nature's refusal to answer old questions prepares the way for new ones that can emerge only through fundamental conceptual reform.

If that much is recognized, then even Toulmin's last bastion of objectivity may not seem entirely impregnable. At that comparatively advanced point in an investigation when he does get to the laboratory or the field, the scientist cannot quite "leave nature to answer his questions for herself, without prompting". The criteria by which he determines whether his apparatus is working properly or not, whether he is confronted by an answer or an artifact, are themselves partly theory-dependent. Both Mr. Polanyi and I have already provided elementary examples; a number of more developed ones are to be found in the reference cited on p. 361, n. 1, above, particularly in its Section III; there will be still others, some of a subtler sort, in the essay from which my paper has been abstracted. That some preformed concepts are necessary for the continuation of research does not neutralize the particular selection made by the profession.

Mr. Toulmin supports his case by suggesting that I confuse a narrow sense of paradigm with a broad one. Certainly he is right that there is far more to be said about which portions of particular scientific achievements come to serve as paradigms, in which periods, and for whom. Those are problems for extended historical investigation only part of which has already been carried through and none of which is reflected in my paper. But such analysis, whether historical or not, will not permit the distinction Toulmin seeks, the one he illustrates by contrasting Newton's corpuscular theory of light with the hard core of his dynamics. Clearly the former was not so strong a theory as the latter. But, though I cannot argue the points here, both derived their strength from the same sorts of evidence. (It is not simply Newton's authority, on the one hand, against observation of nature, on the other.) And both committed scientists to concepts which ultimately had to be given up in order that a more adequate theory could be accepted. That we now think better of one of these theories than the other, provides no basis for describing one as prejudice, the other as objectively scientific. If there is prejudice here it is our own.

Mr. Glass's engaging comments give me the opportunity to make a pair of points that should have been explicit in my paper from the start. First, the incisive distinction, with which his remarks open, between dogmas and paradigms both fits and furthers the purpose of my enquiry. It is a weakness that, until its penultimate paragraph, my paper scarcely hints at the existence of ideological factors which make a scientist *exploit* a paradigm rather than simply *slumber* within it. I am delighted to have had the point brought so effectively to the fore.

Second, though I can now see how it has come about, I did not mean to seem either a defender of or an apologist for the techniques of scientific instruction now so widely deployed in American high schools and colleges. On the contrary, I welcome the reform upon which his committee has embarked, and I agree that the system they aim to change is often no more than a parody of what scientific education should be. But I do insist that it is a parody, i.e., that it is not irrelevent. The fact that it has arisen in the sciences and not in the humanities or social sciences can tell us something about the nature of science. My only possible reservation about Glass's position would be a suspicion, derived from sources which my paper partially describes, that it may not be possible to carry the reform so far as he would wish. In particular, I wonder to what extent the facts (whether "authoritative" or not) can be dispensed with in favour of "methods of investigation". I suspect that students will learn both together as samples of accepted achievement, which is only to say that I suspect they will learn paradigms. Those paradigms may, as Mr. Glass suggests, be upset more frequently in the future than in the past, but I doubt that science will get on without them.

In one other respect, too, I think that Mr. Glass is overly optimistic, though it may only be that biologists behave differently from physical scientists. My experience, both personal and as an historian, is almost exclusively with the latter, and one part of Glass's description scarcely fits them. Very often they do discuss their *hypotheses*. But these are the ideas of an individual, ideas with which he hopes to resolve some particular current problem. Their rejection would not at all upset the *basic assumptions* common to both the individual and his branch of the profession. Those basic assumptions, on the other hand, are in my experience very rarely discussed. Usually attempts to promote their discussion are resisted except when the existence of a recognized crisis makes it urgent. And even then, discussion usually discloses profound disagreement about just what the basic assumptions are. That, as I shall indicate shortly, is why I have talked of paradigms instead of using terms like "basic assumptions" or "conceptual models".

Mr. Polanyi's wise and penetrating commentary I have had reason to leave until last. Since it is generally sympathetic to what is explicit in my paper, the important criticisms it does contain almost all point beyond the limits I had set for my presentation. At best I can deal with only some of them and with those only incompletely. Let me therefore use his criticism, first, to extend the area of agreement he has already mapped and, then, to indicate some of the residual, but I think significant, differences that separate his view of scientific development from my own.

In the first place, I agree that many of my examples of a paradigm's effects were overly negative. Though I hope my concern with the constructive function of paradigms apparent without them, Mr. Polanyi's additions are both to the point and welcome. More important, I entirely agree both that there are no rules for distinguishing an essential anomaly from mere failure and also that some anomalies are recognized for many years without "inducing any scientist to reconsider the current theories with which they conflict". I was concerned not to find a methodological rule for individual scientists (e.g. Mr. Popper's principles of falsification) but rather to characterize the state of the scientific community within which a new theory is invented and accepted. Those points of agreement imply another that is more important still. Having agreed that there are no rules to tell a scientist when to break with established concepts, I can properly be challenged to explain how and why science progresses as it does. Since that problem was deliberately suppressed in my presentation, I concur completely in Mr. Polanyi's closing comment: if my paper is acceptable at all, it can be accepted only as a fragment of a larger work. That, as my first footnote indicates, is what it is. In this respect he and I disagree, I think, only about the shape of the puzzle into which the fragment must be fitted.

I shall turn to that disagreement in a moment but must first point out one other important respect in which Polanyi's views and mine coincide. He suggests that my paper introduces two new terms, "dogma" and "paradigm". My response to Mr. Glass indicates my willingness to surrender the first in favour of something like "commitment to a paradigm". The second seems to me indispensable unless some new and unfamiliar term is to be substituted for it. I doubt that Mr. Polanyi is well pleased with my notion of a paradigm, and I know that many members of the Symposium were not. It therefore seems worth emphasizing that, though I have only recently recognized it as such, Mr. Polanyi himself has provided the most extensive and developed discussion I know of the aspect of science which led me to my apparently strange usage.

In his perceptive and challenging book, *Personal Knowledge*, Mr. Polanyi repeatedly emphasizes the indispensable role played in research by what he calls the "tacit component" of scientific knowledge. This, if I understand him correctly, is the inarticulate and perhaps inarticulable part of what the scientist brings to his research problem: it is the part learned not by precept but principally by example and by practice. Now it is just because I agree that neither the methodological nor the substantive requisites for sound research can be fully articulated that I have avoided the terms urged upon me by Messrs. Hall and Glass, terms like "intellectual framework", "conceptual model", "basic assumption", and "methodological rule". Each of them challenges its user to say what the corresponding framework, model, assumption, or rule *is*, and that proves to be just what neither the scientist, philosopher, nor historian can ever sufficiently discover. Instead I have pointed to what can be discovered: the particular model achievements from which, at any given time, the members of a scientific specialty learn to practise their trade. This they do partly by precept and rule but at least equally by the practice-problem-solving which I earlier called "finger exercises". Perhaps "paradigm" is not the right way to say all that, but I am aware of no word that comes closer.

I turn now to the few points about which Mr. Polanyi and I seem to disagree, but I must say at the start that, with one exception, they arise only by implication and emphasis in either my paper or his critique. When I speak of commitment to a paradigm, I mean commitment to the particular way of doing science that is sanctioned by a given sector of the scientific community at a specified period of time. Clearly such a commitment need not be elicited, though I think it often is, by community authority alone. In the sciences an accepted paradigm always successfully embodies a vast amount of accumulated professional experience: its sanction is pragmatic as well as authoritarian. Nevertheless, though the point cannot be argued here, I draw from history the conclusion that there are other ways to practise the same field of science, some deployed at earlier times and some to be used later. The commitment of every scientist therefore includes an important element of the historically accidental, the temporarily local, and, thus, of the arbitrary. Holding that belief, I could not identify, as Mr. Polanyi does at the close of his second paragraph, the commitments of a scientist with "the holding of the premises of science". Undoubtedly there are such premises, and Mr. Polanyi's published discussions of universal intent, rationality, etc., have wonderfully illuminated them. But however that list is extended, I doubt that commitment to such premises is alone sufficient to make a man a scientist. Commitment to the local, arbitrary, and temporary is also required. And that portion of the commitment is a closing of the mind, one that inhibits, at the same time that it permits, original research. Hence my closing reference to an "acquired tension" in research and also Mr. Hall's remark about the implicit "paradox" of my paper.

Despite their over-condensation these remarks should serve to magnify the importance of the one disagreement that is explicit though muted in Mr. Polanyi's commentary. I have already, in discussing Hall's critique, concurred in Polanyi's judgment that achievements completed within a paradigm are neither "less bold" nor more "circumscribed by the range of hidden possibilities . . . accessible from the position already reached" than are achievements which involve conceptual reform. But Mr. Polanyi also claims that advances within a paradigm are no less "revolutionary" than those that demand a change of concepts. Probably for the reasons suggested in my preceding paragraph, he would like to blur or perhaps eradicate the distinction my paper draws between the two. I cannot see how this is to be done. Polanyi's characterization of Einstein's work on Brownian motion, for example, seems to me entirely apt, but no similar characterization will quite fit the genesis of special relativity. The first of these contributions was a pure construction; the second was a *re*construction and demanded simultaneous destruction of a prior professional commitment Because I believe that such *re*construction goes deep enough to change the "premises" of individual sciences and of their specialties, it seems to me very important to preserve the distinction between normal and revolutionary scientific advance.

I have left to the very last that remark of Mr. Polanyi's which will carry me furthest from what either he or I have made explicit. At the very end of his commentary he speaks of the individual research worker's responsibility and then asks: "But who is he to bear such responsibility? And on what ground should we trust his judgment?" Those questions, if I correctly understand *Personal Knowledge* and, more particularly, *The Logic of Liberty*, Mr. Polanyi would himself answer in terms of the individual's commitment to the premises of science. In ways that I am not the one to explicate it is the depth of that commitment which permits the discovery of "rationality in nature" and which validates such discoveries when they are made. The same reasons, however, which make me sceptical about the existence of "the premises of science" make it hard for me to accept that sort of answer to the questions Mr. Polanyi raises. And another consideration makes me wonder whether the questions themselves are correctly phrased. It is not, after all, the individual who decides whether his discoveries or theoretical inventions shall become part of the body of established science. Rather it is his professional community, a community which has and sometimes exercises the privilege of declaring him a deviant. That being the case I should want to ask: Who are *they* to bear such responsibility? And on what ground should we trust *their* judgment? This is not the place to show why I find that revision of Mr. Polanyi's questions more fruitful than his original. But it may at least indicate that I take the 'social implication' of my views more seriously than his commentary suggests.

PART FIVE

The Making of Modern Science: Factors in Physical Discovery

12

Descartes's Anticipation of a 'Logic of Scientific Discovery'

GERD BUCHDAHL

I

Our estimate of the ideas of earlier thinkers changes with every generation. Our own preoccupations are largely responsible for this, leading not only to the selection of different features and different emphases, but — more important — to a fresh understanding even of some of the most central doctrines. Indeed, not infrequently we may be in a position to understand such doctrines better than their originators. Their statements, once sounding so bizarre, extreme and extravagant, upon further inspection may emerge as important insights that had needed only to be rephrased, and divested of contemporary styles of linguistic expression, in order to yield a novel significance. In this way, the history of scientific thought and, not the least, of scientific methodological thought, can grow into a creative effort in which we may come to understand perhaps more clearly even our own gropings. This is no easy task, for the historian of thought (particularly of the great classical figures) is faced by an immense ocean of traditional responses, framed during earlier periods but still remaining with us. Here, what is needed is a more sensitive awareness of the relevance of the critical issues of our own time with all their unresolved problems.

What are these issues? Most usefully they may, I think, be summarized in the following way: what formulation of the general mode of scientific reasoning can most adequately deal with the problems of the relation of experience to theory, of the relative place and importance of induction and deduction, of the formation of concepts and the links between definitions and the theories into which they enter, of the relations of theories to more general presuppositions of a logical or even aesthetic nature, of the relations of mathematics and physics, and of an adequate analysis of the concept of scientific law; in short: with the problem of scientific truth? Now it seems to me that on all these issues the critical historian himself needs a point of view; at least: an attitude towards contemporary approaches to the problems involved, if he is to bring a new perspective to the discussions on methods that he finds dispersed throughout his historical material. Moreover, since those 'contemporary approaches' themselves are in a state of perpetual flux, the impact on them of the insights obtained from a fresh study of the historical sources may give this whole enterprise a considerable degree of importance; a union between the history and the philosophy of science may here be achieved which is less accidental than the mere coupling of these terms would normally suggest.

It is in this spirit, then, that I want to reconsider the methodological thought of Descartes, hoping that it will throw a significant light on the various facets that I have mentioned in my statement of the general problem. I shall try to steer clear of the more usual interpretations and preoccupations which are thrust upon the student as soon as he approaches the literature. What, then, do we find? Let me list some of the more striking facets:

(1) Descartes's emphatic insistence that methodological accounts, and indeed all accounts of scientific inquiry, should mirror the "method of discovery", paying strict attention to the logical minutiae of that method;

(2) the fascinating spectre of a tremendous tension in Descartes's methodological thought, between the inverse-deductive and the deductive approaches in science, involving a surprisingly clear understanding of the restrictions which the employment of the former places upon that of the latter;

(3) an artful employment of the concept of the 'model' in the construction of some of his scientific theories;

(4) Descartes's mode of *a priori* construction of the major principles of science, that is of dynamics, through an artful combination of logical, conceptual, mathematical and empirical features, thereby initiating the mode of presenting such principles as 'implicit definitions'.

In what follows (for lack of space) no more than a few hints will have to suffice in order to illustrate this reading of Descartes; nor will I be able to provide any sort of extensive documentation, much as that alone would drive home effectively the relevance as well as the freshness of Descartes's approach.

II

I have mentioned Descartes's emphasis on the "method of discovery", not so much for providing us with important hints towards scientific research, but because of the central place occupied in his scientific logic, by a notion which he connects with it, namely the notion of "analysis", a term under which Descartes fascinatingly managed to include three or four totally different ideas without seemingly being aware of it.

Both in the *Regulae*[1] and in the *Discourse* Descartes introduces analysis by reference to certain "ancient geometers", whom he credits with having possessed "certain vestiges of true mathematics", which unfortunately, he says, they craftily kept to themselves! In the *Replies to Objections*, again, he tells us that only "analysis shows the true way by which a matter has been methodically found out and allows us to see how the effects depend on the causes".[2] There, analysis is contrasted with "synthesis", a term roughly equivalent to axiomatics, the proving of a set of theorems by deriving them from axioms already known or assumed to be true. The converse, analysis, ought then to mean the proof of the axioms from the theorems, and that is indeed the most ancient meaning of the term, mentioned by Pappus and again, in Euclid, in the following sense. We may prove an as yet unproven ('unknown') theorem by *assuming* its truth, and then deducing from it some other proposition, theorem or axiom, *already* known or assumed to be true. In this way, we "move" from the unknown, and merely assumed, to the known. The geometrical method furthermore demanded that the analytic step be followed by a complementary synthesis, in which we showed that the "assumed" theorem could in fact be deduced from the axioms in the usual way.

I mention in passing that this method will not help us to discover any theorems; it is only a procedure for proof. Moreover, it assumes that the deductive process will move in either direction, between axioms and theorems.

There was of course a special reason for Descartes to claim a technical proficiency in the application of this method. For in

[1] See *Regulae Ad Directionem Ingenii*, IV, in Ch. Adam and P. Tannery, *Œuvres de Descartes* (Paris, 1956), X, 373, 375–6 (this edition is hereinafter referred to as *A.T.*); also *Discours de la méthode*, II, *A.T.*, VI, 17.

[2] *Meditations, Reply to Objections*, II, *A.T.*, IX, 121–2.

the *Geometry*[1] he had applied it (or rather: something like it!) to the method of 'unknowns' employed in the solution of algebraic equations, using symbols that could be correlated with geometrical lines. Here also, he tells us, we "suppose the solution already effected"; and, of course, the process of discovering a value for the unknown is as powerful as it is automatic.

Now, verbally, these species of analysis as employed in mathematics (let us symbolize them as analysis-M) have a certain superficial similarity (though actually being of a totally different nature) to another kind of "analysis", which we shall denote as analysis-H, which Descartes seems to have included under the general term, analysis. For it must be noted that in the physical sciences an hypothesis that has been proposed may be "proved" by deducing consequences from it which are *already* known, or which may at any rate come to be verified *independently*. Of course, our knowledge of the latter is not 'axiomatic' (as it had been, directly or indirectly, in the previous case). Furthermore, contrary to the requirements stipulated by the "ancient geometers", though the consequences be deducible from the hypotheses, the reverse does not hold. Finally, this method once more is not capable as such of leading to the *discovery* of hypotheses in the sense of helping us to think of them. It only states the minimum logical conditions which hypotheses have to fulfil that are advanced to account for certain data.

But even concerning analysis-H Descartes holds two positions which though related are yet quite distinct. They are positions which have been debated quite recently with considerable warmth. The first of these is what is currently named the 'inverse-deductive' or 'retroductive' method of induction. This involves a form of argument according to which we *infer* that we have reason to believe in an hypothesis H, if it deductively explains a number of verifiable consequences. Formally: if H, then E; but since E, *therefore* (possibly) H.

There is no doubt that Descartes believed this to be a perfectly natural (indeed often the only possible) form of scientific reasoning. In the *Discourse* he tells us explicitly that his method in the *Dioptric* and the *Meteors* has been that of "hypothesis":

The reasonings are so mutually connected in these treatises, that, as the last are demonstrated by the first which are their causes, the

[1] *Géométrie*, I, *A.T.*, VI, 372.

first are in their turn demonstrated by the last which are their effects. Nor must it be imagined that I here commit the fallacy which the logicians call a circle; for since experience renders the majority of these effects most certain, the causes from which I deduce them do not serve so much to establish their reality as to explain their existence; but on the contrary, the reality of the causes is established by the reality of the effects.[1]

Descartes does not explicitly *call* this a form of analysis, but since in the *Replies to Objections* he had specifically said that the synthetic method "proceeds from the causes to the effects", the internal evidence that the reverse procedure was for him a species of analysis is fairly conclusive, and explains the importance that he attaches to it. Of course, this form of scientific reasoning was not new, as one of his correspondents, Morin, reminded him; it had been known since Alexandrian times as the method of "mathematical hypothesis", employed in order to "save the phenomena" — especially, of course, in astronomy, where alternative hypotheses had apparently been capable of explaining identical data. And it had received ample discussion during some centuries preceding the seventeenth. However, with many of these writers, this method had constituted a *pis aller*, which one employed when the "true method" (whatever that might be) could not be applied. And Descartes quite often appears to write as though he shared this view. Thus, immediately following the passage just quoted, he insists that he speaks of hypotheses here in Plato's sense only, according to which such propositions are all deducible from certain "first truths". In biological inquiries, likewise, hypotheses are employed when we have "not as yet sufficient knowledge".[2] Finally, Descartes often uses the conception of "hypothetical knowledge" as a kind of subterfuge in order to evade theological difficulties.[3] Nonetheless, he was when pressed quite capable of realizing that this method was not only perfectly respectable, but indeed in a sense the only possible one to be followed in such studies as mechanics, optics and astronomy. Thus, to a question from Mersenne whether in the *Dioptric* he had "demonstrated" his conclusions, he replies that "to require from me geometrical demonstrations, in a question which concerns physics is to ask me to do the impossible", partly, because in physics, quâ physics, we must always start from suppositions; partly, because the latter are concerned with physical matters, and

[1] *Discours,* VI, *A.T.*, VI, 76.
[2] *Disc.*, V, *A.T.*, VI, 45.
[3] See *Principia Philosophiae,* II, 45, *A.T.*, VIII, 99–100.

thus fall short of the mathematical rigour employed in our formal reasonings.[1]

Of course, it may be said that even in the letter to Mersenne Descartes is only emphasizing the *negative* characteristic of the mere approximation of physics to mathematics, rather than clearly perceiving the existence of a positive and independent method. I do not think that we need be over-punctilious in this matter. Descartes, even in the letter referred to, does clearly insist that physicists reason inverse-deductively, that they *parlent conséquemment*, as he puts it. But furthermore, when questioned subsequently by Morin,[2] he specifically insists that in physical matters the effects are more properly said to be *explained* through their causes, whereas the latter alone should be said to be "proved" by their effects. And the way this happens, he significantly adds, is that we first "prove a cause by several effects already known, and then conversely prove additional effects by means of this cause".[3]

This is as unambiguous a statement of the 'inverse-deductive' form of reasoning as one could wish for; and it seems to me that its existence as a genuine component of Descartes's thinking on scientific logic should never be lost sight of, for our understanding of his more 'rationalist' pronouncements may then perhaps be seen in a different light. Certainly it will no longer be possible to continue writing, as one critic has done only recently, that "Descartes . . . remained unaware of the modern notion of a scientific hypothesis and, indeed, would have rejected it."[4]

"Nonetheless," you might insist, as did some of Descartes's critics, "since alternative hypotheses are always possible, is it not hazardous to speak in such cases of 'proof'?" And in reply, it seems to me, Descartes is shifting towards a second version of analysis-H, a version which seeks to avoid this reference to an explicit notion of inductive 'proof' or 'inference'. For, as a recent writer has explained, in science we do not so much *infer* from successful verifications of consequences *that* the hypothesis is true; rather we *show* that the hypothesis works by showing that it leads to successful verifications of consequences.[5] Now

[1] Descartes to Mersenne, *A.T.*, II, 141–4.

[2] Descartes to Morin, *A.T.*, II, 197–8.

[3] Ibid. p. 198.

[4] A. Wollaston, *Descartes' Discourse on Method and other Writings* (Harmondsworth, 1960), 26.

[5] G. Ryle, "Predicting and inferring", in S. Koerner (ed.), *Observation and Interpretation* (London, 1957), 168.

in the letter to Morin, already mentioned, he not only explains that hypotheses can be said to be "proved" by their effects only if after having been proposed in the light of certain data, further verifiable deductions may be derived therefrom subsequently; he also adds significantly that in order to meet the difficulty of plurality of explanations it is really quite sufficient that one should show that all known effects are clearly deducible from some one given cause, provided that these effects can be shown to range over a very large region of phenomena belonging to widely divergent fields, such as optics, chemistry, meteorology, physics, etc. Of course, there was a weakness in the working out of this programme, for it led to Descartes's attempt to provide a unitary explanation of a vast range of phenomena by means of rather narrow physical principles, aided and abetted by the frequent transgression of his own rule that one should show always *in detail* how effects can be deduced from hypotheses, and by application of the mathematical method. Still, we are now concerned with his thought as a methodologist, not as a practising physicist. And clearly, here he is telling Morin not to worry about the notion of a *proof* of the hypothesis but to consider its fruitfulness alone.

In sum: although Descartes may have been unaware of the vast importance of the method of hypothesis in the ages to follow, there can be no doubt that the concept itself was for him as much a matter of course as it was to be for his more empiricist successors. Indeed, I want to say, how could it have been otherwise? For is not that notion, either in the first or the second version, a mere commonplace? Yet, if so, then the more pronounced deductivist features in Descartes's methodological programme, to which I shall turn presently, the so-called 'a priori' approach, will need a more moderate and enlightened interpretation. It certainly can no longer be viewed as a speculative alternative whereby 'pure reason', as it were, inspires the philosopher towards the vision of physical truth as a kind of exalting fiction!

Too often we are told of Descartes's claim to have deduced the major physical properties of his universe from certain primary and intuitive premises. Yet, in the crucial passage of the *Principles of Philosophy*, where he passes from the laws of motion to the actual physical universe, he tells us in terms whose insistence leaves nothing to be desired that, apart from these laws, all the physical detail is one vast set of contingent facts:

God might have arranged these things in countless different ways; which way he in fact chose rather than the rest is a thing we must learn from observation. Therefore, we are free to make any assumption we like about them, so long as all the consequences agree with experience.[1]

Here, as clearly as one could wish, has the notion of contingency, of empirical physical fact, been related to the method of hypothesis.

III

Nevertheless there remains, as we shall see, a considerable tension between the inductivist and deductivist aspects of Descartes's methodological programme. Instead of seeing these as forms of reasoning totally distinct and serving different purposes, Descartes attempts to relate them; and the form in which this happens, and the resulting conflicts, are once again due to a further expansion and application of this baneful concept of analysis. Already in the *Replies to Objections* previously mentioned, he had referred to analysis as the "method of resolution", there contrasted with "synthesis" or "composition". And this time, analysis (let us symbolize it as analysis-R) does mean what it says; i.e. (in the words of the *Regulae*, V) the method according to which we resolve involved and obscure data step by step into those which are simpler, until we reach the "simplest".[2] Of course, Descartes is not too clear on an adequate characterization of these "things the simplest and easiest to know" (as he calls them in the *Discourse*).[3] Sometimes it is just a 'formal' matter; the "simple" is that which is "viewed . . . as cause . . . as equality, likeness, straight".[4] That Descartes should think of the component elements of the phenomena as "causes" is not surprising; it is a very common idea, still echoed in Newton's famous reference to the method of analysis and synthesis at the end of the *Opticks*, Query 31. There, too, analysis does not denote a real physical analysis into substantial parts, but the regress from effects to causes, from the motions to the forces that produce them. Nevertheless, the verbal suggestiveness of the term "resolution" would tend to conceal from us the difficulty of the task of analysis; of the fact that forces, for instance, are not 'discovered' by analysis,

[1] *Princ.* III, 46, *A.T.*, VIII, 100–1.

[2] *Reg.* V, *A.T.*, X, 379.

[3] *Disc.* II, *A.T.*, VI, 19.

[4] *Reg.* VI, *A.T.*, X, 381.

like chemical elements through an analysis of a compound, but that they are a constructive element of theory.

The reference to equality and straightness may be more baffling, unless we remember the underlying assumptions: Descartes's physics is one of quantity, number, and proportion. More generally (as it is put in the *Regulae*, XIV): physical inquiry proceeds by *comparisons* of things with one another; and these comparisons are grasped in all their clarity and distinctness only when they are reduced to ratios that "can be found to hold between two or more extensions"[1] — always remembering the close relationship that exists (according to Descartes) between extension and number, and again, between matter and extension. In the *Discourse* (II) he is equally explicit; for there he explicitly explains that an example of things "the simplest and easiest to know" are the lines of his analytical geometry, "there being nothing simpler nor what I could represent more distinctly before my imagination and senses".[2]

And now we see how the conception of 'analysis-R', with its attendant slide from the analytical resultant as simple "cause" to that of "mathematical foundation", of a reality as mere geometrical extension, will facilitate (and, at the same time, muddle) the step from the scientific method, considered as the propounding of hypotheses, to its veritable opposite: the perceptive 'intuition' of the 'starting points'. And thus we are led to that second leg of Descartes's methodological programme, according to which a true scientific foundation requires a "clear and evident intuition" (*Regulae*, III): I am "to accept nothing as true which I did not evidently know as such".[3] And we know only too well the history of Descartes's endless search for models of such inexpugnable certainties, generated by the example of mathematics and the search for conceptual clarity. Here, of course, we are concerned solely with the scientific and methodological contexts. Still, these contexts may perhaps enable us to grasp more easily the genuine background as well as the aims of Descartes's more general doctrines.

IV

I shall return to this; for the moment, let us note that an adherence to the programme of analysis brings with it an unexpected veering in the direction of 'intuitionism', where we

[1] *Reg.* XIV, *A.T.*, X, 447.
[2] *Disc.* II, *A.T.*, VI 20.
[3] *Disc.* II, *A.T.*, VI, 18.

had begun so confidently with the method of induction. But before following the path into which the working out of the intuitionist programme leads us, let us first search for some examples of "resolution" in order to test the real significance of this method. Now Descartes actually gives us an example — a precious methodological emblem, worth more than innumerable pages of abstract argument. It occurs in the *Regulae* (VIII) and concerns the problem of the discovery of the shape of a lens that will collect parallel rays into a focal point.[1] Baconian methods had already here been tried, for example by Kepler. And the result had shown that mere curve fitting and mere approximations were quite incapable of providing an adequate solution, or of giving us any insight into the factors involved beneath the phenomenal surface.

The answer to this question, as anticipated, employed "the resolutive method". In the present case, this involved the concept of the refracted ray of light. The degree of refraction depended on the media, that is on the manner in which light passes through matter. This again presupposed "a knowledge of the nature of the action of light", and this, in turn, of the mode of action of a "natural power", that is, a general consideration of a physical process or phenomenon, such as the passage of light. A perception of what is involved simply and absolutely in the passage of light would here give us the intelligible starting point.

Descartes's actual procedure at this juncture has seldom been seen for what it really is; to avoid circumlocution I shall briefly describe it in my own terms, hoping that the extreme sophistication of the approach will nonetheless emerge reasonably clearly.

The "resolutive method" (analysis-R) had seemed to lead us straight to the doctrine of the 'intuitive starting point'. On the other hand, the present problem being one belonging to the realm of physics suggests the employment of hypothesis (analysis-H). The mediation of the conflict is provided (perhaps not surprisingly, in the light of contemporary methodological ideas, but nonetheless revolutionary in the Cartesian context) by a judicious employment of the concept of "analogy" or 'model'.

The discussion occurs in two places. In the *Regulae* (VIII) Descartes says that though our aim ought to be by intuition

[1] *Reg.* VIII, *A.T.*, X, 393–5.

clearly to apprehend the absolute last terms of the resolved whole, this is not usually possible. Thus, to take our present example, if one should be "unable straightway to determine the nature of the action of light", one should "enumerate all the other natural powers, in order that the knowledge of some one of them may help him to understand it, at least by analogy".[1] In other words, Descartes proposes that we should construct a number of models, which will help to "explain" the effects, which after all are already "quite certain".

Now this is of course precisely the method employed in the *Dioptric*. Right at the start he tells his reader that he will not have anything to say about "the true nature" of light, but that instead he will employ

> two or three comparisons, which will help us to understand it in the most convenient manner, in order to explain all those of its properties that experience allows us to know, and to deduce thereafter all the others which may not be so easily noticed. In all this I am using the method of the astronomers who, even though their suppositions be nearly all of them false or uncertain, all the same draw from them many consequences which are perfectly correct and assured, since they agree with the diverse observations which they have made.[2]

In short, the resolutive method, when combined with the construction of models, enables him to slip back again into the employment of inverse deduction. The models he uses in the *Dioptric* are well known: the blind man's stick; the grapes in the vat; and the motions of the tennis ball—models, be it noted, as such mutually inconsistent. But it is by reasoning round these models that he deduces the major laws of geometrical optics. In particular, 'Snell's Law' appears here for the first time in its modern form, relating (though incorrectly) the ratio of the light-velocities in adjoining media to the ratio of the sines of the angles of incidence and refraction.

In 'reasoning round these models', Descartes considers a number of alternative hypotheses. The question considered in particular here is whether the passage of light was to be thought of on the lines of the motion of a body in space, or of the transference of a 'force' through a solid. It should not be objected that this was a completely illegitimate attempt to 'anticipate' facts that ought to have been matters of observation and experiment. Descartes did indeed believe that he had empirical evidence to show that the speed of light was

[1] *Reg.* VIII, *A.T.*, X, 395.

[2] *La Dioptrique*, I, *A.T.*, VI, 83.

"infinite". But it was the purpose of his analogies to create 'conceptual clarity' in a matter that was otherwise opaque, indeed utterly incomprehensible. It will be seen that the 'model' fulfils its function of mediating between the hypothetical and the intuitive elements of the situation by providing us with something akin to 'psychological plausibility'— though not, 'logical transparency', which is what Descartes had led us to expect!

A similar vacillation concerning the status of his models we also find in his biological doctrines, especially as expounded in the *Discourse* (V). He proposes to treat the human body on the lines of the model of a "machine".[1] Working out the "consequences of this supposition"[2] he believes himself able to explain all the relevant phenomena. For him, this explanation has, however, "the force of mathematical demonstrations" since "the motion [of the blood] which I have now explained follows as necessarily from the very arrangement of the parts . . . as does the motion of a clock from the power, the situation, and the shape of its counterweights and wheels."[3] So it is in virtue of the logic of the mechanical model that Descartes believes that he has shown here how "to deduce effects from their causes", by "showing from what elements and in what manner nature *must* produce them".[4] But is the necessitarian force of the demonstration due to anything more than the conceptual clarity produced by the model of the machine? We are not told.

We may distinguish 'models' with respect to the presence or absence of an analogy they have relative to a hypothetical physical structure, which — if real — would explain the phenomena. Let us call them 'diamorphs' and 'paramorphs', respectively. Although the employment of mutually inconsistent models in Descartes's *Dioptric* might suggest that he thought of them as paramorphs, it is more likely that he thought of them as diamorphs, that is as models whose spatial configurations, and more still, whose dynamical relationships as expressed through the laws of motion, mirrored an actual physical structure. His models, then, appear as analogies for and 'interpretations' of putative formal systems intended to treat of a physical structure, which was in fact Descartes's celebrated "second element", the ether of light. 'Intuitional insight', conceptual clarity, hence boils down to the provision of an

[1] *Disc.* V, *A.T.*, VI, 56. [2] Ibid., p. 46.
[3] Ibid., p. 50. [4] Ibid., p. 45.

'interpretation' of a formal structure which is the calculus of a physical theory.

But was it perhaps that the elements of the physical theory, the doctrine of the three elements, involved intuitions, clear and distinct? Not at all! They are purely hypothetical elements, in the formal sense of that term. It is a scholars' legend that Descartes consistently believed that his physics was deducible from first principles, let alone that the postulation of the second element itself was such a principle. For as we have already seen he could surely not have been more definite on this matter than when he told the readers of the *Principles of Philosophy* (III, 46) that whatever might be said of the conceptions of matter and of its laws of motion,

> we cannot determine by reason how big these pieces of matter are, how quickly they move, or what circles they describe . . . [this] is a thing we must learn from observation. Therefore, we are free to make any assumptions we like about them, so long as all the consequences agree with experience,

including, of course, the division into the three elements, and all the vast consequences that follow therefrom! I harp on this so that we may perhaps cease to saddle these rationalist thinkers with absurdities which would seem contrary even to common sense; that we should admit that they regarded as obvious (as did the best of the empiricists) the place of hypothesis in science when it came to the explanation of matters of fact. For only if we do this shall we be in a position to appreciate the place and function of the *a priori* element in their thinking on physical matters.

To sum up, thus far: despite considerable temptation, produced by the multivalence of the term analysis, and the resultant flirtations on the part of Descartes with the concept of an intuitive starting point, we find that in the realms of physical, optical and biological inquiry he continually returns to the hypothetical method, leavened by the employment of models whose minimum purpose is to provide conceptual clarity. It is consistent with this view that we find Descartes harping again and again on the fact that what passes for scientific knowledge at best possesses no more than "moral certainty", that is a certainty belonging to the realm of contingent matters of fact. In particular this is the case as regards our knowledge of the minute constitution of bodies, concerning which (as he explains in the *Principles*, IV, 200–5) he had been constrained to the employment of analogy, giving us a "possible", but not necessarily "actual" idea of the "constitution of nature".[1]

V

Of course, it should not be thought that the tensions between the empiricist and the rationalist approaches are thus resolved. "Moral certainty" is contrasted with "absolute certainty" and this contrast is not to be confused with that which nowadays is drawn between 'physical' and 'mathematical' certainty. Again, as we have already seen, the term "supposition" or "hypothesis" may also be used with Platonic overtones, when Descartes wants to imply that he could deduce such propositions from "primary truths", "from the first principles of my metaphysics", as he puts it in a letter to Vatier[2]. Here, it is the ambiguous use of the notion of hypothesis that enables him to slide almost unawares from an inductive into a deductive position. And I need not harp on the large number of passages in which he proclaims that his primary principles "our minds know by their innate constitution",[3] that they are "such as we see to be self-evident",[4] "clearer and more certain than the demonstrations of the geometers".[5] But let us see how far we can get without inviting or admitting straight contradiction.

We may at once allow that many of Descartes's "suppositions" might well be deducible from higher-level hypotheses. However, in other cases, the most he could surely claim, on his own admission, was that his hypotheses (for example of the three elements) were *compatible* with his general premises, a logical relation easily confused with that of deducibility! Indeed, Descartes emphasizes himself in the *Discourse* (VI)[6] that experiment is needful in order to discover "from the study of effects what are their causes", and in particular, to use crucial experiment to adjudicate between competing hypotheses. So if anything was to be deducible from "primary causes", it could only be some of the most fundamental principles. What these were, we shall consider presently.

Before doing so, we must note a second avenue by which Descartes manages the transition, however strained, from the

[1] *Princ.* IV, 200–205, *A.T.*, VIII, 323–8.

[2] Descartes to Vatier, *A.T.*, I, 563.

[3] *Princ.* IV, 203, *A.T.*, IV, 326.

[4] *Princ.* III, 43, *A.T.*, IV, 99.

[5] *Disc.* V, *A.T.*, VI, 41.

[6] *Disc.* VI, *A.T.*, VI, 50–1.

inductive to the deductive mode of thinking. Let us revert back to the *Regulae* (VIII) where Descartes exemplifies his method of resolution. We have seen how he arrives at a point where he is driven to the consideration of a number of 'models' in terms of which to understand given effects. But it is noteworthy that this Rule is actually *meant* to illustrate not so much a method employing the subterfuge of hypothetical models, but the need to arrive at a starting-point which the scientist "has by intuition clearly apprehended". But what are we to make of a "clear and distinct apprehension" in such a context? (Here the transition from hypothesis to rational starting point is complete!) A hint is provided by the notion of "natural power". For, as Descartes explains in the *Regulae* (IX)[1], our solution should be in terms of what is best understood, and according to him this means that we should devote our "attention to the local motion of bodies, as being of all motions the most manifest". But this we know already to be the ever-recurring theme of Descartes's theory of knowledge: the only ideas on which we can fall back for a clear and distinct apprehension of the physical world are matter and motion — "matter" being understood in its measurable aspect, that is, extension (see above, p. 407). When considering the realm of nature, it is sufficient to consider "only the diverse relations or proportions to be found holding between" its parts; and these proportions are best viewed "as holding between lines, there being nothing simpler and nothing that I can represent more distinctly by way of my imagination and senses".[2] For, as he had said in the *Regulae* (XIV), "what is certain is that whatever differences in ratio exist in other subjects can be found to hold also between two or more extensions"; thus we may consider the difference holding between two shades of colour as a difference that really holds between two forms of spatial configuration.[3]

We see here that "intuition" and "apprehension" are not so much to be considered as mysterious faculties whereby we have an alternative mode of arriving at physical truth; rather it is a question of considering those "objects" which yield the greatest clarity of apprehension when they are contemplated; the paradigm of the contrast between "clarity" and "obscurity" being that of the difference between sensory apprehension of two different shades of colour, and their

[1] *Reg.* IX, *A.T.*, X, 402.

[2] *Disc.* II, *A.T.*, VI, 20 (cf. above p. 407, n. 2).

[3] *Reg.* XII, *A.T.*, X, 414 (cf. above p. 407, n. 1).

metrical determinations. In the light of this interpretation, Descartes's procedure in his example in the *Regulae* (VIII) becomes understandable: alternative models that will explain optical phenomena are indeed possible. But what he is searching after are fundamental models, which will be compatible both with his supreme methodological tenet that natural powers shall yield to mathematical examination, and at the same time with the more general laws of motion, provided always that their application yield verifiable phenomena.

I do not of course deny a deep and systematic vagueness in Descartes' modes of expression. But when in the first of the four rules in *Discourse* II he resolves never to "accept anything as true which I did not evidently know to be such", *need* this be regarded as a criterion of sufficiency, rather than merely the statement of a necessary condition?

It will be replied, no doubt, that Descartes is still involved in the confusion of factual with logical truth. And objectors will point to his putting "enumerative induction" side by side with "intuition" as a mode of reaching "truth with certainty".[1] But I think we need not accept these strictures although their confutation would require arguments transcending both the scope of and the space allowed for this essay. We shall simply insist that the *minimum* interpretation of Descartes's rationalism is always open to us: his demand for 'internal criteria of knowledge' (the doctrine of "innate ideas") need mean no more than that we should know with the utmost clarity what we are about.

VI

But of course, within the scientific context, it means often something more ambitious. Yet even that extra significance we shall (I hope) be able to show yields an interpretation which bestows upon this aspect of Descartes's methodological thought, too, an added significance for our own times. For there can be no doubt that there were parts of scientific knowledge which Descartes (together with almost every other scientific thinker down to the nineteenth century if not later) believed to involve more fundamental positions, which were more deeply rooted in the whole structure of our thinking about mechanics and physics. When, in *Discourse* V, Descartes singles

[1] *Reg.* VII, *A.T.*, X, 389.

out for mention as primary truths "certain laws which God has so established in nature, and of which he has impressed such notions in our souls, that once we have reflected sufficiently upon them, we can no longer doubt their being accurately observed in all that exists or happens in the world",[1] he was almost certainly referring to the laws of motion which he had formulated first in *Le Monde*, and later in the *Principles*. Here we have again admirable material for a study in detail of how precisely Descartes envisaged this process of "reflection" yielding "certainty"; a study which gains perhaps added importance, and requires especially critical comment, when we observe a recent writer on the foundations of quantum mechanics using the words just quoted as a motto for his own approach to reducing the fundamental concept of his science "to simple, almost self-evident ground axioms, so that we can recognize it as a necessity rather than an oddity".[2]

What reflective considerations, then, led Descartes to formulate these laws? Let us consider one only, holding a central position: the Newtonian First Law of Motion, or the Law of Inertia, ascribed by most recent historians to Descartes. Our most valuable information comes from *Le Monde*, Ch. 6, and *Principles*, II, 1–39. I shall only touch on a few essentials. Here again we meet the insistence that matter can be "understood clearly" only when considered under the aspect of length, breadth and depth measurement. The *Principles* (II, 24–9) then considers the proper formulation of the concept of motion: motion, though defined as relative translation, yet is to be considered as a "mode", an attribute, a state of a body. But *qua* "state" (so the argument runs at Section 37), motion is at once subject to the law of causation; all "alterations of state", as Kant was later to formulate it, "take place in conformity with the law of the connexion of cause and effect", the "cause" being conceived of as something that interferes with the preservation of the relevant state of matter, that is as an external force; for Descartes, this is any body acting by impulse.

This then is the famous proof which, starting from "metaphysical first principles", was to yield a fundamental law of mechanics. And it seems indeed to involve no more than a clear intuition of the nature of (or conceptual grammar of the terms) body and motion, together with the principle of causation.

[1] *Disc.* V, *A.T.*, VI, 41.

[2] A. Landé, *From Dualism to Unity in Quantum Physics* (Cambridge, 1960), pp. xv, 41.

But does the law of conservation of velocity follow from this? Not at all. What we need as well is a realization that "motion" is to be interpreted as rate of change of displacement with respect to time. No doubt, heuristic considerations make such a choice obvious, but the empirical element which is introduced at this point into an otherwise relatively formal argument is considerable. Likewise, the fact that "direction" is an aspect of the "state" of a body comes under the same consideration. And here as yet a third element is introduced: for even though "direction" be preserved, and even though "speed" be preserved, I think Descartes's arguments would not be conclusive unless he were not tacitly presupposing the notion of absolute Euclidean space. His reference to the requirements of "simplicity" at this point, though important, is clearly insufficient.

This, then, is what the famous example of a rational deduction of first principles of mechanics comes down to when considered in detail. Yet, I think this does little to undermine the central contentions of Descartes; that is, if my interpretation of his method be accepted, and if we will really try to see that method as a whole, and as a sane attempt to relate rational and empirical, deductive and inductive features in an intimate union. For it is of course still perfectly true that the first law was not, and is not, empirically derivable. Rather, it is a schema for the formulation of Newtonian mechanics; without it, the second law, "Force is proportional to rate of change of momentum", could not be formulated; for we here presuppose that the acceleration referred to is relative to an inertial frame; and that is something which the first law alone can tell us!

The real nerve of Descartes's method of derivation is the intimate union between abstract considerations, such as the demand for quantitative, mathematical formulation of physical problems, and the explicit exhibition of the struggle after a "reasonable" definition of "motion", thus showing how a definition is built into the very formulation of the fundamental laws. If we are becoming more sympathetic in our understanding of the place of regulative principles in the formulation of physical laws, then Descartes's approach here may be viewed as an early groping attempt in this direction; indeed, we gain thus a new perspective on what we thought had been an outworn 'rationalism'. This account is deficient only in its lack of clarity concerning the more specific empirical elements that are being presupposed, and in its inability to give us any very clear statement of the precise relations that hold between the empirical and the rational features. But where these are so deeply embedded in our common procedures, the fault was understandable.

I have claimed that the minimum interpretation of Descartes's procedure might be said to be that of a 'conceptual exploration' of physical possibilities. But no doubt for Descartes it was more; and it is here that he is of course faced by grave logical difficulties. Certainly he is never in doubt that his basic truths must be compatible with experience. The crucial question is whether he would have admitted — a doubtful possibility — that these truths might be falsifiable in a novel context. We have suggested that beneath the unitary language of "intuition" there lie concealed a whole host of the most diverse and often discrepant methods; a fact which emerges the moment the method is applied to concrete contexts. Only the confused notion that there was a single method of "analysis" could have suggested to Descartes the idea that there was a positive and unique path to scientific truth. Yet, the rationalist programme when appearing as the "resolutive method", for instance, is something altogether different from the method of the conceptual foundations of mechanics. What united them, in Descartes's mind, was the associated notion of the clear and the distinct. But the bearing of this notion on the question of physical truth was never to any extent explored by Descartes; the problems it posed, never faced. But despite this (perhaps necessary) lacuna, it is still open to us to see his scientific efforts for what they really were: attempts to trace out conceptual possibilities and plausibilities; the framework within which one might expect any fruitful physical explorations to grow into a solid body of knowledge.

13

Precision of Measurement and Physical and Chemical Research in the Eighteenth Century

MAURICE DAUMAS

It is fairly frequently shown in general accounts of the history of the physical sciences that these entered into the modern phase of their development during the second half of the eighteenth century because scientists had recourse to precise methods of measurement. This affirmation is of too vague a nature to be accepted without qualification. The concept of measurement is probably as old as science itself, but throughout many millenia measurement as a method of investigation has not been employed equally in all scientific fields. For a long time the observer did not have at his disposal any method of measuring very small quantities. If, for example, it was a question of the movement of small particles at great speed for a very short distance, the methods of measurement used for large objects, such as stars, could not be adopted. The speed of light was not accurately measured until the middle of the nineteenth century; formerly, it had only been deduced from apparent motions by means of calculation. But the observer was not often able to extrapolate from the dimensions of interstellar space to the small-scale phenomena with which he was concerned, or to transform a physical observation into an astronomical one.

So it is that the notions of quantity of heat and light, and of the speed of chemical reaction, remained completely indefinable until the last quarter of the eighteenth century. The chemist was able to distinguish, from among the reagents he was using, those which reacted violently and those which reacted slowly. He was, however, only able to classify them in an empirical manner. The first efforts to draw up tables of affinity were deceptive because the observations were subjective; no reference-point could usefully be chosen.

The same applies to the efforts made to measure temperature before the establishment of the constancy of the boiling- and freezing-points of water. Even then, objective knowledge of such phenomena could be obtained only if the physicist already had at his disposal a measuring apparatus, or more exactly some means that would enable him to observe them. It was, in fact, necessary to possess a thermometric tube, even one without a scale, to note that the height of the liquid did not vary during the whole of the melting of a determined quantity of ice. Accordingly, the instrument had to exist before it could become a measuring instrument.

From this example we can see how progress in the knowledge of physical and chemical phenomena is bound up with the existence and degree of perfection of instruments. From being, in the first place, a simple method of making observations, the instrument becomes, thanks to the acquisition of scientific facts which it makes possible, a method of making quantitative comparisons, a measuring instrument. The information it provides can be transmitted, not only from one experiment to another, but also from one observer to another. It acquires an absolute and universal value which enables the instrument to be perfected yet further: not, perhaps, the one which sets the first cycle of progress in motion, but others complementary to it, or which can replace it to advantage. It is necessary to add that the activity of the scientist is no longer the only essential element in the development of such a chain of advances. That of the technician rapidly becomes an equally determining factor. By technician one must understand, for the period with which we are concerned, the maker of the instrument in a form useful to the observer. At first a simple workman, the technician has nonetheless the task of conceiving the physical organization of the instrument, of choosing the materials, and of manipulating these materials properly to obtain the best possible result.

It has always been thus: all measurements, up to the present, have involved either the comparison of an object with a graduated scale, or the observation of a displacement along a graduated scale. Thus, from the moment it became possible to trace curved or rectilinear divisions with equal spaces, scientists began to make use of instruments. Geometry, surveying, geodesy and astronomy were the first to benefit from this advance in instrumentation. The turn of physics and chemistry only came later; that of the biological sciences, later still.

Now, instrument-makers have always displayed in this task the same personal qualities of professional ability. But they have been aided only very slowly by the qualitative and quantitative improvement of materials. In fact, it is precisely towards the end of the eighteenth century that they first began to obtain the preliminary knowledge which was to permit them to make better use of these materials. Thus progress was very slow; so slow to begin with that it only becomes plainly discernible towards the last quarter of the sixteenth century. It suddenly seems to change rhythm towards the middle of the seventeenth, and attains that of the modern age at the end of the eighteenth century.

The acceleration of this progress is due to a great number of factors which have governed the entirety of scientific progress. The most important of these factors are the transmission of information, the growth in number of scientific personnel, the improvement of material methods of research. Only the last factor concerns us here. The invention of new instruments in the seventeenth century: barometers and thermometers, microscopes, micrometers, vacuum pumps, etc., was to a large extent possible only because certain techniques had arrived at a state of maturity sufficient for the instrument to be realized in practice.

It has often been said that the influence of Aristotelian thought, or such of it as still flourished at the end of the sixteenth century, had retarded the progress of observation in physics because it viewed the use of instruments with suspicion. This affirmation would be worth discussing. In this discussion, one would have to make use of data which are, in great part, lacking, on the quality of materials such as iron, steel, brass and glass available in former periods. It would be equally necessary to be able to judge at their true value the methods utilized by the best craftsmen to build the instruments which the scientists asked them to make, almost without the help of models.

The problem of the creation of a model is a very important one. In our own period, special workshops equipped with perfected methods are continuously occupied with them, and a great mastery in this activity has been acquired for all branches of industry. As far as instruments are concerned, it seems that it was towards the end of the eighteenth century that for the first time, in English workshops, people were rationally preoccupied with this problem. But already the task had been long prepared by the work of makers of instruments, and more particularly by English instrument-makers, at the end of the sixteenth and beginning of the seventeenth centuries. Everyone knows that manufacture, where machines or instruments are concerned, begins with a phase in which all the complications are accumulated, the solutions heavy and clumsy. It is only by experimenting with the first model that perfection is slowly attained. This perfection always consists of simplification of either conception or construction. It comes all the more slowly when the occasions for experimentation, the circumstances in which it can be carried out, and experimenters themselves, remain few and with little variation.

In practice, it was towards the end of the sixteenth century that conditions became more favourable for the multiplication of physical apparatus. Their own improvement slowly accelerated to reach a 'productivity' of modern character two centuries later.

By the creation of 'models', we refer to models not only of instruments, but equally of types of machine for manufacturing instruments required in physics. We have, indeed, alluded above to the materials used by the manufacturers; the improvement in the production of these materials, from the point of view of quality as of quantity, was one of the essential conditions for the perfecting of machines as much as for that of instrument-making. The difficulty, for example, of procuring steel of uniform quality, hindered precision engineering until the end of the eighteenth century; the same was true of copper and brass, of which industrial rolling only began to be practised at about the same time. Other materials, such as glass, the importance of which in the manufacture of new instruments of that period can readily be seen, were deficient in indispensable qualities. It is probably the mediocre optical quality of current glass, as manufactured, which for many centuries deterred scientists from using telescopes and lenses, rather than the Aristotelian warning against putting intermediaries between nature and the observer. For as long as no clients showed a particular demand, no attempt to prepare special glass could be envisaged; and the regular production of this type of glass could only be undertaken when there was an assured demand. The whole history of the production of flint-glass between about 1755 and 1820 illustrates in a remarkable way how slowly a satisfactory relationship came to be established between the consumers of special materials and the production of them in the corresponding industries.

In a parallel manner, the creation of instruments and their industrial manufacture were also governed by the progress of applied mechanics. Now, it is precisely from about the middle of the eighteenth century that this was sufficient to enable this new industry really to be born.

Precision mechanics was born of watchmaking. The watchmakers of the end of the seventeenth century created the first machine-tools, which have served as models for all other branches of mechanics. It is true that the lathe is perhaps older in origin than the tools of the watchmakers, which only appeared in the sixteenth century; but until the beginning of the eighteenth century, it was essentially used for working wood or the materials used in marquetry. It is on this model, to a great extent, that the opticians of the seventeenth century constructed their machines for polishing lenses. The making of lathes was completely transformed in a century as a result of the demand from amateurs who wished to produce works of art; it is curious to observe that it was a luxury industry which opened the way for the great machines which transformed industrial mechanics. But these, of which the first prototypes were those of Vaucanson, Wilkinson, Senot and Maudslay, were destined for, or effectively served, industry on a large scale. The makers of instruments borrowed especially from the tools of the watchmakers. These, and among them Pierre Fardoil in the first quarter of the eighteenth century, made not only bench-lathes to cut spindles, machines to cut wheels and pinions to regulate the different pieces of mechanism, but also, for example, machines to make files; moreover, they studied the properties of brasses and steels. It is thus that they were the first to adapt Musschenbroek's pyrometer for industrial usage, which had been only a curiosity of the *cabinet de physique*.

Perhaps the most important novelty which they contributed to spread throughout workshops was the dividing machine. It was an English watchmaker, Henry Hindley, who tried, about 1739, to adapt the machine for cutting wheels with cogs at specified intervals. Later, the duc de Chaulnes used a watchmaker's dividing plate. Ramsden, who made the first dividing machine which could be used in industry, was equally familiar with the watchmaker's divider; he employed the mechanical methods invented and perfected by the watchmakers, such as movement in constant steps by means of reduction screw gearing, which Fardoil had without doubt been the first to adopt for the displacement of a mounted graving-tool. After his machine for dividing circles (1773), Ramsden constructed on the same principle a linear dividing machine. For the first time instrument-makers were provided with machines which executed serially, and at an increased rate, precision work which had previously required long and delicate manual operations. Thirty years after him, all the great workshops used such machines. It had become possible to produce at a better price instruments of quality in significant numbers.

The instruments of chemistry themselves benefited from the progress of precision mechanics. Thanks to it, they passed through a stage which completely transformed the appearance of laboratories and techniques of experiment.

The example of the balance is often quoted. It is, perhaps, balances which least profited from this evolution. The art of the balance-makers was well developed by the end of the seventeenth century for the use of financial houses, money-changers and goldsmiths. Galonde's balance, described in the *Encyclopédie*, which had been made for Rouelle, already possessed the characteristics of a precision balance of the end of the eighteenth century. In fact we already find in Agricola designs for balances which include almost all the features perfected, although not invented, in the period we are discussing. The work of the physicists of the end of the seventeenth century directed attention to certain details of construction which were reformed: the position of the centre of gravity, making the knife-edges parallel, and aligning the planes supporting them. But only the quality of the hard steel available to the mechanics, and especially the development of the art of fine adjustment led to the great precision balances of the eighteenth century. The first of this line was constructed by the famous watchmaker Harrison for Cavendish. But it did not open the way for others. On the contrary, the balances of Lavoisier manufactured first by Alexis Mégnié, then by Nicolas Fortin, and those that Ramsden made after 1788, were the first creations of a new technique. In them are to be found the effects of a new art of adjustment applied to the construction of a traditional instrument. Not only the cutting of the knife-edges, their insertion into the beam of the balance, and the arrangement of the planes benefited from the skill of the mechanics, but equally devices for bringing the beam to rest, damping the oscillations, and regulating the position of the centre of gravity were seen in a new light. The regulating screws, which had been used well before this time, were henceforward constructed with such precision that a spirit-level or a plumb-line was placed on the balance for its adjustment. The oscillations could be read off a graduated sector, and the use of a magnifier became an advantage in taking readings, when it would not have added to the precision of measurements of weighings made on instruments of a former period.

These balances were conceived for weighing fairly heavy quantities with great precision: weights of the order of a kilogramme with an accuracy of the order of one milligramme. The invention of double weighing by Borda gave physicists and chemists an excellent technique for precision weighing which continued to be practised for about forty years. It was the generation of chemists like Berzelius which perfected this technique by operating with weights of the order of some tens of grammes weighed accurately to 1/100th of a milligramme.

The other instruments of physicists and chemists acquired an equally new degree of precision in the second half of the eighteenth century. These were principally thermometers and barometers, pyrometers (or dilatometers*), electrometers.

The attempts of scientists, from those of the Accademia del Cimento to J. A. de Luc, would not have sufficed to make an instrument of scientific measurement out of the thermometer. Even after Fahrenheit and Réaumur, thermometer readings varied considerably from one instrument to another. The manufacturers acquired a certain knowhow, conventional for the greater part of the time; the scales were faithfully copied from types and made by methods unknown to the creators themselves (the principle of two fixed points). It was therefore a simple routine which permitted their standardization. But the construction of graduated rules gained considerably in accuracy. In the last quarter of the eighteenth century the construction of instruments was satisfactory enough for the application of vernier scales to bring further accuracy to the readings.

The improvements to the barometer were made in a similar way. At the suggestion of the physicists, constructors learnt to manipulate mercury, to purify it, to eliminate gaseous occlusions. They devised mechanical systems to enable the level of mercury in the reservoir to be adjusted to a specified zero point. It is symptomatic that the best type of reservoir was invented and made by a mechanic like Fortin. In a word, graduation brought equal benefits in all lines of technical progress.

* The translator has followed the author throughout in using "dilatometry", etc. to refer to all measurements of thermal expansion, although this is a wider usage than that adopted by English scientists.—*Editor*.

It is in the realm of dilatometry that the fruit of collaboration between the scientist and the technician is most readily grasped. Towards the middle of the eighteenth century only watchmakers could construct instruments involving circular motion of a pointer over a scale, by means of pinions and toothed wheels, with sufficient precision to allow, for example, the dilatometric study of rods used in the construction of bimetallic pendulums. Comparisons between standards of linear measure gave rise, before even the establishment of the metric system, to the invention of various contrivances, some of which derive from the principle of dilatometric measurement. We are ignorant of the procedures used by Butterfield and we know hardly any more of those used by Jonathan Sisson. In France, Laplace and Lavoisier in 1781 conceived the idea of a dilatometer, the readings of which were multiplied by a lever arm which altered the inclination of a lens focused on a graduated, fixed target. In 1785, Ramsden was the first to make use of a microscope in the construction of a comparator for thermal expansion. It was for the commission of Weights and Measures that the most accurate comparative devices were made by Lenoir and Fortin. The construction of bimetallic measuring rods, which served as a standard for the base-line in triangulation, revealed Lenoir's singular ability. Not only was there a graduation with a vernier scale, enabling the differential thermal expansion of each rule to be found at any time; also sliding verniers enabled extremely accurate measurement of the small space between two rods placed end to end. For a full-scale study of the behaviour of these rods, and of standard rules, under the influence of heat, Lenoir constructed comparators of which the most perfect model was accurate to the order of a millionth of a *toise* (a linear measure of 6 French feet, roughly $6\frac{2}{5}$ English feet). For the construction of standards of weight, Fortin made a comparator with a dial giving readings to 1/2000 of a *ligne* (an old unit of length equal to 0·225 cm).

To come back to chemical instruments, properly speaking, it is opportune to mention the problems concerned in gaseous measurement. The perfecting of the balance, thermometers and barometers alone would not have sufficed to resolve all these problems. Several other conditions had to be brought about to obtain measures which were exact and precise: the production of pressure vacuums, and gas-tight apparatus; the change from bell-jars to gasometers.

Almost all these conditions were again brought about solely

by the professional ability of mechanical workers. The problem of impermeability, for example, which is tied up with that of the perfection of vacuum apparatus, could only be resolved when mechanics had the means to make perfectly adjusted taps and valves of brass. In this field, the examination of Lavoisier's apparatus for the combustion of oils, fermentation, and the synthesis of water, demonstrates efficiently that the old procedure using cemented joints was thenceforward obsolete. The two successive states of Mégnié's gasometers illustrate, on the contrary, the collaboration of the scientist with the mechanic.

It is Meusnier who determined the characteristics of future gasometers: equlibration of the vessels, compensation for Archimedes's thrust, manometric measurements. Starting with two rudimentary cases made by a tinsmith, Mégnié constructed the first gasometers based on Meusnier's designs (1783). Then, enlightened by this first effort and advised by the two scientists, he constructed, with the aid of more complete and much more elegant mechanical devices, the gasometers of 1787. These constructions were of great importance, for the experiment of the synthesis of water was repeated several times before the end of the century; in each case, gasometers were constructed and Mégnié's solutions profoundly modified, but the principles have always been respected.

It seems that so far we have made many long digressions before coming to the crux of the matter of this communication, the object of which is to discover how accuracy of measurement served to further physical and chemical research in the course of the eighteenth century. It has been suggested that precision was an essential factor in the progress in this field during this period. Such is not my opinion, and what precedes will enable me to explain my view more easily. I take it that the overall picture of progress in physics and chemistry is known, so I will not go over that ground.

At the beginning of this account I said that the idea of measurement was as old as science. It is quite evident that from the moment that scientists began to measure things, they tried to do so with the greatest accuracy permitted by the average materials at their disposal. This consideration has always been present. It gave the best results first in astronomy, then in geodesy, and in all the branches of science concerned with large measurements: topographical elevations, surveying, etc. In physics the first results were obtained in the seventeenth century for phenomena which were relatively easy to measure:

gravitation, weight, ballistics, acoustics, terrestrial magnetism, etc. But a great number of other phenomena, such as those involved in atmospheric pressure, heat, electricity and light, which were much more difficult to assess quantitatively, were the object of merely qualitative researches. It is true that measurement was undertaken in several cases before the beginning of the eighteenth century, but a large margin of inaccuracy remained (except perhaps in barometry) of which those concerned were aware. From the practical point of view, the accuracy of measuring-instruments in physics remained stagnant for almost a century.

But if one considers the various branches of physics during this time, one notes that the idea of measurement had penetrated each of them. In a general manner these measures remained rudimentary ones; but the important fact is that however imperfect they might be, the very existence of these instruments suggested methods of investigation which scientists of prior periods had been unable to envisage for these researches. It was necessary, as demonstrated in the first part of this paper, that there should be much groping in the dark before reaching the stage where the instruments, almost all invented in the seventeenth century, allowed measurements to be taken, of which the accuracy was greater than that of non-instrumental observations. And one may ask oneself who was responsible for the evolution of instruments to this stage: was it the physicists or the instrument-makers? The writings of scientists containing the results of measurement usually simply give the results, without pointing out that a greater degree of accuracy would further advance their field of study. On the other hand, as a profession, the instrument-makers were more concerned to make a better job of their work; thus they put at the disposal of the observers progressively more effective apparatus.

This progress is undeniable as far as it concerns the sighting instruments and angular measures used in astronomy and geodesy, just because the scientists of these disciplines welcomed the technicians' new constructions with curiosity and impatience, and showed themselves demanding in this respect. It is much more diffuse where physics is concerned. If this became an instrumental science, it was hardly a quantitative one. Many initial steps were taken which were not followed up; electrometers, photometers, refractometers, micrometers (except for astronomical instruments), dilatometers, even thermometers, hygrometers and barometers, seemed only to bring a very simple satisfaction to the mind of the scientist before the last quarter of the eighteenth century. If physics remained almost a physics of the drawing-room, that is to say of qualitative experimentation, it was partly because the instruments did not provide measurements sufficiently accurate to permit any elaboration satisfactory enough for quantitative laws; but also because, on the other hand, physicists did not themselves show any great demand for accuracy in measurement. Faced by the great number of phenomena revealed to them, they seem to have shown a naïve satisfaction, or a disturbing confusion of mind. If one excludes the branches of mathematical physics — statics, kinematics, and the dynamics of solids and fluids — the whole of the new physics is permeated with empiricism and subjectivity. Whether it was a question of electricity or magnetism, of heat, optics, or atmospheric phenomena, the quantitative expression of the observations remained at a very low level. What was lacking is a general measurement-based methodology. In its absence, the instrument-maker was subject to only a very weak stimulus, so that during the first six or seven decades, despite appearances, physics remained in a moribund state.

It was between the years 1760 and 1780 that the change intervened. Referring back to what has been said earlier, we can understand that it came about as a result of the conjunction of qualitative knowledge and instrumental possibilities. With Black first of all, then Lavoisier and Laplace, calorimetry was perhaps the first to transform subjective knowledge into quantitative knowledge; then Coulomb in the realm of electricity and magnetism was the first to introduce precise measurement into this domain (the work of Cavendish remained unknown to his contemporaries). These two examples, which are perhaps the only ones one can quote before the end of the eighteenth century, had an important effect.

The vogue of the preceding years for experimental physics had familiarized scientific personnel with the new phenomena and with the new apparatus. The appearance of quantitative data in the fields which had most attracted the attention of that century was to change the attitude of the physicists at the very moment when the manufacturers had become capable of making them more and more accurate instruments. Thus the two currents of evolution meet only at the end of the century, and it is only at that moment that accuracy in physical measurements becomes a really essential factor in scientific progress. In fact it is the needs and results of metrology which have made the desire for precision general among physicists, which have given them this outlook, and which have given rise to corresponding endeavours on the part of instrument-makers to answer the needs of the scientists.

As far as chemistry is concerned, we shall arrive at identical conclusions, but for rather different reasons. We have seen that the chemists only used precision instruments in the last years of the century. Even the equipment of Lavoisier, during the years when his great theories were elaborated, presented no superior qualities, as far as quantitative experimentation was concerned, to that of his colleagues.

Despite appearances, the chemistry of Lavoisier was not so much a chemistry of precision as a chemistry of method. It resulted from a new state of mind, independent of theories current before the discovery of the chemical phenomena of which he was the first to find proof. Before him, chemists, who were all doctors or pharmacists, made constant use of the balance, but in a manner quite different from Lavoisier. Since it was admitted, according to the traditional conceptions systematized in the phlogiston theory, that imponderable principles took part in reactions, there was no need to search to identify them and in particular to use the balance for that purpose. Making abstractions from these conceptions, Lavoisier had the sagacity to understand, perhaps even before beginning his researches, that the whole key to chemistry lay in the balance-sheet of the phenomena of the giving-off and fixation of gases. We know that his first important discovery, the fixation of oxygen by calcined metals, is the result of quite ordinary weighings, but weighings well carried out. And we can say that in almost the whole of the rest of his work precision in measurement (properly speaking) was not an essential feature. Apart from work on calorimetry, which sprang from physics and not from chemistry, there is hardly a great experiment on the decomposition or synthesis of water, from 1785, which necessitated relatively accurate measurement. This is so true that his real precision instruments, balances included, were built in the last ten years of his life, when all his important results had been obtained and his theories constructed.

But Lavoisier's work had a considerable influence in introducing the practice of precise measurement into chemistry. First, it served in some sense as a demonstration for following generations of chemists; it had swept aside a certain part of the traditional methods, and it was becoming evident that to go further into the knowledge of chemical phenomena it was going to prove necessary to be more demanding in the accuracy of measurement. If the chemistry of Lavoisier was more qualitative than quantitative, it implied that that which followed would become quantitative. Moreover, the demands of Lavoisier had led the instrument-makers to adapt their products to the needs of this new stage of chemical research.

It is perhaps from another current of research that the necessity for precision measurements in chemistry was born: that which led from tables of affinity to stoichiometric laws and the atomic theory. These sorts of research necessitated, from the work of Bergman to that of Berzelius, an accuracy more and more directed towards quantitative analysis. The proof of this was given by the results of the celebrated polemic between Proust and Berthollet where the analyst overcame the theoretician. Now, this current of research is quite independent of the work of Lavoisier. The latter was not ignorant of this; he even wrote that he hoped from it for better progress in chemical knowledge; but he judged it would so monopolize his time that he would not allow himself to participate in it. Thus was produced a conjunction of the effects of the two great lines of chemical development at the end of the eighteenth century to give to precision measurement a primary importance in the new stages which were to come.

Our conclusion is that the physicists and chemists of the eighteenth century, unlike the astronomers and mathematicians, did not find it imperative to make use of very great accuracy in their measurements. But they placed scientific research in material and intellectual conditions such that henceforward an ever-growing precision of quantitative observation became indispensable for all progress in knowledge.

Bibliography

M. DAUMAS, *Les instruments scientifiques aux XVIIe et XVIIIe siècles* (Paris, 1953)

M. DAUMAS (editor), *Histoire de la science* (Paris, 1957)

14

Intellectual Factors in the Background of Analysis by Probabilities

C. C. GILLISPIE

On 21 September 1859, Maxwell appeared before the British Association for the Advancement of Science meeting in Aberdeen and read a paper, "Illustrations of the Dynamical Theory of Gases".[1] He introduced it as an essay of the atomic hypothesis in the special case of the kinetic consideration of gases, the velocity of the particles rising with temperature. The argument demonstrates the laws of motion among an "indefinite number of small, hard, and perfectly elastic spheres acting on one another only during impact",[2] and proceeds to compare the properties of such a system to the experimental gas laws. The yield is interesting. One set of equations, for example, entails the surprising consequence that friction is independent of density. Perhaps the most encouraging deduction confirmed Avogadro's law based on chemical information that the number of particles is the same in unit volume of different gases. But what physics prizes most highly is the analysis which Maxwell here employed.

In form, the essay consists in a series of propositions analytical of the laws of motion in the hypothetical system. Maxwell established his mode of reasoning in Proposition IV: "To find the average number of particles whose velocities lie between given limits, after a great number of collisions among a great number of equal particles." Maxwell makes it appear upon analysis "that the velocities are distributed among the particles according to the same law as the errors are distributed among the observations in the theory of the 'method of least squares' ".[3]

In the second part of the paper, Maxwell distinguishes between the motion of translation of the system as a whole, and the "motion of agitation" wherein the "collisions are so frequent that the law of distribution of the molecular velocities, if disturbed in any way, will be re-established in an appreciably

[1] James Clerk Maxwell, *Scientific Papers*, ed. W. D. Niven (2 vols. Cambridge, 1890) I, 377–409.

[2] Ibid. I, 377.

[3] Ibid. I, 380–2.

short time".[1] Thus did Maxwell inaugurate the science of statistical mechanics. The law of errors had itself been introduced as a rule of procedure by Legendre, and clarified geometrically by Gauss before Laplace put it on a rigorous footing in the *Essai analytique des probabilités*, the *Summa* of the early history of probabilities.[2] And the purpose of the present memoir is to survey the intellectual and philosophical elements which preceded and permitted Maxwell's novel application of a probabilistic analysis, not just as theretofore to games or affairs, but to a dynamical problem of matter in motion.

A peculiarity distinguishes the prior intellectual history of probability. The recourse to example was more immediate and frequent than in other modes of mathematical reasoning. Nevertheless, it appears to have been a branch of analysis undernourished by worthy materials. Nor was this for lack of concern in application among the protagonists. Indeed, the school of rational mechanics held high hope of the calculus of probability as an instrument of exact science adaptable (in the complexity if not the contingency of the human condition) to civil and moral matters and to their improvement by administration. Condorcet undertook his probabilistic essay of electoral procedures at Turgot's behest.[3] Laplace from the very beginning of his career divided his main efforts between celestial mechanics and probabilities, the one line concerned with the real world and the other with our procedures for knowing about it. "La courbe", says his famous summary in the *Essai philosophique des probabilités*, "décrite par une simple molécule d'air ou de vapeurs est réglée d'une manière aussi certaine que les orbites planétaires: il n'y a de différence entre elles que celle qu'y met notre ignorance. La probabilité est relative en partie à cette ignorance, en partie à nos connaissances".[4] The dichotomy guided his earlest investigations, and oriented — or perhaps it restricted — his thinking about civil applications toward repairs that might be worked in our ignorance of causes of events.

To "déterminer la probabilité des causes par les événements" was the object of Laplace's earliest memoir of a philosophic character. He describes it as a "matière neuve à bien des égards et qui mérite d'autant plus d'être cultivée que c'est principale-

[1] Ibid. I, 392.

[2] P. S. Laplace, *Œuvres* (14 vols., Paris, 1878–1912) VII, 353.

[3] S. D. Poisson, *Recherches sur la probabilité des jugements* (Paris, 1837) 3.

[4] Laplace, *Œuvres*, VII, p. viii.

ment sous ce point de vue que la science des hasards peut être utile dans la vie civile".[1] Uncertainty in knowledge bears either on events or on their causes. If an urn is known to contain a certain number of black and white slips in a given ratio, and the probability is required of drawing a white one, then the cause is known and the event uncertain. But if the ratio is unknown, and after drawing a white slip one is to say the probability that it is as p to q, then the event is known and the cause unknown. All problems of the theory of chance might be assigned to one or other of these alternative classes. The second, that of inverse probabilities, was the more interesting to Laplace, and his memoir treated it by establishing and exemplifying a rule known under the name of Bayes, who had put it forward less cogently in 1763. It will be clearer to quote the terms in which Laplace couched it in the *Essai analytique*:

> Si un événement observé peut résulter de n causes différentes, leurs probabilités sont respectivement comme les probabilités de l'évènement tirées de leur existence; et la probabilité de chacune d'elles est une fraction dont le numérateur est la probabilité de l'événement dans l'hypothèse de l'existence de la cause, et dont le dénominateur est la somme des probabilités semblables, relatives à toutes les causes.[2]

Other major preoccupations of the *Essai analytique* are apparent in germ in this and in accompanying memoirs — technical problems which led to generating functions; the choice of a correct value among observations (which led to the law of errors); the evaluation of "espérance morale" in games and decisions (out of which economists would later make the principle of marginal utility); the confidence that demographic information might warrant in particular instances. The *Essai* is a summary of all this, notable for the virtuosity of technique and the unity and steadiness of vision in which Laplace held the subject. Nor did he even then move beyond the causal to a statistical treatment of events, and that is the most important limitation to this thinking. His estimates bore upon the chances that we are or are not mistaken about the cause of phenomena and not upon configurations in the data themselves. He studied to know, not the mean about which the barometer varies, but the probability that the fluctuations have a constant cause.

[1] "Mémoire sur la probabilité des causes par les événements", *Mémoires de mathématique et de physique, presentés . . . par divers savans*, VI (1774) 612–56, p. 622.

[2] Laplace, *Œuvres*, VII, 183.

And in the case of minor inequalities in planetary motions, the magnitude of such a probability encouraged him to establish the cause.

Nevertheless, it was primarily Bayes's principle of inverse probability that permitted Laplace his hopes for mathematics as an instrument of social and political amelioration,[1] and the sectors of polity in which he thought to help were electoral procedures, decisions of representative bodies, credibility of witnesses, and the reliability of judicial tribunals. In every case the intent was to know causes from events in order to correct false ones. By "false" causes Laplace meant those that produce events unconformable to principles of morality and justice. "*Vérité, justice, humanité*", he told the *École normale* in the lecture on probability which concluded his course in the year III, "voilà les lois éternelles de l'ordre social qui doit reposer uniquement sur les vrais rapports de l'homme avec ses semblables et avec la nature; elles sont aussi nécessaires à son maintien que la gravitation universelle à l'existence de l'ordre physique. . . ".[2] And though Laplace developed it last, the analysis of judicial decisions aroused greater interest than did other problems. Indeed, it became almost a test-case of mathematics applied to morality, and his procedures may be taken as a paradigm of the entire programme.

In the last article of the first edition of the *Essai analytique*, Laplace treated the judgment of a tribunal pronouncing between two contradictory opinions as he had the problem (already analysed) of the testimony of several witnesses about the extraction of one number from an urn containing only two. If p is the probability that each judge finds the truth, then given r judges the probability of a unanimous verdict will be

$$\frac{p^r}{p^r + (1 - p)^r}.$$

One may compute p from the ratio of unanimous verdicts i to the total number of cases n. Then from the relation

$$p^r + (1 - p)^r = \frac{i}{n}$$

it may be shown that in the case (say) of a panel of three judges,

$$p = \frac{1}{2} \pm \sqrt{\left(\frac{4i - n}{12n}\right)}.$$

Laplace chose the positive root on the ground that it is more

[1] *Mémoires de mathématique et de physique*, VI, 652–3.

[2] Laplace, *Œuvres*, XIV, 173.

natural to assign each judge a greater probability for truth than for error. Let us suppose, then, that we have to do with a court half of whose judgments are unanimous. In that case the probability of the veracity of each judge will be 0·789, and the probability that a verdict sustained on appeal is in fact just will be 0·981 (if the finding is unanimous) and 0·789 (if it is by split vote). "Il y a donc", concludes Laplace, perhaps to exemplify his dictum that probability is only common sense reduced to computation, "un grand avantage à former des tribunaux d'appel, composés d'un grand nombre de juges choisis parmi les personnes les plus éclairées."[1]

An added complication occurred to Laplace for inclusion in a supplement to the *Essai analytique*. Jurors (unlike urn-watchers in this respect) might differ on the fact in perfect good faith. With this consideration in mind, Laplace gave the problem an elaboration which he thereafter addressed to the general public in later editions of the *Essai philosophique*. Taking the condemnation as event, the probability is required that it was caused by the guilt of the accused as opposed to the error of the jurors. As always computation by Bayes's rule presupposed values for the probabilities in play. Laplace assigned $\frac{1}{2}$ as the prior probability that the accused was guilty (thus following a regulative principle laid down in his earliest memoir on causes from events), and assumed that the probability of a truthful juror varies between $\frac{1}{2}$ and 1. This may appear a somewhat dubious construction upon his choice of the positive root in the earlier analysis, and Laplace now justified it on the ground that in an ordered society one cannot well suppose jurors more prone to error than to truth. Even so his computations alarm. In a panel of eight members of whom five suffice for conviction, the probability of error came to $\frac{65}{256}$ or more than $\frac{1}{4}$. On the other hand, Laplace felt that English criminal procedure weighted the odds too heavily against the security of society. It was his considered opinion in the *Essai philosophique* that a majority of 9 out of 12 produced the nicest equilibrium between the protection of society on the one hand and of innocence on the other.[2]

To Poisson as to his master, judicial probabilities appealed as a critical test of mathematics applied to the moral order. He feared lest it fail, however, through insecurity in the *a priori* values which Laplace had assigned to the chance of guilt in the accused and error in the juror. To repair this deficiency

[1] Ibid. VII, 469–70.

[2] Ibid. VII, 520–30.

Poisson put a novel approach in hand.[1] In 1825 the French government had begun publishing annual *comptes généraux* of judicial proceedings. Thereby Poisson could look to experience for the numbers. He assigned a probability of guilt from the ratio of convictions to cases over the years 1825–33 inclusive, and computed the probability of a juror or judge finding in error by analysing the voting records of panel and of bench. Poisson took confidence from what he enounced (none too clearly) as the law of large numbers. In practice, this would appear to have been a reference of Bernoulli's theorems to the phenomenon of statistical regularities.[2] Taken over the whole of France, the rate of conviction was notably uniform: 0·61 for the first six years, varying only to 0·62 in 1826 and 0·60 in 1830. During those years a majority of seven to five sufficed to convict. The rule was changed to eight to four in 1831, and convictions declined to 0·54. In 1832 and 1833 instructions went out to judges to consider extenuating circumstances in fixing sentence, and jurors responded by increasing their severity to a rate of 0·59 in 1832 and staying steady there in 1833.

Statistical treatment, then, was the distinctive departure in Poisson's analysis:

> L'objet précis de la théorie est de calculer, pour des jurés composés d'un nombre déterminé de personnes, jugeant à une majorité aussi déterminée, et pour un très grand nombre d'affaires, la proportion des acquittements et des condamnations qui aura lieu très probablement, et la chance d'erreur d'un jugement pris au hasard parmi ceux qui ont été ou qui seront rendus par ces jurés. Déterminer la chance d'erreur ou d'acquittement prononcé dans un procès connu et isolé serait impossible selon moi, à moins de fonder le calcul sur des suppositions tout à fait précaires, qui conduiraient à des résultats très différents, et, à peu près, à ceux qui l'on voudrait, suivant ces hypothèses que l'on aurait adoptées.[3]

Poisson, indeed, was careful to distinguish between the mathematical and the moral sense of "guilty". It would be more exact, he observed, to substitute "condemnable" for "coupable", since the numbers in play are of those actually condemned, whether or not justly:

> Ainsi, lorsque nous trouverons que sùr un très grand nombre de jugements, il y a une certaine proportion de condamnations

[1] Poisson, *Recherches sur la probabilité des jugements* (Paris, 1837).
[2] Ibid. p. 7.
[3] Ibid. pp. 17–18.

erronées, il ne faudra pas entendre que cette proportion soit celle des condamnés innocents: ce sera la proportion des condamnés qui l'ont été à une trop faible probabilité, non pas pour établir qu'ils sont plutôt coupables qu'innocents, mais que leur condamnation fût nécessaire à la sûreté publique. Déterminer parmi ces condamnés, le nombre de ceux qui réellement n'étaient pas coupables, ce n'est pas l'objet de nos calculs. . . .[1]

Fortunately, there was reason (Poisson felt) to believe the number small, because of the rarity of pardons and of verdicts which offended public opinion. Even in the mathematical sense, moreover, his statistical probabilities appeared far more auspicious for the prospects of justice in France than did Laplace's estimate of the chances in particular cases. Before 1831, for example, the probability that a juror would not be mistaken in his vote was a little better than $\frac{2}{3}$ in the case of crimes against persons and approximately $\frac{13}{17}$ in crimes against property. Taking account of appeals, the probability of guilt was 0·98 in convictions sustained of crimes against persons and 0·998 against property when the court of first instance had voted eight to four. Conversely, the probabilities of innocence were 0·72 and 0·82 respectively when the first findings were reversed. Taking into consideration the initial probability of not being condemned, the probabilities that a guilty person would be acquitted were 0·18 and 0·07. This meant that there were about forty innocent parties among 8,000 found guilty of personal crimes at eight to four, and about eighty-eight out of 22,000 similarly condemned for violations of property. In civil cases, to cite one other result (for the years 1831–3), the probability of a correct judgment at first instance was 0·76, that of correct confirmation on appeal 0·948, that of a correct reversal on appeal 0·64, that of a confirmation of a first appeal by a second 0·75.

Nor did Poisson dodge the objection that the proceedings of revolutionary tribunals invalidated his calculations. There were always two roots to the basic equation, and Poisson followed Laplace in taking the positive root as the solution for the sane society in which judges have a greater tendency to justice than to error: "Mais il n'en est plus de même quand les jugements sont prononcés sous l'influence des passions; ce n'est plus la racine raisonnable des équations, c'est l'autre solution qu'il faut employer, et qui donne aux condamnations une si grande probabilité d'injustice."[2]

[1] Ibid. p. 6.

[2] Ibid. p. 26.

Poisson's "law of large numbers" sometimes seems to reach out towards a statistical mechanics, but he was not the man to find the way.[1] One paragraph, for example, does suggest that "La constitution des corps formés de molécules disjointes que séparent des espaces vides de matière pondérable, offre aussi une application, d'une nature particulière, de la loi des grands nombres". From any point in the interior of a body, one might draw lines measuring the distance to the nearest molecule. Though small in all directions, that distance might be ten, twenty, or even a hundred times greater in one direction than in another. The distribution of molecules would be very irregular around any point and constantly changing with their vibrations. Dividing an element of volume by the number of molecules therein and extracting the cube root of the quotient, one would have a "mean interval" of the molecules, independent of the irregularity of distribution, and abstracting from any compression produced by weight; this mean interval would obtain throughout a body at constant temperature. But Poisson gave no rule for the distribution of molecules around his mean, and he was in fact thinking not of kinetics but of the solid state, not of a way to compute the variations from a mean, but of his law of large numbers as the key:

> De ces exemples de toutes natures, il résulte que la loi universelle des grands nombres est déjà pour nous un fait général et incontestable, résultant d'expériences qui ne se démentent jamais. Cette loi étant d'ailleurs la base de toutes les applications du calcul des probabilités, on conçoit maintenant leur indépendance de la nature des questions, et leur parfaite similitude, soit qu'il s'agisse de choses physiques ou de choses morales, pourvu que les données spéciales que le calcul exige, dans chaque problème, nous soient fournies par l'observation.[2]

Poisson presented the regulative remarks and the numerical results of his investigation of judicial processes in preliminary reports to the Academy of Sciences in 1835 and 1836,[3] and the interest they provoked initiated a philosophical discussion of the prospect for probabilities.[1] To review the main positions will suggest, perhaps, that formation of a statistical mechanics required operations of technique on data in a relation to nature that was by no means obvious. Poisson in his statistical analysis did transcend the Laplacean dichotomy according to which

[1] For example, Ibid. pp. 7–8. [2] Ibid. p. 12.

[3] *Comptes-rendus . . . de l'Académie des Sciences,* I (1835) 473–94; II (1836) 377–80, 395–400.

mechanics describes nature causally and probability repairs our ignorance of causes. Nevertheless, Poisson intended no retreat from the strict determinism of nature itself or from causalism as the grail of science. And it is ironical that Comte, whose philosophy seems most in keeping with the expanding fortunes of the probabilistic analysis, should have rejected the technique while heaping scorn and contumely upon its advocates; whereas Cournot, who alone advanced the idea of an order of chance *per se* and adopted probabilism as an advance upon universal determinism, never laid hold on the statistical assemblage of information or its rationalization about a mean, the which techniques might have bodied his probabilistic philosophy of science into science itself.

From our perspective it appears as if Comte and his disciples might properly have seized on probability and carried it over from the account it gave of error to an account of fact. In their philosophy science knows only for prediction, not by the light of reality, and predicts only for control and not to say truth. And Comte in his phenomenalism and relativism might well have built whatever there was of uncertainty in the observations right into science itself. Instead, he repudiated probability. He wrote, indeed, with violence. He stigmatized it as the illusion "propre aux géomètres" who should seek to render social science positive by "une subordination chimérique à l'illusoire théorie mathématique des chances". The geometric aberration was even more vicious than that of biologists who would create a sociology as appendage to biology. Both would dispense with the indispensable in foregoing historical analysis. That fallacy had been excusable enough in the time of Jacques Bernoulli, less so in that of Condorcet, and impossible to forgive in Laplace's latter years, "when the general state of human reason already began to permit a glimpse of the truly fundamental spirit of a healthy political philosophy". Poisson fared even worse, among "imitateurs subalternes" who are exploiting the just prestige of mathematics in a sort of "manie algébrique, maintenant trop familière au vulgaire des géomètres". The very notion of evaluating probability was radically irrational, except in games of chance where it started and still belongs. It would lead us to reject as unlikely events which, however, are sometimes going to occur. It would lead us to "donner notre propre ignorance réelle pour la mesure naturelle du degré de vraisemblance de nos diverses opinions". And no doubt Comte was himself too close to Laplace to see probabilities in a context other than that of Laplace's philosophy of nature, causal and deterministic.[1]

The temper of Cournot's philosophy is appealing by comparison, and many of the positions which he took have since been firmly occupied.[2] Certainly he intended to lay down a foundation for a probabilistic science, and he identified and clarified elements that later went into the statistical view of phenomena. But it does not appear that his thoughts were heeded or his writings influential. The abortive quality of his career makes a curious study, therefore, and the neglect that was accorded him a sad one. His view of the relations of science and metaphysics was as astringent as Comte's, and far more modest about the function of philosophy. Criticism and analysis of the ideas and procedures of science are the main business of philosophy, which indeed depends on science for materials on which to work. But science does not graduate into philosophy and become historically subservient to a positive sociology and ultimately even obsolete. Science and philosophy retain their identities in a dialogue of matter and form. Cournot appears, moreover, to have been the closest of the French rational school to the empiricism of his British contemporaries, both in knowledge and in spirit. He was the translator of Herschel's *Treatise on Astronomy*, and the inherent compatibility of his interests with Herschel's will appear as significant in relation to his probabilism.

Cournot formed his views from mathematical experience. The problems that attracted him had a common characteristic — they occurred in sectors which invited statistical or probabilistic analysis or both in the combination which would break down in mathematical practice the barrier of principle between physical and civil phenomena. Two of his earliest articles consider the probability that the sequence and inclination of the orbits of comets are determined causally. He treated judicial statistics from a point of view similar to Poisson's, drawing on fuller records in the years after 1835. His first general treatise, *Recherches sur les principes mathématiques de la théorie des richesses*, was a true trailblazer. It is not too much

[1] Auguste Comte, *Cours de philosophie positive*, ed. E. Littré (6 vols., Paris 1869) II, 255 n. (27e léçon); IV, 366–368 (49e léçon).

[2] F. Mentré, *Cournot et la renaissance du positivisme* (Paris, 1908); Jean de la Harpe, *De l'ordre et du hasard* (Neuchâtel, 1936), M. H. Moore, ed. and trans., *An Essay on the Foundations of our Knowledge by Cournot* (New York, 1956); E. Callot, *La philosophie biologique de Cournot* (Paris, 1960).

to describe it as the first full treatise of mathematical economics and the link between the definitions of moral expectation in the theory of probabilities and the mathematization of economic science at the hands of Jevons and Marshall. Here again Cournot figured as an intermediary between French rationalism and British empiricism. His moderation emerges to characteristic advantage from his remarks on economics. Most economists, he observed, set their faces against mathematical expression because they took an overly simple view of its value. They expected numerical results, and if they could not have them, regarded formalization as pedantic. But the object of analysis is not mere computation. It is to find relations between magnitudes which are not numerable and between functions that go beyond algebraic expression. Thus, the theory of probabilities will yield important propositions, even though for lack of information it often happens that numbers can be assigned to contingent events only in cases that are merely curious, and notably in that of games. Rational mechanics is no different in principle. It demonstrates theorems. Nor does their interest depend entirely on the numbers, which have usually to come from experiment. So with economics:

> I am far from having thought of writing in support of any system, and from joining the banners of any party; I believe that there is an immense step in passing from theory to governmental applications; I believe that theory loses none of its value in thus remaining preserved from contact with impassioned polemics; and I believe, if this essay is of any practical value, it will be chiefly in making clear how far we are from being able to solve, with full knowledge of the case, a multitude of questions which are boldly decided every day.[1]

In the expansion of his interests from the mathematical, Cournot moved from comets and judicial statistics through quantification in political economy to the composition of *Exposition de la théorie des chances et des probabilités*. That work advances the ideas which Cournot elaborated into a full philosophy. Its propositions are bound to arrest the attention of anyone interested in the intellectual history of probability. Probabilism was to Cournot what positivism was to Comte, the keystone of a philosophy, notable if not notorious. He, too, took issue with Laplace, not, however, by dismissing probability with dogmatic petulance, but by promoting it and

[1] A. Cournot, *Researches into the Mathematical Principles of the Theory of Wealth* (tr. Nathaniel Bacon, New York, 1927) 5.

assigning chance an objective standing in the world of phenomena. For probability is no mere "calculus of illusions":

> Pendant longtemps on n'a guère appliqué le calcul des chances qu'à des problèmes sur les jeux, problèmes purement spéculatifs ou d'un futile intérêt pratique, et à des faits de statistique sociale dont les causes se dérobent par leur complication à toutes investigations mathématiques, et pour lesquels nous n'avons d'autres données que celles de l'expérience. On s'est peu occupé de l'adapter à des questions de philosophie naturelle, questions pour ainsi dire de nature mixte, où l'on aurait pu espérer de confronter les données de l'observation avec des relations fournies par la théorie.[1]

That chance and order both subsist in objective reality was Cournot's point of departure. Nor did this proposition imply any retreat from causality, but rather a quite novel appreciation of its plurality. Every effect has a cause and may in its turn become the cause of a subsequent event. Such a chain of successive causes and effects forms a linear series of events. There may be any number, an infinite number, of such chains of events running through the world quite independently one of another. One causal chain leads the tile to fall from the roof. Another leads a man to walk by at just that instant. And the chains cross in this, a fortuitous but not an uncaused blow on the scalp. "Events brought about by the combination or conjunction of other events which belong to independent series are called *fortuitous* events, or the results of *chance*".[2] And these intersections are what open the domain of physical phenomena to the calculus of probability.

Mathematical probability is connected to phenomena that happen thus by chance through the notion of physical impossibility. It is physically impossible, for example, that a cone should stand stably on its apex, that a balance should be perfectly precise, or that a sphere should be struck so shrewdly on a line through its centre that no rotation would result. The chances against such an event are logically identical with the improbability of a man in blindfold drawing the one white ball from an urn containing besides an infinity of black ones.

> Consequently it may be said more briefly, in the accepted language of mathematicians, that a physically impossible event is one whose mathematical probability is infinitely small. . . . Thus

[1] Cournot, *Exposition de la théorie des chances et des probabilités* (Paris, 1843) 261.

[2] Cournot, *Essay on the Foundations of Knowledge* (Moore ed.) 41.

mathematical probability becomes the limit of physical possibility, and the two expressions may be used interchangeably.[1]

Cournot developed the comparison into a distinction between what he called the subjective and objective senses of probability. Laplace had confined probability to the former sense, and thereby told — or foretold — only half the story. Given the hypothetical being invoked by Laplace, possessing a sensorium and a mind capable of reporting and knowing all the causes and effects — given those capacities, mathematical probability would disappear for lack of an object. This would not follow from Cournot's conception of nature, wherein even a perfect intelligence would still require its services in computing intersections of independent causal chains. For such a being mathematical probability would fill the office of experiment among ourselves. Far from being a calculus of illusions, therefore, mathematical probability seemed to Cournot precisely that application to phenomena which most widely justified the ancient saying, *Mundum regunt numeri*. And it is not the least interesting aspect of his philosophy that he should have associated it with the limitations of mechanics:

> We have no basis for believing that we can give an account of all phenomena simply by means of the ideas of extension, time, and motion, that is, in a word, simply by the continuous magnitudes on which the measurements and calculations of mathematics rest. The acts of living, intelligent, and moral beings are by no means explained, in the present state of our knowledge, and there is good reason to believe that they never will be explained by mechanics and mathematics. Consequently, these acts do not take their place in the field of numbers on the same basis as geometry and mechanics do. Yet they find their place in this field in so far as the notions of combination and of chance, of cause and of fortune, are superior to geometry and mechanics in the order of abstractions, and apply to phenomena in the domain of living things as to those that produce the forces which activate inorganic matter; to the reflective acts of free beings as to the inescapable determinations of appetite and of instinct.[2]

Is it only in retrospect that this is suggestive? Only in the light of subsequent statistical methods which in fact owe little to Cournot? It may be so. No filiation can be established, at any rate, between the first practice of statistical mechanics, and this, the philosophy which systematically explored the role of chance in natural phenomena. In his classification of the

[1] Ibid. p. 47.

[2] Ibid. p. 50.

sciences, Cournot himself — his views are nothing if not unexpected — regarded political economy as quantifiable and therefore ranking after physics and before biology. Biology would ever remain inaccessible to mathematics, divided in principle from physics and politics and all exact science. And though it is surprising for a mathematician thus to have begun his philosophy in political economy and ended it in vitalism, it seems clear that its inconclusiveness turned on a simple failure. He never hit upon the analytical devices and numerical regularities which might have converted his hypothetical play of chance into a computable order of chance. He never reasoned on the mean, or exploited the law of error, and only occasionally referred in passing to the work of Quetelet, who did just that, and who pieced together the techniques.

It conditioned the pre-history of probability in physics that its protagonists should have had their footing in astronomy and their eye upon society. Founder of the Observatory in Brussels, Quetelet went to Paris in 1823 to study under Laplace, Fourier, and Poisson, became more interested in Laplace's course on probabilities than in those on astronomy, and returned to make his observatory a centre rather of statistical than celestial observation. His career might be taken as a medium for studying the migration of techniques. Popularization fell among his responsibilities, and in 1828 he published *Instructions sur le calcul des probabilités*. The chief interest consists in two chapters explaining Fourier's method of approximating a mean in statistical information by the rule of least squares.[1] He had already in his earliest mathematical paper printed a geometrical study of what he did not then recognize as the binomial curve. From the outset, therefore, he disposed of the two essential elements of which the combination would yield his analytical technique. But he did not as yet see their application to mobilizing the statistical information which all the while he made it his vocation to assemble.

Quetelet's summary of the special statistical studies of those earlier years remains the most famous of his writings — *Sur l'homme et le développement de ses facultés*.[2] The sub-title is *Essai de physique sociale*, and the work wears two aspects, a tabular and a programmatic. Book I contains vital statistics: birth rates,

[1] Joseph Lottin, *Quetelet, statisticien et sociologue* (Louvain, 1912) 118 citing Fourier, *Recherches statistiques sur la ville de Paris*, III (1823) pp. ix–xxxi.

[2] 2 vols., 1836.

taken with reference to population and to marriages; variations thereof with climate, class, economic condition, and habitat; ratios of male to female in town and country, by legitimate and illegitimate status, and according to the absolute and relative ages of parents; death rates by climate and locale, by profession, by age-group, and by sex; scattered information on the incidence of still-birth and certain diseases; estimates of densities of population and rates of growth. Quetelet took his figures where he could find them. He looked to Malthus, Sadler, and Porter, to the publications of scientific societies, to a British peerage, to the French judicial statistics on which Poisson had drawn, to parish registers and urban bureaus, to his own Belgian census returns and to those of Prussia. In Book II Quetelet turned to anthropometry. He gave figures on height and weight and their proportions according to age, sex, and circumstance, and introduced manpower measurements of the force exercised by arm and thigh. Book III deals with the effects of the moral and intellectual faculties. Quetelet chose the drama as a cultural phenomenon to be handled statistically, and made estimates of the comparative productivity of the French theatre. It figures among the findings that tragedy is a secretion of youthful dramatists and comedy of aged ones. What most struck the moralists of the age were the figures bespeaking the regularity of incidence of crimes in any modes. In this connexion Quetelet observed that the difference between speaking of a propensity to courage and a propensity to theft is that the law defines and the state identifies instances of the latter. We have the figures.

All this constituted the prologue to a social physics, his hopes for which Quetelet placed in the identification and specification of man thus measured, man the mean. The flyleaf to Volume II bears an epigraph from Laplace on probabilities: "Appliquons aux sciences politiques et morales la méthode fondée sur l'observation et sur le calcul, méthode qui nous a bien servi dans les sciences naturelles." Statistics contain the evidence for regularities that exhibit the service to law of moral phenomena. There are two conditions for a social science, two conditions and an instrument that brings it within reach of quantification. The first condition is that we should study "les qualités de l'homme qui ne sont appréciables que par leurs effets",[1] and the second that we should abandon as inaccessible to science consideration of man as an individual and take him in the

[1] Ibid. II, 114.

mass. And what gives authority for this procedure is precisely the instrument by which we reduce the laws to numbers. "Le calcul des probabilités montre que, toutes choses égales, on se rapproche d'autant plus de la vérité ou des lois que l'on veut saisir, que les observations embrassent un plus grand nombre d'individus." But the inacccessibility of the individual derogates not a whit from the rigour of the laws. Physics offers the analogy of statical analysis, which employs the centre of gravity rather than considering all the points distributed through the figure of a body. In just such wise will the *homme moyen* figure in the laws of social physics:

> L'homme que je considère ici est, dans la société, l'analogue du centre de gravité dans les corps; il est la moyenne autour de laquelle oscillent les éléments sociaux; ce sera, si l'on veut, un être fictif pour qui toutes les choses se passeront conformément aux résultats moyens obtenus pour la société. Si l'on cherche à établir, en quelque sorte, les bases d'une *physique sociale*, c'est lui qu'on doit considérer.[1]

Nevertheless, social physics was at best a qualitative science in *L'homme et ses facultés*, for Quetelet had devised no useful way of assigning numerical values to the faculties or dimensions of his human mean, who as yet was nothing more determinate than the average man. For example, in his discussion of the weight of a population of 10,000 souls (or bodies), Quetelet multiplied the average weight at certain ages by the proportion of the population within those limits, and computed the mass of men and women between the years of thirty and forty, forty and fifty, etc. The population of Brussels he estimated at 4,572,810 kilograms, which was to say four and a half times the weight of a cube of water ten metres square. Indeed, the entire human race would not balance thirty-three cubes of water 100 metres on a side.

So much for *Sur l'homme et ses facultés*. The phrase "social physics" was little of a novelty, and the vein is humanitarian and uncritical, not to say naïve. Ten years later Quetelet published a further general work, *Lettres à S.A.R. le Duc régnant de Sax-Cobourg-et-Gotha sur la théorie des probabilités appliquée aux sciences morales et politiques*.[2] The title seems to promise even less than *Sur l'homme*. At this date one does not expect to find an important treatise masquerading under the conceit of letters to an enlightened princeling. The book contains neither new

[1] Ibid. I, 21–2.

[2] Brussels, 1846; citations are to the English translation (London, 1846).

compilations nor mathematical novelties, and it must be admitted that not all the examples satisfy. Nevertheless, this volume is no mere exhortation. Rather, it is a synthesis, a real synthesis in which probabilities and statistics met in that relationship of language and subject which opened the way to a statistical account of nature. It seems to me, indeed, that the difference between this social physics and Maxwell's statistical mechanics is in the objects rather than the methods. The latter distributes velocities instead of deaths or births about a mean, but the distribution is similar and the mean is what counts. Consider Quetelet himself on his conception of statistics as a science:

> Collecting statistics is generally verv well understood. But it is not so with the definitions of this science: there is almost always a tendency greatly to confine its domain. I think that the definition which I propose, and which moreover varies little from that given by many modern scientific men, sufficiently circumscribes the attributes of statistics, for it not to be confounded with the historical sciences or the other political and moral sciences which is the nearest approach to it. *It only considers a state during a determined period: it only collects the elements connected with the life of this state, applies itself to make them comparable, and compares them in the manner which is most advantageous with a view of showing all the facts they can reveal.*[1]

The argument turns upon the distinction which Quetelet now introduces between an average and a mean, or as he says an arithmetical mean (that having been his criterion of *l'homme moyen*) and a true mean. Since writing *Sur l'homme* he has found out how to represent the distribution of deviations from the "true" — i.e. most probable — value. The technique resolved the situation under study into two sorts of occurrence, complementary and equal in probability, which might come about in groups distinguished by the combinations — for example, the drawing of black and white balls two at a time, or five at a time, or 999 at a time. Quetelet chose the deaths of men and women in a city where equal numbers die, and showed that the combinations of male and female deaths taken in groups of one, two, three, and up to thirteen may be represented by Pascal's triangle, which was to say by the binomial expansion.

This was rather a case of recognition than of discovery. A memoir of 1844 contains Quetelet's first construction of this

[1] Ibid. p. 182.

"échelle de possibilité".[1] Like the least square rule, which he had expounded in 1828, a "courbe de possibilité" figures in Quetelet's earliest work, without his having then imagined its identity with the "binomial law" by which he would situate his mean amid the data.[2] *Sur l'homme* itself contains tables of meteorological observations and of human stature which might have been graphed to represent the distribution of positive and negative deviations from the mean. But Quetelet did not then see the opportunity: "Je ne déterminai d'abord pas la véritable nature de la courbe qui se rapportait à ces lois (relatives aux facultés de l'homme); mais je reconnus plus tard que c'était la fameuse formule de binome de Newton."[3]

What was novel, therefore, was not the mathematics, but the analytical idea that exploited it and permitted the combination of a distribution according to the binomial expansion with the least square rule for prediction of probable error. The latter is the basis of Quetelet's "modulus of precision", a measure of the contraction of the curve of possibility towards the mean. That diminution varies as the square root of the number of observations (or possibilities). And now perhaps we may identify the elements of Quetelet's synthesis. Hitherto (unless I am wrong in this) Pascal's triangle or the binomial expansion had governed combinations of events equal in chance and opposite in nature, whereas the least square rule had governed the distribution of mistakes and inaccuracies. The very phrase "law of errors" restricted application to departures from the truth or target. Thus, the crucial idea that permitted Quetelet his synthesis was that measurements themselves may be taken as events subject to equal chances of error in excess or in defect. The difference in sign disappears when the magnitude is squared to compute the probability. One must cite his favourite illustration. He took it from the thirteenth volume of the *Edinburgh Medical Journal*, where there appeared a compilation of the chest measurements of 5,738 Scottish soldiers of various regiments. The figure for the puniest was 33 and for the huskiest 48; and

> The mean of all these measurements gives a little more than 40 inches as the average circumference of the chest of a Scotch soldier:

[1] "Sur l'appréciation des documents statistiques", *Bulletin de la commission centrale de statistique*, II (1845) 205–86.

[2] "Sur une nouvelle théorie des sections coniques considerées dans le solide" (14 October 1820), cited in Lottin, p. 14.

[3] Quoted in Lottin, p. 155.

this is also the number which corresponds to the largest group of measurements; and, as theory points out, the other groups diminish in proportion as they recede from it. The probable variation is 1·312 — a value of which we should not lose sight.

I now ask if it would be exaggerating, to make an even wager that a person little practised in measuring the human body would make a mistake of an inch in measuring a chest of more than 40 inches in circumference? Well, admitting this probable error, 5,738 measurements made on one individual would certainly not group themselves with more regularity, as to the order of magnitude, than the 5,738 measurements made on the Scotch soldiers; and if the two series were given to us without their being particularly designated, we should be much embarrassed to state which series was taken from 5,738 different soldiers, and which was obtained from one individual with less skill and ruder means of measurement.[1]

In uniting the distribution of binomial combinations with the law of errors, Quetelet may all unwittingly have done more for positivism than its founders, for this step abolished in practice the distinction between phenomenon and error, between nature and science, or (in Cournot's terms) between subjective and objective probability. No difference of treatment remains between a magnitude and a measurement, between an error of nature and an error of science. Thus, he liberated the analysis from its relativity to Laplace's ignorance of causes, and in effect opened the way to a probabilistic description of nature itself. "A chemist", he writes,

would have the greatest chance of arriving at results in conformity with truth, were he perfectly sure of his analyses. In drawing a glass of water from a pure spring, the atoms of oxygen and hydrogen would be found in an infinite number, and consequently in the ratio fixed by the Creator in the composition of water. This case corresponds with the extraction of an infinite number of balls from the urn.[2]

And in another passage, "The urn, then, which we interrogate is Nature."[3]

How far did Quetelet see down this, the vista he helped to open? Not far, perhaps — his gaze was fixed on social physics, not on physics, nor did he effect the transfer to mechanics of the bell-shaped curve. One who did see further was Herschel, who appreciated the prospect from the standpoint of British empiricism. Quetelet's *Letters on Probabilities* commanded little attention until Herschel took the English translation as occasion

[1] Quetelet, *Letters on Probability*, 92–3. [2] Ibid. p. 75. [3] Ibid. p. 20.

for a splendid essay in exposition of the entire subject of probabilistic analysis, an article which the *Edinburgh Review* published at the head of the journal in July, 1850.[1] I do not know whether Maxwell read and was instructed by this fine piece. He may well have been. Herschel republished it in a collection of his occasional essays on philosophy of nature in 1857, two years before Maxwell introduced statistical mechanics to the British Association. But I have nothing to go on beyond this *post hoc* relationship and Maxwell's well known familiarity with Herschel's work and admiration for his standing. And even if the connexion were established, the transmission of ideas in nineteenth-century science occurred along a front of communications broader than person-to-person filiation of influences.

In any case, Herschel's essay brought before the public explicitly that appreciation of the role of probabilities on which statistical mechanics did in fact depend. His own background of interests and values suited him to play the mediator — his studies of the distribution of stars in space, his support for liberal rationalization in political and economic affairs, his natural theology which recognized the contingency of the physical creation. In this last he was at one with Cournot, who had translated his *Astronomy* and who shared his astronomical and economic interests. Nor did Herschel's interest in Quetelet begin with the *Letters on Probability*. They had corresponded for some years, and Herschel actually prompted Quetelet to define the law of distribution from which he constructed his first curves. But with all this, what fundamentally informed Herschel's essay was his agreement with the philosophy of science of John Stuart Mill.

"Experience", he begins, "has been declared, with equal truth and poetry, to adopt occasionally the tone, and attain to something like the certainty of Prophecy."[2] Out of this confidence in the uniformity of past and future, Mill has constructed a philosophy of logic, a philosophy which amounts almost to a "discovery" in showing that all reasoning is from particulars to particulars, and that the business of inductive science is to determine what are the really relevant circumstances, what the uniformities which it then calls laws of nature. But what security have we for the truth of anything asserted about a fact that we have not observed? What measure is there of such security as may be found? For inductive philosophy

[1] *Edinburgh Review*, XCII (1850) 1–57. [2] Ibid. p. 1.

contents itself "with *practical*, as distinct from *mathematical*, certainty in all physical inquiry, and in all the transactions of life".[1] Probability is only the expression of that security and that certainty. Its theory gives the measure of it. It is, therefore, "as a practical auxiliary of the inductive philosophy that we have chiefly to contemplate this theory".[2]

Into its procedures, "its delicate and refined system of mathematical reasoning", no metaphysics intrudes and no pre-occupation with causation.[3] Cause means only the occasion for occurrence of a result with greater or lesser frequency. It may just as well consist in taking away some obstacle as in an efficient agent. Nor is the result variable in intensity or extent proportionally to the degree of the cause. A result is only an event that does or does not happen, of which the theory studies the frequency, whatever may be the physical or moral agencies at work within the system. Herschel knew the strain on ordinary habits of thinking about the civil and physical world imposed by so radical a reversion to common sense. To mitigate it was the purpose of his essay:

> There still remains behind, however, this inquiry — which we have known to occur as a difficulty to intellects of the first order — *Why* do events, on the long run, conform to the laws of probability? What is the *cause* of this phenomenon as a matter of fact? We reply (and the reply is no mere verbal subtlety), that events do not so conform themselves — the fact to the imagination — the real to the ideal — but that the laws of probability, as acknowledged by us, are framed in hypothetical accordance with events. To take the simplest case, that of a single contingency — the drawing of one of two balls, a black and a white. We suppose the chances equal, in theory; but, in practice, what is to assure us that they are so? The perfect similarity of the balls? But they need not be similar in any one quality but such as may influence their coming to hand. And, on the other side, the most perfect similarity in all visible, tangible, or other physical qualities cognisable to our tests is not such a similarity as we contemplate in theory, if there remain inherent in them, but undiscernible by us, any such difference as shall tend to bring one more readily to hand than the other. The ultimate test, then, of their similarity in that sense is not their general resemblance, but their verification of the rule of coming equally often to hand in an immense number of trials: and the observed fact, that events *do* happen according to their calculated chances, only shows that *apparent* similarities are very often *real* ones.[4]

One would not, indeed, wish to argue that Maxwell *had* to

[1] Ibid. p. 3. [2] Ibid. p. 29. [3] Ibid. p. 2. [4] Ibid. pp. 30-1.

read this essay. It is more impressive, perhaps, to take it as an epitome of the adaptability of probability in the medium of British liberalism and empiricism to important preoccupations of nineteenth-century science. Let me simply, by way of conclusion to what is meant most tentatively as an introduction, allude to two of the many further notes which Herschel strikes in his exposition, and which echo in familiar fashion.

The first may suggest the reflection that neither did Darwin really need to read Malthus. Herschel moves from the passage just quoted on the relation of probability to the world to a consideration of what we mean by tendencies observed in experience. Were we to ask why the strong win out and the weak get nothing, we would reply that this does not happen in every case, and that although we cannot go into the dynamics of every competition, nevertheless we see what happens in a number of instances and observe a "visible enough *tendency* to the defeat of the weaker party". Contrariwise, when we say that success is proof of ability, what we mean by ability is simply some undefined collection of qualities which has a tendency to success. We may not be able to identify all the qualities, or in very confused or obscure circumstances any of them, and have to fall back on our experience of the tendency itself:

> And it may further happen that this tendency, which we are driven to substitute in our language for its efficient cause, may be so feeble — whether owing to the feebleness of the unknown cause, its counteraction by others, or the few and disadvantageous opportunities afforded for its efficacious action (general words, framed to convey the indistinctness of our view of the matter) — as not to become known to us by long and careful observation, and by noting a preponderance of results in one direction rather than another.
>
> And thus we are led to perceive the true, and we may add, the only office of this theory in the research of causes. Properly speaking, it discloses, not causes, but tendencies, working through opportunities — which it is the business of an ulterior philosophy to connect with efficient or formal causes; and having disclosed them, it enables us to pronounce with decision, on the evidence of the numbers adduced, respecting the reliance to be placed on such indications. . . .[1]

And the second passage to be quoted evokes the approximation of social to physical science — or vice versa in the case of statistical mechanics — in a common method:

[1] Ibid. pp. 31–2.

Whether statistics be an art or a science . . . or a scientific art, we concern ourselves little. Define it as the way, it is the basis of social and political dynamics, and affords the only secure ground on which the truth or falsehood of the theories and hypothesis of that complicated science can be brought to the test. It is not unadvisedly that we use the term Dynamics as applied to the mechanism and movements of the social body; nor is it by any loose metaphor or strained analogy that much of the language of mechanical philosophy finds a parallel meaning in the discussion of such subjects. Both involve the consideration of momentary changes proportional to acting powers — of corresponding momentary displacements of the incidence of power — of impulse given and propagated onward — of resistance overcome — and of mutual reaction. Both involve the consideration of time as an essential element or independent variable; not simply delaying the final attainment of a state of equilibrium and repose — the final adjustment of interest and relations, and, in effect, rendering any such final state unattainable. . . .

Number, weight, and measure are the foundations of all exact science; neither can any branch of human knowledge be held advanced beyond its infancy which does not, in some way or other, frame its theories or correct its practice by reference to these elements. What astronomical records or meteorological registers are to a rational explanation of the movements of the planets or of the atmosphere, statistical returns are to social and political philosophy. They assign, at determinate intervals, the numerical values of the variables which form the subject matter of its reasonings, or at least of such 'functions' of them as are accessible to direct observation; which it is the business of sound theory so to analyse or to combine as to educe from them those deeper-seated elements which enter into the expression of general laws. We are far enough at present from the actual attainment of such knowledge, but there are several encouraging circumstances which forbid us despair of attaining it.[1]

[1] Ibid. pp. 40–1.

15

Physical Concepts that Cannot be Assimilated to Instrumentation

D. H. WILKINSON

I am writing these notes as an experimental physicist without knowledge of philosophy other than what has rubbed off in the course of casual contacts with colleagues, and without knowledge of the history of science. I am simply putting down raw evidence about the way practising physicists regard the conceptual background of their subject. Many of us do not think about it at all from one end of our career to the other and I am not prepared to say whether I think this is a good thing or not. I confidently anticipate that the whole of what I shall now say will be regarded as reprehensible if factual, trivial if true, and false if interesting. I take comfort in, but do not comment on, the general anti-correlation between the interest experimental physicists take in the philosophical implications of their work and the advances made in their subject by their endeavours.

Experimental physicists by trade deal only with observables. An actual measurement must be made in the macroscopic world and so the final manifestation linking the equipment with the experimenter must be classical. This does not mean that quantum phenomena do not have immediate macroscopic consequences as witness measurements of the specific heat of solids at low temperatures, the difference between the specific heats of metals and non-metals, the quantization of rotation in liquid helium and our inference of e/m for the electron from the current in a space-charge limited diode. These are macroscopic, classical measurements directly dependent on the quantization of the energy of oscillators, the antisymmetrization of fermion wave functions, the quantization of angular momentum and the value of atomic constants. Although these are striking examples in that they are each dominated by a single quantum effect and so may in some sense be (falsely) thought directly to demonstrate that effect they are only inferences from essentially macroscopic and classical properties and may alternatively be held to be no more essentially quantum in character than any other classical measurement such as that of the elastic constants of copper since that too in the last analysis of course is determined by atomic properties. It is the linking of the phenomena to our consciousness that imposes the definition of classicity on all observations and, despite some appearances, interposes inference between us and the quantum world. Should we not then admit in our description of nature only those attributes that are susceptible of observation in this sense? Can there be any place in our structure of physical theory for aspects of nature that are in principle inaccessible to observation? Probably the answer to the last question used to be 'No'. But today the answer is 'Yes'. The wave nature of matter bases our description of atomic structure and of elementary particles in general on the representation of a particle by an amplitude. All measurements are of the particles themselves; the probability or square of the amplitude has to be taken before we make an observation. Yet the underlying amplitude is crucial to our account of how the particle happened to turn up at that place and quantum mechanics could not be constructed without it. We should surely be much happier if we could measure this amplitude and not be restricted to its square. Quantum mechanics denies us this possibility, however. A clear difficulty is that to measure an amplitude directly we must have a frequency for the wave that it represents. There is no definite frequency for the particle wave of wave mechanics, and we can add and subtract arbitrary constants to it and from it. This situation is to be contrasted with the case of light where the corresponding wave has a definite and experimentally-determined frequency and the amplitude is directly measurable in a macroscopic experiment. The wave-particle dualism is different from the two ends. In the case of light we can do an experiment to determine the amplitude but cannot hold it in our fingers; in the case of particles we can hold them in our fingers but cannot measure their amplitude. This distinction which leads to the often quoted remark to the effect that the electron is of course a particle and its wave is the property of the mathematics used to describe it is a very clear one and is merely another way of saying that if we seek the nature of quantum objects in the classical limit by letting $\hbar$ tend to zero then everything becomes either a particle or a wave. Is not this utter dependence in our description of nature on the particle amplitude, something that we can never verify, rather worrying? I think that I ought to find it so. Here then is a vital concept that cannot be assimilated to instrumentation by the rules of the game and for which it is a silly question to ask 'Does it exist?'. The huge and uniformly successful edifice of quantum theory convinces us that the representation of a particle in terms of an amplitude is 'right'. We sometimes make the most astounding and non-commonsensical predictions about particle behaviour which are always correct. We have with wave functions the familiarity of confident use and yet we can never get at them. We feel that here is truth permanently beyond our powers of verification because part of that truth denies us the possibility.

Situations like this, being convinced of the 'truth' of something that we cannot check, are found at all levels in quantum physics, some of them quite homely. Consider the quadrupole moment of a nucleus, the degree to which it is spheroidal. It is a trivial result that if a nucleus has zero total angular momentum then we cannot observe it as other than spherically symmetrical because there is no means in the absence of a spin of defining an orientation in space. Now certain nuclei possess level schemes that agree with great precision with the hypothesis that they are strongly ellipsoidal and can rotate in a quantized fashion about a minor axis (for prolate nuclei with the major axis being that of symmetry) without any change of internal structure (shape) thereby generating this very characteristic 'rotational spectrum'. This way of talking implies that these nuclei, in their ground states, are ellipsoidal, even though they may in the ground state have zero spin. It is impossible in the face of this evidence, to resist thinking of such nuclei as being ellipsoidal even though we are rigorously forbidden from demonstrating any non-sphericity in a direct measurement because their lack of spin will not permit us to specify an orientation for the nucleus. Here again is a 'truth' that remains inaccessible to verification, a concept that cannot be assimilated to observation.

Another very useful but observationally wholly inaccessible concept is that of the virtual state. The uncertainty principle allows us effectively to violate energy conservation for short periods of time and so we speak of particles and photons as being emitted 'virtually' by particles and charges in a manner violating energy conservation by ΔE and so having to be reabsorbed very quickly within Δt where $\Delta E \,.\, \Delta t = \hbar$ so that the embezzlement should not be detected. This virtual state enables the temporarily emitted entity to be exchanged between two particles and to constitute the communication between them by which a force is transmitted. In this way we describe the electrostatic force between two charges as being due to the exchange of virtual photons and the nuclear force between two nucleons as due to the exchange of π-mesons. This concept is basic to and wholly satisfactory for our description of such interactions and we know of no other way of doing it. And yet the virtual state is by definition not accessible to observation: to detect a photon communicating between two electrons or a π-meson between two protons it must be real, have a finite energy and so imply the permanent non-conservation of energy.

Another class of inaccessible concept of a different kind is that of the 'bare' particle. Elementary particles are thought of as having a sort of inner existence in which they subsist wholly in their own right without interaction of any description. In such a state for example the g-factor of the Dirac electron is precisely 2. However, they must in fact always interact if only with the vacuum that surrounds them. The vacuum is rich in capabilities and when for example we 'allow' the bare electron to interact with it, it can recoil by emitting virtual photons into the vacuum and reabsorbing them with or without a flipping of its spin. This is the case of the interaction of the electron with the vacuum modifying the electromagnetic properties, and the theoretical g-factor becomes

$$2(1 + \alpha/2\pi - 0{\cdot}328\,\alpha^2/\pi^2 + \ldots) = 2(1 + 0{\cdot}001160) \qquad (\alpha = e^2/\hbar c).$$

The experimental value is $2(1 + 0{\cdot}00116)$. The very close agreement in this and other properties calculated using this concept gives strong confidence in the correctness of the procedure and yet we can never, of course, deal directly with the underlying 'bare' basic particles.

Quantum physics abounds in such illustrations at all levels, concepts that are crucial to our description of nature or, more shallowly, to our way of speaking of her, and yet which in principle elude our direct observation, and cannot be assimilated to instrumentation. Some of them can be denounced as error, and it is easy to explain how not to worry about the illustration of the ellipsoidal nucleus that can only be seen as a sphere. It is a different matter to follow the advice. Some of them are fundamental and we do indeed seem to be stuck with many concepts that must remain perhaps on some level that we might call belief and certainly cannot be elevated to fact.

Commentaries

Commentary by N. R. Hanson

"History of science without philosophy of science is blind. Philosophy of science without history of science is empty."[1]

Since this sentiment is built into Buchdahl's paper, I need only develop it to express my approval of his approach.

It is difficult to understand the occasional mock-antagonism between historians and philosophers of science. It *is* dialectically useful for an historican occasionally to refer to an opponent as 'a mere philosopher'. This will suggest an indifference, or an incompetence towards the facts underlying the issue in dispute. It is equally effective for a philosopher to characterize his antagonist as 'a mere historian'. This will suggest a molelike preoccupation with minutiae and marginalia when, it is hinted, what is really needed is the analysis of an argument or the illumination of an idea. Although such references are handy in debate is it not risky to press the contrast? For history of science at its best is history of scientific ideas and arguments. Philosophy of science at its best is analysis of scientific ideas and arguments.

The historian is concerned with the genesis and evolution of scientific concepts; but he must be able accurately to delineate such concepts when the developmental story is told. When he succeeds in this he is doing what philosophers think themselves to have been trained for. The philosopher is concerned with the logical structure of scientific concepts and arguments; but he *must* ask whether any scientist, past or present, ever entertained the concept or argument so analysed. When he successfully answers this he is doing what historians think themselves to have been trained for.

Where lies the intellectual advantage in an historical account of, say, the concept of the *electron*, when the writer is basically unclear about the logical function of this term within different types of scientific theory? It is part of a definition for Stoney who coined this term to refer to the basic *unit* of electrical charge, positive or negative. *Electron* is an observational term in J. J. Thomson's papers, where it refers to the particle *carrying*

[1] I owe this aphorism to Mr. Imre Lakatos.

only the negative variety of this basic unit of charge. For the early work of Schrödinger *electron* is a theoretical term, designating packets of the maxima of interfering phase waves in mathematical configuration space. Any lack of awareness of the diverse logical functions of this term can vitiate the efforts of the most industrious historian.

On the other hand, what makes a philosophical analysis of concepts and arguments into philosophy *of science*? Surely it is the fact that the concepts and arguments analysed have *in fact* played some significant role in past or present science. Lose this contact with the data of scientific practice and thought, and the result becomes an exercise within logical space. There the ideas examined are usually prefaced with a phrase like 'someone might consistently have believed that' or 'it is conceivable that a scientist might argue that'—these are incantatory references in the writings of some philosophers.

Consider the superiority of recent work on the origin and evolution of Euclidean geometry as against comparable studies in the eighteenth and early nineteenth centuries. The change is directly connected with a sharp increase in our philosophical understanding of the nature of axiomatic systems. This is due to the work of Saccheri, Lobachevski, Bolyai, Gauss, Riemann, Dedekind, Weierstrass, Frege, Peano, Hilbert, Russell and Gödel. By considering precisely which aspects of an axiomatic system make it 'go', how it gets its meaning, what determines its completeness, its consistency, its criteria for well-formedness, its rules of transformation, substitution and proof—we are now better placed than were Mill, Whewell, Kant or Leibniz for appreciating which parts of Euclid's proofs are strictly defensible, and which are not. In short, histories of geometry are more sound now than were those of our predecessors because we are now better able to say what geometry *is*. And undertaking to say what geometry is, is again doing what philosophers of science think themselves to have been trained for, although admittedly historians of mathematics have more often shed light on this problem. In any case, we are now better able than were our great grandfathers to distinguish what is and is not relevant to such a history of geometry. This insight is due largely to relatively recent philosophical and logical clarifications of geometrical concepts, whether these were carried out by philosophers or by historians does not matter.

Similarly, the transformation in studies of the Scientific Revolution is connected with the heightened interest in concepts like 'explanation', 'prediction', 'infer', 'justify', 'verify'; in expressions like 'deducing laws from phenomena', 'the observational basis of the mathematical philosophy' and 'rendering laws general by induction'; and in arguments such as those of Galileo in 1604, of Beeckmann's correspondence with Descartes, and of Newton in the Scholia of the *Principia*. Had Mr. Koyré not directed us to the *arguments* of Galileo and Descartes — had he not disclosed how the geometrical mode of representing instantaneous velocity controlled the thinking of these men — this corner of the history of scientific thought might have remained unlit. Every historian of science feels the power of a logical distinction between concepts or arguments. When such a distinction is well drawn the facts of history are clearer.

Moreover, philosophers are more conscious than ever that when the facts of history are clear, conceptual distinctions can be better drawn. Mr. Buchdahl realizes this: his paper is an admirable example of history of science illuminated by sharp conceptual distinctions, and of philosophy of science infused with content by a patient reading of Descartes.

This concludes the amiable part of my paper.

Beyond this use of philosophical analysis and logic in the description and evaluation of scientific arguments, there is a more comprehensive, and less laudable, exploitation of philosophy by historians. This consists in importing pre-formed philosophical 'isms' into a reading of the literature of science, finding there support for one's intellectual posture. This usually precedes some sweeping generalization about the objectives and tendencies of science.

The result is distortion. Consider a recent book in our discipline in which the author, having decided in advance that true science consists in slow, patient, Baconian collection of generalizations tortured from nature by slow, patient observations exacted from minutely-engineered experiments, then proceeds to read Newton's *Principia* as if it were a summary of just such an approach — as if it were a kind of laboratory technician's record book. Indeed, Newton has at times been cast as a neo-Kantian by Whewell, Cassirer and Pap, as a Baconian by Mill, Broad and Russell, and as a positivist by Mach, Schlick, Carnap and Reichenbach. And if there is danger of atomizing a scientific concept by too much logical analysis, there is also the danger of swamping it in too much systematic philosophy.

Next to the service Buchdahl has done us in revealing as myth-eaten the picture of Descartes as a naïve Cartesian rationalist — lacking any empirical proclivities or sensitivities — the following will be a small complaint indeed. Nonetheless, this excursion is necessary to understanding in what sense Descartes was concerned to expound a 'Logic of Scientific Discovery'.

One preliminary point: scarcely any reputable philosopher has ever used the expression 'logic of discovery' directly to designate a manual, or a compendium, of *rules*, by the application of which mediocre talents can make great discoveries. As Bacon, Mill — and Mr. Polanyi — have said, there could be no such manual. The most that is ever intended, by Buchdahl, by Popper, by Peirce, and (if you will pardon the conjunction) by myself, is an analysis of arguments generated during research leading to discoveries. Inferences *are* made during discovery: more bluntly, scientists very often use their heads while solving their problems. *How* they use them is a legitimate area for historical and logical inquiry. Buchdahl and I will quarrel about the correct analysis. But please do not saddle us with theses we would reject as readily as anyone. We are not concerned with recipes for discovery — our own, Descartes's, or anyone else's. Still, do not throw the whole problem of discovery too quickly into those large, dark receptacles called 'intuition', 'inspiration', 'guesswork' and 'hunch' — or even 'paradigm'. It is possible both to be driven by intuition and at the same time to reason carefully. Most scientific discoveries, indeed, result from just such an intertwining of headwork and guesswork.

On p. 402 Mr. Buchdahl writes:

> The first of these [two positions] is what is currently named the 'inverse-deductive' or 'retroductive' method of induction. This involves a form of argument according to which we *infer* that we have reason to believe in an hypothesis *H*, if it deductively explains a number of verifiable consequences. Formally: if *H*, then *E*; but since *E*, *therefore* (possibly) *H*.

Mr. Buchdahl is just plain mistaken here; he identifies the 'retroductive' technique described by Peirce with the quite different 'hypothetico-deductive' technique elaborated by Mill, Popper and Braithwaite. Peirce did not express the formal structure of retroduction as do these philosophers, and as does Buchdahl. Peirce argued: *E, but if H then E, therefore* (*possibly*) *H*. The philosophers present will mark this presentation as logically equivalent to what I quoted from Buchdahl. The change consists in nothing but a reordering of the two premises. Here is where Buchdahl trips up. It does not follow from the fact that two arguments are equivalent in logical structure, that there are therefore no conceptual differences between them. Let me explain.

Imagine yourself in a logic classroom (i.e. in a classroom in which logic is being taught). There are, notoriously, two different kinds of question the teacher can pose. He can say: "here are premises P^1, P^2, and P^3 — generate from them some theorem". But he can also say: "here is a theorem; find three premises from which it can be generated". The latter undertaking is vastly more difficult, as every mathematician and scientist knows. Being presented with an anomalous phenomenon E and then being charged to discover an H from which E follows is a different conceptual task from being given premises *if H then E*, and E, and concluding that H is (insofar) confirmed. Nor is this difference merely psychological. Yet the logical criteria for evaluating answers to these two different questions are identical. If E follows from H, and if E obtains, then both the retroduction and the hypothetico-deduction are sound. But this identity does not fuse the retroductive undertaking with the inverse-deductive. Arguing from three premises at the top of a page, down to a conclusion at the bottom, as a mathematician may do, is a fundamentally different conceptual undertaking from beginning with a conclusion at the bottom of a page and constructing the argument upwards towards the three premises at the top — as natural scientists often do. These are distinct, even though the formal criterion of validity is the same in each case — namely, is what is at the bottom deductively (i.e. formally) connected with what is at the top?

This distinction is built into nineteenth-century astronomy. The classical problem of perturbations is always distinguished from the 'inverse problem of perturbations'. If one knows a planet's mass and orbital elements, one can easily determine (via the laws of celestial mechanics) the disturbance it produces in another body. But one might proceed by first describing the observed disturbances in a planet, for example Uranus, and then attempt to infer from this, via the same laws, the mass and orbital elements of some disturbing planet. Whether or not one gets the right answer in either case is subject only to the criterion that an observed disturbance in one planet can be shown to follow (via celestial mechanics) from the assigned mass and orbital elements of some other planet. But anyone who insisted that there was therefore only a psychological difference between the two tasks would not be taken seriously by any astronomer. Knowing Venus's mass and elements, and calculating therefrom Mercury's perturbations is a different kind of problem *conceptually* from that of knowing Uranus's perturbations and calculating therefrom the mass and elements of some as-yet-unobserved planet.[1]

Determining an argument's validity *ex post facto*, justifying it, constitutes inquiry only into the soundness of deductions. But this does not mean that everyone who argues is deducing. The way a Descartes, a Newton, or a Leverrier actually argued is best characterized as 'retroductive'. The simple expression 'Descartes's argument' often conflates these two issues. It can fuse the actual order of Descartes's moves as he reasons his way out of some perplexity in dioptrics, with the logical order which formally structures his final report. This expression has a different force depending on whether it is 'Descartes' or 'argument' which is stressed. But although premise-unpacking and premise-hunting are subject ultimately to the same criteria of validity, they constitute different intellectual activities; they have distinct conceptual roles. This point is even more apparent in the expression 'Descartes's deduction'.

Analogously, the traveller's question, 'Where do I go from here?' is not just psychologically different from his question, 'How will I get back here from over there?' These questions reflect distinct conceptual sets. But the criteria for appraising the traveller's answers are the same — purely cartographical: 'Is there a geographical route connecting these two positions?' Similarly, the logical criteria for good scientific argument are

[1] That the difference between *deducing* and *retroducing* is conceptual and not merely psychological is easily shown. Given three consistent premises, P^1, P^2 and P^3, if any two theorems θ^1 and θ^2 follow from these, then θ^1 and θ^2 must be consistent. But in retroducing we are given the theorem θ^1, and urged to infer to a cluster of premises from which it follows. The cluster P^1, P^2 and P^3 may do the job: but so may the cluster P^4, P^5 and P^6. It does not follow that these premises-clusters will be consistent with each other: Huygens *v.* Newton on the explanation of refraction is a case in point. In general, a deduction from consistent premises will entail a potential infinitude of consistent theorems. But a retroduction from consistent (yet anomalous) theorems will terminate in a potential infinitude of premise-clusters many of which will be inconsistent with other clusters. Therefore the difference is conceptual — not psychological — although the logical criteria for the validity of the argument are constant for both processes.

purely deductive: 'Is there a logical route connecting these two propositions?' But the queries 'What follows?' and 'From what does this follow?' remain conceptually distinguishable.

Here two different conceptions of what a 'logic of scientific discovery' might be, split apart. We might understand this in Popper's sense, wherein the schema is: if *H* implies true observation-statements then *H* is (possibly) true. This, clearly, has nothing to do with discovery as such. It is, rather, a criterion for evaluating suggested explanations of phenomena. But one might also understand 'a logic of scientific discovery' in Peirce's sense, wherein the schema is this: these anomalous phenomena fall into an explanatory framework when *H* is entertained, therefore *H* is (possibly) true. This seems to have more to do with the *de facto* conceptual considerations involved in making discoveries. It is no more a rule for making discoveries than is Popper's version. But it does provide a framework of language and inference which can be shown to figure in research leading to some important discoveries in the history of science. Just contrast Kepler's account of his own argument in *De Motibus Stellae Martis* with the account of planetary motion to be found in any school text-book on astronomy. The latter may indeed have the 'hypothetico-deductive' form. The former certainly does not! One further point of clarification: what I have been calling 'retroduction' is not an alternative *logical form* of argument. It is, rather, an alternative logical description of the way scientists (often) argue. The strictly formal connexions between premises and conclusion are abstract, context-neutral and time-independent. They have nothing to do with the way people argue in fact. A description of how *mathematicians* actually argue — sometimes from premises down to conclusions — is quite distinct from a consideration of these abstract formal connexions. How a mathematician may actually deduce (from the top of the page down) is not a context-neutral and time-independent question. As such, this kind of description is also distinguishable from the strict question of logical form. A merit of the retroductive elaboration is that it shows that descriptions appropriate to a mathematician deducing may be inappropriate to a (natural) scientist when actually arguing. My point is that the hypothetico-deductive elaboration is not always appropriate to describing how scientists actually reason towards their solutions, although many '*H–D* theorists' certainly pretend that it is. What I have set out here as 'retroduction' is much more often realized in the *de facto* arguments of scientific discoverers. But this does not reduce the conceptual importance of retroduction to being a matter of 'mere history' or 'mere psychology'. Because, as philosophers and historians, we do not *understand* what scientific discovery is if we do not understand how scientists actually use their heads when discovering the previously unknown.

How does this affect Mr. Buchdahl's reinterpretation of Descartes, and his claim that Descartes was not a naïve Cartesian rationalist? It may affect it profoundly. Buchdahl means but one thing by a 'logic of discovery', namely — the formal structure of the finished research report. This is apparent from his interchangeable use of 'retroduction' and 'inverse induction'. Thus from Buchdahl's account we cannot know whether Descartes was offering only a logician's analysis for the *ex post facto* appraisal of discoveries, or whether he was offering a logician's general description of the actual argumentation, step by step, which terminates in discoveries. Very probably Descartes was not always clear about which enterprise he was engaged in. Indeed, at times he even seems to be offering 'general rules of the recipe-book conception of a logic of scientific discovery' which Buchdahl and I — and, I suppose, almost everyone today — would reject. But that Descartes did not always reject it is perhaps a significant datum for the historian of scientific thought.

Buchdahl has shown that Descartes's philosophy of science was not slavishly deductive, as one might have gathered from the standard — and secondary sources and their mischievous chapters on 'rationalism'. He reveals Descartes as one who realizes as well as we do that, in empirical science (as opposed to geometry), the most one can do is increase the plausibility of hypotheses as one increases the probability of the observation statements those hypotheses imply. This is particularly clear in Descartes's letter to Morin. But, as I have argued, it remains unclear whether Descartes's 'logic of scientific discovery' was concerned primarily with the general logical analysis of hypothesis unpacking, or rather with the general logical description of hypothesis hunting. It is significant that almost every line of Descartes quoted by Buchdahl is compatible with either interpretation. Thus, in the *Principles*, we read: ". . . we are free to make any assumptions we like . . . so long as all the consequences agree with experience" (III, 46). And in the *Discourse* he says: ". . . the causes from which I deduce [the effects] do not serve so much to establish their reality as to explain their existence. . . ." (VI, 60). My own further reading of Descartes, moreover, has turned up no clear-cut resolution of this interpretative problem.

All that I am clear about is that Descartes was not himself clear about whether he was (1) analysing *ex post facto* the finished arguments of discoverers — as a pure logician might do, or (2) describing the structure of the actual steps in the reasoning of scientists struggling towards discoveries — as an historian or a philosopher of science might do, or whether he was (3) providing rules to guide the perplexed towards making scientific discoveries — as no one ought ever to do. It is within category (2) that conceptual excitement will seize the scholar whose academic concern is with the history and structure of actual scientific discovery. Mr. Buchdahl has shown us that Descartes was such a scholar, and in doing this he has revealed himself also to be such a scholar.

Commentary by I. Bernard Cohen

Mr. Daumas's attractive communication evokes an historical and analytical contemplation of that close link between concept and operation that so often seems to characterize modern exact science. Indeed, does not the very use of the word 'exact' in relation to science at once bring to mind the allied concept of 'precision' which has been studied by Mr. Daumas? Precision, furthermore, may be applied equally to scientific thought itself and experimental technique — both being necessary to the production of significant measurements. Mr. Daumas's perceptive analysis of these subjects permits us, while agreeing with his theme in general, nevertheless to pose a number of questions which may help to illuminate the role of precision measurement in the advancement of physical science in modern times, without limiting ourselves strictly to the eighteenth century. If I draw my examples primarily from physics and astronomy, may I hope to provoke our author to make comparisons from his own field of chemistry? And perhaps to stimulate others to address themselves to the role of quantification in general and of precision techniques in other parts of science, notably biology in its several aspects?

It is a commonplace today to assume that precision measurements may lead directly to advances in the physical sciences, and that the introduction of new techniques are thus of paramount importance for understanding the rise of modern physics. Whenever this problem is discussed, recent examples come to mind. A 'classic' of this sort would appear to be the Michelson–Morley experiment — new experimental techniques making possible a high precision test of the 'aether drift' or 'aether wind' which in its results may have made of it the most important experiment of the century (although at least one member of this Symposium would deny its importance in the development of Einstein's thought). But it is in accord with Mr. Daumas's conclusions that such examples (at least in physics and chemistry) — in which sudden vast theoretical consequences may follow from a single precise measurement or a group of such measurements — tend to date from the nineteenth and twentieth centuries and do not characterize the founding (sixteenth and seventeenth) centuries of modern science, nor the eighteenth century which saw the development of instruments of precision. One must, of course, keep in mind that in astronomy things were different and that in those physical problems related to astronomy (for example, geodesy), precision measurements such as the length of a degree along the meridian — related both to the accurate size of the earth and the shape (prolate or oblate) of the earth — could be and were of striking importance. Nevertheless, it is not the least of the merits of Mr. Daumas's paper to warn us not to read back into the scientific revolution of the seventeenth century and its eighteenth century aftermath conclusions that apply to chemistry and physics only much later.

My first comment on this paper deals with the concept of 'precision' itself. Nowhere in his paper does Mr. Daumas define 'precision'. And although at first glance this would seem to be a wise procedure, it does imply — perhaps too arbitrarily — that nothing can be said in this regard. Clearly, whatever may be the case for 'precision', there is a very distinct sense to 'greater precision', for example more accurate knowledge to the last decimal point or a numerical result repeatable to within a smaller percentage of error, or a gain of knowledge to the next decimal point. And the question arises as to whether such an increase in precision is always, and necessarily, beneficial to the advance of science. Mr. Daumas, although not declaring himself specifically for one side or the other, never once raised so much as a suspicion of doubt as to whether increasing precision was necessarily good for scientific progress. In the face of such 'optimism', may I suggest that the contrary view is also valid?

A primary 'pessimistic' example may be seen in the work of Tycho Brahe in relation to Johannes Kepler. It is well known that Tycho introduced so great a degree of precision into astronomical measurement that the work of Copernicus (and of other predecessors) appeared to be rough schemes, at best calculated to give some crude approximations. It is also well known that these precise data enabled Kepler to discover the elliptical planetary orbits: nay, forced Kepler to abandon the circles and combinations of circles that since Platonic times had always been part of astronomical theory. When Kepler thanked the divine providence for the accuracy of Tycho's data which had led to the ellipses, he spoke truer than he knew! For it was not only a question of how accurate Tycho was, but of how accurate Tycho was not. Tycho's observations were, fortunately, *not precise enough*. Just think of the consequences if this had not been so and if then Kepler would have had to discover the real truth — that there are no planetary elliptical orbits save in an ideal Platonic sense! — in that case no Newton, no *Principia*, no law of gravitation in 1687, and perhaps no modern science or at best a delayed modern science. Fortunate physics, that truly precise observations came into planetary observations considerably after Newton and not before Kepler!

In the seventeenth century, the degree of precision of Tycho made possible the *Principia* of Newton, but before long it was seen that the planets do not have elliptic paths, a fact which challenged gravitation theory and produced the theory of perturbations. Eventually, the observed departure of Uranus from its predicted path led to the discovery of a new planet, Neptune — a victory of theoretical prediction in physics that is one of the triumphs of nineteenth-century science, comparable only to the prediction and subsequent discovery of conical refraction and of the existence of electro-magnetic radiation. It is also a matter of record that Newtonian dynamics could not equally well account for the advance of the perihelion of Mercury, small as this quantity proves to be, a matter unresolved until the general theory of relativity.

Examples of the beneficial role of a delayed high precision are not limited to the early days of modern science (Tycho to Kepler, sixteenth and seventeenth centuries). A more recent case may illustrate not only the way in which lack of precision is important for the growth of modern atomic and nuclear physics, but may also help to clarify the role of the increase of precision in advancing science. J. J. Thomson's experiments on cathode rays, made at the end of the nineteenth century, led to apparently precise determinations of the ratio of charge to mass (e/m) of these particles. The numerical result accorded with the concept that these particles must be smaller than hydrogen atoms, as might be expected of particles that could pass through thin metal foil. But the astonishing theoretical result was that e/m was constant, no matter what gas was present in the discharge tube or what metals served as electrodes. The inescapable conclusions were sensational: the atom is composite, all atoms are built of electrons plus some positive matter.

So much for the constancy of e/m; now for its variation. Shortly after Thomson had shown the consequences of the same value of e/m for all materials, Kaufmann and Bücherer found that for higher discharge voltages, and thus for electrons of higher energy or higher speed, e/m changes in a regular fashion. The relation of this result to the concept of electromagnetic mass and "the electrodynamics of moving bodies", to use the title of Einstein's 1905 paper, is well known to students of relativity theory and to the world at large in the equation $E = mc^2$. But think of the difference our history might show if Thomson's results had not preceded Bücherer's and Kaufmann's!

This example also illustrates the way in which in our modern physics a single numerical result (e/m) may alter the basic structure of physics. Why is this so recent a quality of physics? Why is it that only in the last century or so has it become a regular feature of the history of physics to find such vast consequences of but a single measurement or observation? Can the reason be that this is an aspect of scientific development that arises only when there is so great an advancement and interrelation of data, concept and theory that, like a great complex engine, a slight motion of one part may cause a violent upheaval of the whole structure?

I do not wish to disparage in any way Mr. Daumas's concentration on the makers of instruments and the role of the skill of artisans in relation to increases in precision of observation and measurement. Yet I fear a little that a happy optimism may trap the unwary neophyte and it is for this reason that I dwell perhaps overmuch on the fortunate effects that error and lack of precision may have on the progress of science. There are examples to support this view from every branch of science in the last four hundred years. A famous one is 'the law of Hooke, Townley, Boyle and Mariotte', an approximation that could not long withstand the scrutiny of precision measurement in the nineteenth century. But in the meanwhile look at the significant and beneficial results for science of incorrect laws based on wrong (because imprecise) experimental results. This law of gases led Newton to an erroneous theory of gases when he was able to show that a necessary and sufficient condition for this law was the assumption of gas particles repelling one another according to a force varying inversely as the distance between their centres. Newton's erroneous theory was of crucial importance in the formation of Dalton's atomic theory — which, we must admit, was built on a series of bad measurements which Dalton fortunately altered ('cooked' or 'doctored') in order to advance and maintain a theory that has been of undeniably great importance for the rise of all the sciences (physical and biological) in the last 150 years! Compare the work of Dalton with his contemporary Coulomb. The latter made experiments and measurements on friction with a degree of precision never before achieved but which led to no theory. Even Coulomb's beautiful measurement of electric and magnetic force, yielding an inverse-square law, did not of themselves notably advance electrical and magnetic theory. These examples may show how dangerous it is to assume a simple one-to-one correspondence between increase in precision of measurement and the progress of science.

Mr. Daumas calls attention to the importance of precision in chemical measurements just after Lavoisier, notably in the atomic theory: one thinks at once of the law of Gay-Lussac and its consequence in Avogadro's hypothesis. Of a like character is the Faraday constant of electrolysis. It is difficult, however, to think of a major polemic in physics of the early nineteenth century solved in the manner of the Proust–Berthollet polemic, in which "the analyst overcame the theoretician". The reason may lie in the fact that in physics often even simple measurements had to be based on advanced theory: for instance in electricity, one needed a solid theory indeed to distinguish effects of charge, potential and capacitance. Eighteenth-century electrical theory did not remain qualitative only because it was a "physique de salon" which ignored measurement; rather, it seems to me, theory itself was not yet ready for measures. At the century's end, Coulomb did make precise measurements of the law of electric force, but from these results — as I have just mentioned — there flowed forth no striking theory. But the qualitative theory developed by

Franklin and others, though not quantitative and not based on measurement, was nevertheless *exact* in the sense that it yielded unequivocal and verifiable predictions about the outcome of laboratory manipulations. In the new branches of physics mentioned by Mr. Daumas on p. 428, therefore, it seems to me that the need was not so much for "a general measurement-based methodology" as to achieve a wholly new level of concept and theory which would make measurements meaningful. Advances in optics, for example, did not come simply from new instruments, new measures, or even a new method of investigation, but rather from the new concept of 'interference' which showed how a whole class of phenomena could be explained by the concept of wave and not by particle. It was the success of Young and Fresnel in explaining what we call 'interference' phenomena that established the wave theory with all of its consequences for nineteenth-century physical science. And it is significant that for Young the old precision of Newton, for instance in measuring the rings that today bear his name, was sufficient.

Perhaps, therefore, there may be a difference between chemistry and physics which may somewhat invalidate Mr. Daumas's general conclusions. But is it not true in chemistry, as it is in physics, that the importance of increase in precision in measurement for the advancement of science has been — until fairly recently at any rate — controlled by the state of theory and concept as much as, if not more than, by the experience and technical skill of artisans? And may not the role of the instrument-maker and designer in the advancement of the physical sciences be greater — or at least just as great — in the opening-up of wholly new ranges of experiment and experience (on both the small and the great ends of the scale) than in achieving a greater precision in ranges already subject to scientific exploration? Mr. Daumas has illuminated these questions for the eighteenth century. I hope that he and other members of the Symposium may care to examine further the validity of his conclusions for the nineteenth and even the twentieth century.

Commentary by Mary B. Hesse

Mr. Gillispie again puts us in his debt by his facility in seeing below the surface of that most difficult area for the historian of science, nineteenth-century physics. He gives a penetrating analysis of the antecedents of statistical methods in the dynamical theory of gases. It is universally agreed that Maxwell's law of distribution of velocities is the first successful application of these methods in dynamics, since the essence of a statistical method is the use not merely of mean values, but of the distribution of values about the mean, and Maxwell was the first to exploit this. Gillispie makes some perceptive distinctions between the views of Maxwell's predecessors on the analysis by probabilities of the data of science. These views may be summarized as follows:

(i) That the world is causally determined, but our knowledge of it is subject to error, therefore statistical analysis must be used to discover true causes from our data. This is the position of Laplace.

(ii) That the world is causally determined, but our knowledge is incomplete, therefore statistical analysis may be used to discover relations in nature which are less than complete causes, and depend on the law of large numbers. In other words, nature is subject to statistical as well as to deterministic laws. This is the position of Poisson and many of his contemporaries among physicists, and, as I shall argue, also that of Quetelet, Herschel, and, with a significant extension, of Maxwell.

(iii) That the world is not causally determined, but subject to some element of chance. This position may be held in a weak or a strong form. The weak form is the assertion quoted by Gillispie from Cournot, to the effect that events are linked in deterministic causal chains, but that the intersections of these chains are fortuitous. The strong form is the view now held almost universally but which make no appearance in Gillispie's period, namely that there are no deterministic, but only statistical, laws.

As far as I understand him, Gillispie's more controversial theses arise out of the circumstances surrounding these three views. He notes that although Poisson overcame the dichotomy between the world and our knowledge of the world, which characterized Laplace's use of probability, he never moved from the statistical analysis of society to that of mechanical systems, and never retreated from a belief in strict determinism. Gillispie therefore suggests that the application of the statistical method to mechanics "requires operations of technique on data in a relation to nature that was by no means obvious", and looks for the antecedents of Maxwell's method rather in the probabilism of Cournot and the human statistics of Quetelet.

In commenting on this I want to concentrate on three main points:

(1) Quetelet's discussion of the average and the mean does not abolish the distinction between phenomena and errors as Gillispie claims, neither does Herschel interpret it as doing so, and hence these two writers cannot be regarded as important influences on Maxwell.[1]

(2) The essential conceptual elements of a statistical mechanics are to be found in Clausius, and this is the direct inheritance of Maxwell, explicitly acknowledged by him.

(3) The difficulties which Maxwell overcame were not those of statistical technique, but rather of complexity in the physical model.

(1) First, Gillispie shows signs of having fallen into a confusion about the views which he describes on the relation of probability to the world. A distinction must be made between, on the one hand, the notion of a deterministic nature in which there are causal laws and also statistical regularities among large numbers, and in which statistical laws can be discovered even when all determining causes are not known; and, on the other hand, a conception of nature which is *irreducibly* statistical, that is, where some or all events are not causally determined. Only the first conception is required for a statistical mechanics. It is therefore not clear why Gillispie quotes Cournot's statement of a weak form of the second conception among the antecedents of Maxwell's theory. It is indeed by no means clear, as Gillispie himself points out, that Cournot even grasped the significance of the law of large numbers, for he nowhere reduces his fortuitous intersections of causal chains to numerical analysis.

Thus, in asking where Maxwell's inspiration may have lain, it is necessary to ask where are the first applications of the law of large numbers in physics, not as a theory of errors only, but as yielding statistical laws of the events themselves. Gillispie's answer to this is that Quetelet had the essence of the matter, for he first assimilated the Laplacean subjective law of errors to the objective chances given by the binomial distribution for large populations of physical events.

Here I must differ. This interpretation of Quetelet does not

[1] Although Maxwell almost certainly read Herschel's essay in 1857 or 1858, see his letters to Campbell and Litchfield: L. Campbell and W. Garnett, *Life of J. C. Maxwell* (London, 1882) 210, 217.

yield the requirements of a statistical mechanics, any more than does Poisson's, and not even Herschel is able to furbish it up to do so. To see this, we have only to look at the use to which both Quetelet and Herschel put Quetelet's example of the chest measurements of the Scottish soldiers. This example does not *abolish* for them the distinction between natural events and errors, but rather shows that some natural events, namely those following the same distribution law as that of errors, *can be regarded as* nature's own errors in aiming at a 'type'. Quetelet is quite explicit about this. In a paragraph next but one after that quoted by Gillispie on the chest measurements he writes:

> Of the admirable laws which Nature attaches to the preservation of the species, I think I may put in the first rank that of maintaining the type. In my work *La Physique Sociale*, I have already endeavoured to determine this type by the knowledge of the human mean. But if I mistake not, what experiment and reasoning had shown me, here takes the character of a mathematical truth.[1]

Herschel is equally explicit in identifying probability with the analysis of errors: probability is, he says, "a term having reference to our ignorance of the analysis of events, and of the efficient causes which really *necessitate* the successive steps by which they arise".[2] There is for him a clear distinction between the probabilistic analysis of partial data, and the subsequent establishment of causes, which is the work of physics. And in giving examples of this physical discovery of causes, both Quetelet and Herschel make it clear that it is concerned with detecting *deviations* from the Gaussian law of error, that is to say, statistical analysis first tells us what errors are to be expected, due both to observation and to nature's own bad shots at a 'type', namely, those satisfying the error-law, and then, if the data do *not* fit this law, a determining physical cause for the deviation can be looked for. Thus, Herschel gives as example the mean level of the sea, which is disturbed by fluctuations of wind according to the error-law, but which also shows periodic disturbances superimposed on this, for which a determining cause can be found in lunar and solar attractions.

To relate statistical distributions to physical causes in this way is not yet to take the step essential to statistical mechanics, for this does not interpret the data as error-like variations about

[1] Quetelet, *Letters on Probability*, p. 93.

[2] J. Herschel, *Essays from the Edinburgh and Quarterly Reviews* (London, 1857) 368.

a mean in order to distinguish these variations from those due to superimposed causes, and then to neglect the 'errors'. It rather exploits the so-called errors by describing their own regularities. The method of Quetelet and its interpretation by Herschel is essentially the same as that adopted by the physicists of the period, Poisson, Stokes,[1] and others, who in their investigations of the elasticity of fluids and solids remark that the irregular density and motions of molecules can be neglected compared with their average density and average velocity, if sufficiently large volumes are taken. Here the law of large numbers is applied to physics, but only as an excuse for adopting mean values, not as the basis of a science in its own right.

(2) Thus, the idea of smoothing out small-scale irregularities is commonplace in both physics and human statistics at this period. But the next step beyond this in considering a distribution about the mean in physics must be ascribed not to Maxwell but to Clausius, in the paper of 1858 which was the direct inspiration of Maxwell's researches in the theory of gases.

This paper of Clausius, entitled "On the mean length of the paths described by the separate molecules of gaseous bodies on the occurrence of molecular motion",[2] was provoked by an objection to his previously published mechanical theory of gases, on the grounds that if molecules move in straight lines, gases must speedily mix with each other, and yet smoke clouds are observed to persist for long periods in the air, and noxious gases emitted in one corner of a room do not immediately make themselves felt at another. Clausius replies to this objection by calculating the mean free path of a molecule between collisions with other molecules, and showing that this mean is very short compared with macroscopic distances, and that individual cases of free paths much longer than the mean are rare. This calculation already involves statistical consideration of a distribution about a mean, moreover the distribution in question is *not* that of the law of errors. In this paper the emancipation of statistical physics from the law of errors is complete.

(3) What then was the essential novelty of Maxwell's

[1] "On the theories of the internal friction of fluids in motion, and of the equilibrium and motion of elastic solids" (1845), *Mathematical and Physical Papers* (Cambridge, 1880) I, 78.

[2] English trans., *Philosophical Magazine*, 4th series, XVII (1859) 81.

achievement? To answer this it is only necessary to compare the extreme crudity of Clausius's gas-model in his early papers, particularly that of 1857,[1] and indeed of those of his predecessors, from Bernoulli to Joule, with the technically difficult derivation of the law of distribution of velocities by Maxwell. Clausius first considers the highly simplified case of molecules having no interactions with each other and all moving with the same velocity. Then in order to calculate an upper limit to the mean free path, he considers all the molecules as being at rest except one, and finds the mean free path of this, remarking that if all are moving, their mean free path will certainly be less than if only one is moving. Maxwell on the other hand plunges with great facility into a model of finite elastic spheres moving with any velocity and colliding in any manner, and sets out, in the case of a collision between two spheres, "To find the probability of the direction of the velocity after impact lying between given limits". In 1862 Clausius pays tribute to this feature of Maxwell's paper: "In this memoir, which is remarkable for the elegance of its mathematical developments, the motion of small bodies is regarded from very general points of view. . . . The mutual action of two impinging elastic spheres is very comprehensively treated by Maxwell."[2] Having been shown the way, Clausius goes ahead to correct some of Maxwell's assumptions regarding gas diffusion, with, one feels, physical insight the equal of Maxwell's, but with greatly inferior mathematical equipment. It was generality of mechanical argument that had at first eluded Clausius, not application of statistical technique. But Gillispie is right that both eluded the other physicists, including Poisson and Stokes, who were content to remain on the firm foundation of the theory of solids rather than trust themselves to the cloudy diffuseness of gases.

I conclude that we cannot find the *detailed* influence of "social physics" on physics that Gillispie suggests, although of course it is beyond dispute that the formative debates on the nature of probability took place among the games and insurance statistics. But in considering their transfer to mechanics, it must not be forgotten how important a place sheer mathematical difficulties and the difficulty of finding the right initial model have among the intellectual factors.

[1] English trans., *Phil. Mag.*, 4th series, XIV (1857) 108.

[2] "On the conduction of heat by gases", English trans., *Phil. Mag.*, 4th series, XXIII (1862) 420, 423.

Commentary by David Bohm

Mr. Wilkinson raises some very interesting and important points concerning the possibility of linking the fundamental concepts of physics to observation and experiment. Although he raises the question in a general sense all of his examples have to do with the quantum-mechanics, in which there are a great many basic concepts that are not observable (for example, the amplitude of the wave function, the appearance of 'virtual' states, etc.). As pointed out by Wilkinson, such concepts, although not corresponding to anything directly observable, play a key role in making the results of the theory intelligible to us. This appears to disturb him, at least sufficiently to make him ask the question of whether we are not "stuck with many concepts that must remain perhaps on some level that we might call belief and certainly cannot be elevated to fact". I can say that the majority of physicists are disturbed in a similar way when they first learn the quantum theory. Eventually most of them get so used to the situation that it no longer bothers them (as we can get used to practically anything). Nevertheless, every now and then, any one of us may awaken with a start and ask what it all means. If this is what Wilkinson is doing, then I must say that I sympathize with him.

It is not an accident that the examples cited by Wilkinson come from the quantum theory. Of course, it does happen that unobservable concepts are introduced into other theories too, but their unobservability is usually only incidental. On the other hand, in the quantum mechanics, the incomplete observability of the basic concepts is built into the structure of the theory itself so that, far from being incidental, it is essential. The root of this essential unobservability lies in an objective and basic characteristic peculiar to the laws of the quantum theory, namely the *indivisibility* of the quantum process.

According to classical physics, all movement is *continuous*, and can therefore be analysed into indefinitely small steps. But in the quantum theory, there are *discrete* levels of energy, momentum, etc., of any system, with the implication of a discrete jump in these properties in a transition. This in turn implies *discrete movement*, not analysable into indefinitely fine steps. Each step in a given process is indivisible, and in a peculiar sense. It is potentially divisible by means of some external disturbance, but if it is actually divided, it becomes another process — as an egg can be divided by breaking it, but then it must become something else and cease to be an egg. Similarly, in order for a given quantum process to be what it is, a division of the process must not be taking place.

In a quantum jump, energy, momentum and other properties are exchanged between a system and its surroundings. Since the process is indivisible, the quantum serves as an indivisible link between any system and its surroundings. Everything that exists is linked in this way to everything else: to the *total process* of the universe. This linkage is either direct, by means of a single quantum, or else indirect, through a series of such linkages.

Since observation is a special case of a natural process, it follows then that there must be quantum links between the observing apparatus and what is observed. And according to Heisenberg's well-known analysis, the existence of such links results in an irreducible disturbance, reflecting the fact that in every observation process, there is a significant participation in the very mode of existence of what is observed. If a given system (for example an electron) is to be what it is, it therefore cannot be taking part in a process of linkage to the rest of the world in general and to the observing apparatus in particular of a kind that would permit observations of indefinitely great detail to be carried out on it. And this is at the root of the questions raised by Wilkinson. For the incomplete observability of the basic processes which are going on in any quantum system seems to be reflected mathematically and theoretically in the necessity for using concepts that likewise do not correspond to properties that are observable in full detail.

Now, in classical physics, we have got used to a very different way of thinking of things. We imagine the world to be constituted of separate parts, each existing in its own region of space and time. These parts interact, to be sure, but the interactions are supposed to be continuous and infinitely divisible. As a result, we can in principle analyse the world, *at least conceptually*, into infinitely fine parts. If we do this, we can treat interactions as producing minor changes — also called perturbations — in the basic elements out of which the world is supposed to be constituted. In the process of observation, it is in principle possible to use interactions so weak that they have no significant effect on the observed system; and as a result, observations of indefinitely fine detail can be carried out.

The quantum theory plainly implies that these classical

assumptions are not true, and that instead, all parts of the world are indivisibly linked by discrete quanta of action of magnitude equal to Planck's constant. From this, it follows of course that classical ideas on observations cannot be correct at the micro-level. At first sight, one might be led to ask 'Why not develop new quantum theoretical ideas concerning the process of observation?' At this point one meets with the fact that physicists generally accept the conclusion that this is impossible, because the human mind is supposed to be capable of thinking only in terms of classical concepts. Wilkinson's statement may be taken as typical of this point of view: "The linking of phenomena to our consciousness imposes the definition of classicity on all observations." That is to say, we can become conscious only of that which fits into the general conceptual scheme of classical physics, involving the assumption of a continuous and infinitely divisible world.

It is evident that at the large-scale level of everyday experience, in the laboratory or outside, individual quanta are too small to have an appreciable effect, so that the approximation of continuous divisibility is good enough for practical purposes. Therefore, the use of classical concepts to think of the observable results of experiments will introduce no significant error at this point. But these results must be connected to the micro-level, which is the subject under investigation. And these connexions actually take place through indivisible quanta. Classical concepts are therefore not good enough to permit us to understand the relationship between the observable experimental results and what goes on at the quantum mechanical level.

How is this problem treated now? This is done (for example by Heisenberg, Bohr, von Neumann, and others) by introducing a conceptual 'cut' between the classical level and those systems which are essentially quantum mechanical (for example atoms). Everything on the classical side of the cut is thought of as satisfying classical laws, involving continuous movement, while what is on the other side of the cut is treated by the laws of the quantum theory, involving discontinuous process. Although there is some arbitrariness in the placing of the cut, it is shown that the net results are not sensitive to just where it is placed, as long as it is not pushed too far into the quantum mechanical side of the process.

Plainly this cut is not only imaginary, but it also denies the laws of the quantum theory, which assert that *every* process is indivisible, so that it is wrong to regard any aspect of the process whatever as divided (even if this is done only conceptually). As a result, a contradiction arises when one introduces such a cut, which implies a division in the quanta that are involved in the process of interaction between what is on the two sides of this cut. Of course, for a certain limited range of practical purposes, this contradiction does not bring about any serious errors in the results. In mathematics a similar situation frequently arises. For example, the self-contradictory statements, $x = 2x$, and $y = 2y$, will introduce no error in the calculation of the ratios, such as x/y, but will lead to errors in other operations. We can expect that by introducing a cut contradicting the indivisibility of those quantum processes which cross the cut, we may be limited in a similar way in the domain of problems that can be treated correctly, namely that in which this contradiction produces no important results.

We can make an interesting comparison here. Thus, roughly speaking, a man's thought processes take place in his brain, which is above his neck. We may therefore introduce a conceptual 'cut' in the form of an imaginary plane through the man's neck. Of course, as long as the plane is only imaginary, the man will not be unduly disturbed by our cut. For a certain limited range of practical purposes, this will work. But it is well known that the functioning of the body cannot really be understood without the nervous system, of which the brain is an integral part, while evidently the functioning of the brain likewise cannot really be understood without a consideration of the rest of the body. All sorts of essential factors depend on processes taking place across this cut. The cut is therefore really of no help to us in understanding man, but it is actually a serious hindrance, because it denies the basic fact that a man is an integral whole — a totality who cannot be understood by juxtaposing his parts and considering their interaction.

Is not the situation that I have just described very similar to that in quantum mechanics, where there are always indivisible quantum links across the imaginary cut between classical and quantum levels? And is it not likely that in quantum mechanics too, there will be an important range of problems which will become hopelessly confused as long as we think in terms of such cuts, namely problems arising in connexion with those processes in which linkages across the supposed cut are playing an essential part? The success of quantum mechanics in the limited domain of problems to which it has been applied is then no assurance that it is providing us with a correct treatment of relationships that go across the cut. In fact, these relationships simply have not been investigated as yet, and indeed could not be investigated within a conceptual framework in which they must be regarded as contradicting the basic laws of quantum mechanics (just as relationships depending in an essential way on processes crossing the plane in a man's neck could not be considered in an intelligible way until it was recognized that the plane is both imaginary and irrelevant).

Now, do we have to think only by beginning (as we do in classical physics) with assumed parts, then putting them together in continuous interaction, in the way that has been described here? It seems clear that the notion that such a procedure is necessary is no more than an undemonstrated conclusion, largely philosophical in nature. Indeed, in the light of previous discussions in this Symposium, it would seem that we have here a clear case of what has been called a 'paradigm', namely an unproved set of conclusions which people generally would prefer not to discuss. Is there not a danger that to begin with such conclusions will close the door to further inquiry? The danger is particularly great at present, when the modern quantum-mechanical field theory faces serious internal contradictions, which suggest the need for a radical revision of our basic concepts. (There is indeed good reason for suspecting that these contradictions arise in part just from the uncritical acceptance of the notion that all thinking must be in classical terms, but I have no time to enter into this aspect of the subject here.)

Is it not possible, then, to begin in an entirely different way, with the notion of a totality, the total process of the universe, which includes all that exists; namely the natural world, man, his laboratory apparatus, etc.? If we begin with such a total process, the parts will appear as sides, or aspects developed in the process, and not the other way round. That is to say, the process is not treated as a change from one part into another, but the parts are generated in the total process itself.

Lack of time prevents me from explaining this suggestion in more detail, but I shall give here a rather simple example. One could study circles empirically and establish various relationships approximately (for example, circumference, diameter, chords,) tabulating them in a log book. If one understands a circle as a movement of a given point that remains equidistant from a fixed point, and in a similar way, the straight line as a movement of a segment in its own direction, then one can develop a geometrical theory in which all of these relationships come out as sides of a total process. When the theory is explained, at first the listener tries to follow, and then suddenly he says, "I see". By this, he means that he perceives the circle, the straight line, and all of the various relations that have been mentioned here as following from — and in a sense generated by — a total process, so that he is no longer trying to comprehend these relations in terms of the various parts. When one says that he perceives these relations as sides of a totality, he does not mean that he sees them all at once, in detail, and exhaustively, but only that he has understood the essential process, in which they are all generated and from which they all follow.

Similarly, in physics, may we not try to understand the world as a total process, in which all parts (for example, the system under observation, observing apparatus, man, etc.) are aspects or sides whose relationships are determined by the way in which they are generated in the process? Of course, in physics, man can, in an adequate approximation, probably be left out of the totality, because he obtains his information from a piece of apparatus on the large-scale level, which is influenced in a negligible way by his looking at it. But at a quantum-mechanical level of accuracy, the apparatus and the system under observation must be recognized to be linked indivisibly. Should not the theory be formulated so as to say that this is so, and to do it without contradiction (that is, without introducing imaginary 'cuts' which deny the indivisibility of the quantum connexions between small-scale and large-scale levels)?

In a total process of the kind that I am talking about, an observation is regarded as a particular kind of movement, in which some aspects of the process are, as it were, 'projected' into certain large-scale results which are visible in the apparatus. This process of projection is, however, an integral part of the total process that is being projected. In other words, we do not have a universe, plus an observing apparatus, plus a process of interaction of the two. There is only one process, and it is this total process which is projected into the directly observable large-scale results of an experiment. Now this process of projection is what must be described in the theory. In other words, as long as, by our customary habits of thinking, we try to say that in an experiment, some part of the world is observed, with the aid of some other part, we introduce an element of confusion into our thought process. Indeed, even the very word 'observation' is misleading, as it generally implies a separation between the observing apparatus and the object under observation, of a kind that does not actually exist.

It is perhaps illuminating to consider a problem that exhibits a certain partial analogy to the quantum mechanical situation that I have just described; namely that of trying to understand an experience in which a part of what we observe is a reflection or a projection of ourselves. Thus, we habitually think of ourselves as separate entities, who are observing a world that is wholly other to us (this may be compared with the classical conception of an observation process in which there is no significant participation in what we observe). In fact, however, we are in the world and inseparably related to it. (This may be compared to the situation in quantum mechanics, where the observer's proxy — that is his apparatus — must likewise have an irreducible participation in the world which it is designed to observe.) Suppose now that we try to understand the fact of our inseparable linkage to the world as a whole. Beginning with our habitual modes of thinking, we first try to observe ourselves to see what is really going on. As one looks at oneself, either outwardly in a mirror, or inwardly, by observing one's thoughts, feelings, desires, etc., it seems that the being who observes is separate from the one who is being observed. Indeed, one could quite accurately say that *in one's thinking* there is a cut, such that all that is on one side is labelled the observer, while all that is on the other side is labelled the observed. In reality, it is evident that the cut is wholly imaginary, and indeed illusory, and that across it there is a continual and inseparable linkage. This illusory separation of the observer from what he observes can introduce the utmost confusion into our thinking. Thus, suppose we say that everything should be observable. Do we mean by this that the observer should be able to observe the very process of observation itself? As long as he imagines that he is wholly separate from what he observes, and from the process of observation, he will be trying to do the impossible. For as he tries to observe the process he will introduce a further imaginary split between himself and the process; and in this way, he will always bring in another part that he cannot observe.

Is it not possible to avoid this kind of confusion by keeping in mind the fact that the world is a totality, and that we, including our process of observation, are sides or aspects of this total process? For example, as one looks in a mirror, one understands that one is observing a part of the world containing a mirror and light linking us to the mirror. This linkage is such that the movements of the image in the mirror can reflect not only our own actions but also the total process by which we are brought into relationship with the world as a whole and with the mirror in particular. (This fact could be brought out more clearly if the atmosphere had a bit of smoke in it, so that it could show up the paths of the light rays that link us to the mirror and to the whole world. Such paths could not only be seen directly, but they would also be reflected in the mirror.)

Failure to realize what was going on in the process could then make it impossible to interpret the results of an observation in a consistent way. Suppose, for example, that the observer thought that he was seeing a wholly separate man behind the mirror. He would then discover that this 'man' seemed to be 'disturbed' whenever the observer moved so as to obtain a more detailed view of him, and indeed, disappear altogether whenever the observer looked behind the mirror. Would not the observer be tempted to consider an imaginary cut between a 'classical' world on his side of the mirror and a 'non-classical' world on the other side (as Lewis Carroll did in his *Alice Through the Looking Glass*)?

In order to avoid the introduction of irrelevant problems of this kind, it is necessary to keep in mind that we are in the world, and that a certain *part* of what we observe is therefore either a reflection or a projection of our own actions. This does not mean that the world has no existence outside of ourselves, but only that we must recognize that we exist in the world, and that serious confusion can result if we forget this fact. Similarly, in physics, we can introduce unresolvable paradoxes if we forget what the quantum mechanics itself has shown us, namely that the results of an observation are a projection and a reflection of the totality, and do not correspond just to some hypothetical world that is wholly other to the physicist, his apparatus, the processes which he uses in his experiments, etc. To deal with a situation of this kind, our traditional, habitual and 'classical' modes of thought will not be adequate. But from this there is no reason to conclude, either in physics or in everyday experience, that there is no way at all to understand what is going on when the observer participates significantly in what he observes.

With this situation in mind, let us return to the questions raised by Wilkinson concerning the need to introduce concepts into our theories which do not correspond completely to something that is observable. First of all, let us ask, "Why do we consider observations to be so important?" Is not this emphasis on observation perhaps already somewhat misleading? Let me give an analogy: anyone making a cursory inspection of how typical students work in a university might easily get the impression that the main purpose of university work is to prepare the student to pass his examinations. But such an impression would be wrong, since the main purpose of examinations is (or should be) to test how well the student *understands* the subjects. Similarly, the scientist immersed in his daily work can easily get the impression that observation is the essence of science, whereas, in fact, the main purpose of observations is to help show us how well we really understand what we are investigating. Therefore, our requirement should be, not so much that everything must be observable, but rather that it should be *understandable*, that is, that we should be able to conceive it as a coherent total process in which everything that is significant appears as a side or aspect developed in the process itself. Of course, the physicist must then use his ingenuity to devise appropriate experimental tests for showing how correct this understanding really is. If it is good enough, there is no visible reason why he should not be able to find an experiment that could either confirm, or deny, any particular aspect of the theory. But before he can do this on the experimental side, it is important that the theory be understood adequately on the conceptual side, for confused thinking on the part of the physicist will in general result in the presentation of confused questions to nature, which will of course lead to confused answers that are not very helpful. (For example, if the observer imagines that there is another man behind the mirror, his experiments designed to study the behaviour of this 'man' are likely to present him with more and more paradoxes, until he sees clearly that he has not understood the situation in which he is working.) That is to say, before we require that everything be observable, we must be sure that the general conceptual framework defining what is meant by an observation is both understandable and relevant.

If we look at the quantum theory as it stands today we must agree that its general conceptual framework is not fully understandable and probably not entirely relevant. One of the main points that cannot be understood is the relationship between large-scale and small-scale levels, assumed to be separated by an imaginary cut which denies the property of indivisibility that is most basic to the quantum theory as a whole. As long as we think in terms of such contradictions we will have to regard the theory as being at bottom nothing more than a technical device, which enables us to calculate a rather wide (but nevertheless limited) range of numbers that agree with corresponding numbers coming out of experiments. But the theory does not furnish a comprehensible insight into the world as a totality. And without this, there is no way to obtain a clear understanding of what can actually be meant by an observation, within the framework of the theory itself. Without such an understanding, how can we hope to frame relevant questions concerning the observability of all concepts that appear in the theory? We have not yet arrived at the stage where problems of this kind can properly be considered. It therefore seems important that more work must be done on this phase of the subject, and that it be studied in new ways. I have been engaged on this kind of work for some time, but there is, of course, no time to discuss it here in any detail. The results will appear elsewhere.

Discussion

J. W. Herivel

I suggest that perhaps Mr. Buchdahl and Mr. Hanson attach too much importance to the role of the inductive-deductive process in science. Consider Newton's theory of gravitation. It is presented in Book III of the *Principia* in a wonderfully persuasive philosophical manner in terms of an ascent and descent of Bacon's ladder. But what has this to do with the *actual* process (what we are concerned with surely in this Symposium) extending over the period 1665–85 which finally led to the completed theory? This process consisted of a number of specific questions posed by nature herself to which in each case Newton gave the correct answer. There was a further element certainly, and you can if you wish term it inductive, though I should prefer not to since this might give the impression it had something to do with Aristotle, which it certainly had not. This further element is best illustrated by Newton's first test of the law of gravitation during the plague years. The story is well known: how he discovered the law of centrifugal force and applied it to the motions of the planets about the sun. Kepler's third law then showed that the centrifugal forces of the individual planets varied inversely as the squares of their distances from the sun. Then Newton must have made a great discovery. He must have realized that there was no such thing as centrifugal force, only *centripetal* force towards the sun, that it was this pull towards the sun which prevented the planets flying away from the sun along their natural inertial paths. It was at this point that I think the further element entered. I think he then said, "What is good for the sun will be good for the earth." In this case the force[1] on the moon will be so much less than the force on the stone at the earth according to the self-same law. There is here, I think, no question of induction but rather the appreciation of that principle of uniformity, known to the pre-Socratic philosophers, made conceivable again by Copernicus and popularized by Galileo. The same principle is applied (almost unconsciously of course) by the astrophysicist who, seeing what *seems* to be the spectrum of helium from the sun, assumes that there *is* helium in the sun. Nothing, of course, will ever prove that there is.

[1] Though *really* acceleration.

We shall never be able to go and see. And philosophers can argue the point to their hearts' content. But the scientist is not concerned. He believes with Descartes that God is no deceiver and gets on with his work.

But there *is* one other thing. The scientist, as Mr. Vernant has so brilliantly reminded us, has still one bitter task to perform. He must now go into the *agora* and communicate his results to the city. And at this point, if he happens to be not only a scientist, but also a philosopher, then he will use his philosophy to clothe his thought and present it as a great persuasive work of art, such as Galileo did in the *Dialogue* or Newton in Book III of the *Principia*.

G. J. Whitrow

I should like to supplement what Mr. Buchdahl has written and what Mr. Hanson has said about Descartes's anticipation of a 'logic of discovery' by drawing attention to one or two facets of a question that has long puzzled me. The problem is this: how was it that Descartes, a man of consummate intelligence living in one of the most important centuries of scientific advance and, moreover, a great mathematician who believed in using both mathematics and experiment to further the advance of science, nevertheless failed to anticipate the decisive breakthrough which we rightly associate with Newton?

No doubt there were a number of reasons why Descartes failed in this respect. I will mention only two. First, I would stress the fact that time played a very minor role in Descartes's natural philosophy, whereas Newton raised it to a concept of major importance — and indeed went even further than was really necessary by regarding it as an absolute concept existing in its own right, independently of material things. Second, and I believe no less important, was the fact that Descartes, unlike Galileo, seems not to have grasped the crucial role in science of the method of piecemeal and limited inquiry. On the contrary, it is well known that Descartes actually criticized Galileo on this very score. On the other hand, Newton in the *Principia* deliberately isolated certain factors and skilfully side-stepped others of which he was ignorant. For example, he had no more knowledge than Descartes of the 'mechanism' or mode of operation of gravitational attraction, but unlike Descartes he avoided it, at least in the *Principia*, and concentrated on those factors which were required for the purposes of what came to be called 'celestial mechanics'. Newton was, in short, a supreme master of the 'black box' technique, of ignoring those factors about which one knows nothing while exploiting to the full a limited number of significant and testable principles. Thus, in his theory of gravitation, he concentrated on the idea of central forces operating between point-masses in three-dimensional space so as to yield the inverse square law, and revealed the power of this limited approach to the study of celestial motions. I submit that this difference between Newton's method and Descartes's is vital for a proper assessment of Descartes's role in the evolution of scientific method.

M. B. Hesse

I want to put in a word for Descartes, because the image of him that we are given in the general histories, and which Mr. Whitrow has partly repeated, does not seem to me to do him justice. It may be that at that time in the seventeenth century it was necessary for the development of science that someone should take a universal view. If he had been another Galileo he might have done some things that would now appear in our elementary text-books, but then the progress of science might well have been much slower. It is very remarkable in reading his contemporaries and predecessors, even Gilbert and Gassendi, who are described as founders of science, the reviver of atomism, and so on, to see how their discussions take place in an atmosphere of all kinds of spiritual emanations and quasi-vital and animistic entities, and how they are wrestling unsuccessfully with the problem of what are the essential qualities of bodies which should enter a theory of matter. It required Descartes to cut all this away, and come out clearly with the primary qualities of extension and motion, indeed he cut it down too far, since mass had to be re-introduced, but it may well be that a prerequisite for Newton was the establishment by Descartes of a universal framework, or paradigm, of the mechanical philosophy.

D. Speiser

I should like to ask Mr. Daumas a question. But first let me draw attention to another link between the development of theories and the art of measurement. This is the effect which the theories and the investigation of their consequences have on the construction of measuring devices. Neither the apparatus of Michelson nor the equipment of J. J. Thomson, mentioned by Mr. Cohen, would have been possible without most of the theories already developed. And this is certainly not merely a technological question. It is a specific and characteristic property of modern science, that effects predicted by formulae belonging to very different fields may be combined such that completely new questions can be asked by the physicist. Moreover, old questions can be answered with a much greater accuracy. The history of nineteenth-century physics and of contemporary physics both display numerous examples, and this as I said is characteristic of modern science.

The question then is the following: when and how did physicists begin to invent and to construct experimental devices, which were more than trivial applications of discovered laws but were the products of ingenious apparatus based on theoretical results combining different specific effects? I know one example from the middle of the eighteenth century — in the field of optics, but I am sure Mr. Daumas knows many more.

If this is not a central property of modern physics, it certainly is a very typical one, and the development of modern physics cannot be completely described without it. But also we might feel here the pulse of early physics particularly well, since it marks the meeting point of theory and experiment. Moreover the best part of the experimentalists' activity is devoted to imagining such devices. I suggest that it would be worth while investigating the history of physics systematically from this point of view.

J. R. Ravetz

I would like to ask Mr. Daumas a question. The rapid rise in the standard of the craft of precision instrument-making towards the end of the eighteenth century would seem to have causes outside science itself. It would be tempting to ascribe it to the 'industrial revolution', but the technology of heavy industry of that period made little use of such instruments. Was there some special factor involved in this development?

N. R. Hanson

Since I have been rash enough to have published spirited defences of the Copenhagen Interpretation of Quantum Theory against its critics, my expectations were that I would be aligned with Wilkinson against Bohm. But my first point is concerned with a debatable contention in Mr. Wilkinson's paper.

In his second paragraph he writes: "The huge and uniformly

successful edifice of quantum theory convinces us that the representation of a particle in terms of an amplitude is 'right'." I cannot agree. Quantum theory, as an algorithm, is not a 'uniformly successful edifice'. My assumption is that quantum field theory is a major part of 'quantum theory'; moreover, radiation effects in general are an experimental microphysicist's responsibility. Indeed, one might argue that quantum field theory is the logically more fundamental discipline; it includes 'elementary quantum theory' as a sub-theory.

From the formal point of view, quantum field theory has been spectacularly unsuccessful. There are many radiation phenomena which, when they involve high energies, cannot be consistently described via any 'unadjusted' quantum theory. The wave-equations for the microparticles involved within such experimental contexts are such that their constituent integrals diverge radically as energy increases. This results in a potential infinitude of possible solutions to each wave-equation. This is mathematically intolerable. So, through an algebraic technique called 'renormalization' (due to Bethe, Schwinger and Tomonaga) the theoretician draws from this infinitude a small number of solutions for further examination. This he does on grounds which are formally quite extraneous. That is, the principles of choice built into 'renormalization' are not purely algebraic: they involve some rather slippery physical assumptions as well. It all suggests something like forcing observational facts from land-surveying into critical steps within a formal proof of Pythagoras's Theorem.

Not only is the formal rationale and procedure of renormalization somewhat dubious, the actual intra-theoretical results are physically scandalous. An immediate effect consists in the rendering of the S-matrices ('scattering matrices') for the particles in question as non-Hermitean, or non-unitary. This means that the theoretician cannot formally justify his natural assumption that there is *at least one* particle present within the experimental volume-element dx, dy, dz, with which he is concerned, and which particle's coordinates or energy he is trying to determine. Indeed, non-unitary S-matrices force one to entertain the 'negative probability' of a microparticle's location at coordinates x, y, z, t. The 'physical interpretation' of this negative probability forces the physicist to speak of the 'ghost states' of particles — a shadowy concept which, so far as I know, has never made much sense.

Now here is a fundamental structural difficulty within the

algebraic design of quantum theory. The point may be put even more strongly, by urging that, as a well-formed algorithm, *quantum mechanics does not even exist yet.* How long would the great physical theories of the past have lasted were they riddled with formal inelegancies and inconsistencies of the sort embodied in both renormalized and unrenormalized quantum theory? Not very long, I submit.

However, lest this be thought too much to lend colour to Mr. Bohm's general programme, permit me one parting note of caution. It is true that, for such reasons as those set out above, quantum theory is conceptually imperfect. As an algorithm it is very far from being 'uniformly successful', as Mr. Wilkinson has suggested it is. Nonetheless, whatever success modern physics has had with sub-classical particles, and this success is considerable, it is entirely due to the powers of the only extant theory capable of dealing seriously with micro-phenomena. One must distinguish those moments in the history of physics when two equally well-developed theories have competed to furnish the 'best' explanation of a phenomenon, from those quite different periods during which scientists have available to them but one workable theory *without even an intelligible alternative anywhere nearby.* Such is the present state of quantum theory. Let me develop this.

When, in the seventeenth century, the problem of explaining the nature of light radiation seriously perplexed physicists, there were two well-made theories actively in competition. Arguments might then have proceeded profitably over the vexed question of whether light propagation was fundamentally an undulating phenomenon, or fundamentally a particulate phenomenon. The explanatory and predictive power of either theory was roughly comparable to that of the other. The issue, therefore, turned on the physical interpretation of the formal parameters involved in the two calculi.

Contrast that situation with the slow collapse of classical celestial mechanics in the later half of the nineteenth century. Leverrier's discovery of a secular advance of Mercury's perihelion 38″ *in excess* of what Newtonian theory could explain, contained the seeds of the decay of that very theory Leverrier had been instrumental in raising to its highest pinnacle in 1846 — the year in which Neptune was discovered. But although the walls of the theory were cracking over this fault, there was no alternative theory to which to turn. No intelligible way of thinking of planetary motions and perturbations, other than the Newtonian, was available to astronomers just after 1860. It would have been one thing then to urge that efforts be redoubled to patch up the theoretical damage done by Mercury's precessions. It would have been quite another thing incessantly to remark the shortcomings of the only available theory, hinting thereby that the theory be abandoned for the time. This would have been tantamount to abandoning planetary astronomy altogether. No serious astronomer could have taken this seriously.

To return to the present: if the frequent criticisms offered by Bohm, Vigier and Feyerabend of orthodox quantum theory are construed only as energetic ways of remarking its formal and interpretative shortcomings, *à la bonne heure*. Most quantum theoreticians are as concerned with these shortcomings as are Bohm, Vigier and Feyerabend — and they are doing their best to shore up the imperfections from 'inside' quantum theory. If, on the other hand, the suggestion is that quantum theory, in the light of its structural weaknesses, should be scrapped *in toto*, the answer must be "not quite yet, thank you very much!" When Bohm, Vigier and Feyerabend manage to supply a fully articulated, algebraically detailed and physically intelligible alternative to orthodox quantum theory, then they shall have won the day — *provided* that their new theory generates all the 'observational numbers' supplied by the present theory. One wants sharp quantitative predictions of the properties and elements not only of electrons, protons and neutrons, but also of phonons, hyperons, leptons, photons, anti-neutrinos, etc. When this is forthcoming experimental physicists will go down on their knees in thanks. And perhaps this prospect in itself fully justifies the continued efforts of Bohm, Vigier and Feyerabend. But until then Wilkinson's attitude will not only prevail, it will remain the philosophically *most reasonable* attitude for physicists to adopt.

In sum: it is not the case, as Wilkinson's words might incline us to think, that the present state of quantum theory is wholly healthy, and "uniformly successful". On the other hand, we should not, because of this *malaise*, bury orthodox quantum theory in the cemetery of dead and useless theories — as Bohm sometimes leads his readers to understand. Speculations about alternative theories *should* be encouraged to continue. But until one of these fully succeeds in displacing orthodox quantum theory as an instrument of prediction and measurement, they must continue to be described as 'speculations'. This is not an unworthy appellation. Some speculations have changed the course of the history of science.

D. Bohm

Mr. Speiser raised the question whether the work of von Neumann does not solve the problem of the relationship of what is observed to the observing apparatus and to the wave function.

The answer is that von Neumann makes essentially the same assumption of a 'cut' between classical and quantum domains as is made in other treatments of these problems. His treatment differs in various details, but in the last analysis he is forced to assume that there is a classical domain satisfying classical laws, and that observations are made in this domain. The relationship between the classical domain and the quantum laws is not treated in a unified way as a total process, so that the problem of understanding what is meant by an observation within the framework of quantum laws is, in my opinion, not adequately faced.

G. Buchdahl

I want to single out for discussion the question which Mr. Hanson has raised in his comment on my paper, namely whether 'inverse-deduction' and 'retroduction' are different forms of *reasoning*, or whether they are two different words for the same thing.

We are, as far as I can see, agreed that, *formally schematized*, it is all one whether I say: 'If *H*, then *E*; but since *E*, therefore possibly *H*'; or: 'Given *E*, and given that *H* would imply *E*, then (possibly) *H*'; or even: 'Given *E*, to find that *H* which, because it implies *E*, is possibly the *H* we are looking for', etc., etc.

But, Mr. Hanson tells us, *materially* there is a very great difference, because the time relation is inverted, or because (as he puts it) the retroductive formulation symbolizes a different conceptual role. I confess I do not understand this last remark; at least, I do not understand its significance. I will admit that the relevance of high-lighting the usefulness of the retroductive schema is greatest in examples from applied mathematics and physics. Thus, consider the following: given the observed perturbation of some given planetary orbit, what would be the mass and position, etc., of a hypothetical planet in order to cause such a perturbation? Here certainly we are enjoined to 'move from effect to cause', to use an archaism; moreover, we are here in a position to obey this command because we can *calculate* what the masses ought to be, in order to be capable of producing the observed perturbations.

But it seems to me that this is only because we are already availing ouselves of a number of known hypotheses. Consider to this end an even simpler example: given the length of a shadow, solve the problem: What would the height of the sun in the sky and of the neighbouring wall have to be to cast such a shadow? Now here also we move from effect to cause. But surely this is because in such a case we do not really have to do with the request to compute an hypothesis but rather to apply an already known deductive schema or method of representation. Where the example is mathematical, this is a most important element in our reasoning but it is nonetheless solely an application of a deductive schema.

So, short of the interpretation just given, I must stick to my position, which is, that to say, 'given *E*, find or fit the hypothesis that will explain *E*' differs from the other way of talking only in the time sequence. This being the case, I must also stick to my strictures on Descartes which were to the effect that although he suggests that the "method of analysis" moves from effect to cause, this is not of course a new mechanical method, let alone a new logic — apart from being an oblique reference to inverse-deduction: what I called "analysis-H" in my paper. He has not got a new conceptual tool for the discovery of causes.

Mr. Hanson wondered whether Descartes's method of analysis did not after all embrace a distinctive mode of 'retroduction'; and he said it was not clear to him whether Descartes was confusedly sometimes hankering after the latter, sometimes after inverse-deduction. In trying to answer this question, let us once more look at Descartes's derivation of Snell's law. For it is here in particular that he claims that his presentation follows the "analytic method", which he says mirrors the method of discovery. I have tried to say a few words about this in my paper but I want to consider this with Hanson's question in mind. In other words, since Descartes claimed that here we have a method whereby we move from effect to cause, perhaps we are dealing therefore with what Hanson wants to call "retroduction" specifically, as distinguished from inverse-deduction.

Now it is fairly universally accepted that Descartes did *not* discover Snell's law in the way in which he presents this in his *Dioptrique*. In this respect, his account is quite different from the more genuinely autobiographical one which Kepler gave in his *Paralipomena ad Vitellionem*, where he carefully describes the steps that eventually led him to the discovery of a formula which tolerably accounted for the observations.

Now the hypothesis, so-called, to be 'derived' here, is Snell's law. Therefore our retroductive schema should be: given a set of values for the angle of inclination *i*, and the angle of refraction *r*, find the form or formula that will yield this set of values, subject to certain conditions. How does Descartes pretend to derive this formula? (And short of biographical speculation, we can of course only study his published work.) As I have indicated in my paper, he does it by the application of a certain kind of resolution, and by what (to be brief) we may call the addition or insertion of additional hypotheses. For instance, we add that the angles *i* and *r* are formed by physical light-rays; that these rays are the orbits of physical disturbances which have complex velocities such that the horizontal component of these velocities are undisturbed by the passage of light in different media, etc., etc. Given then that there *are* these angles (and this fact is of course given in the statement of the phenomenon to be explained), and given the supplementary hypotheses, then the main hypothesis proper may indeed be 'derived'.

The use of the term 'derived' here is deliberate. For Hanson is of course perfectly correct in saying that the formulation of our hypothesis in the light of the phenomena is not just simply 'guess-work', or 'psychological intuition', but that it involves a complicated process in which, furthermore, is implicated a considerable amount of reasoning. On the other hand, we must be clear that this term "derive" does easily mislead us into forgetting that it conceals a considerable element of hypothesis — as my example will have shown.

One might indeed go further and say: does not the insertion of the supplementary hypothesis itself involve 'guess-work'? Well, as far as Descartes's reasoning is here involved, I have shown in my paper that the supplementary hypothesis is in turn suggested (or should we once more say "derived"?) from Descartes's general account of the material constitution of the universe. But it is nonetheless the case, that these hypotheses (in the paper I have spoken indeed of the "employment of a model or models") constitute what one might call 'supplementations from without'. They are not implied by the major hypothesis, nor by the data for which the latter is meant to account; they are simply fitted into the argument in the way in which hypotheses are generally fitted to cover the phenomena; the 'logical gap' indicated is in no way different from that suggested by the inverse-deductive schema. Now, fitting hypotheses to facts is not a new logical operation; it is, materially speaking, whatever it is scientists are creatively engaged in when looking for considerations relevant to the solution of their problems; and in my paper I have stated in some detail the considerations that motivated Descartes in this particular instance. But *formally*, we simply have inverse-deduction, despite the original appearance of a 'derivation' of Snell's law.

However, what is important and useful about Hanson's strictures is that to concentrate our attention overmuch upon a perfectly obvious logical schema (however many interesting philosophical problems this may raise) often conceals the much more exciting forms or ways whereby we 'derive', that is formulate, hypotheses, through the employment of models and subsidiary schemas. To this extent his critical remarks form a valuable supplement to my paper.

M. Daumas

We have now reached a point in the chronological sequence of this Symposium at which it is appropriate to examine the problem of scientific instruments. The question of the invention, construction and diffusion of apparatus was becoming at this time an increasingly important factor in the progress of knowledge. It is perhaps inappropriate to talk of precision measurements; the word 'precision' is a snare. We understand it as from our twentieth-century point of view, but it certainly meant something quite different in the eighteenth century. Concerning the remarks of Bernard Cohen, I think that for that period it would be more appropriate to speak of exact measurements. In the field of physics and chemistry it was in fact the main achievement of this whole period (which we must define as beginning with the early seventeenth century) to create conditions in which exact measurements could be made, and when tested by different observers invariably give the same result. From one period to the next, the increase in precision to which more and more stress was given, brought gradually modified measurements, and so modified also the determination of phenomena, and consequently there was an evolution in concepts which attempted to give a more universal interpretation of them. But, as others have pointed out, and as I have said myself, the need for great precision was felt at a much later period than that which we are considering. This period only opened the way and made it possible. The problem would have been quite different if we had also had to consider astronomy. The evolution of astronomical instruments was determined very early on, that is to say, from the sixteenth century, by the great accuracy of measurements made possible by the continually improving techniques of instrument-makers. In this field, technical progress went hand in hand with the growth of theory and scientific knowledge. There is always a certain interdependence between scientific theory and instruments of observation; there is a constant interaction between one and the other which leads to continual progress and explains the accelerated rate of progress.

Mr. Speiser has asked which was the most ancient instrument based on a known scientific principle. The oldest is, without doubt, the balance, which later became a scientific instrument. For the modern period one may point to optical instruments; they were first born of empirical research, but were perfected with the discovery of the laws of geometrical optics; the works of Young and those of Fresnel gave birth to a whole new category of instruments. But without doubt one of the first examples of the application of a known scientific principle in the construction of an instrument was the regulation of chronometers by the pendulum designed by Huygens. Clocks had been up to then things in everyday use.

Thanks to Huygens's invention, they became instruments of scientific value; the researches into clocks for the construction of naval time-pieces contributed to the development of precision chronometers.

It has also been asked if the development of workshops was originally a question of supply and demand. Certainly from the end of the seventeenth century, there was a demand which grew greater during the last quarter of that century. Demonstration instruments apart, it was primarily astronomy, followed by geodesy, that provoked the largest demand for new instruments, a demand proportionate to their degree of accuracy. So a new industry was born.

Similarly, as time went on, the character of certain sciences was transformed. This occurred for example in chemistry.

There is a difference of character, as Mr. Greenaway has indicated, between chemistry and physics when, from the end of the eighteenth century, the new laws of physics were applied to chemical research and led to the emergence of such new methods as those of spectroscopy, polarimetry, cryoscopy, ebulliometry, etc.

In conclusion, I will simply add that in my paper I have especially sought to draw attention to the technical problems involved in creating the material means of observation, for they are, in my opinion, the least known and the most often neglected in the history of science. I have said very little about the effect of the use of these instruments on the measurements themselves and on the evolution of theory, partly because the subject was too vast for a single paper, and partly because I was persuaded that Bernard Cohen's comments would rectify the omission. I would add that I am in perfect agreement with the views he expressed.

C. C. Gillispie

Miss Hesse's criticism is interesting and important, and on re-reading the sources and reflecting, I agree that the paper (which appears as written) goes too far when it attributes to Quetelet and Herschel an identification in concept of errors and events on the grounds that the distribution of either might be governed by the mean square law. Indeed, I venture to hope that to be thus corrected will rid the paper of an error and embarrassment and clarify the argument, which it does not seem to me necessary to abandon. And there are a few additional observations to put before the reader before he decides what weight to accord the model which social statistics may have afforded in the circumstances in which physics found itself in Maxwell's time. It will be well to take advantage of the clarity of the alternatives which Miss Hesse defines on the relations that may be thought to obtain between the calculus of probabilities and the world, for these categories are more evident in retrospect than they were in times past.

As to the first alternative — that the world is causally determined, our knowledge subject to error, and statistical analysis to be used to discover true causes — Miss Hesse describes this as the position of Laplace. But Laplace did not employ statistical methods. He only employed the calculus of probability and quite without statistical information. It was left to Poisson to look to statistical information unavailable to

Laplace in order to determine *a priori* probabilities for use in Bayes's theorem.

As to the second alternative — which works out that nature is subject to statistical as well as deterministic laws — there may also lie in this category the risk of confusing statistics with probabilities — the data with the combinatorial analysis — before the junction was firm, as it became in Quetelet's work and Maxwell's. Certainly Poisson did think this to be true of society. It is not clear to me that he was so definite about nature.

As to Miss Hesse's third alternative, she wonders why I treat its "weak" form in the person of Cournot. The answer is that it is for historical reasons. There is a considerable literature on Cournot as the founder of probabilism. He thought himself to be occupying new ground. It seemed worthwhile to review the position taken by the one philosopher of science who espoused probabilism (even if weakly) in advance of its systematic introduction into physics as an analytical technique. Nor was it for technical reasons that Cournot's probabilism proved irrelevant to the development of physics. A footnote to the *Théorie des chances* explicitly acknowledges the near coincidence of the curve obtained from the distribution of errors with that from the binomial distribution.[1] But he made nothing of it, perhaps because he lacked interest in the fruitful problems, but mainly because he saw it as an issue in the structure of nature rather than in scientific method.

Indeed, it was because Herschel did see probabilities relative to Mill's "inductive philosophy" rather than relative to nature that he could appreciate the technique. Nor in agreeing that my discussion presses the assimilation of errors to events too far towards modern positivism, do I think the relation of the binomial distribution to the law of error to have been devoid of historical interest. Quetelet did not think so. It was at Herschel's urging that he pursued the question, recognized the binomial distribution in his data, and went on to write his most important treatise, the *Letters on the Theory of Probabilities.*[2] True, Quetelet did regard his distributions as governing deviations from a type. But the notion of mistakes by nature (this has nothing in common with some ancient idea of a *lusus naturae*) was a step beyond Laplace's determined world order. Practically, though not ontologically, it was a longer step than

[1] Cournot, *Théorie des chances*, pp. 60–1.

[2] Lottin, *Quetelet*, pp. 154–5.

Cournot's, for we may see it as tacitly employing a frequency conception of probability. Nor was Quetelet concerned simply to get the parameters, the initial probabilities, as Poisson had done in his analysis of judicial returns, but rather to describe the state of things in situations accessible to numerical analysis. For Quetelet, a degree of probability is the measure of the frequency with which a property occurs in some certain class. It would be interesting to discuss whether the same may be said of Clausius's application of probability to the mean free path. It would be interesting, too, to know whether his conception of the mean distinguished it from the average, as did Quetelet and Herschel, and as Maxwell's treatment presupposed. These are delicate questions, the import of which I may have misconstrued. It is safer to raise them than to pronounce with dogmatism. But I do not think these things may be said of Clausius's paper.

It is well known that that paper started Maxwell on the dynamical study of gases, and it formed no part of my intention to slight its importance either physically or intellectually. Rather, the theme of this conference made it seem appropriate to take that for granted and to look about outside of physics for techniques, methods, inspirations, and models that might have played their role. One would like to know by what routes the migration of probabilities from social studies to physics did occur. Certainly there was more than one. I thought to have singled out a likely possibility in observing that though Maxwell found his problem in Clausius's discussion, he resolved it by employing a mean as Quetelet had already done and as Clausius did not do. Clausius did not employ the distribution from the law of errors to define his mean free path. He did not turn to the mean square. Maxwell did. Not only did he define the mean in the same way as Quetelet, but he then used this value, not simply to average out variations, but to compute the kinetic energy of the system. It is the velocity of mean square which figures in his equations as the mean man would ideally figure in Quetelet's social physics. And it is precisely this role of the mean which Herschel emphasized as the main point of his essay on the relation of indictive science to probabilities, an essay which concludes with a summons to compare the methods of mechanics and social studies.

As to what Miss Hesse calls the "strong" form of the belief that the laws of nature are statistical, I agree that it would be most unfortunate if the discussion were to leave the impression that any of the persons who figure in this paper intended to eliminate determinism from physical nature in order to introduce a statistical mechanics. Maxwell himself never went so far, and it is, therefore, irrelevant that neither did Herschel nor Quetelet. Statistical mechanics could and no doubt much later did contribute to the notion of a nature in which all laws are statistical. But there was no *a priori* vision of a statistical nature, comparable (say) to Galileo's of a geometrized nature. Cournot's chance was not amenable to statistical treatment. The argument, then, should convey, and is intended to convey, that the opportunities for combining probabilities and statistics existed first in social studies and then in physics; that the techniques for doing so could be transferred from one to the other; that Quetelet and Maxwell, but not Clausius, had the same concept of a mean as distinct from an average and computed the distribution about it by the same law, to wit the mean square law of error; that Quetelet in effect did this before Maxwell; and that the flashover may have occurred via Herschel's timely article. Nowhere should the argument imply that Maxwell's treatment depended on indeterminacy, or that Quetelet caused Maxwell's dynamical theory of gases, any more than one would say that Malthus caused Darwin's theory of natural selection. It may be that Miss Hesse refutes a "stronger" form of historical causalism than was intended. The paper does say that one would not wish to argue that Maxwell had to have read Herschel's essay. Nevertheless, I am pleased to learn from Miss Hesse, and it is generous of her to point out, what had escaped me — that in fact it is almost certain that he did.

D. H. Wilkinson

First, I would like to repeat and perhaps clarify a little what I wrote. I have not made sufficiently clear that there are two ways in which we as practising physicists talk about things that in principle are unobservable. One is that on which Mr. Bohm spent his time, the very deep unobservability of the starting-point of our description of nature. This is the present situation. Whether it should and will be modified in the way Mr. Bohm suggested I do not know and it is not my business to discuss this. The other way is the more practical one which I think historians of science and students of methods of discovery might be interested in: even when we are wrong in so doing we have continued as practising scientists to use ordinary language to "describe" things that we know in fact have no direct observable significance. The illustration I gave was the distorted nucleus which in fact we cannot possibly observe as other than spherically symmetrical. This sort of procedure we find has great heuristic value and many important developments in the last few years have come from what one might call completely improper and unallowable starting-points. Of course as in many of the cases here discussed when it is finally written up it is not presented in this way at all. When you go and talk with the people who have done it, you find that they have started out with a mechanical model or a physical picture which is strictly illegitimate. I think this is interesting. The way in which one actually gets one's ideas is often based on things that are strictly incorrect, even if the way in which they are finally presented is always legitimate.

Secondly, I think I should point out that I do not regard quantum theory as in any way a closed book, very far from it. My rash remark about the huge and uniformly successful edifice was more concerned with the chemical and almost macroscopic aspects of quantum theory, namely our ability to calculate atomic and molecular structures. There are, I agree, very considerable residual uncertainties of the sort that Mr. Hanson has mentioned. We do not have a closed description of any field aspect of quantum theory. Quantum-electrodynamics is I think our nearest approach to it and there we do appear to be able to calculate anything we have the energy to calculate as accurately as we wish. At the same time one can demonstrate, as has been done by Landau, that if you do a calculation with sufficient energy, which nobody has, again you must get the wrong answer. So it is a paradoxical situation where if we carry the calculation to a small number of degrees of approximation, which already is a task beyond us, we get an answer which converges more and more to the experimental answer; and yet we can prove that if only we continued we would begin to get the wrong answer again. This is obviously an unsatisfactory situation and one which very rightly Mr. Hanson draws my attention to. We should certainly worry about it from the point of view of formulation of the subject. It is not a worry from the point of view of the application at the moment. The question is possibly connected with a remark made earlier by Mr. Speiser, that the infinite extent of the co-ordinates, so to speak, that were used — the ghost states to which Mr. Hanson referred — are found only in very remote regions of these co-ordinates of energy and it is fashionable in certain circumstances to impose a 'cut-off' which we do not understand. This is a way of concealing our ignorance of the true situation, which simply removes the problem in a very *ad hoc* and highly unsatisfactory manner, but a manner which does not impinge on our ability to make calculations of practical problems. So when I made my rash statement I was referring chiefly to less precise and delicate matters — just to the fact that we can calculate properties of matter, we believe to as high a degree of approximation as is interesting in the laboratory, using the inverse-square law of electro-static force and the rules of wave-mechanics, which basically are the representation of a particle in terms of an amplitude. And the success has been huge and uniform. The whole of chemistry and most of physics is based directly upon it. I do not think one can doubt the success if one contemplates the scale on which modern science is now carried out, and all this is based on the representation of particles in terms of amplitude. So let me just sum up and say that this practical application of quantum theory is uniformly successful. When we push it to the limits which are these high energies and high degrees of approximation, it breaks down, it is wrong, it is not a complete theory, and if it were there would be nothing to discuss.

PART SIX

The Making of Modern Science: Factors in Biological Discovery

16

The Role of Analogies and Models in Biological Discovery

GEORGES CANGUILHEM

It is not easy to agree on the role and significance of models in the physical sciences. Boltzmann did not hesitate to claim that Maxwell's formulae were entirely the consequence of his mechanical models. But Pierre Duhem believed that the same Maxwell could only have created his theory by renouncing the use of any model.

It seems to be even more difficult to agree on the role and significance of models in the biological sciences, and even to agree on the definition of such models. In fact, sometimes this word refers to a group of corresponding analogous features between a natural object and a manufactured one, and sometimes to a system of semantic and syntactical definitions, set up in a mathematical type of language, concerning the relationship between the constituent elements of a structure and their formal equivalents.

Without doubt, it would seem that in biology analogical models have been and still are more frequently used than mathematical models. The fact is that explanation by reduction is more naive than explanation by formalized deduction. It is also a fact that biological phenomena the study of which is susceptible of direct formalization are few in number. First among them are the relationships involved in heredity. But these relationships have no functional character and, as opposed to most biological phenomena, they do not pretend to any appearance of completeness. The models studied in genetics make, therefore, no pretensions to aetiological description. On the other hand, the reduction of organic structures and functions to forms and mechanisms which are already more familiar, the use in biology of aetiological analogies borrowed from the realms of mechanical, physical or technological experiment, has had for a long time, and still has, a breadth of usage directly proportional to its age. There can be no question here of going back to the origin of such an intellectual leaning. But it seems to me that the concept of *organs* provides of itself, and by the very fact of its etymology, a directing principle for the understanding of the permanence of a method.

It has not been sufficiently noticed how full the vocabulary of animal anatomy in Western science is of nomenclature for organs, viscera, segments or regions of the organism expressing metaphors or analogies. Sometimes the nomenclature only serves to disguise a morphological comparison (*scaphoid bone* and *trochlea of the femur*, for example). Sometimes the name also indicates analogous function or role, which is not present in the structure (*cornea*, *vessel*, *anastomosis*, *sac*, *canal*, *axis*, for example). The Greek and Latin nomenclature of macroscopic structures makes it apparent that technical experiment informs the observation of organic forms, while, in reverse, technical objects and tools are often designated by words of anatomical origin (*arm*, *wing*, *neck*, *knee*, *elbow*, *teeth*, *claw*, *finger*, *foot*, etc.). As a result of this fact, would it not be possible to consider the explicit use of models in biology as the systematic and considered extension of an outlook inherent in the way man sees organisms? When he compares the vertebrae to door-hinges (*Timaeus*, 74a) or the blood vessels to irrigation canals (*Timaeus*, 770), is not Plato knowingly making use of a summary procedure for explaining physical functions which originates in a technical model? Is Aristotle doing anything other than this when he compares the bones of the fore-arm, flexed by the movement of the 'nerves' — i.e. the tendons — with the arms of a catapult, drawn back by tightened cables (*De motu animalium*, 707b 9–10)? Physiology was first of all, and remained for a long time, an *anatomia animata*, a discourse *de usu partium* apparently founded on anatomical deduction, but in fact drawing its knowledge of function from that of tools or mechanisms suggested by the form or structure of the anatomical features which were identified with them.

One must admit that the use of mechanical models in zoology, and in the study of the peculiarly animal functions of locomotion, is first justified by the fact that in vertebrates the organs of local movement are articulated. If one understands by articulated a kind of mechanism of which the constituent parts are moved while two of their extremities always remain in contact, it must be admitted that articulation is practically the only type of mechanism presented by living organisms. The explanation of the peculiar features of locomotion has thus been able to proceed by the establishment of analogies with human techniques, taken as models in the wide sense of this term. It is thus that Borelli,[1] then Camper,[2] explained the swimming action of the fish by comparing the movements of the caudal fin with those of an oar used as a rudder. The criticisms put forward by Barthez[3] of this explanation constitute a 'model' of the objections, vitalist in inspiration, which are periodically raised against the use of reductive models in biology; criticisms which have not prevented the resuscitation and use by Marey[4] and by J. Gray,[5] more recently, of the Borelli–Camper model.

This crude use of the technical model in biology is so spontaneous and so implicit that it has been possible, as I have noted above, to misunderstand for a long time its presence in the methodology of anatomical deduction. Cournot, writing in 1868, drew attention to the fact that Harvey had noticed so clear an analogy between the valves of veins and mechanical valves (in fact Harvey said: lock-gates) that he had been irresistibly led to induce the law of circulation. "In this case", added Cournot,[6] "the organ is so precisely appropriate to its function that one is able to pass without hesitation from the organ to its function. . . ." Yet, a dozen years previously, Claude Bernard had cleverly refuted the false simplicity of this methodological outline. To the mistaken theory of the embodiment of a function in a structure, he opposed the impossibility of deducing from an anatomical examination knowledge of a functional nature other than that which had been introduced into it:

> It was already known by common experience what was meant by a reservoir, a canal, a lever, or a hinge, when, as a simple comparison, it was said that the bladder must be a reservoir for the purpose of containing liquids, that the arteries and veins were canals destined to conduct fluids, that the bones and joints played the part of scaffolding, hinges, levers etc.[7]

[1] J. A. Borelli, *De Motu Animalium* (Lugduni in Batavia, 1685) pars prima, prop. ccxiv.

[2] P. Camper, *Œuvres qui ont pour objet l'histoire naturelle, la physiologie et l'anatomie comparée* (Paris, An XI–1803) III, 364–6.

[3] P. J. Barthez, *Nouvelle méchanique des mouvements de l'homme et des animaux* (Carcassone, An VI–1798) 157–77.

[4] E. Marey, *La machine animale* (Paris, 1878) 208.

[5] J. Gray, *How Animals Move* (London, 1953).

[6] A. Cournot, *Considérations sur la marche des idées et des événements dans les temps modernes* (Paris, 1934) I, 249.

[7] C. Bernard, *Leçons de physiologie expérimentale appliquée à la médecine* (Paris, 1856) II, 6.

At the time, the term 'model' had not yet gained a place in the normal vocabulary of epistemology, but the formula by which Bernard summed up the preceding examples can be accepted as an early definition of the term: "analogous forms were brought together and similar functions were inferred".

It would evidently be an exaggeration to attribute great heuristic efficiency to this use of a summary technological model. To return to the discovery of the circulation, Harvey's seizing upon the anti-retrograde function of the valves of the veins only constitutes one of the arguments for his thesis, the confirmation of his third supposition.[1] The systematic use, in the seventeenth and eighteenth centuries, of references to mechanisms analogous to organs, inspired by Galilean and Cartesian science, in a new image of the world, cannot be credited with decisive discoveries in biology, even if it did not remain merely a philosophical or literary theme. It is worth noting that recent apologists for the heuristic efficiency in biology — especially in neurology — of cybernetic mechanisms and of feed-back models, consider the construction of classical automata (that is to say those lacking some sort of feedback mechanism) capable of simulating, within the limits of one or more rigid programmes, animal behaviour or human gestures, to be just a craze, without any scientific interest; merely a pastime. And yet, in a very original study of the history of biomechanism, A. Doyon and L. Liaigre have revealed the connexion, in the eighteenth century, between medical research and the construction of mechanical apparatus, "moving anatomies" or "automatic figures" according to the terms used by Vaucanson.[2] The quoted texts, taken from Quesnay, Vaucanson and Le Cat, do not indeed leave any doubt that their common plan was to use the resources of automatism as a dodge, or as a trick with theoretical intent, in order to elucidate the mechanism of physiological functions by the reduction of the unknown to the known, and by complete reproduction of analogous effects in an experimentally intelligible manner.

The Cartesian animal-machine remained a manifesto, a philosophical war-machine, so to speak; it did not constitute the programme, scheme, or plan of construction of any particular description of function or structure. On the contrary,

[1] W. Harvey, *Excitatio anatomica de motu cordis et sanguinis in animalibus* (Frankfurt, 1628) 56.

[2] A. Doyon and L. Liaigre, "Méthodologie comparée du biomécanisme et de la mécanique comparée", *Dialectica*, X (1956) 292–335.

the attention given by Vaucanson and Le Cat to the elaboration of detailed plans with a view to the construction of simulators, and the spectacular public success of the efforts of the first of these biomechanics, must allow us to carry back to the eighteenth century, at least, the explicit recognition of an heuristic method using, under the name of imitation, recourse to analogical models of function. Condorcet, in his *Eloge de Vaucanson*,[1] grasped perfectly the difference between a simulation of effects, sought as a sort of game or means of mystification, and a reproduction of means of action — today, one says a construction of pattern — with the aim of obtaining experimental evidence of a biological mechanism. Speaking of Vaucanson's first automaton, the Flautist, Condorcet writes:

> Some of these men who believe themselves to be wise, because they are suspicious and credulous, saw in the Flautist only a bird-organ, and considered as quackery the movements of the fingers which imitated those of a man. Eventually, the Academy of Science was charged with examining the automaton, and decided that the mechanism used to give forth the sounds of the flute rigorously executed the same operations as someone playing a flute, and that the mechanic had imitated at once the effects and the methods of nature, with an exactitude and perfection that even people most accustomed to the prodigies of art would not have imagined to be attainable.

One will doubtless not deny Condorcet a sort of intuition of the ulterior possibilities of construction, or even only of theoretical conception, in the field of mechanisms acting on information as distinct from those simply using energy. He affirms, indeed, that the genius of a mechanic "consists principally in imagining and disposing in space different mechanisms which must produce a given effect and which serve to regulate, distribute, and direct the motive force". And he adds: "One must not look upon the mechanic as an artist who owes his talents or his success to practice. One can invent mechanical works of art without having made or worked a single machine, just as one can find methods of calculating the movements of a star that one has never seen."

This enunciation of a possible evolution of models towards a mathematical theory is the theme of a story which we must go over rapidly. For almost twenty years it has gradually become more and more commonplace to claim that the invention of

[1] Condorcet, *Eloges des Académiciens* (Brunschvick–Paris, 1799) III, 203–32.

Watt's governor provided physiologists with the initial model, albeit a non-premeditated one, of a feed-back circuit between an effector organ and a receptor one. In fact, for there to be noticed in Watt's arrangement an analogy with a reflex circuit, it was necessary for the methodical exploration of the properties of the nervous system to be made possible by progress in electricity, starting from the observations and experiments of Galvani. It is not from the steam engine but from the battery and induction coil that were born, by means of technical epigenesis, the electronic assemblies recently promoted to the dignity of feed-back models of the functions of the nerves and nervous centres.

The first stages of positive neurology are a kind of counterpart to the discovery of the circulation of the blood.[1] Galvani's discovery and Volta's invention established the analogy of the nerve with a conductor of current. Even Galvani's error concerning the existence of animal electricity is explained by the analogical necessity of finding a source of current in the organism. The Bell–Magendie law and the distinction of the functions of the spinal nerve assigned to the propagation of intranervous current a centripetal and a centrifugal direction. The concept of reflex action (Marshall Hall, 1832; J. Müller, 1833) and the schema of the reflex arc (R. Wagner, 1844) furnished the elements of a functional system, no longer merely a morphological one.[2] Whilst electricity was becoming, with Ampère and Faraday, a science of dynamic fields and currents, the experiments and polemics of the physiologists (Du Bois-Raymond *v.* Matteucci) were leading to the renunciation of the concept of the passive nerve conducting the impulse, and to the presentation of evidence that its activity is accompanied by the production of electricity. In these conditions, recourse to electrical models in neurology became a familiar practice. And by means of this example, we can understand the reasons why research tends to make use of models. On the one hand, nervous fluid is hypothetical, not something observed like the blood; thus a model is necessary as a representational substitute. On the other hand, electric current was first used for the transmission of messages, not of energy, and the priority of this application contributed more than a little to the popularity of

[1] K. E. Rothschuh, "Aus der Frühzeit der Elektrobiologie", *Elektromedizin*, IV (1959) 201–17.

[2] G. Canguilhem, *La formation du concept de réflexe aux XVII*[e] *et XVIII*[e] *siècles* (Paris, 1955) Ch. 7.

the electrical model in neurology. Finally, before the establishment and consolidation of the cellular theory, neurophysiology could not be a physiology of constituent parts, but could only consider the totality of an arrangement; accordingly we must make use of a model for the investigation of a phenomenon whose complexity cannot be broken down.

Herein resides the difference between the fields of application and validity of the model method and those of the classical method of experimentation taking its departure from an hypothesis of a functional law. Experimentation is analytical and proceeds by discriminating among the determining conditions by varying them, all other factors being supposed unchanged. The model method allows the comparison of entities which resist analysis. Now, in biology, analysis is less a partition than a liberation of entities of a smaller scale than the initial one. In this science, the use of models can legitimately pass as being more 'natural' than elsewhere.

Before the era of cybernetics, one could believe in the inadequacy of mechanical models of biological systems which are characterized by their completeness and internal autoregulation.[1] Today, this opposition seems to have been overcome, and L. von Bertalanffy can maintain, on the contrary, that the model method can be applied to the study of organisms because they present the general properties of a system.[2] It is known that Bertalanffy introduced into his General Theory of Systems the distinction made in the last century by comparative anatomists, between analogues and homologues, that is to say between apparent similarities and properly analogous functional correspondences, in the mathematical sense of the term. According to this vocabulary, it is on homologues that rests the elaboration of conceptual models and the possibility of the transference of structurally similar laws outside the initial domain of their verification.

By this approach, we can perhaps observe how the construction of electrical (physico-chemical) models in neurophysiology constitutes an intermediary, at once historical and logical, between the mechanical model, a reproducer of pattern rather than a simple simulator of effects, and the model of a

[1] L. Asher, "Modellen und biologische Systeme", *Scientia*, LV (1934) 418–21.

[2] L. von Bertalanffy, *Problems of life* (New York, 1952); "Modern concepts on biological adaptation" in *The Historical Development of Physiological Thought* (New York, 1959) 265–86.

mathematical or logical type. The spirit of mathematical physics, itself progressively educated by a new mathematical knowledge, that of structures, has found an accessible path into biology, thanks to Maxwell's work in the field of electromagnetism. In modern mathematics, to construct a model is to translate one theory into the language of another, to set up a correspondence between their terms while retaining structural relationships. This implies the isomorphism of the theories. In mathematical physics, as it has become following the work of Joseph Fourier, mathematical theories are taken as an object of study, from which analogies arise in experimental fields which are *a priori* unconnected. These analogies prove the polyvalidity of mathematical theories in relation to physical reality. To reconsider the examples which struck Fourier, the propagation of heat, the movement of waves, and the vibration of elastic laminae are intelligible by means of mathematically identical equations.[1] But, in mathematical physics, the construction of a model in one field of phenomena, in order to understand phenomena of a different field, does not in any way confer a privileged character on the field chosen as a reference of intelligibility. The choice of phenomena for analogical reference depends only on one of the two following requirements: either the knowledge of these phenomena has already reached the stage of being a theory; or these phenomena lend themselves particularly easily to experimental investigation. In neither case does the concrete realization of a model claim to have the validity of a literal representation of the phenomena which the model aims to explain. Maxwell used to say that the physical analogy serves, starting with a partial similarity between laws, to *illustrate* one science by means of another.[2] Illustration is not representation.

Now, in biology, it seems more difficult than in physics to resist the temptation to confer a representational value on a model. It is perhaps not only the scientific vulgarizer who has a tendency to forget that a model is nothing more than its function. This function consists in lending its type of mechanism to a different object, without imposing itself as axiomatic. But has it not sometimes happened that the analogical models of the biologist have benefited from an unconscious validation

[1] J. Fourier, "Théorie analytique de la chaleur" in *Œuvres*, publiées par G. Darboux (Paris, 1888) I, 13.

[2] J. Clerk Maxwell, "On Faraday's Lines of Force", *Scientific Papers* (Cambridge, 1890) I, 156.

having as its effect the reduction of the organic to its analogy mechanical, physical or chemical? Despite their great degree of mathematical complexity, it does not appear that cybernetic models are always safe from this accident. The magical aspect of simulation is strongly resistant to the exorcism of science.

It is true that the feed-back model, for example, has shown itself fruitful in the exploration and explanation of the organic functions of homeostasis and of active adaptation.[1] One can, however, believe that the process of nervous regulation is not really represented by it. As Couffignal has noted, when one labels as feed-back the parts of the nervous system for which the mechanical mode of regulation serves as a model, one seems to give the impression that organic feed-back is part of the same class of objects as mechanical feed-back.[2] In fact, one has created, by bringing these together, a new class of objects whose definition would be able to retain only the operational characters common to regulatory organs and mechanical regulating arrangements. In other words, the use of an object as model transforms it, inasmuch as one takes explicit cognizance of the analogies with the undetermined object for that it is a model. A model only becomes fertile by its own impoverishment. It must lose some of its own specific singularity to enter with the corresponding object into a new generalization. When some kind of machine becomes a valid model for an organic function it is not the machine in its entirety that becomes the model, but only the pattern of its operations such that it can be expressed in mathematical terms. Here light is shed on the great difference between the model method in physics and in biology. It consists in the fact that one cannot, at the present time at least, speak of a mathematical biology in the sense in which, as we have seen, one has for a long time spoken of mathematical physics. In physics, in using a model — for example, a flow of electricity in a metal plate as analogous to a hydrodynamic phenomenon with a horizontal component — we suppose that we can use the results of measuring the phenomenon which occurs *in concreto* for the description and prediction of the characteristics of the undetermined phenomenon. What guarantees the validity of this transference of metric results is the correspondence, established by a special mathematical

[1] A. Rosenblueth, N. Wiener and J. Bigelow, "Behavior, purpose and teleology", *Philosophy of Science*, X (1943) 18–24.

[2] L. Couffignal, "La mécanique comparée", *Thalès*, VII (1951) 9–36.

study, between the general laws of distinct orders of phenomena.[1] That is what does not exist in biology. It is true that there exists an arithmetical or geometrical biology of fairly long standing, and a more recent variety of statistical biology, but we hardly find ourselves in a position to speak of an algebraic biology. Therein lies the profound logical reason for the specific role of models in biological research. They lead to the establishment of analogical correspondences solely on the level of concretely designated objects, structures or functions. They are unable to show the identity of the general laws of the two fields of phenomena which are brought together. It will doubtless remain so as long as mathematics in biology is allied more closely to that of an engineer's formulary than to theories like those of a Riemann or a Hamilton.

Biological epistemology must, then, attach the greatest of importance to the counsels of prudence that biologists address to each other inside their working community. Adrian's remark is valid not only for the type of research at which it aims: "What we can learn from the machines is how our brain must differ from them!"[2] A study by Elsasser has since culminated in parallel conclusions: an organism does not spontaneously fulfil any of the conditions of stability required for the correct functioning of an electronic machine, in which an increase in information can never appear.[3] In his general theory of automata,[4] von Neumann has underlined a fact never yet disputed:[5] the structure of natural machines (organisms) is such that failures of function do not affect general behaviour. Regenerative functions, or, failing this, the supplementing of the insufficiency of one organ by another, compensate for the destruction or the breakdown of certain elements. A lesion of the organism does not necessarily abolish its plasticity. The same cannot be said of machines.

We can, therefore, ask ourselves if the employment of

[1] Suzanne Bachelard, *La conscience de rationalité, étude phénoménologique sur la physique mathématique* (Paris, 1958) ch. 8.

[2] E. D. Adrian, *Proc. Roy. Soc. B.*, CXLII (1954) 1-8. Cited by J. B. S. Haldane, "Aspects physico-chimiques des instincts", in *L'instinct dans le comportement des animaux et de l'homme* (Paris, 1956) 551.

[3] W. M. Elsasser, *The physical foundation of biology* (London, 1958).

[4] J. von Neumann, "The general and logical theory of automata" in *Cerebral Mechanisms in Behavior* (New York and London, 1951) 1–41.

[5] A. Liapounov, "Machines à calcul électroniques et système nerveux", in *Problèmes de la cybernétique étudiés aux séminaires de philosophie de l'Académie des Sciences de l'URSS, Voprosy filosofii* (1961) No. 1, 150–7.

electrical and electronic models in biology represents, on the level of heuristic logic, of *ars inveniendi*, as radical a mutation as the construction of such machines seems to be on the technological level. In analytic experimentation of the classical type, one of the conditions favouring discovery resides, we know, in the divergence between the results of prediction based on the hypothesis, and the facts of observation. A good hypothesis is not always that which leads rapidly to its own confirmation, which allows at the first attempt the description of a phenomenon in an explanatory schema. It is that which obliges the researcher, by dint of an unforeseen discord between the explanation and the description, either to correct the description or to reconstruct the schema of explanation. Could not one say, similarly, that in biology the models which have the chance of being the best are those which halt our latent tendency to identify the organic with its model? A bad model, in the history of science, is that which the imagination evaluates as a good one. The imagination is inclined to believe that to construct a model is to borrow a vocabulary and so obtain an identification of two objects. When the cellular boundary had been named a membrane, the laws of osmosis and the making of semi-permeable barriers seemed to provide a language and a model. It seems, on the contrary, that it is in the interest of the biologist to retain the lesson of the mathematical physicist: what must be required of a model is the provision of a syntax to construct a transposable but original discourse.

By saying that the extension of the model method does not perhaps constitute a revolution in the biological heuristic, we wish simply to say that the criteria of validity of research by models remain in conformity with the schema of the dialectic relationship between the experiment and its interpretation. What validates a theory is the possibility of extrapolation and prediction which it permits in directions which the experiment, keeping to its own level, would not have indicated. Similarly, models are judged and tested one against another by the completeness of the accounts they give of the properties to which they direct attention, in the object of study, and also by their aptitude for revealing properties hitherto unnoticed. The model, one could say, predicts. But mathematical theories in physics do so also.

We will not contest Grey Walter's view of the importance of the results obtained in the study of the superior functions of the brain and of learning, by the construction of functional models which do not claim to imitate elementary structures. Yet, despite a discreet humour at the mutual expense of the patterns of experimentation recommended by Claude Bernard, Grey Walter, when he fixes the rules of a legitimate usage of models, rediscovers, scarcely altered, the classical criteria for the criticism of experiments.[1] It is legitimate to study the model of an undetermined process if three conditions are fulfilled: some characteristics of the phenomenon must be known, the undeterminism cannot be total; to reproduce what is known of the phenomenon, the model must include only the strictly necessary operating elements; the model must reproduce more than the initial amount known, whether this enrichment of knowledge be foreseen or not. To illustrate these rules, the chosen example is that of the models of the nerve. It is an excellent example, which enables us to follow the successive identification of the nerve with a non-isolated, passive electric conductor (submarine cable), then with an electro-chemical assembly (Lillie's artificial nerve, 1920–2) simulating the propagation of an impulse and the establishment of an insensitive period, and finally with a model of an electric circuit, combining a battery with a grid-leak condenser, capable of exhibiting the equivalent of eighteen properties of nerves and synapses. One sees, by this example, that the succession of models, for the same object of research, obeys the norm of dialectical substitution of theories, with the obligation for a new theory to account at once for all the facts which the antecedent theory explained, and for those which could not be brought within its jurisdiction. As for the material technically put to work in the model itself, it is for its role that it is chosen, at a given moment, and not for its intrinsic nature. The electrical model of the nerve, says Grey Walter, does not prove by the fact of its greater efficiency, that the activity of the nerve is electrical in nature. From the point of view of the theory, the model is nothing other than the equivalent of a series of mathematical expressions. This last affirmation seems to us to be a very important one, insofar as it allows us to see the shape of the future rather than the details of the past. The model method will really cause a revolution in biology when, without equivocation, the biologist borrows from other sciences not so much particular sorts of model, as models which are examples of structures unaffected in themselves by the mathematical constructions which unify their phenomenal disparity.

[1] W. Grey Walter, *The Living Brain* (London, 1953) Appendix A.

The model will no longer then be the electronic arrangement as such, but rather the common function of such-and-such electronic, thermodynamic, or chemical arrangements (function of rectifier, valve, etc.).[1] This supposes, as we have already said, the formation of a mathematical biology, which does not necessarily mean an analytic biology, but a biology in which non-quantitative concepts, like those of topology for instance, permit not only the description of phenomena, but the enunciation of theories involving them.

To sum up, the use of models in biology has shown itself more fruitful in the study of function than in the investigation of structure and the relation of structure to function. It has been possible to study analogies of general performance between models and organs, without assuming analogies between the constituent elements and between the elementary functions. When 'neural nets' had been constructed as a method of mathematical approach to the properties of the neuron, one might have believed that a model of the neuronic relay had been proposed. But the neurophysiologist did not recognize in this model the relative independence of the functions of the brain with respect to the integrity of its structure.[2] On one hand, the nerve-cells are not interchangeable relays; on the other, their partial destruction does not bring about, necessarily, the loss of total function.

In these conditions, we may ask ourselves if the concept of a model, of which it daily becomes more difficult to propose a definition,[3] has not retained a few traces of the ambiguity of the initial intention in constructing it. I have indicated, at the beginning of these reflections, that a certain technological and pragmatic structure of human perception in the matter of organic objects showed up the condition of man — an organism, but a maker of machines. I have only sketched out the stages by which a naïve tendency to identify organisms and machines lost what this naïveté may have had that was magical or puerile. But perhaps a more radical naïveté, an attitude of cognizance, scientific or not, in the face of life, fundamentally inspires new attempts made to exhibit in a model such-or-such organic causalities.

[1] W. M. Elsasser, op. cit. ch. 1.

[2] A. Fessard, "Points de contact entre neurophysiologie et cybernétique", *Structure et évolution des techniques*, V (1953) 25–33, 35–6.

[3] J. W. L. Beament (editor), *Models and Analogues in Biology* (Cambridge, 1960).

The model has for a long time simultaneously resembled the type and the scale model, the norm of representation and the change in scale of size. It seems to us today that the explanatory model, an integral replica, be it concrete or logical, of the structural and functional properties of the biological object, has been relegated to the rank of myth. On the side of function, the model tends to be presented as a simple imitator, which reproduces a performance, but by methods of its own. On the side of structure, it can at the most present itself as an analogy, never as a double. It is, then, on analogy that the model method in biology rests, whether the models be mechanical or logical ones. In all cases, the only valid analogies are to be found at the heart of a theory.

Whilst waiting to promote a revolutionary heuristic tomorrow, the biological model uses today the resources of a revolutionary technology. But it would be quite unjust to forget the progress that biology made yesterday thanks to methods of experimental analysis; to forget, for example, that scientists like Sherrington and Pavlov did not work by constructing models. And to conclude, it is ironical to remember that the discovery, by Sherrington and Liddell, of the myotactic reflex (1924) furnished, in the most classical manner, a weighty argument for those who, since that time, have not been able to study an organic regulatory function without seeking to build a model of servo-control.

17

The Establishment of Modern Genetical Theory as an Example of the Interaction of Different Models, Techniques, and Inferences

BENTLEY GLASS

I

Eighteenth-Century Genetic Models

In the eighteenth century two controversies dominated biological thought. One of these related to the origin of the individual, the other, to the origin of the species. The former was the sharp dispute between adherents of preformation and adherents of epigenesis. The latter was the rather less vigorous opposition of those believing in the fixity of species to those believing in evolution. It was no accident that those who believed in the preformation of the embryo within the egg — by mid-century Charles Bonnet's discovery of the occurrence of parthenogenesis in plant-lice had discountenanced the spermists, who had believed in preformation within the sperm — believed also in the fixity of species; while those who believed that the embryo takes its origin from formless, dissociated matter had no difficulty in believing that species may change with time. Both of these antithetical pairs of genetical ideas were furthermore related to a third great biological controversy of the time, that over spontaneous generation in contrast to strict biogenesis. If living things may be generated spontaneously in mud or slime or filth, or from organic nutrients, then why indeed might not the lesser miracle of change of species occur? But if living things arise only from parents of their own species, there must be a material basis in the germ. Charles Bonnet was thus, naturally enough, a friend and correspondent of the Abbé Spallanzani, and they must frequently have discussed the relation between the theory of preformation that so occupied the thoughts of the former, and the disproof of spontaneous generation that so claimed the efforts of the latter.

Charles Bonnet and preformation

The preformation theory of Charles Bonnet is often today dismissed with mere ridicule. The modern student of biology is likely to forget that in the mid-eighteenth century the idea that an animal, or even man himself, is from a scientific viewpoint a machine was still a daring hypothesis. La Mettrie's *L'homme machine* had appeared only in 1747 and gave its author notoriety in Europe second to none.[1] The mechanistic or materialistic view was nevertheless readily seen to be more scientific, as leaving less to be accomplished by mysterious entelechies and affinities which could not be observed. In explaining the origin of an individual from a parent like it in species, although differing in minor characteristics, Bonnet eschewed what he felt to be the nebulosity and vitalism of epigenesis, either in the form of the old Aristotelian view tainted by the assumption of the entelechy, or of the new *vis essentialis* of Caspar Friedrich Wolff. Heredity must be material, Bonnet felt. That is to say, there must reside within the egg the material form of the new individual, an embryo needing only nourishment to swell it and model it into the typical form and stature of the adult parent.

Although at first Bonnet thought in terms of crude *emboîtement*, embryo within embryo in recognizable form but diminishing size *ad infinitum*, he grew in the maturity of his thought to replace this idea of the germ by one somewhat different. It was the observations of the budding of hydra that led him to this new version of preformation. The bud on the side of a hydra is not like the bud of a plant, a bud with miniature parts all ready to expand and unfold. The hydra's bud is a mere bump, an excrescence on the parent's body. Yet, as it grows in size, it puts forth tentacles, opens up a mouth between them, and becomes a fully formed hydra before it drops from the side of the parent. Here, said Bonnet, although there is no preformed miniature hydra in the bud, there must still be something material and present from the beginning to guide development, "certain particles which have been pre-organized in such a way that a little polyp results from their development".[2] And since a new polyp can regenerate from any piece

[1] J. O. de La Mettrie, *L'homme machine* (Leyden, 1748); A. Vartanian, *La Mettrie's L'Homme Machine* (Princeton, 1960).

[2] C. Bonnet, "Tableau des considérations", Art. XV, in *La Palingénésie philosophique* (1769), in *Œuvres*, VII, 68. For a discussion of Bonnet's

of a hydra that is cut into fragments, the pattern of particles must exist in every part of the whole polyp. This "preordination", this "preformation of parts capable by itself of determining the existence of a plant or of an animal",[1] is what Bonnet meant by the *germ*. Assuming as the fundamental principle that nothing alive is generated spontaneously, but that always there must be the preformed germ, he postulated that

> all organized bodies derived their origin from a germ which contained *très en petit* the elements of all the organic parts . . . [that] the elements of the germ [were] the *primordial foundation*, on which the nutritive molecules went to work to increase in every direction the dimensions of the parts . . . [that] the germ [was] a network, the elements of which formed the meshes. . . . The primitive organization of the germs determines the arrangement which the nourishing atoms must take in order to become parts of the organic whole.[2]

It would seem that to have arrived at a thoroughly modern view Bonnet lacked only the conception that the 'germ', this primordial foundation or pattern, can replicate itself. Lacking the concepts of the cell theory — the knowledge that cells arise only from pre-existing cells, chromosomes only from pre-existing chromosomes, and DNA only from pre-existing DNA — Bonnet nevertheless saw the necessity for the existence of the primordial pattern of each species, existing somehow within each material, reproductive part of the organism. Hereditary differences within the species, he thought, represent minor and probably temporary impressions made upon the essential germ of the species, which in all individuals of the species is quite the same. The only reasonable mechanism for such a conceptual model, lacking the ability of the intricate germ to replicate itself in all essential details of pattern, is preformation — the existence of innumerable individual copies of the pattern from the beginning. In the course of generations these are sorted out, but there is in fact 'no new generation'. The pattern, the germs, have existed from the beginning. If a fact this would, of course, also exclude any true evolution of the species, though not a certain progressive improvement, supposing the Creator to have made the germs of succeeding generations superior to those that had gone before.

conceptions, see B. Glass, "Heredity and variation in the eighteenth-century concept of the species", in *Forerunners of Darwin 1745–1859*, ed. B. Glass, O. Temkin, and W. Straus, Jr. (Baltimore, 1959) 164–72.

[1] Bonnet, ibid. [2] Bonnet, op. cit., Pt. VII, Ch. 4, p. 205.

Particularly repugnant to this frame of thought was any suggestion that out of separate organic nutritive particles there might arise a living organism belonging to some definite species, as Buffon proposed; or that the particles might find the way to their right places by virtue of mysterious chemical affinities or some reminiscence of their former places in the pattern, as Maupertuis conjectured. No, said Bonnet, we know of no such forces in nature. The pattern that characterizes a species is a whole, and in the form of the germ it must have been present from the beginning.[1]

Maupertuis and particulate heredity

Maupertuis was led to his views of heredity by his conviction that the theory of preformation was nonsensical.[2] Already in 1744 he emphasized the significance of biparental heredity, including the mixed inheritance of hybrids between two different species. A study of polydactyly in a family in Berlin demonstrated to him not only that the defect (*monstre par excès*) was inherited, but that it could equally well be transmitted by a male or a female parent. The albino Negro whose appearance in Paris in 1744 had excited Maupertuis's consideration of heredity had on the other hand been born of parents both of whom were black. It was therefore necessary to abandon the preformationist systems of the spermists and ovists, who could readily postulate only a unilateral type of inheritance, and instead to conceive of a material system capable of embodying in the foetus either maternal or paternal traits, or on occasion even those seen only in a more remote ancestor and not evident in either parent. Maupertuis thus conceived of a system of hereditary particles conveyed from one generation to the next by way of the semen of the male and female parents. He rejected the idea, put forward by Bonnet and other preformationists to account for hereditary influences derived from both

[1] Bonnet, op. cit., "Tableau des considérations", Art. XIV, p. 64.

[2] P. L. M. de Maupertuis, *Vénus physique* (Leyde, 1745), in *Œuvres*, II, 1–134; published anonymously as *Dissertation physique à l'occasion du nègre blanc* (Leyde, 1744). For a fuller account of Maupertuis's arguments against preformation, his genetics, and his evolutionary theory, see B. Glass, "Maupertuis, pioneer of genetics and evolution", op. cit. pp. 51–83. See also A. C. Crombie, "P. L. Moreau de Maupertuis, F.R.S. (1698–1759), précurseur du transformisme", *Revue de synthèse*, 3ème série, LVIII (1957) 35–56; and P. L. Maillet, *Pierre-Louis Moreau de Maupertuis (1698–1759) pour le bicentenaire de sa mort*, Conférences du Palais de la Découverte, Série D, No. 69 (Paris, 1960).

parents, that some sort of essence or spiritual virtue, or other vaguely defined immaterial influence, coming from the semen of one parent, could modify inheritance. Thus, in the Ruhe family, polydactyly was first known in a female and her daughter, from whom it was transmitted to a son, who then transmitted it to two sons. In each of the semens, Maupertuis conjectured, there must be many particles, corresponding to each part of the embryo to be formed. For the most part, these would represent the characteristics of the parents (in the *Système de la nature*[1] Maupertuis suggested that they actually come from the organs of the parent and retain a memory of their state there); but there would also be particles representing characteristics present not in the parent but in a grandparent or some remoter ancestor; and even sometimes particles of a novel sort might arise, "forgetful" of their past. Drawn by chemical affinity, like particles from male and female parent would unite two by two, and the right particles would find adjacent places. Rarely one might find at some point a union of three particles, giving rise to a monster with an extra part; and, again rarely, maybe a failure of the particles to form a pair or to align themselves properly with adjacent particles, whence might arise a monster with a deficiency of some part.

Maupertuis's model of hereditary elements thus differed from Bonnet's principally in that the hereditary particles making up the fundamental germ are separable, swimming freely in the semen, and finding their right places by virtue of strong affinities between identical particles and weaker affinities between less similar particles. This remarkable model, which must surely remind us of the pairing of corresponding maternal and paternal genes in the Mendelian model, has the merit of permitting biparental heredity to occur as the general rule rather than the exception. It also provided for the origin of monsters and mutations (although the latter term was not used by Maupertuis), and became the basis of Maupertuis's ideas regarding the modification of species and the origin of new species. For he was led on to postulate that by deviations from the normal and by novel alterations of hereditary particles new kinds of organisms would arise, perhaps through the action of the environment, and that if these were isolated in different parts of the earth and subjected to the elimination of the unfit, new and viable species would in time come into being —

[1] Maupertuis, *Système de la Nature* (1751), in *Œuvres*, II, 135–84.

though perhaps only imperceptibly even over the span of centuries.

Consequently, just as the essential nature of Bonnet's model forced him to view the species as inalterable, Maupertuis's model led him to the development of crude but reasonably accurate evolutionary conceptions. It is perhaps fair to say also that Bonnet was more of the armchair natural philosopher than the maligned Maupertuis. Bonnet's growing imperfection of eyesight led him to rely principally upon pure reason for reaching conclusions, whereas Maupertuis carried out both the remarkable study of the inheritance in man of polydactyly, the first adequate genetic study of its kind, and in addition conducted parallel breeding experiments with an unusual type of Iceland dog, having a slate-coloured body and a yellow head.[1] First observed in a female, the pattern was recovered, after several matings and litters of normally coloured pups, in a single male offspring, which subsequently produced, among normally coloured offspring, a second male having the same pattern. (The character seems to have been of a dominant type.) Maupertuis rightly concluded that this transmission, like the human inheritance of polydactyly, demonstrates equal freedom of transmission by either the male or the female parent.

Linnaeus and the fixity of species

Linnaeus's often quoted view that there are only so many species as were created in the beginning underwent a profound change as the naturalist grew older. The characteristics of *Peloria*, a newly discovered form of the common wildflower (*Linaria*) variously known as toadflax or butter-and-eggs, led Linnaeus in 1742 to consider it a new species, since it formed perfect seeds and supposedly bred true to type. Linnaeus, upon comparing its parts with *Linaria* and other flowering plants, came to the conclusion that it was produced by hybridization. During the next fifteen years Linnaeus and his students found a number of other supposed new species that had originated by hybridization, although only one of these (a *Tragopogon*) was actually produced by Linnaeus in his garden, from a cross made artificially between two species. Linnaeus concluded eventually (in 1762) that the work of God in the creation had stopped with providing the common source of each genus, or even of each order, and that diversification within these systematic

[1] Maupertuis, *Lettres*, XIV, in *Œuvres*, II, 185–340.

categories had arisen partly by hybridization and partly through the action of the environment.[1]

Linnaeus's views regarding the origin of new species were shortly subjected to experimental test, through the careful and extensive work of Joseph Gottlieb Koelreuter and Michel Adanson. Koelreuter's work, more widely known at the present day, consisted in attempting to cross many species and obtain hybrids between them. His results, published in 1761–5,[2] indicated that only closely related species may be crossed at all, although Linnaeus had postulated some very distant crosses. Furthermore, in general Koelreuter found interspecific hybrids to be self-sterile, and consequently they could not be regarded as new species. The few cases of fertile hybrids, on the other hand, might be taken to indicate that the parent forms were not truly distinct species. Linnaeus's *Tragopogon* hybrid was dismissed by Koelreuter as being no real hybrid plant, but only a "half-hybrid" that had a tincture of foreign parentage but was mostly pure *T. pratense*, the maternal species. Koelreuter's work was widely accepted as invalidating Linnaeus's views of the origin of new species, but an even more devastating attack was accomplished by Adanson.

In a painstaking series of researches,[3] Adanson examined each of the species reputed by Linnaeus to have arisen as hybrids. Every one of them, including the *Peloria* and a new four-ranked barley bred by Adanson himself, turned out to be inconstant varieties, tending to revert to the original form. In *Peloria*, the peloric and the usual *Linaria*-type flowers even appeared on the same stalk. The conclusion was clear that these forms were "monsters" — or, as we would say today, mutants — and represented no transmutation of species. They were the deviations of nature which, according to Adanson, had their laws and their limits. Such monstrosities and varia-

[1] C. Linnaeus, *Amoenitates academicae* (1762); quoted by J. Rostand, *L'Evolution des espèces* (Paris, 1932) 24. For a fuller account of Linnaeus's evolutionary views and their refutation by Koelreuter and by Adanson, see B. Glass, "Heredity and variation in the eighteenth-century concept of the species", op. cit. pp. 144–63.

[2] J. G. Koelreuter, *Vorläufige Nachricht von einigen das Geschlecht der Pflanzen betreffenden Versuchen und Beobachtungen, nebst Fortsetzungen 1, 2, und 3* (Leipzig, 1761–6).

[3] M. Adanson, "Examen de la question, si les espèces changent parmi les plantes; Nouvelles expériences tentées à ce sujet", *Histoire de l'Académie Royale des Sciences* (Année 1769) 71–7; *Mémoires*, 31–48.

tions occur within a prescribed latitude, and return in time to the nature of the species to which they belong.

These researches tended to confirm the concept of the fixity of species, from which Linnaeus himself had somewhat departed. They thus retarded the consideration of the problem of the origin of species for at least a half-century. Perhaps of more immediate effect was the impact of Koelreuter's studies on the prevailing acceptance of preformation. J. von Sachs, in the late nineteenth century, stated in his *History of Botany* that the effect of Koelreuter's hybridizations on the preformation theory was even more decisive than the famous studies of Caspar Friedrich Wolff.[1] The best of Wolff's work, after all, was done in St. Petersburg and was not translated into German until 1812. Its most notable influence was delayed until it bore fruit in the work and ideas of Meckel and von Baer. But Koelreuter's many hybridizations, especially the crosses between plants with different flower colours, clearly revealed the significance of biparental heredity, and the influence of the pollen parent extended to seemingly every portion of the hybrid plant.

II
Nineteenth-Century Genetic Models

The nineteenth-century hybridizers

The problems of heredity remained, during the early part of the nineteenth century, almost exclusively the province of the plant hybridizers, although a few practical animal breeders were slightly concerned about them. Karl Gärtner performed some ten thousand crosses and produced three hundred and fifty different hybrids, and other plant hybridizers whom Charles Darwin was later to cite (W. Herbert, T. A. Knight) were almost as assiduous. Their aim remained the elucidation of the degrees and causes of hybrid sterility, or the purely practical objectives of the plant and animal breeder. Perhaps simply because of the great number of genetic differences commonly involved in the interspecific crosses they attempted, they seem not to have advanced beyond the general conception of heredity as a biparental mixture which had satisfied Koelreuter. Even Knight's discovery of the dominance of certain characteristics over the alternative traits, and the evidence of segregation in the F_2 generation following a hybridization,

[1] C. F. Wolff, *Theoria generationis* (2nd ed., Halle, 1774).

already evident in Koelreuter's experiments and very well established by Alexander Seton and John Goss, alike failed to lead to any altered conceptual model of heredity, particulate or non-particulate.

Yet notwithstanding the intractability posed by the problem of analyzing species hybrids, by mid-century M. C. Naudin, one of the most noted of the hybridizers, was reaching the significant conclusion that there is no qualitative difference — only a quantitative one — between species, races, and varieties. This conclusion was supported by evidence that continued breeding of hybrids, whether originally between different species or only between races or varieties, leads to a gradual reversion of the hybrid population to one or the other, or both, of the original ancestral types. In exceptional cases, as Koelreuter and Gärtner reported, the original hybrids may quite closely resemble one parent species rather than the other. Yet in these cases, too, there is generally a regression of the later generations to the parent types. Nevertheless, in some crosses, hybrids are produced which are fertile and breed true. Gärtner describes a number, and Wichura added the hybrids among willow species to this group. Gärtner's conclusion was that the species has well-defined and fixed limits; but Naudin on the contrary saw between races and species only a difference in degree of contrasting characters. If so, species might enjoy stability, but not real fixity.[1]

The nineteenth-century particulate model of hereditary elements

Considerations of the kind just discussed led Mendel to begin his famous intervarietal crosses of peas. He was very interested in the work of Koelreuter, Gärtner, and Wichura and describes how it led to his own experiments, undertaken because

> among all the numerous experiments made, not one has been carried out to such an extent and in such a way as to make it possible to determine the number of different forms under which the offspring of hybrids appear, or to arrange these forms with certainty according to their separate generations, or definitely to ascertain their statistical relations.[2]

[1] M. C. Naudin, "Nouvelles recherches sur l'hybridité dans les végétaux", *Nouvelles Archives du Museum d'Histoire naturelle*, 1re ser., I (1865) 1. See E. Perrier, *La philosophie zoologique avant Darwin* (Paris, 1884) 279–80.

[2] G. Mendel, "Versuche über Pflanzenhybriden", *Verhandlungen des naturforschenden Vereines, Brünn*, IV (1865) 3–47; trans. in *Classic Papers in Genetics*, ed. J. A. Peters (Englewood Cliffs, N.J., 1959) 1–20.

It is quite clear that in Mendel's case it was the existence of a tantalizing and hitherto insoluble problem that led him to undertake the particular kind of experiment he designed, and not the existence in his mind of any conceptual construct to which he was committed and for which he might have desired support.

The particulate conception of heredity derived from Mendel's experiments is too well known to need description here. It suffices to emphasize that Mendel himself spoke only of alternative "elements"[1] for each pair of alternative characteristics, elements existing singly in the pollen and egg cells and combined in pairs in the fertilized egg. These elements were seen to segregate and recombine according to the laws of chance, but nowhere is there any suggestion on the part of Mendel that these elements are represented by material particles in the reproductive cells. Perhaps, indeed, he thought so. But he seems carefully to have refrained from committing himself to any material basis for the behaviour of the inherited traits he was studying. This reluctance is indeed most remarkable, whether seen against the nineteenth-century background of idioplasma and ids, or against the twentieth century's chromosomes, genes, and DNA.

In contrast to Mendel, Carl Nägeli was the ultimate devotee of the conceptual model. In his early theoretical work (1844) he laid down, as the aim of natural research, two objectives: first, to discover new facts; and second, to create new laws of thought.[2] The approach is distinctly Hegelian, a fact not strange, since Nägeli in his youth spent two years studying Hegelian philosophy in Berlin. Nägeli was thus, according to

[1] The first application of the term 'factor' to Mendelian units seems obscure. Bateson, in his English translation of Mendel's paper, translated *Elemente* quite literally as "elements", e.g. in the passage (W. Bateson, *Mendel's Principles of Heredity*, Cambridge, 1909, p. 356) which reads: "This development [of a new individual] follows a constant law, which is founded on the material composition and arrangement of the elements which meet in the cell in a vivifying union." But Mendel himself for the most part referred to the *Merkmalen* or "characters" as remaining pure and segregating in definite ratios. The term "allelomorph", introduced by Bateson to refer to the segregating characters, was also applied to the Mendelian elements which determine the unit-characters (see Bateson, op. cit. p. 11). Very soon, however, Bateson is referring to the fact that "the development of characters in animals or plants depends on the presence of definite units or *factors* [italics added] in their germ-cells . . ." (pp. 16–17). This usage rapidly increased and became general.

[2] C. W. von Nägeli, "Über die Aufgabe der Naturgeschichte" (1844); see E. Nordenskiøld, *The History of Biology* (New York, 1942) 553.

Nordenskiøld, "ever seeking to create fixed categories of thought, preferably with reference to mathematical deductions. Above all, he strives to create 'absolute ideas', in which the various phenomena are to be defined".[1] Later, his fine work on the nature of starch granules in cells, a fundamental contribution to plant cytology, led him to the conception that cells are composed of ultimate particles which he called "micellae". Years later, he developed his theory of heredity (1884), which he based on two principal considerations: first, that the undifferentiated egg cell is in actuality as complicated as the creature that develops from it; and second, that since egg and sperm cells have equal hereditary potency although so different in size, the hereditary material of the egg cannot comprise the entire egg but must be some part of it which by segmentation could be transmitted to every fresh cell formed in the development of the organism. This material Nägeli called the "idioplasma". It was conceived to be a solid body, and all evolution took place by changes of the micelles of the idioplasm.[2]

Mendel, of course, lacked the advantage of knowing the nature of the fertilization process, the union of the male and female pronuclei observed in full detail by Oscar Hertwig only in 1875; nor was the entire matchless story of mitotic cell division, high-lighting the role of the chromosomes, to be pieced together through the labours of Fol, Bütschli, Oscar Hertwig, Strasburger, Flemming, and van Beneden until the 1880's. But it is certainly astonishing that Nägeli, writing in 1884, made no effort to relate his conceptual model to the developing realization of the chromosomes' significance. Edouard Strasburger, Oscar Hertwig, and August Weismann announced almost simultaneously, in 1885, that the chromatin of the nucleus — the assorted group of chromosomes present there in the nucleus — must be the material basis of heredity. Weismann, in his *Vorträge über Descendenztheorie*, later pointed out that however wrong Nägeli was about the netlike nature of the idioplasm, which he thought must extend in strands throughout each entire cell, he was nevertheless profoundly right in distinguishing between the hereditary substance of the cell (the idioplasm) and the rest of the protoplasm.[3]

[1] See Nordenskiøld, ibid.

[2] C. W. von Nägeli, *Mechanisch-physiologische Theorie der Abstammungslehre* (Münich and Leipzig, 1884).

[3] A. Weismann, *Vorträge über Descendenz heorie* (2nd ed., Jena, 1904) I xvi Vortrag, 277–8.

Nägeli's *Mechanisch-physiologische Theorie der Abstammungslehre* is to the modern scientific mind a strange mixture indeed of physical constructs and vitalism. Nägeli charged Darwin with failure to supply specific physical and chemical causes for evolutionary change — surely a fatal defect in the Theory of Natural Selection! Instead, Nägeli conceived that evolution must proceed more directly from inside the organism. He writes: "According to the theory of direct action, on the contrary, the structure and function of the organism in its principal characteristics is a necessary consequence of forces dwelling within the substance and thereby independent of external chances".[1] This "perfecting force" (*Vervollkommnungskraft*), as he termed it, is the evolutionary counterpart of Goethe's and Haeckel's "inner formative force", and derives by direct lineage from the *vis formativa* of Wolff and the *nisus formativus* of Blumenbach. Carried into more modern times, it reappears in new guise in Hans Driesch's *Entelechie* and Henri Bergson's *élan vital*.

It would seem that the consequence of Nägeli's thinking in such a mode, of fitting the organism into his own conceptual pattern, was to lead him to despise the work of Mendel as purely limited and empirical; and he said as much to Mendel in one of his letters in response to the latter's humble request for aid and advice.[2] This tendency appears to have carried over into the thinking of August Weismann, Nägeli's most eminent pupil. In spite of the brilliant development by Weismann of the theory of the ids, which relates the idioplasma of Nägeli to the material basis of heredity in the chromosomes, vehicles for their transmission from generation to generation through the isolated, continuous germplasm, Weismann somehow failed to see the relation of his conceptual model to the Mendelian analysis of inheritance, when this was rediscovered in 1900. In spite of the triple confirmation by Carl Correns (the last student of Nägeli), by Hugo de Vries, and by Erich von Tschermak, and in spite of the almost immediate and independent realization, by Theodor Boveri in Germany and W. S. Sutton in the United States, that the behaviour of the Mendelian factors exactly parallels the behaviour of the

[1] Nägeli, op. cit. p. 294.

[2] "Gregor Mendels Briefe an Carl Nägeli", 1866–73, published by Carl Correns, *Abhandlungen der königlichen Sächsischen Gesellschaft der Wissenchaften* (mathematische-physikalische Klasse) XXIX (1905) 189–265. Translated into English, *Genetics*, XXXV (1950), No. 5, Pt. 2, pp. 1–29.

chromosomes in sexual reproduction,[1] we find Weismann writing in 1902 with considerable reserve:

> This led to the discovery that similar experiments had been published as far back as 1866 by the Abbot of Brünn, Gregor Mendel, and that these had been formulated as a law which is now called Mendel's law. Correns showed, however, that this law, though correct in certain cases, did not by any means hold good in all, and we must thus postpone the working of this new material into our theory until a very much wider basis of facts has been supplied by the botanists. There is less to be hoped for from the zoologists in regard to this problem owing to the almost insuperable difficulties in the way of a long series of experiments in hybridization in animals.[2]

As I have said elsewhere:

> How lacking in foresight this was, Thomas Hunt Morgan was soon to show by the commencement of *Drosophila* breeding. Not all Weismann's insight and his knowledge of the similarity of mitosis, meiosis, and fertilization in plants and animals, from high to low, enabled him to see that Mendel's discovery was valid as far and wide as the prevalence of sexual reproduction.[3]

Probably far greater than any influence of a master's experimental work upon the development of his pupils is generally that teacher's way of looking at things, his basic philosophy of nature, his fund of conceptual models. Certainly this was true in the relation of Nägeli to his students. What magnificent irony, therefore, that it was chiefly the elaborations of the concept of the idioplasma by Nägeli's student Weismann that laid the essential basis for understanding the discoveries of Mendel which Nägeli had slighted and failed to comprehend. And what further irony that it was the student of Nägeli's old age, Carl Correns, who rediscovered and verified the work of the Augustinian prelate.

[1] T. Boveri, "Über mehrpolige Mitosen als Mittel zur Analyse des Zellkerns", *Verhandlungen der physikalisch-medizinischen Gesellschaft, Würzburg*, XXXV (1902); *Über die Konstitution der chromatischen Substanz des Zellkerns* (Jena, 1904). W. S. Sutton, "On the morphology of the chromosome group in *Brachystola magna*", *Biological Bulletin*, IV (1902) 24–39; "The chromosomes in heredity", *Biol. Bull.*, IV (1903) 231–51.

[2] Weismann, op. cit. II, 49.

[3] B. Glass, "The long neglect of a scientific discovery: Mendel's laws of inheritance", in *Studies in Intellectual History* by George Boas and others (Baltimore, 1953) 160.

III
Twentieth-Century Genetic Models

The triumph of the gene and chromosome theories

The first three decades of the twentieth century saw the birth and triumph of the theory of the gene and the chromosome theory of heredity. The former, in its abstract form, is the lineal descendant of Maupertuis's hereditary particles, particles contributed equally by the two parents and having an organic memory relating some part in the parent's body to the corresponding part to be produced in the offspring. Darwin's pangenesis theory, with its postulated "gemmules", was essentially the same idea, though more definite in its derivation of the particles from all parts of the parent's body. De Vries's "pangenes" and Weismann's "ids" are models of the same sort, the latter somewhat more realistically posited to be parts of the chromosomes. From this point in the history of the idea to the concept of the gene is but a step, made ere long when the investigation of linkage and crossing over in the fruitfly *Drosophila melanogaster* demonstrated that any Mendelian factors which are linked may be mapped in linear series by means of the frequencies with which they recombine in the offspring. On the other hand, the chromosome theory grew from the marriage of genetics and cytology, first from the growing realization that the chromosomes are the bearers of the hereditary material, and subsequently from the beautiful parallels drawn between the behaviour of the Mendelian factors and the behaviour of the homologous maternal and paternal chromosomes during meiosis and fertilization. Beginning with the inspired work of Sutton and Boveri, this conceptual development reached its peak in Calvin Bridges's studies of the genetic and cytological parallels occurring in cases of non-disjunction of homologous chromosomes, in Mrs. Morgan's discovery that inseparably linked genes on two sex-chromosomes were due to physically united X-chromosomes, and finally to the prediction and verification of cytological crossing between specially marked chromosomes, on the basis of genetic crossing over between genes known to lie on those chromosomes. This was accomplished for maize and for *Drosophila* almost simultaneously in 1931 by Harriet Creighton and Barbara McClintock, and by Curt Stern, respectively.[1]

[1] H. Creighton and B. McClintock, "A correlation of cytological and

Most significant is the contrast between these two closely related theories, which may clearly be regarded as conceptual models, and all the earlier models, which were derived by pure reason. For the first time in the history of genetics it became possible, not simply to produce a model that would fit known facts, but also, on the basis of the model, to make predictions which could be put to an experimental test and be verified or disproved. Sutton indeed made one such prediction: that in any species the number of linkage groups into which the genes would fall should correspond in number to the number of pairs of chromosomes in the somatic cells of the organism (or the number of individual chromosomes in the mature reproductive cells). It was hard to demonstrate the truth of this, because a species must be studied genetically for several — or even many — years before the linkage groups can be identified with some certainty. (What at first appear to be genes belonging to different groups may later be found to be linked, through linkage to some gene at an intermediate point between them, although they are themselves so distant that they recombine virtually at random.) Even today, Sutton's prediction is verified for only a small number of species which have relatively few chromosomes. But in Bridges's work, and in the cytological demonstration of crossing over, one could predict that certain genetic types would upon examination turn out to have certain chromosome types, or the converse. The difference between a model that yields verifiable predictions and one that does not is, in modern eyes, the essential difference between scientific method and speculative natural philosophy. The previously indicated, adverse effects which have flowed from the adoption of untestable models in the history of genetics may consequently not apply at all to the present-day use of models. We must examine the matter afresh.

Before considering the later history of the theory of the gene, certain developments in the chromosome theory of heredity may claim attention. No biologist today doubts the general validity of the chromosome theory, unless it be Trofim Lysenko and his coterie of Russian agriculturalists. Attention has consequently shifted largely to problems of the evolution of genetic, and specifically chromosomal, systems. In this area

genetical crossing-over in *Zea mays*", *Proceedings of the National Academy of Sciences of the United States of America*, XVII (1931) 492–7; C. Stern, "Zytologisch-genetische Untersuchungen als Beweise für die Morgansche Theorie des Faktorenaustauschs", *Biologisches Zentralblatt*, LI (1931) 547–87.

no work of recent years has had greater influence than C. D. Darlington's *Evolution of Genetic Systems*.[1] It has superbly drawn together and clarified the relationships existing between the various cytogenetic systems of plant and animal species. Yet precisely because it deals with broad evolutionary trends, past changes, and relationships between uncrossable species, the conceptual system tends to share the untestable and unverifiable aspects of the earlier genetic models of the eighteenth and nineteenth centuries. It would certainly be a mistake to decry such an effort to synthesize our knowledge of evolutionary processes, even if no way of testing hypothesis and theory presents itself in the near future; for from bold, suggestive thinking of this sort workers derive interest, stimulation, and perspective. New lines of investigation open up in consequence. Yet ever and again we must beware the insidious charm of the undemonstrated and unverifiable model. Accept it as fact, fall in love with it, and like Nägeli or Weismann we may blind ourselves to the sober reality of an experiment like Mendel's that leads elsewhere or denies some fond conviction.

The triumph of operationally defined elements

Early discussions of the concept of the gene clearly adopted an abstraction. The gene was often described as 'a bead on a string', the string being the linear constitution of the chromosome. It was probably not even realized that the model implied not only discrete and separable units based on molecular discontinuity, but also independence of primary gene functions, and identity of the genetic unit regardless of the methods used to study it. During the 1930's questions regarding the applicability of the model to reality came to be asked. I well remember the reaction which first greeted Richard Goldschmidt's suggestion, based on studies showing that the activity of a gene depends upon its material relations to neighbouring segments of the chromosomes, to the effect that perhaps one might better conceive of the chromosome as a chemical continuum, maybe a single giant molecule, and that the so-called 'genes' represent only changes introduced at one point or another in this continuum.[2] The reaction was not merely one of incredulity — it varied from pity that a great geneticist had gone crazy to one of actual personal hostility.

[1] C. D. Darlington, *The Evolution of Genetic Systems* (Cambridge, 1939; revised ed., New York, 1958).

[2] R. B. Goldschmidt, *Physiological Genetics* (New York, 1938) 309–16.

Yet this new model, as Goldschmidt conceived it, in no way conflicted irreconcilably with the experimental evidence then available. Gradually, into the minds of at least some geneticists, prominent among whom was Louis Stadler, the need for adopting operational definitions of the gene became apparent.[1] One may define genetic units within the chromosome on the basis of mutation, or on the basis of recombination by crossing over, or on the basis of gene function. There is not the slightest reason to suppose that these three operations define precisely the same units in a material sense, although of course the three sorts of units must be related in some way. Evidence, first found in studies of certain loci in *Drosophila melanogaster*, that the unit of function and the unit of recombination do not correspond was found in the late 1930's and 1940's in the investigation of the phenomenon of pseudoallelism. The standard genetic test held to demonstrate that two recessive mutants are alleles, that is, occupy the same locus on homologous chromosomes, is to introduce them in heterozygous state, one in each chromosome of the pair, and see whether they express themselves in the phenotype. If so, they were considered to be alleles; if not, they would represent different genetic loci even though closely linked. But M. M. Green and E. B. Lewis, working independently, demonstrated that when recombination is studied on a sufficiently large scale, genes considered to be alleles because of the interaction test proved to be separable by conventional crossing over, and consequently could not be at the same chromosomal locus.[2]

The development of microbial genetics in the 1950's added to the mounting evidence that a gene is only to be defined in terms of the particular operation being used and that the employment of different operations to define the same conception leads only to confusion. Seymour Benzer, in particular, working with mutation and recombination in bacteriophages, found increasing evidence of the fine structure of genetic loci.[3] Changes originating by mutation within a single unit of function could undergo genetic recombination, and in some cases the material changed by mutation was larger in extent

[1] L. J. Stadler, "The gene", *Science*, CXX (1954) 811–19.

[2] M. M. Green, "Pseudoallelism and the gene concept", *American Naturalist*, LXXXIX (1955) 65–72; E. B. Lewis, "Some aspects of position pseudoallelism", ibid. pp. 73–90.

[3] S. Benzer, "The elementary units of heredity", in *The Chemical Basis of Heredity*, ed. W. D. McElroy and B. Glass (Baltimore, 1957) 70–93.

than the smallest recombinable units, in other cases not. Benzer therefore proposed the terms "muton", "recon", and "cistron", for the smallest units definable by mutation, recombination, and function, respectively. (The particular operation defining the unit of function in such studies is too complex to describe here.) Even among geneticists who do not approve of the use of these terms, the validity of the distinction between the 'gene' as defined by different operational concepts is freely admitted. At least in such bacteria as *Escherichia coli* and in bacterial viruses (bacteriophages) the genetic material within the limits of the individual units of function appears to be a molecular continuum. It remains to be determined whether or not the bounds of a cistron represent a discontinuity of some sort. Perhaps there is some genetically inert, or 'non-gene' material inserted between the functional units. Yet at least in the case of bacteriophage there is now evidence that the entire chromosome is one long, uninterrupted molecule of deoxyribose nucleic acid (DNA).

The genetic trinity — DNA, RNA, and protein

Within the past decade geneticists far and wide have come to accept what is not infrequently called the dogma of the holy trinity, DNA (deoxyribose nucleic acid), RNA (ribose nucleic acid), and protein. The dogma — another term for an accepted model — takes the following form: in all organisms, except a few viruses in which there is only RNA, the ultimate store of genetic information which is replicated and passed on from generation to generation lies in the DNA of the chromosomes contained within the nucleus of each cell. DNA not only replicates itself, but also passes on to RNA a code of information in the chemical form of a specific sequence of the nucleotides making up the nucleic acid molecule. RNA moves from the nucleus into the cytoplasm and there presides over the synthesis of protein molecules, in such a way that a specific sequence of nucleotides in the RNA molecule becomes translated into a specific sequence of amino acids in a polypeptide molecule; and polypeptides are combined into protein molecules of specific sorts. The most important proteins are the enzymes that govern the almost innumerable chemical reactions that must go on in each cell to maintain life, and the differences between which constitute not only the differences between different kinds of cells in the same organism but also the differences between species.

This conceptual model originated from the union of two lines of experimental evidence: the one, evidence that DNA is in fact the basic genetic material of the chromosomes, the molecular stuff that contains the information which controls the chemistry and the course of development of the cell; the other, evidence that alteration of a particular gene by mutation in general leads to the blocking of a particular metabolic step by inactivation of the specific enzyme controlling the step. The former line of evidence is based on experimental demonstrations in viruses and bacteria that genetic information is transmitted through transfer of the DNA but not through transfer of the protein of the chromosomes. The second line of evidence involves a gradual refinement of the original hypothesis of George Beadle and Edward L. Tatum that each gene controls the nature of a single enzyme — the 'one gene–one enzyme' hypothesis.[1] As difficulties developed in adhering to this simple view, it became first transformed into a 'one gene–one biochemical step' hypothesis, and is at present in course of a second metamorphosis into a 'one gene–one polypeptide chain' hypothesis.

The important thing to note in this connexion is the effect of the overwhelming, well-nigh universal acceptance of a conceptual model that explains satisfactorily all — or nearly all — of the scientific data now known. One must recall that the doctrine of the 'billiard-ball gene', the conception of the 'chromosome as a string of beads', likewise had a tremendous weight of experimental evidence in its favour and little to render it invalid or even slightly dubious, until evidence of a new kind began to accumulate in the past twenty years. Today, graduate students and young geneticists, like those of a generation ago, accept without question the current dogma, mould their thinking round it, and most importantly, plan their experiments in accordance with it. Is it not conceivable that, for all its virtues, the blind acceptance of a conceptual model may once again, as so repeatedly in the past, hinder the advancement of science toward a deeper appreciation of genetic relationships?

Mendelian populations and the concept of the species

In the study of the nature of biological species a similar transformation of concepts has grown out of Mendelian

[1] See, for example, G. W. Beadle, "The genetic control of biochemical reactions", Harvey Lecture, XL (1944–5) 179–94; "Genes and biological enigmas", *Science in Progress* (1949) 184–249, esp. 198–9.

genetics. The first important new conceptual model grew out of the independent demonstration, in 1908, by G. H. Hardy and W. Weinberg, that, assuming Mendelian behaviour of genes and chromosomes, hereditary variability in a population does not diminish with intermating but is conserved undiminished, unless specific forces act to make one allele rarer and a competing allele commoner.[1] From this demonstration there grew on the one hand a recognition that the evolutionary forces are those that can alter the frequencies of alleles in a population, namely, differential mutation, differential selection, differential movement of genes between populations, and in very small populations the random effects of what Sewall Wright has named "genetic drift". In the second place, there emerged from the Hardy–Weinberg principle the conception of the gene pool, comprising all the alleles at all the loci in an interbreeding population — in other words, the collective genotype of the population. Virtually all evolutionary genetical studies are now based implicitly on acceptance of this model. Experimental studies show that often, in actual situations, gene frequencies do behave in accordance with a Hardy–Weinberg equilibrium. Very often, of course, they do not, and such findings lead to a search for some force or condition that in the particular situation can disturb the calculated equilibrium. Often such searches are highly illuminating. Be that as it may, here again the blind acceptance of a model is not only fruitful in stimulating specific lines of research, but undoubtedly exercises constraint upon the direction in which scientific advance progresses.

If this is true of the overwhelmingly accepted Hardy-Weinberg principle, it is clearly even more true of newer conceptual models in this area of genetics, such, for example, as the model of the coadapted gene complex which must maintain a certain degree of *internal* genetic harmony and balance if the population is to remain well adapted to its environment. But limitations of space prevent more than a mention of this example.

[1] G. H. Hardy, "Mendelian proportions in a mixed population", *Science*, XXVIII (1908) 49–50; W. Weinberg, "Über den Nachweis der Vererbung beim Menschen", *Jahreshefte des Vereins für vaterländische Naturkunde in Württemberg*, LXIV (1908) 368–82.

IV
Conclusion

Our currently accepted views of the relation of heredity to the formation and development of the individual embrace both the concept of replicating particles and also that of the existence in the egg of a preformed pattern controlling the paths of development. The pattern is molecular and is made of elements which can segregate and recombine in the ways of Mendelian heredity; yet the pattern is an entity, an assemblage of each and every kind of necessary gene in at least a single dose, and more usually in a double dose. In a very real sense, the epigenetic view of heredity and development has come to terms with concept of the preformationists. The modern view of the relation of heredity to development is not Bonnet's, but neither is it Maupertuis's. It has something of both, and something of neither. The two views, once held to be irreconcilable, have merged in a higher synthesis.

As for our current views of heredity and the species, much the same may be said. There must be a certain stability about the genetic composition of a species or it could not endure and maintain its adaptation to the existing environment. The Hardy–Weinberg equilibrium provides this stability, although not an absolute fixity of type. The existence of mutation, of natural selection, of gene exchange between differently adapted populations, and of chance shifts in gene frequency will certainly prevent the fixity of species. And a changing environment requires modification within the gene pool if adaptation to the altered conditions is to transpire. Natural selection is stabilizing and tends to promote uniformity; but natural selection also, in the face of new circumstances, promotes change and diversification. Nature is full of such paradoxes, the reconciliation of irreconcilables.

The irreconcilability, naturally, lies in the human mind, not in nature. No conception is absolutely true, although most conceptions contain something of the truth. It is in the dedication to a conceptual model which may seem to hold true, but cannot in fact describe nature in its fullness, that we find both the highest stimulus to current scientific investigation and the greatest barrier to ultimate knowledge.

18

Complexities, Advances, and Misconceptions in the Development of the Science of Vision: What is being Discovered?

VASCO RONCHI

The study of the history of the theories governing the mechanism of vision and the growth of the science of vision in general is, I believe, one of the most important topics within the terms of reference of this Symposium at the University of Oxford. For, of all the means by which we come to know and appreciate the outside world, that of sight is undoubtedly the most immediate and comprehensive, and scientific progress has always been, and still is, integrated with our deepening knowledge of the sense of vision.

Even a glance at the course of scientific progress from ancient times to our own day is enough to reveal a most interesting tendency. Down to the seventeenth century progress was slow, thereafter becoming ever swifter and more impressive. Indeed, down to the seventeenth century men had only the vaguest notions about the mechanism of direct vision and strictly speaking did not possess accurate optical instruments. It is not until the beginning of the seventeenth century that we get an adequate explanation of the actual mechanism of vision. At this time optical instruments began to be used, and since then they have continually been perfected and put into practical use.

I believe, therefore, that it will be useful to trace the stages of this development in order to display the effects this has had on scientific and philosophical progress in general.

The study of the mechanism of vision goes back to the earliest times, certainly before the fourth century B.C., the century to which we can trace the earliest complete treatise on optics still available to us, which we attribute to Euclid.

At that time the question that engaged the attention of the most eminent philosophers was precisely that of the means by which the 'I' comes to know the external world. From that period it was recognized that the human organism has its own peripheral sense organs which receive external stimuli and transmit messages along nerves to the brain, where they are received and represented by the mind. The sense of touch was easily explained through the contact of external bodies with the skin of sentient man; likewise that of taste by the contact of bodies placed in the mouth with the organs situated therein, whose function is the creation of flavour. Similarly the sense of smell was explained by the passing of exhalations from outside bodies to the nose which represented them in terms of scent and smell; and that of hearing by the response of the ear to vibrations set up in the air, and represented in terms of sounds and noises. But when it came to inquiring into the means whereby man was able to register the visual world, enormous problems arose which it has taken over 2000 years to solve.

Let me point out first that the major difficulty arose from the fact that the observer sees at the same time innumerable objects distributed at various distances in space and all with different colours and brightnesses. It was indeed very difficult to discover a process that would explain how shapes and colours might be registered simultaneously, and how each was allotted its place with an almost magical precision: particularly when the objects seen were often an enormous distance away from the observer. The problem was to establish a relationship between the object and the eye, and to discover how this process included the necessary constituent elements which in their complex and precise manner permitted the mind to reconstitute the forms, the colours and the varied positions. It had also to be explained how all the visual elements entered the eye itself, how they stamped their impression upon it, and how everything was finally transmitted to the mind. Truly a problem of frightening proportions.

The efforts made to solve the problem are well known: whether by the mathematicians who evolved their theory of *visual rays*, which were supposed to issue from the eye to explore the outside world; or by the physicists, who advanced their theory of *simulacra* or *eidola*, which allegedly carried to the eye the forms and colours of the object seen, by which they were projected. But the visual rays, even if they effectively solved the problems of perspective, left many problems unsolved, notably that of the means by which they transmitted the elements explored to the eye. They were, in short, credited with truly acrobatic communicative properties.

And even if the eidolas seemed more practical as a means of transmitting the forms and colours, in spite of the need for contraction en route so that they could enter the small pupil no matter where the latter was situated, they could not satisfactorily explain how the mind managed to grasp the distance they had travelled.

It is idle to dwell on criticism that is easy enough for us today, and was as easy for the philosophers of centuries gone by. It was generally agreed that the mechanism of vision was still a mystery.

Many observations were made with the intention of finding the key to the workings of the organs of sight, and inevitably the conclusion was drawn that the eye is often fallible, permitting shapes to be seen by no means corresponding to the objects, as far as it was possible to judge by means of touch; and not infrequently permitting images to be seen where no objects at all are to be found. This phenomenon can be demonstrated by numerous examples of what have come to be known today as optical illusions, as well as by experiments conducted with the simplest form of apparatus available, such as a plane mirror, or, even more strikingly, with spherical, cylindrical and conical mirrors or others more complicated in shape. And observance through plate glass and other transparent substances of complex shape reveals strange images that have little or no connexion with the real object seen, either in position or shape.

An organ that resisted explanation in this way, and was so consistently proved wrong, could hardly shake the traditional beliefs of the philosophers. And, in fact, the doubtful validity of the sense of vision was an accepted commonplace in scientific circles throughout Antiquity and the Middle Ages. It became an accepted dictum that: *Non potest fieri scientia per visum solum*; that is, no scientific value should be attached to anything observed by sight alone. Visual observation could never be considered valid unless confirmed by touch.

Clearly if this practice shielded the investigator from any possible misconception due to an optical illusion, it also represented, conversely, a total obstacle to the use of the simplest optical instruments, for touch cannot confirm either the shape or the position of what is seen through a plane, spherical, convex or concave mirror, prism and lens.

It is generally thought that in ancient and medieval times there were no optical instruments: an opinion not borne out in fact. The ancients possessed not only plane, but also spherical, concave and convex mirrors, and various forms of refractive apparatus. Euclid, in his *Catoptrics*, paid special attention to spherical mirrors, and Ptolemy, too, gave a very accurate account of them. They (and other scientists along with them) proved conclusively that images seen in a spherical mirror are larger than life-size, and Ptolemy in particular evolved a very accurate mathematical theorem in explanation of this phenomenon; but no one used these enlarged images as the basis of a microscope. The reason for this essential fact is clear: nobody believed what he saw in a mirror, once he realized that he could not confirm it by touch.

The same reason must account for the totally negative response of every philosopher and mathematician without exception to the application by craftsmen working in glass (glaziers) of convex lenses to the correction of long sight. Not one gave the matter any thought, and not one studied these practical attempts in detail. This all took place at the end of the thirteenth century A.D.; seventeen centuries had passed since Euclid had published his *Optics* and *Catoptrics*, but the fundamental ideas on the subject had remained static. In the meantime the study of the mechanics of vision had progressed considerably, but, we must add, in the East, through the school of Ibn al-Haitham, this work had as yet had no impact on the Western world. When it finally did strike a response this took the form of an additional confusion of ideas which merely made worse the already critical state of the science of optics. The multiplication of research and observations had added still further to the known examples of optical illusions. Thus geometrical analysis of the optical behaviour of spheres and hemispheres achieved little more than to make it even more difficult to understand how a small image might be seen through them, recalling the surrounding objects of the outside world, but always appearing either larger or smaller, nearer or further away than reality, sometimes even upside down, and frequently distorted and iridescent. Instead of approaching a solution the mystery deepened.

Hence the corresponding decrease in confidence in observations made with optical instruments. When the Florentine, Giovanni Rucellai, published his account of the anatomy of the bee in 1523, on the basis of observations with a spherical concave mirror, it is not surprising that nobody followed him in adopting this technique. The learned academicians greeted a work so devoid of meaning, according to them, with amused contempt.

Even the lenses for the benefit of long-sighted people — which the craftsmen continued to produce from the end of the thirteenth century, mainly for older persons — might be regarded essentially as microscopes: a very slight alteration to the curvature of the surface was needed to make the lens more powerful and achieve a greater magnification, as in essence was done in the seventeenth and eighteenth centuries. If this practice did not become general, the cause must be sought in the same scepticism, that had by now hardened into a by-word, towards observations made through optical instruments in general. It was still the notorious saying: *Non potest fieri scientia per visum solum*, that defiantly hamstrung all research work, which might already have been able to make progress with the optical instruments available. This has been one of the most damaging principles in the annals of scientific, and for that matter of human, progress. Clearly no further progress could be made until it had been totally refuted.

As we have shown elsewhere, the fundamental change that was to determine the final collapse of the old optical tradition and usher in a new approach to optics began in the last decades of the sixteenth century and was concluded in the first decade of the seventeenth. In this short space of time — considering the two thousand years and more that had already passed — two basic developments took place: first, the key was discovered to the mechanism of vision; and second, classical scepticism was replaced by the most complete faith in observation by the naked eye and through optical instruments.

Let us now briefly summarize this great development, marking all the most significant dates.

There is no doubt that the experiments and theories of Ibn al-Haitham — which had become known in the West thanks to the rarely bettered translation made by Witelo from the Arab master's manuscripts — contributed considerably to this development; as did the work and theories of Francesco Maurilico of Messina, a mathematician of great distinction and reputation. It is worth noting that Maurilico, himself a native of Messina, was the son of a refugee doctor who had fled from Constantinople at the time of the Ottoman invasion. His ideas certainly reflect the influence of those circulated by the Arab school. But when he died in 1575 his writings were hardly known and had achieved no practical results. But from now on the time was ripe for reform and matters were coming rapidly to a head.

1589: this is the date of the new edition of the *Magia naturalis* of the Neapolitan, Giovan Battista Della Porta, the seventeenth volume of which is the first printed book ever to carry a reference to lenses, albeit described as *magie naturali*. In the same volume earlier scientists were explicitly accused of not having paid any attention to them, and of being unable to explain their function. This fact is of great historical, if not of scientific, importance, standing as it did for a complete break with the conspiracy of silence maintained, for three centuries, by mathematicians and philosophers concerning lenses. Nor is it without importance that the *Magia naturalis* had a tremendous success and was translated into all the known languages of the time.

1590: an unknown Italian built the first recorded telescope using a diverging eyepiece; a telescope which we now know was taken to Holland.

1593: the year of G. B. Della Porta's *De refractione*. This remarkable work was the first in which an attempt was made to formulate a theory of lenses. Della Porta, who was not a scientist, attempted a scientific text-book on optics, and dealt with the question of refraction, at that time a very living issue in the field of scientific research. Having studied refraction through a plain surface, then through spherical, concave, and convex surfaces, he wrote a chapter in Book VIII which attempted to explain the behaviour of lenses. Here he declared that everything is perfectly clear: that on the basis of the principles of classical optics he had succeeded in fully explaining the function and behaviour of lenses. In fact, the lack of logical reasoning in his argument only serves to demonstrate a very important fact precisely the opposite of the author's declared intention: it emerged quite clearly that the principles of classical optics are irreconcilable with the behaviour of lenses, and that there is not room for both of them in the same world. Today we can safely say that, whereas the classical system of optics was a theoretical construction, and moreover a very disjointed and incomplete affair, lenses were an experimental reality. Not only were they real, but, as they were continuously being perfected by craftsmen who were the very opposite of theorists, the writing was on the wall so far as the old system was concerned.

1604: the date of the publication of the *Ad Vitellionem para-*

lipomena of Johannes Kepler. In this work the basis of the new science of optics was laid down and the key was given of the mechanism of vision, an explanation which still holds good today. It was demonstrated for the first time that the rays coming from each point on the observed object are refracted by the optical system of the eye in such a way that an image of the object is formed on the retina. This wonderful discovery will be examined in greater detail in the following pages. We need only remark now that 1604 is a memorable date in the history of science. Naturally we must not imagine that its effects were felt immediately. On the contrary, no one took any notice of this work when it was published, or recognized the importance of its contents. So startling was the revolution it propounded, that generations were to pass before the new views became officially adopted. But this was the genesis of modern optics, and from that time forth it only remained to wait on events. Even in the field of science a slow process of penetration and conditioning is usually necessary before a new discovery is accepted and recognized at its face value. Only in exceptional cases does the older generation give up the ideas on which it has based its scientific principles in youth, and with which it normally dies. It is to young men alone that one must look for a new assessment of ideas, and this re-orientation of thought generally demands a great deal of time.

1604: in the same year Dutch craftsmen put into circulation telescopes with diverging eyepieces, put together with spectacle lenses, following the Italian model of 1590. Thus even this new instrument began to make itself known. It is well known that it was not favourably received, being ill-made by the craftsmen responsible. We now know that we cannot construct a practical telescope with spectacle lenses. The telescope, like spectacle lenses, came up against the combined opposition of the mathematicians and the philosophers who condemned it as an inaccurate instrument unworthy of consideration as a means of scientific research, and consequently paid no attention to it. Once again it was the old school of thought that hindered the development of scientific inquiry, through its own lack of confidence in the means of observation.

1609: this year marks the conclusion of the revolutionary break-through, the advent of a new man who, on his own initiative, snapped the chains that had hitherto prevented scientific advance, the chains of the notorious scepticism of former times. This man was Galileo Galilei. He re-modelled the telescope (and it is a matter of indifference whether it was his own invention or whether he reproduced a model from abroad); but he understood the one essential question: that the telescope had to be *good*, and to be good it could not be made with spectacle lenses, but must be made with new lenses manufactured with new techniques. He was in short the founder of what has come to be known today as *ottica fina* (precision optics). The first result was an amazing increase in the power of the instrument. Before this opticians had never managed to achieve more than three magnifications of the object: beyond that the image became indistinct and the instrument useless (and in any case a telescope capable of only three magnifications, and inaccurate into the bargain, has no practical value, as the contemporary public had recognized). Galileo managed to produce an instrument that magnified more than thirty times, and he obtained from it new and unexpected results. On 24 August 1609 he wrote to the Doge of Venice announcing that the telescope was an instrument of "inestimable advantages". This was the first time that a man of science had personally and unhesitatingly guaranteed the practical value of a telescope. We may say that on that day modern science was born, a science that no longer shied away from the idea of direct sight and direct observation through optical instruments. Henceforth the terrible dictum: *Non potest fieri scientia per visum solum*, can be regarded as dead.

We should recall what happened to Kepler's new and revolutionary optical theory. Galileo was the *one* man in contemporary academic circles to share this new belief in the validity of vision. The most positive proof we have of this assertion is precisely the unanimous reaction of the academics of the time to the publication of Galileo's astronomical discoveries — and notably his discovery of the satellites of Jupiter — based on his telescopic observations, and included in his *Sidereus nuncius*, the first copies of which (still hot from the press) began to circulate on 10 March 1610. All without exception rushed to the attack on Galileo, accusing him of allowing himself to be led astray by his telescope — a notoriously unfaithful instrument and one unworthy of consideration as a means of scientific research.

It is well known that many of his opponents turned down Galileo's insistent invitations to observe *through his own telescopes* — the only existing models that permitted such observations to be made — what he himself had seen, and refused to have anything to do with the instrument. They denied in advance any possible substance in whatever they might see, even though it might bear out all that Galileo had affirmed. And those who decided to accept the invitation did so with the full intention of declaring the observations by telescope null and void and of underlining its defects. This was not difficult, considering that Galileo's telescopes — despite their improvement on those made by the opticians — still fell considerably short of perfection. The tremendous argument that broke out in 1610 between Galileo on the one hand, armed with nothing but his telescope, and the whole scientific world on the other, barricaded in behind scepticism and prejudice, ended, as is now clear, with the total victory of Galileo. But it was generations before Galileo's faith and confidence came to be shared by all men of science.

Particularly interesting was the reaction of Kepler. We must remember that Kepler had specialized in the study of optics, and furthermore that he was at the time probably the most learned, if not the only, scientific optician. Galileo on the other hand was totally ignorant of the science of optics, and it is not too bold to assume that this was a most happy accident both for him and for humanity at large. When he started to build his telescopes, his mind was completely free of any philosophical preconceptions about the theory of vision and the need for the confirmation by touch. It is quite possible that, had he fully studied the classical theories of optics, he would not have found the necessary intellectual initiative to rid himself of the grip of that scepticism that had characterized previous generations.

Kepler by contrast was the author of the *Paralipomena* of 1604. At that time he did not yet believe in lenses. In fact, in the *Paralipomena* he hardly gave them a mention. Although he had thoroughly studied the optical behaviour of transparent *spheres* (which interested him as corresponding to the eyeball), and although he had very clearly given the foundations of the new concept of the image as the place of concentration of the rays refracted by the sphere, he only deals in one short page with lenses, in order to show how converging lenses correct long sight and diverging lenses correct short sight. And even for this he almost apologizes; he says that he did it only in order to satisfy the pressing wish of Ludwig L. B. von Dietrichstein, who had asked him for *three whole years* to make a study of spectacle lenses.

After the bombshell of Galileo's telescope, the whole of the scientific world turned to Kepler for his opinion. But he made no positive statement either way. He attempted to build a *good* telescope for himself — without success. In August of 1610 — fully a year after Galileo had stated his case — he came into possession of one of the Italian's telescopes which had been sent by him to the Elector of Cologne, according to a subtly pre-arranged plan which permitted Galileo to side-track the hostile efforts of the mathematicians. With this telescope Kepler undertook a series of minutely accurate observations, some with the help of other observers, with the precise intention of finding out the shortcomings or, as they were then called, 'fallacies', of the instrument. After experiments conducted over a period of ten days he concluded that Galileo was right. The greatest optician of his day had been converted to belief in the validity of lenses and from that time forth the days of the old system were numbered. No more *visual rays*, no more *simulacra* or *species*, but instead *geometrical rays*, which, emitted from every point of every body in all directions, arrive, in part at least, at the base of the human eye, where they form an image on the retina which is then projected into, and localized in the outside world by the mind of the observer.

The first effect of Kepler's conversion to the new faith in direct observation and optical instruments was not long to come. In a *few weeks* he produced the theory of lenses and telescopes, starting from the principles expounded in his *Paralipomena* (1604); and in the first months of 1611 he published the wonderful booklet which carries the title *Dioptrice*: it is the first book of *geometrical optics*, the very same geometrical optics that we study today.

Thus lenses became accepted by science as indispensable research apparatus. The most distinguished men of science of the age devoted their energy to studying them. The uses found for them multiplied day by day, notably through the efforts of the younger generation and of some older people who had escaped the prejudices of the old school. But it is not to be wondered at if Galileo himself never appreciated the importance of Kepler's new optical discoveries, but continued to perfect the technique of lens manufacture, training a body of young craftsmen in the work who became famous in their own right. He was in fact preoccupied primarily with the structure of the solar system and with mechanical problems in general. These were the main concerns of his work even when he was concentrating on his telescope. Evidently his interest was not that of an optician, but arose simply because the telescope was for him a means of exploring the universe.

We should not be surprised by the fact that about 1660 a famous French mathematician, De La Chambre, published a treatise on optics which completely overlooked Kepler's work and proceeded along the lines of the theory of *species* and *visual rays*. Nor should we be surprised that the father of the microscope was a certain van Leeuwenhoek, a man of such modest education that he never managed to put adequately into writing his numerous important discoveries made with his rudimentary apparatus. The fact that he was a minor Government official, an usher of the States General, rather than a university professor proves quite conclusively that what was needed in order to exploit the new optical instruments to the full was a completely new generation. We might say that the study of academic texts at the time did more harm than good.

We pointed out at the beginning how the scepticism of ancient science was largely due to the lack of understanding of the mechanics of sight and how it rested on a broad knowledge of various optical illusions. The logic of this line of argument in ancient science is not easy to break down. We are here up against an extremely interesting historical and philosophical phenomenon, which illustrates the possible harm that can be caused by logic and reason, while pure faith — for all its unreasonableness — may bring about the most fruitful results. The truth is that Galileo's faith in his observations through the telescope owed nothing to his reading and appreciation of Kepler's theory of the mechanics of vision, a theory he always considered too 'hermetic'. He pursued his own ideas because he was a man of faith which could not be destroyed by the seemingly irrefutable logic of the schools. The tremendous impact of pure faith in scientific research is borne out by the advances made in the field of optics during the three and a half centuries since Galileo.

Kepler had explained the mechanics of sight by means of a theory that was both admirably simple and organic. He had succeeded in demonstrating the projections on to the retina of the retinal image, as it is now called, and had considered the means by which the mind of the observer might reconstruct the outside world, on the basis of the information collated by the mind itself from the retinal stimuli.

Taking a point-object emitting rays in all directions towards the eye of the observer, he demonstrated for the first time that the cone of rays that has its apex at the point-object (today called the radiating point) and its base at the pupil of the eye, is transformed by the optical system of the eye into another cone, with its base at the pupil, but with its apex at the retina. When the object is composed of very many points — that is, is extended — the same construction is repeated for each point. The locus of the apical points of the cones on the retina is precisely that which we now call the retinal image (figs. 1, 2).

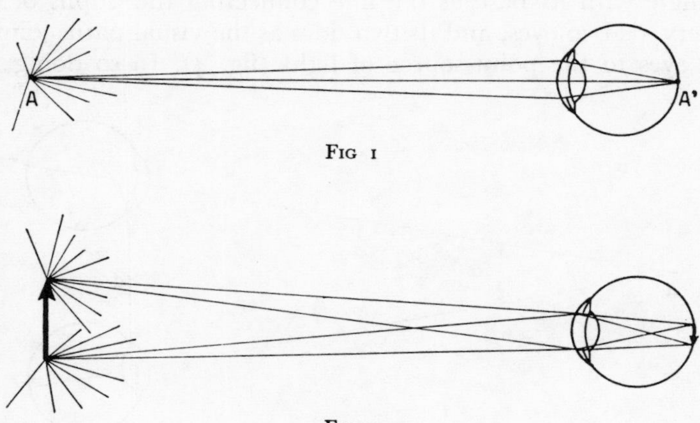

FIG 1

FIG 2

Now when the object consists of only one point-source, the retina can only be stimulated at one point itself, or rather over a very small area. From this the mind draws the conclusion that the object must be represented by a *luminous point*, or starlet. The task for the mind is now to localize the starlet at the place where the radiating point is situated. Does the stimulus received by the retina furnish a sufficient number of clues?

Kepler went into the problem with extraordinary insight. He immediately perceived that the position of the stimulated point on the retina determined the direction in which the luminous point must be localized (fig. 3). This is determined very precisely, because the structure of the eye allows for the

FIG 3

very accurate tracing of such a path. Once the direction has been decided, it now remains to determine the distance from the eye at which the luminous point must be localized. Kepler realized that this was a very difficult problem for the mind to deal with, and that the optical means it had available for the solution of the problem were inadequate. In an attempt to measure the distance of the radiating point from the eye, Kepler conceived of a triangular structure, and imagined a triangle with its base as the line connecting the pupils of the observer's two eyes, and its two sides as the visual paths joining the eyes to the point-source of light (fig. 4). In so doing, he

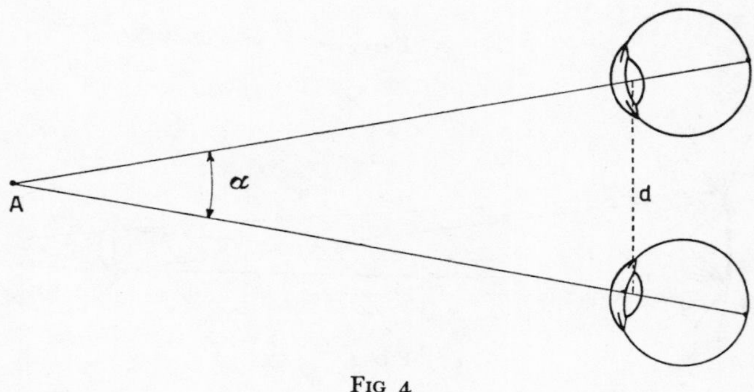

FIG 4

made reference to binocular vision. Thus, he found a rather simple solution to a very difficult problem.

But Kepler also correctly observed that one eye alone was sufficient for the observer to see the luminous and coloured figures in visual space. Hence even with one eye the mind was capable of estimating the distances of the point-sources, and of localizing the luminous points correspondingly. How could the mind measure the distance of the point-source with one eye alone? Kepler again attempted to perform triangulation; he looked for another triangle and found it: a triangle with the point-source as its apex and the diameter of the pupil as its base (fig. 5). He called this "the triangle for the measurement of distance" (*triangulum distantiae mensorium*). He could now

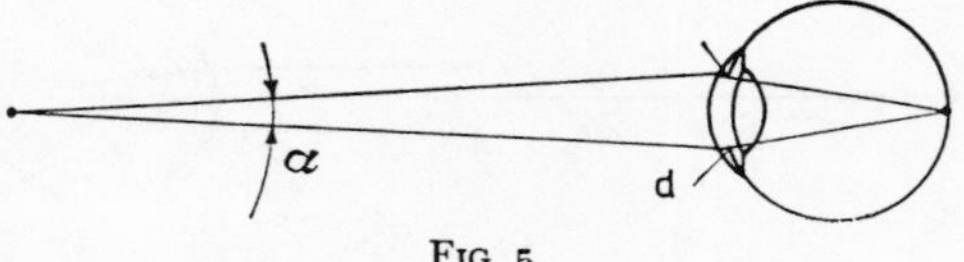

FIG 5

draw up the following rule: that the mind localizes — that is, sees — the luminous point at the apex of the cone of rays that penetrate into the eye. This is a fundamental principle, sufficient in itself to immortalize the name of the man who discovered it. It is the foundation of geometrical and physical optics from the age of Kepler down to the present day. This is the rule that brought order and clarity into the inextricable jumble of ideas that had frustrated the science of optics before Kepler's time. And it is the rule that opened the door to the application of mathematical formulae — whether geometrical or algebraic — to the solution of optical problems.

But the very importance of this principle, on both the historical and the practical levels, does not mean that it necessarily corresponds to an experimental reality. In effect, it is no more than a marvellous *working hypothesis*, all the more useful because it has made possible the simplification and definition of the very complicated mechanics of vision. Nowadays we can easily understand that things are not as simple as Kepler represented them. In modern terms, Kepler's rule of the triangle as a measuring rod is as much as to say that a single eye is capable of fixing the position of the point-source by the means of its accommodation device. There are still those today who maintain that this is true; but anyone who has conducted experiments on these lines has been obliged to state that accommodation is an extraordinarily inefficient means of measuring distance. The most recent conclusions deny point blank that accommodation can possibly discriminate between the distances of two point-sources at more than four metres from the eye. Even when one or more points are within this radius from the eye, accommodation can never register their position with a reasonable accuracy. A definitive examination of this very complex problem would require a very long and detailed discussion, beyond the scope of this Symposium. The conclusion which concerns us here is briefly summarized: the rule of measurement by the triangle is hardly ever borne out in fact. One can say that those cases which do bear it out are truly exceptional, and in any case these apply only to point-sources very close to the eye.

The historical phenomenon which merits discussion at this point is truly remarkable and unknown to the great majority of even optical specialists. As we have said, the rule of measurement by the triangle is the basis of geometrical optics. No one speaks of this rule as an hypothesis, furthermore a working hypothesis hardly ever borne out in practice. If anyone says that geometrical optics is not an ideal mathematical representation of optical phenomena as verified in practice, but is a purely mathematical science, being merely a collection of deductions drawn from a working hypothesis — he will find very few people to agree with him. And yet the proof that the laws of geometrical optics do not, in fact, correspond to the results of specific experiments is very simple to come by, requiring no specialized apparatus, for in fact the difference between theoretical calculations and observed data is enormous. We are faced with a very disturbing fact: numerous students of the subject, including many of the most distinguished men of science, have believed that the laws of geometrical optics represent a final and absolute truth, and have closed their eyes when faced daily with contradictory phenomena. If we start to believe that things are, in fact, different from all that theoretical evidence reveals, and begin to observe everything we see with an open mind, we will discover precisely what we discovered above: that the cases that prove the rules of geometrical optics are very few and far between. The triangle as a measuring rod has no control over the positioning of the mental images that correspond to the stimuli received by the retina.

A brief discussion of this matter may be of some value. Once he had formulated his rule of measurement by the triangle Kepler used it to explain how an observer looking into a plane mirror sees in it the exact images of the objects that stand in front of it (fig. 6). This, too, was a phenomenon

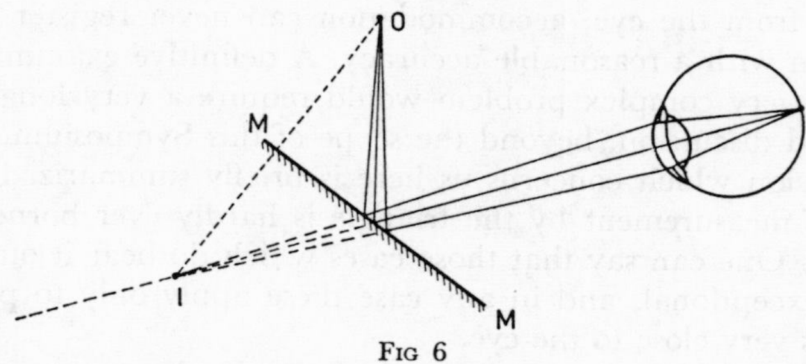

FIG 6

that had remained unexplained before him, and, as we have pointed out, had contributed considerably to the strengthening of the scepticism of ancient science.

While on the subject, let us now consider reflection in a

spherical mirror, or the passage of an image through one or more lenses (figs. 7, 8). The following is the point-by-point description of the phenomenon: a radiating point transmits a cone of rays to the optical system; these, following a series of reflections or refractions, emerge to form another cone, at a different position from the position of the point-source. From this new point the rays diverge again and fall upon the eye, where they undergo the normal process of refraction to produce the retinal image. Finally the observer must see a luminous point; but he will not see it where the point-source actually is:

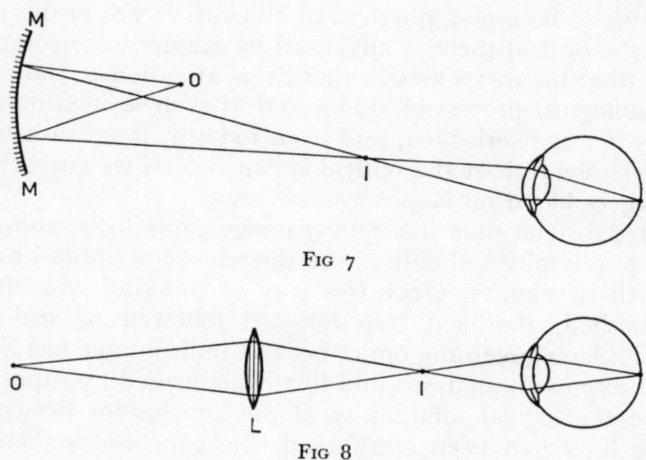

FIG 7

FIG 8

rather he will see it (according to the rule of measurement by the triangle) at the apex of the cone of the rays that penetrate the eye. Thus the luminous point is localized in a different position from that of the point-source. In other words, what is seen is not the object itself, but what has come to be known as its *image* given by the optical system through which the rays of light penetrating the eye have passed. This is the definition of the image, a term still current in the field of geometrical optics today. However arguable this definition, let us for the moment take it as valid, as is generally accepted at present. But the historical circumstances through which it passed are extremely interesting.

There is no doubt that the nature of the image *seen* at a different point from the point-source is clearly psychological, for the luminous point is localized at that precise spot by the mind of the observer. But once the rule of measurement by the triangle has been accepted, the fact that the luminous point is localized by one means or another becomes irrelevant, since it *must be* localized, come what may. Hence in our survey of the images projected by the optical system we can omit the whole physio-psychological process of vision. All that need be discussed is the *position of the apices of the cones of rays emerging from the optical system.*

This conclusion was the result of an inevitable tendency in research during the course of a century in which the renown of physics grew without ceasing and captured the admiration of the whole scientific world, to the extent of persuading every scientist to become a physicist at all costs. It was in this period that the optical theories advanced by Kepler were completely forgotten: his was a system that drew attention to the physio-psychological process of vision, and as such seemed outdated. Thus it was overlooked, and even today it is difficult to find anyone aware that the optical system which we currently use is largely based on Kepler's discovery.

At the same time the optical image came to be considered as a purely physical entity, and the science of optics itself as a branch of physics. Once this way of thinking was officially established, the next step forward followed naturally: the *physical* laws governing optics became indisputable fact, having been discussed, analysed and finally confirmed by experiment. Once the logical infallibility of the conclusions drawn from these laws had been established, the conclusions themselves became a physical *truth*. Individual observation lost all meaning: either it coincided with the conclusions drawn from the rules mentioned above, thus adding to the evidence in their support; or else it differed from them, in which case truth became the theoretical truth, whereas what had been revealed by observation was no more than the result of the imperfect and subjective means of observation at our disposal.

But to accept this line of argument one had not to insist too much that the laws of geometrical optics were based on deductions from a hypothesis and hence conditioned by the truth of this hypothesis. Insistence on the hypothesis became conspicuously less, until it was finally dropped altogether. But eventually the hypothesis was re-discovered and then it was found that it hardly ever verified in fact. This collapse in the system proved to be disastrous. All of a sudden the laws of geometrical optics were shown to be worthless. And today optics has taken a new direction. The classical system, hitherto regarded as a simple and admirable truth — surely one of the most reliable keystones of scientific enterprise — suddenly came to be considered as no more than a formal mathematical analysis — far too simple to give a complete account of actual optical phenomena. No longer was it possible to count on a connexion between the conclusions drawn from the theoretical laws, and the results of experiment.

If we look at the development of the history of optics before the great revolution initiated by Kepler and Galileo, and compare it with what came afterwards, we discover a common tendency, even if it produced quite contradictory results. First, reactionary scepticism fought shy of optical instruments, and even welcomed observation by the naked eye, fearing exaggeratedly objective interference on the part of the observer. Then came an exaggerated trust in both direct observation and observation through optical instruments, which attributed physical reality to many phenomena that are purely mental creations of the observer, such as light, colour and imagery. Related sciences have grown up round this physical basis — for example photometry and colorimetry, whose purpose is the study and measurement of specifically psychological phenomena with physical means and techniques.

It is extremely interesting to look critically at the method followed by many physicists when faced with intractable phenomena such as the perception of light, colours and also of images, and to watch the efforts they are forced to make in order to reach some repeatable conclusion. Again we are struck by the results that can be obtained by a faith which no one discusses or disputes, a faith which, in this particular case, amounts to a preconception.

It should be noted that even today the vast majority of scientists are still under the influence of this preconception. Even today scientists talk of the 'velocity of light' as though light were something that travelled to us from the stars at 300,000 kilometres per second, and not, on the contrary, a mental creation in the minds of all of us — the eyes being stimulated by electro-magnetic waves which themselves travel from the stars to us at 300,000 kilometres per second. But, if a large proportion of the scientific world still labours under the delusion that it has found a science of optics purely physical in essence, there is a new generation of opticians who have returned to the right road. They consider every true optical phenomenon as the impact of a physical agent on the organs of sight: a physiological intervention with a psychological conclusion.

Today the visual world is considered as a psychological phenomenon: a mental reconstruction, the product of all the mental faculties and experiences of the observer. Those who believed in optics as physics finally blinded themselves into considering the world as seen as an objective entity which remains the same even when the observer shuts his eyes, or else remains static where it was seen for the first time, its luminosity, its colours and its spatial distribution unchanged. Today much of this belief has gone. When an image is seen, we are confronted with the problem of getting down to the roots of what actually exists and of what has produced the simulacrum of the object. This is a far more tenable philosophical approach than that which preceded it; and it is precisely this new approach that we must thank for the discovery that it is incorrect to call the *point-source* the *luminous point* — as is still the general practice almost all the world over — because it implies acceptance of the rule of the triangle for measuring distance. Today the problem is to localize the radiating point, once the luminous point has been seen in a certain position, because in principle the two points do not coincide: at least not in depth.

We must thank this new approach, too, for making it possible to demonstrate what was always perfectly clear but never appreciated — that the apparent world we see is much smaller than the real world. It has also made it quite clear that the numerous optical illusions so familiar to us these days, with our swifter means of transportation, are the direct and unavoidable consequence of this contraction of the visual as against the real world — a contraction which, being far greater vertically than horizontally produces the most extraordinary effects in a mountain landscape or a view from an aeroplane in flight.

I will close this very brief survey of the long and controversial history of optics in ancient, medieval and modern times as I began: with the remark that this study can provide us with invaluable lessons about human behaviour in face of the arduous task of exploring the physical world and of advancing science along the road that will lead as easily and as directly as possible towards truth.

Bibliography

VASCO RONCHI, *Il cannocchiale di Galileo e la scienza del 1600* (Torino, 1958)

VASCO RONCHI, *Histoire de la lumière* (Paris, 1956)

VASCO RONCHI, *Optics: The Science of Vision* (New York, 1957)

19

Clinical and Objective Psychology: A Problem of Scientific Method

B. A. FARRELL

In the middle of the nineteenth century it was taken for granted that 'the mind' of a person was made up of an inner stream of events, which could only really be known and studied by the person himself; and that the study of mind was the proper, if not exclusive, business of philosophy. Kant had argued that the mind could not be investigated in the proper scientific way. His chief grounds reduced to: (i) that mathematics is not really applicable to the manifold of inner sense, as this has one dimension only, namely, time; and (ii) that the items in the manifold of inner sense cannot be separated and connected again at pleasure, and cannot, therefore, be subject to experiment.[1] This argument cast its forbidding shadow well into the nineteenth century.

But by the second half of the century, this Kantian view came to be rejected. Though it was still taken for granted that the mind was a stream of inner events, knowable only to the person concerned, the work of Fechner made it plain that the manifold of inner sense had another dimension, namely, intensity; and that this dimension could be varied, and in a way that enabled us to apply mathematics to it.[2] In 1879 Wundt founded the first psychological laboratory at Leipzig and proclaimed the collapse of the traditional position. He argued that experimental investigation of mind was not merely a possibility, but was the *only* way in which it could be studied. For mental events are not things but processes, and while things can be just observed, processes can only be observed by experimental means.[3] Under the stimulus primarily of Wundt and his many eminent pupils, scientific methods came to be widely and seriously applied to psychological phenomena.

[1] Kant (1786), *Metaphysische Anfangsgründe der Naturwissenschaft* (*Gesammelte Schriften*, Berlin, 1910) IV.

[2] G. T. Fechner, *Elemente der Psychophysik* (Leipzig, 1859).

[3] W. Wundt, *Grundzüge der Physiologischen Psychologie* (Heidelberg, 1874), *Grundriss der Psychologie* (Leipzig, 1896).

Nineteenth-century optimism led these workers to take it for granted that the laws of mental functioning would be discovered by the application of scientific methods; and a great development of psychological studies actually took place, both in Europe and in the United States.

This programme for psychology ran into difficulties about the beginning of the twentieth century. The difficulties centred round the fact that, in using introspective observation to try to discover the ultimate constituents of mental processes, psychologists arrived at quite conflicting results.[1] The realization grew that the introspective method was being asked to carry a load that it could not bear. Under the stimulus chiefly of the psychological work being done on animals, psychologists rejected the dominant nineteenth-century view of psychology and its objectives. The aim of science now became the study of the activity of organisms, human and infra-human. The mental phenomena connected with an individual were now no longer regarded as an inner process, open only to observation by himself. They were regarded as aspects or part of his own reactive activity as an organism, which could best be investigated by studying him as a third person, or as an animal with the capacity for speech. This investigation was to be prosecuted by methods that were strictly objective, just like those used in the other natural sciences. The generalizations, laws, and principles which underly man's behaviour were to be arrived at by the study of stimulus and response.[2]

This change in the objectives and methods of psychology was a revolutionary one. But in spite of the radical character of this departure, one central assumption of nineteenth-century psychology was retained. Psychologists continued to assume, and with added strength, that what they were doing represented *the* scientific way of investigating the field; and that by carefully and objectively applying scientific methods to the behaviour of organisms, they would discover the laws governing this behaviour. Now psychologists have indeed discovered an immense amount in the course of the past fifty years or so; and

[1] E. B. Titchener, *Experimental Psychology of the Thought Processes* (New York, 1909).

[2] J. B. Watson, "Psychology as the behaviorist sees it", *Psychological Review*, XX (1913), *Psychology from the Standpoint of a Behaviorist* (Philadelphia, 1919); A. P. Weiss, "The relation between functional and behaviorist psychology", *Psychological Review*, XXIV (1917); W. S. Hunter, *Human Behavior* (Chicago, 1919).

they have cleared the air in all sorts of ways about human and infra-human functioning. These are achievements of which the outsider is apt to be very ignorant. But what psychologists have not done is to succeed in fulfilling the high romantic hopes of the pioneers. The objective application of scientific methods in this field has not yet yielded a body of scientific knowledge comparable to the bodies of knowledge that have been developed in fields such as biochemistry, genetics, and physiology. Every generation of objective psychologists starts out imprinted with, and enthusiastic about, some captivating analogies that guide them in their work. But every generation so far has lived to see these analogies exhaust their fertility without revealing the secrets concealed in the behaviour of organisms. In this respect the history of objective psychology has been a disappointment.

At the very time that Wundt and others were fighting themselves free of the thralldom of nineteenth-century philosophy, and applying what they took to be scientific methods to psychological phenomena, a development of quite another sort was getting under way. It is well known that our knowledge of neuro-anatomy and neuro-pathology grew in a remarkable way in the course of the nineteenth century. Concurrently the medical world began to look upon and to study the disorders of mental functioning in a way that we recognize today as psychiatric.[1] The critical or turning point for our purposes was reached with the study of hysteria. When, for example, a patient complained of anaesthesia in his limbs, was this the manifestation of some organic injury, of some neural lesion, or not? If it was not, then neurologists were inclined to regard it as a symptom of malingering or imposture. The clinical study of hysteria by Janet, Breuer, and Freud led them to reject this view and to put forward the hypothesis that these cases were very genuine disorders of mental functioning.[2] This hypothesis would have been quite unimpressive if it had been offered by itself. But it was presented along with techniques which, it was claimed, were able to treat and cure these disorders. These were, in particular, the techiques of hypnotism and free association. It was clear that these modes of treatment were

[1] See, for example, J. Bucknill and D. Hack Tuke, *A Manual of Psychological Medicine* (London, 1858), and D. Hack Tuke, *A Dictionary of Psychological Medicine* (London, 1892).

[2] P. Janet, *L'État mental des hysteriques* (Paris, 1893–4) and J. Breuer and S. Freud, *Studien über Hysterie* (Leipzig and Vienna, 1895).

different from those current in ordinary medicine, as they were plainly psychological in character. It was also clear that their apparent therapeutic efficacy did lend some weight to the hypothesis that we were here concerned with disorders of a mental or psychological kind. In short, this work on hysteria led to the discovery of the neuroses. This, in turn, proved to be the key to the development of psychopathology and twentieth-century psychiatry, to psycho-analysis and to most forms of psychotherapy.

This whole development, and more especially the contribution of Freud, has transformed our view of human nature in the West in the course of the last sixty years. Indeed, it is perhaps not too misleading to oversimplify the situation and say that, just as our sociological outlook is predominantly post-Marxist, so our psychological outlook is predominantly post-Freudian in character. One social consequence of this development has been the rise of another, second group of workers in the psychological field. The first group stems, as we have noted, from Wundt and prosecutes its inquiries by methods that are strictly objective. This group is housed in academic institutions, research institutes and places of this kind. The other second group arose out of the developments in medicine that we have just discussed. Its members are housed for the most part in and around hospitals and medical bodies, and their work is connected in some capacity or other with the treatment of patients.

When objective psychologists came to notice, somewhat belatedly, that these clinical workers were claiming to study mental functioning and to make psychological discoveries, there was an initial tendency among them to reject this clinical work, and especially the work of Freud and the psycho-analysts, as quite unscientific.[1] Their reasons for doing so are quite easy to understand. This work was based on methods that were clinical in character. Thus, for example, when Freud startled the world at the turn of the century by announcing that infants have a sex impulse, which goes through various stages, his generalization was based largely on the data obtained in a clinical type of situation, namely, the psycho-analytic session. Now the central defect of clinical methods lies in the fact that it is difficult to determine how reliable and

[1] H. L. Hollingworth, *The Psychology of Functional Neuroses* (New York and London, 1920); A. Wohlgemuth, *A Critical Examination of Psycho-Analysis* (London, 1923).

valid they are, and hence difficult to assess the weight to attach to the data they produce. This defect had become more obvious in the course of the nineteenth century as the result of the development of the natural sciences; and medicine began, in consequence, to lose the high standing that it had enjoyed as a science for centuries. Moreover, whatever the difficulties of clinical methods in general, these became much more obvious and serious in the field of psychological medicine. For example, when a patient is being analysed, the data he produces differ from those produced by the ordinary patient on a hospital ward round, in that they are private, non-reproducible, and probably, in part, the product of suggestion. Further, it seemed clear that Freud's own theories, and those of others in this field, were not scientific in character, since they were not open to empirical investigation in the usual way. So some objective psychologists rejected as unscientific the psychopathology, and what one might call the clinical or dynamic psychology of that time, by pointing to the differences between the methods of clinical workers and the objective methods of science, as well as to the differences between the sorts of theories developed in the two fields. The result was to produce a situation that seemed paradoxical. The branch of psychological studies that has disappointed — as we have noted — is the branch in which a stenuous effort has been made to apply scientific methods to psychological phenomena. On the other hand, the branch of psychological study that has revolutionized our view of human nature is one that uses methods, the validity of which is uncertain, and whose concepts and generalizations are of uncertain status also.

Now let us examine this initial or early response by some objective psychologists to the development of clinical, or dynamic, psychology. That is to say, let us examine the contention that it was an unscientific enterprise. Though this was an early view of the situation, it is one that is still apt to move objective psychologists today; and hence it also has contemporary relevance.[1] For the sake of brevity let us take as our talking-point the contribution that Freud made to the development of what we have called Clinical Psychology. There is no doubt that the differences which objective psychologists pointed out between the work of the psycho-analyst and that of the ordinary scientist are good reasons for rejecting

[1] For a more recent expression of this view, see H. J. Eysenck, *Uses and Abuses of Psychology* (London, 1953) Ch. 12.

psycho-analysis as unscientific. These differences did, and still do, serve to maintain the intellectual conflict between the analysts and the objective psychologists. But there were, and are, other and deeper sources of this conflict and schism which we are all apt to overlook, and which serve to maintain the tension all the more strongly just because we are unconscious of them. Let us now go on to pick out *one* such deeper source of the trouble and examine this alone.

Suppose we challenge the objective psychologist in the following way. "You said (or say) that psycho-analysis is unscientific. Now please tell us: when is a procedure or method unscientific?" He may be tempted to meet the challenge by giving us some criterion that he considers sufficient to distinguish a scientific from an unscientific procedure. Much work in the philosophy of science has emphasized the important role played by hypotheses and generalizations that are refutable. Suppose our objective psychologist picks on this feature of science, and suggests, as his criterion, that a procedure is scientific if it does in fact give us testable generalizations. The procedure of analysts, he could then go on to say, is not scientific because it does not in fact produce testable generalizations for us.

Now let us ignore this last contention and not inquire whether it is correct that psycho-analytic methods fail to yield testable generalizations.[1] Let us notice instead that, in meeting the challenge in this way, the objective psychologist takes it for granted that we can draw a *sharp* line between a procedure that is scientific and one that is not, and he offers us a certain criterion that he takes to be sufficient for this demarcating purpose. Well, does this certain criterion answer the challenge successfully? Obviously not. It runs into the immediate objection that it is far too wide. For it allows *any* procedure or method to count as scientific provided that its use gives us testable generalizations. So if Jimmy, the new lab-boy, finds that by looking into a crystal, or by tapping in a certain way on a window of the laboratory, he can produce testable generalizations for the Professor, we shall have to describe his crystal-gazing or window-tapping as a scientific procedure. Which is absurd.

But this single and immediate failure is probably not enough to make the objective psychologist give up his compulsive wish

[1] Cf. B. A. Farrell, "Can psychoanalysis be refuted?", *Inquiry*, I (1961) 16–36.

for a sharp demarcation line between the scientific and the unscientific, and for some criteria sufficient to mark it. He may still want to draw a line, and to offer us criteria. How is he to do this? Suppose we try to come to his rescue. What we could do on his behalf is to choose a procedure that is admittedly scientific and contrast it with procedures that are admittedly not scientific at all. We could then exhibit their mutual differences and attempt to formulate criteria sufficient to distinguish between them. But this is a long-winded way of coming to the rescue. Accordingly, we shall choose a briefer but analogous method of rescue. It is one that makes use of the imaginary situation, a device with which Wittgenstein's use of language games has made us familiar.

Let us, then, imagine the following situation.[1] An empty room, with a long table at the end, a chair, and a sink and a tap. On the table are five bowls (or containers) in a row. Four of them contain colourless liquids. The fifth, on the extreme right, contains a deep red liquid. On the table there are also some empty beakers, a burner, matches, and some paper and pencils. A person is led into the room and told that he will be left alone in it and the door locked; and that, if he wants to have the door unlocked to allow him to escape, he has to solve the following problem. He has to turn the red liquid of the fifth bowl (or a sample of it) into a colourless liquid.

Now it is possible to imagine different people behaving very differently in this situation. Consider Mr. A. Let us imagine that he tries to solve the problem in the following way. He turns to the window, starts tapping on it for a time in a certain fairly regular manner, and utters series of muttered remarks between each of his short periods of tapping. Then he stops altogether, and either looks round confidently at the red bowl, or, briskly and with an air of confident expectation, takes a sample of the red liquid and mixes it with a sample of one of the other bowls. When his first attempt fails, he goes through the window-tapping routine again, apparently with more seriousness and care than he showed the first time. Let us speak of A's procedure as being an instance of a type which we shall call Method I. Next consider Mr. B. Let us suppose that he goes down at once on his knees and prays aloud to God for help. He then rises, looks at the red bowl — apparently to see

[1] I wish to thank Mr. John Andrews for calling on his knowledge of chemistry to provide me with a problem that satisfied my logical requirements.

if it is still red, and then tries the handle of the door. On finding the colour of the liquid unchanged, and the door locked, he seats himself on the chair for some time in what appears to be gloomy and abstracted rumination. He then starts praying again. Let us speak of B's procedure as an instance of a type we shall call Method II. Now consider Mr. C. He inspects the bowls, and starts using the red liquid to make mixtures, both heated and unheated, with samples from the other bowls. He notes the results of all his attempts. At last he discovers that, when he mixes roughly equal amounts of the first bowl on the extreme left and the third from the left with the red liquid, and heats the mixture, the red colour vanishes. Let us call this whole procedure an instance of a Method III. Lastly, let us look at Mr. D. He inspects the liquids by look, smell and taste. He then writes down the following :

1	2	3	4	5
?H_2SO_4	Alkali	Acid Catalytic agent?	H_2O	?Pot. Permang.

D then ignores bowl 4, uses trial and error systematically, with note keeping, on samples from 1, 2 and 3, and solves the problem more quickly than C. did. Let us call this an instance of a Method IV.

The distinctions we have just exhibited between Methods I, II, III, and IV may give the appearance of being quite artificial and absurd. For we may feel strongly inclined to say that, while it is quite easy to imagine Messrs. C and D using Methods III and IV, it is just laughable to think of anyone actually using Methods I and II. But this appearance of artificiality is quite misleading. All we need do to remove this appearance is to make the problem situation a stressful one for A and B (for example, we can suppose that A and B are political prisoners under very harsh conditions, and they are told that the correct solution will be rewarded by better treatment, or freedom). If A and B were under stress in an actual problem situation, we should have good reason to anticipate that they would exhibit any one or more of a range of odd and bizarre types of response, and that Methods I and II might be among them. Indeed, they might begin by using Method III, and then, after a period of unsuccessful effort, revert (or regress?) to Methods I and II, or some combination of them. Under stress, therefore, the behaviour of A and B is not all artificial and absurd, but something to be expected.[1]

What, now, are the outstanding characteristics of these four Methods of trying to solve the problem?

In using Method I Mr. A does not withdraw from the problem, as he would do by, for example, a passive escape into fantasy. He appears to be trying to solve it. But he does not try to solve it by making use of any of the observable properties of the liquids, or any actual experience, past or present, with the liquids. He appears to be trying to transform the red bowl in the way he wants by means of his window-tapping. He appears to treat this performance of his as causally connected with the liquids in a non-observable and paranormal way, such that, by doing his finger tapping correctly and by uttering the right remarks in connexion with it, he will succeed in decolourizing the red liquid. In short, A's way of dealing with the problem is to use magic. Method I is a magical type of procedure. In using Method II Mr. B resembles Mr. A, in that he too deals with the situation by trying to master it. But B differs from A in that he does not try to master it himself. He tries to get someone else to do so for him, rather like a child is apt to do when it cannot deal with a situation — it turns aside for aid to a grown-up person and tries to get him to come to the rescue. In our imaginary situation God is the person whom B turns to for aid. Following standard practice, we can call this a religious way of trying to deal with the situation, and Method II a religious type of procedure. In doing so we are not suggesting that everything normally covered by the term 'religious conduct' is also exhibited by B. We are merely pointing to the similarity between B's way of dealing with the situation and a typical sequence of religious activity. What they both have in common is the pattern of supplicatory behaviour towards some superior or more powerful being or beings.

Mr. C, like Messrs. A and B, tries to master the situation. Like A but unlike B, he tries to master it himself. But he differs from A in that he does not try to transform the liquids by magic, but tries to do so by discovering what actual operations

[1] J. R. Patrick, "Studies in rational behavior and emotional excitement", *Journal of Comparative Psychology*, XVII/XVIII (1934); R. R. Grinker and J. P. Spiegel, *Men under Stress* (Philadelphia, 1945) Ch. 6; E. V. Rickenbacker, "Pacific mission", *Life Magazine* (1942); E. A. Cohen, *Human Behaviour in the Concentration Camp* (London, 1954).

with the liquids will solve the problem. He tries to make this discovery by a crude, empirical trial and error, in which he relies solely on a repertoire of concepts and generalizations from his commonsense knowledge about the world. A failure does not deter him. He keeps pegging away at the problem in a persistent, reality-facing way. D's way of responding to the situation is like C's, except in one important set of respects. D does not only rely on the concepts of common sense. He also makes use of technical concepts — ones that are found in textbooks on Chemistry. For example, H_2SO_4, alkali, acid, catalyst. He appears to use the generalization, "Water dilutes potassium permanganate, and does not decolourize it", and hence ignores the bowl of water. C does not do this. D also seems to make use of his past experience and special training in the solution of problems of this sort — something that C does not appear to possess. But it is important to note that there was something D *failed* to do. Let us suppose that the bowls of liquid in fact contained, from left to right, the following solutions, each of normal strength: sulphuric acid (H_2SO_4), sodium hydroxide (NaOH), oxalic acid ($(COOH)_2$), water (H_2O), and potassium permanganate ($KMnO_4$). Now it is known that if potassium permanganate is heated in a mixture with oxalic acid and sulphuric acid (in approximately equal amounts), the potassium permanganate is decolourized. If it is heated alone, or with sodium hydroxide alone, a dirty brown precipitate is formed. What D failed to do was to make use of the relevant generalization, namely, if potassium permanganate is heated with a mixture of approximately equal amounts of sulphuric acid and oxalic acid, it is decolourized. We do not know whether he failed because he did not have this generalization in his repertoire at all, or because he just failed to make use of it on this occasion for some reason or other. Clearly, if he had made use of it, he would have solved the problem straight away. He would then have exhibited very little trial and error, and his procedure would have differed from C's much more than it did.

We can now return to the challenge confronting the objective psychologist. How is he to distinguish between a procedure that is scientific and one that is not? What criteria will be sufficient to enable him to lay down the sharp line of demarcation between them which he wishes to draw?

A procedure that was admittedly scientific would resemble Methods III and IV more closely than it would resemble

Methods I and II. Yet it is clear that procedures of types III and IV, even in the simplified form they take in our imaginary situation, are very complex indeed, and that our brief description of these procedures fails to do justice to their complexity. This strongly suggests that, in so far as a scientific procedure resembles methods of types III and IV, it will be very difficult to find any single set of criteria that distinguishes between this scientific procedure and a non-scientific one. If we wish to distinguish adequately between them, we seem likely to be forced into giving a long psycho-sociological narrative, in which we fully describe the two procedures — the scientific and the non-scientific, and exhibit their likenesses and differences in detail. So, when we long for a neat set of criteria, it would seem that we are being moved by a wish that is naïve and inappropriate.

But though we may not be able to demarcate the distinction between a scientific and a non-scientific procedure by means of a set of sufficient criteria, our discussion of Methods I to IV does suggest that the distinction between I and II on the one hand, and III and IV on the other is a very clear cut and obvious distinction. In so far, therefore, as a scientific procedure resembles III and IV, it looks as if the distinction between it and the use of magic and religion will be very sharp and marked. And this is, indeed, the case. A scientific procedure — like those of types III and IV — is a reality-facing method, which helps the user by helping him to discover the actual facts and invariances of the problem he is confronted with. The procedures of magic and religion do not possess these features; and the contrast is both abrupt and obvious. This marked difference helps to explain why we reject window-tapping as a scientific procedure, even if it *does* lead on certain occasions to testable generalizations. We reject it because it is like a piece of magic, and does not form part of a reality-facing procedure. It is for this very reason that we could use it as an example to object to the sufficient criterion of a scientific procedure that was originally proposed.

But does this marked distinction between a scientific procedure, on the one hand, and the use of magic and religion, on the other, help the objective psychologist? No, it does not. For when he rejects psycho-analysis as unscientific, he does not normally wish to say that the procedure of the psycho-analyst is unscientific because it is like the procedures of magic or religion. The psychologist does not normally have this contrast in mind — however much he may tend to think of psycho-analysis as a cult. He wants to say that psycho-analysis is unscientific in some other sense altogether.

What is this sense? The objective psychologist might reply as follows. "When Mr. D deals with the problem by using a procedure of type IV, he is behaving in a way which, in a very simplified form, is rather like the sort of behaviour we all agree about calling scientific. When, however, the psycho-analyst is confronted by a patient, he does not behave in way IV at all. He tackles his problem in a manner that could be described, at best, as crudely empirical, and that is, therefore, quite unlike the procedure used in science." Now this is a very reasonable answer. The difficulty about it is that, if we accept it, we are then unable to draw any sharp line at all between the procedure of the analysts and the procedure of the ordinary scientific worker. For, if we distinguish between them by saying that the analyst is just 'crudely empirical', and hence 'unscientific' in this sense, we are saying that the procedure of the analyst resembles Method III, and the procedure of the ordinary scientific worker resembles Method IV. But it is clear that no sharp line can be drawn between procedures of Method III and those of Method IV. This strongly suggests that no sharp line can be drawn between the crudely empirical activities of the psycho-analyst and the careful, hard-headed, objective work of the ordinary scientist.

It is not difficult to see that, and why, no sharp line can be drawn between Methods III and IV. When we first introduced these two types of method, we distinguished between them by saying, for example, that Mr. D resorted to technical concepts in using IV, whereas Mr. C did not do so in using III. Suppose we take the use or non-use of technical concepts as a defining difference between III and IV. We then have to ask: when is a concept technical and not commonsensical? For example, is the concept of an acid technical and not commonsensical? And what of the concepts of water and potassium permanganate? Mr. C might have met the latter liquid before (perhaps as a gargle!). Clearly it is quite pointless to try to delimit precisely the distinction between technical and commonsensical concepts. Suppose, moreover, that C had acquired and used the generalization that the addition of water will only dilute the red liquid further, and not decolourize it. C's procedure in the imaginary situation would then have resembled D's rather more closely than it did. We could now go on to make yet further suppositions, which would bring it closer still. But to do so would be to labour the obvious. There is no sharp line to distinguish between what we have picked out as Methods III and IV. What, then, is the relation between the two? It may help us if we think of all problem-solving procedures that are reality-facing, and imagine them placed on a continuum or spectrum. At the one end would be procedures that are at the extreme of crude empiricism. At the other would be the procedures that are at the extreme of rigorous, systematic empiricism. We shall now have to place procedures of the type we called Method III near the end of crude empiricism, and procedures of the sort we picked out as Method IV, closer, but not very near to, the other end of systematic empiricism. This picture of the relation between Methods III and IV is vague and incomplete and only a first answer. But it may also strike us as quite artificial and remote. We should then do well to note that this picture presents, in a very simplified way, the well known and widely accepted thesis that science is a development from common sense.

When, therefore, the objective psychologist is moved to reject psycho-analysis as unscientific, he does so partly because he assumes that we can draw a line round Scientific Method, which is both sharp and relevant, and which we can demarcate by means of sufficient criteria. This assumption seems to be a mistake. Scientific Method is not something around which it is appropriate to try to draw lines in this way. Hence it is inappropriate and misleading for the objective psychologist simply to maintain that psycho-analysis is an unscientific enterprise. Hence, also, it is quite inappropriate and misleading for psycho-analysts to maintain the opposite — to claim, or take it for granted, in the naïve way they are apt to do, that psycho-analysis is 'a science', and that what they are doing is perfectly respectable. Of course, these claims and counter-claims have their point and their uses. But they also go to foster and sustain the current intellectual conflict and schism between clinical and objective workers in the psychological field. In so doing these claims are a nuisance and a bore.

If we wish to contrast psycho-analysis with objective psychology, we should not resort to demarcating boundaries. Let us remember that psycho-analysis is a much more refined and subtle affair, both in theory and in methods, than anything we find in ordinary common sense. Yet psycho-analysis is, nevertheless, a manifestation of crude empiricism. It falls near this end on the spectrum of reality-facing procedures. Studies that we would all agree to call 'scientific' fall towards the other end of our spectrum or continuum. If we wish to contrast the two current approaches to the psychology of human functioning — the clinical and the objective — this would seem to be the safer way of doing so. The same conclusion applies, perhaps, *mutatis mutandis*, to the way we should contrast the use of clinical methods as a whole in psychiatry and medicine with the use of methods that are admittedly 'scientific'.

Our discussion also seems to suggest that the paradox of the present situation in psychology is not a genuine one. There is really nothing paradoxical at all in the fact that the branch of psychological inquiry whose methods are impeccable has disappointed, whereas the branch whose methods are uncertain has revolutionized our view of human nature. For the important methods developed by Freud and the clinicians were new, and a great refinement on common sense. The use of these methods succeeded in drawing our attention to features of human functioning that may or may not be genuine, but which had not been emphasized or even mentioned before this time, and which were very surprising and revolutionary in character. This achievement would only have been extraordinary if the methods of analysts and clinical workers generally were unlike scientific ones in the way that the use of magic is. But this is not the case; their methods are examples of an empiricism that is more or less crude. Now why should not methods that are crudely empirical startle us and revolutionize our view of human functioning, especially when some of the methods are new ones, as was the technique of free association? And what is there puzzling about the fact that the careful, piecemeal and rigorous work of the objective psychologists has not yet made a similar impact upon us? Just because their findings are more securely grounded, they accumulate and are integrated much more slowly.

What we have been examining is an initial or early response to the rise of clinical or dynamic psychology by objective psychologists. It is important to note that, though this attitude is still apt to affect them today, it has been supplanted to a large extent by other and different views of the matter. Thus, at the present time, perhaps, a more widely held view among them can be summarized by saying that "in comparison to the physical and biological sciences psycho-analysis is, at the best, a poor science and its procedure makes use of the weakest and most unreliable of scientific methods".[1] Clearly this view presupposes that there is some continuum between the poorer and the stronger sciences, and places psycho-analysis at the poorer end. This is in full accord with what has emerged from our examination of the early response of objective psychologists to the work of Freud. What we are confronted with today, therefore, is not a paradox, but two sets of procedures, the one much more crudely empirical and poorer than the other, operated by different groups of workers, and each closely connected with two different bodies of doctrine and ways of talking. This schism is the outcome of a certain historical situation, which we have outlined. This outcome is no doubt unfortunate, but it is quite natural and understandable. At the present time the business of the objective psychologist in this field is to sift the contribution of the clinical worker, and to absorb it into the corpus of scientific knowledge. This task is not part of the business of the psycho-analyst, or the ordinary clinical psychiatrist. He is not trained for the job, and it is silly to ask him to do it. His role in this connexion is a very different one. He has to learn to appreciate the uncertainties surrounding his own methods, concepts, and theories, and so learn to understand what the objective psychologist is up to. He may find this difficult when it requires him to surmount the limitations of his medical training. He also has to come out of his seclusion — whether in hospital or clinic or private consulting room — and learn to co-operate with the objective and hard-headed scientific investigator. Such joint efforts will help, and indeed are helping today, to mitigate the present schism in the psychological world. They may also help to take us a little further along the road towards a unified and generally accepted picture of human functioning.

[1] C. Landis and M. Bolles, *Textbook of Abnormal Psychology* (revised edition, New York, 1950) 561.

20

Changing Views of Behaviour Mechanisms

R. C. OLDFIELD

Mr. Farrell has drawn attention to a particular form of controversy which seems to some people to stultify contemporary psychology. But I think we ought to be careful to distinguish the terms in which an argument is conducted when logic (sometimes sharpened by contentiousness) is the watchword, from those which allow one to make a rough and provisional, yet significant sketch-map of the general territory within which detailed explorations are going on at a particular time. Such a sketch-map may be dissatisfying to the logician and unrewarding to the intelligent layman who seeks definitive conclusions about questions of interest or importance to him. But it forms an indispensable element in the cumbrous and rickety machinery of scientific progress. I shall suggest, not as counterblast to Mr. Farrell's handling of his subject, but by way of supplementing it, that within the context of a biological psychology this general sketch-map has undergone a profound change in the last 150 years, and in the sense of gaining unity and continuity without sacrificing articulation. But I must emphasize again that this chart — personally I dislike the term 'model' — is a piece of research equipment, not a resumé of established knowledge. This, however, can be said for it, that conceptions as apparently disparate as those of clinical and experimental neurophysiology on the one hand, and of Freudian psycho-analysis on the other, can find a place in it.

I

The reflex as paradigm

At the outset of the nineteenth century there existed four elements whose later development and interaction eventually generated the kind of picture which now underlies psychological research. These were the Cartesian dualism, the presentationism deriving from Locke, the reflex, and a growing scientific interest in the abnormalities of mental function. The history of the concept of the reflex has been admirably traced by Canguilhem[1] so far as the seventeenth and eighteenth centuries are concerned and by Liddell[2] for the nineteenth century. For our present purposes we may note in the first place that the reflex as envisaged at the beginning of the nineteenth century is *specific* — a definable stimulus gives rise, reliably, to a definable action. Secondly it is *automatic*, and thirdly it is particularly associated with that part of the central nervous system which is still present and active when an animal has been decapitated. These features served to set the genuine observable reflex action rather apart from the rest of behaviour. Though of manifest scientific interest, it could be regarded as something of limited significance. In a setting of Cartesian dualism its impact on views about what in general governs behaviour was softened. It is true, of course, that speculation had long been current in many quarters as to the possibility of regarding behaviour at large as determined by mechanisms resembling the reflex in being automatic, though of a different order of complexity.[3] But even among men who had themselves made observations upon reflex activity and other of the simpler features of behaviour, such thinking remained at a speculative level. For a fresh start, a clear experimental demonstration was needed of behaviour which, mediated by a central nervous system deprived of its foremost part, was seemingly automatic, yet much more complex and flexible in its relation to an external environment than the simple classical reflex. Such a demonstration was provided by Pierre Flourens and reported in 1824.[4] He showed, for instance, that a pigeon, from which he had removed the cerebral hemispheres (supposedly the seat of the bird's soul — if any), would fly effectively, if rather

[1] G. Canguilhem, *La formation du concept de réflexe aux XVIIe et XVIIIe siècles* (Paris, 1955).

[2] E. G. T. Liddell, *The Discovery of the Reflex* (Oxford, 1960).

[3] e.g. R. Descartes, *De homine* (1662), T. Willis, *Cerebri anatome* (1659), *De anima brutorum* (1672), and (not exclusively with scientific or philosophical intent) J. G. de la Mettrie, *L'Homme machine* (1748).

[4] Pierre Flourens, *Recherches expérimentales sur les propriétés et les fonctions du système nerveux dans les animaux vertebrées* (Paris, 1824). The demonstration in question is reported on p. 32 in the second edition of 1842. Previous experimenters had, of course, noted the survival, and capacity for locomotion, in other decapitated animals. Flourens's demonstration had a more powerful impact because it was presented in a systematic series of experiments designed to determine the functions of different parts of the cerebrum. He was probably moved to these by impatience with the *a priori* tone of the phrenologists' declarations.

clumsily, when thrown into the air. Some features of behaviour, such as complexity and flexible interaction with the external world, which had previously seemed dependent on the powers and intervention of mind, were now associated with the apparently automatic activity of a portion of the nervous system intermediate between the spinal cord and the cerebral hemispheres.

A third feature of the reflex as envisaged at the beginning of the nineteenth century — one of notable significance for future development — was that to which Wakley[1] drew attention in 1846. He pointed out that until Marshall Hall suggested in the 1830's that reflex action essentially involves influences travelling *from* the motor organs *to* the central nervous system, the conception of the reflex consisted in no more than the idea of an *act*, and involved no postulation of, or inquiry into, a *function*. From then on, growing knowledge of the fine structure of the central nervous system (made possible by rapid strides in the development of microscopy), the accurate style of physiological experiment initiated by Claude Bernard, and the demonstration in 1850 by Helmholtz of the finite velocity of nervous influence all tended to concentrate attention upon the spinal reflex and its underlying mechanisms. In the course of these investigations the adaptive and relatively complex character of some of these reactions were appreciated, even to the extent of giving rise to the strange conception of a *Rückenmarkseele*.[2] But towards the end of the nineteenth century the intensive investigations of Sherrington and his school[3] so illuminated the reflex functions of the cord that a firm basis for advance up the neural axis and for informed conjecture about the functions of its upper components was established. Magnus[4] and his colleagues established the role of the midbrain, together with the labyrinthine, muscular and visual organs which feed their information to it, in the maintenance and control of posture and locomotion. An almost complete paradigm for the explanation of one aspect of

[1] See Liddell, op. cit. p. 65.

[2] Ibid. pp. 68 ff., p. 86. One of the most forthright statements was that of Pflüger in 1853, who said that if he divided the spinal cord of a cat into two parts, the cat acquired two souls. According to Liddell, the *Rückenmarkseele*, though not immortal, lingered on till the close of the century.

[3] C. S. Sherrington, *Selected Writings*, ed. Denny-Brown (London, 1939).

[4] R. Magnus, *Körperstellung* (Berlin, 1924).

complex everyday behaviour, exhibiting the hierarchical organization of its underlying mechanism, emerged. The spinal cat exhibits in the stretch reflex an elementary basis for postural stability and in the flexor and crossed extensor reflexes an underlying pattern of the alternation required for walking. The decerebrate animal, in which the centres of the medulla are spared to exercise their control over these simple spinal functions, shows exaggerated anti-gravity activity and stands rigidly, not proof against contingent disturbances of its postural stability. By a higher cut which preserves mechanisms at the midbrain level, the exaggerated tone of the decerebrate animal disappears and normal stance capable of maintenance in the face of adventitious disturbances is present. Remove only the cerebral cortex and a vastly more complex control system comes into play which allows locomotion but fails to make provision for initiative or the use of past experience. So are revealed the essential features of organization in the central nervous system. At each level there are purposeful adjustive mechanisms, the contribution of each becoming manifest as the machinery is stripped down. Each level higher than the last not only makes use of the wider range of sensory information available to it, but, by exercising control over the levels inferior to it, utilizes them to promote effective adaptive behaviour in the organism as a whole.

II
Dissolution as "the great analyst"[1]

These same basic features of neural organization may be discerned by observation of the 'dissolution' effected by disease, and it is in this connexion that a second theme enters the story. This theme is particularly associated with the name of John Hughlings Jackson,[2] the obscurity and repetitiveness of whose verbal formulations effectively concealed from his contemporaries the remarkable insight which contemporary neurology so fully acknowledges. Jackson's clinical acumen was fully appreciated by his immediate colleagues, but the force and incisiveness of his interpretive principles seem to have impinged almost alone on Sigmund Freud and a little later on two other neurologists with psychological interests — Arnold Pick and

[1] Sherrington, op. cit. p. 497.
[2] J. Hughlings Jackson, *Selected Writings*, ed. Taylor (London, 1931).

Henry Head.[1] The multifarious ramifications of these principles developed by Jackson make it impossible to give any but the most cursory account of them here. We may try to express their essence as follows.

In his clinical observations, Jackson concentrated on the analysis of disturbed function, refusing to join his contemporaries in a search for cerebral localizations. Whether in the field of dysphasia, of epilepsy, of the degenerative diseases of the nervous system or of the insanities, he envisaged the breakdown as a 'dissolution' of a hierarchical organization, thus foreshadowing in a wider field the more precise findings of later nineteenth-century neurophysiologists. The most elaborate, least automatic functions — those most recently evolved — are the first to suffer in disease. The symptoms, often apparently bizarre, represent the activity of lower levels of the neural hierarchy which are now the only ones left to the organism, uncontrolled by those superior levels which the disorder has rendered inactive. When Jackson first expressed these views, Sherrington had not yet demonstrated decerebrate rigidity, but the activity of the spinal animal is analogous to that of the cerebrally impaired patient. The dysphasic, for instance, is often unable to put out his tongue as a voluntary act in response to the command to do so, and may, indeed, seek to comply by pulling it out with his fingers. Yet a minute later he protrudes it spontaneously and without difficulty in order to lick his lips. The patient who has lost all power of effective propositional speech may yet, when spurred by feeling, utter crude expressions of a stereotyped character. Such 'inferior speech' represents the activity of a more automatic, less voluntary, level of the speech mechanism than that which operates in voluntary propositional speech. The phenomena of epilepsy, chorea and paralysis agitans all illustrate the same principle. There is a tendency for those parts of the body which are normally most concerned with the most voluntary — least automatic — functions, and controlled by the highest functional level of the nervous system, to be the first, and at any given stage of dissolution the most severely, affected. Thus the thumb and index finger, the hand, the arm, the leg and

[1] S. Freud, *Zur Auffassung der Aphasien* (Wien, 1891). Pick dedicated his *Die Agrammatische Sprachstörungen* (1913) to Jackson — 'The deepest thinker in neuropathology of the last century'. Head's exposition of Jackson's principles is almost indispensable in getting a sound start on his writings: H. Head, *Aphasia and Kindred Disorders of Speech* (2 vols., Cambridge, 1926).

the trunk are affected in that order. In the insanities, delusions, hallucinations and confabulations are all the positive results of the activity of lower functional levels released from higher control. The patient who misrecognizes his nurse as his wife does so as a result of the positive activity of the remaining functional levels. The inactivity of the highest level is responsible only for the negative fact that he fails to recognize her as his nurse. The same principles may be applied to the interpretation of dreaming. In sleep there is a natural temporary dissolution. The dream represents the positive activity of the highest level remaining in action. Jackson did not hesitate to extend the same conceptual framework to an analysis of the psychology of joking, in which punning represents the lowest functional level!

Jackson's *schema* of hierarchically organized 'levels' was devised primarily in the interests of bringing order into clinical observation. He hesitated to define their number, their interrelationships or their whereabouts in the central nervous system. As regards number, he was generally inclined to speak in terms of three, or sometimes four, main levels, but emphasized the complexity of their interconnexions. On one aspect of their functional relationship, however, he is fairly explicit, if somewhat forbidding. As regards, for instance, the representation of motor functions in the three levels:

> . . . the middle motor centres represent over again in more complex, etc. ways, what the lowest motor centres represented in simpler ways and by intermediation of those lower centres; by re-re-represent I mean that the highest motor centres represent over again what the middle motor centres (re-representative centres) have represented and by intermediation of those middle motor centres in most complex, etc. ways.[1]

Jackson's general theoretical position naturally brought him to consider the relationships of the voluntary and the automatic. Leaning heavily, as he did, upon the formulations of Herbert Spencer, it cannot be said that he reached a view about this which would stand up to philosophical analysis. But for his practical intent to advance neurology and psychology it will serve.

> The expression 'most voluntary' when used in contrast to 'most automatic' is very objectionable [he writes], it is a compound of a psychological and a physiological term. Instead of it, I suggest the

[1] Jackson, op. cit. II, 432 f.

expression 'least automatic', which is rigidly equivalent to what is called 'most voluntary'.

He continues:

. . . we say that the progress in evolution is from the most to the least automatic, and thus that the highest centres are the least automatic. It is not a mere question of words. The substituted expression does not imply an abrupt division into the voluntary and the automatic, but implies degrees from most to least automatic, and that a man, physically regarded, is an automaton, the highest parts of his nervous system (highest centres) being least automatic; the substituted term does not bring the will, a psychical state, into a purely physical sphere.[1]

Later, Henry Head was to re-phrase this idea more cautiously when he wrote: "There is no separation of mind and body so long as we are examining the consequences of disintegration."[2]

Head, a profound admirer and ardent exponent of Jackson's views, had the advantage of close acquaintance with the work of Sherrington and his school during the time when clearer conceptions of spinal function were at last rapidly emerging. His own contribution includes an attempt to clarify and define more closely than Jackson succeeded in doing the relationship of consciousness to the organized neural mechanisms subserving behaviour. He is at one with Jackson in rejecting the Cartesian dualism. Consciousness is not a self-contained entity or form of activity which, supervening over the highest neural level, performs tasks which the nervous system alone is incapable of. Which features of the environment and of the activities of the organism find representation in consciousness at any given time depends upon a number of factors. Head points to many examples in the fields of sensation and of skilled motor activity. Thus in binocular rivalry there is complete suppression of the incoming impulses from one eye. Similarly in homonymous hemianopia occasioned by damage to a cerebral hemisphere, there is in most cases a complete lack of awareness of the absence of half the visual field. Other examples may be adduced from the bodily sensations and pain. In the same way, many highly complex skilled acts may be carried out without the intervention of consciousness, which may at the same time be fully occupied with other matters. These are the *secondary automatisms* first clearly described and discussed by

[1] Jackson, ibid. p. 68. [2] Head, op. cit. I, 495.

David Hartley.[1] Of greater import, in a scientific sense, than the degree of conscious awareness attaching to any particular activity, is the physiological question of the state of 'vigilance' manifested by that level of the nervous system which is involved in its performance. To say that any given part of the nervous system is in a high state of vigilance is to say that its physiological efficiency in mediating the most elaborate and adaptive functions which are proper to it is at or near its maximum. Thus the spinal animal which is still in a state of shock following the transection of the cord, or under narcosis, manifests only primitive reflex activity. As the shock or the narcosis passes off, more and more elaborate reactions are shown until in the chronic spinal animal there are present all those more complex reflex patterns of which it is capable. In the same way, the intact human organism, whose cerebral cortex is affected by fatigue, narcosis, disease or even anxiety, exhibits behaviour of a less refined, skilful or discriminative kind. This condition may involve increased conscious awareness of activities, such as walking, writing or speaking which normally can proceed automatically while the attention is directed on other things. And not only is the perfection of the highest level activity thus diluted, but partial loss of control over lower levels may result in the emergence of forms of behaviour which are to be attributed to these lower levels:

> Consciousness stands in the same relation to the vigilance of the higher centres as adapted and purposive reflexes to that of those of lower rank in the neural hierarchy. When vigilance is high, mind and body are poised in readiness to respond to any event external or internal. But if it is lowered by injury, want of nutrition, chloroform or any other toxic influence, these high grade functions may suffer in general or in part, whether they are associated with consciousness or not. *There is no absolute criterion by which an external observer can distinguish conscious from unconscious behaviour*[2] [my italics].

III
Retrogression from consciousness

For all his excursions into the psychology of language, dreaming and the insanities, there might seem superficially to be a great gap between the speculative interpretations of

[1] D. Hartley, *Observations on Man, his Frame, his Duties and his Expectations* (2 vols., 1749).

[2] Head, op. cit. I, 496.

Jackson and those of Freud. Freud is commonly regarded as having early abandoned the hope of achieving continuity between physiology and psychology. This view, however, is not accurate. What Freud abandoned was the hope that he himself might arrive at any fresh integration of the physiological and the psychological.

> I have no inclination [he wrote in 1898] to keep the domain of the psychological floating, as it were, in the air, without any organic foundation. But I have no knowledge, neither theoretically nor therapeutically, beyond this conviction, so I have to conduct myself as if I had only the psychological before me.

And in 1917:

> Psycho-analysis hopes to discover the common ground on which the coming together of bodily and mental disturbance will become intelligible. To do so it must keep free of any alien preconceptions of an anatomical, chemical or physiological nature, and work throughout with purely psychological auxiliary hypotheses.[1]

The operative word is 'alien'. There is no reason to suppose that Freud ever abandoned this position. His clinical work, and the varying provisional conclusions he drew, form the culmination of increasingly intensive interest in what might be called the non-Cartesian aspects of mind which date from the late eighteenth century. Mesmer excited Europe with curious demonstrations; humanitarians such as Pinel, Hack Tuke, and Benjamin Rush, radically revised the treatment, and recommended the scientific study, of lunatics; and the liberating surge of the romantic movement encouraged exploration of mental phenomena of a kind which did not obviously conform with the tidy pictures of the mind favoured by James Mill and the Scottish philosophers. A flood of excited speculation and empirical dabbling in hypnosis, hallucination and the occult spread throughout the educated classes of Western Europe, especially in France. Bernheim and Liébault, bent on the cure or alleviation of mental disturbance, turned up many surprising things which could hardly be viewed as a breakdown of the mind envisaged by Descartes or Locke. Herbart[2] took the first

[1] Quoted by E. Jones, *Sigmund Freud: Life and Work* (London, 1953) I, 433.

[2] J. F. Herbart, *Psychologie neu gegründet auf Erfahrung, Metaphysik und Mathematik* (1842–5). In drawing his basic psychological stock-in-trade from Herbart, Freud was more fortunate than was Hughlings Jackson with Herbert Spencer. Leibniz's original contribution to the notion of unconscious processes is well known.

formal steps towards theoretical acknowledgement of unconscious processes. As Jackson embarked on the study of disturbances of higher nervous function, Charcot was engaged on his classical comparison of the organic anaesthesias and paralyses with those which, failing to comply with the requirements of known anatomical structure, came to be called hysterical. He thus stirred Janet and Freud to a whole-hearted study of more elaborate eruptions of the unconscious in the shape of amnesias, phobias and automatisms.

Freud, starting with the study of hysteria and the anxiety neuroses by the methods of hypnosis, was soon led by his invention of analysis to a more effective way of uncovering the background of consciousness. A certain measure of exploration of the human organism from above downwards, to supplement the physiological approach from below upwards, was thus made possible. The psycho-analytic method soon brought the study of the dream into prominence and in connexion with this Freud was led to introduce his concept of regression. There seems little doubt that he got the idea for this from Hughlings Jackson, and amid all the changing emphases of his theoretical formulations and all the twists and turns of interpretative principles he used as his clinical experience widened, this notion remained central.

In 1891 Freud wrote a short monograph on aphasia.[1] In this, avowedly basing his treatment on Jackson's principles, Freud attacks the localizationist doctrines then almost universal amongst his contemporaries and urges the need for psychological analysis:

> In assessing the functions of the speech apparatus under pathological conditions [writes Freud] we are adopting as a guiding principle Hughlings Jackson's doctrine that all these modes of reaction represent instances of functional retrogression (disinvolution) of a highly organized apparatus, and therefore correspond to previous states of its functional development. This means that, under all circumstances, an arrangement of associations which, having been acquired later, belongs to a higher level of functioning, would be lost, while an earlier and simpler one will be preserved.[2]

The German word used by Freud for "retrogression" (disinvolution or dissolution) is *Rückbildung*. The term *Regression* was first to appear in the *Traumdeutung*.[3] In this work the concept of regression is expounded in a theoretical setting

[1] Freud, op. cit. (1891). [2] Ibid. p. 87.

[3] S. Freud, *The Interpretation of Dreams* (1900), in *Complete Psychological Works of Freud* (London, 1953) V.

deriving from the unfinished *Project for a Scientific Psychology* (1895). This fulfils ". . . a requirement with which we have long been familiar, namely that the psychical apparatus must be constructed like a reflex apparatus. Reflex processes remain the model of every psychical function."[1] Intervening between the perceptual input to the apparatus and the motor output are a succession of memory factors. These do not represent separate memories but separate ways in which memories are organized. In a paragraph added in 1914, Freud remarks,

> . . . regression plays a no less important part in the theory of the formation of neurotic symptoms than it does in that of dreams. Three kinds of regression are thus to be distinguished: (a) *topographical* regression, in the sense of the schematic picture of the ψ-systems which we have explained above; (b) *temporal* regression, insofar as what is in question is a harking back to old psychical structures; and (c) *formal* regression, where primitive methods of expression and representation take the place of the usual ones. All these three kinds of regression are, however, one at bottom and occur together as a rule; for what is older in time is more primitive in form and in psychical topography lies nearer to the perceptual end.[2]

Freud's analysis of the mechanism by which perceptual presentations are thrown up in dreaming and in hallucination is almost identical with that of Jackson.

While it is clear that in many points of detail Freud's general formulation does not coincide with that of Jackson, both advocated, for use in a biological psychology, a sketch map in which the subject matter, from the highest to the lowest levels, is delineated in terms of function. Neither would have thought of denying the indispensability of studying structures and the mechanics proper to them as a way of advancing understanding of function. Freud, as we have seen, himself abandoned such a study when he saw a vast territory of fresh phenomena open before him. Today, new technical resources and rapid advances in the understanding of physiological mechanisms by ascent from below have rather tended to induce a phase of development opposite to that of Freud.

Until recently, the experimental psychologist might reasonably have been accused of too narrow a preoccupation with the problems of a single, namely the highest, level of the neural hierarchy. This was partly due to the towering prestige of the work of Pavlov, and partly the result of a failure to shake off

[1] Ibid. p. 538.

[2] Ibid. p. 548.

the traditional dualism. The cerebral cortex alone seemed necessarily the seat of consciousness, of the 'highest' capacities of the organism, such as learning, perception and intelligence, with which psychologists were supposed to concern themselves, and of the conditioned reflexes in terms of which it was hoped the mechanisms underlying these capacities might be analysed. But latterly, partly through a general widening of interest and partly by reason of an increasingly close relationship with physiologists, psychologists have been led to study a variety of matters, all of which demand consideration in terms of different functional levels and their interactions. Perhaps most outstanding in this connexion has been the stimulus deriving from cybernetics to view the control of human activity in terms of a system of mechanisms, broadly speaking hierarchical, but with multiple interconnexions between them. Anatomical advances have shown how complex is the system of interconnexions which must be taken into account in interpreting function.[1] It is abundantly evident that the simple kind of scheme proposed by Hughlings Jackson is hopelessly inadequate in detail. But current trends of work cannot dispense with the general principle of hierarchical organization. We might instance contemporary interest in the role of sensory stimulation in the maintenance of consciousness; developments in the analysis, behavioural and physiological, of appetitive, instinctive and emotional processes; the effort which is at present being put into the unravelling of the mechanisms of selective attention; the attempt to understand that form of perception which has been called '*sub*ception', that is, of the demonstrable effects of stimuli too feeble to evoke a threshold judgment; and the experimental analysis of the breakdown of manual and other bodily skills. These by no means exhaust present-day themes in experimental psychology and related scientific fields. Many problems, that for instance of the neural mechanisms of visual pattern-discrimination, can at present be tackled without hypotheses involving more than one level. But the general sketch-map, which everyone who is actively working to try and understand behaviour must willy-nilly create for himself, can no longer be an adequate one unless it incorporates features we owe to Pierre Flourens, to John Hughlings Jackson, to Charles Sherrington and to Sigmund Freud.

[1] A good example is afforded by the cerebral structures (the limbic lobe, hypothalamus and prefrontal cortex) now being intensively studied in connexion with temperament and emotion.

We have traced one, though I think a central, theme in the history of scientific thought about the behaviour of the organism. What can be said in this connexion about the questions this Symposium is supposed to be specially concerned with — about the origins, social, personal, technical and historical of the kind of model involved? It is not difficult to point to a number of particular factors which, on a superficial view at any rate, might be held of causal significance. But whether to do this is to go very far in unravelling the complex aetiology of scientific change may be doubted. A discovery or a fresh formulation is not a symptom of an exogenous disease-entity. It is the reaction of an individual to external *and internal* circumstances, events and needs. I hope that some of these which are external to the individual may have emerged from my account. The internal factors, about which we can generally say little, remain, to me at least, by far the more interesting.

Commentaries

Commentary by K. E. Rothschuh

On the Importance of Models in Physiology

In his carefully thought-out paper Mr. Canguilhem* has drawn attention to the fundamental shortcomings of certain cybernetic models of nervous actions. Indeed — if I understand him correctly — his misgivings predominate to such an extent that he regards the whole enterprise of constructing and carrying out research by means of such models as an inadequate method for the explanation of complex neurophysiological processes. On the one hand I share his misgivings about their uncritical application, but on the other hand I can see the general advantages of such models in physiology. This requires further analysis.

To begin with, on the topic of *the classification of models*, let it be said that we can distinguish between 'thought-models' (*Gedankenmodelle*) (or theories) and concrete or 'real models' (*Realmodelle*), and further between analogous and homologous models.

I
Thought-models

The empirical sciences[1] are at pains to transfer their verified experience into a system of definitions which conflict neither with experience nor with themselves. This body of experience, taken as a whole and including the connexions between its different aspects, forms a mental image of scientific knowledges. While observing a certain formalism in research, science endeavours to approach this picture of the world. It is the

* Mr. Canguilhem was prevented by illness from being present at the Symposium.

[1] C. Bernard, *Introduction a l'étude de la médecine expérimentale* (Paris, 1865; English trans. by H. C. Green, Dover Publications, New York, 1957; German trans. ed. K. E. Rothschuh in *Sudhoffs Klassiker der Medizin*, Leipzig, 1961).

'pentodos' of the inductive, experimental and empirical method.

It comprises the following steps:

(1) Observations form the stimulus and the starting-point for reflections (=starting-point).
(2) We try to understand the observation by means of a theoretical model or hypothesis (=an inductive generalization).
(3) From the hypothesis we derive a logical conclusion which can be tested by an experiment (=deduction).
(4) We plan the method of testing for these conclusions and carry out the experiment (=test).
(5) We interpret the results for the judgement of our model. The assumption is either confirmed (verified) or not confirmed (disproved) (=evaluation).

The results of these methods are examined to see whether they contradict the known results. Then they are fitted into the picture of relationships. In this way science endeavours to establish *an isomorphous thought-model of reality* with a growing accuracy of description. Thus science is employed on the one hand in the extension of experience and on the other in the theoretical mastery of it. 'Correctness' in science lies in the conformity of the thought-model and the conclusions drawn from it with the experienced reality. Consequently the thought-model is abstract and poorer in details than reality. It strives to attain knowledge of the relations which are decisive in the interpretation and mastery of this experienced reality. Abundance of details, convergence and proof determine its value. If we view comprehensive generalizations in this sense as models of reality, then all scientific work is work on a thought-model.

In physiology a model or a theory can contain either a small section of reality, for example the process of nerve-stimulation, or a wide field, for example a 'theory of the organism'.[1] According to this distinction all theoretical work in the empirical sciences can be termed 'model-work'.

II

Real models of physiological functions

All real, artificial models of physiological processes are imitations. The more they resemble the original in their

[1] K. E. Rothschuh, *Theorie des Organismus* (München, 1959).

structure or their functioning the better they are. The material of which they are made is almost always different from that of the original. Amongst the models which are constructed for the purpose of imitating physiological processes we can distinguish between two types with regard to form: (*a*) the analogous model, and (*b*) the homologous model. The boundaries are not completely clear, since it is possible that certain parts of the same model can be termed analogous and others homologous.

(*a*) *Analogous models* are homoeomorphous, that is they have in some respect (shape, structure of the process) a great resemblance to the original. They are made of extraneous material, and because the processes imitated 'in spite of all formal similarity of effect' consist of other materials, they are furthermore mostly hetero-causal. The model produces effects resembling those of the original by means of different cause-and-effect relationships. Physiology possesses several such homoiomorphous but heterocausal, analogous models, for example Lillies's model of nerve excitation (1923)[1] and Gerstner's model of the nerve-cell rhythm (1950). Other examples are the 'feed-back' models of 'animals' built by technicians, for instance Grey Walter's tortoise and Brunisma's dog.[2] Such models are valuable as a means of demonstration. They contain no explanations, but are 'imitations' as Canguilhem rightly says.

(*b*) *Homologous models* are more or less isomorphous and isocausal, and are made so far as possible of the same materials as the original. They are a combination of links with similar actions (isofinal) and properties, and operate according to similar cause-and-effect relationships. Physiology also possesses such homologous models, for example in E. H. Weber's rubber-tube model (1825) and Rollett's improved model of the circulation of the blood (1880),[3] and further in Donder's model of respiration (*c.* 1860).[4] In the models of the circulation, the movement of the blood is studied in an *elastic* system, also the pulse-wave and the behaviour of the pressure when a certain

[1] For the models of Lillie, Weber, Rollet, Marey, Ludwig and Cyon, see Rothschuh, *Entwicklungsgeschichte physiologischer Probleme in Tabellenform* (München, 1952).

[2] A. H. Brunisma, *Roboter-Schaltungen* (Eindhoven, 1958).

[3] See K. E. Rothschuh, "Über Kreislaüfschemata und Kreislaüfmodelle seit den Zeiten von William Harvey (1578–1657)", *Zeitschrift für Kreislaüfforschung*, XLVI (1957) 241–49.

[4] H. Drischel, "Untersuchungen über die Dynamik des Lichtreflexes der menschlichen Pupille", *Pflügers Archiv,* CCLXIV (1957) 145–69.

volume is transported against a variable resistance. Another model is that of Marey (1857) in which, by means of the elasticity of the walls of the blood vessels, an intermittent flow is changed to a continuous flow.

In physiology real models have a didactic, methodical and heuristic importance. In every case they assist demonstration and are good visual aids, as for example Donder's model of the respiratory mechanism. They help research in many ways. In certain cases, as in that of the models of the circulation of the blood, they allow the variation of conditions (e.g. modulus of elasticity, volume) which we cannot alter at will in the body or which we cannot influence *separately* in isolation from the accidental conditions in the body. Finally, real models occasionally reveal parts of processes, which stimulate a closer analysis of the natural processes. In this way the oscillation of the technical regulators in the reaction of the pupil to light could be demonstrated.[1] Lillies's model proved itself to be especially interesting for research.

III

The theory of the control circuit and cybernetic models

In modern neurophysiology the use of technical principles and of the idea of the model have proved themselves fruitful in two fields: first in the observation of certain regulating mechanisms as technical regulators, and secondly in the interpretation of central nervous actions through the application of cybernetic principles.

(a) *Physiological regulation as the product of control circuits*

The organism contains manifold organs, which automatically keep functional values constant by means of reflexes, as for example in blood pressure, body temperature, blood sugar and so on. Thus we speak of regulation of the blood pressure, temperature regulation, etc. Recently, under the influence of the regulator technique, interest in this field has greatly increased. In an age of automation, of machines and instruments, technicians are equipping themselves to an ever-increasing extent with automatic, regulatory devices, which replace human direction, supervision and control. It was not long

[1] B. Hassenstein, "Die bisherige Rolle der Kybernetik in der biologischen Forschung", *Naturwissenschafthiches Rundschau*, XIII (1960) 349, 373, 419.

before the analogies between the automatic regulations of the organism and the technical mechanisms of the control circuit were noticed.[1] The analogy lies in the first place in the total action of the biological and technical control mechanisms, and further in the role of the parts. In spite of entirely different causal mechanisms (biological, electrical and mechanical), the components of the control circuit mechanism play essentially the same role. Thus the physiologists considered it useful to take over the vocabulary of the regulation-technicians, because in this way many biological processes can be formulated more uniformly than hitherto.

We distinguish between *steady-state regulators* and *follow-up regulators*. Common to both is the automatic control, the function of which is to see that deviations from the prescribed value are automatically corrected. For example, every refrigerator contains a *steady-state regulator*. The deviation from the prescribed value itself controls the mechanism which brings it back to this value, thus forming a control 'circuit'. In the organism there are receptors and afferent and efferent paths, with corrective links, which are similarly connected in a circuit, as a reflex-arc with information of the result and 'feed-back'. The analogy is good. As examples I would name the depressor reflex in the regulation of blood pressure[2] and the reaction of the pupil to the maintenance of a constant intensity of illumination on the retina.[3]

In the *follow-up regulators*, the action of a dependent mechanism automatically follows a continuously changing prescribed value. Similarly in the organism muscular strength follows the varying power requirements. The participation of a 'feed-back' mechanism was first recognized by R. Wagner.[4] The exact method of operation of the muscle spindle as a measuring gauge (dilator receptor), the role of the afferents, and so on, was clarified by Matthew and Granit amongst others. Thus the analogies then between technical and biological regulators in their effect and in their structure are in fact astonishing. Furthermore the imitation of biological function by the goal-directed functioning of the follow-up regulators is theoretically interesting. Amongst other things they disclose that in the organism something expedient, something teleological can be attained by means of a causal 'feed-back' process. This does

[1] See p. 592, n. 1. [2] See p. 593, n. 1.

[3] R. Wagner, *Probleme und Beispiele biologischer Regelung* (Stuttgart, 1954).

[4] Ibid.

not of course explain the existence of this process of regulation, merely its mechanism.

The control circuit theory is of considerable importance for physiological regulation. As a closer analysis shows, certain examples of regulation, for instance the regulation of blood pressure or the reaction of the pupil, have operative parts and processes similar to those of the technical regulators (receptors, transformation of signals, centres of measurement and regulation), namely, effectors for the correction of the value of regulation. The diagrams of the control mechanisms are isomorphous models of the structure. This permits the adoption of the technical conceptions of the model of the control circuit, and gives this heuristic importance for research. It is theoretically remarkable that the example of the control circuit shows that a decidedly teleological and biological process is to be understood as a causal connexion of this kind. *The danger of the control circuit theory* lies in the transference of this concept to every biological occurrence, even when the elements mentioned above are definitely not present, for example in the self-regulation of cell dimensions,[1] in the formation of antibodies in tissues, or in the development of leucocytosis or of granulation tissue in the healing of a wound.[2] The drawing of analogies is meaningless here. And it must not be overlooked that biological control circuits are closed, and yet are woven into the whole system of the organism, in which a multitude of control circuits operate together. Often the control element of one control circuit is at the same time an effective valve in another control circuit.[3] Technical control circuits are as a rule open, that is their prescribed value is adjusted from without, while biological control circuits are part of a closed system.

(b) *The cybernetic thought and control models*

A very special group is that of the cybernetic models. By cybernetics we mean the science of information and its reception, transmission, storage and use by systems for the evaluation of this information. Cybernetic apparatuses are therefore technical arrangements, which receive and use information. To this group belong for example calculating and other such

[1] A. C. Drogendijk, "Der kybernetische Krankheitsbegriff", *München. Med. Wschr.* (1960) 2577.

[2] H. Schaefer, *Die Stellung der Regelungstheorie im System der Wissenschaft* (in Mittelstädt, *Regelungsvorgänge in der Biologie*, München, 1956) 26 ff.

[3] N. Wiener, *Cybernetics* (Paris, 1958).

machines. The structural elements of these cybernetic instruments are tubes, condensers, rheostats, valves, cables, etc. There is no affinity between them and neurophysiological processes, nor do they operate with an isocausal mode of action. But as far as the total field of action is concerned, they have a resemblance to certain actions of the central nervous system. For the organism — or to be more precise its nervous system — is likewise continuously receiving information from the environment. These environmental stimuli become excitations of sense and nerve, that is they become information. Thus the sense organs are organs which receive and filter out information, the nerves being connecting links transmitting the information, and the central nervous system the centre where the information is used. Further analogies come from the fact that in both cases, the technical and the biological, qualitative phenomena are transformed into quantitative values, and that the storage of information corresponds to memory. The formal analogy is considerable. But we are dealing with heterocausal and heteromaterial analogies of the functioning of the nervous system.

The cybernetic models of Grey Walter and Brunisma amongst others, which imitate the behaviour of animals, are without doubt analogous models. Their apparatus is extremely ingeniously equipped, eyes and ears are imitated by means of photocells and microphones, and the nervous system by means of cybernetic arrangements. These models show phenomena analogous to spontaneity, memory, use of environmental stimuli and experience, and so on. Even if they are rather more technical playthings than scientific instruments, yet they give a strong stimulation to research into the problem of making intelligible the functions of the nervous system including the sense organs, as a system which receives, stores and uses information. Herein lies the value of these models. Of course it must not in the meantime be forgotten that the organism-like action of the cybernetic models owes its origin to a human designer.

In conclusion, I consider the thought- and real-models in physiology as neither dangerous nor misleading, if we are informed about their nature and limits. It is not necessarily a fault that they operate with a reduction of the complexity present in real life. Each grasp of a complexity has begun with insight into its elements. So let us wait and see where the research with models will lead us.

Commentary by J. S. Wilkie

Mr. Glass writes (p. 533):

> Probably far greater than any influence of a master's experimental work upon the development of his pupils is generally that teacher's way of looking at things, his basic philosophy of nature, his fund of conceptual models. Certainly this was true in the relation of Nägeli to his students.

Since Mr. Glass mentions only two students of Nägeli (Weismann and Correns) and since he seems clearly to exclude Correns from the class of those adversely influenced by Nägeli, we must assume (what is already reasonably clear from the context) that it is Weismann's behaviour which is being attributed to Nägeli's influence. Indeed, this has already been made clear in the passage (p. 532) which reads:

> It would seem that the consequence of Nägeli's thinking in such a mode, of fitting the organisms into his own conceptual pattern, was to lead him to despise the work of Mendel as purely limited and empirical. . . . This tendency appears to have carried over into the thinking of August Weismann, Nägeli's most eminent pupil. In spite of the brilliant development by Weismann of the history of the ids . . . Weismann somehow failed to see the relation of his conceptual model to the Mendelian analysis of inheritance, when this was rediscovered in 1900.

Mr. Glass attributes Nägeli's "way of looking at things, his basic philosophy of nature" to the circumstance that Nägeli "in his youth spent two years studying Hegelian philosophy in Berlin". We have here, then, the assertion of a most interesting causal sequence: Hegel infects Nägeli with a mistaken view of the nature of scientific investigation, and Nägeli infects Weismann, and so Weismann in 1900 is as incapable of appreciating Mendel as was Nägeli in 1866. Such extraneous influences in the development of scientific thought are always of major interest, particularly when they stem from the thought of a great philosopher. But such chains of influence are notoriously difficult to demonstrate.

What is the evidence for this particular chain? In the first place, there seems to me to be a far more probable cause of Weismann's inability to appreciate Mendel's work. It seems to me indubitable that the reason why it was Sutton who first produced a consistent theory linking chromosome-behaviour with Mendelism was this: Sutton was the first observer to *see* the diploid chromosome set as a set of pairs of which each pair differed from every other pair.[1] This is essential to the theory. Weismann, who had considerable authority in this field, had early denied that the chromosome set (of somatic cells) consists of a set of dissimilar pairs; and this idea, consistently and tenaciously maintained by Weismann, could only be negated by actual observation.

Weismann's theory enabled him to produce a mathematical expression, of a rudimentary kind, for multifactorial determination, but was not able to assimilate the idea of determination by factor-pairs. This, surely, is a natural reason for Weismann's inability, at the age of sixty-six, to adjust his mind to the new theory; and it seems to me an axiom of the writing of the history of science that, if an internal factor, that is, one within his set of scientific ideas, can account for a scientist's behaviour in the execution of his task *as* scientist, then no external factor should be appealed to, unless the evidence for it is overwhelming.

Now, what is the evidence for the chain of influence starting with Hegel? I have scrutinized the standard biographies of Nägeli and of Weismann[2], and I cannot find any evidence that Nägeli and Weismann were ever together in the same university. Moreover, although neither was a person of narrow professional interests, Weismann was as clearly a zoologist as Nägeli was a botanist. And what is the evidence for the tenacious myth that Nägeli was an Hegelian? I cannot deal indulgently with Mr. Glass's assertion that Nägeli studied Hegelian philosophy in Berlin for two years; for the time was in fact one *Semester*, and, at the age of twenty-five, there is a world of difference between a *Semester* and two years. If this is to be accepted as sufficient evidence for Nageli's Hegelianism, how many young men in Germany at that time would have to be accused of a lifelong bias to one or another philosophy, on the strength of a *Semester's* study?

Cramer, who was a pupil, a collaborator and a lifelong friend of Nägeli, tells us that Nägeli explicitly denied being an

[1] It appears from the discussion (below, p. 619) that I did not make clear that what I suppose Sutton to have seen for the first time is not the mere association of chromosomes in pairs, but their association in pairs in such a way that each chromosome might normally be expected to have one, and only one, possible partner among all the other chromosomes.

[2] C. Cramer, *Leben und Wirken von Carl Wilhelm von Nägeli* (Zürich, 1896); E. Gaupp, *August Weismann, sein Leben und sein Werk* (Jena, 1917).

Hegelian. But perhaps a careful reading of his works might show that he was an Hegelian without knowing it? I have just spent at least two years reading the works of Nägeli and of those who were his pupils and his pupils' pupils, and I have not perceived anything in them which seems to me to give any hint of Hegelian influence. I have also spent a great deal of time reading the works of other biologists and I should say that Nägeli's writings, at least in his maturity, show unusually little evidence of any philosophical influence. Certainly, I have not read his earliest productions, but the fact that he went directly from Berlin to Jena to study microscopic techniques under Schleiden and that he found Schleiden's work with the microscope "insufficiently methodical"[1] seems to militate against the idea that he was obsessed by general and philosophical notions at this time.

But I wonder what would qualify as a specifically Hegelian mode of thought? I cannot pretend to an intimate knowledge of the works of Hegel, yet I seem to glimpse something Hegelian about the following expression:

> The modern view of the relation of heredity to development is not Bonnet's, but neither is it Maupertuis's. It has something of both, and something of neither. The two views, once held to be irreconcilable, have merged in a higher synthesis.

The author of this passage is not, however, Nägeli, but Mr. Glass (p. 541).

It seems to me that Mr. Glass has omitted one extremely important factor in the change of heart which made possible the appreciation of Mendel's work in the early years of the present century. This factor is the growing appreciation of the possibility of discontinuous variation and of discontinuous inheritance. I intentionally invert the natural order of words, because in the last decades of the nineteenth century far more interest attached to evolution, and hence to variation, than to inheritance. But it is possible to discern a continuous, though small, stream of work directly on heredity during this period. This small but extremely important stream has its source in the work and speculations of Francis Galton.

Galton himself, though naturally greatly interested in the theory of evolution propounded by his cousin Charles Darwin, was able to keep his attention fixed upon heredity and variation

[1] S. Schwendener, *Berichte der deutschen botanischen Gesellschaft*, IX (1891) 28.

as a distinct field of study. He made important empirical observations and first-order generalizations; but he also considered the subject of variation theoretically, and pointed out, in 1889, that it is extremely difficult to see how variations which are *not* discontinuous could become heritable: he also, though briefly and somewhat incidentally, remarked upon the importance of discontinuous variations as the raw material of evolutionary change.

Most of his English followers, of whom the most distinguished was Karl Pearson, preferred to ignore these theoretical conclusions, and to believe that Galton's work supported their doctrine of universally continuous variation: their interests being principally in ideas relating directly to the theory of evolution, and hardly at all in the pure problem of heredity. But Bateson, who advocated the new heresy of discontinuous evolution, fully understood the value of Galton's theorizing, as also did de Vries, who, it will be remembered, was one of the three workers who simultaneously 'rediscovered' the work of Mendel. The particulate theory of variation received powerful support from de Vries's studies of mutation, elaborated in his book written and published at the turn of the century (1900–3). But since mutations had in fact been recorded in the eighteenth century, de Vries could do no more than produce new arguments for their significance in evolution.

Of far greater importance was the work of Johannsen, published in 1903, which showed that even the most classical examples of continuous inheritance could be interpreted as special cases of discontinuous inheritance. Johannsen, who dedicated his paper on this topic to Galton, is the originator of the concept of 'pure line' which J. B. S. Haldane has described as "fundamental to modern genetics".

Anyone who reads the controversies of the first year of the present century, between the advocates of Mendelism and discontinuous inheritance on the one side, and the *Biometrika* school under Karl Pearson on the other, will understand with what extreme difficulty prejudices in favour of continuity were eradicated, and how great was the resistance to the notion that a fundamental biological process might be treated as particulate.

This aversion from the particulate in biology is a circumstance of the greatest importance in the historical study of the work of Mendel and of his contemporaries. I am far from wishing to suggest that it is altogether unjustified: it is certain, for example, that Galton's speculations on particulate inheritance represent a point of view which is quite untenable; for the factors or carriers of heritable characters cannot possibly be represented as a heap or swarm of independent entities: "a swarm of flies" as Galton says. All I wish to say is that heredity cannot be treated as *in no sense* particulate, and that, for the first stages in the elaboration of Mendelian genetics, it was necessary to stress the particulate aspect of inheritance.

If, after these considerations of the history of genetics about 1900, we turn to the work of Mendel and compare it with that of Nägeli and that of Weismann, we perceive, much more clearly than, I think, Mr. Glass has been able to do, certain essential features of the situation.

Mr. Glass writes (p. 530):

> The particulate conception of heredity derived from Mendel's experiments is too well known to need description here. It suffices to emphasize that Mendel spoke always of alternative elements for each pair of alternative characteristics . . . nowhere is there any suggestion on the part of Mendel that these elements are represented by material particles in the reproductive cells. Perhaps, indeed, he thought so. But he seems carefully to have refrained from committing himself to any material basis for the behaviour of the inherited traits he was studying. This reluctance is indeed most remarkable, whether seen against the nineteenth-century background of idioplasm and ids, or against the twentieth century's chromosomes, genes, and DNA.

In fact, the contrast between Mendel's presentation and that of the other persons and schools referred to by Mr. Glass is much greater than this passage would lead us to suppose: for, in the whole of his elaboration of data and theory, Mendel does not in fact mention "elements for alternative characteristics", *but always* speaks *directly* of *Charaktere* or *Merkmale*; and the symbols he uses are always class-symbols, so that, for example, where we should now expect him to speak of an organism having the elements *AAbb* in fact he always speaks of an organism of the *class*, or having the *Merkmal A* and the *Merkmal b*; and so consistently does he do this that the germ-cells receive the same notation as the adult (in this case *Ab*), and are also said to "belong to the class *Ab*", which becomes quite confusing to a modern reader. Especially when Mendel calls the germ-cells "of the permanent class *Ab*".

So scrupulously does Mendel adhere to a class-notation that even when he broaches the subject of multifactorial determination (as we should probably now call it) he fails to find any way of distinguishing what can only be distinguished by recourse to the language and symbols of particles, and so fails to give a considerable increase of generality to his theory.

It is only in his *Schlussbemerkungen*, after the completion of his theory, that Mendel allows himself to speak of *Elemente* (not *Faktoren*) in the germ-cells; which *Elemente* we may conclude to be particulate, though I think he nowhere says that they are.

Now, if we ask why Mendel behaved in this way, we can also, I think, explain why neither Nägeli nor Weismann, though they *had* a particulate theory of heredity, contrived to excogitate Mendelian properties in the distribution of their particles. The answer is partly that they had not the notion of chromosome *pairs* and partly that they had not the courage of their particles. For Weismann *every* character was a multifactorial character, determined, that is, by a host of particles in the germ-plasm; and when Nägeli discusses what we now call mutations, he timidly suggests that a long process of elaboration involving a large number of invisible particles must be supposed to precede the sudden overt appearance of the new character. The fact is that it is still extremely difficult to believe that each character is determined by just one particle, and this is hardly what we mean when we associate a character with just one gene. I believe that Mendel perceived this pitfall and evaded it by eschewing particles altogether. He could assert from empirical observation that his *characters* behaved as discrete units in inheritance, and so long as he spoke only of *characters* he did not have to face the impossible task of convincing his readers that so elaborate a thing as a character could be correlated with so simple a thing as a particle.

Consider the following description given by Mendel of one character behaving as a heritable unit: *die graue . . . Farbe der Samenschale, in Verbindung mit violett-rother Blühte und röthlicher Mackel in den Blattachseln* ("the grey colour of the seed-coat, together with violet-red flowers and reddish spots in the axels of the leaves").

There now seems no improbability in the assertion that such a character-complex is associated with one gene (if we are still allowed to talk about genes), but this is at least in part due to the fact that a 'gene' is the name of something which is itself relatively complex. To say, however, in 1865 "this character-complex is caused by (or associated with) a single particle" would almost inevitably have led to the supposition that something complex was being causally derived from something essentially simple: because the particle would have been a mere hypostasis having no known properties other than its relation to the character, so that any image of the particle would have to be as simple as possible: it would have had to be a mere piece of geometry; probably a sphere. The scepticism of those who did not see how such an entity could account for such a character would have been amply justified. And this, I suggest, was apparent to Mendel, who only speaks of *Elemente* (which *may* mean particles) after he has completed the formal exposition of his theory.

Commentary by G. J. Warnock

My comments on Mr. Ronchi's paper will be very brief, as I do not, I think, differ from him — it would, indeed, be presumptuous of me to do so — on any point of substance.

After his account of the vicissitudes of the theory of vision in the ancient and medieval periods, Mr. Ronchi comes to the crucial period of the work of Galileo and Kepler. Kepler, as he points out, may be said effectively to have perfected the classical account of the geometry of optics; but — as is natural enough, and indeed usual in the history of ideas — he did not resist the temptation to try to make his theory do too much. In particular, as Mr. Ronchi makes admirably clear, he offered an account, in terms of 'triangulation', of visual judgments of distance which is plainly and grossly at variance with the facts. And no doubt it is true that many of his successors have similarly attempted to make use of geometrical optics, quite inappropriately, in the explanation of visual phenomena and of judgments of perception in general. On this point I have just two comments to offer.

First, realization that there are many visual phenomena on which geometrical optics throws little light, if any, is not, I think, so recent as Mr. Ronchi's paper might seem to suggest. Berkeley's *New Theory of Vision* (1709) was largely devoted precisely to pointing out that visual judgments of distance and size could not be accounted for within the terms of that theory, and that such arguments as Kepler's on this topic involved a fundamental misapplication of the classical (geometrical) doctrine.

But secondly, Berkeley did not suggest, as Mr. Ronchi seems

to me to do, that this shows the classical doctrine to be *wrong* in some way, or 'worthless'. It is a question rather of its correct application. One might say that Kepler's results, and the whole 'classical' doctrine of geometrical optics, have really to do with the propagation of light, with such phenomena as reflection, refraction, and magnification — with, in effect, what goes on in vision *in front of* the retina. In this field, surely, the geometrical theory (with its associated physical interpretation) gives perfectly correct results. From this we must distinguish the neuro-physiology of vision, what goes on *in and behind* the retina; and then we must further distinguish the psychological and philosophical problems that arise when we consider the way things look to the observer, and the judgments he makes. Here geometrical optics certainly helps us very little; but the realization that it does not supply us with answers to *these* questions should not lead us to deny that there are *other* questions which it answers most admirably.

At this point I am tempted to think that what Mr. Ronchi's remarks amount to is an insistence upon a particular *definition* of 'optics'; if, he seems to say, a certain theory does not cover the field of visual phenomena comprehensively, *including* the explanation of visual appearances and perceptual judgments, then it is merely a piece of mathematics, or physics, or perhaps physiology: it is not *optics*. I would not particularly wish to dissent from this view. But it seems to me of much more importance to distinguish accurately from one another the different *kinds of inquiry* that arise or may arise concerning vision, than to decide just how much or how little of this general area the name 'optics' should be made to cover. Scientists should leave purely verbal disputes to philosophers!

Commentary by C. A. Mace

I
On the history of psychology in general

There are two sorts of 'philosophy of history'. One is the philosophy that there *is* a philosophy of history — that the historians can discern causal sequences or at least patterns in history, for example the pattern described by Hegel and Marx as the dialectical progression — thesis, antithesis, synthesis. The other philosophy of history is that there is no philosophy of history. The historian is content merely to ascertain what actually happened in history, when what happened was just one thing after another. There is no philosophy of geography — the geographer just describes *what* is *where*; so the historian just describes *what* happened *when*. What happened when, what so-and-so did or thought, may well have been due to a fortuitous combination of genes which determined his personality and to the accidents of the situation in which that personality was placed.

Both these theories are correct — if stated with care. There *are* patterns in history but these patterns are distorted and complicated by the chance combinations of genes and by the accidents of circumstance. The disentangling of the pattern from the chance circumstances is one of the difficult things in writing a history of science.

The Hegelian dialectical progression becomes enlightening if it is not treated metaphysically but is translated into terms of the psychology of fashion or the homely concept of the swing of the pendulum, a cardinal principle of the British political philosophy but equally relevant to the history of science. In psychology we are living through a new reversal in the swing of the pendulum. In the philosophy of Descartes the pendulum had swung to its extreme in the direction of dualism. The rise of scientific psychology during the last hundred years has coincided with a swing to the opposite extreme as represented by positivism in philosophy and behaviourism in psychology. The pendulum is now again reversing its direction of movement. This was one of the important points made by Koestler in his recent articles in the *Observer* (23 and 30 April 1961) which provoked such strong reactions in some quarters. Basing his thesis largely on some remarks of Wilder Penfield, Koestler stressed the reaction — but in an unfortunate way. He seemed to imply that the pendulum was swinging back to something like the old dualism. This is not the case. The image of the pendulum is less apt than that of a spiral progression. We are returning to a dualism but to more than one dualism — not to the dualism of 'the ghost in the machine'. The situation as I see it today — as represented in the position of psychologists such as Oldfield and philosophers like Farrell — is something far removed both from Cartesian dualism and from the physicalism of the positivist philosophers and the behaviourism of psychologists. We have in fact:

(1) The dualism of science in general — of physics and chemistry concerned with the visible spectrum and sensible tastes and smells;

(2) The dualism of psychology in particular, which is a science which includes the scientist himself as part of its subject matter and in which the scientist's self-observation contributes to the advance of his science.

The pendulum is a paradigm, a model, an analogy from physics. There is another from biology equally useful to the historian of science — the concept of *differentiation*. Among the points made during the first session of this Symposium was that the transition from Greek to modern physics was essentially a transition in which science became differentiated from philosophy.

Roughly speaking, this differentiation occurs in time in an order corresponding to the complexity of the phenomena treated in science or rather the positions of the particular sciences in the hierarchy of science. It occurred first in physics, next in chemistry, then in biology and last of all, up to date, in psychology. Perhaps we are now witnessing a similar transition in sociology.

This brings me to the papers before us. In complementary ways these two papers illustrate and illuminate the process of differentiation between scientific psychology and the philosophy of mind. In Oldfield's paper we see certain fundamental and general concepts — philosophical concepts — being translated into the language of the natural sciences. We see the scientist extricating himself from philosophy. In Farrell's paper we have an example of the way in which a constructive philosopher can assist the scientist in so extricating himself both by the analysis of basic concepts and by the analysis of scientific method.

II
Oldfield

Here is a very pretty example of the way in which the scientist takes a 'philosophical' concept and reduces it to terms in which it can be treated in the natural sciences — the concept of 'hierarchical order'.

We could start with Aristotle and his account of the hierarchy of 'souls' — vegetable, animal and human. Much of what Aristotle said about hierarchical organization could be translated into contemporary language in the form of statements about the 'mechanisms of behaviour'. The concept of hierarchical organization runs continuously through the history of the philosophy of mind. We meet it again in Bishop Butler's illuminating sermons on human nature with the hierarchy of the particular impulses, the principles of cool self-love and benevolence and the supreme function of conscience. We have met this hierarchy again in our own life in McDougall's hierarchy of instinct, sentiment and 'master sentiment', and we have met it in a new form in Freud. What the scientists are doing, what Oldfield is doing, is to explicate this concept and its historical development in its neurological application in the work of Hughlings Jackson, Sherrington and others who have positions of unquestioned eminence in the natural sciences. If we can get clarity in the concept of hierarchical organization in the nervous system and the 'neural mechanisms governing behaviour' we shall be on the way to getting clarity in talk about the 'mechanisms' discussed by Butler, McDougall and Freud.

A second point to be noted in Oldfield's paper is that it illustrates *one* way in which psychology becomes a science by establishing connexions with better established sciences.

In the history of psychology there are many examples of the attempts of psychologists to become 'scientific' by accepting models from other 'more advanced' sciences. The outstanding case is that of the sensationist and associationist psychologies which were modelled on chemistry. Examples could be given of psychologies modelled on physics, mathematics or engineering.

Much more promising are the attempts not to 'model' psychology on other sciences but to *integrate* psychology with nearly related sciences, physiology, neurology and the biological sciences generally. This is the line taken in Oldfield's paper.

There are, naturally, a number of points in this paper on which I would take a different view. But these are domestic questions. My present purpose is merely to stress points of agreement not only between Oldfield and myself but among, I think, the majority of psychologists today about the relation of psychology to the other natural sciences.

III
Farrell

In Farrell's paper, too, I find statements on which I could join issue, but again the issues are domestic. What I want to stress now are the more fundamental matters on which we agree — points made by Farrell which contribute to the advancement of psychology as a science, and to the integration of psychology with the well-established sciences, and the differentiation of the science of psychology from the philosophy of mind. It illustrates the kind of service which the philosophers, the logicians, and the methodologists can give in telling the scientist what he is doing. There is perhaps something a little odd about this 'service'. What exactly does the physicist, the chemist or the psychologist get out of the philosophy of science from being told what he is doing? The physicists and the chemists can give their own answers to this question. My impression is that some do get something and that others get along very well without any commentary from the philosophers of science.

In the case of psychology my impression is that the scientific psychologist, whether he *feels* the need or not, *has* a need for the sort of guidance which methodological philosophers, like Farrell, can give. For one thing, psychologists rather more than other scientists are apt to confuse empirical questions with questions of analytical philosophy. Titchener is an example.

It is indeed helpful to make the positive point that there are some criteria by which to distinguish scientific procedures from those of magic and religion, but in my view it is even more helpful to make the negative point that no sharp distinction can be drawn between so-called 'clinical' and so-called 'objective' procedures. I am inclined to go further than Farrell in support of a liberal and tolerant concept of scientific procedures. Indeed to accept the antithesis 'clinical' versus 'objective' is in my view to concede too much. Clinical observation can be as objective as a laboratory experiment.

While accepting distinctions between science on the one hand, and magic and religion on the other, I am again inclined to use Farrell's concept of a continuum and to concede that science can grow out of magic and religion. The change from magical rainmaking to scientific meteorology is an example.

To conclude, I return to Oldfield's paper. The intriguing but cryptic concluding paragraph might, I suggest, be developed to disclose some of the sociological or psychological forces which produce the doctrinaire and restrictive concepts of the science against which Farrell's arguments are directed. Consider the anxiety of so many psychologists to establish scientific status for themselves and their science. It is not clear whether this is to be regarded as the effect of external pressures or of internal pressures. The advanced sciences in setting a model of rigour can be regarded as an external force. The psychologist's willing acceptance of this model, his urge to attain full scientific status, is an inner force. This force can operate through a conscious and rational endeavour to integrate psychology with the other natural sciences. Such I should say is the line taken by Oldfield. On the other hand there are quasi-pathological, obsessional and neurotic impulses which find expression in the elaboration of superfluous technical terms, the use of refined statistical procedures with crude data, and in the arbitrary restriction of the concept of science of the kind which Farrell's paper helps to correct.

Discussion

J. Needham

At this conference I have been a little puzzled by the great use that has been made of the terms 'conceptual model', 'paradigm' and 'dogma'. When I was young we used to talk about accepted bodies of theory, which were superseded and outmoded when new facts demanded the formation of new hypotheses, these themselves becoming for a while accepted bodies of theory. If any special meaning could attach for me to a 'conceptual model', it might however reasonably be what I should have called the faculty of imaginative visualization, possessed in high degree by certain rare individuals. Here I think particularly of my own teacher Sir Frederick Gowland Hopkins, P.R.S., the *fundator et primus abbas* of biochemistry in this country. How many times have I heard him talk of "the geography of the cell", and the "cell as a chemical factory". It was in 1919, I think, that he defined the cell as a "dynamic equilibrium in a polyphasic system". With profound intuition, he visualized the "polymer molecules" like Nägeli's micellae, held in active orientation, with enzymes located thereon like the shaping machines in a machine-shop with a planned flow-sheet. His recognition of the great importance of small molecules, not only the mass materials of carbohydrates, protein and fat, led directly to the great discovery of the accessory food substances, the vitamins. In a word, Hopkins possessed a prophetic vision of the sub-cellular biochemical morphology, and it was elaborated by many of those whom he inspired, such as Sir Rudolph Peters and David Green, among whom I also hope to be numbered. This is why we are always so full of regret that Hopkins never lived to see the wonderful pictures which the electron-microscopes are today so abundantly producing. He would have delighted in the enlarged mitochondria with their complex 'battery-plate' structure, or in those curtains which fill the cells with the endoplasmic reticulum, or in the microsomes, virus liquid crystals, and fibrils set in strict parallel order in the single cilium. But it was not to be; like Harvey, who knew that there must be capillary vessels but never saw them, so Hopkins knew that there must be a realm of order intermediate between histology and biochemistry, but the electron microscope came just too late. Still, if I can attach any sense to the term 'conceptual model', this is it.

J. Toulmin

I wish to deal with one small point raised by Mr. Glass in the two main paragraphs on p. 535. In these two paragraphs Mr. Glass talks about models and theories in a way which leaves the relation between them unclear. In the first paragraph he gives a tough criterion for distinguishing between a genuinely scientific model and a "piece of speculative natural philosophy". His criterion, which he seems to apply universally, is that the model should be capable of yielding "verifiable predictions". Presumably what he means is that the appropriateness of the model should be capable of being checked in the laboratory by suggesting questions and experiments which lead to coherent and quantitative results.

The trouble arises when, in the next paragraph, he applies this criterion not to a Bateson beads-on-a-string model, but to an overall embracing theory such as Darlington's. In Darlington's theory the mechanisms of contemporary genetics are applied to historical processes so as to improve our understanding of evolution. Mr. Glass seems to refer to this too as just another model, and warns us to beware of the "insidious charm of the undemonstrable and unverifiable model". But if there are elements in Darlington's theory which are unverifiable this is not because they involve bad scientific models but because they are concerned with historical processes, and you cannot experiment with history.

As a touchstone, what would Mr. Glass say about Darwin's theory? This was one of the most complete and illuminating theories ever to be offered in biology, and it would be a brave man who would say now that it was unscientific. But the theory that species 'originate by variation and natural selection' has never yet been the subject of a verified prediction.[1] Variation has been observed occurring, but no one has ever got around

[1] Mr. Glass's reply to this point was that new species had been predicted and observed to be created by alloploidy; and this does not meet my objection for, in this case, the species originated by mutation but was never exposed to the processes of natural selection with which Darwin was primarily concerned. Moreover, Darwin's theory was recognized as a good scientific theory at least fifty years before predictive techniques in genetics were possible.

to predicting successfully the appearance of a new species. So Darwin's theory has many of the features of what Bentley Glass calls speculative natural philosophy.

I would be grateful if Mr. Glass would establish a little more clearly just how far he feels the criterion of verifiable predictions should be generally applied to biological concepts, and what particular value it has there.

I suspect this is just one more example of the phenomenon to which Mr. Mace has referred: the intellectual inferiority-complex that biologists and psychologists have about their concepts when compared with those of physics and chemistry. I feel that Mr. Glass has fallen for the insidious and fatal charm of certain philosophical theories derived from a study of the inanimate sciences. I am not myself convinced that predictive criteria are of universal importance in physics, still less in biology. In any case, it is surely unwise to import these concepts from physics into biology solely because they have been successful in other fields. As Claude Bernard said last century, biology has its own special problems and its own attitudes; it utilizes the tools of other sciences but not the concepts. If my interpretation of Mr. Glass's motives is correct, then I would like to inject into him — and in other psychologists who share his timidity — a little courage. Biologists of the world arise and throw off your inhibitions — you have nothing to lose but other people's paradigms!

M. H. Pirenne

The following comments are made from the point of view of a sensory physiologist primarily interested in the mechanisms underlying such functions of the eye as its absolute and differential sensitivity, visual acuity, and colour vision. First it may perhaps be remarked that, since the study of vision has been pursued for so many centuries and constitutes such a complicated field, it is useful to read old writings simply in order to obtain a clearer understanding of the subject. The first man to discover a new fact or a new idea often explains it better than any of his successors. This applies for example to Newton's optical writings and even to Euclid's *Optics*. (I believe that the less valuable book on *Catoptrics* is no longer ascribed to Euclid.)

'Saving the appearances': a great deal of attention has been devoted to this aim of the Greek astronomers. Now the 'appearances' for which a Ptolemy wanted to account were primarily the angular positions of celestial bodies; they were indeed objective facts, valid for all observers. Astronomy taught us that there are laws, said Poincaré. First it taught us that visual appearances may contain objective elements.

There is an element in the visual appearance of stars which must have been dismissed as irrelevant already in Ptolemy's time. Because of the defects existing in the dioptric system of the eyes of most observers, stars as a rule seem to have 'points'. This purely subjective effect, similar for all stars and planets in any given observer, changes when he uses either one or the other eye.

The problem encountered by sensory physiologists is a special one, for their studies do relate to subjective appearances. First they must deal with truly objective facts as far as the physical conditions of the experiments they perform on human subjects are concerned. Circularity of argument must be avoided when, say, colour, as seen, is to be correlated with the physical properties of the stimulus. Then the question arises: can subjective phenomena be investigated in an 'objective' manner, to give results having general validity like those of physics? Further: what is the theoretical framework to be used to interpret experimental results? In my opinion the sensory physiologist can use a method dealing with bodily processes alone, both in experiments and in theoretical explanations. On this point I am not sure how far I am in agreement with Mr. Ronchi.[1]

The problem might require development too long to be given here.[2] First the sensations, the perceptions, the consciousness of the subject are not directly observable by the experimenter. He can only record what are sometimes called the physical manifestations of consciousness. Secondly, the experimenter uses such concepts as electromagnetic radiation, the dioptric system of the eye, quanta of energy absorbed by the retina, and nerve impulses — which concepts are derived from observations of an objective kind. He should logically go on using physico-chemical and neurophysiological concepts in the

[1] V. Ronchi, *Histoire de la lumière* (Paris, 1956).

[2] M. H. Pirenne, *Vision and the Eye* (London, 1948); "Descartes and the body–mind problem in physiology", *The British Journal for the Philosophy of Science*, I (1950) 43–59; "The mind–brain problem", ibid. V (1954) 153–9; M. H. Pirenne and F. H. C. Marriott, "The quantum theory of light and the psycho-physiology of vision", *Psychology: A Study of a Science*, ed. S. Koch (New York, 1959) I, 288–361.

elaboration of his theory and entirely leave out mental concepts, which belong to a different category.

This method of approach may be considered as having merely heuristic value. It is becoming increasingly used, at any rate by isolated workers, some of whom developed it quite independently of cybernetics. Nevertheless such concepts as sensations keep creeping back into physiological theory. One of the advantages of the purely mechanistic approach is that it removes such intractable concepts as mixtures of sensations from the study of colour vision and of binocular vision. Almost a century ago, the physiologist Aubert, who was a consistent follower of Descartes and of Johannes Müller, and who did not use a purely mechanistic approach, gave almost a cry of despair which must have found an echo in many a reader of physiological textbooks: "Was heisst überhaupt: Mischung von Emfindungen?"[1]

On the other hand I do emphatically agree with Mr. Ronchi that we must ascertain experimentally what the visual system actually does, instead of merely speculating on what it should do. And we must take the utmost care to prevent such speculations from influencing, even unwittingly, our experimental results; this is more easily said than done.

To turn to another matter, Mr. Ronchi in his paper said, rightly in my opinion, that the problem of linear perspective had effectively been solved by the ancient doctrine of the visual rays — as used by Euclid. Now theories[2] have been put forward, by an important school of art historians, on the evolution of linear perspective as used in the art of painting. They seek to explain this evolution mainly on the basis of changes in theoretical conceptions of space. It is not clear whether these theories accept that there are *any* empirical elements involved in visual perception which remain permanently valid, independently of theoretical conceptions. But in any case, Mr. Panofsky, their leading exponent, has stated that "perspective construction as practised in the Renaissance is, in fact, not 'correct' from a purely naturalistic, that is, a

[1] H. Aubert, *Physiologie der Netzhaut* (Breslau, 1865).

[2] E. Panofsky, "Die Perspective als symbolische Form", *Vorträge 1924–5 for Bibliothek Varburg* (Leipzig–Berlin, 1927) pp. 258–330, translated with other writings as *La prospettiva come "forma simbolica", e altri scritti* (Milan, 1961); *The Codex Huygens and Leonardo da Vinci's Art Theory* (London, 1940) 106. P. Francastel, "La perspective de Léonard de Vinci et l'expérience scientifique au XVIe siècle", in *Léonard de Vinci et l'expérience scientifique au XVIe siècle* (Paris, 1953) 62–72.

physiological and psychological point of view".[1] According to this, the solution of the problem of perspective given by the doctrine of visual rays, namely central projection perspective, which is essentially the construction of the Renaissance, would be fundamentally wrong.

These theories have been criticized by other art historians and by students of optics.[2] Their rejection, however, does not make the problem simpler. Euclid's *Optics* deals primarily with perspective in the natural, direct, vision of the external world, not with the use of perspective as a mode of depiction. Before the seventh century B.C., artists never drew according to the system of central perspective, even though they were certainly aware of many optical facts which lie at the basis of it.[3] It may be added that the subject has been bedevilled by the failure to realize that the projective relationship of linear perspective is *not* a relationship between the actual scene depicted and the artist's psychological percepts; but that it is a relationship between the objects constituting the actual scene, on the one hand, and another object which also belongs to the external world, namely the picture itself, on the other. It would be valuable to have Mr. Ronchi's opinion on these complicated problems.

D. Speiser

I am not sure whether as a physicist I should comment on Mr. Ronchi's paper for, deliberately perhaps, it is being discussed in the biological and psychological session. What I now shall say may, therefore, be beside the point, but Mr. Ronchi uses the terms 'classical optics' and 'geometrical optics'. We are certainly indebted to him for having reminded us that the whole process of vision still remains a challenge to physics or, as I should probably say, to science. Now geometrical optics since Newton and Huygens (and maybe even earlier) had been conceived as a *theory of the propagation of light.*

[1] *The Codex Huygens and Leonardo da Vinci's Art Theory*, p. 106.

[2] D. Gioseffi, *Perspectiva artificialis*; *per la storia della prospettiva*; *spigolature e appunti* (Trieste, 1957), reviewed by M. H. Pirenne, *Art Bulletin*, XLI (1959) 213–17; E. H. Gombrich, *Art and Illusion* (London and New York, 1960); M. Zanetti, "Una proposta di reforma della prospettiva lineare", *L'Ingegnere* (September, 1951); M. H. Pirenne, "The scientific basis of Leonardo da Vinci's theory of perspective", *Brit. J. for Philos. of Science*, III (1952) 169–85; G. ten Doesschate, "De Schilderperspectief", *Euclides*, XXXVI (Groningen, 1960) 33–50.

[3] H. Schäfer, *Von agyptischer Kunst* (2 vols., Leipzig, 1919).

In practice, it centred round the theory of lenses, microscopes, etc. It was not conceived as a theory of vision and the scientists always were aware of the fact that they had not solved the puzzle of the eye. On the contrary, Euler, on grounds of the example offered by the eye, believed that an achromatic lens system ought to be possible, whereas a superficial investigation of the theory seemed to contradict this. It is also interesting to observe that in Euler's view the eye even seemed to lend some support to the teleological principles proposed by Maupertuis. Euler felt that new principles were needed to explain the growth of the human eye, apparently so much superior to every lens system constructed at his time.[1]

We should keep separate classical optics and the theory of vision. It is indeed very questionable whether this problem should and could be attacked in the framework of physics. It seems that much more is needed. Mr. Pirenne alluded to the example of the classical perspective. I think we are on the wrong track if we try to find a justification of the rules of classical perspective, and what is more, an explanation of its significance and function in the arts, simply on the basis of the construction of the human eye, though as a heuristic principle this certainly played a decisive role!

P. Alexander

(1) Mr. Farrell, in his very interesting paper, shows that there is a continuum in scientific method between the crudely empirical and the fully scientific, and I agree with this. But surely his characterization of Methods III and IV as 'reality-facing methods' is question-begging. Too much knowledge, in this context, is a dangerous thing. We, watching the men in Farrell's imagined situation, can see that the window-tapper is unlikely to succeed and so we regard his method as unscientific and akin to magic. But is Method I really so distinct from III and IV? Note that when Method I fails the subject goes through the procedure again "with more seriousness and care". He is trying to get it right. He is trying to discover *what* affects the liquids and he may be engaged in trial and error, even if we eventually decide that he is a magician rather than a scientist.

What is involved here is the difficult question of how we

[1] Cf. L. Euler, "Examen d'une controverse . . .", *Mémoires de l'Académie des Sciences der Berlin* (1755), in the forthcoming volume of Euler's *Opera omnia*, III, 5.

judge *relevance*. Given *no* knowledge of the properties of liquids and what affects them, is it ridiculous or unscientific to try window-tapping? Starting from scratch we only discover which are the reality-facing methods by trying and rejecting those which are not. Magic involves crude empirical methods and trial and error and I doubt if we could infallibly decide whether the subject was using magic or science just by watching his behaviour, even over a long period. We should perhaps have to know something about the previous state of his knowledge and the intentions behind his actions. A procedure which in relation to one body of knowledge is unscientific may be scientific in relation to another body of knowledge.

Is it then impossible to distinguish between magical and scientific methods? Might it not have something to do with a desire to show *how* things work? Suppose we find that window-tapping does work, then is not the difference between the magician and the scientist that the scientist goes on to attempt to establish a connexion or at least works on the assumption that there is a connexion to be found? At most he seeks a testable connexion and at least a plausible one. We should at least have to watch Farrell's subject's behaviour *after* the initial problem was solved. Could we say that the magician does and the scientist does not rest satisfied with remote correlations and that the scientist goes on to try to connect what has been correlated either, in the cruder situations, by filling in a physical gap by further empirical investigation or, in more complex ones, by filling in a conceptual gap? While magic *primarily* aims at getting things done, science *primarily* aims at explaining how things get done. Of course this needs explanation: magic, too, has its body of theory, but I think these are the lines on which we must work if we are to distinguish between them.

(2) This leads me to wonder why Farrell has dwelt so largely on the empirical side of clinical psychology and so little on the theoretical side. It is perfectly true that for certain purposes it is desirable to separate within psycho-analysis, on the one hand, a heuristic and technical aspect from, on the other, a theoretical and explanatory aspect. The first may be crudely empirical but to argue that this puts it safely on one end of the scientific spectrum is not to answer some of the most serious criticisms that it is unscientific. Much of this criticism depends upon objections to the effect that the theory is untested and untestable and, moreover, not explanatory. The heuristic and technical aspects would not, I think, have

come in for so much criticism if they were not inseparably connected with the theory, on the one hand because they are determined to some extent by that theory, and on the other hand because the findings and the successes of the clinicians are regarded as support for the theory. Moreover, there are several widely divergent, and so competing, theories and, most seriously of all, the holders of different theories tend to obtain different results in their crudely empirical investigations.

There are many other and dependent difficulties. *Can* there be a body of fact agreed between the advocates of different theories? What is to count as a test for a theory? Is the kind of explanation put forward comparable to scientific explanations or is it more like other sorts of acceptable explanations; or is it perhaps no kind of explanation at all? Moreover there are ingredients in the crude empirical situation which distinguish it from others on Mr. Farrell's spectrum. The psycho-analyst is *involved* in the phenomenon under investigation in a way in which the chemist, for example, is not: the chemist is not in the test tube along with the precipitate, the psycho-analyst *is*. Moreover, an essential reagent in psycho-analysis is *meaningful talk* and an essential reaction is the understanding of that talk.

Although I have been critical, I am on Mr. Farrell's side in thinking that the criticisms of clinical psychology are often unwarranted, confused or avoidable; I think, however, that he has insufficiently stressed the main point and strength of such criticisms.

J. P. Vernant

It is difficult for me to accept the picture painted by Mr. Farrell of present-day psychology. He portrays it as being divided between two great tendencies: on the one hand, what he calls objective psychology, but which he reduces somewhat artificially to the level of simple behaviourism; on the other, Freudianism. One would suppose, on reading him, that there is nothing between these two. It is, however, in this 'no man's land' that the true nucleus of contemporary psychology is, in my opinion, to be found. The psychologists have attempted to found their discipline, avoiding both this narrow positivism which claimed to be applicable to man in the same way as to nature, and equally the nebulous metaphysics, of biological inspiration, on which the Freudian theories rest. They have compelled themselves to build up a truly objective science, progressively taking into account, in its methods, only those human factors definite enough to be objective. Thence derives the importance attributed, in the various branches of research, to such notions as structure, system, construction, differentiation, and level of differentiation. Is it necessary to recall what brought Gestalt-psychology into existence? It was thought that it was going to renew psychology and make its mark in the field of physiology itself, through work like that of Goldstein, the writings of Cassirer on symbolic forms and the echo they found in the psychologists, the phenomenological current whose influence is manifest today even in the vocabulary of psychopathological studies, and finally the historical and comparative psychology of M. I. Meyerson. This studies psychological functions, their genesis, their transformation through the corpus of work which men have continually created during the course of their history: languages, religions, institutions, arts, techniques and sciences. There — in this double rejection of both behaviourism and psycho-analysis — is to be found, it seems to me, the living psychology of the twentieth century.

B. Glass

I indeed regret having erred in the matter of Nägeli's relationship to Hegel. At the same time I must emphasize that the reference to Hegel is a matter solely of a single sentence. It was not at all my intention to imply the existence of a chain of influence running from Hegel to Weismann, whether that in fact exists or not. But in respect to Nägeli's influence on Weismann and upon applying Mr. Wilkie's own criterion that "no external influence should be implied unless evidence is overwhelming", I shall firmly stand my ground.

In another matter I regret to say that Mr. Wilkie is himself clearly in error. Sutton was not at all the first observer to see pairs of chromosomes. Neither he nor his professor E. B. Wilson (in the monumental work *The Cell in Heredity and Development*) ever claimed that. What Sutton actually did was to postulate that the paired Mendelian factors (or alleles as we now call them) segregate in the formation of germ cells because they lie respectively in homologous chromosomes that segregate during meiosis. The demonstration that the chromosomes do occur in pairs, each pair being composed of a maternal and a paternal homologue, we owe to the cytological researches of Flemming, van Beneden, and Strasburger in the 1880's; and August Weismann was fully acquainted with this when he predicted the occurrence of meiosis.

As to the question of whether more interest attached to the study of heredity or of evolution in the final decade of the nineteenth century, I consider the matter problematical. One's answer may well depend on whether one views the situation from Great Britain or from Germany. Clearly, on the one hand there was some waning of hope for any speedy demonstration of natural selection — it was accepted rather than demonstrated — while on the other hand the great cytological studies of Oskar Hertwig, Fol, van Beneden, Flemming and Strasburger on the nature of the fertilization process and the role of the chromosomes had led to Weismann's great theory of the isolation and continuity of the germ plasm and to Boveri's matchless studies of the individuality and continuity of the chromosomes.

As to Mendel's avoidance of any use of the term 'particle' for his units of heredity, in this Mr. Wilkie and I are in full agreement. Let me say only that Mendel does use the term *Elemente* in his concluding discussion, which may well be regarded as more definitive of his idea than the exposition of the experimental data; and that he had a very clear idea of the relation of the *Elemente* to the production of the *Merkmale* or *Charaktere*. It therefore seems to me that Bateson's choice of the word 'factor' to translate *Elemente* is, to say the least, permissible.

Finally, may I express my regret that Mr. Wilkie did not see fit to comment upon the main thesis of my paper, namely the harmful as well as advantageous consequences to scientific advance of the acceptance of conceptual models, especially those that are experimentally untestable.

With Mrs. Toulmin's comments I find myself in virtually complete agreement. But I would distinguish between the entire conceptual system of Darlington's *Evolution of Genetic Systems*, and certain specific untestable and unverifiable models which form a part of it. The former indeed resembles the Theory of Natural Selection in scope; but the individual models, in so far as they are unverifiable, represent in my opinion what may blind our vision of reality by their "insidious charm". For the Theory of Natural Selection we can at least point, after a century has elapsed, to certain allopolyploid species of plants whose origin and establishment in nature by means of natural selection are experimentally and observationally verifiable. Perhaps in due course of time "the evolution of genetic systems" may be similarly established by observation and experiment. But that every individual model employed in the theory will stand up seems to me no more likely than in the case of Darwin's achievement, where his specific model of 'pangenesis' has clearly proved to be incorrect.

V. Ronchi

In reply to Mr. Warnock's remarks, I should like to say that, in fact, some of Berkeley's criticisms are very similar to mine, as far as the geometrical theory of vision is concerned. A detailed study on this subject has been made by C. M. Turbayne of the University of Rochester, who also gave a paper on "Berkeley and Ronchi in optics" at the International Congress of Philosophy at Venice in 1958. But two important points must be kept in mind in this connexion. The first is that Berkeley's criticisms are two-and-a-half-centuries old and have had no echo whatever: nobody has discussed them, and they have been forgotten; no specialist of optics knows them. I myself became aware of them only after meeting Mr. Turbayne. I have emphasized these criticisms precisely because they are very important and must be taken into account by every student of optics.

The second point concerns the range of Berkeley's criticisms: they are confined to the province of direct vision, and do not take account of vision by means of optical instruments. My criticism goes much deeper. The development of geometrical optics since the time of Berkeley has been very extensive, but has taken no notice of Berkeley's criticism and reservations; in consequence, there is a universally accepted *faith* that the images calculated by means of formulae of geometrical optics correspond perfectly with experience. That this attitude is dictated by faith and not by scientific truth is proved by the fact that any experimental check shows it to be wrong in every case — with a few exceptions of simple and special cases, such as reflection in a plane mirror near to the observer — and that the differences between the images reckoned by means of formulae and those seen with the eyes can be enormous. But this faith is so deeply established that nobody carries out any check; and if occasionally one is forced to observe differences, a 'disturbance' is promptly suggested to explain the result. If I had more space I could give decisively-demonstrative examples.

I should also like to say to Mr. Warnock that defining optics is not only a question of words "to be left to the philosophers" as he wittily says: it is a question of scientific — and also philosophical — import, precisely because it is connected with the process which I discussed in my paper. It is impossible to go on studying a science which completely abstracts from human eyes, and still call it *optics*: this would be optics also valid for blind men. What happens *in front of the retina* is not optics, but just physics: the study of waves, whether mechanical or electromagnetic, does not specifically concern optics, but also acoustics, radio, even earthquakes. Only inertia makes us go on considering as optical phenomena the phenomena of reflection, refraction, interference, etc. Here again I could add many arguments in favour of my thesis: I must confine myself to referring, for further clarification, to the writings cited in my bibliography.

My answer to Mr. Pirenne must also be kept within too short a compass, since he touched upon two questions on which, as he said himself, there should be much to discuss. The first question concerns 'saving the appearances', namely the building of theories — optical, mechanical, astronomical — fitting what we actually see; the second concerns perspective. On the first point I shall only say that such theories will be the more scientific and rational, the more we realize that appearances are created by the mind of each observer and so are not constant but vary from one observer to another.

If what one sees is not 'reality', as most people believe, but the image that each observer makes for himself of what is the case, according to the information he receives through his eyes and other senses, and from previous experience stored — not always faithfully — in his memory, the task of 'saving the appearances' is much simplified; and any theoretical conception can be received and taken into careful account even though it does not save the appearances.

This is specially true concerning Pirenne's second argument: on the controversial question of perspective. Many geometers wanted to apply Euclidean geometry to representation of space, and 'believed' themselves to have been on the right road, provided space is really Euclidean. But artists who followed this attitude found themselves in an awkward position, because their task is not to represent in painting what is real, but to represent the representation of reality as it is 'made' by each observer; they do not have to paint the real world (this is today the task of photography), but the world of appearance, which is *always different*, in geometrical terms, from the real world, if one excepts the immediate neighbourhood of the observer.

In order to prove this statement, which many would consider heretical, I shall touch briefly upon a question which will also serve as an indirect answer to Warnock's and Pirenne's remarks.

Everybody has noticed that objects are seen as smaller when they are far away than when they are near. This experience is so common that nobody gives it a minute's thought. It is in fact a demonstration of my view, because, if the world of appearances coincided with the real world, things in this world should have the same size as things seen, as happens in the observer's immediate vicinity. But we can go further than this. The question: why are objects seen the smaller the farther away they are? has been answered for more than two thousand years geometrically: because they are seen under a smaller angle. This answer is based on the hypothesis that the size of shapes seen is proportional to the angle under which they are seen, or, in modern terms, to the dimensions of the retinal image. But this is false: objects near to the observer — a chair, a book, a hand — are seen equally large even though their distance from the eye varies between 1 and 10 times or more.

I believe myself to have been the first to break with this old tradition, by stating that the angle under which the object is seen has no influence whatever on the size of the shapes seen by the observer. The proof can be given in many ways: I shall follow a very brief one.[1]

In Fig. 1, let O be the observer and ABC the horizon with the *real* mountains AB and BC. These mountains appear to the observer as being, for example, three times *smaller* than the real mountains, as $A'B'$ and $B'C'$. Now it is clear that the observer must also see the two apparent mountains three times *nearer*. If the *shapes seen* were localized at the same distance from O as the real mountains in fact are, they should be in the positions $A''B''$ and $B_1''C''$: but in this case the horizon could not be continuous, and there would be a gap between B'' and $B^{1}{}''$. Since nobody sees this gap, we must conclude that the only way of getting a continuous horizon with shapes smaller than the objects on the real horizon is to localize the shapes on a circle of smaller radius, proportionally to the size of the shapes seen on it.

This means that the shapes seen are not the real objects (if somebody says he sees the object he is wrong); they are phan-

[1] Vasco Ronchi, "Does what we see coincide with what exists?", *Atti della Fondazione Giorgio Ronchi*, XVI (1961) 6–17.

tasms, similar to the objects but smaller and nearer. Only this will explain many strange and frequent appearances.

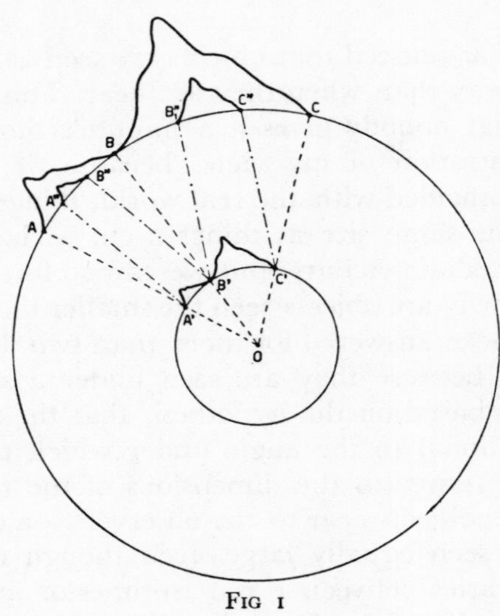

FIG I

These remarks may clarify my answer to Mr. Pirenne's question on perspective: painting aims at representing the apparent world and its geometry is very complex.

Before concluding, it may be interesting to remind ourselves of the case of Nicolò Tartaglia, which shows how powerful faith can be even in the domain of so-called exact sciences. Tartaglia was a famous *mathematician*, who wrote, among other things, a book on ballistics which was studied by Galileo: some notes in Galileo's own hand are preserved in a copy of that book in Florence. According to the theory obtaining in Tartaglia's times, the movement of projectiles was composed of two parts (Fig. 2): the first was *violent motion* (*AC′*); the

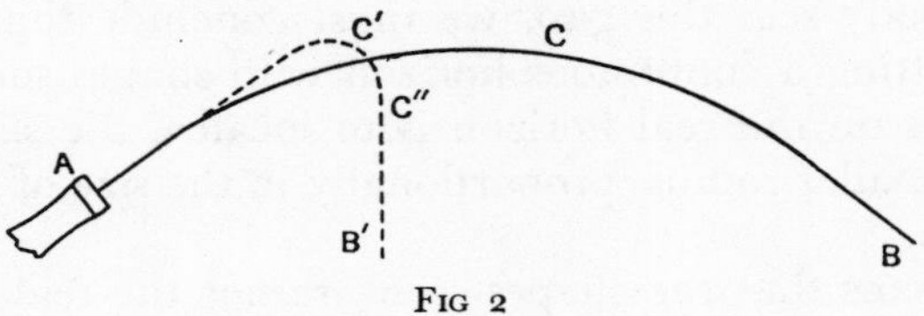

FIG 2

second, *natural motion* in a vertical direction (*C″B′*). It is clear that the author of this *physical* theory had 'saved the appearances' as seen from near the gun: these appearances correspond to those I have mentioned concerning the contraction of the apparent world as compared with the real world. It is also clear that, had the observer been in another place, for example near the landing place of the missile *B*, he would not have said that the trajectory had that shape, because the victims of shelling never see the projectiles coming from above their heads. Philosophers had warned that one should not trust one sense without the help of the other senses; Tartaglia did not listen to them, and suffered in consequence. Still, nobody doubted his theory of the trajectory of projectiles, and his book on ballistics was held in great esteem. But as soon as Galileo — starting from revolutionary conceptions — proved that the trajectory of the projectile must be a parabola (*ACB*), Tartaglia's demonstration was immediately forgotten: it was not refuted, simply forgotten. Nobody spoke of Tartaglia's 'experiment'. What is then the use of *mathematical demonstrations* if they can be altered so easily without a fight and without a discussion?

What happened can be described, in short, as follows: Tartaglia and his contemporaries observed the missile from near the gun: what they saw, they considered as true, as 'reality', and tried to give a physical explanation of it. What they were seeing from their place was so 'true' that they did not feel the need of watching the projectile from any other position, either from the rather dangerous landing-point, or from the side. Only a man who doubted what he saw would have planned such other observations.

After Galileo launched the new theory, a new *faith* took the place of the previous one. Nobody any longer observed the trajectory from near the gun; if at all, they observed it from the side. Nobody any longer tried to 'save the appearances'; faith in the new demonstration was so complete that observation was omitted.

That this was again *faith*, and not demonstrated truth, is clear from the well-established fact that missile trajectories such as can be obtained in the air, on the earth, are not parabolas but much more complicated curves, affected by the change in the acceleration due to gravity at different heights above sea level, by changes in the direction of gravity, by air resistance, winds and so on.

This example of Tartaglia's theory is typical of the reciprocal relations between faith, experience, and science.

B. A. Farrell

I would like to thank Mr. Mace for his helpful comments. One of his main points is that the distinction I have drawn between clinical and objective psychology concedes too much. I agree that the distinction as I have presented it is far too sharp. There are indeed many psychological workers in the clinical field who are prosecuting their inquiries by objective methods. Moreover, I could be accused with justification of having used the term 'clinical psychology' in a way that diverges from its normal use in this country, and which is misleading in consequence. But any other currently used term would raise similar difficulties. I used the term 'clinical psychology' in the way I did solely to exhibit an aspect of the historical controversy in this field.

I shall now touch on two points raised by Mr. Alexander.

(1) I tried in my paper to exhibit the difficulty of drawing a sharp, neat line between procedures that are scientific and those that are not. Now the ordinary scientific worker, including the student of human behaviour, uses the ordinary naturalistic way of talking about the world in the course of his work. This way of talking embodies an implicit distinction between a procedure that is scientific and one that is superstitious and magical. When a psychologist is faced with the problem of describing the differences and likenesses between the behaviour of Mr. A and Mr. D in the problem situation I outlined, it will be quite proper for him to *use* the ordinary, naturalistic distinction between magic and science to exhibit these likenesses and differences. This is what I have tried to do in this paper. I have tried to *use* this distinction to exhibit the character of the behaviour of Messrs. A, C and D, in order thereby to help to show how it is difficult to draw a neat line between procedures that are scientific and those that are not. But if I were challenged to *elucidate* this ordinary naturalistic distinction between science and magic, then I should be involved in the sort of complications to which Mr. Alexander drew attention. Thus, I may find myself forced to agree that I am using certain criteria of relevance when I class Mr. A's procedure as a magical one and irrelevant to the solution of the problem. But it is obviously not part of my concern in this paper to elucidate the distinction between a procedure that is magical and one that is scientific. This is an additional philosophical task. Nor is there any genuine doubt that I am applying the naturalistic

distinction correctly in this instance when I class Mr. A's procedure as a magical one. But if I *am* challenged about this, the appropriate move for me to make is not to try to meet the challenge, but to find another example that we would all agree was an instance of a magical procedure.

(2) A strong case can be made for the view that psycho-analytic *theory* is unscientific in character, and that for this reason alone psycho-analysis is to be treated as an unscientific enterprise. Mr. Alexander is quite right to stress the defectiveness of the theory. It is also quite fair to say that I have not stressed it in my paper; and that my paper fails to convey the strength of the case that can be brought against psycho-analysis and cognate contributions. I hope that no one will go away supposing for a moment that he has had the case against psycho-analysis fully presented in this paper.

But Mr. Alexander's point is not quite as apt and weighty as it may seem. (*a*) In suggesting that objections to the *theory* of psycho-analysis are more important than objections to the *method*, Mr. Alexander supposes that when I speak of 'procedures' I am speaking of what are normally called 'methods' in a discussion of scientific method. But this is not so. I use the word 'procedure' widely enough to include 'theory making and using'; and when I place psycho-analysis at the crudely empirical end of the continuum, I do so in respect of the quality of its theory as much as of the quality of its methods. I do not make this clear in the paper; and Mr. Alexander's objection does us the service of drawing attention to the wide sense in which I use the word 'procedure', and to the possible confusion this may cause. (*b*) In so far as it is apt to say that I have concentrated on 'method', it is necessary to remember that my paper is concerned with a certain controversy in the history of psychology. I am inclined to think that the objections to psycho-analysis on account of its unscientific methods were more important historically than objections based on its defective theory. Hence, in fact, my stress on method in this paper.

R. C. Oldfield

I agree with much Mr. Vernant said. For the purpose of this Symposium, which is to draw lessons from history, the two contributions relating to psychology were arranged so as to cover separately two trends in the subject which are to some extent mutually opposing. It would not be surprising if, as Mr.

Vernant says, the interaction between psychophysiology and "metaphysics, of biological inspiration" led to exciting advances which at present we cannot foresee. But the aim of my communication was not a speculative one.

I am also in sympathy with Mrs. Toulmin in her plea that psychologists should not allow themselves to be tied by a compulsion to construct their science in accordance with models from the older established, primarily physical, sciences. Indeed I would go further and suggest that much preoccupation with methodology, and with complex logically structured theories, and the prevalance of jargon are not merely hindrances to real progress but an unconsciously motivated way of avoiding it.

21

The Scientific Approach to Disease: Specific Entity and Individual Sickness

OWSEI TEMKIN

I

This paper should perhaps be described as the thoughts of an historian of medicine on a subject that is not, in itself, historical. We are not dealing here with the historical development of the concept, or of the typology, of disease, for which we can refer to a series of competent publications.[1] Nor shall we try to evaluate the interplay of external and internal factors, since this has been done by Mr. Shryock[2] whose comments appear below. Rather we shall discuss some historical illustrations of the role which the notions of specific entity and individual sickness have played in the scientific approach to disease.

The basic situation involved is a perennial one. When a man is ill, that is when he feels dis-ease, he has experiences which are partly his own, partly open to others. This is his individual sickness which in exactly this particular form with all its details will never repeat itself in others or even in himself. But the sick man, his family, and neighbours, the physician (if there is one), all will try to understand what is happening to him. When Job was smitten by Satan he complained:

[1] Of the very large literature dealing with, or related to, this subject, I name here Emanuel Berghoff, *Entwicklungsgeschichte des Krankheitsbegriffes* (2nd ed., Vienna, 1947); Friedrich Curtius, *Individuum und Krankheit, Grundzüge einer Individualpathologie* (Berlin, 1959); Lester S. King, "What is Disease?", *Philosophy of Science*, XXI (1954) 193–203; Richard Koch, *Die ärztliche Diagnose* (Wiesbaden, 1917); L. J. Rather, "Towards a Philosophical Study of the Idea of Disease", *The Historical Development of Physiological Thought*, ed. Chandler McC. Brooks and Paul F. Cranefield (New York, 1959) 351–73; Walther Riese, *The Conception of Disease, its History, its Versions and its Nature* (New York, 1953). A few additional items will be cited below, with my apologies to the very numerous authors whose publications I am unable to mention.

[2] Richard H. Shryock, "The interplay of social and internal factors in the history of modern medicine", *The Scientific Monthly*, LXXVI (1953) 221–30.

> . . . wearisome nights are appointed to me. When I lie down, I say, When shall I arise, and the night be gone? and I am full of tossings to and fro unto the dawning of the day. My flesh is clothed with worms and clods of dust; my skin is broken, and become loathsome. . . . When I say, My bed shall comfort me, my couch shall ease my complaint; Then thou searest me with dreams, and terrifiest me through visions: So that my soul chooseth strangling and death rather than my life. I would not live alway: let me alone; for my days are vanity.[1]

This is part of the way in which Job, the sick man, tries to express what he feels, sees, and thinks when being diseased. The narrator of the book puts it more briefly: "Satan . . . smote Job with sore boils from the sole of his foot unto his crown."[2] This is the diagnosis of a disease: generalized sore boils caused by Satan.

Speaking of 'sickness', or 'illness', or 'disease', we have introduced a conceptual denominator uniting many such individual events. The individual may not think of himself as being ill or dis-eased. By thus labelling him, his friends, physician, or society, have classified his experience. From here on it becomes possible to approach the matter scientifically. But the introduction of the label has also determined the reply. The person's experience has become the sickness of X. Use of the term disease raises the question of the nature of disease. Here we may avail ourselves of the observation of Lord Cohen of Birkenhead that two main ideas have been dominant: disease as an entity that befalls a healthy person, and "disease as a deviation from the normal", where a number of factors have influenced a man so as to make him suffer. To this observation Lord Cohen adds:

> Many terms are used to cover these two concepts — e.g., *ontological* — indicating the independent self-sufficiency of diseases running a regular course and with a natural history of their own, as opposed to the *biographical* or *historical* which records the history of the patient. Other names arise from the founders of the schools of thought which appear to have given these concepts birth — e.g., *Platonic* and *Hippocratic*; from the philosophies from which they are primarily derived — the contrasting *realist* and *nominalist*, *rationalist* and *empirical*, *conventional* and *naturalistic* schools. The names are of little importance. The two notions varying a little in content and occasionally overlapping have persisted, the dominance of the one or the other at different epochs reflecting either the philosophy of

[1] Job, vii, 3–5 and 13–16. [2] Ibid. ii, 7.

the time or the influence and teaching of outstanding personalities.[1]

Without inquiring into the historical emergence of these two ideas which, for brevity's sake, we shall here refer to as the 'ontological' and the 'physiological', I shall make a few comments on their interplay, and this will also lead us to other aspects.

II

Ontologists find themselves hard pressed when asked what exactly they mean by the existence of specific diseases. In the case of 'demoniac possession' the answer is reasonably clear. The demon which has entered a person struggles with his personality: it speaks out of the mouth of the possessed; it makes him commit unusual acts, it inflicts pain which causes the possessed to cry or to wrestle with the demon.[2] Ontologists have, therefore, been suspected of clinging to a demoniac aetiology of disease, even if the demon was replaced by a bacterium. Indeed there are analogies between the demonistic and bacteriological interpretation, at least where bacteriology appears in the crude assumption of a specific micro-organism as *the* cause of the specific disease. In both cases the entrance of a certain living being is made responsible for the disease, and the expulsion or killing of this being is considered the essential part of therapy. In both cases there is a clear-cut difference between health and disease.

But even the extreme bacteriologist of the nineteenth century had to deviate from this ideal of medical ontology. The bacterium might be made responsible for all the symptoms of the disease, yet it could cause the symptoms only by damaging parts or organs of the body or otherwise interfering with their normal functions. The disease was represented by the injured organism which the bacterium had poisoned. With the elimination of crude and one-sided modes of thinking, the bacteriologist had to visualize the relationship between parasite and host as an interaction, and it was this interaction which manifested itself as the disease.

In the history of medical ontology, specific aetiology is not a constitutive element. The ancient Empiricists, a sect founded in the third century B.C., did not believe that nature could be

[1] Henry Cohen, "The evolution of the concept of disease", in *Concepts of Medicine*, ed. Brandon Lush (Oxford, 1960) 160.

[2] T. K. Oesterreich, *Possession, Demoniacal and Other* (London, 1930).

understood, and they rejected aetiological research beyond such evident causes as hunger and cold. They concentrated on "pathognomonic syndromes" as Galen tells us.[1] A Greek author of the sixth century indicates that the Empiricists thought of diseases as species. "Of symptoms," he writes,

some constitute species of the diseases and definitely appear together with them. The Empiricists call them 'pathognomonic' as characterizing the nature of the species (*idea*) of the diseases: for instance, cough, fever, dyspnea, and stabbing pain in pleurisy. Other symptoms, foreign [to the idea of the disease] appear later. . . .[2]

Since the scepticism of the Empiricists regarding the comprehensibility of nature reflects the scepticism of the Academy, as Edelstein has shown,[3] their belief in species of disease as Platonic ideas would not be improbable.

Sydenham, the arch-ontologist of modern times, also disparaged the search for the remote causes of diseases. He claimed that "Nature, in the production of disease, is uniform and consistent; so much so, that for the same disease in different persons the symptoms are for the most part the same . . .".[4] On the other hand,

a disease, however much its cause may be adverse to the human body, is nothing more than an effort of Nature, who strives with might and main to restore the health of the patient by the elimination of the morbific matter.[5]

Put together, this amounts to the definition of diseases as uniform patterns of the organism's attempt to restore its health. The "concatenation of symptoms"[6] is nature's method for the elimination of the peccant matter. This is not very far removed from a very recent statement that "physicians now consider most diseases to be distinct from one another insofar as they

[1] The passages are conveniently available in Karl Deichgräber, *Die griechische Empirikerschule* (Berlin, 1930), see Index *s.v. syndrome.*

[2] Stephanus, "Commentarii in priorem Galeni librum therapeuticum ad Glauconem", *Apollonii Citiensis, Stephani, Palladii, Theophili, Meletii, Damascii, Ioannis, aliorum scholia in Hippocratem et Galenum*, ed. F. R. Dietz (Regimontii Prussorum, 1834) I, 233–344 (p. 267).

[3] Ludwig Edelstein "Empirie und Skepsis in der griechischen Empirikerschule", *Quellen und Studien zur Geschichte der Naturwissenschaften und der Medizin*, III, 4 (1933) 45–53.

[4] *The Works of Thomas Sydenham, M.D.*, trans. R. G. Latham (London, 1848) I, 18.

[5] Ibid. p. 29.

[6] Ibid.

represent patterned responses or adaptations to noxious forces in the environment".[1]

The difficulty inherent in the ontological idea of the separate existence of diseases is matched by the difficulty of making the diseases or patterned responses conform to the variety of individual sickness. Sub-divisions that made the distinction between disease and symptom illusory had to be assigned in the nosological schemes of Boissier de Sauvages, Cullen, and Pinel. In the first half of the nineteenth century, pathological anatomy helped to weed out a number of diseases and to secure the position of others. But many contemporary investigators recognized that the anatomical changes, though they might account for a number of clinical symptoms, were products of the disease rather than the disease itself.[2] This led to a discussion of the nature of the disease behind anatomical and clinical symptoms. In this discussion ontologists fared badly until bacteriologists were believed to have discovered the source of disease outside the body and geneticists inside it.

The hope that bacteriology would allow a reliable classification on the basis of specific causes, at least in the realm of infectious diseases, also proved doubtful. If this principle were pushed to the logical extreme, there should be as many specific diseases as there are pathogenic organisms, or even strains.

The weakness of a bacteriological definition of specific diseases is shared by the definitions based on other aetiological classifications. There should be as many specific deficiency diseases as there are substances whose absence can affect the body adversely. Finally, there should also be as many hereditary diseases as there are different genes representing abnormal submolecular chemical structures. A person with haemoglobin-C genes, we are informed, will suffer from so-called homozygous haemoglobin-C disease. If he has one haemoglobin-C gene only, while the other is a haemoglobin-S gene (sickle-cell-anemia gene) "he suffers from a disease that has been given the name haemoglobin-C: sickle-cell anemia".[3] Since about twenty kinds of abnormal human haemoglobin are said to exist, the number of combinations and possible 'specific diseases' in this one province seems very large. In short, if based

[1] Stewart Wolf, "Disease as a way of life: neural integration in systemic pathology", *Perspectives in Biology and Medicine*, IV (1961) 288–305 (p. 288).

[2] Knud Faber, *Nosography* (2nd ed., New York, 1930) 53.

[3] Linus Pauling in *Disease and the Advancement of Basic Science*, ed. Henry K. Beecher (Cambridge, Mass., 1960) 3.

on causative principles such as micro-organisms, absence of nutritive substances, or inherited genes, danger arises lest specific diseases be postulated which have no clinical reality, or, vice versa, that clinically important entities like appendicitis have no logical place in the nosological scheme.

III

The weaknesses of ontology are avoided by the physiological idea of disease. This has been cultivated by Hippocrates and his scientific (in contrast to the purely empirical) successors from Galen to our own times. When we turn to the Hippocratic *Epidemics*, it is true, disease entities are accepted as a matter of course and referred to by names, such as "phthisis", which had probably been in common popular usage. Hippocrates, or whoever the physicians were whom this name connotes, is outstanding for having seen disease as a process in time, not as a mere stationary picture.[1] The book *On the Sacred Disease*, that is epilepsy, is probably the earliest monograph on a disease, describing its pathogenesis, symptoms, pathological physiology, and prognosis. Diseases have their nature; but they are seen as rooted in the general nature of man. There is neither a studious exclusion of disease entities nor a one-sided concentration on them. In judging diseases we are told to take into account "the peculiar nature of each individual".[2] Most of the patient's activities, mental and physical, are considered, from thoughts and dreams to eructation and flatulence. The list of things to be observed included diseases and symptoms as well as functions and discharges such as respiration and urine. This allows the gathering of a very large number of data in each case. Since the totality of these data will vary from patient to patient, each will have a description of symptoms fitting him only.

But the ancient followers of Hippocrates did not believe that Hippocrates had given them a science of the individual. Galen, the last of the ancient Hippocratics, and Galen's Byzantine successors ended on a sceptical note.[3] They thought Hippo-

[1] Owsei Temkin, "Greek Medicine as science and art", *Isis*, XLIV (1953) 213–25 (p. 223).

[2] Hippocrates, "Epidemics", I, 10, *The Genuine Works of Hippocrates*, trans. Francis Adams (London, 1849) I, 367.

[3] For the following see Galen, *Ad Glauconem de medendi methodo* I, 1, *Opera*, ed. C. G. Kühn (Leipzig, 1821 ff.) XI, 1 ff., and the commentary on this work by Stephanus, op. cit.

crates right in demanding that the nature of the disease as well as of the individual be studied. The nature of disease was to be found in man's temperament, the structure of his parts, his physiological and his psychological dynamism. Thus the nature of disease was grounded in the nature of man. All men have humours and divers parts and organs; they all digest and possess sensation and mobility. Consequently, they also have diseases in common. But no two men will be completely alike. The individual differences are "ineffable and cannot be subjected to concepts".[1] Therefore, it was concluded, there is no science of the individual, and medicine suffers from a fundamental contradiction: its practice deals with the individual while its theory grasps universals only.[2]

Ancient medicine had a particular reason for this scepticism.[3] The physician possessed an approximate picture of the behaviour and appearance of healthy individuals.[4] He could compare his patient to this picture of the normal and decide what was "according to nature" (*kata physin*) and what "against nature" (*para physin*). But just because of the physician's strongly individualizing inclination, such a comparison was considered insufficient. For instance, his patient's face might indicate a morbid discolouration. If the patient's colour always had been like this, the finding was meaningless, while in a new patient, the physician had nothing to refer to. It was advisable that the doctor be his patient's friend and know him intimately.[5] Such intimate knowledge was possible in private practice only, and, according to Celsus, where it was impossible, medicine of an inferior kind was practised because it relied on the features common to many diseases:

> For in like manner those who treat cattle and horses, since it is impossible to learn from dumb animals particulars of their complaints, depend only upon common characteristics; so also do foreigners, as they are ignorant of reasoning subtleties, look rather to common characteristics of disease. Again, those who take charge of large hospitals, because they cannot pay full attention to individuals, resort to these common characteristics.[6]

[1] Stephanus, op. cit. p. 235. [2] Ibid.

[3] The nature of the medical scepticism of the Hippocratic authors as rooted in their individualistic approach has been brought out by Edelstein, op. cit.

[4] Celsus, *De medicina*, I, 2, 4. [5] Ibid., Prooem., 73.

[6] Ibid., 65; Celsus, *De medicina*, with an English translation by W. G. Spencer (London, 1935 ff.) I, 35.

Celsus made this remark in discussing the ancient sect of the Methodists who judged disease according to whether it exhibited a *status strictus, laxus,* or *mixtus*. Thessalus, a Methodist of the time of Nero, boasted of teaching medicine to anybody within six months.[1] Methodism was popular in the Roman Empire, and it would be of interest to find out whether it had its social roots among military surgeons and in the latifundia, since such hospitals (*valetudinaria*) as existed in Antiquity were for soldiers and slaves.

Few things mark the chasm between ancient and modern medicine as impressively as does the different character of the hospitals. The ancient hospital, just because it housed many patients, was looked down upon as neglecting individual sickness. The modern hospital, just because it houses many patients, has developed into an institution where individual sickness can be described with some degree of precision.

In the hospitals of the nineteenth century it became possible to observe many cases of the same disease, clinically as well as anatomically, and thus to strengthen the diagnosis of 'diseases'. At the same time, it became possible to establish standards of what was normal, and to elaborate tests which expressed numerical agreement with, or deviation from the norm. The norm here was a value found in a smaller or greater number of healthy persons. Without this norm, measurements were of little avail. The ever lengthening chart of data accumulating in the course of medical examinations, from pulse rate and temperature curve, to X-ray pictures, chemical, physical, bacteriological and immunological tests, mirrors this development which has been traced admirably by Knud Faber for the nineteenth and early twentieth centuries. A modern physician has at his disposal infinitely more objective data concerning a particular patient than the Greek doctor could ever dream of. Ophthalmoscope, bronchoscope, etc. allow him a direct view of the conditions of many parts. Experimental medicine enables the physician to interpret his findings so as to translate the language of symptoms and tests into the language of physiological processes. Here then is a scientific approach to individual sickness.

Thus it might appear that modern medicine has succeeded where ancient medicine failed. This success is due to giving statistical attention to what is normal and abnormal. The

[1] Galen, *De sectis ad eos qui introducentur*, VI, refers to Methodists in general, but seems to have Thessalus in mind.

Ancients did not evaluate statistically what was "according to nature" and "contrary" to it. Still, there is a significant parallel between their attempt to explain certain diseases as an imbalance of qualities or humours and our numerical occupation with the normal and abnormal. The parallel can be formulated in the question: what deviation constitutes sickness? We know that 'the normal individual' is a construct, not to be found in nature. Likewise, the Galenists realized that a complete balance of the four humours and their qualities represented an ideal temperament. We allow variations within the normal;[1] the Ancients conceived of temperaments where the predominance of one or the other humour characterized the still healthy organism. But where exactly was, and is, the line to be drawn where imbalance or variation becomes disease?

Galen defined health as a condition "in which we neither suffer pain nor are hindered in the functions of daily life".[2] In as far as this definition is concerned with impeded function, it leads to the equation of disease with *functio laesa*, popular among the academic physiologists of modern times. "The condition of the living body whereby the ability of exercising any one function is abolished, is called disease," writes Boerhaave in his *Institutions*, and he adds the following comment to the word disease: "we correctly define it as 'functio laesa'. . . ."[3] In speaking of the functions, Boerhaave had in mind the traditional natural, vital, and psychic functions, all of which could be diminished to the point of disappearance.

But, if the ontologist was rightly challenged by the demand that disease must be understandable as a process of life, the physiologist was challenged to show cause why the endless variations of form and gradations of function should somewhere admit classification as healthy and diseased.[4] It is a truism to designate 'health' and 'disease' as medical categories. It is not easy to decide whether these categories themselves, though relating to biological phenomena, still belong in biology. Following in the footsteps of Broussais,[5] the young Virchow

[1] John A. Ryle, "The meaning of normal", *Concepts of Medicine*, op. cit. pp. 137–49.

[2] Galen, *De sanitate tuenda*, I, 5.

[3] Hermann Boerhaave, *Praelectiones academicae in proprias institutiones rei medicae*, ed. Albertus Haller (Turin, 1742 ff.) V, 4 and 10.

[4] This problem has been dealt with very lucidly by G. W. Pickering, "The concept of essential hypertension", *Concepts of Medicine*, op. cit. pp. 170–6.

[5] Erwin H. Ackerknecht, *Rudolf Virchow* (Madison, 1953) 50–1.

referred to disease as life under changed circumstances. But Virchow himself later admitted that a man in prison also lived under changed circumstances without therefore necessarily being ill.[1] The answer may depend on the biologist's philosophical orientation. If he excludes all teleology, he may, with Ricker, believe that health and disease are not scientific terms.[2] If he does not mind using teleological notions, he may find it pertinent to pay attention to those states where nature fails in two of its main aims, as Galen had them, assurance of the life of the individual and of the species.[3]

But disease does not necessarily threaten life. To supplement his teleological biology, Galen added nature's aim of assuring a "good life".[4] A blind man might be able to live and to have progeny, yet he would not live well. But there are no limits to the "good life". For man, the good life extends far into his mental and social well-being. This is best illustrated by Galen's reference to pain in his definition of health and in his explanation of the functions of daily life as our ability "to take part in government, to bathe, drink, and eat, and do the other things we want".[5] Participation in government and frequenting the bath were activities of the member of the ancient city state. In another civilization, different functions might be required for health, or, if absent, mark disease.

Examples for this are most easily adduced from the field of mental abnormalities. Theologians of the Renaissance persecuted witches as confederates of the devil, and the worldly authorities executed them because of their alleged danger to society. The defence of witches could claim that the devil was powerless to bring about the evil deeds ascribed to witches, themselves victims of the devil who caused their illusions. This argument was a theological one,[6] which explains the accusation made against Weyer, the defender of witches, that he meddled

[1] Virchow, "Über die heutige Stellung der Pathologie", in Karl Sudhoff, *Rudolf Virchow und die Deutschen Naturforscherversammlungen* (Leipzig, 1922) 77–97 (p. 91); see also Paul Diepgen, "Die Universalität von Rudolf Virchows Lebenswerk", *Virchows Archiv.*, CCCXXII (1952) 221–32 (p. 228).

[2] Ricker distinguishes between medical and scientific thinking; cf. also Claudius F. Mayer, "Metaphysical trends in modern pathology", *Bulletin of the History of Medicine*, XXVI (1952) 70–81.

[3] Galen, *De usu partium*, VI, 7; ed. G. Helmreich (Leipzig, 1907) I, 318.

[4] Ibid: *τὸ καλῶς ζῆν.*

[5] Galen, *De sanitate tuenda*, I, 5.

[6] Gregory Zilboorg, *The Medical Man and the Witch During the Renaissance* (Baltimore, 1935) 117.

in things which were none of his, the physician's, concern. Instead of being victims of Satan, witches could be declared to suffer from a natural disease, preferably hysteria. Similarly, convulsions, often taken as demonstrations of demoniac possession or of divine enthusiasm, were diagnosed as *grande hystérie* by the school of Charcot.[1]

In contrast, Charcot's own time tended to refuse recognition to disease where it existed. It is not so very long ago that people who felt ill, or who suspected illness, would consult a physician to be told after a thorough physical examination that there was nothing wrong with them, and that they could go home. Thomas Huxley who suffered from "the blue devils and funk" could not make out what it was and suggested "liver".[2] Disease in the second half of the nineteenth century meant somatic disease, if one disregarded the frank psychoses. This attitude reflected the prevailing materialistic philosophy which Huxley himself had helped to shape. It also reflected the conviction that there is a science of disease separable from medicine as the art of healing. Men of this persuasion might have much human sympathy for the sick, but they were not easily influenced in their scientific work by vague subjective complaints. A whole realm of disease was in danger of losing the right to existence because of the dissociation between the sick person's complaint and the physician's philosophical outlook.

Functio laesa is not a self-explanatory definition of disease in man. The ontologist avoids this difficulty by accepting entities which are set apart from health or 'normal' functioning. However he may define disease, it is something strange to man in his ordinary life: it enters or befalls him. In this respect, the ontologist's weakness is also his strength. There is a tendency in ontology to consider disease entities as persistent and to corroborate the specific nature of a disease by tracing its existence through the ages. Bretonneau said of diphtheria, "because during a long series of centuries it remained so constantly the same that in each of the epochs where it appeared it was recognized in the admirable description of Aretaeus",[3] giving this among the arguments for diphtheria as a specific

[1] Owsei Temkin, *The Falling Sickness* (Baltimore, 1945) 321.

[2] Leonard Huxley, *Life and Letters of Thomas Henry Huxley* (New York, 1901) II, 112–13.

[3] Pierre-Fidèle Bretonneau, *Traités de la dothinentérie et de la spécificité*, publiés, etc. par le Dr. Louis Dubreuil-Chambardel (Paris, 1922) 309.

affection. Since, according to Charcot, *grande hystérie* was "a perfectly well characterized morbid entity", his school tried to prove its existence long before its scientific discovery.[1]

The ontological bias of the perennial existence of the specific diseases can express itself moreover in a reluctance to admit the appearance of new diseases or the existence of specific diseases during a short period of time. The plague of Thucydides has challenged diagnostic acumen and has been variously interpreted as plague, smallpox, typhus, measles. Without denying the possibility of identifying it with some disease of our modern nosological catalogue, I still fail to see proof of the necessity. Similarly, the "sweating sickness" which appeared in epidemic waves, chiefly in England, between 1485 and 1551, is but reluctantly acknowledged as a disease unknown to modern nosology.

The ontologist thus avoids a difficulty which the radical physiologist must face. The difference in attitude between the two is expressed in the encounter between Michel Peter and Pasteur as told by René Dubos. Peter claimed that "Disease is in us, of us, by us", whereas

> Pasteur emphasized that contagion and disease could be the expression of the living processes of foreign microbial parasites, introduced from the outside, descending from parents identical to themselves, and incapable of being generated *de novo*.[2]

Pasteur made it clear that contagious disease was the expression of a foreign life. But if disease has to be looked for in our own nature it has to be accounted for differently. If we attribute it to genes we still have recourse to ontology, as I indicated previously, an 'internal' ontological orientation in contrast to the external of the bacteriologist. It is probably neither possible nor advisable to renounce ontology completely. The wisdom of Hippocrates documents itself in accepting such popular disease entities as were known, rather than denouncing them. The danger which the physiologist faces, as well as the consequences which may ensue, are illustrated by Freud's work — if it is permissible to broaden the term physiology so as to admit his psychological method.

In the meaning of our context, Freud offered a physiological explanation of neuroses by explaining them as the result of a reaction between psychic urges and restriction imposed upon

[1] Cf. above, p. 639, n. 1.

[2] René J. Dubos, *Louis Pasteur, Free Lance of Science* (Boston, 1950) 246.

them. He believed himself to be dealing with psychological phenomena like the one symbolized as the Oedipus complex, necessarily engendered in all civilized human beings. This being the case, everybody was fundamentally neurotic, the intensity and particular turn of the neurosis depending on the experiences of the individual's life. Psycho-analysis thus succumbed to the danger of what the Greeks called *aeipatheia*, perpetual illness.

Psycho-analysis insisted upon a minute scrutiny of the patient's life in order to find, and to make conscious, those experiences with which the patient had been unable to cope successfully. This meant that the disease was not due to some accident. More than others, Freud and his followers leaned on the biographical approach, on the detailed case history of the patient. Finally, as the name indicates, psycho-analysis originated from Freud's therapeutic activity. Freud gained his insight into neuroses while treating patients. Since the contact between patient and psycho-analyst invariably involved an emotional engagement (on the patient's side at least), the psycho-analysis had to affect the patient. Thereby Freud ran counter to one of the scientific ideals of his time: the study of an object without interfering with it.

Whatever the merits of psycho-analysis may be, I believe that it was consistent (though possibly wrong) in imputing neurosis to everybody, looking for the vicissitudes of man's neurosis in his biography, making the judgment of manifest disease dependent on the patient's inability to cope with the aims of society or of himself, and avoiding a gulf between the diagnostic and therapeutic activity of the physician who deals with individual sickness.

Consistency is not necessarily a virtue, but it has the advantage of laying bare what may otherwise pass unnoticed. I believe that Freud elucidated the part played by the case history and therapy in the comprehension of individual sickness.[1]

IV

Case histories form one of the glories of Hippocratic medicine; they mark the appearance of the form by which the physician

[1] In thus summarily dealing with Freud and psycho-analysis, I am conscious of some degree of historical and material oversimplification for the sake of brevity.

tries to deal with an individual illness. The Hippocratic case histories are remarkable for what they contain, a passionless description of the symptoms and outcome of the case, and for what they largely lack, details as to the patient's diet and therapy.

In course of time, the case history changed, especially with the introduction of the new clinical teaching methods in Leyden. The diagnosis, usually meaning a disease entity, was incorporated, the treatment was registered, and, if available, a post mortem report was added in cases with fatal outcome. Detailed case histories emanated from the hospitals of the Old Vienna School of the eighteenth century. In the nineteenth century, a separation between the subjective history of the patient and the objective examination by the physician became noticeable. The objective signs of percussion and auscultation were the early core of the examination; temperature curves, and the results of the ever increasing tests and special examinations, followed. Thus the case history has come to incorporate all the data obtained through the scientific progress of medicine.[1]

As the member of a profession, the physician has used case histories to contribute to the spread or advance of medical knowledge. This, probably, was already the function of the Hippocratic case histories. All cases that are unusual because of the patient's illness, or its outcome, or the treatment employed, reveal new possibilities regarding human disease. The case history therefore has played a great role in the history of medicine. As casuistic material in combination with the post mortem protocol, it led to the rise of pathological anatomy for reasons which become clearer when this development is compared with the rise of normal anatomy.

The study of anatomy as based on dissection did not derive from the opening of many bodies. Both Galen and Vesalius described the structure of *the* body (of animal or man). They were aware of variations which, it is true, could be established as such by repeated autopsies only. Yet it is fair to say that both expected an immediate insight into the body, as God or nature had willed it, that is into the norm. This insight was then cleared by discounting individual variations or morbid changes.[2]

[1] On the history of the case history see: Pedro Lain Entralgo, *La historia clinica* (Madrid, 1950); Walther Riese, "The structure of the clinical history", *Bull. Hist. Med.* XVI (1944) 437–49; O. Temkin, "Studien zum 'Sinn'-Begriff in der Medizin", *Kyklos*, II (1929) 43–59.

[2] William L. Straus, jr. and O. Temkin, "Vesalius and the problem of variability", *Bull. Hist. Med.* XIV (1943) 609–33.

Although some of the ancient physicians had the idea of a pathological anatomy, pathological anatomy, as we know it, began with the medieval *anatomia privata*. This was a dissection performed in an individual case to establish the cause of death, especially if foul play was suspected. It differed from the *anatomia publica* where the fabric of man's body was demonstrated to a large audience. Benivieni's little book of 1507 from which we conventionally date the literary beginning of pathological anatomy, was named significantly: "On Some Hidden and Singular (*mirandis*) Causes of Diseases and Cures", the causes being revealed by the autopsy. Bonet's *Sepulchretum* of 1679 was a huge collection of casuistic material culled from the literature. Morgagni's *De sedibus et causis morborum* was to be a revised edition of Bonet's *Sepulchretum*, and the work as it finally emerged in 1761 still shows its descent. Its backbone is the hundreds of case histories elucidated by post mortem findings. It differs from its predecessors by having overcome the limitation of the singular and remarkable. It systematically applies the method to diseases in all parts of the body, *a capite ad calcem*, and tries to draw generally valid inferences. Thereby it marked the beginning of something new. After Morgagni, it became more convenient to envisage the pathological anatomy of disease processes, a trend that culminated in Rokitansky's *Manual* of the 1840's. Here too a huge casuistic material was utilized, yet it was integrated into a work which dealt with disease entities.[1]

It is not immediately clear why the anatomical interpretation of disease had to follow the road from case histories to disease entities. The idea of an anatomical substratum of disease was not unheard of. Pneumonia and pleurisy, as their names indicate, were differentiated by ancient authors according to the organs involved.[2] Dysentery was described by Aretaeus as due to ulcers of the intestine.[3] Medieval textbooks named quite a number of diseases. Conceivably, one might have started out by describing the anatomy of disease after disease, following the example of normal anatomy. One or a very few cases should have sufficed to give an insight into the particular disease; nor is it likely that such private anatomies would have met with

[1] Strictly speaking it deals with the pathological anatomy of tissues and organs.

[2] Cf. Galen, *Opera*, ed. Kühn, op. cit. XI, 77.

[3] Aretaeus, *The Extant Works*, ed. and trans. Francis Adams (London, 1856) 353.

external obstacles. The obstacles were of a different nature. It was assumed that diseases were sufficiently known, so that only the unusual was worth investigating. Moreover, the traditional disease entities were not sufficiently suited to such an anatomical analysis.

The role of the case history in a particular phase of medical development elucidates further the notion of the abnormal in medicine. Even if expressed in numerical values it retains the character of something that is not as nature or man would have it. To bring a person back to normal, therefore, means to bring him back to where he should be. But where should he be?

To this query the old formula of complete curative success gave a superb answer: *in integrum restitutus est*, he has been restored to his former condition. The formula leaves it undecided whether this connotes health or simply the state before the physician was called in. In either case the answer is a doubtful one; treatment may have made the patient 'a changed person' as the saying goes. The sickness which brought the patient to the doctor may even reveal a lack of previous health, and the cure of a neurotic patient may consist in not restoring him *in integrum*. Each patient's sickness is truly individual in the role it plays in his life; it has a meaning for him. But here where disease melts into the patient's whole life, science finds its limits. In bringing a patient back to health the physician will take as his frame of reference what is commonly considered as health. The patient is cured when he feels well, when his life is not in danger, and when he can safely do what healthy people generally do. This will often require far-reaching adaptations. If a person who was close to death undergoes a religious conversion, this in itself is outside the physician's concern. The physician traditionally is not supposed to judge his patient's morality or to influence his religion.[1] The case history is the form in which the physician links the science, which does not deal with the unique directly, and the patient, who requires attention as an individual. Replete with scientific data and possibly utilized to serve the advance of medical science, the case history documents the physician's art. It is the closest approach to an individual's sickness, yet it does not become the whole life story of a person while sick. Job fell ill and was

[1] O. Temkin, "Medicine and the problem of moral responsibility", *Bull. Hist. Med.* XXIII (1949) 1–20.

restored to health and wealth. But the *Book of Job* is not a case history: the 'meaning' of Job's illness is not of medical concern.[1]

V

Nevertheless, the interdependence of treatment and of the idea of disease is a very real one. It is by no means true that treatment is always adapted to the nature of the disease. Treatment can determine how disease should be considered. The rise of pathological anatomy at the turn of the eighteenth to the nineteenth century was stimulated by the growing influence of the surgeons and of their localistic point of view.[2] Ontologists have been inclined to favour the treatment of diseases and to look for possible specifics. Sydenham hoped for plants with specific actions on specific diseases, such as cinchona upon malaria.[3] While localized pathology was favoured by surgeons, specifics were favoured by the apothecaries who liked to sell drugs that promised cures of symptoms, syndromes, or diseases. By contrast, the physician of the physiological school opposed the routine use of standard treatments. At the end of the fifteenth century, Leoniceno warned doctors against trying to cure the French disease with the same medicine in all cases, in imitation of "a bad cobbler who tries to fit everybody with the same shoe".[4]

Similar notions are at the bottom of the maxim to treat the patient, not the disease. This is reinforced by the declaration that only sick individuals exist, that diseases are mere abstractions. Most physicians are likely to subscribe to this declaration, even if they find the abstractions useful. It is not altogether by chance that Hippocrates figures as the author of the case histories of the *Epidemics* and of the Hippocratic *Oath*. There is reason to doubt this authorship, especially that of the *Oath*.[5] But the fact remains that the *Oath* formulates classically the ethics of the doctor-patient relationship. Until not so very long

[1] For arguments against the metaphysical interpretation of sickness by the physician see Curtius, op. cit. and his "Hippokrates und die moderne Medizin", *Tägliche Praxis*, II (1961) 1–9.

[2] O. Temkin, "The role of surgery in the rise of modern medical thought", *Bull. Hist. Med.* XXV (1951) 248–59.

[3] Sydenham, op. cit. I, 23.

[4] Karl Sudhoff, *The Earliest Printed Literature on Syphilis*, adapted by Charles Singer (Florence, 1925) 172.

[5] Ludwig Edelstein, *The Hippocratic Oath* (Baltimore, 1943).

ago, 'medicine' was the domain of the physician who treated patients, privately or in the hospital. The medical sciences too were cultivated by men nearly all of whom were engaged in medical practice. Somewhat over a hundred years ago, a change took place: medical scientists, chiefly professors at German universities, began to separate themselves from practical medical work and to devote themselves 'full time' to anatomy, physiology, or pathology. The change set in at about the same time as the abandonment of the traditional therapy. Therapeutic nihilism and autonomy of the full-time medical scientist are, in my opinion, but two aspects of the same movement.[1] Therapeutic nihilism was a passing phase, while the growth of the basic sciences was accelerated with the development of bacteriology, immunology, and experimental pharmacology, and the increasing alliance with industry. As a result, medicine ceased to be the exclusive domain of the physician who treated patients. The contributions of the chemist Pasteur were fundamental, as well as symbolic, for the things to come.

Pasteur invented an anti-rabies vaccine the effectiveness of which he tested in dogs. In the scientific part of this discovery the rabies virus and the possibility of counter-acting it were under consideration. But from the practical point of view it was the disease embodying a well-known course with fatal outcome that was to be combated. In the background there was Jenner's discovery of the prevention of smallpox by vaccination with cowpox. In contrast to Jenner, who was a physician, Pasteur was not qualified to vaccinate; the boy Joseph Meister, who had been bitten by a mad dog, was vaccinated by physicians associated with Pasteur. Although the actual treatment, preventive or therapeutic, may still be applied or supervised by the physician, there is behind him a growing organization of persons and institutions who are screened from individual patients, yet work towards the cure and prevention of disease. In the scientific part of their work, 'the disease' may play no role at all; their minds may be occupied with bacteriological, immunological, and chemical details. Yet the work is directed against diseases as the public health officer, rather than the practitioner, sees them. There are laws aimed at preventing smallpox, and Jenner discovered a means of preventing it. Thousands of children are vaccinated against a disease which, at the time, may not show a single sufferer in the country.

[1] I have dealt with this matter in more detail in my Josiah Trent Lecture at Duke University, 1960, which now awaits publication.

In all this work and in campaigns to eradicate this or that disease, the picture of the disease as an entity devoid of individual features has a very real existence, though we must leave it to the metaphysician to determine the nature of this particular form of existence.

We began with a denunciation of ontology and end with its reassertion. In between we discussed the strength and weakness of the physiological approach and the case history in which the physician's art comes closest to individual sickness. We would like to draw the inference that in the scientific approach to disease the notions of both specific entity and individual sickness play their roles. The question: does disease exist or are there only sick persons? is an abstract one and, in that form, does not allow a meaningful answer. Disease is not simply either the one or the other. Rather it will be thought of as the circumstances require. The circumstances are represented by the patient, the physician, the public health man, the medical scientist, the pharmaceutical industry, society at large, and last but not least, the disease itself. For our thinking about disease is not only influenced by internal and external factors, it is also determined by the disease situation in which we find ourselves. Sydenham, the ontologist, lived at the time of the great plague of London, and the plague, I understand, has little concern with individual variations. In contrast, the practitioner of our time, who has to deal with degenerative disorders and neuroses demanding much individual attention, may have little use for disease entities. He may be inclined to leave them to the laboratory or the public health man for prevention.[1] With the changing disease situation our thoughts about disease change too. As Hippocrates said, "The art consists in three things — the disease, the patient, and the physician."[2] To the historian's mind, the histories of all three are bound up in the history of the art itself.

[1] For concepts of disease in social medicine see Iago Galdston, *The Meaning of Social Medicine* (Cambridge, Mass., 1954) 73 and *passim.*

[2] Hippocrates, *Epidemics* I, Sect. 2, 5, in *Works,* op. cit. I, 360.

Commentaries

Commentary by Sir George Pickering

Mr. Temkin has given us a learned and very comprehensive survey of one aspect of this vast subject. I ought to introduce myself. My hobby is dealing with the sick and trying to understand disease. I am glad to say that the University of Oxford pays me to enable me to indulge my hobbies. Now I am not going to say anything about my hobbies, about the practical handling of the sick or how the understanding of disease is advanced by observation and experiment. I am going to take as my text a passage from an essay called "The place of general ideas in medicine" by Wilfred Trotter.[1] Wilfred Trotter was one of the most remarkable men of this century. He operated on King George VI and was finally made Sergeant-Surgeon to His Majesty, a very ancient office—one of the duties of the Sergeant-Surgeon being to accompany the monarch into battle. He was also elected a Fellow of the Royal Society, because of his contributions to psychology. He was chiefly responsible for the idea of the 'herd instinct'. May I recommend this essay, and another entitled "Has the intellect a function?"? Trotter is talking about the seventeenth century and he writes:

> The characteristic feature of the period was the exuberance with which doctrine flourished. . . . Early in this period there is George Ernest Stahl, whose life almost exactly corresponds with the interval between the death of Harvey and the birth of Hunter. He taught an animism which regarded the body as a mechanical puppet, whose functions were maintained by the direct action of the soul. Misbehaviour of the soul was therefore the cause of bodily disease. It seemed to be a necessary consequence of this theory that drugs could have no action on the body, and like a good rationalist Stahl denied that they had. His responsibility for the many animists and vitalists who followed him is perhaps less heavy than for the phlogiston theory with which he burdened chemists, for this theory is perhaps the most perfect example in the world of ideas of the mysterious viability of the false. Then there is John Brown, whose life coincides roughly in time with that of Hunter, and who was the author of the famous Brunonian system. This

[1] Wilfred Trotter, "The place of general ideas in medicine," *The Collected Papers of Wilfred Trotter,* F.R.S. (London, 1941) 143-63.

product of reason is said to have been remarkably complete and consistent: it divided diseases into sthenic and asthenic, and treated them respectively with opium and alcohol, drugs to which Brown himself, less tough than his system, early succumbed.

The air of caricature never fails to show itself in the products of reason applied relentlessly and without correction. The observation of clinical facts would seem to be a pursuit of the physician as harmless as it is indispensable. Reason, however, could scarcely stop at so elementary a phase as this, and it seemed irrestibly rational to certain minds that diseases should be as fully classifiable as are beetles and butterflies. This doctrine found its most eminent cultivator in the great Sydenham, but bore perhaps its richest fruit in the hands of Boissier de Sauvages. In his *Nosologia Methodica*, published in 1768, the year of Hunter's appointment to St. George's, this Linnaeus of the bedside grouped diseases into 10 classes, 295 genera, and 2,400 species. Towards the end of our period, these particular developments met an opponent in Broussais, who lived till Lister was 11 and Pasteur 16. For Broussais disease in the sense of the nosologist had no existence. Diseases were for him consequences of local irritation and resulted in gastro-enteritis, which was the essential pathological lesion of all maladies. Broussais's quality is shown by his aphorism "La nature n'a aucun pouvoir de guérison naturelle"; believing this, he knew that recovery depended solely on the exertions of the physician. Since the condition he had to contend with was always an irritation and could be met by reducing the patient, he set himself to starve and bleed with a dreadful rigour. The lapse of a hundred years has made this doctrine seem no more than gruesome balderdash, but it was not without plausibility for the contemporary world. In fact, no less a surgeon than the great Dupuytren was a believer, and was accustomed to add to his mere surgical powers of reducing his patients the sterner measures of his colleague.

If these instances give a fair sample of what the intellect was doing for medicine for 200 years, it is not perhaps surprising to find Hunter about the middle of that period exclaiming impatiently, 'Why think?'

Now I chose this text because it brings out three points: the first point is that medicine like religion cannot tolerate ignorance. If it does not know the answers it has to invent them. There is an irresistible urge to have a rational system that explains everything. It is very interesting. There is a group of diseases whose nature is unknown. When I was a medical student these diseases were all due to focal sepsis. I am sure that there must be a large number of people who have sacrificed their teeth or tonsils on the altar of this hypothesis.

Then of course focal sepsis became unfashionable and these diseases became psycho-somatic. Now as you know they are all disorders of adaptation due to stress.

The second point is that these general ideas are unfortunately not entirely harmless, because, as Trotter has brought out so clearly, they determine treatment. Since the doctor does not know what the treatment is he draws on what are known as general principles, that is to say, his treatment is based on a rational hypothesis about disease, as you will have noticed with Stahl, Brown and Broussais. Of course teeth and tonsils are a recent example.

The third point is Hunter's reaction to this "Why think?". Why not try experiment? And it is a very remarkable thing that the experimental approach to clinical science is a product of the last 50 years. Now this really is extraordinary because treatment is by nature an experiment. If you take a patient, and you alter his diet, or you give him a drug, or you remove part of his anatomy, or you subject him to certain kinds of rays, you are in fact performing an experiment, and you might think that it would be interesting to find out the results and also to plan your experiment in such a way that you learn something. Curiously enough this has only just dawned on the minds of the doctors. It happened fortunately because R. A. Fisher became interested in testing chemical manures. The principle of finding out whether chemical manures affect the growth of plants is exactly the same as trying to find out whether drugs affect the course of disease. Fisher's book *The Design of Experiment* has led to the controlled use of therapeutic trial which has enormously increased the precision with which we gain knowledge of the action of drugs. The recent control of pulmonary tuberculosis by the new drugs streptomycin, isoniside and the like was accomplished with great precision in a remarkably short space of time, with the waste of the fewest possible human lives thanks to the use of this method.

The last point I want to make, which is a different one, is that nowadays most doctors, when they think of the nature of disease, think in qualitative terms. And this is natural because up to now the diseases that we have understood have all been characterized by some specific fault: bacterial diseases due to the invasion of the body by a specific micro-organism, the deficiency diseases due to a deficiency of a specific factor in the diet, diseases due to poisoning, heredity diseases due to single gene defects, and even malignant diseases all have quite clearly recognizable histological fault. However, I believe that there is a disease, essential hypertension, in which the deviation is not qualitative but quantitative. I will not go into the evidence. I think that medical science suffers very greatly from the contemporary fragmentation of knowledge, that all our disciplines tend to form closed intellectual societies, and that this tendency is perhaps the greatest in medical science, because of this the very exacting nature of being a doctor and tending the sick, and also because of the doctor-patient relationship. The difficulty of course about closed intellectual societies is that they tend to lack intellectual humility and clarity of thought. These I think are the difficulties with which we have to contend.

Commentary by Richard H. Shryock

Mr. Temkin has provided an interesting analysis of these two concepts — specific entity and individual sickness — with historical illustrations of the role played by each in the scientific approach to disease. The difference between them seems disarmingly simple. One may, first, think of disease in terms of diseases; that is, in relation to specific realities which are in a sense distinct from the patients who harbour them. This is clearly the easiest way in which to conceive, for example, of smallpox — which is much the same in all bodies and which can be traced as an entity in both epidemiology and history. Here one has the so-called ontologic concept.

In contrast to this view, how are we to conceive of a type of illness which is described in English as 'being all run down'? The patient is not 'well' but no specific diagnosis is possible. Such a condition seems internal and even peculiar to the given patient; it is a matter of the behaviour patterns of his particular body and/or mind. Here one has what Mr. Temkin terms the 'physiological' concept. In between such obvious cases, most illnesses exhibit some aspects which suggest the role of a specific entity but also other phenomena which imply behaviour patterns peculiar to the individual patient. As Mr. Temkin puts it: when a man is ill, his experiences are "partly open to others" (ontology), and also "partly his own" (physiological). And he notes that the Hippocratic literature early envisaged illness in both of these ways.

But actually one observes throughout subsequent medical history opposing tendencies to emphasize one of these concepts at the expense of the other — or even to the exclusion of the other. In some cases, emphasis was not as extreme as is often assumed. Thus, Sydenham in the seventeenth century declared that disease entities were as real and objective as biological species — a view which suggests medieval realism. Yet, as Mr. Temkin notes, Sydenham also left room for behaviour internal to the patient. More extreme was the view of early bacteriologists, *c.* 1875–90, who are said to have declared that tuberculosis was basically the same regardless of the particular bodies which it inhabited. Conversely, certain medical leaders of about 1800 went to the other extreme of 'physiological' thinking. They held that *all* illness was a matter of internal body patterns, and that it made no difference what external factors 'stimulated' these patterns into action. For such physicians, there were no disease entities and even common names for diseases were useful only in distinguishing forms of bodily response.

The history of alternating emphases on one or the other of these concepts is an intricate one which Mr. Temkin mercifully avoids, though he makes illuminating comments on certain of the factors involved — as in the analysis of the relation of anatomical approaches to a subsequent trend towards ontology. What impresses me in the historical background is not only the recurrent swing from one emphasis to the other, but more especially the verve and confidence of those who pushed in each direction.

It must be remembered that opposing theorists were not just playing an intellectual game; they were in deadly earnest because lives apparently were at stake. If one accepted a 'physiological' view he employed a therapy thought to affect body processes in general; for example, bleeding. Conversely, if one were an ontologist, he sought for specific drugs against specific diseases — a practice which was not necessarily less heroic than that of the opposing 'school'.

Each group thought that it alone offered helpful treatment; and in some cases even believed that it had provided for the first time a sound basis for both thought and practice. They either did not know or ignored history, inasmuch as they failed to recognize the recurrent pattern of alternating views into which their own doctrine fitted nicely as we now see it.

Thus an American, Benjamin Rush, in 1800 was sure that he had at last provided "the most perfect system the world had yet known" by denying the existence of any distinct diseases. Yet only fifty years later, Bartlett — expressing the ontology of the 'Paris school' — focused attention on specific entities and declared that there was more "unqualified absurdity" in the writings of Rush than in those of any other physician in history! In the presence of such conflicts and apparent dogmatism, two interrelated questions emerge. What circumstances led physicians to proclaim new emphases and, having done so, why were they so sure of themselves?

Mr. Temkin quotes Lord Cohen as stating that the dominance of one view or the other at a given time reflected the influence either of great personalities or of "the philosophy of the time". We may take for granted the role of leaders, but this only pushes the question back to the influences which impinged on *them*. As for the part played by prevailing philosophies, this may have been important prior to the seventeenth century but would, I should think, be more difficult to demonstrate thereafter — and particularly so after 1850. Thus, although ontology suggests Platonic ideas or medieval realism, it would certainly have surprised the bacteriologists of 1890 if they had been accused of harbouring any such notions.

Mr. Temkin himself suggests that the type of illness most encountered by physicians at a certain time may have determined their outlook. Thus Sydenham dealt with bubonic plague, and its uniformity and externality made him something of an ontologist. Present-day physicians, confronted with so much degenerative and mental illness — neither of which now can be well envisaged as an external entity — are driven back to 'physiological' concepts. But public health officers, still 'plagued' by the plague or other apparently external infections, continue to think as ontologists.

One may perhaps read into Mr. Temkin's statement (about illnesses encountered) all that medical scientists had learned about these conditions up to a given time. It was not only the prevalence of pulmonary tuberculosis between 1800 and 1900 or the uniformity of its symptoms which promoted the view that it was an entity. Also involved was new evidence, in terms of common lesions and then of a common causal factor, which encouraged ontology. We need not enter here into the intriguing discussion of whether a disease entity can be distinguished from 'its' symptoms, lesions, and 'cause', or from all of these criteria combined. But, clearly, new evidence may point in some cases toward entities and in other cases towards the reverse. Thus, in recent decades, it has been biochemical or biophysical discovery which has led such a scientist as Hans

Selye of Montreal into a re-emphasis upon 'physiological' bases of illness. Once again, we are employing non-specific remedies intended to improve the general state of the 'system'.

Prior to the last two or three centuries, new evidence was very slow in emerging and positions could be long maintained on more or less speculative grounds. But as data accumulated more rapidly, reorientations resulted whenever one concept or the other had been pushed to extremes. As Mr. Temkin points out, ontology which ignored body processes was bound to be checked by discoveries concerning these very processes. In like manner, the most extreme 'physiologists' had to recognize *some* role for external stimuli; and any discoveries about such stimuli might restore recognition of their significance. Perhaps the accelerated shifts from one perspective to the other since 1800 have made it easier today to realize that neither view can claim exclusive validity. But there are no grounds for complacency here if we recall that we — the heirs to all the ages — are simply returning in this respect to Hippocratic wisdom.

The final question, as to why medical thinkers of the past were so sure of themselves, has already been answered in part. Unless one was an extreme empiricist, a theory was needed in order to guide practice or just to bring order into thought. Once adopted, the theory was applied in practice, most patients then recovered, and what better proof of the theory could be had? Or, in the recent era, valid new evidence revealed the weaknesses inherent in a dominant view and thus justified a reaction against it.

There were, of course, various other factors of a subsidiary nature which made for over-certainty in medical outlooks. Some of these were professional or philosophical in nature, rather than scientific. There were times, for example, when professional reputation depended on proclaiming a sweeping and supposedly consistent 'system' of medical thought and practice. Under these circumstances, a leader would defend either ontology *or* physiology — but no half-way compromise between them. And one can readily understand why. There is no nice consistency in resorting first to one concept and then to the other, as we now are apt to do. Certainly such procedure leaves the ultimate metaphysical question — whether a disease *can* be viewed as a thing in itself, or whether sick bodies are after all the only realities — quite 'up in the air'! That is where most of us today would be inclined to leave it, but this no doubt reflects the preconceptions of our own, non-metaphysical age.

One final question remains. What was the actual role of these alternate concepts in what has been called here "the structure of scientific change"? Did they serve merely as frames of reference, into which physicians fitted either speculations or evidence? Or did they serve as dogmas which determined a man's reactions in advance, or even as hypotheses which aided in formulating questions addressed to nature? I have not looked into this question carefully, but my first hunch would be that these notions were employed in all of these ways. If space permitted, illustrations could be given of each of these operational roles.

Discussion

E. Heischkel-Artelt

I should like to add only some details to Mr. Temkin's paper. On pp. 632 and 647 he speaks about Sydenham, the arch-ontologist of modern times, and of the ontological idea of the separate existence of diseases. On this point one may draw attention to the so-called *naturhistorische Schule* in Germany. The opinion of the physicians belonging to this group was that the diseases are born, grow up, flourish and die like an individual organism. This was, in my opinion, an extreme manifestation of the ontological idea during the romantic phase of the history of medicine, and these physicians merit too the name of arch-ontologists. On p. 646 Mr. Temkin mentions a very interesting connexion between the therapeutic nihilism and the autonomy of the full-time medical scientist, and one can look forward to his paper dealing with this matter in detail.

J. Needham

There are two things which I should like to say. First, is not the ontological–physiological antithesis in the philosophy of pathology a special case of the fully generalized biological situation of specific stimulus on the one hand, and cell reactivity on the other? I seem to have lived through so much of this personally. After the classical discovery of the embryonic organiser-region by Hans Spemann in the twenties, and the no less classical discovery ten years later that the active principle of the gastrula's dorsal blastopore lip was stable to boiling, a stream of research started which is yet far from exhausted. Some (including myself) have always been convinced that in normal development a specific chemical substance, a *Wirkstoff*, is primarily involved, but many biologists have preferred, and still prefer, in spite of the demonstrations of the Finnish and Japanese schools, to place most of the emphasis upon the reactivity of the overlying ectoderm, hence on the cell-proteins of this germ-layer, which must convert it into neural tissue as development goes on. In the end, Hippocrates must always be right — we cannot do without both of the factors, external and internal; the only problem is to know just how they interact.

Secondly, since all the discussion has taken place within the realm of Greek and Western medicine, I should like to ask, especially as we have with us so fortunately Mr. Huard and Mr. Wong Chu-Ming, what was the situation in Chinese medicine regarding the ontological–physiological antithesis? My impression is that the great classical work, the *Nei Ching*, of the second century B.C. approximately, which summarizes the experiences of physicians during five or six previous centuries, emphasizes the physiological side, disease depending on the state of the patient's *yuan chhi* and other properties. But in the Han, with such brilliant physicians as Shunyu I, there comes in a tendency to classify diseases as entities, and this increases to a climax in the wonderful book of Chu Yuan-Fang, the *Chu shih Ping Yuan Hou Lun* written about A.D. 610. We may trace it in all subsequent writings, such as the important *Wai Thai Pi Yao* of a little over a century later. But when we come to the Ming (the sixteenth century A.D.) the great systems of medicine then written seem to return to a more physiological view. I shall look forward with great interest to tracing the evolution of this antithesis in Chinese thought as our work in Cambridge proceeds. In the meantime, I should be very glad to hear what Mr. Huard and Mr. Wong might have to say on this question.

P. Huard and Wong Chu-Ming

Modern Western work has taken the form of translations into English (e.g. by Ilsa Veith) or French (e.g. by Chamfault); or else of essays in chronology, like Bridgman's recent study, to which we have already referred. The translations (which are, really, adaptations) have not been made from a philosophical angle. Until we possess a good critical edition, in some Western language, produced in collaboration with sinologists, we shall not be able to discuss the doxology of the *Nei Ching* except with reserves. It would be necessary, too, to draw considerably upon the new editions and commentaries recently published in China. We believe it to be perfectly legitimate to compare the *Nei Ching* with the Hippocratic collection and we are full of admiration for the brilliant fashion in which Mr. Needham has made use of comparative methods on this occasion.

But we will excuse ourselves for not being able to discuss this *ex tempore*. A hasty reply to the important question he asks would be of little value.

J. R. Ravetz

The 'ontological' and 'physiological' conceptions of disease seem to have had one feature in common, down through most of medical history: ignoring the full 'case history' of the patient. Although the 'physiological' conception might seem to be more closely related to the individual, it would appear that it was in eighteenth-century nosology that the strongest attempt was made to base a theory on close observation. Was there no theory of disease based on the 'Hippocratic' conception of the medical art?

O. Temkin

The actualities of medical life are very complex. It is, therefore, essential for a discussion of the relative roles played by the concepts of specificity and individual illness to have the views of such an experienced clinical investigator as Sir George Pickering. The complexity also withstands any neat chronological or sociological arrangement: in the same year, 1679, we have Bonet's casuistic pathology, Sydenham's ontological approach, and the iatrochemists and iatrophysicists who try to base medicine on the inorganic sciences. The importance of the sociological factor is very great in our closely knit modern society, but a loosely meshed society may assign greater roles to individual thought. It has also to be remembered that the present discussion deals with the scientific approach to disease from a particular point of view, one that is much too limited to explain the entire progress of modern medicine. The metaphysical question as to what is disease still remains with us. But the suggestion that disease is not to be considered an object like a molecule or an animal, but must be viewed within the context of prevention, prognosis, and therapy, seems to shift the question and to deserve further critical thought.

PART SEVEN

The Making of Modern Science: Organization of Science and Technology

22

The Development of Scientific Research in Modern Universities: a Comparative Study of Motives and Opportunities

D. S. L. CARDWELL

I
Introduction

Francis Bacon, the quatercentenary of whose birth fell this year, was the first sociologist of science; not only by virtue of his descriptions of the social and psychological hindrances to the pursuit of science: the Idols of the Theatre etc., but also by virtue of his clear analysis of the modes of innovation. The mariner's compass, firearms and the printing press are, he says, the inventions which established the supremacy of Europe. An acute observation, no doubt, but Bacon goes further and points out that whereas the introductions of the compass and of firearms depended on the prior discoveries of the properties of the lodestone and of gunpowder — on science, if you like — there was no such precondition for the invention of the printing press. There was, in his view, no reason in principle why the ancient Egyptians or the Greeks could not have invented it.

This distinction between invention which depends on prior science, or discovery, on the one hand, and 'straightforward' invention[1] on the other, is one which runs through the history of technology from ancient times to the present day: it may be commended as a useful framework for prospective historians of technology. In the Baconian scheme the relationship between science and inventions based on science is one good reason for encouraging the advancement of science. Certainly Bacon's ideas helped to inspire the foundation of the Royal Society; but, as I understand him, he went even further in hoping that science, both pure and applied, would become a broadly based national and social institution. This did not begin to be the case until the end of the nineteenth century.

[1] There appears to be no generally accepted expression for this mode of invention.

Bacon has often been criticized for his suggestion that quite ordinary people should be able to undertake scientific research. If we think of science as a succession of 'big names' — Galileo, Descartes, Newton — it is easy to believe that Bacon was wrong. But he was not wrong; he was clearly right: every large modern research laboratory is a confirmatory instance. In fact, the great discovery of the nineteenth century that ordinary talents can be effectively harnessed for the process of discovery is a vindication of Bacon's judgment in this matter.

It was not unfitting that the nineteenth century opened in England with the foundation of the, apparently quite Baconian, Royal Institution. The intention was that it should further scientific investigations and seek to apply them to useful ends,[1] should disseminate scientific and other useful knowledge, and should have a library and museum of models. But it soon became clear that these intentions were not to be fully realized. Davy and Faraday established a tradition of research, but no fertilizing school of science was set up,[2] the lectures were not given to industrial technicians but to the wealthy and fashionable, the museum was never started and the great problems of relating science to industry were not tackled. It would be difficult, therefore, to sustain any claim that the Royal Institution was the first of the modern teaching and research laboratories.

The Royal Institution reflected the temper and traditions of English science: those of the amateur or devotee. In much the same way the Royal Society was, at that time, an association both of men actively and of men passively interested in science. If there were relatively few really professional scientists in the Society, that was because there were few indeed in the country; and if some of the Fellows were influential non-scientists, that was not necessarily to be deplored.

Correlative with the amateurism of English science, the universities took it to be their duty to conserve and to transmit the established liberal education based on classical literature and Newtonian natural philosophy. Interpreted by a man like Whewell this philosophy of education could be persuasive, and

[1] Early supporters of technical education in England favoured the teaching of the 'sciences underlying the arts'. Apparently this meant teaching the 'public', or carefully edited science of learned journals, text-books, etc. This is science at its most general and with little or no reference to the particular instances which may be the main concern of technicians. This possibly impeded the development of scientific technical education.

[2] A proposed "Davy School of Practical Chemistry" did not materialize.

criticism was, in fact, usually restricted either to matters of standards and syllabus or to the exclusiveness of English university education. The intending scientist would be advised, on this philosophy, to postpone his researches until his liberal education was completed, when the clarity of his thought and the soundness of his judgment would be fully developed. Accordingly, university reform in England during the first half of the nineteenth century was devoted to securing the inclusion of modern sciences in the syllabuses and ending unfair discriminations. The roles of scholarship and research in the university were hardly considered at all.

It was different in Germany. From the beginning of the century and more particularly from the foundation of Berlin University, free research was regarded as the ideal means of higher education. Wilhelm von Humboldt, a Kantian humanist, established the doctrine that the autonomy of reason was fundamental to the nature of the university. The university professor is an original scholar whose students help him in his work, acquiring their education and love of learning in the process. Beneath these academic ideals there were strong social currents: in times of defeat and political fragmentation the German universities were the acknowledged strongholds of aspirations for political and social unity: symbols of a common national heritage. This gave them an honoured place in the centre of German public life. The geography and history of England demanded no such role of the English universities. There were enough separate German states to ensure the existence of a number of competing, non-centralized universities. The ideal of free research was from the beginning impartial and non-utilitarian: it applied equally to classical philology and chemistry, to history, law, philosophy and physics, indeed to all branches of systematic knowledge. Engineering and technology were excluded from the university.

The German system was set up in very conscious opposition to the French. In 1808 Napoleon had unified all higher education in France under one central university. This in the event was unfortunate: it established the scientific domination of Paris over the provincial cities, prevented the development of autonomous 'schools' of science and, thanks to the parsimony and indifference of the state, led to the neglect and under-endowment of research and scholarship.[1] Much later, after 1870,

[1] S. d'Irsay, *Histoire des universités* (Paris, 1935) II, 290 ff.

Pasteur attributed many of France's political ills to her persistent neglect of science.[1]

France, in fact, has as good a claim as any country to have pioneered the systematic application of science to industry. The advance of French mathematics in the eighteenth century had been accompanied by advances in application to mathematical engineering — civil and military — to hydraulics and shipbuilding. These were really the main applied sciences of the eighteenth century. During the Revolution heroic efforts were made to develop new industries and to put the older ones on a scientific basis. In 1794 the Ecole Polytechnique was established; here, among other things, training in practical chemistry was given and students were allowed to carry out their own experiments and investigations. This practice was, in fact, copied from the much admired mining college at Schemnitz (Štiavnica, in Czechoslovakia) founded in 1760 during the reign of Maria Theresa — the first of its kind.

Great though the achievements of French and British science were during the nineteenth century, neither country, and this is especially true of Britain, proved able to turn out research students — the rank and file of science — in the numbers and of the quality that Germany achieved. T. H. Huxley put it aptly when he likened British science to any army consisting solely of officers.

In the new century systematic experimental science and later systematic applied science were pioneered in Germany. Early in the century Strohmeyer at Göttingen and Gmelin at Heidelberg had teaching laboratories, but it was really the opening, in 1825, of Liebig's famous laboratory at Giessen that marked the start of organized scientific research as well as the emancipation of chemistry from medicine. Not only was there a constant stream of highly trained scientists from this laboratory, and from that of Wöhler at Göttingen, but new sciences were to be developed: organic chemistry, biochemistry, agricultural chemistry (interest in organic chemistry was much stimulated by its practical possibilities in agriculture and medicine). Following the successes of these laboratories, others were instituted at Marburg (1840), Leipzig (1843 and 1868), and elsewhere in the 1850's. In the 1860's extremely well equipped laboratories were opened at the universities of Berlin

[1] R. Vallery-Radot, *The Life of Pasteur* (London, 1906) 196.

and Bonn. The latter had accommodation for over sixty students.[1]

But the development of the German schools of chemistry may not have been so smoothly effected as a simple chronology of events might suggest. As late as 1840, Liebig himself made a sharp attack on the neglect of experimental chemistry by the six Prussian universities; they offered, he said, no place for the training of the teacher of experimental science, the way was blocked by "an overgrown humanism".[2]

The other sciences followed chemistry in setting up research and teaching laboratories from the late 1830's onwards. (In a sense, of course, physical and biological laboratories have always existed in the forms of observatories, botanical and zoological gardens, etc. And learned academies often carried out specified researches — Victor Regnault's investigations into the properties of steam are a classical example. But in the first case the institutions are very specialized and limited in number; in the second, as soon as the particular inquiry has been completed all research has stopped.) The development of biological laboratories has been closely tied to the medical faculty in which, at the beginning of the nineteenth century, the dominant scientific disciplines were anatomy and botany. But the influence of Liebig and other chemists together with the tremendous development of medicine — first in France and then in Germany[3] — led to the foundation of systematic laboratories for physiology and other sciences related to medicine. Prominent among these were those of Purkinje and Claude Bernard. The Pasteur Institute was opened in 1888.

It was not until the sixties and seventies that physics laboratories were established more or less simultaneously in most universities. It is not clear why physics should have lagged some forty years behind chemistry in this respect. Maxwell gives the rather negative reason: "it will take a good deal of effort to make Exp. physics bite into our university system which is so continuous and complete without it."[4] It might be

[1] For the chemical laboratories at Berlin and Bonn, see: *Report of the Department of Science and Art* (1866). For practical chemistry in the early days of the École Polytechnique, see: G. Pinet, *Histoire de l'Ecole Polytechnique* (Paris, 1887) 366.

[2] *Annalen der Chemie und Pharmacie*, XXXIV (1844) 97, 339.

[3] C. Newman, *Evolution of Medical Education in the Nineteenth Century* (London, 1957).

[4] Lord Rayleigh, *John William Strutt, Third Baron Rayleigh* (London, 1924).

that while the heart of physics — Newtonian mechanics — held little scope for experimental investigations, and while subjects like heat and electricity were regarded as branches of chemistry, the development of the physics laboratory would necessarily be retarded.[1]

II
A particular instance

It will be clear that the development of university laboratories represents a complex and far ranging subject. From this point, then, I must limit my discussion to one important topic only, and I must apologize for the serious omissions this will necessitate.

Only if the admission of students to a laboratory is recognized as a permanent practice can we talk of the laboratory as a systematic research institution. Judged by this standard, systematic research chemistry was taught for the first time in England when, in 1845, the Royal College of Chemistry was opened in London. Public recognition of the importance of Liebig's work for agriculture and medicine inspired the foundation of this institution, and the first principal, A. W. Hofmann, was in fact a nominee of Liebig's. For the first twenty-five years of its existence the College was small — numbers varied between thirty and fifty-two, indicating that the 'need' was not so great as its founders may have hoped — but in that time some 140 original papers were published.

The study of organic chemistry was now being pursued all over Europe. In France, a chair in the subject was created in Paris in 1853, and men like Chevreul, Dumas and others worked in collateral subjects at about that time or earlier; but the main centres of research were in Germany. It was therefore almost an accident when, in 1856, W. H. Perkin discovered the first of the aniline dyes. Perkin, a student of Hofmann's at the Royal College, had been working on his own in the Easter

[1] British chemists who made important contributions to the studies of heat and/or electricity include Black, Cavendish, Dalton and Davy. Through the work of men like Joule, Kelvin and Maxwell these subjects became part of natural philosophy. But public recognition of 'physics' did not come immediately, and a curious example of what we should regard as a misuse of the word is provided by Walter Bagehot's *Physics and Politics* (1873). Here by "physics" was meant natural selection. The word *physics* was imported either from France (cf. Biot, *Traité de physique*) or from Germany.

vacation, attempting to synthesize quinine, when he made this discovery. Realizing its significance and encouraged by the report of a firm of dyers, Perkin, his father and brother launched into manufacture of the new dyestuff. Technologically the moment was propitious: Mansfield, a student of Hofmann's, had just discovered a process for separating benzene from coal tar, Zinin, a student of Liebig's, had reduced nitrobenzene to aniline and Béchamp greatly improved the latter process. But all this hardly detracts from the credit due to Perkin for what Sir Robert Robinson calls "his active, forceful pioneering" in the new manufacturing techniques of coal tar colours.[1] For seventeen years Perkin's firm prospered until, in 1874, he sold it and returned to chemical research.[2]

Thus a number of conspicuous threads from Giessen were woven into the pattern of an important scientific industry. And the new enterprise was not limited to England: factories were set up very quickly in Germany, Switzerland and especially in France where important contributions were made by Verguin, Girard, De Laire and others, and where there was a great tradition not only in scientific chemistry but also in the art of dyeing. In Germany one important firm which manufactured the new aniline dyes had formerly made natural dyestuffs;[3] curiously, in England, no old dye works seem to have taken up the manufacture of the new dyes. Firms were either founded specially to make the new dyestuffs, like Ivan Levinsteins, started in 1864, or else they were like Read Hollidays of Huddersfield, tar distillers started in 1830 who took up aniline dyes in 1860.

Levinsteins and Hollidays were, by the end of the century, the largest and most active manufacturers of aniline dyes in Britain. There were very good reasons why they should be: they were located near their markets, in the textile areas of Lancashire and Yorkshire, raw material — coal tar — was readily available from gas works, and in both areas there was a traditional interest in scientific industry.[4] To these assets we should add the commercial experience of these localities, the

[1] Sir Robert Robinson, in *Endeavour*, XV (April, 1956) 94.

[2] S. Miall, *A History of the Chemical Industry* (London, 1931) 66 ff.; L. F. Haber, *The Chemical Industry during the Nineteenth Century* (London, 1957) 80, 128, 162.

[3] Leopold Cassella & Co.

[4] South Lancashire and the West Riding of Yorkshire strongly supported the Mechanics Institute movement between 1825 and 1851.

availability of capital and, in the case of Levinsteins, who were near Manchester, proximity to the largest and most active school of chemistry in England. It is therefore the more surprising that, by the end of the century, the aniline dyes industry had migrated to Germany, where about 90 per cent of the world's manufacture was carried out. In England the growth of the industry had been very slow indeed.

To revert to the question of systematic scientific education in England: the University Commissions of 1850 and 1854 paid little attention to research training in science, and the ideal continued to be a liberal education. The committee set up by London University in 1858 to consider the inauguration of science degrees similarly paid little attention to research: 'science in education' meant knowledge about science rather than the art and practice of science. An emphasis reinforced by the nature of the written examination system.

The change began in the late sixties and early seventies, and it came through two distinct, although related, movements. Grove, in his Presidential address to the British Association in 1866, asked for Government endowment of research, and this plea was taken up by others in the following years. The aim seems to have been that men of science should have available public research laboratories in much the same way that scholars were provided for by the British Museum Reading Room. This suggests that in the early seventies the typical British scientist was still thought to be an amateur; but now, thanks to the growing complexity and national importance[1] of science, his work was to be officially helped. The second movement began with the criticisms of conventional liberal education and its instrument the written examination by Matthew Arnold and Mark Pattison. An added impetus was given to this movement by a young philosopher, C. E. Appleton, who had studied in Germany and who, by the early seventies, had won the support of a number of men of different disciplines. Thus, of the eight contributors to the volume *Endowment of Research* (1876), only two were scientists (and of these, one, H. C. Sorby, was a distinguished amateur). This movement was therefore inspired by the achievements of German learning and scholarship in general, rather than by the practical achievements of German science. In fact, in 1873 the Devonshire Commission reported

[1] Among the sciences thought to be of the greatest national importance were surveying, meteorology and solar physics. See *Royal Commission on Scientific Instruction and the Advancement of Science* (Devonshire Commission).

that on no subject were academic witnesses so united as on the desirability of research training in scientific education. In America, this same belief led to the foundation of Johns Hopkins in 1876.

How did German and English universities compare in the matter of training in scientific research at this time? At Owens College, Manchester, H. E. Roscoe had built up what was certainly the biggest and very probably the best school of chemistry in this country. Roscoe, trained under Bunsen, believed that research should have a place in scientific education. He was a member of the Appleton group, and a paper he published in 1874[1] contained the observation that German chemical manufacturers were by then insisting that the chemists they employed should have had a research training. Thus the ideals of pedagogy and utility concur! In 1869 new chemical laboratories for Owens College were designed following the best German practice, and by 1871 they accommodated some sixty students. In 1874 the — for England — unprecedented step of appointing a second professor of chemistry was taken, when Carl Schorlemmer was made professor of organic chemistry. In the twenty years the College had existed, 1851–71, some 84 original papers in chemistry had been published.

But Owens College, in chemistry the best that England could achieve, was the only university institution in the great textile areas of the north. In 1865 A. W. Hofmann had returned to Germany, and for nine critical years there was no higher teaching of organic chemistry in England. So when Kekulé's theory came out in 1865 there were few in this country competent to understand it, and very few of these indeed would be in industrial occupations. In comparison with the achievements of Owens College, in the six years 1866–71, some 80 papers were published from the chemistry department at the University of Leipzig (or 89 in the seven years 1866–72). Indeed, some six times as many papers on chemistry were published in Germany in 1866 as in Britain, and this highly unfavourable ratio was maintained until the end of the century: in 1899 some two-thirds of the world's original chemical research came from Germany.[2] As early as 1872 Kolbe had

[1] H. E. Roscoe, *Original Research as a Means of Education* (1874).

[2] F. Rose, *Report on Chemical Instruction in Germany and the Growth and Present Condition of the German Chemical Industries, Miscellaneous Series, Diplomatic and Consular Reports* (Cd. 430–16) (1901).

claimed: "Why is German chemical industry now at a higher level than that of England and France? Because in England and France government policy does little for chemical education and Germany has outstripped both countries in that respect. Indeed it is through the scientific laboratories that the chemical industry of Saxony has contributed so much to the wealth and prosperity of the state."[1] A point of view in interesting contrast to Liebig's observation of 1844 that England was not the land of science, for "only works which have a practical tendency command respect, while the purely scientific works, which possess far greater merits, are almost unknown . . . in Germany it is quite the contrary".[2]

Statistics can be produced to show not only that Germany endowed its universities much more generously than did England, but also that there were disproportionately more students in Germany than in England. But of course the social arrangements in the two countries were not the same, and great caution would be necessary in interpreting such statistics. Here I will merely observe that in 1890 there were twice as many German academic chemists as there were British (101 : 51), while by 1900 the proportion had dropped slightly in favour of Britain: 16 Germans to 10 British, or, taking account of populations, 12 Germans to 10 British — a rough indication which would suggest that the founding of new universities in Britain was tending to redress the balance. But, as the German technological universities have been excluded from this comparison, the case in favour of Britain has been overstated.

III
The practical consequences

There is, then, a general relationship between the numbers and quality of higher education in chemistry on the one hand and the development of advanced industrial techniques, such as systematic applied science, on the other.

The adoption of the simplest laboratory techniques by British industry began, it seems, only after the Exhibition of 1851. The first step appears to have been taken by a somewhat obscure ironmaster of Dudley, Samuel Blackwell, who was

[1] H. Kolbe, *Das Chemische Laboratorium der Universität Leipzig* (Braunschweig, 1872) xlv.

[2] Letter to Faraday.

responsible for the introduction of analytical, or control, chemists into iron works. It is true that the simple control, or standards, laboratory may develop in the course of time into a research laboratory, as for example the National Physical Laboratory has done. But this process is by no means inevitable and we must ask in which industry and for what reason the systematic research laboratory originated.

Systematic research means the employment of salaried research scientists engaged solely or substantially on research, on a permanent basis and to be replaced by others when they leave. Scientific research, in the form of an attack on one or two definite problems, to be wound up when the problems are solved, has been carried on in industry for a long time; there was, indeed, much of it during the eighteenth century. But this *ad hoc* procedure is not the same as institutionalized research which is a permanent feature, a continuing activity.

On this definition it seems certain that systematic industrial research began in the synthetic dyestuffs industry. The exact date is uncertain, but it must have been about 1870, and the location must have been one or more of the German firms which were, by 1900, to dominate the industry. At the end of the century one of these firms employed scores of graduate chemists on research, while many others worked on production, development, sales and services. There was no such scope for the employment of research scientists in the mechanical engineering industries, such as power generation, machine tools, textiles, etc. It is not evident, on the face of it, why this should have been so. The industries related to the biological sciences, such as agriculture, fishing, etc., were similar to the mechanical industries in this respect.[1]

When Perkin retired, in 1874, from the industry he had founded, it was prospering. He later gave as his reason for retirement his desire to return to chemical research. But, "a much more weighty consideration than this" was, said his son W. H. Perkin, the recognition that the firm could only be carried on successfully if a number of trained chemists could be recruited and employed in the all-important work of making new discoveries. "I remember", he says,

that enquiries were made at many of the British universities in the

[1] Edison's famous laboratory at Menlo Park, set up in the 1870's, and the well-known agricultural researches carried out at Rothamsted by Lawes and Gilbert were both highly individualist enterprises, and can therefore hardly be taken as typical.

hope of discovering young men trained in the methods of organic chemistry, but in vain. There cannot be any doubt that the manufacturer of organic colouring matter during the critical years 1870–1880 was, owing to the neglect of organic chemistry by our universities, placed in a very difficult and practically impossible position.[1]

According to F. M. Perkin, another of Perkin's sons, the original firm was in the early 1870's faced with the problem of rapidly expanding production in order to meet a sharp increase in demand. This meant more research chemists: "research chemists however could not be obtained".[2] True, German chemists were available, but they tended, after a while, to return to Germany, where their English experiences naturally made them much sought after. In the new dyestuffs industry the pressure of rapid change was very great: it was a matter of new colours, of new processes and the improvement of old ones.

This rings only partly true: the inevitable problems of growth in size and complexity are certainly familiar to students of management; but, as regards the absence of suitable scientists, it may be wondered why Perkin & Son were apparently unable to train their own research workers.[3] Surely, the opportunity of training for research under the leading English organic chemist of the time, who was also the founder of a unique industry, should have brought in a number of able young men. In this respect a comparison between Perkin and James Watt is not inapt: both were brilliant scientists and technologists, both founded revolutionary new industries, both had brilliant sons. Nearly a century before, Watt, with his partner, Matthew Boulton, had faced the same problem — shortage of talent — in an even more acute form. But whereas Watt and Boulton succeeded in attracting able men from all quarters — Southern, Clegg, Peter Ewart, Murdoch and others, so that the firm was called the "science school of Soho",[4]

[1] W. H. Perkin (Jr.), "The position of the organic chemical industry", *Journal of the Chemical Society*, CVII (1915) 557 ff.

[2] F. M. Perkin, *Journal of the Society of Dyers and Colourists*, XXX (10 November 1914) 339 ff.

[3] There was a good precedent: R. Calvert Clapham told the Parliamentary Committee on Scientific Instruction (London, 1868) that the alkali works on Tyneside commonly took apprentices into their laboratories for training as (presumably) control chemists. The facilities for scientific training at Durham University were, he said, very inadequate.

[4] Conrad Gill and Asa Briggs, *History of Birmingham* (London, 1952) I, 109.

Perkin apparently sold his firm when the universities were unable to supply trained research chemists. Watt's son, James Watt, junior, later managed his father's firm with great success; Perkin's two elder sons were academics all their lives, and his youngest became a consultant. I conclude that Perkin and his sons lost, or never acquired, a taste for chemical industry, and so they sold the firm. I infer that the shortage of trained chemists was not so critical.

Brooke, Simpson and Spiller, who bought Perkin's firm, were in fact able to recruit two leading colour chemists: Raphael Meldola, who was with them from 1877 to 1885, and A. G. Green, who stayed from 1885 to 1894. But both men considered that their talents were being wasted and resigned disappointed.[1] Brooke, Simpson and Spiller eventually went bankrupt early in the twentieth century.

Levinstein's, the Manchester firm, were more successful and achieved a reputation for scientific innovation. It would have been remarkable if no firm in the area of Roscoe's large and active school of chemistry had been able to achieve a competitive position in this field! Ivan Levinstein himself was a life governor of Owens College, wherein he endowed a bursary and made donations to the physics and chemistry laboratories. This support for scientific education was manifestly only in the late 'nineties, and it has been reported that during much of this period this firm lacked a research atmosphere.[2]

On the Yorkshire side of the Pennines the firm of Read Holliday also achieved modest success together with a somewhat better record in scientific innovation. This firm recruited such scientists as they could find — the majority appear to have been Germans — and by 1890 they had a research laboratory in which about four or five scientists were continuously employed upon research. They may well, therefore, have instituted the first systematic research laboratory in Britain, some years before those at Widnes (1892) and Ardeer (1896).[3]

"It is characteristic of the synthetic colour industry that it is subject to continuous change through the introduction of new

[1] James Marchant (ed.), *Raphael Meldola* (London, 1916) 4, 65. A. G. Green later said that his employers told him that his discovery of Primuline was a "pretty experiment" and he should show it to the Chemical Society!

[2] For much of my information about the industry in the north of England I am indebted to Mr. C. M. Mellor, a student at Leeds University.

[3] D. W. F. Hardie, *A History of the Chemical Industry in Widnes* (Birmingham, 1952); F. D. Miles, *A History of Research in the Nobel Division of I.C.I.* (Birmingham, 1955).

products: this was true at the start and remains true today."[1] In an industry like this the advantage must be with the organization which has a good supply of trained research chemists to pioneer new products and chemical engineers to ensure their efficient production and sale. The balance of advantage then would lie with Germany. And the sound Baconian point was made, by Sir James Dewar in 1902, that: "It is in the abundance of men of ordinary plodding ability thoroughly trained and methodically directed, that Germany has at present so commanding an advantage".[2]

Many reasons can be found to account for the very slow development of the industry in England: patent laws, alcohol duties, trade discrimination, the tendency of investors to favour such sound securities as Consols, railways, coalmines, etc. But to produce reasons like this is merely to explain things away. In America and France, too, where patent laws, duties, etc., were presumably very different, the industry failed to develop. The only point clearly established is that Germany had more research scientists than England, America or France and certainly more chemical engineers than England. Only those firms which could recruit, without much difficulty, research chemists and chemical engineers could hope to keep up with what had become, by 1914, a veritable flood of new dyestuffs.

Systematic research was one of the necessary factors that gave Germany the lead in this industry; and this in turn was made possible by a supply of research scientists; the final product of an admirably developed education system.[3] But, and this is very important, the English manufacturers *apparently* made no attempt to overcome this handicap by training their own men. And even when men like Meldola and Green were recruited they were not given a proper chance to employ their talents. Towards the end of the century the numbers of graduate and research scientists in England increased rapidly. However, and here I must use parochial evidence, during the first twenty years of the University of Leeds Dyeing Department each one of the four largest German firms made more donations of

[1] Sir Robert Robinson, op. cit.

[2] Presidential Address to the 1902 British Association.

[3] An important feature of the German system was the number of schools of chemistry in mutual competition. In England there were, with the possible exception of Roscoe's at Manchester, no schools of this sort between 1865 and 1901. And, if we are to believe contemporary reports, German scientists were very successful in imparting a love of learning and a zeal for research.

dyestuffs than the two largest English firms combined. The English firms did not contribute to the funds of the University, nor did their members serve on advisory committees or similar bodies. It should be added that the Department of Dyeing had a high standard from the beginning; A. G. Perkin joined the staff in 1882 and later became Professor. In view of the unenterprising attitude of the industry, it is not surprising that at the end of the century Perkin found it difficult to get students to do research in this subject. Very briefly, the English dyestuffs firms do not seem to have appreciated the value of scientific education and research experience, from the time that W. H. Perkin, senior, left the industry up to the outbreak of the 1914 war.

A short quotation from a report made by Meldola in 1902 indicates the way in which the industry had been penetrated by German firms:

> The manufacturers of colours are themselves — especially the Germans — not only keeping the dyers supplied with a constant succession of new colouring matters, but it is the custom of the German firms to send round their own experts to teach the dyers how to use these new products or to issue such detailed instructions that practically nothing is required of the dyer in the way of scientific knowledge.[1]

The tentative conclusion is that while systematic research was a necessary ingredient of German success, short-sighted management sealed English failure. Generally speaking the difficulties encountered by inefficient organizations are the consequences of their inefficiency and not the cause of it. Of the two best English firms in the industry, Levinstein's took eighteen years to acknowledge the fact that there was a scientific department of dyeing at Leeds University; Read Holliday, being nearer at hand, took only twelve years; the four biggest German firms took at most two years.

My conclusions here must be very tentative, and it seems to me that there is considerable scope for detailed studies of the internal development and external relations of English firms during this time. Such studies should be comparative, taking full account of foreign experience as well as the development of the relevant sciences.

The importance of studies of this sort for the histories of both

[1] A private report on the Dyeing Department at the Yorkshire College (Leeds University).

science and technology (and one cannot separate them) is that here, in the coal tar colour industry, for the first time systematic applied science made its impact: the 'invention of the method of inventions', a Baconian ambition, was made when, in Germany, industry borrowed from the universities the distinctive institution of research laboratories and recruited from the same source the men to staff them. A developed educational system ensured a supply of research scientists and other men technically qualified to staff the industry. This first successful attempt at systematic applied science constituted an enormous object lesson, and no really progressive industry could thereafter afford to neglect applied science. In fact, one could not write the history of the application of science in the electrical industry without some reference to the triumphs of the dyestuffs industry. At some unknown date the majority of students under training in chemistry laboratories must have intended to seek an industrial career and not one in the teaching professions. In Germany this probably occurred before 1914; in England certainly after 1918. I do not know when it happened in America or France.

The specialization of higher scientific education in England arose as an administrative consequence of the educational system, and I have tried to show elsewhere[1] that it had nothing to do with industrial demand. I have no reason to believe that the specialization of scientific education in Germany was any more a product of industrial demand. If any practical applications were expected of German academic chemistry in the earlier days, those applications would be in medicine or agriculture; the scientific development of the coal-tar colour industry was an unlooked-for bonus. I have tried to show in this paper that at no time before 1914 did the industry in which science was most readily applicable significantly influence English scientific education.

IV
Conclusion

It seems that whether our emphasis is on research or on liberal education, the end is specialization. How does such specialization affect the development of science? No doubt large numbers of scientists in institutions can, sufficiently

[1] D. S. L. Cardwell, *The Organisation of Science in England* (London, 1957) 116-18.

endowed and well led, produce original papers indefinitely.[1] But is there no danger that an essential component of science, the endeavour to achieve unity, may be lost in a welter of detailed papers?

The older specialization did not at any rate impel the student to make a career for life of his undergraduate discipline. No one thought it unusual if a graduate mathematician subsequently became a lawyer, a clergymen, a naturalist, and so on. But the rise of the modern research institution has in effect consolidated specialization and made it almost a life-long discipline. It is very hard for the individual, especially in his formative years, to escape from such social sanctions, from what is explicitly expected of him, yet demonstrably much of science has been built up by men who, following their scientific intuitions, have abandoned one discipline for another. How then, in the face of these institutional difficulties, to secure the welfare of science without prejudicing the benefits of applied science is a problem which is worthy of the attentions of a modern Francis Bacon![2]

[1] F. Paulsen was referring to much the same thing when he used the expression "pseudo-productivity": *The German Universities* (London, 1906) 173.

[2] There remains the more general question of the relationship between scientific and non-scientific education. It should be remembered that the mutual exclusiveness of scientific and literary education was explicitly condemned by H. G. Wells and Sir J. J. Thomson, and before them by a long line of educational thinkers. It is satisfactory that the existence of this gap (as Wells termed it) should now be under criticism, but it is depressing that the same criticisms have, apparently, to be made in every generation.

23

Economic Incentives for and Consequences of Technical Invention

C. F. CARTER

"There can be no doubt that an over rigid insistence upon definition would immediately bring all discussion of invention, and of the part it plays in changes of ways of living, to a dead stop."[1] Nevertheless it is nice to know what one is talking about. If 'invention' is narrowly defined so as to relate to the first point at which one can discern as having an independent existence what is judged as being the most essential element of a new idea, this paper would be almost impossible to write. To ask what economic incentives will produce an Edison or a Whittle is much like asking what incentives will produce a Shakespeare; and, even if we concern ourselves with lower levels of ability, it has to be admitted that the first steps of invention are often a by-product of some other activity, and have little relation to the incentives and sanctions of the economic system, so long as that system allows freedom for the inventive activity.

I therefore propose to define *invention* as relating not merely to the conception of an idea, but to its birth as a marketable product (or as a process which can yield a marketable product). A product is 'marketable' if it can over a substantial period be sold in a free market to willing buyers at a price which covers its costs, together with such profits as are necessary to persuade the producer to continue making the product. Since few markets are really free, and many things (for example guided missiles) have only a single buyer within a given country, the question of when an invention has proved its economic worth by yielding a marketable product is large and complex. I propose to evade it.

The general answer to a question about economic incentives for innovation is to be found by considering the central problem of economics, the problem of the best use of scarce

[1] John Jewkes, David Sawers and Richard Stillerman, *The Sources of Invention* (London, 1958) 13.

resources. The elements or factors which enter into production are often classified as land, labour and capital, but for the present purpose it is more relevant to describe them as:

(*a*) Natural resources and natural processes — coal seams, rivers which provide power, the combination of land and climate which yields a growth of grass, and so on;

(*b*) Man-made capital and improvements, together with the stock of ideas. The essential element in these is that they yield opportunities of creating wealth over a period;

(*c*) Applied human energy, skill and organization.

With very few exceptions (such as the air we breathe), all these factors (in their innumerable forms) are in short supply, relative to possible human needs; even in the most affluent society they mostly command a price. The effective supply of natural resources is increased by discovery or by new means of exploitation, but is reduced by prodigal use — the cutting down of forests, the exhaustion of coal seams, the over-farming of land. On the whole it seems likely that during the next two generations the shortage of natural resources, in relation to the world's population, will become a much more serious matter than at present. The potential supply of human energy and brain-power rises with rising population, and it can be increased if people work harder; but on the whole the object desired by mankind is to work less, not more. Thus it is the increase in the second group of factors — the piling up of capital goods and the accumulation of ideas — that provides the hope of a rising standard of living.

At any time, therefore, there are two related types of choice to be made. One is the choice of what to produce and how to produce it, so as to meet human desires best from a given supply of factors of production; the other is the choice of what to set aside from current resources to add to physical capital or to make possible an increase in the stock of ideas. The more resources are thus set aside, the less human needs can be met in the present, and the more fully they can be met in the future.

With this framework of analysis, it is possible to distinguish five different situations which may give rise to invention:

(i) With given resources and desires, an invention may be stimulated by a desire to improve the utilization of resources. Thus a lift in an office, or a coffee machine in a factory, release for productive use time and energy which would otherwise be spent walking up stairs or 'brewing up'.

(ii) The relative scarcity of resources changes through time, and an invention may be stimulated by the need to avoid using some particularly scarce factor. Thus synthetic rubber was first created to avoid dependence on natural rubber.

(iii) Human desires change through time, and the change may stimulate invention. It is true that to a considerable extent we desire, or can be made to desire, whatever is produced; but even if a primary desire has been created by example or advertizing, it often gives rise to secondary or derived inventions. The mounting desire for a car gives rise in due course to the invention of improved fuels and lubricants, and seat belts to attach the ardent motorist to his dangerous machine.

(iv) The accumulation of technical ideas constantly creates new 'conjunctures', new opportunities of invention which are formed by the meeting of ideas. Thus the gas turbine was 'capable of being invented' when the design principle of the turbine could be matched by metallurgical knowledge sufficient to enable it to withstand the effects of the hot gases.

(v) By deliberate choice, more resources may be set aside for research and development, thus making conditions more favourable for invention. Investment in research is an investment in the creation of ideas, and thus of opportunities for physical investment.

These are situations which may stimulate invention. The degree to which they will do so depends on the size of the stimulus, the effectiveness of its communication to those who make business decisions, the sensitivity of the decision-makers to the stimulus communicated to them, and their ability to react in a rational manner. These factors I discuss in turn.

(1) The size of the stimulus. Large changes in the relative scarcity of resources, such as occur through the interruption of supplies in wartime, are a powerful stimulus to inventions; this is seen not only in deliberate research programmes on subjects such as synthetic rubber, but in countless minor examples of ingenuity in using unfamiliar materials. I have already pointed out that a change in human desires, though it may be the consequence of a major invention rather than its cause, often gives rise to derived or associated inventions — and in general the more the major invention alters the established pattern of consumption, the more likely is it that significant associated inventions will be called for.

The most interesting influence of the size of the stimulus

may be expected from the setting aside of more resources for research and development. It is true that for more than a century the influence of science on invention and industrial progress has been obvious — though if we were to look back two centuries, we would have to give chief place to the artisans and 'practical men' rather than to the scientists. But the influence of science a hundred, fifty or even thirty years ago was on the whole haphazard and on a small scale; the growth of organized research and development as a major and widespread industrial activity in this country has been recent but rapid. The resources set aside for research and development may have doubled between 1930 and 1938, and doubled again between 1938 and 1950;[1] I would guess that there was a further increase of 50 per cent or more between 1950 and 1955, by which date British manufacturing industry was spending on research 3·1 per cent of its contribution to national production. In 1958 the corresponding proportion was 4·2 per cent, and it is now certainly higher. A large part of the spending in 1955 was financed from defence contracts, and, since these were less important in 1958, it appears that expenditure on purely 'civil' research and development doubled between 1955 and 1958.[2] Expenditure for civil purposes in Government research stations shows a rapid rate of increase; and fragmentary evidence from other developed countries suggests that many of them also show a rapid rise in research expenditure.

It is not of course certain that by increasing the amount of *organized* research and development one will increase the flow of useful inventions. Some have argued quite the opposite: "The industrial laboratory does not appear to be a particularly favourable environment for inducing invention".[3] But it seems to me a common-sense conclusion, and one supported by observation, that as the frontiers of science are pushed outwards and scientists necessarily become more specialized, the importance of the team will rise relative to that of the individual. Thus, although there can be no doubt about the past importance or the present value of individual inventors, the trade of the individual inventor may well be becoming more difficult, and in some areas of technology (for example nuclear

[1] C. F. Carter and B. R. Williams, *Industry and Technical Progress* (Oxford, 1957) 45.

[2] Department of Scientific and Industrial Research, *Industrial Research and Development Expenditure, 1958* (H.M.S.O., London, 1960) 1.

[3] Jewkes et al., op. cit. p. 132.

physics) it is already impossible. I would find it odd, too, if there were to be no connexion whatever between the number of people looking for a thing and the speed of its finding; and I therefore conclude that the very large increase in industrial research and development is certainly significant as creating conditions favourable to invention — though other favourable conditions may have to exist before the promise becomes performance.

The early stages of organized research are often concerned with such things as the accurate measurement of the properties of materials, and it may well be more than ten years before there is a significant output of commercially usable ideas. Thus no evidence from the past will be of much help in testing a hypothesis about the recent rise of research expenditure, nor is it conclusive to point to an apparent lack of major inventions during the last year or so (except in the field of space research and rocketry). The steep rise in the 1950's would not be expected to yield obvious results before the late 1960's.

(2) THE COMMUNICATION OF THE STIMULUS. Two quite different problems are here involved. One is the communication of scientific ideas; the efficiency of this communication affects the results to be expected from research and development, and it affects most vitally the opportunities for invention which are created by a meeting of ideas. On this well-worn subject I have little to add to what I have said elsewhere.[1] There is probably room for considerable advance in the techniques of scientific communication, notably by the use of computers for translation and as an index store; but it is a mistake to give too much attention to the form of the message, and to forget the characteristics of those who send and receive it. The sender and the receiver must be sensitive to each other's ways of thought, and this is no easy matter if they have been educated in two quite different cultures.

The other aspect of communication is the way in which the economic system makes known to decision-makers the existence of a shortage or misuse of resources, or of a change in the desires of consumers. Such knowledge may be communicated through a free price system and a competitive process, or by the decisions of planners. In practice the communication of the stimulus is often imperfect, and worth-while invention is thus delayed or inhibited. Thus

[1] Carter and Williams, op. cit. pp. 30–7.

(i) State interference with prices, directly or through taxation, may give a false impression of supply or of demand. Thus the high tax on petrol relative to kerosene encourages the development of the kerosene-burning tractor, which is relatively inefficient:[1] and at one time it could be argued that the price policy of the National Coal Board failed to reflect the shortage of high-grade coals, and therefore did not encourage the invention of better ways of using low-grade coal.

(ii) A firm may remain in ignorance of high costs, arising from a misuse of resources, because it has no competitors sufficiently lively to demonstrate how costs can be reduced. In consequence it will feel no incentive to seek or sponsor inventions which might enable it to use its resources better.

(iii) Planners find it hard to admit error. Thus it can be argued that some of the resources devoted to research on nuclear energy would be better used elsewhere, and would never have found their way into the nuclear energy programme if there had not been a fundamental error of forecast of energy needs.

Imperfections of communication of this kind may thus distort the pattern of invention.

(3) THE SENSITIVITY OF THE DECISION-MAKER. The particular definition of invention which I have chosen on p. 678 implies the existence of two kinds of decision. The first is the decision that a particular field for invention is worth exploring — that it is worthy of the interest of an individual inventor, or forms a proper part of an organized research programme. The second is the decision that the first outlines of an invention, commonly rough and imperfect, are worth developing to the point of commercial application. Both types of decision involve an assessment of needs and of the background of technical possibilities. But in both cases it may be possible, even after a strong and well-communicated stimulus, to delay decision or to avoid it altogether.

The reasons for this are to be found in the laziness of individuals and in the inertia of organizations. Some of us enjoy change more than others, and by a process of natural selection those who dislike change tend to be found in the slowest-moving parts of the economy, which are often those parts most in need of the upsetting effect of new invention. Anyone who moves about industry will be conscious of the contrast

[1] Ibid. p. 150.

between those who are proud of tradition and suspicious of innovation, and those who are proud of a record of innovation and contemptuous of tradition. The differences in individual attitudes to change are reflected in differences in the inertia of organizations, which take their tone from dominant executives; but it is important to realize also that invention frequently upsets the organization of production and the structure of management, and there are limits to the speed at which organization and management structure can change. Sometimes it is possible to devise an organization which is inherently flexible, for example one based on a collection of 'project groups'; but more often an organization (particularly if it is large) gathers round it rules about responsibility and seniority of a kind which, however well adapted to the past work which the organization had to do, make its members unwilling to contemplate the upsetting influence of a new idea.

Fortunately there are pressures which force us to admit the possibility of change, most notably those of competition. Therefore among the incentives for invention we must include a sufficient degree of competition. This need not be the commercial competition of a free enterprise economy; a competition in prestige for technical excellence may suffice. Thus some have thought that it was better to have four separate main-line railways, each with a Chief Mechanical Engineer and his staff applying their inventive ability to the improvement of locomotives: that such a rivalry of ideas helps to overcome resistance to change, even though the direct commercial competition between the railways was very slight. If a firm is subject to the competition of the market, there is an important point to be remembered: technical progress depends on a favourable balance between competition and safety, and a severe degree of competition, though perhaps creating an urgent desire for successful invention, may cause such doubt and uncertainty as to remove the possibility of its commercial application. Thus it does not follow that all measures against monopolies, cartels and restrictive practices will, by substituting the sharp prod of competition for the feather-bedded ease of restriction, favour invention; they may succeed only in making the life of an industry so unsafe that invention is frustrated.

(4) THE ABILITY OF THE DECISION-MAKER TO MAKE A RATIONAL RESPONSE TO THE STIMULUS. Under this heading I

discuss two related matters. One is whether the decision-maker of a firm, being responsive to pressures which favour invention, will make the right choices; the other is whether, even if he does make the right choices, he will be allowed by his environment to do what he has chosen. The first of these is concerned with the efficiency of management at its economic task of making the best use of scarce resources. Thus it sometimes happens that the directors of a firm regard its research staff as back-room boys, clever but inferior in status, who can be banished to some quiet country house and left to get on with their work with hardly any contact with the current operations of the firm. In consequence the direction of research becomes unrelated to the commercial objectives of the firm; and (though there may be a flow of inventive ideas) they will not be applied because they are found to be irrelevant. Some firms also, though forced by competition to realize the need for innovation, have such a poor costing system or so ineffective a means of assessing their markets that they cannot define the points at which action is needed.

But even if a need for invention is felt and accurately assessed, the stimulus may not lead to action. For instance:

(i) The structure of the industry may be inappropriate to the scientific possibilities which lie before it. If there were a large number of independent small local generators of electricity, it would be difficult to make progress with the development of nuclear power, since the minimum scale of its operation is so large. Inventors of new techniques of building have to face the frustrating fact that most of the industry is organized in small firms, which command neither the financial resources nor the technical knowledge to make use of expensive or elaborate new methods. It is true that technical possibilities may lead to a change of organization (as has occurred in the development of 'consortia' for atomic energy projects); but such a change usually occurs only slowly.

(ii) It may be impossible to attract scientists, technologists, managers and technicians of the right kind or in the right numbers — because the educational system has not in the past trained such people in adequate numbers, or because they have been directed into inappropriate types of technology, or because the particular firm or industry is unattractive to them. Britain's failure to build a structure of invention and application on the pioneer work of Perkin on synthetic dyestuffs, which between 1860 and 1880 caused us to lose first place to Germany in this field, was due to a shortage of industrial chemists; and many later examples of similar failure can be quoted. In interpreting them it must be remembered that no country can be in the forefront in all kinds of science and technology at the same time, and that behind all complaints of local shortage lies the problem of the absolute shortage of high ability, which is the most fundamental of all limits to technical progress.

(iii) The development and application of inventions requires capital; and it may be that inventors are frustrated by the conservatism of the lenders of money or by high taxation. It is clear that many *individual* inventors believe this to be so, but this is usually because they have made a questionable assessment of the commercial value of their invention. Many industrial firms also feel that they would be more enterprising in making new developments if they could overcome difficulties about the raising or retention of money. There is some truth in these assertions, but I doubt if in British conditions they have anything like the importance usually claimed for them.[1] What appears to be a financial difficulty is often an unwillingness to accept the conditions which naturally accompany financial help; there seems little evidence that lenders as a class are more cautious about inventions than those who seek to develop them, nor that a practicable recasting of the tax system would greatly affect the speed of technical progress. But I do not know whether such judgments are applicable to other countries.

Let me sum up the argument to this point. I have been concerned only with the way in which economic incentives or hindrances influence the probability of the occurrence and full application of an invention. It remains true that invention still requires in some degree the flash of genius. We cannot provide a particular invention to order; we can (I believe) influence the statistical probability of invention in general. The factors which influence this probability are numerous and complicated, and they differ in relative importance in different industrial and technological situations. Therefore there is no easy path of generalization which will tell us how to maximize invention.

I turn now to the economic consequences of technical invention. One consequence is to stimulate further invention.

[1] Ibid. pp. 136–53.

This may be done by creating new demands: for instance, an improved design of motor-car engine, giving rise to higher speeds, stimulates the invention of improved designs of brakes. Or the stimulation may occur because the primary invention alters the relative scarcity of factors of production; perhaps a curious example of this is about to occur in the invention of new methods of teaching mathematics, because invention in other fields has created a shortage of mathematics teachers. The most interesting possibility is that the primary invention may create new opportunities for the interaction of ideas between different types of technology — it may turn out to be the missing element which makes a practical possibility of something which was previously only a theoretical dream. Thus the invention of electronic computers of great capacity and speed has made possible many new kinds of scientific inquiry; and the possibilities of the electronic computer not only influence the sheer quantity of arithmetical work done, but also (and most significantly) influence the forms of thought which lie behind that work. Previously these forms were designed for the capacity of a human brain; now they can be designed in a new way, to suit an instrument whose capacities can to some extent be suited to its tasks.

There is therefore a momentum about the inventive process; changing the metaphor, the seed of scientific inquiry, once planted, grows and throws out branches continually. It does not do so without any food. It has a considerable appetite for all the resources which go into research and development, and in particular for the services of able men. If we could regard the whole world as a single unit for scientific purposes, there would still be a limit to the fruitfulness of invention, set by the limits of human ability and of the amount of that ability which can be spared from other uses. It is apparent that national boundaries are still highly relevant to the progress of invention. The curse of Babel is still upon us — indeed, we have gone backwards since the days when many scientific papers were written in Latin. The variety of languages and the sheer complexity of the scientific field combine to make it likely that the diffusion of new ideas through the world will be slow and imperfect. In any case, much effort is required to adapt new ideas to the circumstances of each country; a new strain of wheat, admirably suited to the climate of Canada, may be wholly inappropriate for the frequent rains of Ireland. Therefore the growth of the tree of invention, for a particular country, is to some extent related to the resources available for research and development in that country. It is difficult to get all the invention one needs by being parasitic on other countries — and, indeed, a country without its own active and inventive scientists and technologists will not be able to understand what is going on in other countries.

Two consequences follow. First, it is an advantage to be rich; a rich country will be more able to spare resources for research and development, and also for the development of the educational system which is essential to provide a supply of trained scientists, technologists and technicians. Second, it is an advantage to be large; ideas move more freely within national boundaries than across them, and the large country gives more opportunity for the profitable interaction of ideas. These two consequences support that perverse economic law, "unto every one that hath, shall be given, and he shall have abundance";[1] unless contrary action is deliberately planned, the nature of invention is to increase the disparity between the rich and strong and the poor and weak.

But this is not the end of the story. Particular inventions may reduce the call on scarce products, and may indeed have been designed for this purpose; but the general effects of invention are associated with those of the higher standard of living which invention has helped to create, and the two together lead to a higher rate of exploitation of a wider range of natural resources. The consequences for particular areas of poverty may be enormous. Consider, for instance, the riches which have been heaped on the Arab world (or, at least, on its rulers) by the invention of the internal combustion engine; or the dependence of Malaya and Indonesia on the motor tyre, which is the great source of demand for rubber. Under favourable circumstances, the strong draught of export demand created by an invention may be enough to fan the slow economic activity of a country into a flame of active development. But such a result depends on luck — luck which in the mid-twentieth century has rested on the owners of oil, while passing by those who have only the fruits of agriculture to offer; and those who have had the luck have often failed to make good use of their opportunities.

It is commonly supposed that most inventions are labour-saving. This is not necessarily intentional; but in proceeding from simpler to more complex uses of science, invention tends

[1] Matthew xxv, 29.

to increase the need for physical capital and to displace labour. Yet there are cases in which invention is capital-saving (for example radio communication as compared with the use of a submarine cable); and on occasion it can save both capital and labour — this is said to have been the result of the introduction of transfer machines in a certain motor car factory. It is probably increasingly true that invention displaces labour because the human being is limited, crude and unreliable, either in the provision of power or of control. Thus Old Joe, who could tell when a mix was hot enough by looking at it, is first replaced by a man who watches a temperature recorder, and then by a fully automatic thermostatic control.

History does not support the natural prejudices of workers displaced by a new invention; there is no doubt that the general effects of invention are to raise the standard of living and to make possible a shortening of working hours. But these effects are not achieved without hardship to individuals, and they are not achieved uniformly and steadily through time. It is quite possible that for a period the hardship will be widely spread, and the fruits accrue only to a few. For instance, the group of inventions which come under the vague title of 'automation' has the capacity to produce heavy unemployment of the less skilled forms of clerical labour. In the long run, no doubt, people will cease to enter the depressed clerical occupations, and the benefits of the change will be taken in higher production or in shorter hours; but since the careers of workers are often determined at a very early age, the period of adjustment could be long and painful.

If we look forward at the effects of automation on factory processes, a grave and more permanent problem can be seen. Many past inventions have tended to eliminate skilled workers; for instance, the specialized machines on the motor car assembly line make possible the use of semi-skilled labour. But the tendency of automation is to eliminate the unskilled as well as the skilled, leaving responsibility with a few highly trained technicians. This implies a contraction of opportunities of employment for the least intelligent and the least fortunate members of the community, and (although there will remain many areas of economic life in which automation is inappropriate) it may be difficult to avoid continuing unemployment of those of low intelligence.

It is particularly difficult to foresee the effects of invention over the next exciting century of economic history. Conflicting tendencies are at work. The vast increase in population numbers promises in time to bring much of mankind back to starvation level — unless it is checked by the invention of a simple, safe and acceptable contraceptive. The prodigal use of raw materials must begin to outrun new discoveries on this limited earth; but at the same time invention is giving us new materials, most notably for the generation of power. Under the pressure of these great tendencies, the balance of economic power will shift, and new rivalries and dissensions will appear. It could well be that the problems of affluence, which now trouble the advanced countries, will prove to be problems for the present century only; it is at least certain that if mankind wants to exist on earth for a thousand years in reasonable comfort, a way of limiting population growth must be found quickly.

"When time shall have revealed the future progress of our race, those laws which are now obscurely indicated, will then become distinctly apparent; and it may possibly be found that the dominion of mind over the material world advances with an ever-accelerating force." With these cautious words Charles Babbage[1] looked forward from a time when the latest news of science was that "machinery has been taught arithmetic". But if this "dominion of mind" does indeed for a period seem to solve our material problems, what will be the effect on our long-run ability to meet the changes of economic circumstance? "An easy and luxurious existence", wrote Samuel Smiles,[2] "does not train men to effort or encounter with difficulty; nor does it awaken that consciousness of power which is so necessary for energetic and effective action in life"; and, again, "Necessity, oftener than facility, has been the mother of invention; and the most prolific school of all has been the school of difficulty." Such ideas suggest that the inventive faculty may be in the long run self-defeating; at least it is right to stress the economic significance of the effects of invention on the habits and energies of human beings.

[1] *On the Economy of Machinery and Manufactures* (3rd ed., London, 1832) 390.

[2] *Self-Help* (centenary ed., London, 1958) 50, 141.

24

The Organization of Science in Russia in Relation to the Development of Scientific Thought in the Eighteenth and Nineteenth Centuries

A. T. GRIGORYAN and B. G. KUZNETSOV

In attempting to connect the organizational forms of science in Russia in the eighteenth and nineteenth centuries with the content and style of scientific thought and specific features of the Russian historical process, we reach the following conclusions.

In the course of a period practically coinciding with the eighteenth century, from the reforms of Peter I to the time immediately preceding the war with Napoleon, experimental and theoretical science in Russia was practically wholly concentrated in the Academy of Sciences founded in 1725 in Petersburg. Anything done outside the Academy cannot compare with the atomic theory of Lomonosov, the work of Euler on mathematics, or with the results of the Academy expeditions, which had accumulated vast amounts of geographical, geological, botanical and zoological information about the huge territory of the Russian state.

In looking for the historical reasons for such organization of scientific research in Russia in the eighteenth century, we must first of all take into account the general features of scientific progress in that period. An outstanding characteristic was the tendency to apply the mechanical regularities of the world, found in the seventeenth century, to all fields of astronomical, mechanical, physical, chemical, biological and geological knowledge, that is the construction of mechanical theories and models embracing all fields of science. It is true that in the eighteenth century the physics of Descartes did not satisfy the new demands. With Newton's mechanics came phenomonological regularities in science without kinetic explanations, but which resulted in giving a more universal character to the mechanistic conception of nature. In those fields where the mechanistic conception did not bring positive results, a systematization was applied which epistemologically had much in common with Newton's phenomenological tendency. This tendency to synthesize science on a mechanistic basis went hand in hand with differentiation and with the accumulation of factual material within the different fields of science. In these separate fields facts were just accumulated, while any attempt at theoretical discussion and generalization was mostly in terms of the accepted all-embracing mechanism. The time had not yet come for the systematic activity of special scientific bodies which limited their interests to definite fields. The eighteenth century was a period in which scientific academies and universities attempted to take the whole of science for their field of study.

Such, as a first approximation, is the scheme of characteristic traits of the science of the eighteenth century, on which essentially depended the organization of original scientific work. The specific traits of the historical process in Russia in the eighteenth century we shall also enumerate in a first approximation.

The vast territory of the Russian Empire of the eighteenth century, the rapid pace of its economic development, and the military and administrative problems of the state all demanded intensive centralization of scientific research for the discovery of natural resources, the creation of new fields of production, and the provision of supplies for the army and navy. The Church could not influence scientific development here as it could in the West. During the reign of Peter I the struggle of the Church against the anti-theological tendencies of the new sciences was carried on mainly in hidden forms. When Christian Wolf refused to go to Russia, for fear of persecution by the Church, the president of the Russian Academy of Science wrote: "The clergy here has no such power as Wolf imagines. He may safely ignore the priesthood as the Emperor is the head of the church and rules without taking the church into consideration, which is wholly subordinate to him."

Peter himself edited the translations of scientific books, his nearest associates often combated Church opposition, and the attempt of reactionary Church circles to oppose the new science usually had no important results. The Russian Church schools which existed in the eighteenth century did not play an essential role in the development of science and their significance was limited mainly to elementary teaching of the young men who later became the first Russian scientists. Under such conditions the St. Petersburg Academy of Sciences founded by Peter I became the state centre of scientific research. The idea of founding the Academy first came to Peter in 1715, and in later years he returned to it again and again. In the early 1720's Peter charged his representatives to begin negotiations for inviting Western European scientists to Petersburg. In 1724 he ratified the Statute of the Academy of Sciences and the university attached to it. This Statute laid down the necessity for Russia's having a research and teaching institution united in one. Later the organizational forms of the Academy of Sciences, as expressed in its statutes, reflected the fluctuations of the policy of the government, but, in the main, the Academy continued to be a centre for experimental science and for the elaboration of mathematical principles, and it also sponsored a number of large expeditions exploring the natural resources of Russia.

The most active members of the Petersburg Academy were the 'polyhistors', scientists who united in their creative work the most varied fields of theory and practice. To their number belonged Euler and Lomonosov. The universal scope of astronomical, mathematical, physical, chemical and technical problems was not only affected by the specific particularities of the Russian historical process, which demanded state centralization of science. Such scope was affected also by the characteristic particularities of the science of the eighteenth century. These connexions are especially clearly seen in the activity of Lomonosov — the creator of the atomistic conception of the world in which the mechanics of particles was to explain the whole sum of astro-physical, chemical, geological and other facts.

At the end of 1764 or at the beginning of 1765 Lomonosov drew up a proposal for a new Statute for the Academy of Sciences, in which is clearly seen the connexion of organizational forms of scientific research with the basic trend and style of the science of eighteenth century. In determining the duties of the members of the Academy, Lomonosov laid down that everyone must know his own speciality, but at the same time must not estrange himself from related sciences. Commenting on this requirement, Lomonosov shows its connexion (and the connexion of his proposed structure for the Academy) with the characteristic role of mechanics in eighteenth-century science. A physicist must know chemistry, anatomy and botany because these subjects "help to explain the physical cause of effects",[1] that is they provide for the reduction of complex regularities to simple laws of mechanical displacements.

Comparison of Lomonosov's organizational proposals (more than the official statutes they express the objective demands of the science of those times) and his scientific views make it possible to see the connexion of the leading scientific ideas with the organization of scientific research.

At the same time the statutes of the Academy of Sciences in the eighteenth century and Lomonosov's proposals reflect the connexion of the organization of science with the specific requirements of Russia. This can be seen particularly in the projected and partially realized arrangements for connecting the Academy of Sciences with state-organized research into the economic resources of the country and with the training of specialists for industry, administration, the army and the navy.

Continuing this general characterization of the organizational forms of scientific research in Russia, we may say that the nineteenth century was a time of the gradual transfer of much of the scientific research to the universities. In the first half of the century, the universities as scientific research institutions had just come into being. In the second half of the century the number of universities increased and it was from the universities that the most important ideas emerged. The greater part of scientific research came from the university faculties, which had become in the scientific sense comparatively independent. This evolution was to a certain extent connected with the development of the sciences in the nineteenth century.

Looking back on the second half of the nineteenth century, one might say that the most characteristic features of the science of that period were the considerable broadening of precise quantitative experimentation and the increase in the number of people engaged in scientific research. The appearance of the steam engine and scientific progress connected with its invention turned the attention of scientists towards new regularities, which came into sharp contradiction with the mechanistic explanation of nature (the key concepts were those of entropy and of statistical regularities of physics in general). New biological facts displayed the specific features of the regularities of living nature (especially cell theory). Purely mechanistic conceptions of the world are met with on all sides.

[1] See Lomonosov *Complete Works*, (Moscow and Leningrad, 1957) X, 140.

The type of scientist changed — more and more thinkers clearly saw the limits of their knowledge, which basically depended on the transition in certain fields to a type of regularity new in principle. The further and rapidly growing differentiation of science was not opposed by the unifying tendency of the mechanistic conception of nature. The collective discussion of scientific problems was transferred to departments of the Academy more independent than formerly, and also to special scientific societies. A considerable separation of the faculties took place in the universities.

Decentralization of scientific research connected with specific regularities, and the differentiation of the sciences, was related to the political situation of the times. Scientific thought reflects at the end of the eighteenth century the contradictions of serfdom in Russia. In the first half of the nineteenth century one may find many examples of the connexion of scientific interests with anti-governmental opinions. But this was just a rehearsal of the colossal — in its consequences — synthesis of social ideas and scientific knowledge in the second half of the nineteenth century. At the beginning of the nineteenth century science in Russia received a strong impulse from industry, which developed very quickly after the Continental blockade and wars with Napoleon. These influences may be seen in the work of the universities. New universities were founded at the beginning of the century. They were founded by the government, which gave them a certain autonomous power, but at the same time tried to 'rein in' the scientific circles and to hinder the progressive ideas which had grown from the generalization of scientific knowledge. In the history of the relations between the government and the universities one may follow all the zigzags of governmental policy from the comparative liberalism of the first years of the reign of Czar Alexander I down to the Arakcheyev tyranny and reactionary obscurantism of Nicolas I. Magnitsky — one of the most reactionary figures of the reign of Alexander I — said that the universities were the personification of revolutionary tendencies in science and proposed the suppression of the Kazan University. The University was not suppressed, but was placed completely under the control of Magnitsky. With the development of productive forces, the government's obscurantism became all the more of a hindrance to industry and to the social and cultural progress of the country. Science was on the lookout for new organizational centres, comparatively independent of the government, and tried to find them in the universities. The situation in these institutions differed sharply from that in the Academy of Science.

The beginning of the new period of organization of science in Russia comes at the beginning of the nineteenth century. In the course of the eighteenth century only one university was founded in Russia — Moscow University (1755). At the beginning of the nineteenth century a university was founded in Derpt in 1802. Yuriyevsky University, which is now called Tartu University, was founded in the sixteenth century and existed until the beginning of the eighteenth century; Vilna University was founded in 1803 (based on the Main Lithuanian school, founded in the sixteenth century); then followed Kazan University (1804), Kharkov University (1805), Petersburg University (1819), and Kiev University (1834). Observatories were founded at these universities (in 1808 at Kharkov, in 1809 at Derpt, in 1830 at Moscow, in 1838 at Kazan, in 1845 at Kiev), along with laboratories and botanical gardens. The next important event in the history of Russian science of the nineteenth century was the beginning of round-the-world tours of Russian scientists. Observations made during these expeditions included astronomical and geophysical measurements, which were combined with the observations made in Russia at the astronomical observatories founded in Russia at that period.

New scientific problems arose from the technical problems worked out in the old and new higher technical schools (in 1814 a building school was founded, in 1819 the Main engineering school, in 1828 the Petersburg technological school, and in 1830 the forestry school and many others).

In the second half of the nineteenth century a rapid economic and ideological improvement took place in Russia. The 1860's left a great impression on all aspects of the development of Russian society. During this period Russia gave world culture a pleiade of outstanding thinkers in different fields. The work of these thinkers is in some cases clearly and directly, in others obscurely and indirectly connected with social conditions.

Social improvement in Russia coincided with the beginning of a new period in the development of world science. In order to approach an historical explanation of the organization of Russian scientific thought in the second half of the nineteenth century, it is necessary to characterize this new period in the development of world science.

The new period began in the middle of the nineteenth century. In the 1840's the law of the conservation of energy ceased to be just a law of mechanical processes, and became a universal principle of physics. At the same time the idea of entropy showed the irreducibility of the more complex regularities of nature to the regularities of classical mechanics. The theory of natural selection included organic life in a general causal scheme and at the same time illustrated the specific character of the laws of biology. Science became all the more differentiated and at the same time general principles developed, opposing teleological ideas and closely connected with the progressive tendencies of social thought. The reforms of the 1860's, and above all the abolition of serfdom, caused a great social improvement. Large-scale industry, the railroads, the post-reform economy of Russia in general, forced the building of new educational and scientific institutions. Not only the universities but technical colleges also became scientific centres. At the same time the social rise and upward flight of revolutionary democratic thought directly influenced science. The universities did not satisfy the needs of science as organizational centres, for science now not only looked to the government for independence but, at the end of the century (as exemplified by Sechenov, Timiriazev and many others), went against the government. Along with the universities, social, scientific and educational institutions appeared. The prerevolutionary evolution of organizational forms of Russian science came to an end with the almost symbolic picture of Lebedev's research work in a laboratory founded with the help of social donations following his expulsion from the university, after he had discovered the pressure of light.

There was only a slight increase in the number of universities in the 1860's. In 1865 Novorossiisk University was founded in Odessa, and Tomsk University followed in 1888. A new form of higher education appeared — the higher women's courses. Courses of this type were organized in Moscow in 1872 and in Petersburg in 1878. The higher women's courses, besides being considerable political and cultural influences, sometimes also became centres of scientific research work.

One of the most characteristic features of university life, beginning in the 1860's, was the organization of scientific societies. In the first half of the century the attempts to organize such societies seldom succeeded because of governmental opposition. Now the dam was breached in many places. The nature of science itself after the discovery of unifying principles uniting all scientific fields required systematic contacts between scientists apart from official gatherings. The ever-increasing connexions of science with society made the demands of the scientists more urgent. During the years of the new rise of social thought and enhancement of scientific interests, societies of naturalists were organized at the universities of Yuriev (1853), Moscow (The Society of Lovers of Natural Science, Anthropology, and Ethnography, 1863), Petersburg (1868), Kazan (1869), Kiev (1869), Kharkov (1869), and Tomsk (1889). Along with them were organized at the universities physical-mathematical societies (1890 in Kazan and Kiev). Scientific societies were organized not only at the universities. In addition to the already existing Free Economic Society (founded in 1765), appeared the Moscow Society of Naturalists (1805), the Mineralogical Society (1817), the Geographical Society (1845), the Russian Entomological Society (1859), the Russian Technical Society (1866), the Russian Mathematical Society (1867), the Russian Astronomical Society (1890), and others. Periodical congresses of natural scientists also became an important organizational means of facilitating the growing contacts between scientists from various cities and with different specializations.

The contacts of the scientists in the forms mentioned above reflected the main tendencies of the 1860's. The word 'naturalist' in the titles of scientific societies was already not a logical abstraction. Mathematicians, physicists, chemists, zoologists, botanists, and physiologists, all considered themselves 'naturalists' using general methods in the study of nature.

The problem of the organization of science in the first half of the twentieth century and at the present time is not included here. We shall limit ourselves to a short outline.

A planned system for scientific research is characteristic of Soviet science. It took on a planned nature after the October revolution. At the present time main natural scientific problems, as well as philosophical, historical, economic and juridical problems, are investigated at the Academy of Sciences of the U.S.S.R. and through corresponding chairs in colleges, while problems of the practical applications of science are studied at the corresponding institutes, which come under the organs directing the national economy. This system is the result of the historical development of Soviet society and Soviet economy, which now embodies the greatest achievements of science in new techniques. It is necessary to point out that the planning of science is deeply connected with its internal regularities. Planned organization of science directs its development along the paths determined by its internal logic. The characteristic features of contemporary organization of scientific research in the U.S.S.R. are closely connected with the evolution of world science and with the evolution of practical applications of science in the first half of the twentieth century — with a new synthesis of scientific knowledge and with social conditions created in the U.S.S.R. Scientific synthesis and social conditions do not stand in opposition to each other; social conditions in this case fully allow for the fulfilment of the demands based on the content and style of contemporary science. This epistemological and historical problem can be no more than indicated here.

At the end of the nineteenth and the beginning of the twentieth centuries, the scientific revolution connected with the discovery of particles of the atom took place. At the beginning of the twentieth century the theory of relativity radically changed ideas about space and time. At the end of the first quarter of the new century the elementary particles showed their dual corpuscular-undulatory nature. The development of radio techniques, X-rays, applications of electronic apparatus, and the extensive electrification of the economy have led to a new kind of link between science and practice. The middle of the century demonstrated the connexions between the new physical ideas and the radical technical revolution, including the application of atomic energy, the development of cybernetics, and the beginning of the systematic study of cosmic space with the help of artificial sputniks and interplanetary ships. During this period the organization of scientific research has changed considerably. Giant experimental apparatuses have made their appearance, the construction of which is often a great state, and sometimes international, enterprise. The most abstract theories are comparatively quickly put to application. New links between various scientific subjects appear. Cosmological and cosmogonical pictures are related to the picture of the movement and changes of the elementary particles in the ultra-microscopical spheres. These generalizations acquire direct practical application. Accordingly the connexions between scientists of different specialities grow closer. In the technical laboratories of different branches, such abstract spheres of knowledge as information theory are being developed, and on the other hand, from purely theoretical problems from the universities and academical institutions come discoveries of more practical importance. In the middle of the twentieth century the institutes concentrating their forces on the most highly advanced problems of science become most important for scientific and technical progress.

Planned organization of scientific research, which may be consistently put into effect under planned organization of the national economy, opens many possibilities to the scientific tendencies determined above.

25

The Interaction between Scientific Research and Technical Invention in the History of Russia

N. A. FIGUROVSKY

The important role of the interaction of science and technology throughout their historical development hardly needs to be debated. Most of the scholars interested in the history of scientific development have undoubtedly always believed such an interaction and interdependence to be the basis of the progress of science and technology. As an example we might quote a statement made by M. Lomonosov in his well-known work, *A Discourse on the Use of Chemistry* (1751) which says: "The sciences show the way to industries while the latter accelerate the progress of the former. Both serve one and the same purpose."[1]

It must be noted with regret that historians of science have been far from strict in adhering to this principle in their works. For instance, in the voluminous monographs and textbooks on the development of chemistry which started with Gmelin[2] and Kopp[3] the development of chemistry is treated completely apart from technological advances and from the requirements of manufacture. But a thorough analysis of the correlation of science and technology, at least during the periods of their intensive simultaneous development, could promote a clearer understanding of the actual reasons and prerequisites both for some particular scientific discoveries and for the rapid progress of scientific research in certain branches of science.

In his time Friedrich Engels wrote:

> If a society experiences a technological need, this fact will help scientific advance much more than ten universities. The whole of hydrostatics (Torricelli and others) was brought into being by the necessity of regulating mountain streams in Italy in the sixteenth and seventeenth centuries. We began to understand electricity only after its technical applicability had been discovered. It is regrettable

[1] М. В. Ломоносов, *Полное собр. сочинений* (Москва - Ленинград, 1951) II 351 (Lomonosov, *Complete Works*, II).

[2] J. F. Gmelin, *Geschichte der Chemie* (Göttingen, 1797–1799) I–III.

[3] H. Kopp, *Geschichte der Chemie* (Braunschweig, 1843–1847) I–III.

that in Germany there is a tradition of describing the history of science as if it had dropped from the sky.[1]

Throughout the history of Russia and the Soviet Union the interaction and interdependence of science and industry (technology) can be traced quite distinctly in the course of many a century. To simplify the examination of this correlation we shall indicate roughly the main periods in the history of Russia and the Soviet Union according to production methods and scientific development. These periods are as follows:

(1) The ancient period (up to the beginning of the seventeenth century);
(2) The period of the development of handicrafts and manufactures (seventeenth century to the end of the eighteenth);
(3) The period of the advent and initial development of capitalism in Russia (from the end of the eighteenth century until 1861);
(4) The period of rapid development of capitalism in Russia (1861–1917);
(5) The period of socialism (beginning with 1917).

(1) *The first period (to about 1600)*

The process of economic development in Russia during the ancient period (till up to the seventeenth century) somewhat differed from that of the countries of Western Europe. The Russia of those times was exceedingly thinly populated. The vast expanse of eastern and north-eastern Russia and Sideria was covered with virgin forests and had few settlements. Even in central Russia the number of cities and towns, in relation to the territory as a whole, was not great, compared with the West. Natural economy was the principal mode of production.

Enormous damage to the handicraft manufacture of ancient Russia, which had absorbed many traditions of Byzantine handicrafts, was done by the Tartar invasion and the ensuing 300-year long Tartar yoke, which lasted from the thirteenth century to the fifteenth. The Russia of that period had practically neither scientists nor prominent specialists, except perhaps for building specialists and architects. In the sixteenth century there appeared in Moscow and in the cities and towns of western Russia doctors with a European education and such specialists as gunsmiths, founders who cast guns and bells,

[1] К. Маркс и Ф. Энгельс, *Письма* (Москва, 1931) 407 (K. Marx and F. Engels, *Letters*).

mining and metal-workers, and the like. Handicrafts and commerce during that period reached quite a high level. Manufactures appeared and began to develop. During the reign of Ivan the Terrible trade routes were established between Russia and Great Britain and Holland via Archangel. Thus the fifteenth and the sixteenth centuries were for Russia what might be called a sort of Renaissance.

Feudalism, which was more long-lived in Russia than in other countries of Europe, as well as the exclusive domination of religious ideology, did not stimulate traditions of scientific research. The existing handicrafts and petty manufactures catering for the primitive demands of the population aroused practically no large-scale problems for scientific research.

(2) *The second period (about 1600–1800)*

The beginning of the seventeenth century in Russia was a time of political unrest and Polish intervention. But even during that period Czar Boris Godunov followed the example of his predecessor Ivan the Terrible in trying to found a university in Moscow. A considerable development of trade and manufactures at that time had already confronted Russia with the problem of prospecting and utilizing the immense natural resources she possessed.

The year 1613 saw the beginning of a considerable flourishing of medicine and pharmacy[1] in Russia. The Pharmaceutical Department founded as far back as the end of the sixteenth century developed by the first half of the seventeenth century into not only an administrative medical centre, but an educational and research institution as well. The establishment solved a large number of medical and pharmaceutical problems. To cater for the needs of the army and the population the Pharmaceutical Department collected and revised foreign pharmacopoeias and medical books. Russian herbals and medical books recommended over 2,000 medicinal herbs of the Russian flora. In the middle of the seventeenth century there was introduced the scientific degree of Doctor of Medicine.

Prominent representatives of medicine of the Leyden, the German and the British schools had extensive practices and did scientific research in Moscow. It was in Moscow that the British physician Arthur Dee (1579–1651), physician in

[1] Н. Новомергский, *Врачебное строение в до-Петровской Руси* (Томск, 1907) (N. Novomergsky, *The Organization of Medicine in Russia before Peter the Great*).

ordinary to King James I and later on to Charles I, wrote his first book on chemistry (or rather on alchemy) *Fasciculus chemicus*, in 1629, which was published in Paris in 1731.[1]

The seventeenth century in Russia saw great developments in the production of such chemicals as potash (for export),[2] saltpetre and gunpowder, in the glass and paper industries, alcohol distilleries, and other industries.[3] Defence and industrial requirements necessitated the foundation of a number of departments — administrative bodies to supervise the production of guns, arms, powder, prospecting for metal ores, etc. Some of these departments had assay laboratories attached to them.

The manufacturing of woollen and linen fabrics, tanning, chemicals and other products continued to thrive throughout the latter half of the eighteenth century. Especially noteworthy was the rapid progress of metallurgical industries and above all, iron-ore mining and processing in central Russia (Tula, the Moscow area), and especially in eastern Russia and the Urals.

The reign of Peter I (1682) brought a further fresh lease of life to thriving manufacture industries.[4] Engaged in warfare and realizing the economic backwardness of his vast country, Peter I in every way encouraged the advent of various new industries, particularly the metallurgical and shipbuilding industries. He initiated the large-scale building of new cities — Petersburg was founded by him in 1703 — as well as a number of ports and fortifications, among them Kronstadt, Asov and Taganrog. Peter I devoted great attention to the industrial development of the country. Early in the eighteenth century he organized systematic prospecting for the natural resources of the Urals and Siberia and established copper smelting, the processing of silver ore and other industries.

It was from this sufficiently strong economic and industrial foundation, which Peter I had laid in Russia for the first time in her history, that the necessity again arose of establishing a

[1] Arthur Dee, *Fasciculus chemicus abstrusae hermeticae Scientiae* (Paris, 1731).

[2] *Акты хозяйства боярина Б. И. Морозова, ч.I и II*, Изд. Института истории Академии наук СССР (Москва-Ленинград, 1940-1945) (*The Economic Activity of the Boyar B. I. Morozov*, Parts 1 and 2).

[3] П. М. Лукьянов, *Краткая история химической промышленности СССР* (Москва, 1959) (P. M. Lukyanov, *A Short History of the Chemical Industry in the USSR*).

[4] П. Т. Любомиров, *Очерки по истории русской промышленности XVII, XVIII и начало XIX века* (Москва, 1947) (P. G. Lyubomirov, *An Outline of the History of Russian Industry in the 17th, 18th and early 19th centuries*).

university in the country. This time the ground was more favourable than during the reigns of Ivan the Terrible and Boris Godunov. The advisers of Peter I recommended him for a start to found an academy of science so as to establish scientific research and the training of scientists in the country. It is very typical of Russia that unlike most of the academies of Western Europe, which were started as scientific societies (for instance, the Royal Society in Great Britain), the Academy of Petersburg was established by an act of government in 1725.

The foundation of the Petersburg Academy should not be regarded as a mere act of patronage springing from the desire of the Czar to have at his disposal a group of learned men to glorify the grandeur and luxury of the court. The founding of the Russian Academy of Sciences was a logical consequence of the economic progress of the country. It was made necessary by the vital needs of the developing industries, an acute demand for prospecting and utilizing the country's enormous natural resources, and by the need to stimulate the education and cultural growth of the population. The difference between the ways of coming into being of the academies in Western Europe and the Petersburg Academy of Sciences proved to be historically immaterial. In the Russia of that time there were no scientists who could have established a scientific society, while there existed a definite need for one.

The Petersburg Academy of Sciences started its glorious activity after the death of Peter I, in the reign of his successors who were far from being as eager as he had been to encourage the progress of learning in the country. During the early days of its existence the Academy could not boast of any Russian scholars. At the same time among the foreign learned men invited to work at the Academy there were no 'celebrities', men of European renown who could have at once made the Academy famous both by their previous work and by their new research. The first members of the Petersburg Academy of Sciences were for the most part young men without any name in the world of learning. For instance, Daniel Bernoulli arrived in Petersburg at the age of twenty-five, the historian G. F. Miller at the age of twenty, the naturalist I. G. Gmelin was but eighteen, while the famous L. Euler, when he came to Petersburg in 1727, was also merely twenty years old.[1]

[1] П. Пекарский, *История императорской Академии наук в Петербурге* (СПб., 1870) (P. Pekarsky, *A History of the Imperial Academy of Sciences of Petersburg*, I).

From the earliest days of its existence the Petersburg Academy could boast extremely favourable conditions for the fruitful activity of the young scientists in the various fields of learning. There was no end to work to be done on the absolutely virgin soil in all fields of science and its applied branches, all of which were suffering from an acute shortage of hard-working hands and minds. The vast country's demand for scientific research could be satisfied only to an insignificant degree. The growth of industry made it necessary to solve a whole series of problems, first and foremost among them being prospecting for and mining of the natural resources, study of the flora and fauna, research into problems of astronomy and geodesy, and elaboration of a number of questions in the field of applied mechanics and mathematics, physics and chemistry, mineralogy and other sciences. It was no wonder therefore that the first academicians of foreign descent, in spite of finding themselves in alien conditions and without the necessary scientific equipment at their disposal, proved to be exceedingly successful in the research. The works of D. Bernoulli, L. Euler, I. G. Gmelin and other scientists at once attracted the attention of men of learning and in the course of some ten years after its foundation brought the Academy extensive and honourable fame.

Speaking in terms of the history of science, the eighteenth century might be called a century of scientific expeditions, travels, and geographical discoveries. It was in the course of that century that system was first introduced into the examination of the principal types of minerals, as well as into descriptive botany and zoology. Scientific expeditions were essential for the Russia of that time, for the vast expanses of Siberia and north-eastern Russia still remained *terra incognita*. The Far East and Siberia were practically little more than mere names. Fragmentary reports of certain discoveries and findings of new species of plants and animals, rich deposits of ores and the like led to the fitting out of a number of large-scale expeditions on the initiative of the Russian government and the Academy of Sciences. Some of those expeditions lasted a long time. For instance, D. G. Messerschmidt travelled for about nine years, and I. G. Gmelin and S. P. Krasheninnikov explored Siberia and Kamchatka for over eleven years.[1]

[1] *История Академии наук СССР*, I. *1724-1803* (Москва-Ленинград, 1958) (*A History of the Academy of Sciences of the USSR*, I, *1724–1803*).

Quite characteristic of the activity of the Academy of Sciences of the middle of the eighteenth century was the work of M. V. Lomonosov (1711–65), which reflected as in a mirror the need of the Russia of that time for scientific research.[1] Lomonosov was the first scientific academician of Russian origin. He is known to have been one of the most prominent atomists of the eighteenth century and a pioneer in the solution of many a problem of physics and chemistry. The pressing need for scholarly research into various questions closely connected with the scholarly and cultural progress of the country turned Lomonosov's attention to a variety of problems in linguistics, philology, poetry, history, geography and meteorology, astronomy, cartography, economics, statistics and other fields of knowledge. He experimented with atmospheric electricity together with G. W. Richman, designed projects for sea routes across the Arctic Ocean, examined the causes of Aurora Borealis, and conducted many activities in other fields as well. In 1748, he built the first state scientific research and teaching chemical laboratory, in which he carried on his work. He took part in working out plans for expeditions to the north-eastern part of Siberia, and solved many technological problems connected with the production of mineral paints, porcelain, stained glass, etc. Lomonosov's twenty-five years of activity is the best possible example of the close connexion existing between the scientific research done in Russia and the requirements of the growing industry and the needs of the national economy at large.

In 1755, on Lomonosov's initiative, and in accordance with his project, Moscow University was founded.[2] This was Russia's second great centre for science and culture. For a long time it built up resources for conducting large-scale research in the field of natural sciences, while confining its activities during the first few decades after its foundation to the training of highly skilled specialists for public services and medicine. But even in the eighteenth century its role in the advancement of Russian national culture and science was tremendous. It goes without saying that in the course of its work the University met the important requirements of life and production and satisfied the country's acute demand for cultural progress.

[1] Б. Н. Меншуткин, *Жизнеописание Михаила Васильевича Ломоносова* (Москва-Ленинград, 1947) (B. N. Menshutkin, *A Biography of Mikhail Vasilevich Lomonsov*).

[2] *История Московского Университета* (Москва, 1955) I (*A History of Moscow University*, I).

It is in place here to say a few words about scientific progress in Russia towards the close of the eighteenth century. According to many historians, the period of capitalism in Russia started in the third quarter of the eighteenth century. It was, indeed, during that period that rather large-scale enterprises of capitalist type sprang up and rapidly flourished especially in the mining and metallurgical industries with hired workers and these industries gradually replaced manufactures manned by serfs. In spite of Russia's still continuing to be mainly an agricultural country, the needs of growing industry greatly influenced the choice of the fields of scientific research conducted at the Academy of Sciences. For instance, the chemists of the period following Lomonosov's time — I. G. Leman (in the field of metallurgy), I. I. Georgy (traveller and practical chemist),[1] T. E. Lovits[2] (who discovered absorption from solutions and many methods of analytical chemistry), N. N. Sokolov, Y. D. Zakharov, V. M. Severgin (practical chemists), K. G. Laxman (traveller and chemical technologist), the physicist V. V. Petrov (who discovered the electric arc in 1805)[3] and others — closely connected their activities with the vital needs of the growing capitalist industry of Russia. Many of them were talented and prominent scientists who in chemistry adhered to the anti-phlogistic theory of Lavoisier.

From the above it follows that during the second period of Russia's scientific and industrial development the entire activity of the Petersburg Academy of Sciences and of the University as well as of the first scientific society — the Voluntary Economic Society founded in 1765 — was closely connected with the requirements of industry and the vital needs of a country rapidly developing after a prolonged economic stagnation.

(3) *The third period (about 1800–61)*

The rapid growth of capitalist industry which was to be seen during the eighteenth century somewhat slowed down at the beginning of the nineteenth. The Czarist government, par-

[1] *История Академии наук СССР* (Москва-Ленинград, 1958) I, 375–377 (*A History of the Academy of Sciences of the USSR*, I).

[2] N. A. Figurovskij, *Leben und Werk des Chemikers Tobias Lowitz* (Berlin, 1959).

[3] For earlier investigations into this problem by Humphry Davy, see *Nicholson's Journal*, IV (1800) 326 and *Journal of the Royal Institution*, I (1802).

ticularly during the reign of Catherine II, was supported by the feudal nobility, and used every means at its disposal to build up the domination of landlords based on the slave labour of serf peasantry. The domination of the feudal and landlord system restricted the growth of capitalist elements. Under such circumstances Russia continued as an agricultural country as before. Naturally this slowing down of the development of capitalism in Russia could not but affect scientific advancement as well. Nevertheless, the needs of the capitalistic sector of the country's economy were becoming quite tangible. One result of this was the foundation in the early nineteenth century of several universities: Kazan University in 1804, Kharkov University in 1805, Petersburg University in 1819, as well at other institutions of higher learning and for the advancement of culture.

The early part of the nineteenth century was not very promising for Russia's scientific advancement. The governments of Alexander I and later of Nicholas I not only did not encourage research into natural sciences, but rather hindered it, regarding it as a source of what was called "free-thinking" (progressive ideas). Nicholas I, fearing the spread of "the infection of free-thinking" from Western Europe, at one time even suspended the customary visits of Russian scientists to European cities.

In spite of the efforts of the Czarist government to preserve the country in a system of feudal serfdom and to keep the population in a state of ignorance, science spontaneously broke out of its embryo stage and Russia produced a number of outstanding men of learning even during the first half of the nineteenth century. Among them was the famous mathematician N. I. Lobachevsky of Kazan (1792–1856).[1] It was in the same town that the first Russian school of chemistry was established. In 1842 K. K. Klaus, in trying to solve the problem of utilizing the waste from refining platinum, discovered a new chemical element — ruthenium. The mathematician and astronomer, N. N. Zinin,[2] who later devoted himself to chemistry, in the same year discovered his famous reaction of reducing nitrobenzol to aniline, which was of great theoretical and practical importance. But his greatest service

[1] В. Ф. Каган, *Лобачевский* (Москва-Ленинград, 1944) (V. F. Kagan, *Lobachevsky*).

[2] Н. А. Фигуровский и Ю. И. Соловьев, *Н. Н. Зинин* (Москва–Ленинград, 1959) (N. A. Figurovsky and Yu. I. Solovyev, *N. N. Zinin*).

consisted in bringing about the establishment in Kazan of the well-known school of chemistry, which presented world science with a whole galaxy of scientists with A. M. Butlerov at the head. It is characteristic of the history of Russian science that it was not the University of Petersburg, nor even the old Academy of Sciences, that turned out to be among the first large centre of research of the nineteenth century, but the university of the provincial town of Kazan. The reasons for this lie in the same phenomenon — that is, the close connexion between the work of the Kazan scientists and the practical requirements of growing industry, the vital needs of the country and her people.

The spontaneous development of Russia's industry, despite the hindrance on the part of the still dominating system of the feudal and landlord rule and serfdom, brought about tangible economic changes in the structure of national economy even in the 1830's and 1840's. Capitalism during that period was rapidly gaining ground in the field of industry, particularly in mineral ore processes, which immediately resulted in the appearance in Russia of prominent scientists and scientific schools in various fields in many Russian cities and towns. Especially rapid and noteworthy was this progress in scientific research in Petersburg — Russia's chief political centre. It was here that the middle of the nineteenth century saw the rise of prominent mathematical schools led by M. V. Ostrogradsky (1801–61), P. L. Chebyshev (1821–94), the astronomer V. Y. Struve (1793–1864), also a founder of the Pulkovo Observatory, the chemists H. I. Gess (1802–50), A. A. Voskresensky (1809–80), N. N. Zinin (1812–80) and J. F. Frietsche (1808–71), the physicists E. C. Lents (1804–65) and B. S. Jacobi (1801–74), and many other representatives of other natural sciences. Research groups were formed in other towns as well — such as Moscow, Kharkov, Kiev, Tartu.

In summary, the first half of the nineteenth century in Russia saw the inauguration and flourishing of the capitalist mode of production. Immediately resulting from that was the rapid development of research into various fields of science. It should be noted here that in this case, as throughout the history of science, it is not always possible to trace a direct connexion between the technological advances and theoretical research. Nevertheless, certain examples undoubtedly prove that such a connexion does exist even in cases of what might be called purely theoretical investigations.

(4) *The fourth period (1861–1917)*

The period of the rapid growth of capitalism in Russia was accompanied by a simultaneous flourishing of natural science. The year 1861 saw the so-called release of the peasantry from serfdom. Though this liberation amounted in fact to a new form of bondage for the peasants, nevertheless, the change in the economic structure of the country brought about by the reform was not slow in making itself felt in all spheres of life including science and technology.

The changes caused in industry and technology can be clearly seen from several figures quoted from the well-known work by V. I. Lenin, *The Development of Capitalism in Russia*,[1] in which the author collected and studied extensive statistical data characterizing the rapid development in the various branches of Russian industry during the period following the Reform. Quoted here are just fragmentary data out of Lenin's work. For instance, the production of cast iron and coal extraction in Russia increased as follows:

Year	*Production of cast iron (in thousands of poods)*	*Coal extraction (in millions of poods)*
1867	17·028	26·7
1877	24·579	110·1
1887	37·389	276·8
1897	114·782	683·9
1902	158·618	1,005·21

From these figures [Lenin writes] it can clearly be seen what a technological revolution is taking place at the present time in Russia [the first edition of the book was issued in 1899, the second edition in 1908] and what a tremendous capability for the development of productive forces is possessed by large-scale capitalist industry. . . . We can see the mining industry in Russia making more rapid progress than in Western Europe, in some ways even more rapid than in North America. In 1870 Russia produced 2·9 per cent of the world's cast iron (22 million poods out of the total 745), while in 1894 it was 5·1 per cent (81·3 million poods out of 1,584·2) (*Vestnik Finansov*, 1897, No. 22). In the course of the past decade (1886–1896) the production of cast iron in Russia increased threefold (32·5 and 96·5 million poods respectively), while in France, for instance, it took 28 years (1852–1880), in the United States 23 years (1845–1868), in Great Britain 22 (1824–1846), and in Germany 12 (1859–1871) (see *Vestnik Finansov*, 1897, No. 50).

[1] В. И. Ленин, *Сочинения* (Москва, 1) 194 III, 428–429 (V. I. Lenin, *Works*).

These figures for the growth of heavy industry are characteristic of other fields of the economy as well. For instance, the year of 1861 saw in Russia the beginning of a rapid growth of railways, commerce, water transport, etc. Naturally these changes in the economy of the country led to changes in the entire way of life. The natural economy prevailing heretofore began to yield. Historically it is very significant that at the outset of the rapid growth of capitalism in Russia the natural sciences staged a veritable revolution in their progress and reached their prime in the 1880's and 1890's. Scientific research in various fields was done in various parts of the country and important theoretical schools sprang up. Applied natural sciences also flourished. For instance, considerable success was achieved in electrophysics. Scientist-inventors, among whom were P. N. Yablochkov (1847–94) and A. I. Lodigin (1847–1923), were engaged in the application of electricity to lighting. The physicist A. G. Stoletov of Moscow (1839–96) made great advances in research into photo-electricity. The well-known physicist A. S. Popov from Petersburg (1859–1906) in the 1890's invented the radio and demonstrated the first radio-broadcasts in practice. The physicist P. N. Lebedev of Moscow (1866–1912) discovered the pressure of light, and so on.

Particularly great was the success attained by the Russian chemists of that period. In 1861 A. M. Butlerov put forward his theory of chemical composition. In 1869 D. I. Mendeleyev (1834–1907), already well known for his earlier research into physical chemistry and chemical technology, discovered the periodic law of chemical elements.[1] Petersburg produced a whole galaxy of prominent chemists, among them L. N. Shishkov, A. P. Borodin, G. G. Gustavson, N. A. Menshutkin, and F. F. Beilstein. The Kazan school of chemistry sprang up at Kharkov, where as early as the 1860's the world's first course of physical chemistry was delivered by N. N. Beketov. Scientists P. P. Alexeyev, M. I. Konovalov and others successfully worked at the problems in Kiev. The flourishing of chemical science in Russia at that period is not at all fortuitous. In spite of many discoveries (such as the periodic law, theory of structure, laws of distillation discovered by D. P. Konovalov, and others) being of a purely theoretical nature, many of the Russian chemists devoted a great deal of attention to problems

[1] Н. А. Фигуровский, *Д. И. Менделеев* (Москва-Ленинград, 1961) (N. A. Figurovsky, *D. I. Mendeleyev*).

of applied chemistry. The birth of the chemistry of oil dates back to that period. Markovnikov discovered a new class of hydrocarbons of oil — naphtha. Mendeleyev and Beilstein solved chemical and technological problems of the chemistry and refinement of oil. Many chemists directed their efforts to such applied fields as the chemistry of coals, explosives, by-products of wood, etc. Many prominent chemists were not merely 'arm-chair' scientists and would leave their laboratories to deal with practical problems of technology, to search for new ways of processing the natural resources, and point out ever-newer ways of utilizing the country's wealth.

Needless to say, it was not only chemistry that contributed to the scientific progress in Russia at the close of the nineteenth century which placed her in the first rank of European countries in this field of science. A great contribution was made by other natural sciences scoring important results as well. Such names as those of the mathematician P. I. Chebyshev (1821–94) and of his followers, A. A. Markov and A. M. Lyapunov, are well known in the scientific world for the calculus of probability. Of great importance for future technological advancement and particularly in the field of aircraft construction were the investigations done by N. E. Shukovsky (1847–1921) and S. A. Chaplygin (1869–1942) in mechanics and aerodynamics. A. N. Krylov (1863–1945) became famous for his theory of the stability of ships.

Geographical and geological expeditions also grew in scope, to embrace such explorers as P. P. Semenov of the Tien Shan, A. P. Fedchenko, I. V. Mushketov, N. I. Przhevalsky, V. A. Obruchev, A. P. Karpinsky and many other participants of expeditions who helped to fill in many a blank on the maps of Central Asia. An acute shortage of metals for industry necessitated the numerous geological expeditions whose number especially increased in the 1880's.

Biology must not be overlooked, and it owed its considerable progress to the distinguished scientists A. O. Kovalevsky, I. I. Mechnikov (1845–1916), I. M. Sechenov (1829–1905), K. A. Timiryazev (1843–1920), S. N. Vinogradsky, I. P. Pavlov (1849–1936) and others.

We have had to confine ourselves merely mentioning the scientists' names in the hope that each of these names will be associated in the minds of the historians of science with respective discoveries and contributions to science. The rapid growth of capitalist industry in Russia continued into the early part of the twentieth century. All the way through it was accompanied by scientific advances. In spite of Russia's considerable economic backwardness in comparison with Western Europe and the United States during that period, science stimulated by the needs of production was rapidly reaching the level of Europe's scientific development and producing ever greater numbers of prominent men of learning. The scientists of pre-revolutionary Russia did not confine themselves merely to research into applied branches, but foreseeing, as it were, the broad technological vistas of the country's future development solved numerous theoretical problems. During the period under consideration the interdependence of technological development, the growth of the industrial potential and the prospect of research can be traced both in the great upsurge of all the natural sciences, and in the examples of the immediate effect of the practical requirements of technology (in metallurgy, oil and coal extraction, and other fields) on the subjects of research.

Soviet Russia inherited from pre-revolutionary Russia a whole galaxy of prominent scientists and even whole scientific schools whose activity reflected specifically Russian scientific traditions. This circumstance proved to be of great importance for the future advancement of science in the country, and was, indeed, one of the prerequisites for the rapid and many-sided progress of science in the Soviet Union.

(5) *The fifth, or Soviet, Period (from 1917)*

This period of the development of science in the U.S.S.R. might be subdivided into several phases: (*a*) economic rehabilitation, (*b*) the development of science during the early years of socialist construction and industrialization of the country, (*c*) World War II, and (*d*) the post-war phase.

During the October Revolution and the years immediately following it Russia found herself ravaged by post-war devastation. Most of the mills and plants were idle. Transport was disrupted. The population was starving. Yet it was during these grim years of the civil war and foreign intervention (1918–21) that very important steps were taken to lay the foundation for the future limitless flourishing of science.

The head of the Soviet State, V. I. Lenin, and the Soviet government were well aware that the country's industry and science formed the sole basis for the progress of the country and the only way of raising the living and cultural standards of the people. V. I. Lenin wrote the following words during those years:

> Formerly the human brain, the human genius of all mankind created everything only to place all the wealth of technology and culture at the disposal of one group of people and to deprive the others of such elementary necessities as education and advancement. Henceforth all the wonders of technology, all the gains of culture will become the property of the people at large, and henceforth never shall the human brain and genius be turned into a means of violence, a means of exploitation.[1]

Science in pre-revolutionary Russia developed to a large extent spontaneously, without the backing of the government. From the first years of Soviet power in Russia scientific development, for the first time in history, was included in the general state plan. At that time to many West European scientists, even some prominent ones, the very idea of planning scientific work seemed to be a quite impracticable fantasy. It is known that even in the 1930's this principle was criticized in the scientific literature of Western Europe, above all in the light of the theory attaching the main role in the development of science to intellect.

Under the conditions of building up of a new socialist Russia on the ruins of the old world, the planning of all branches of the national economy, including science, was to form the basis for the development and strengthening of the new socialist state. As far back as April 1918 — the hardest time of post-war devastation — V. I. Lenin drew up an *Outline of the Plan of Scientific and Technological Work*,[2] in which he suggested ways of developing the country's scientific research which were to be closely connected with the solution of important technological problems. In the *Outline of the Plan of Scientific and Technological Work* were raised the questions of a rational distribution of industry in the country, electrification of industry and agriculture, the search for new power resources and many others. Science and scientists were faced with tasks connected with the most vital practical problems of the country.

Sponsored by V. I. Lenin and the Soviet government, in 1918 and 1919, certain large-scale scientific investigations were launched. For instance, oil prospecting was started in the Volga

[1] В. И. Ленин, *Сочинения* (Москва, 1949) XXVI, 436 (V. I. Lenin, *Works*).

[2] В. И. Ленин, *Сочинения* (Москва, 1950) XXVII, 288–289 (Lenin, *Works*).

area in Bashkiria; 1919 saw the beginning of a thorough investigation into the Kursk magnetic anomaly, which resulted in a discovery of enormous resources of iron ore. The same period saw the construction of the first few hydro-electric power stations, and in December 1920 the Congress of the Soviets approved the state plan for the electrification of the country (the G.O.E.L.R.O. plan). Some scientists devoted their attention to the utilization of local raw-material resources for the production of the necessities of life.

At the same time, in 1918, new research centres were established in the country. Prior to the revolution Russia had merely laboratories under the academies of sciences, and under universities and institutions of higher education. Scientific research institutions as such did not exist. From the very inauguration of Soviet power a plan was drawn up for the development of a network of research institutions. There sprang into being the Nizhni Novgorod Radio Laboratory, the State Optics Institute, the Physics Technological Institute, the Karpov Institute of Physical Chemistry, the Central Aero-Hydro-Dynamics Institute, the Institute of Applied Chemistry, the Institute of Fertilizers, and other institutions. Also founded were several universities and institutions of higher learning among them the Universities of Tbilisi, Nizhni Novgorod, Tashkent, and others. This network of scientific institutions was continuously improving and expanding, and by the beginning of the period of industrialization (1927–29) it flowered in a number of scientific discoveries and solutions of numerous important theoretical and technological problems. The system of planning of scientific effort, and a close contact between the activities of scientific institutions and industry, made it possible to create new industries in the country which but shortly before had seemed to be quite unfeasible.

The year 1927 ushered in the period of industrialization in the U.S.S.R. The carefully planned construction of several heavy industry plants opened up the glorious march of the country towards complete economic independence. It is also a well-known fact that the 'industrial revolution' in the Soviet Union brought about a veritable leap in scientific research. Numerous examples might be quoted of the solution of important technological problems by scientists during the early years of industrialization. Among these can be mentioned the brilliant way of producing synthetic rubber discovered in 1928 by S. V. Lebedev (1874–1934), the solution of the problem of optical glass, a method of processing apatites into fertilizers, and the potassium problem.

Rapid industrialization revealed an acute shortage of specialists and scientific workers in the various branches of technology. In view of this a total reform of higher education was carried out in 1929. Around the few universities and institutions of higher learning was created an extensive network of special higher institutions whose number to date has reached 1,000. At the outset there was an acute shortage of competent teachers, but that difficulty was soon overcome with the help of the younger generation. Fresh groups of young students from worker and peasant backgrounds entered higher schools between 1929 and 1933 and eagerly absorbed knowledge, applying and perfecting it at the mills and plants after classes. The problem of training skilled workers for all the branches of industry and science is known to have been successfully solved even before the war, but later on the Soviet Union is also known to have occupied the first place in the world in the number of trained specialists employed in industry and science.

As it is impossible within the scope of this one article to give even a brief account of the scientific development in the Soviet Union after 1927, we shall have to confine ourselves to considering only some general features and factors of scientific progress, devoting most of our attention to the prerequisites and conditions for training a large staff of specialists in this country.

As has already been mentioned above, Soviet Russia has inherited a certain number of very skilled scientists who followed old Russian traditions in their methods of research. By no means all of these men of learning were quick to adapt themselves to the new requirements and problems which arose in the early years of Soviet power. Differences arose between scientists which resulted in the emigration of a certain group of them. In spite of that, immediately following the October revolution a group of old-time intelligentsia actively joined in building up a new Russia. In the 1930's the grandiose scale of creation and construction captivated the entire body of the old Russian intelligentsia. There is no risk of exaggeration in stating that many professors at the institutions of higher learning of that time not only delivered daily lectures, but simultaneously supervised the work of post-graduates, gave scientific advice to the industrial enterprises, did research at scientific institutions, wrote text-books and articles, and so on. There was hardly any other country where intellectual work was as strenuous as it was among the Soviet scientists during the period of industrialization. But then it was a period of transition. A genuine revolution in the field of science in the Soviet Union was brought about by the following generation of scientists reared under Soviet power in an atmosphere of strenuous creative labour by the entire Soviet people.

During the period of industrialization in the Soviet Union there were particularly favourable conditions for creative work not only for professional scientists, but also for engineers and workers as well. New inventions and the rationalization of technological processes were carried out on a large scale. And though the path that many inventors and self-made technologists had to cover before reaching some tangible results was far from being a bed of roses, their combined activities, with those of prominent scientists and engineers, made it possible to settle a great many questions which arose daily from the practice of construction. Technological processes fully made up for lack of technological experience and traditions of research in certain new branches of science which were not to be found in old Russia.

Generally speaking, the success of Soviet science during the period preceding World War II was greatly enhanced by the fact that the problems solved by the research institutions and higher schools were closely connected with the vital needs of industry and national economy. In the 1930's a system of research under contracts with industrial enterprises was widespread, in accordance with plans made by state planning bodies. This by no means implied that no theoretical investigations were made in the country. For they went on, and not without considerable success, at the Academy of Sciences, which by the middle 1930's had considerably grown numerically and extended the network of its scientific institutions.

There were 44 research institutions (including museums and committees) under the auspices of the Academy of Sciences in 1918, 57 in 1931, 75 in 1934, 97 in 1938, and in 1940 as many as 102. Apart from those, in 1932 in a number of Union Republics branches of the Academy of Sciences were established numbering 10 before the outbreak of World War II. Central academies of sciences proper existed at that time in the Ukranian Republic, the Bielorussian Republic, the Georgian Republic and the Armenian Republic.

The growth of the Academy of Sciences in the years of industrialization can be seen from the following figures showing its staff increases and its publications:[1]

Year	*Total staff of the Academy*	*Scholars among the staff*	*Printed matter (in quires)*
1918	220	109	697
1925	873	363	940
1932	2,143	1,021	2,809
1935	3,881	1,775	4,700
1937	5,954	2,719	7,295
1941	10,213	4,582	12,773

At present the staff of the Academy of Sciences of the U.S.S.R. exceeds 60,000 persons.

To ensure a closer contact between the activity of the Academy of Sciences and the requirement of socialist construction, in 1934 the Academy of Sciences was transferred from Leningrad to Moscow and placed directly under the auspices of the Government of the U.S.S.R. Naturally this step opened up new and brilliant vistas for the further progress of scientific work in the institutions under the Academy.

From the example of the Academy of Sciences of the U.S.S.R. which since 1935 had been transformed into what might be called a "Department of Science" in the U.S.S.R., one can clearly see the peculiarities of scientific organization in the country. The planning of research work by the government is certainly the chief peculiarity. This planning has in no way ever restricted the initiative of any scientist despite the fact that each one of them works in accordance with a plan approved by the head of research and the board of directors of the scientific institutes. The state plan for the principal problems merely canalizes the respective research institutions into the necessary fields, leaving both to the heads of the research and to the individual scientists under them the greatest possible initiative. It is quite groundless to say that any persons in the planning bodies or in the scientific administration act as guardians of this or that research group or interfere in their course.

The second important peculiarity of the development of science in the U.S.S.R. lies in the close connexion between the basic problems of research and the needs of socialist industry,

[1] *Материалы к истории Академии наук СССР* (*1917-1947*) (Москва -Ленинград, 1950) 304, 448 (*Material for a History of the Academy of Sciences in the USSR, 1917–1947*).

agriculture and other spheres of the country's life. This connexion is not always direct. It does not at all imply that a scientist working at an important theoretical or technological problem is to be regarded as merely a rationalizer of production or an inventor. Though at times Soviet scientists really are engaged in settling purely technological questions, which is quite inevitable, their main duty lies in investigating theoretical problems in this or that branch of production. For instance, the problem of building up the country's aircraft could be solved as a result of settling a whole number of complex questions of aerodynamics, mechanics of solid bodies and theory of electricity. The problem of launching new branches of chemical industry has always required scientists in the field of chemistry to develop new kinds of compounds, to carry out research into the thermodynamics and kinetics of the processes and to investigate questions of stable materials for the apparatus as well as a number of other problems.

The third peculiarity of scientific advancement in the U.S.S.R. lies in the planned training of the staff of specialists and scientists. The history of science has hardly any examples similar to that of the Soviet Union, which boldly put forward and successfully solved the problem of training scientific personnel in a very short time. Scientific institutions are manned by graduates of the institutions of higher education. All the apt young people have an opportunity to perfect their knowledge in a branch of their choice. There is a broad network of postgraduate and doctorate courses under the auspices of first-rate scientific institutions and institutes of higher education, which greatly contribute to the solution of the problem of personnel training. The scientific degrees of Candidate and Doctor of Science in the U.S.S.R. are not formal scientific distinctions easily accessible to any graduate of a university. Getting a scientific degree requires long and strenuous work. The preparation of a Candidate's dissertation takes about three or more years, while the preparation for a Doctor's dissertation takes from five to ten years. There is quite a strict system of supervising the conferring of scientific titles. The possessors of scientific degrees are well off. The scientific degree of Doctor of Science is the highest scientific title in the country and entitles its possessor to hold a chair at institutions of higher education, and to a leading position at research institutions. But there are some exceptions for very experienced teachers and specialists in technology.

In 1955, the scientific staff of the country numbered 7,014 Doctors of Science and 54,365 Candidates of Science.[1] To date this number has increased by approximately one-third. At present the total number of scientific workers in the U.S.S.R. is 4,000,000 or 1·8 persons per 1,000 inhabitants of the country. 'Scientist' in this country is an honourable and respectable title, but this is not the only stimulus for young men. The very prospect of creative work, great opportunities for important scientific discoveries, and — which is the main thing — serving the motherland in one of the most important walks of modern life — these are the principal considerations to stimulate a person into choosing the career of a scientist in the U.S.S.R.

Soviet scientists are not infrequently asked the question of how the Marxist ideology affects the successful advancement of science in the U.S.S.R. This is a question of no small significance. The Marxist doctrine of the development of society, the laws of materialistic dialectics are unreservedly and fully accepted by all Soviet scientists and at the present time by many foreign scientists as well. These laws, which naturally embrace the development of science as well, form, I should say, a clear understanding of both the methods and aims of scientific research. The Soviet scientist clearly realizes to what end he works. He is entirely free of doubts and disillusionments caused by contradictions between his intellectual aspirations and the ideals of humanism. The Soviet scientist is not tortured by the idea that his discoveries might be used for the enrichment of others, for the exploitation of people and the annihilation of people. He works in the name of the ideals of 'Soviet patriotism' and he is constantly aware that even the slightest success he achieves in his work is a contribution to the common cause of building up a future communist society.

There is hardly any need to say that fables of the ideological pressure on the minds of Soviet scientists are somewhat ludicrous fiction. At scientific institutions of the U.S.S.R. debates are often held on various philosophical problems of principle in connexion with scientific development, and certain discoveries and ideas are evaluated. No matter what might be individual opinions and points of view, these discussions contribute to the progress of scientific thought. It is known that it is impossible to confine science to any ideological limits.

The last thing for me to do is briefly to describe the post-war

[1] *СССР. Большая Советская Энциклопедия* Изд. II, (Москва, 1957) L, 436 (*The Great Soviet Encyclopaedia*, 2nd ed.).

period in the development of science in the U.S.S.R. As is known, it was during this period that Soviet science, perhaps for the first time, caught the attention of Western European scientists and politicians. Until 1945 many people in the West questioned the real capacities of Soviet scientists. But by 1950 the Western European political leaders at last seemed to realize that science is one of the most important spheres of modern social and state life and that it cannot but be the focus of the attention of statesmen.

The U.N.E.S.C.O. report of 1960, *On the Principal Trends of Development in the Natural Sciences*,[1] compiled under the supervision of P. Auger, contains a statement to the effect that at present science is developing eight times as rapidly as any other sphere of human activity. This statement, confirmed by some data on the increase in the number of discoveries, in the number of scientists in various countries, and in the number of scientific periodicals must be quite authentic. The report states among other things that the number of scientists walking our planet today amounts to 90 per cent of the total number of scientists who have ever lived until our days.

If these data apply to the chief countries of the modern world it follows that they apply above all to the Soviet Union. During the post-war period Soviet scientists have scored tremendous results, which lie not only in mastering atomic power and research in this field, and not only in the achievements of jet-propulsion. There is an enormous upsurge in the field of theory as well. Mathematical investigations and diverse computations are now done in the U.S.S.R. with the help of most rapid computers. These machines have been introduced into all the principal branches of science and technology and are gradually becoming part of the daily routine of all research institutions.

Quite characteristic of post-war development are great strides in the design of instruments, and the equipment of scientific institutions with physical and physical chemical instruments of great precision. Just twenty years ago such a progress in the field of instrument construction was considered by many foreigners quite an unattainable fantasy for the Soviet Union. Today many instruments manufactured by Soviet plants are superior to the same types of foreign-made instruments. During the post-war period Soviet physicists and

[1] UNESCO NS/ES/19, by Pierre Auger (Paris, 1960) (lithographic edition).

chemists have solved most important problems connected with the structure of substances, thereby advancing our knowledge in this important field to a considerable degree. Soviet biology is concentrating on the adjacent fields of science — biochemistry and biophysics. Geologists can boast tremendous achievements in both purely practical work in prospecting for new natural resources and in the theoretical elucidation of mining problems. Today the Soviet Union is in a position to appraise and solve the immense problems of deep (abyssal) prospecting for natural resources.

Within the scope of this article it is certainly very difficult to give even a few examples to illustrate scientific progress in the U.S.S.R. But one thing must be mentioned — that all of these achievements have been brought about as a result of exceedingly close co-operation between science and industry in the U.S.S.R. This contact is extremely beneficial for both scientific progress and technology. It is reflected in the rise of new branches of production, in the automation of technological processes, in an increase in the productivity of labour and in streamlining of production. The Soviet period of scientific development in Russia is a brilliant illustration and proof of the advantages of the interaction and interdependence of science and technology. It goes without saying that these beneficial advantages are many times more powerful than in the capitalist world. The reason for this lies in the socialist way of organizing scientific work and the entire activity of the gigantic force of scientists and specialists in all walks of life.

Commentaries

Commentary by Sir Eric Ashby

It is a commentary on the magnitude of the intellectual revolution in the last 100 years that the title of this session would have been almost meaningless in 1861. Organization of scientists, perhaps, in bodies like the Royal Society or the British Association; but not the organization of science: that would have sounded as superfluous as the organization of lyric poetry or visual art.

We are, therefore, dealing with a new problem; one so recent that the study of it is (I suppose) regarded as journalism rather than history. Mr. Cardwell in his paper — and still more in his fascinating and important book[1] — has given us a record of one part of the problem in Britain. Mr. Carter has analysed the contemporary anatomy of another part of the problem. Mr. Grigoryan and Mr. Kuznetsov have outlined the organization of science as it arose in Russia and Mr. Figurovsky has set out evidence from Russia that technological needs there have been the spur to scientific education and research.

I should like to open this discussion by commenting on two related themes which run through all four of these papers and indeed hold them together in one pattern of thought. One comment concerns the channels of communication through which science is influenced by society and society by science. The other is a variant on this theme, namely the nature of what we now call 'feedback' from society to universities and other institutions of higher learning.

First of all I must define what I mean by society in this very restricted context. I mean organized communities of people whose interests are bound up with scientific research. A century ago there were very few such communities; today the list includes not only universities and learned societies but industry, the public services, Parliament itself. And that is how the problem of organizing scientific work has arisen: organization has been necessary to open up communication between science and social activities which are dependent on science, with the

[1] D. S. L. Cardwell, *The Organisation of Science in England* (London, 1957).

unexpected result that today science has come to depend on some of these social activities.

Now a few words about each of the two themes. Mr. Carter has reminded us that the anatomy of the two-way communication between science and society is a well-worn topic. Nevertheless I think that we still do not understand it in depth. The channels of communication are familiar: books, scientific papers, libraries, lectures, memoranda, the Press. It is the dynamics of communication which need further analysis. What constitutes skill in transmitting and receiving information through these channels? What are the forces which drive information from science to society, or money and support from society to science? Mr. Carter and Mr. Figurovsky have analysed in their papers the incentives which industry offers for research and invention. This is one driving force for one particular channel. Do other social groups beside industry possess analogous driving forces? Or do all the driving forces in the end resolve themselves into the incentives of economics?

I think it is true to say that skill in transmitting the results of science to groups in society is far more efficient than skill in receiving these results or in transmitting back to scientists the reactions (and needs) of society. From the early days of the Royal Society emphasis was laid on (as Thomas Sprat called it) "a close, naked, natural way of speaking". It is indeed easy for a layman to read with understanding all but the mathematical papers of eighteenth-century scientists. In the eighteenth century the receivers, too, were efficient. They were a small compact élite who — when science needed patronage — were able to give it without red tape or fuss. When the dissenting academies and later the mechanics' institutes widened the population of receivers it became evident that communication could fail through lack of skill on the part of the receivers. This problem is still with us. One of the reasons why science was so slowly incorporated into education and government enterprises was the lack of adequate education on the part of the receivers, not the transmitters, of ideas: managers administrators, controllers of policy.

But the more serious shortcoming is over communication in the opposite direction. There has arisen over the last century a greatly increased need to transmit ideas and needs from groups in society to groups of scientists; and this need has not yet been met efficiently. A hundred years ago this inefficiency was not important for scientists because research did not depend on support from social groups outside science. Darwin and Faraday did not have to convince faculty boards or government committees before they could get on with their work. But now nearly all science depends on support from outside its own ranks. Even if the channels of communication do not have to carry ideas from the institutions of society into scientific institutions, they have to carry money; and many of those who give the money like to feel they have some control and direction of it, and in any case to understand the purpose for which they are giving it. Hence the need has grown up for machinery to transmit ideas and needs from society to science. Management in industry was the first to learn how to do this, and (as Mr. Cardwell's paper showed) even industry learnt it dangerously late. Governments (except for purposes of war) have not yet learnt how to do it well. In brief the process of transmission from society to science lacks vigour and clarity. There are various reasons for this, but there is no opportunity to mention them here. Each country has its own techniques for trying to overcome these difficulties of communication. The British solution, which was invented in the nineteenth century but was developed on a large scale only after the First World War, has some great merits and some drawbacks. It is to use scientists to represent those groups of society which support science and technology; in other words to bring some scientists from the receiving end of the channels of communication and to put them at the transmitting end, with the duty of formulating needs, generating ideas, and deciding priorities. This is the way some £75 million per annum are administered on behalf of the three British Research Councils and the University Grants Committee. The majority of members of all these bodies are, or have recently been, active scholars or scientists. It has great virtues for the organization of pure research because it relies for incentives not upon economic criteria of the kind mentioned by Carter and Figurovsky — nor even upon financial rewards — but upon the incentives of prestige. If a research worker has any overriding ambition outside the satisfaction of his own curiosity it is to earn the recognition of his peers. Scientists have so vividly impressed their image of the successful scientist upon the public that social groups outside science now accept the scientist's own criterion of success. The public estimate of the distinguished scientist is not the man who has earned profits or satisfied governments: he is the man who has been elected into the Royal Society.

Unfortunately I have no time to mention the place of the administrator in this communication system. Some scientists regard him as a troublesome parasite. But, like the bacterial flora in the gut of a cow, he has become essential. The problem for which there is no historical precedent was to make these parasites symbiotic; and that was accomplished only by educating the administrators.

I have a few words in which to mention the second theme running through these three papers: the feedback from science to education. Mr. Cardwell shows in his paper that the teaching of chemistry was developed in London and Manchester in advance of a demand from industry. This is one of many similar examples which could be given; often in the latter half of the nineteenth century it was the market for graduates, and not the production line, which needed to be stimulated. This is true, I think, of the circumstances Mr. Figurovsky describes too. But this must not obscure the fact that institutions of higher education in this country are resistant to change and tend to be self-insulated from outside pressures. There is an interesting unwritten chapter in nineteenth-century history here. Universities founded in the nineteenth century were not constitutionally insulated from the outside world. They did not copy the constitutions of Oxford and Cambridge nor those of the pre-1858 Scottish universities. Their constitutions provided for government by a predominantly lay body consisting of representatives of industry, commerce, and local public life. Under these circumstances one might have expected a vigorous feedback into the new universities from those groups of society which made use of them. But this did not happen. What happened was an adoption by the new universities of the balance of power characteristic of the old universities: initiative came from the teachers, from oligarchies of professors, not from the lay councils.

We are not concerned in such a conference as this to decide whether this ideological mimicry of Oxford and Cambridge is good or bad. We are concerned with its consequences, which are that the content of higher education in Britain is determined by men many of whom are insulated from the pressures of social groups outside the university. They tend, therefore, to make decisions based largely on their own educational experience. At the beginning of the nineteenth century, when the needs and interests of society changed relatively slowly, a lag of a generation between university curricula and the needs of society did not matter. But in the mid-twentieth century some more direct feedback from society to university is desirable. It is not to be inferred from this that universities must always be adjusting themselves to forces from society. But it is desirable that they should be receptive to these forces and should understand them, and the point which is perhaps relevant for this discussion is that in the nineteenth century our new universities were given constitutions designed (among other purposes) to accomplish just this end. An organization for feedback to institutions of higher education was deliberately devised. It has not worked as its founders expected it to work.

Commentary by Richard H. Shryock

Mr. Cardwell has contrasted the success of German institutions, as compared to those in France and particularly in England, in applying science to technology during the nineteenth century. This contrast is ascribed to several circumstances. Stated negatively, in the case of English developments, there was persistence of the amateur role in science, the long failure to secure governmental or industrial support for systematic research, and especially the limitations of an educational tradition which failed to produce 'quite ordinary' scientists in such numbers as were needed in nascent industries. In other words, the English universities — like English industry — failed for some time to adjust to new opportunities in the German manner.

In looking more closely at the educational factor, Mr. Cardwell suggests that one of the handicaps in England was the concentration of higher education in the two universities, which denied such advantages as Germany derived from variety and competition among many institutions. While such advantages were apparent, I doubt if multiplicity of universities was in itself of great significance, since there were other countries possessing this advantage where the record was no more promising than in England. In proportion to population, Scotland had quite a number of universities, but I do not recall that research training and contacts with industry advanced any more rapidly north of the border.

Perhaps one could ascribe conservatism at Oxford and Cambridge to sheer age — combined with the absence of political upheavals during he preceding century. But here again, a comparative perspective raises doubts. The majority of American arts colleges, in the years 1800–75, were relatively new institutions, yet their attitude towards research training in science was not unlike that of university colleges in England A number of technological schools were also founded — chiefly, as in the case of most arts colleges, on the basis of private endowments. In one or two special areas, notably in geology, one can see in these schools the beginning of education for applied research; and in any case it is interesting that some Americans were willing to give funds for technical education. But by and large these institutions trained men for routine practice; and the same thing can be said of the many medical schools of the same era.

American attitudes towards basic research, either in science or other fields, did not change greatly until the German-speaking university model was imported — ready-made, as it were — in the 1870's. The Americans, like the British, were said to be a practical people, which presumably meant they were disinclined to support science which could not be obviously applied. If the German universities first supported research in principle, as Liebig held in a statement quoted by Mr. Cardwell, then later practical results were just the reward of virtue. But Americans did not import this model until such results could already be envisaged.

Ironically enough when real universities appeared in 'the States', they did not at first have as much practical impact on technologies as universities were already exerting in Germany. Some influence, of course, was exerted in areas like medicine and agriculture; but the products of new, research-based industries could still be imported more cheaply from Germany than they could be made at home — even after scientific guidance became available. And the first generation of research-trained scientists went largely into academic positions.

These circumstances alone do not entirely explain the fact that American industrialists were as slow or slower than their British counterparts in appreciating the possibilities of applied science. I cannot document this statement in the detailed and illuminating manner which Mr. Cardwell applies to British experience in the dyestuffs field. But little applied research was accomplished in American chemical industries before the present century; in pharmacology, for example, dependence on newer German products persisted until 1914. In the electrical field, independent laboratories — such as those of Edison and of Elihu Thomson — did feed ideas into industry during the

1880's and 1890's, but the first corporation laboratories were not set up until 1900 or shortly thereafter.

On the eve of World War I, American industries equalled or excelled the German in fields based primarily on empirical skills and the exploitation of national resources — as in iron and steel to some extent and more especially in food and textiles. But they were far behind the German in areas such as chemicals and optical products, which evolved from applied science.

This situation may supply a clue to the contrasts between the German industrial record on the one hand and the British and American on the other.

Mr. Cardwell reminds us, at the beginning of his paper, of Francis Bacon's distinction between technology growing out of applied science and that which depends simply on 'straightforward' or empirical invention. The Industrial Revolution, coming early in England and somewhat early even in France and the United States, saw the development of major industries which owed relatively little to applied science. By the 1870's, such industries were doing well without benefit of research — especially in America with its abundant resources. It is hardly strange, under these circumstances, that British and American corporations were indifferent at first to the possible implications of advances in physics and chemistry. Mr. Cardwell notes the frustrated attempts of a few English dyestuff firms to find research-trained chemists, but I do not know that any American concerns even looked for such personnel.

In Germany the industrial revolution was roughly concomitant with pertinent advances in the physical sciences, so that new industries were probably more open-minded about seeking aid from these disciplines. In the fields most successfully developed, indeed, industries owed their origin to science and were fully aware of their indebtedness from the start.

Behind this situation was the development of systematic investigations in German universities and, more especially, the recognition that men could be trained through and for research. There was research in England, of course, as at the Royal Institution; but, as Mr. Cardwell notes, no school for future scientists developed there. Beaumont, one of the few Americans who did basic work on medical problems before 1880, was never even invited to a post in a medical school. In other words, both the British and Americans were quite aware of research as such, but seemed willing to leave this function to chance as far as education was concerned. Out of this *laissez-faire* situation emerged outstanding, individual scientists, but not that rank-and-file personnel important in the long run to science itself as well as to industry.

I am not prepared to explain just why the Germans brought research and universities together so early to their mutual advantage, whereas the British and Americans usually left the first of these functions to independent individuals or to special institutions isolated from universities. But one can at least ask preliminary questions which may clear the way for a study of the sources.

Should we, to begin with, seek answers in the nineteenth century or go back earlier than this? My colleague Mr. Temkin reminds me that Haller was already providing laboratory instruction to students in the eighteenth century, although we often think of this procedure as having been first introduced in Liebig's famous laboratory.

Whatever our temporal focus, should we first examine the more general social and political circumstances; for example, the effects of the Napoleonic upheaval on German education which Mr. Cardwell notes; or again, the implications of the relatively paternalistic attitude of German governments toward higher education? This meant support for science as well as other fields, at a time when the British Government did little, and the Federal Government in America almost nothing for the stronger universities. As late as 1900, W. H. Welch of Johns Hopkins assured Congress that all medical science asked of the national government was to be left alone.

Perhaps, on the other hand, we had best look into the history of universities themselves — into their curricula and especially into their teaching methods. One is reminded that seminar procedure in humanistic subjects was analogous to laboratory teaching in the sciences, and German institutions seem to have been the first to use seminars systematically. Did laboratory teaching follow the example of seminars or vice versa, or was there some common factor here which expressed itself in both of these connexions?

Much has been written on the history of universities and some of the answers may be imbedded in this literature. Or perhaps members of this Symposium can throw light on these themes. Of one thing we can be reasonable certain, there is no one simple explanation: doubtless all aspects of the matter merit consideration.

Commentary by H. J. Habakkuk

The papers of Mr. Carter and Mr. Cardwell and certain sections of the paper by Mr. Figurovsky raise two problems of general importance for the history of technology: how far has (1) the character and (2) the volume of invention been determined by economic incentives? How far, that is, has technical progress been a response to the needs of the economy? How far, on the other hand, has it followed an autonomous path, the result of the evolution of scientific ideas or of pure chance, to which the economy has had to adapt itself?

(1) *The character of technical progress.* It is easy to see how, in theory, this might have been adapted to the relative scarcities of labour, finance, capital goods, and natural resources in the economy. When, for example, labour was particularly scarce in relation to capital, inventors searched for new ways of saving labour, and entrepreneurs picked out from the flow of new ideas those which saved labour, even if they were expensive in capital. If the adoption of these more mechanized methods raised the cost of machines, this gave businessmen an additional motive to try to find ways of cheapening them or making them last longer. A similar argument would apply where it was natural resources which were particularly scarce. Thus invention edged forward in response to the changing relative scarcities of the factors of production.

There are three points to be made about this argument:

(*a*) It implies that there was no overriding technically necessary bias in invention, that is that invention could be steered one way or another by economic circumstances. It is, as Mr. Carter says, commonly assumed that invention has, from its very nature, a strong labour-saving bias. But looking at the historical record, I think that improvements which saved capital or natural resources have been as common features of technical change as those which saved labour. Quite apart from inventions which directly saved capital per unit of output, for example Cort's puddling process, there have been important improvements in the manufacture and in the performance of machines the effect of which has been to save capital over the economy as a whole.

(*b*) A good deal of the technical progress of the eighteenth and nineteenth centuries can be interpreted as the result of such market pressures. Thus it was high labour costs which led to the invention and adoption of the devices of Hargreaves, Arkwright and Crompton. Similarly the mechanization of American industry in the nineteenth century has plausibly been attributed to the scarcity and high cost of American labour as a result of its high productivity in agriculture. This explains why the method of manufacture by interchangeable parts, developed by Simeon North and Eli Whitney, was widely adopted in the U.S.A. and became the 'American System'. The idea itself was French in origin and something like the method was devised in England by Samuel Bentham and Brunel for the manufacture of wooden blocks during the Napoleonic wars. But manufacture by interchangeable parts did not catch on in Europe because the need to save labour was less urgent than in the U.S.A. The contrast between American and European technological development in agriculture can also be interpreted in terms of relative factor scarcities. "In Europe", said Jefferson, "the object is to make the most of their land, labour being abundant: here [i.e. in the U.S.A.] it is to make the most of our labour, land being abundant." Hence Europeans specialized in developing new rotations and in applying chemistry to agriculture to increase the yield per acre, while Americans developed the combine harvester, etc., to increase the yield per man.

(*c*) But even in the nineteenth century, there were cases when pure research or the accumulation of technical ideas produced new methods quite independent of market pressures — new methods so superior to the old that they were adopted whatever the relative factor scarcities. Perkin's discovery of the first aniline dyes is a case in point. And the dynamo and the internal combustion engine were the result of attempts to explore a body of technical ideas, not of attempts to alleviate stringencies in the supply of particular resources.

At first sight one is tempted to say that the influence of market pressures on the character of inventions was greater in the last century than it is in this: because in the nineteenth century technical progress was still more empirical than scientific and therefore more likely to take the form of slow modifications of detail in response to immediate problems of industrial practice. The systematic application of science and the growth of organized research, which are, as Mr. Cardwell emphasizes, relatively recent developments, are much more likely to produce spectacular and unpredictable leaps in technology unrelated to immediate economic circumstances. It is difficult to relate space research and rocketry to any terrestial factor scarcities. The character of developments in atomic energy may still reflect the relative importance attached in different countries to new supplies of industrial power. But in general, technology has become less responsive to market forces, and now forges ahead under its own steam; more problems of adaptation are now thrown on the economy.

(2) *The volume of technical progress.* Does invention "follow investment like a shadow" as one economist put it? Or was it autonomous invention, the resolution of certain purely technical problems, which gave rise to investment?

A strong case can be made for the first point of view. Fruitful inventions are most likely to be made and adopted in an expanding industry. An expanding industry is most likely to be able to command capital and skill, and to afford opportunities for trying out new ideas. Since it is by applying new ideas that the technical possibilities of further advance can be identified, these are the industries where technical progress is most continuous. Thus, though depression may sometimes sharpen the wits of industrialists, a high level of investment is the circumstance most favourable to invention.

There are also several episodes in the history of technology which can be explained in these terms. Thus the textile inventions in England in the eighteenth century occurred in an industry the output of which had been growing rapidly for several decades previously. The slower rate of technical progress in a number of British industries in the later nineteenth century, compared with their American and German counterparts, can also be explained by the fact that industrial capacity in Germany and America was growing more rapidly than in England, simply because they were later in industrializing. Take for example the electrical industry. The British lag can be accounted for, briefly, by two circumstances. In the first place, demand for lighting was principally an urban demand, and the urban population was growing more rapidly in America and Germany. In the second place, on the eve of the introduction of electric lighting, Britain was better lit than the other two countries because it had an old-established and efficient gas industry, against which electricity had to compete. For these reasons, the economic circumstances were much more favourable to technological progress in Germany and America than in Britain.

On the other hand, the economic influences on the volume of investment obviously work within limits set by purely technical considerations. Thus the commercial application of electricity long after the discovery of the principle of electro-magnetic induction by Faraday was held up by the intrinsic difficulties of perfecting the dynamo. Similarly the application of steam to sea-transport was delayed because of the difficulty of developing compound engines. The principle of compounding was patented as early as 1781, but it was not until the 1880's that compound engines were widely applied. This was not due to any lack of economic incentive: the installation of more powerful engines in ships had to wait for the development of open-hearth steel which was cheap and strong and suitable for ships and boilers. There are other instances where, despite strong economic incentives, technical progress along particular lines was held up until solutions to specific technical problems were forthcoming from independent improvements in other industries.

One is tempted to say that the volume of technical progress, like its character, is now much less directly influenced by economic incentives than it was in the century or so before 1914. In that century the factory was all the research laboratory there was in almost all industries, and it was only by creating new industrial capacity that ideas could be tested and developed, and further ideas suggested. Today the research laboratory can be relied upon to turn out new ideas in a marketable form, and it is much more plausible than it was earlier to argue that it is the flow of such new ideas which in the long run determines the volume of investment. It is true, of course, that expenditure on research, and the willingness of businessmen to put to practical use the results of research, depend on profits and market prospects. It is true also that many improvements are made to a new product or process only after the prototype stage. Nevertheless, the volume of invention and of technical progress is much less dependent than it used to be on the volume of industrial investment. The spectrum of strictly technical possibilities within which economic incentives operate has become increasingly narrowed.

Commentary by A. R. Ubbelohde

Communication of new knowledge and invention: With reference to the paper presented by Cardwell, scientific discovery and technological invention both constitute an extrapolation from existing knowledge. Successful development of this knowledge depends upon (i) communication of information, and (ii) the availability of a matrix of achievement which the new idea can fertilize. It may be argued that the relative failure of British inventive genius towards the end of the nineteenth century in making adequate application of scientific knowledge was partly due to inadequate communication. Men with the power to make economic and political decisions were not sufficiently educated in science to appreciate all the potentialities of technological application. It is illuminating to consider how we now ensure communication between the men responsible for adding knowledge, and those who are responsible for making decisions about its application. This dichotomy of functions takes different forms in different social environments — British, European, American or Russian. It may be doubted whether this diversity of functions ever can be avoided in the ideal state, or even should be avoided. What are the optimum relations that might have been realized at any period of history still remains to be defined. Actual relationships were often far from ideal; historical studies of the communication between those who added to science and those who made decisions to apply it are scanty.

In the seventeenth and eighteenth centuries those who made decisions were probably wealthy amateurs, but in the nineteenth century capitalist managers played an increasingly important role. Decisions inspired by political as well as economic considerations become more prominent. Though its emphasis may have shifted, one suspects that problems raised by the dichotomy have not evaporated in any of our contemporary social and scientific environments.

Cardwell's assessment appears to under-emphasize the effectiveness of value judgments as incentives determining the actions of prominent individuals. It seems to be well established that Michael Faraday (and other eminent successors in British science) turned down lucrative consultancy opportunities presented by contemporary industry, in order to devote themselves to the advancement of pure knowledge. In counterpart, the impressive German drive for education in science appears to have aimed quite deliberately at the training of managers for industry, at least in the second half of the nineteenth century, regardless of any philosophic enthusiasm for scientific knowledge which was so prominent at the end of the eighteenth century.

Carter's review of the incentives for making scientific ideas generate economic values — the incentives in fact for invention — is so closely woven that it is slightly invidious to emphasize any particular aspect by giving it special comment. So far as we can determine, the physical opportunities for successful invention have usually been available many years before some of the more far-reaching applications of new knowledge emerged. Obviously physical opportunities provide a necessary condition, to use mathematical language, but seldom have they provided a sufficient condition. Scientific knowledge has always been a necessary condition for effective invention, but the time lag between additions to knowledge and successful applications is considerable. Great scientists have seldom or never been great inventors.

Conflicts between the new and the old: In the same general theme, what Carter has termed the sensitivity of the decision maker involves matters of special interest. Conflict between ideas and practices that are tested and established, and new emergences, seems inevitable and is always present in the history of science and technology. But nations at phases of very rapid growth and with large unexploited resources tend to escape some of the major problems of growth raised by this inevitable conflict between the old and the new. Once the national tempo becomes more stabilized, the replacement of one activity by another involves major decisions both with regard to its intellectual demands, and its demands on physical resources. Such decisions can be postponed but not indefinitely avoided by rapidly growing communities of scientists and inventors. Carter's discussion (section 3, p. 683) is thus particularly vital for the established communities.

A quite different social pressure, which is obviously very real, and of which there are numerous examples in history, arises from the conflict between the Frankensteins generated by each new application of science, and the human beings whose activity they displace. Some of the problems introduced by automation are of this kind. To some extent, modern hindrances to new growth from existing organizations that have already proved themselves viable include the Frankenstein antipathy. We do not know how such conflicts are dealt with in phases of very rapid technological and scientific growth, as in Russia — but one suspects they are perennial and the ways of recognizing, of anticipating and of dealing with them obviously warrant discussion.

Social organization and the growth of knowledge and its applications: Grigoryan and Kuznetsov give an interesting review of the relationships in Russia between social organization and the development of scientific thought. They do not deal with what many people regard as almost a Siamese twin, the relations between social organization and the applications of science. We are grateful to these contributors for their review and will want to consider it in conjunction with the contribution by Figurovsky, which deals more specifically with this second aspect of scientific growth. His comprehensive paper presents quite clearly the contemporary enthusiasm for scientific knowledge and for its application, which harnesses so much talent in Russia at the present time. Like a bird of passage, but not I hope a bird of prey, I will pick out some points that seem to me to warrant discussion with the warning that my selection of nutritive grains must by its very nature be incomplete.

Many of us would regard the contributions of the British experimentalist Michael Faraday and the British mathematical physicist Clerk Maxwell in plain contradiction with the opinion of Engels that we began to understand electricity only after its technical applicability had been discovered. In the earlier developments the role of educated curiosity was certainly prominent in the advancement of science. Although most scientists are now in one way or another professionals I think — indeed I hope — that the role of scientific curiosity about nature is by no means extinguished in our own age, despite the fact that other incentives, such as those discussed by Engels, have certainly grown in importance.

Most of us will find the comments by Figurovsky on the activities of foreign scientists who flourished in Russia interesting, and will hope that this aspect of the history of science will be enriched by further research.

I suppose (p. 705) the Académie Française and the Institut de France can be regarded as successful organizations sponsored by government comparatively early. In Britain the organization of the Royal Society was certainly much more a spontaneous movement by individuals though it did receive essential support through the personal interest of King Charles II.

Those who are less familiar with Russian history would find it helpful (p. 708) to know who paid for the livelihood of the various leaders mentioned in this section of the paper. Were they supported by government or other patronage or by private means? Forms of patronage for scientific work throughout the ages are of perennial interest for the history of science.

Obviously many of us are going to be particularly interested in the flux of innovations and incentives discussed in the last part of Figurovsky's paper (roughly from p. 718 onwards). Presumably it is a little too early to decide, as a matter of historical observation, which centres in Russia will prove to be the most fertile in innovation, and which types of organization lend themselves most effectively to new and worthwhile applications of science. We are certainly most interested to follow these essays in human activity and human co-operation.

As a matter of comment (p. 720) it is worth noting that in most Western communities scientific work for the highest scientific distinction — the Doctor of Science — involves about the same number of years of application as in Russia. But with us its attainment does not result in quite as automatic promotion to the highest or most influential positions, which usually appear to require other qualities as well. Is this difference in standing due to the unusually rapid growth of Soviet science? If so, one would anticipate some readjustments of assessment in due course. It would be most interesting to learn how far those corresponding with men whom we would call senior executives in the West hold the highest scientific degree in Russia, and indeed what academic degrees they hold at all. Considerations of this kind concern both the policy-making and the communications aspects of the growth of science. Both the growth of knowledge, and the growth of its applications to industry, are affected by current attitudes to the importance of university training and university degrees.

Discussion

W. A. Smeaton

The situation in Russia in 1918 was in some ways similar to that of France in 1793, when the country was seriously weakened by revolution and war, and it is interesting to note that in each case intervention by the state led to rapid advances in science and technology. In Russia, as Mr. Figurovsky has shown, the state controlled scientific developments through the Academy of Sciences. This did not happen in revolutionary France, for the Paris Academy of Sciences was suppressed in August 1793 by the Jacobin government. But it was replaced almost immediately by a number of *ad hoc* committees set up by the Committee of Public Instruction to investigate specific technical and scientific problems, the most urgent being the work leading to the institution of the metric system, which was already well advanced. It may be noted that although the Academy was dissolved, nearly all its active members took part in the research projects organized by the Committees of Public Instruction and Public Safety. This state control led for a short time to considerable scientific and technological advances in France, as has been shown by C. Richard,[1] though his book leaves plenty of scope for further exploration in this field by the modern historian. But when the Institut was founded in 1795 the control of scientific activities almost stopped. The powerful Jacobin government had fallen, and the Directory relaxed most controls, especially when the country was no longer in military danger. This is in contrast to the situation in the U.S.S.R., where state control continued and led to very considerable progress. Had some form of central organization with full support from the government been retained in France greater progress might also have been made there.

Here I think I must disagree slightly with Mr. Cardwell, who believes that after the Napoleonic reorganization of education in 1808 science failed to develop in France for two reasons: the scientific domination of Paris and the parsimony of the state. In my opinion the second of these factors was alone responsible, for it had been shown in the late 1790's that science

[1] C. Richard, *Le Comité de Salut public et les fabrications de guerre sous la Terreur* (Paris, 1922).

and technology could develop rapidly when the leading scientists were concentrated in Paris with ample financial support, and, indeed, most of the considerable advances made in France before the Revolution took place in Paris. Much of the development in the late 1790's occurred in the Ecole Polytechnique, whose importance has, I think, been underestimated by Cardwell. If we agree with him (p. 662 of his paper) that we can only talk of a laboratory as a systematic research institution when the admission of students is recognized as a permanent practice, then surely we must give this status to the Ecole Polytechnique, at least in its first ten or fifteen years. Initially about 100 students per year were admitted; as Cardwell points out, they were all supposed to do practical chemistry, and some stayed on after graduating to do research. Gay-Lussac and Thenard were the most distinguished academic chemists to come from this school, but it also produced industrial chemists, such as Bernard Courtois. The Ecole Polytechnique was, in fact, founded in order to provide scientists and engineers for industry and the army. After about 1808 practical chemistry declined there but in its early years the Ecole Polytechnique was certainly functioning, at least in part, as a systematic research institution, and not only in chemistry. When the Ecole Polytechnique was opened, Berthollet, Fourcroy and Guyton de Morveau were all professors. Berthollet soon left, but the others remained and were eventually succeeded by Gay-Lussac and Thenard. The succession of students to the chairs of their former masters later became quite common in research institutions.

I should like also to comment briefly on Mr. Carter's paper, and on a point raised by Mr. Habakkuk. I feel that Mr. Carter has not attached sufficient importance to the incentive given to technological progress by the needs of the armed forces. This frequently leads to the development of an invention without regard to such factors as the cost of labour and the difficulty of raising capital. As Figurovsky has pointed out, defence as well as industrial requirements led to technological progress as early as the eighteenth century, and this does not apply only to Russia. Finally, it is surely the military applications of the subject that first led to the development of space research, in Germany and later in the U.S.S.R. and the U.S.A., though commercial applications of artificial satellites are now possible. National prestige is another very important cause of progress in this and other fields.

D. W. Singer

No mention has so far been made of the advantage enjoyed by German students because of the ease with which they have always passed from one university to another. It is true that graduates from Scottish universities have often passed to further study at Oxford, and that today it is common for graduates of Commonwealth universities to pursue research for higher degrees at Oxford, a process for which facilities were enacted I think in 1912 or 1913. Few people now living can recall the envy expressed by our students in the early years of this century for the undergraduate in Germany who could (if duly accepted) study a part of his subject with the professor of his choice and then pass to another university for the subjects required to complete his undergraduate course.

My second point concerns the briefing of those who produce or direct the stream of support for scientific research. We have heard that the incentive to such persons is sometimes economic, sometimes pure interest in scientific problems. But no one has mentioned the passion to prevent the loss of scientific achievement. A good example is Sir John Pringle, President of the Royal Society at the end of the eighteenth century. He was not a great scientist but he was imbued with this passion. Thus there was a modest Irish general practitioner, David Macbride, who evolved the proper regime for seamen on long voyages. Macbride's brother was a commander in the Royal Navy and permitted him to carry out this regime on the crew of H.M.S. *Jason* commanded by him during a voyage of two years from 1765 to 1767. Dr. Macbride had the enthusiastic support also of the ship's medical officer, and throughout the voyage there was not a single case of the scurvy that had decimated crews on previous long voyages. Macbride published his happy experience in a slender volume which was sent by another physician to Pringle who immediately entered into correspondence with Macbride. Now Pringle was a great friend and patron of Captain Cook. I am quite sure that he gave him this book, and it was for that reason that Cook was able to prepare and insist on the careful regime for his crews that enabled the great voyage of three years and eighteen days from July 1772 to be accomplished without a single case of scurvy.

Similarly in the matter of ventilation. When Pringle had realized its importance and had seen the ventilator invented by Hales, he spared no pains until he had succeeded in getting these ventilators installed in hospitals, in jails, and finally after infinite trouble he even persuaded the Admiralty to install them in the ships of the Royal Navy. Pringle was impelled by a passion to promote human welfare through the utilization of knowledge.

S. Galin

Objections have been raised against the idea that discovery and invention have as their incentive economic advantage or profit. Would these objections be urged against the statement that social pressures may be the cause of inventions and discoveries or may provide an atmosphere for these researches? For example the early history of the steam engine is the history of attempts to rid mines of flood water by pumps. Eventually Watt, about 1780, was successful in using steam to drive his pumps. Watt derived some of his theoretical knowledge of the properties of steam from his association with Professor Black of Edinburgh.

Watt and his contemporary inventors inaugurated the Industrial Revolution in England; but after their work was finished in the eighteenth century, the laws of thermodynamics were discovered in the nineteenth century by people like Mayer and Sadi Carnot. Now these laws were necessary to help the new industries to flourish; but personally Carnot and Mayer derived neither profit nor prestige. At first Carnot's work was declared of no value by his judges and Mayer was driven to commit suicide. Both were urged by an unflinching search for truth, yet the social pressures of their time may have provided an atmosphere for their work.

In the case of people like Mme. Curie, the sole motive force behind the researches was the pursuit of truth in the face of dreadful difficulties and obstacles.

R. Taton

I read Mr. Cardwell's report with much interest. A study of the general conditions of scientific progress in the nineteenth century is a vast subject, and a particularly important one. I believe that a special Symposium should be dedicated to it. But Mr. Cardwell seems to me to have imposed somewhat artificial limitations on its study. His account in fact deals essentially with German influence on the evolution of scientific teaching in Great Britain. The problem is certainly an interesting one, but it leaves untouched other important aspects in the evolution of scientific teaching during the nineteenth century. A comparative study of its evolution in different countries would be the best approach to this vast subject, for it would enable fruitful comparisons to be made and lead to a better understanding of what caused major successes and failures. In any case one must avoid adopting an 'a priori' thesis and attempting to manipulate the facts to suit it; the only valid method is to describe these facts in all their complexity, before attempting any kind of explanation.

A first examination makes it obvious that it was during the course of the nineteenth century that science gained its increasing social importance, and led the most perspicacious governments to adopt a proper scientific policy. This new state of mind had its first significant manifestation in France during the revolutionary period and I am sorry that Mr. Cardwell has not indicated sufficiently clearly the value of its effort as as example. In fact the re-examination of scientific teaching in its higher branches undertaken during the French Revolution was to bear fruit almost immediately. The momentum given to scientific research enabled French science to enjoy a period of great brilliance though in the long run less favourable political and social conditions compromised some of the results obtained. But the results of this experiment were to spread in a variety of forms to different Western European countries. During the whole of the first half of the nineteenth century, the French example was to have a symbolic value and all the liberal and national movements tended to be inspired by it, connecting it to the great revolutionary tradition.

The Ecole Polytechnique was the most brilliant product of these legislators of the French Revolution in the realm of scientific teaching. This school furnished France with a magnificent pléiade of men of science and technicians of high standing. Its influence in different countries was felt either through the creation of similar schools, or by the direct help of engineers graduating from the school itself. I do not believe that one can accurately describe scientific progress in Western Europe at the beginning of the nineteenth century without stressing the outstanding role that this school played.

I would like to conclude by expressing my disagreement on a point of detail. It seems to me to be misleading to affirm that the German system was codified in conscious opposition to the French system. Certainly the political and philosophical outlooks of these two countries were very different and the creation of the University of Berlin marked an important stage in the cult of German nationalism in opposition to the Napoleonic regime. But several of the men responsible for the new scientific teaching in Germany were too deeply impregnated with the spirit of the revolutionaries to set up any effective opposition. A characteristic example is that of Alexander von Humboldt who played such an important part in the development of his country's scientific institutions, while keeping, at the same time, in close contact with the French scientists with whom he had been in touch during his long sojourns in Paris, and also appreciating the efficiency of the teaching of the Ecole Polytechnique.

B. Glass

I should like to comment on Mr. Cardwell's statement that Francis Bacon suggested that "quite ordinary people should be able to undertake scientific research". No one is likely to disagree with the statement of Sir Eric Ashby that administrators of science are essential to science, as the bacterial flora in the cow is essential to the cow. This assumption has been demonstrated by an ingenious experiment showing that the cellulose-digesting protozoa in the gut of a termite are essential to the life of the termite, since the feeding of an antibiotic to the termites killed all their symbiotic protozoa, whereupon the termites then starved to death. But the question of real importance, it seems to me, is not whether the administrator is essential — as indeed he is — but rather an understanding of the nature of scientific advance, on the part of both the administrators and general public, is necessary or important to the continuation of scientific advance. I wish I had heard this question discussed.

Margaret Mead, the American anthropologist, has, with several colleagues, been studying the popular image of the scientist in the minds of American teenagers. There are two common images. The one, derived from science fiction, is that of the scientist as the white-robed wizard, possessed of mysterious and miraculous powers. This image is scarcely different from the superstitions once felt by the ancient man in the presence of the medicine-man, or astrologer. Science is here equated with magic. The second image is that of the scientist as a shabby, unsocial recluse, so abstracted from real life that he continues to count the hairs on the back of a cockroach while the roof is falling on his head. Will our future administrators of science, who may come largely from the general public rather than the ranks of the scientists themselves, administer wisely if they harbour such opinions? Will the general public continue to support the advancement of science intelligently on the basis of such distortions? Is this not a major problem of education in a democracy?

I would furthermore like to emphasize that the problem is one requiring solution at the level of the secondary schools rather than at that of the universities, which Mr. Cardwell discusses. The objective of changing the attitude towards science through an understanding of its true nature and methods has been foremost among the objectives of the Biological Sciences Curriculum Study, for which I am responsible, in the United States. To this end, we have prepared new textbooks, laboratory programmes and what we call laboratory 'blocks', in order to avoid the connotations of other terms. During the past academic year teachers in 118 schools have tried out these materials on an experimental basis. The modernized textbooks proved too difficult for the lower 75 per cent of the students — although not as difficult for the students as they were for some of the teachers. The concurrent laboratory work consisted of exercises, in part illustrative of the subject matter considered in the classroom and textbook, in part investigatory in character — true experiments for the laboratory or the field. This part of the programme was generally successful. About three-fourths of all students participating seemed to profit greatly and were enthusiastic. But the greatest success was achieved by the laboratory 'blocks'. These were arranged so as to occupy a full six-week block of the time allotted to biology during the school year; that is, the block replaced the regular classwork, laboratory exercises and home assignments. Each block consisted of a co-ordinated sequence of experiments relating to a particular biological area, such as microbial nutrition or animal development. The students worked in teams of two to four, pooling their results and learning to handle quantitative data mathematically and graphically. Teams supplemented each other, and each experiment was duplicated by two or more groups. Quite rapidly the students acquired the necessary skills, began to analyse 'unknowns' and eventually were doing experiments the precise answers to which were unknown to the teacher and the scientist as well as to themselves. Time was taken to total the results and discuss them, failures equally with successes. Even the weaker students quickly responded to this challenge.

The interest and high morale would have to be seen to be believed. Asked what they had learned from such an experience, the students replied: "We have learned what science is really like"; "We are doing the experiments, not just being told"; "Anyone can take part in science like this."

Here is evidence to substantiate Francis Bacon's belief that quite ordinary people can undertake scientific research! Will a populace educated along these lines not possess a better understanding of science, and more willingly and fully support it?

M. Daumas

I would like to make two comments. The first relates to the foundation of the Academy of Sciences in Russia. Contrary to the view expressed by Mr. Figurovsky, I do not believe that the circumstances in which this foundation was made differed fundamentally from those obtaining in scientific foundations in other European countries. Apart from the British and French academies which arose from the desire among certain scientists to form themselves into a group, the other academies were formed by the will of a sovereign wishing to enhance his own prestige. Moreover both the kings of England and France were anxious to give official recognition to their countries' academies. In France, under the influence of Colbert, it was planned to make use of the Académie des Sciences to further the development of industry or of certain technical processes. But in fact, apart from the knowledge of hydrodynamics required to irrigate the gardens at Versailles, the government required nothing of the Académie for a long time. It was not until the middle of the eighteenth century and after the publication of the *Encyclopédie* that the government gave the Académie the financial means to complete and to publish its *Description des Arts et des Métiers*, whose preparation, begun towards the end of the seventeenth century, had been long neglected. For a long time, in all countries, the life and work of the academies kept itself aloof from economic and industrial activity. If Peter the Great called upon the services of little-known young men, it is purely because no other scientists were available on the 'international market'. Later, the rivalry between Frederick and Catherine to attract to their courts scientists of great repute showed that it was merely a question of prestige.

My second remark concerns the fact pointed out by Mr. Figurovsky that Russian scientists of the seventeenth century, and particularly the chemists, were preoccupied with industrial techniques. These facts also are generally applicable to all the industrial countries of the period. Already in the sixteenth and seventeenth centuries the bounds of chemistry had been partly defined by the mineralogists and the metallurgists. In the nineteenth century, the appearance of the coal-gas industry and later of synthetic processes enabled chemists to find lucrative employment, thereby bettering their conditions of work and increasing the number of scientists. The same was true in other branches of technology as, for example, in the railways or telegraphy where engineers began to make careers and at the same time were able to carry out scientific research.

V. P. Zubov

The task of any symposium consists not only in resolving, but in posing problems. Now, it seems to me, that the papers read during the course of this session have posed problems for a comparative study of scientific and technical progress in different countries throughout the course of the centuries — in America, Western Europe, in Russia, etc. I would like to draw attention to a few points relevant to the old Russia.

(1) Russia in the eighteenth century was faced with an important problem non-existent for America at the same period — that of the elaboration of a scientific language. American scientists made use of English; Russian scientists had to create a new scientific language. The activities of foreign scientists in the heart of the Academy of Sciences during the eighteenth century was by no means the main reason why Latin continued to be used. The Russians themselves were obliged to use it. By comparing the Russian resumés of the Latin "Memoirs" of the Academy made during the first half of the eighteenth century, with the Russian scientific writings towards the end of the same century, after Lomonosov, one can see the tremendous progress made by Russian scientific language. It is unnecessary to say how important this progress was for education and for the dissemination of scientific and technical knowledge.

(2) One of the practical tasks imposed on eighteenth-century Russian science was the exploration of the country's natural resources over an immense territory. It was this task which prompted the great expeditions to the north, the east and the south of the empire, organized after the foundation of the Academy in 1725. The founding of new universities at the

beginning of the nineteenth century inevitably not only contributed to the progress of scientific and technical instruction and education, but made possible the country's exploration. The activities of the University of Kazan were characteristic: a stable base was created for the systematic exploration of a great territory in eastern Russia. To some extent, this was true also of the nineteenth-century institutes for higher education.

(3) We must not forget that all the Russian universities founded during the course of the eighteenth and nineteenth centuries were purely secular institutions. There were no faculties of theology. Teaching in this field was limited entirely to ecclesiastical schools and academies. This created an ideological climate different from that of most Western European universities, and at the same time made them appear suspect in the eyes of university professors of science. The evolution of Russian scientific ideas cannot be understood without some consideration of these special factors.

(4) Much has been said on the subject of economic influence on scientific and technical inventions. I would prefer to draw attention to the influence of economic conditions on the *marketing* of these inventions, their application and their construction. Eighteenth- and nineteenth-century Russia produced striking examples of this when the thinking of inventors developed in step with the progress of science and world technology. But they were unable to obtain enough support from society for them to be able to produce their inventions on a greater scale. One need only mention Polzunov and Kulibin, two eighteenth-century inventors. The steam engine, built by Polzunov, remained unused; Kulibin was obliged to apply his technical ingenuity to inventions which often did not appreciably differ from the automatic toys of Hero, whilst his greater inventions were never built. One could also cite the case, this time in the sphere of agriculture, of a whole series of innovations which were introduced only on a reduced scale possible under the economic conditions of Russia in the first half of the nineteenth century, before the abolition of serfdom.

D. S. L. Cardwell

There are two brief comments that I would like to make in response to Sir Eric Ashby's kind remarks about my paper. In the first place, the nature and aims of provincial universities were admirably defined as long ago as 1872 by Lyon Playfair in his address: "Teaching Universities and Examining Boards".

I believe this can be read with profit even today and I would like to commend it for attention. The second point I wish to make is that the two-way traffic in ideas, the mutual feedback, between science and society must be affected in some way by educational specialization which, in this country, has resulted in what Sir Charles Snow calls "two cultures". The experience of other countries who face the same problem is clearly important here.

I am very grateful to Mr. Shryock for filling in some serious gaps in my paper. From the time of the McCormick reaper and the turret lathe onwards the pace of mechanical invention and innovation in the U.S.A. was, as we all know, astonishing. But it seems, to me at any rate, that science played a less important role in American than it did in German industrial development. Mr. Shryock has, I think, thrown much light on this question. I am also grateful to him for reminding me that a multiplicity of universities does not, of itself, ensure vigorous research and scholarship. His question whether seminars or laboratories came first in the order of things is most suggestive. I am afraid I do not know the answer.

Much technological history is still, as far as I can see, at the 'great man' stage: it does not try to account for a particular series of inventions; it describes them as they were handed down by the 'great man'. This, I think, may be relevant to one of Mr. Habbakuk's points: I would like to suggest that if you examine the main researches of James Watt you will find that at practically every stage his work was governed by cost considerations.

The word 'technology' is often used in a very indiscriminate fashion. May I, therefore, enter a plea here that we give it a more precise and restricted interpretation. I would like to suggest that we use it to describe only those branches of technics (to use Lewis Mumford's word) which depend on science. This, I hasten to add, is quite in accord with the dictionary definitions.

Mr. Ubbelohde raised a very important point when he mentioned state intervention on behalf of science and scientific industry in nineteenth-century Germany. I did consider this factor, but, apart from the field of higher education, I found it a very difficult one to evaluate: so many of the 'subsidies' are necessarily hidden or disguised. I should, of course, have mentioned this in my paper and I would like to thank Mr. Ubbelohde for calling my attention to it. The whole topic of the intervention of the state in science merits study in its own right.

Mr. Taton reproves me for my failure to discuss a number of important topics. But I was quite aware of these omissions, indeed, in my paper I apologize for them. They were the inevitable consequence of a compromise between an intensive and an extensive study. But I would like to comment on one point of his: I am aware of the importance of the Ecole Polytechnique, that is why I mentioned it. Also, I did not say that the Ecole Polytechnique was modelled on the mining school at Schemnitz; I know that it was not. What I did say was that the course in practical chemistry was derived from Schemnitz.

C. F. Carter

I will limit myself to a few headings. My paper was of course concerned with a view of affairs from here, that is in the United Kingdom, and now, not looking backwards to any appreciable degree. But it does suggest some wider applications. I am particularly grateful to Sir Eric Ashby for underlining the point (with which I fully agree) about alternative incentives and in particular the incentive of prestige; and also to Mr. Smeaton for mentioning the very great importance of the needs of military defence. I would say that on the whole the difference between the incentives to technological change is not very sensitive to differences in the structure of the social system. I think we would find that when we had got over the difficulties which are simply created by words, the kind of framework which I have set out would apply with very little change in the U.S.S.R., as it does in the U.S.A., or Britain or France. On the other hand if one seeks to carry the ideas not to other countries but backwards in time, then I think that one has to take account of the fact that large-scale organized research and development is a relatively new thing. This must limit the extent to which the lessons of the present can also be seen in the past. The existence of the present scale of activities of the Soviet Academy of Sciences with its 60,000 employees must bring an entirely new element into the situation. I was very interested in Mr. Habakkuk's point about the relation of the volume of invention to economic activity in the nineteenth century and his suggestion that this relation might not now be so close because we have passed from the stage where the factory is, so to speak, the inventive unit, to the stage where the research laboratory is that unit. On the other hand one has to remember that research and development are very expensive activities and that the pressure to undertake them is much greater in the expanding and changing industries. I would say that you would certainly find in the statistics of present-day activity, that there is still a strong correlation between economic activity and the volume of resources devoted to trying to create change. Of course there is also still the chance element which may mean that change is in fact created with only a small expenditure of resources. But I do not think that one must suppose that by better administration and by giving large resources to the creation of change one can increase the pace of growth without limit. There is a limit to the rate of change of organizations. However well your administrators are trained there is a limit to the rate at which they can make decisions. And I have recently been concerned with decisions about scientific matters where the rate of making decisions is almost exactly equal to the rate at which each successive change of scientific method occurs. For example, by the time a decision has been taken to install Mark I, Mark II has been invented and therefore a decision has then to be taken because one has to decide whether it would not be better to install Mark II rather than Mark I, and by the time this has been taken Mark III will have been invented. This is a rather foolish example, but it indicates the kind of limit to the pace of change which is set by the way in which decisions are taken.

A. T. Grigoryan

There have been many valuable publications in the U.S.S.R. dealing with science in Russia in the eighteenth and nineteenth centuries. There is also a history of the Academy of Sciences which includes comparisons with other academies and accounts of the works of scientists of other countries than Russia. It seems that the Russian people are more familiar with the work of other European countries, America and the East, than the people of those countries are with Russian work.

N. A. Figurovsky

I am grateful to all the commentators for their remarks. They extend the basis for our discussion of the organization of science in Russia.

In the rapid flow of science and social progress today, the current of science is only one of many which meet in whirlpools and eddies so complex as to be difficult to distinguish one from another. Although it looks as if there are cut-and-dried separate departments of science in Russia, in fact there are many discussions on interrelationships between administrators and scientists and how best to direct the resources available. There are some cases where the older scientific disciplines still command the greatest proportion of financial support, but there are others in which newer disciplines are becoming predominant.

There is under way at the present time a reform of the organization of scientific organization in Russia. Hitherto the Academy of Sciences has been dominant, with some thousands of smaller institutions pursuing independent lines. There has now been set up a national coordinating and organizing committee which will exert an influence not only on the Academy of Sciences but also on the organization of particular institutes.

In reply to Mr. Ubbelohde, the U.S.S.R. inherited from old Russia a fine group of famous names and pioneer workers who carried on their work under the new regime. In the U.S.S.R. the scientists have constantly to urge their needs on the administrators.

Concerning Mr. Habakkuk's comments, I think that it is not mainly in day-to-day or short-term invention that economic pressures are principally significant, but in the very big long-term problems like the utilization of the sun's rays to provide energy.

In reply to Mr. Daumas, it has to be pointed out that the Academy of Peter the Great differs from that of all other European academies in that it was founded in a void, a wilderness devoid of intellectual precursors.

The centralizing of scientific research at the present time is a progressive force — whether this will always be so I am not prepared to say. Periods when there was no centralization have produced good work also.

The present state of scientific organization in the United States of America needs careful study. Some features of it are undoubtedly progressive. I think pure and applied research are pretty well co-ordinated in the U.S.S.R.

Scientific progress comes not only from intellectuals: the minds of administrators, technicians, laboratory workers, engineers and rank-and-file operatives all play their part in putting new ideas into effect. Science is now embedded in society and in the whole history of science one must be careful to take account of sociological factors.

PART EIGHT

History of Science as an Academic Discipline

A Note on History of Science as an Academic Discipline *

A. C. CROMBIE and M. A. HOSKIN

What is the purpose of including the history and philosophy of science among academic studies? In the most general terms, it is to give to the student — whether his main interest is historical, philosophical, or scientific — an informed and critical awareness of the scientific tradition that has grown up in our midst, and of its numerous links with many other aspects of our thinking and conditions of life. For scientists it has also the more intimate purpose of providing an approach to the critical examination of what they are themselves doing. In all this the study of the historical development and the analysis of the principles and assumptions of scientific thinking are linked together. The results of scientific inquiry may be to a large extent impersonal and timeless, but the activity that produces them is an activity of particular men sharing in the conditions of life, opportunities, and much of the intellectual outlook of a given society and period. To think of science apart from the human imagination and forms of reasoning that create it and the institutional, technical and economic conditions that make it possible is to misunderstand its character and position profoundly. Studied in the context of the period a scientific writer of, say, the seventeenth century can provide a valuable exercise in taking us out of ourselves. We find that technical efficiency in solving problems can be combined with a conception of the world, and of those problems in relation to it, very different from ours. The comparison throws light in both directions. The materials for the analysis of scientific thought, which is most illuminating when it is comparative, are provided by the past as well as the present. Conversely it is clearly impossible to understand the history of science without a knowledge of science and its principles. Similarly the comparative method can throw light on the conditions that may, in different societies, favour or discourage the growth of science

* This contribution is based on an article by A. C. Crombie published in *The Oxford Magazine*, 12 June 1958.

and its applications, for example, in medicine and in industrial and military power.

Interest in these subjects in its modern form dates at least from the scientific revolution itself when, for example, writers such as Francis Bacon and Voltaire appealed to historians to include the history of science and of technology in the general study of history.[1] It scarcely needs mentioning that philosophers since Descartes have found many of their major problems in contemporary scientific thought, and the greatest scientists have always shown that thinking *about* science can be as integral a part of scientific thinking as thinking *in* science. The eighteenth and nineteenth centuries produced some remarkable specialized scholarship and analysis in history of science, philosophy of science, and history of medicine. During the last hundred years these disciplines have acquired their own learned organizations and journals. The tenth International Congress of the History of Science is being held in 1962 and there has been a section for "L'histoire des sciences et de la technique" in the International Historical Congresses since 1900.

The introduction of the history and philosophy of science into university curricula, and the establishment of academic posts in these disciplines during the present century, have been the result of two decisions made by universities. They recognized first that these subjects are interesting and illuminating in themselves, and secondly that they require in those who teach them special combinations of knowledge and skills which must be acquired if proper standards and continuity are to be maintained. The first decision has led to the spread of the history and philosophy of science in examination curricula and the second to the making of provision for postgraduate training.

A pioneering chair in the history of science was established at the Collège de France in 1892 and, also before 1900, Ernst Mach held a chair in the History and Theory of the Natural Sciences at the University of Vienna. Further chairs in the

[1] Cf. Herbert Butterfield, "The history of science and the study of history", *Harvard Library Bulletin*, XIII (1959) 329–47; A. C. Crombie, "Historians and the scientific revolution", *Endeavour*, XIX (1960) 9–13; and for medicine F. N. L. Poynter, "Medicine and the historian. The Fielding H. Garrison Lecture", *Bulletin of the History of Medicine*, XXX (1956) 520–35; Owsei Temkin, "An essay on the usefulness of medical history for medicine", ibid. XIX (1946) 9–47, "The study of the history of medicine", *Bulletin of the Johns Hopkins Hospital*, CIV (1959) 99–106, and "Scientific medicine and historical research", *Perspectives in Biology and Medicine*, III (1959) 70–85.

history and the philosophy of science were established at the University of Paris at the beginning of this century and at London and Harvard between the wars. The Leipzig Institute of medical history under Karl Sudhoff was founded in 1906. Even earlier, a chair in history of medicine was founded in Paris during the Revolution and at Pisa in 1846, and at some German universities in the nineteenth century professors of chemistry were officially required to teach the history of their subject. These chairs in history of science have been followed since the Second World War by others at Amsterdam, Leiden, Utrecht, Frankfurt, Hamburg, Moscow and the Hebrew University of Jerusalem, lectureships in Danish, Swedish and Polish universities, and chairs at some dozen major universities in the United States. The total number of American universities and colleges with undergraduate examination courses in history and philosophy of science is now over forty and the majority have established teaching posts. Harvard, Wisconsin, Cornell, Princeton, the University of Washington, the University of California at Berkeley and at Los Angeles, Minnesota, Indiana and Yale also provide for postgraduate training, and the list is doubtless already out of date. During the same period further lectureships or readerships have been established in Great Britain at London, Cambridge, Oxford, Aberdeen, Leicester, Leeds, Belfast and Hull; several other universities plan teaching posts; in Australia there is a notable department at Melbourne; and a recent article by W. Mays in *The British Journal for the Philosophy of Science* (xi, 1960, pp. 192–211) shows that almost every British university and many of those in the Commonwealth give at least some instruction in history and philosophy of science. There has been a similar growth of interest and a parallel increase in academic posts in history of medicine[1], and a beginning is being made — in the U.S.A. and in Britain — with the establishment of posts in history of technology.

[1] According to the report of the Committee to Survey the Teaching of the History of Medicine, published in the *Bulletin of the History of Medicine*, XXIX (1955) 525–44, there were at that date 23 organized departments or divisions of history of medicine in universities in the U.S.A. and Canada and courses were offered in 52 medical schools. For a general discussion of the subject see F. N. L. Poynter, op. cit. In Britain there is as yet no chair in the history of medicine. There are honorary lectureships at Edinburgh, Birmingham and Guy's Hospital Medical School and, on the initiative of the Faculty of History of Medicine and Pharmacy of the Society of Apothecaries, honorary lecturers have recently been appointed at other London medical schools.

Discussion of such a practical problem as the teaching of history and philosophy of science ought to deal with actual situations as well as with generalities. The general aim of teaching — to provide an opportunity for students of both the sciences and the arts to think *about* science as an intellectual and social phenomenon — has been achieved in practice only by making history and philosophy of science an integral part of examination curricula. The natural way of doing this is to stress the aspect of the subject related to the student's other knowledge, whether for a scientist the analysis of scientific thinking or for an historian the relating of science to intellectual and social history. These studies may start early and they grow naturally with other knowledge; in fact the subject is regularly taken as early as the General Certificate of Education in some English schools. The main practical problem is that conventional divisions of subjects may make it difficult to find a place for a discipline going beyond normal science curricula and at the same time requiring more knowledge of science than is usually offered to students of arts. In this the relative rigidity of the British university system contrasts strikingly with the more flexible American possibilities, especially for combining major and minor subjects. (For some details see the papers by Dorothy Stimson, Henry Guerlac, I. Bernard Cohen and others in *Critical Problems in the History of Science*, ed. Marshall Clagett, Madison, Wisc., 1959, pp. 223–53.) In Britain some interesting comparisons are provided by the three universities where regular postgraduate courses as well as undergraduate courses are held: London, Cambridge, and Oxford.

The oldest centre is at University College, London, where there is a department with a professor, two readers and three lecturers, who give mainly postgraduate instruction but also some undergraduate courses. The postgraduate teaching is for the four written papers constituting Part I of the M.Sc. examination: one paper on the history of science from Antiquity to the seventeenth century; two on the history of either the physical or the biological sciences from 1650 to 1900; and one on the philosophy of science. A fairly exacting scientific qualification, a good first degree in science or medicine or engineering, is normally required of candidates. A dissertation of research standard forms Part II of the M.Sc. examination. Candidates for the Ph.D. degree are required to take the M.Sc. first. Lectures are given also by two honorary lecturers in the history of medicine and the history of technology. And in the

Faculty of Arts the history of science is recognized as one of the optional subjects in the final examination for the B.A.(Hons.) degree in history.

At Cambridge, by contrast, the main undergraduate course in history and philosophy of science, taken annually by some forty undergraduate scientists in Part I of the National Sciences Tripos, gives equal emphasis to history and philosophy, and in history the particular sciences are studied chiefly as they affect the *general* development of Western science from 1400. Candidates for the more advanced Certificate in History and Philosophy of Science, normally a one-year course for postgraduate students, choose four papers out of six, one of which is purely philosophical (principles of scientific thinking), one largely historical (origins of modern science, 1500–1800), while four contain varying emphasis on each (society and civilization in the Middle Ages, with special reference to natural philosophy and science; a special subject, currently the origin and development of Cartesianism; philosophy of science — the seventeenth- and eighteenth-century sources; philosophical aspects of some topics in nineteenth-century science). Candidates new to history and philosophy of science must take the first two papers mentioned, but otherwise candidates are free to choose the more historical or the more philosophical papers. There is, however, no attempt to separate history from philosophy, and each is used to illuminate the other.

As at London, a good degree in science is the normal requirement for the Cambridge Certificate, but arts graduates may be accepted and have on occasion made up half the class. The Certificate lectures provide a focal point for all postgraduate studies, while the undergraduate courses give the subject a position in the main stream of university teaching. The obstacle to further expansion at undergraduate level lies in the 'Tripos' system whereby a student is restricted in any year to one of the traditional fields of study. Students may transfer from one Tripos to another at the end of the year, but this does not solve the problem of a bridge subject with no obvious home in any existing Tripos. One solution might be to have an independent Tripos in history and philosophy of science, but with a staff of only three such a step is difficult.

At Oxford, in contrast to Cambridge, the history and philosophy of science has developed so far as a subject for examinations at the fourth-year and postgraduate levels. The main obstacle to expansion at undergraduate level is to be found in the system of examinations divided into different Honour Schools each with a relatively rigid syllabus, and in the reluctance of examiners and college tutors to extend the standard syllabuses by introducing new subjects. This particular experiment is in its early stages in Oxford, but the immediate result has been that although the subject is represented in various undergraduate examinations, it is in research and postgraduate examinations that the main expansion has taken place. One innovation that has proved notably interesting is that candidates for Chemistry Part II can spend their whole (fourth) year in preparing a research thesis on a topic in the history of science. But the most substantial recent development at Oxford has been in courses of postgraduate training tested by examination, in addition to straightforward research whether for the D.Phil. or a lower qualification. This development has been greatly encouraged by the prominence at Oxford of postgraduate training in philosophy leading to the B.Phil. Papers on the history of scientific thought are included in the philosophy B.Phil., and in addition a special postgraduate Diploma in History and Philosophy of Science has recently been established. Here the Oxford method which emphasizes teaching by guided reading, classes and tutorials more than lectures has allowed a wider variety of subjects to be offered as options than at either Cambridge or London. The Diploma examination consists of three parts: (*a*) the general history of science studied in relation to the general history of thought and to social history, with papers on science in Antiquity and on the origins of modern science down to about 1800; (*b*) a special period of scientific thought studied in original sources, the present options being Greek science, medieval science, seventeenth-century physics and physiology, and nineteenth-century biology, physics or chemistry; (*c*) principles of scientific thinking with special topics in either the physical or the biological sciences. The Diploma has thus been designed both for a general survey of the history of science in which the comparative method can be used, and for penetration of limited topics in depth. It has also been designed to be sufficiently flexible so that graduates in, for example, classics or history or philosophy or science can follow the natural routes opened to them by the subjects of their first degrees while at the same time acquiring a broad knowledge of the general history of science. In recent years about half the students taking these postgraduate courses have been arts graduates and half science graduates (out of a present total of about twenty). In the whole teaching of the subject at Oxford history and philosophy are used to illuminate each other, with emphasis on each as an analytic discipline, and the cooperation of colleagues in a variety of cognate scientific, philosophical and historical disciplines has made it possible to increase the range of instruction given far beyond the competence of the present limited specialist staff.[1]

It may be that the history and philosophy of science will eventually find a substantial place among undergraduate studies at Oxford as part of a scheme such as was first proposed as long ago as 1923 for a new combined honour school that became known as 'Science Greats' — a combination of science and philosophy including history and philosophy of science. But perhaps such proposals are always doomed to failure by the legitimate demands of specialization within the limits of three undergraduate years. For the immediate future the expansion of the subject at Oxford is likely to continue to be at the postgraduate and fourth-year levels, with possibly the introduction of a special B.Phil. in the History and Philosophy of Science as the most efficient means of helping to meet the rising demand for university teachers in the subject — a demand recognized by the Ministry of Education and the Department of Scientific and Industrial Research, both of which include the subject among those for which grants for postgraduate study are made.

In the end it may be argued that education can begin only through specialization. To know anything at all one must know something in particular well. It may also be argued that one may begin at any of a fairly large variety of the specializations into which the sheer increase of knowledge has divided both the arts and the sciences, provided that this is related to a widening circle of human thought and experience. In any educational system, such as the British, in which serious study is based on specialization the widening of the circle becomes an immediate problem. The study of the history and philosophy of science is often offered as a solution to this problem. It is also a specialization in its own right. Thus it may be held to satisfy both criteria for a good academic discipline. But having convinced everyone on this point, the real difficulties begin. Many of these are purely administrative and political, such as persuading institutions and colleagues to make room for it in

[1] The syllabuses of the Oxford Diploma and the Cambridge Certificate are published in *History of Science*, ed. A. C. Crombie and M. A. Hoskin (Cambridge, 1962), I.

examinations. But there are also problems of principle which not everyone may believe to have been finally solved. History and philosophy of science draws on several different disciplines in science, history and philosophy: how much previous training in each of these disciplines is necessary in both teacher and taught? This question is frequently raised when new proposals are made for examinations and teaching posts. It is a serious question, but in part at least it has been answered in practice by the experience of the last few decades. The present is an occasion for considering it further in the light of that experience and of the possible — something determined, as the Anglo-American contrast shows vividly, as much by the established habits of particular institutions as by the nature of the discipline itself.[1]

[1] Some special problems of certain subjects "which have received recognition in British universities only in recent years, and are still incompletely or insufficiently recognized" (p. 47) are considered in the Report, made by a special committee of the British Academy under the chairmanship of Sir George Clark and of Sir Maurice Bowra, on *Research in the Humanities and the Social Sciences* (published for the British Academy by the Oxford University Press, London, 1961). The Report includes History of Science in this group of subjects, and recommends that "immediate policy should be directed towards building up a few strong centres for each study, equipping them adequately with teaching material and research facilities, and attracting new entrants by providing research studentships tenable at these selected centres. In our view it is the only way that these subjects can develop, as they should do, into accepted academic disciplines" (p. 48; cf. p. 68).

Discussion

Asa Briggs

In opening this discussion I confess that I have some initial difficulty in deciding what constitutes an 'academic discipline'. It is easier in practice for seasoned academics to consider subjects in terms of jurisdiction and status (the number, for instance, of departments, chairs and conferences) than in terms of content. Clearly at this Symposium — and particularly in the preceding enlightening session on the history of technology — we have been considering not so much a single subject as a field of impinging and interrelated studies where different insights and disciplines converge and incidentally where converging insights and disciplines are necessary. To me this is the fascination of the history of science and technology and one of the reasons why it should figure in university curricula.

From this starting-point the first aspect of the history of science as a university study which I want to touch upon is its value precisely as a link between different disciplines. It provides a means of interesting non-scientists or half-scientists with a knowledge and understanding of the methods and results of scientific inquiry in human history. It provides scientists with an understanding of other factors besides science in the development of thought and practice, if you like with some sense both of the shape and themes of history and of the intricate and controversial combinations of particular factors and circumstances at given moments or periods of history.

I think that the demand from students for the inclusion of the history of science in university curricula, a vociferous demand in Britain today, springs from considerations such as this, however untidily they may be expressed. Students are not asking for the addition of another specialism to the curriculum, but for an antidote to the specialization which exists within the contemporary university curriculum. I base this assessment on information collected as a member of the University Grants Committee. It is the custom of this committee to collect views of students on their own universities. This custom, not universally popular among university professors, involves the preparation of initial memoranda. In nine universities in Britain the demand for the inclusion of the history of science as a subject figured.

Now, leaving on one side the question of the 'reliability' of this demand, it is easier to state it than to satisfy it. First, there is a shortage of people, in this country at least, with the right qualifications to teach the history of science. To teach it effectively some knowledge of both history and science is necessary — I do not think that the history can be taken any more for granted than the science, or treated simply as a background or a residue. It must be understood. To treat it simply as background means selecting a number of more or less relevant features of the past and failing to understand the climates of opinion, the states of mind and the guiding experience of scientists at particular times. Scissors-and-paste history is bad history in the history of science as in the history of anything else. To treat it as residue — a bundle of general 'external' explanations about society which are made to do when no other 'internal' explanation is forthcoming — is to fail to wrestle with the complexities of historical explanation. Historians bring arts to the study of the history of science, and the arts go much further and deeper than the mere handling of sources and evidence. So much, all too briefly, for the history component. On the knowledge of science which is necessary, others will be more able to speak than I, but it is obvious enough that the word science covers even more specialisms than the word history, and that histories of technology tend to be written by teams of particular technologists. Given the shortage of people, there is a natural tendency to envisage the concentration of studies in the history of science in particular universities. I have complete sympathy with this view if it reflects a feeling that this is merely the first necessary phase of the development of the history of science in this country (studies can be given a proper base and specialists will not be isolated) but acceptance of it entails a serious lag in the reform of existing university curricula. And malaise about curricula is not confined to students: it is one of the features of the existing mood in British universities today.

Second, and the point is not without its delicacy, there is a tendency for some among the strictly limited number of practitioners of history of science to concentrate on the minute and the remote. The relevance of their studies to what might be called the structure of educational change is not apparent. Of course, this tendency is not confined to the history of science: it certainly affects history and it is said to affect science. I do not want what I am saying to be misunderstood. I am not denigrating pure research. I believe, moreover, that it is essential in the history of science, even as an undergraduate study, to examine details — details of particular people, particular problems, particular experiments, particular developments. It is only when a certain level of detail is reached that the pattern illuminates and satisfies either the historians or the scientists. What I do suggest, however, is that the significance of the research needs to be considered if only by the researcher himself. This Symposium has shown that there are many big problems which deserve fuller study as well as small ones. As an academic 'subject' develops, research which is necessary to its development often too quickly loses itself in the thickets. Two things then happen. First, the appeal of the subject changes in relation to the appeal of other subjects and, second, it often splits into further sub-subjects. To my mind the drawing of boundary lines between the history of science and the history of technology is or would be disastrous. I believe that for these reasons it is necessary to develop wisely directed postgraduate schools where historians of science meet other historians and other scientists, and where the direction involves at least the good will and, if possible, the co-operation of different faculties. These schools must necessarily be in a limited number of places.

Third, when the demand for the history of science is met, the customers are not always thereby satisfied. This may not be the fault of their teachers. The people who make the demand may not know quite what they are asking for. They may have little or no prior scientific understanding. The system of educational specialization in schools is relevant at this point. The history of science may present difficulties to them or be an inadequate substitute for the teaching in universities of some science to non-scientists. Even non-science students with prior knowledge are sometimes disappointed because the history of science which they are taught stops short in time at the point where their own real interest begins. This is again sometimes a weakness of the teaching of history itself, and it can only be got round by instilling some real sense of the relevance — not necessarily, of course, the immediate contemporary relevance — of what is being studied. The teaching of the relatively recent history of science to non-scientists does, of course, pose all kinds of intellectual and practical problems.

I have talked so far of the history of science as a link, but I believe that we should also discuss the history of science as an element in existing studies. Rather than talk in general terms, I would like to say a little about the way in which we have thought about this problem in my own department — a history department — in my own university. Case studies are valuable, as Mr. Crombie and Mr. Hoskin have shown: they are perhaps particularly valuable when they concern one's own experience. Most history departments in this country expect their students to do what is called somewhat intimidatingly a 'thought' paper. We introduced in Leeds the history of scientific thought as an option instead of political thought or economic thought. A small but on the whole above-average minority of students have chosen this option. Most history departments in this country have what is called a 'special subject', a subject which is studied in depth and with careful scrutiny and analysis of basic source materials. We introduced in Leeds as one of our special subjects two papers on the history of science and technology, *Scientific and Technical Change in Britain from 1780–1830*, where source materials are available and where fortunately, living in a centre of what is now called the 'classic industrial revolution', local materials, some of them untapped, were also available. Very few students have chosen to do this option, but those who have have been well above average. These developments within the history department have been associated with earlier developments in the philosophy department, which provides us with tutors. Indeed many historians do a first-year subsidiary course in the philosophy of science, which is a valuable prelude to the more concentrated work on the history of science which a small number of them pursue in the later stages of their undergraduate work.

The place of the history of science within undergraduate history courses in foreign universities may be much bigger than this, but this Leeds attempt has this to be said for it — that it fits in the history of science, as of other approaches to history, in a natural way. Against it may be said that it depends on options and, therefore, does not lead all historians to study the history of science. On this point it should be added that some attention to the history of science, however inadequate, is, of course, customary in broader history courses in Britain as elsewhere, although my own hunch, as a nineteenth-century historian, is that while historians of the seventeenth century seldom leave it out (thanks largely to Messrs. Butterfield and Hall), nineteenth-century historians seldom put it in.

What I have said about history could also, of course, be said of other subjects. How, when, and how much history of science can or should be included in science courses? How and where can or should the history of science be related to social studies courses? There are two obvious lines to follow here — first, the study through economic and social history and organization of the role of science, and second the comparative examination of methods and procedures in natural sciences and social studies. Both these lines imply academic links of the kind about which I spoke earlier.

I have deliberately related what I have said to a narrow segment of British experience. In other countries, where the educational and social context is different from our own, the development of academic subjects may follow quite different lines. In all countries, however, the scope and approach to the history of science as a university subject rests not only on what the universities do but on what the schools do first. There is a problem of transmission and communication here which cannot be ignored in the context of this discussion any more than it could be in the preceding session or can be in discussions of the shortage of mathematicians or physicists.

On the universities themselves, I have left out one question which it may well be unprofitable to discuss in general terms, but which often creates difficulties in particular places. Where are historians of science to be located in a university if their knowledge is to be effectively deployed? It is unfortunate that weaknesses of university structure often make this question important. Perhaps it best lends itself, however, to gossip rather than to discussion.

I. Bernard Cohen

One of the major differences between the rise of the history of science as an academic subject in America and in Europe stems from a difference between the over-all organization of American and European universities. In America, generally, the separation of arts faculties and science faculties is not rigid; thus students — both undergraduates and graduates — are not restricted to courses offered by the particular faculty in which they are enrolled. The result is that science students may take courses in the history of science, which are offerings of the department of history or of philosophy, while arts students (say, of history, philosophy, or literature) are not so bound that they may not take courses in the history of science which are sponsored by a strictly scientific department and may even be designated as a physics, chemistry, or biology course. It is, in fact, this feature of the organization of American universities that has enabled historians of science, even though a major part of their students may be scientists in the making, to function effectively as members of history departments. The recent growth of the history of science as an academic discipline in America is in no small measure due to the increasing recognition by the general historian that this subject is truly a part of history, to be studied along with such traditional branches as political and diplomatic history and those of more recent recognition, such as intellectual and social history. The fundamental question — whether the History of Science *is* an arts subject or whether it is properly speaking a part of science — is not resolved by the form of organization of the curriculum of the university and is a topic for endless debate. I shall return to this topic presently, but at the moment I should like to say a little more about diverse ways in which the History of Science has been established in American universities.

In 1960, as one of the features of the commemoration of the 400th anniversary of the birth of Francis Bacon, organized by the American Philosophical Society (in conjunction with the University of Pennsylvania), there was held an informal round-table discussion of the administrative features of the history of science as it exists in American colleges, technological institutes, and universities. All the participants found that their experience confirmed the opening statement of the chairman, Richard H. Shryock, that as the history of science "has been introduced into American higher education, it has followed no common pattern in its structural allocation within the university programs". For example, at my own university, Harvard, the subject, though closely affiliated with the history department, is autonomous, under the control of a faculty committee drawn equally from historians and scientists, with representation from philosophy. At Wisconsin, there is a wholly separate and independent department of history of science, while at Cornell the historians of science on the faculty are members of the history department. At Yale a single department combines the history of science and the history of medicine, while Indiana has a department of the history and logic of science, comprising equal numbers of historians of science and philosophers of science. Princeton offers a combination of history of science and philosophy of science, with a choice of emphasis on one or the other and a consequent degree in either history or philosophy. These are the chief patterns, adopted with major or minor variations by universities in which the history of science has been successfully launched as a subject for higher degrees (A.M. or Ph.D.) including the University of California (at both Berkeley and Los Angeles), The Johns Hopkins University and the Universities of Oklahoma and Washington.[1]

The history of science is not only a graduate subject but is also taught in many American colleges and technical schools, often being a 'second' subject for a faculty member whose 'primary' (or 'bread-and-butter') course may be general history, philosophy or even one of the sciences.[2] In some technical or scientific schools, of which the Massachusetts Institute of Technology and the Case Institute of Technology are examples, the history of science is a part of a department of history or 'Humanities', where it may be associated with the history of technology.

Just before the Second World War there were two major centres of graduate study in the history of science at an advanced level in America: Columbia and Harvard. In the years after the war's end, Harvard's programme continued but Columbia's was dropped, while new graduate programmes were inaugurated at Cornell and Wisconsin. At the present time the list of institutions where the history of science is a major subject of research and instruction is rapidly expanding in America, and there are more and more universities seeking to inaugurate the subject. We have, thus far, not produced enough young scholars to fill all of these newly created posts, which include not only university professorships but also teaching positions in colleges. Thus the major brake on expansion at the moment is the shortage of trained personnel — a situation that will undoubtedly get worse before it gets better. As far as one can see, for a number of years immediately ahead

[1] At Brown, higher degrees are offered in the history of mathematics with emphasis on the exact sciences in the earlier periods. It is to be observed, furthermore, that my presentation does not include institutions for the sole study of the history of medicine.

[2] In America, since World War II, there has been a rise of historically oriented introductory science courses of the 'General Education' type, often planned so that the history may make the science more palatable and more meaningful for arts students. A number of such courses are taught by men of genuine ability and distinction in the history of science. These are science courses, not courses in the history of science — nor can they serve as substitutes for courses in the history of science.

the desire to have history of science taught in yet more academic institutions will create a demand that will far outstrip our supply.[1]

Let not these statements about numbers give the impression that I would ever measure the worth of America's contribution to scholarship in such purely quantitative terms. Yet it goes without saying that the 'job situation' is a very important element in the general health of any academic discipline. The fact of the matter is that, except for one or two occasional rare and dedicated men and women, young scholars of ability are *not* apt to be drawn to fields of learning unless they see some prospect of good posts and at least regular academic preferment after completion of the doctorate. Those of my generation may well remember the difficulty in attracting top-grade students in the days when there were no posts in history of science for them to fill, no matter how meritorious they might have proved themselves to be in their studies and graduate research. The significance, therefore, of the existence of good academic posts in the history of science is their role in the recruitment of young scholars.

In the years just before and after the Second World War, when we were struggling to establish a permanent place in the academic scheme for our subject, historians of science grasped at any possible opportunity to demonstrate to colleagues and to university deans and presidents how essential to a college curriculum the history of science actually was. In our propaganda, we would lay stress on the unique role an historian of science might have as a mediator between the arts and the sciences, and on the consequent importance of giving a teaching post to an historian of science in either an history department or in one of the science departments. A favourite expression used to describe the history of science in those days, to be found in many of the essays by George Sarton, was that it was 'a bridge' between the sciences and the humanities. Valuable as this slogan was, I think we must admit that as bridge-builders we were failures. Scientists today are not generally concerned with the humanities nor do humanists tend to have any profound

[1] This refers to academic posts only. It should be added that there have been opened up a large number of opportunities for government employment as well, chiefly as historians of scientific projects and as archivists; there are also many parascientific posts in government, and in industry and in libraries and academic institutions — embracing such posts as editors, museum curators, librarians, archivists, and deans.

appreciation of the sciences. It is consoling to realize that no other group has been able to build the much-desired bridge between the sciences and the humanities. I mention this topic because the slogan of the 'bridge' still haunts us. Yet I believe we have reached the day when the basic concern of historians of science — and I know I speak here not only for myself but for most of my colleagues — lies in advancing our chosen subject, not in becoming the bridge between the subjects of others.

At the present time, it is surely no longer necessary to justify the study of history of science. We need seek no 'excuse' for our inquiries into the origins and development of any activity which for more than two millennia has attracted to itself some of the best minds the world has known! From such studies it is always possible that there will emerge foundations for some kind of bridge between the sciences and the humanities: for example, a close examination of the creative aspects of scientific discovery may demonstrate similarities between the creative arts (so-called) and creative science. Should this happen, we will be pleased, of course, even though we do not give it an undue importance and certainly do not make the search for it our *raison d'être*. If I seem to linger overly on this topic, the reason is not only that I am weary of being considered a bridge between disparate groups, but that I cannot avoid such a discussion in relation to my assigned topic: the history of science as an academic discipline. For if history of science is not merely to be a bridge, what shall it be and to whom shall it be addressed? Shall the works in history of science be addressed to other historians of science? To historians, and to philosophers who may be historically minded? Or to scientists? This question of audience is basic to the quality of our researches, the level and tone of our writings, the technical demands we make upon our students and — in short — it actually becomes one of the defining features of every aspect of our professional careers.

With the continued growth of the history of science as an academic profession, the number of competent readers who can fully appreciate works in the field daily becomes greater. Not far off is the time when historians of science will be so numerous that they may produce scholarly works which need satisfy only the members of their own profession, the only requirement being that of high standards. But it is clear that the most important contributions to the history of science will always make demands upon the reader of a severe kind, since of necessity these inquiries will combine aspects of old and new science, philosophy, an historical point of view, and in some cases social and economic history.[1] As a result the need for scholarly communication will require that some writings on the history of science be addressed to other academic colleagues — including other historians of science. The history of science contains so many different specialties that technical works by some members of the profession will of necessity be always far removed from the interest and comprehension of others. It must be kept in mind that some historians of science specialize in aspects of science in modern Europe, or in modern America or Asia, others in the age of the Renaissance or Reformation, still others the Middle Ages, or Antiquity. One cannot expect a man whose basic concern is the impact of evolutionary ideas upon American education in the nineteenth century to follow carefully a work on the astronomical methods of ancient Mesopotamia. Nevertheless, it will always be important for all historians of science to be aware of what is going on in the field as a whole, and to appreciate the general significance of each major piece of research insofar as it alters in a major or minor way our ideas about the development of science as a whole. Because historians of science thus have a dual obligation — to produce the technical works so necessary for deepening our knowledge, and to write books and articles of a general character to inform the other members of their own profession — they also produce works of interest to general historians, to scientists, and to philosophers. Thus by ensuring that the advances in the history of science are not disseminated wholly by means of amateurs and popularizers, historians of science will make a contribution to our understanding of the very nature of the historical process, and illuminate every period and area of historical knowledge.[2]

Every historian of science, some time in his career, inevitably encounters the question: "How can anyone do work in the History of Science without being a scientist?" This question is

[1] What follows is true to some extent of every subject of specialization. Nevertheless, the history of science differs from most other academic subjects in the extent to which it calls upon competence in contemporary science as well as a knowledge of early science, and appeals to both science and history.

[2] There will always be a danger, as in every field of specialization, that these less technical works, because they are available to a larger and more general public than the technical works of scholarship, may by attracting mass admiration tend to distort the values of a growing field.

very misleading, and actually makes no more sense than, say, asking, "Does being a scientist qualify a man as an historian?" Obviously, scientific training is a necessary condition for studying the History of Science, as history is — but neither is wholly sufficient by itself. The literature of both science and history is filled with errors that no well-trained historian of science would make. These errors prove again and again both how foreign the canons of historical scholarship are to most scientists, and how impossible it is to expect historians to approach a scientific problem with the insight of a man of scientific training. It must be emphasized that in many notable cases a scientist will produce an historical analysis, of a topic within his own speciality, of enormous value. I would go one step further to say that few historians of science can ever bring to the understanding of scientific issues of the past those particular insights that appear to an imaginative scientist of the highest order confronting the primary documents of his own subject.

The general historian without scientific background does best in the history of science on topics where his historical training may compensate for his lack of science, as when dealing with an area in which the job is to study a vast secondary literature, select the best works of modern commentary, and then evaluate the various points of view. Nevertheless, to trace the history of scientific ideas and even to understand the evolving impact of science on society, it is necessary for the historian to have had training in the sciences, and the more the better! Yet, even for such an historian, the case is like that of the scientist to the extent that there can be no substitute for that essential and particular historical sense that is developed by graduate or post-graduate study and training in the History of Science.

Without any question, it is vital for historians, say of seventeenth-century mathematical physics, to know what developments came from the work on which they are concentrating, which means that they must be acquainted with mathematical physics as it was formed in the eighteenth and nineteenth centuries, and as it is being pushed forward today. It would be a pity, certainly, to present a view of late eighteenth-century and early nineteenth-century dynamics without being aware of the fact that certain aspects of the subject have assumed a new and special importance in current physics — which argues for a need of knowing some contemporary science even in presenting scientific ideas of an earlier day. Yet we must also admit that a complete distortion would result if the presentation of late eighteenth-century and early nineteenth-century dynamics were to be limited to only those topics which have a current importance for quantum mechanics; for such topics may not reflect the major interests of the men of the nineteenth century, and — we must admit — may not prove to represent the major topics ten, twenty, or thirty years from now! Certainly, a sound training in science is required of an historian who wishes to trace the history of scientific ideas, and the more science he can learn the better; but scientific training by itself — however necessary — is not sufficient unless accompanied by a sound historical sense, such as may be developed by actual training in the history of science.

I prefer to think privately of the history of science as a branch of history in which the primary subject-matter is science. This no doubt raises a major question because the methods of science and those of history are not necessarily the same, and it means in the first place that to do any history of science you have to start out with a background in science and yet your method has to be an historical method. But, however much we may affiliate ourselves with historians, it is not the methods of ordinary history but rather the methods of history of science that we must use, and these are respectable enough now in their own right.

The very introduction of this topic is a reflection of the day in which historians of science were overly sensitive to criticism on the part of scientists. At that time, unrecognized by general historians, historians of science often found themselves closely allied with the scientists, and took whatever criticism scientists gave very seriously. All too often, those scientists would criticize a piece of historical research in terms of the prior scientific training of the author, rather than the demonstrated merits of the result of the inquiry. Fortunately that day is past; now it is clear that the major determinants of the paths in which the history of science should progress must come from other historians of science. If not, the situation would be dangerously analogous to the acceptance by historians of art of a direction of their studies indicated by such men as Picasso, Henry Moore, and other modern artists.

Any consideration of the history of science as an academic discipline must take into account the contacts it makes with other disciplines. Foremost among these is philosophy. Most of us are in agreement that historians of science should have a philosophical orientation, so as to gain an insight into the general significance of the ideas they study. One of the problems that arise here is the dual need of having some comprehension of the philosophy or logic of science as well as some understanding of the history of philosophy. It is often assumed that the history of science will actually grow best when properly allied with a department of the philosophy of science. But it can also be argued that there is more sympathy to be found in an alliance between the history of science and the history of philosophy, since both are concerned with problems of the development of ideas in historical perspective, and since the methods of analysis employed are very similar. The philosophy of science, or logic of science, is of obvious importance for the historian of science who wishes to analyse scientific concepts. Care must be taken to prevent the rise of a distorted 'applied' history of science, in which certain historical aspects of the sciences are studied only to provide examples for a particular view of the philosophy of science. In particular, it would be especially valuable for the student of history of science to address himself to the philosophy of science itself in historical perspective.

In the degree programmes in most American universities, young historians of science are made to undergo rigorous training in history, often being required to prepare themselves in as many as two of the four purely historical fields required of ordinary graduate students in history. This means taking the same courses and research seminars and even taking the same examinations as history students. One result has been that many of our students, on receiving their Ph.D. degrees, have become members of an history department, part of their job being to give some course instruction on a purely historical subject as well as in their chosen field of history of science. In America one reason why so many of the new posts in history of science are created in history departments may be purely administrative, perhaps only demonstrating the reluctance of deans and presidents to create new departments. It is also possible that there is a truly growing awareness that whatever its special virtues and qualities, the history of science *is* a kind of history. This topic was debated with a particular intensity at the Philadelphia meeting referred to above. One man expressed the fear that history of science might be in danger of becoming "regarded as a province within history". The reply was: There is nothing wrong with being a good historian. The point was then made that with limited funds, a university dean might prefer to place the subject — at least at first — within a history department and allow it to grow naturally with a rise in the response of the student body. In the ensuing discussion there was no dissent concerning one danger of having the history of science established within an history department: the competition for funds for a second or third appointee. For instance, might not a history department decide that it needed another man in modern European history far more than a second historian of science?

This discussion led to another topic of great consequence: the passing of the 'one-man show'. Any university appointing an historian of science, everyone agreed, had better be reconciled to having within a short time at least one and very likely two (or even more) additional historians of science. In view of the increasing professional competence within this field, such a conclusion is not surprising. It is difficult, indeed, to conceive of a first-class training given today in the history of science by a single individual. The bare minimum requirement would seem to be three men, one specializing in the development of the physical sciences in modern times (say, seventeenth to nineteenth centuries), and another with a major interest in the biological sciences in the same period. The third man ideally should specialize in one of the earlier periods of science, which might mean that his primary concern was in Greek, Islamic, or Latin medieval science, either the biological or the exact sciences. Such a group of minimum size could be increased by one or more scholars, perhaps of other faculties, for instance specialists in the history of medicine, or the history of pharmacy. Other welcome additions would be historians of mathematics, historians of technology, social historians concerned with, say, the development of science in America, and even literary historians interested in the influence of science on literature. In addition, specialists in the development of science in the Far East would be valuable members of the group.

While the foregoing remarks indicate that in American universities historians of science establish contact with scientists, historians, and philosophers, it should be added that in many circumstances — particularly important for those concerned with the development of science in America — there are also valuable contacts to be made with people in the fields of economics, government, and public administration. This is a natural reflection of the ever-growing importance of science in the national life and in international affairs, with a consequent wish to understand the historical origins of current problems.

No presentation of the history of science as an academic subject in America would be complete without some mention of the very valuable support given to this subject by the National Science Foundation. Now past its tenth year, the National Science Foundation is the central agency for the distribution of federal government funds for the advancement of basic science. Although the chief fields of concern of the National Science Foundation are scientific education, the biological sciences, and the physical sciences and engineering (including mathematics), a small but ever-growing part of the foundation's activities has been concerned with the social sciences, including such fields as anthropology and archaeology, mathematical economics and certain parts of sociology, and also the history and philosophy of science.[1] The effect of the National Science Foundation on the last has been notable in various major ways: (1) in providing fellowships for graduate students who are working for the Ph.D. in history of science; (2) in offering post-doctoral and senior post-doctoral fellowships for men and women who have already obtained the Ph.D. degree, but want a year of study and research, free of all academic duties; (3) in making research grants to active scholars, to aid them at every stage of their research, including such diverse matters as research assistance, travel, microfilming, secretarial help, and even some salary during periods of research; (4) in supporting summer institutes, where college teachers are brought together and given the opportunity to learn some history of science; (5) and in giving aid to international scientific meetings

[1] Reports on various courses and programmes in the history of science in America may be found from time to time in *Isis*. An investigation into the first courses in history of science in America is reported in F. E. Brasch, "The teaching of the history of science", *Science*, XLII (1915) 746–60.

For a syllabus of a history of science course within a history department, see Henry Guerlac, *Science in Western Civilization* (New York, 1952). On the establishment of the programmes in the history of science of the National Science Foundation, see: "Conference on the history, philosophy, and sociology of science", *American Philosophical Society*, XCIX (1955) 327–54 (papers by R. H. Shryock, H. Alpert, H. Margenau, B. Barber, I. B. Cohen, P. G. Frank). The teaching of the history of science is discussed by H. Guerlac, D. Stimson, M. Boas, D. H. D. Roller, and I. B. Cohen in *Critical Problems in the History of Science*, edited by M. Clagett (Madison, Wisc., 1959) 223–53. A report on the teaching of history of science in America was given by Duane H. D. Roller at the IXth International Congress of the History of Science, Barcelona–Madrid, 1959.

(chiefly by providing travel for scholars) — including this one.[1]

Since, until fairly recently, few of the most significant contributions to the advancement of science originated in the New World, most of the research in the history of science done in America is not limited to a study of American contributions or the disseminations of European science in America. Hence, American historians of science regard the true test of the worth of their work to lie in its critical reception by their colleagues throughout the world.

W. P. D. Wightman

It may be remembered that my department of the History and Philosophy of Science in the University of Aberdeen was the first in the British Isles to be concerned largely with undergraduate teaching. From this 'unique' position I offer a few remarks on my experiences during the ten years of the department's existence.

Whereas in the Faculty of Arts, apart from a very few short 'infiltration' courses, the response even to a specially devised course has been virtually non-existent, in the Faculty of Medicine and even more so in the Faculty of Science there has been every year a significant response to similar courses. But even in these cases the appeal has had to be made through the philosophical analysis of the data, concepts and procedures of modern medicine and science. Once this appeal had been established the audiences generally respond readily to historical treatment of the problems raised. I therefore support the view advocated in the paper by Mr. Crombie and Mr. Hoskin, namely that the divorce between history and philosophy is to be deplored; but I do so with the reservation that at a more mature level investigations of the greatest importance may be made by individuals temperamentally allergic to either the philosophical or the historical standpoints.

In regard to the teacher himself, I should like to urge the importance of serving an apprenticeship in minute study of topics, which though in themselves trivial in respect of their strictly scientific importance are indispensable for the just appreciation of the climate of opinion and the actual conditions

[1] Support to a limited extent, in the history of biology and medicine, is also available through another federal agency, the National Institutes of Health. Fellowships, funds for research, and travel grants are also available to historians of science from their own universities and from private foundations.

of the historical process. The application of labels like 'revolution', 'renaissance', 'scientific revolt', based on traditional myths and ideological value-judgements, are just as likely to obscure and distort as to clarify a complex situation.

In conclusion, while admitting that scientists cannot hope to write history without undergoing a long and arduous apprenticeship, I myself would view with grave misgivings the control of the history and philosophy of science either by historians or philosophers, unfamiliar with the realities of experiment or the waywardness of the genius for discovery.

G. Buchdahl

I want to emphasize one or two points made by Mr. Cohen and Mr. Wightman. I should particularly like to emphasize Mr. Cohen's insistence that history of science desperately needs the assistance of philosophy of science, and I can do this best perhaps by drawing attention to the approach taken to this matter at Cambridge, and considering the syllabus for the Certificate in History and Philosophy of Science. This can be taken either as an independent third-year course in the three-year tripos or as a postgraduate course in one year. People can spend equal time, if they so wish, on history and on philosophy of science. The examination includes (as Mr. Crombie and Mr. Hoskin have already mentioned in their introductory paper) Society and Civilization in the Middle Ages, the Origin and Development of Cartesianism, etc., but also, among the philosophical papers, one on Philosophy of Science: The Seventeenth- and Eighteenth-Century Sources. Mr. Cohen especially mentioned the possible need to include the history of philosophy in the history taught, and there can be no doubt that the sharpening of intellectual weapons through a discussion of the philosophical ideas enveloping scientific questions of this period would be most valuable.

Here I want to comment on a remark made by Mr. Wightman, to the effect that a thorough training in laboratory science, and a considerable familiarity with its methods and procedures, is a *sine qua non* of a successful historian of science. I do not wish to dogmatize in any negative fashion, but if we want to say this, then I must insist that with equal force and justification a philosophical training is likewise an essential prerequisite. Consider indeed an example from a session during this Symposium. At one moment Mr. Southern attempted to lynch Mr. Crombie's account of Grosseteste's notion of science by insisting that for Grosseteste the verdict of experiments was only acceptable in so far as it moved within the orbit of his primary principles. In this argument, however, it is already assumed that a clear meaning can be given to the terms involved, particularly that we know what was there meant by 'first principles'. More important, the issue is considerably complicated by the fact that in order to offer a just and critical interpretation of this remark we have to use our knowledge of the subsequent development of this concept; we have to understand how in general the relationship between experiment and concept or principle appears. Now this can be done only by a critical appreciation of fairly complicated, more or less recent developments.

To return to our Certificate: the syllabus shows that the study and teaching which it requires need considerable time; these cannot be achieved in a few hours; what we demand (and get) is a full year of devoted effort on the part of our students. This reflection reminds us of perhaps the most important issue in this whole complex of questions, the conception that the main value of history and philosophy of science is as a 'bridge-subject'. At an informal discussion during this Symposium by university teachers of the subject in Great Britain there was emphatic agreement that this approach, with all it entails, was highly undesirable. For a lecturer to be constantly limited to giving a more or less extended course of lectures to students whom he will see only occasionally and during a single year, and for whom such a course is merely a random activity (however interesting and rewarding), with or without examination, is utterly frustrating. I emphasize this point of examinations, for it highlights the issue: history of science needs sustained participation on the part of every student; treatment of subjects must carry over from one lecture to the next; essays must be written, and the intellectual difficulties that arise must be taken seriously. And this is unfortunately only possible given the institution of examinations. A lecturer in any subject will gradually become demoralized if he is unable to argue and discuss the issues of his discipline with students who have gone on to an advanced level, whom he sees day after day, who look at the subject as one focal point of their university career, and who in this way — as it were — are enabled to sharpen their intellectual teeth.

My last point arises out of this: for if it is frustrating to lecture day in, day out, on merely elementary matters, it is equally invidious to be expected to cover single-handed the huge field presented by the history, let alone the philosophy, of science. Yet time and again universities concerned with the problem of the celebrated cultural gap appoint a single lecturer to serve in the capacity of the putative bridge. This is an intolerable situation and can only help to bring the subject into disrespect. I should say that it is absolutely essential, when a university decides to set up departments or teaching posts in history of science, that it should aim from the start at creating at least a small band of teachers with complementary interests and abilities, with relatively different backgrounds and specialized training. One of the important by-products of this is the satisfaction of the absolutely essential need for mutual discussion and intellectual exchange in one's subject. It is necessary to be stimulated not only by the labours of the scientists and the historians, but also by that of one's own colleagues!

One final point: the creation of a body of advanced students at undergraduate level will also do something to overcome the difficult problem of staffing new and unfilled posts in the subject. For then we shall be able to pick future research workers and teachers from among students who have actually received training in, and who have at least some insight into, the methods and objectives of the history of science, instead of employing the present haphazard system (in Britain) of drawing candidates from the fields of pure history, or science, or philosophy — a situation hardly designed to increase the respect in which this field deserves to be held by the academic community at large.

W. A. Smeaton

I should like to amplify the account given by Mr. Crombie and Mr. Hoskin of the courses at University College, London, in the Department of History and Philosophy of Science.

The course for Part I of the M.Sc. degree extends over two years, and is given in the evenings to classes composed mainly of part-time students, many of them teachers in secondary schools. A third of the lectures and one of the three historical papers in the Part I examination are devoted to early science (to 1650). The fourth paper is concerned only with the philosophy of science, so all students have to spend a considerable amount of time studying that part of the subject, in which they take a great interest. However, when they choose a topic for a dissertation for Part II of the M.Sc. examination, or for a thesis for the Ph.D. degree, they nearly always choose an historical subject.

The undergraduate courses are still embryonic. These courses are of two kinds. First, the necessary lectures will be given by members of our department to students from all colleges of the University who choose the optional subject for the B.A. (Hons.) in history. There will be a course of one lecture per week for two years, with a seminar, and the period covered will be approximately 1550 to 1750. This course will probably include a discussion of the relation between the history of science and the general intellectual and social history of the period, an aspect of the subject which does not figure largely in our M.Sc. course. Secondly, there may be a short course on the history of science in one of the science departments of University College; this is not intended to lead to an examination.

I. Lakatos

The article by Mr. Hoskin in *The Times Educational Supplement* (7 July 1961) has made it clear that the history-cum-philosophy of science is now passing through a rather critical stage of its rapid growth because of the shortage of teachers. I should like to re-emphasize this point. Indeed I wonder whether the brakes should not be applied to diasporic provincial appointments and to the establishment of degree courses all over the country. Our subject is an extremely difficult one, being a boundary subject between logic, scientific method, philosophy, science, and history, and many may be tempted to think that a boundary subject has no area and that one can try rope-walking this boundary without being competent in the fields which it 'bounds'. We cannot tolerate a situation where historian-cum-philosophers of science learn their mathematics, science and history from popular expositions. This is why I think that we should pay due attention to building up *centres of research* to *educate* historians and philosophers of science besides *appointing* them, and to *building up* this new field of knowledge before, or at least simultaneously with, *spreading* the gospel.

My second point concerns the evaluation of the recent increase of interest in the subject. The undergraduate clamour for courses in history-cum-philosophy of science is not an argument for the granting of their wishes. They clamour not because they have suddenly become passionately interested in problems, such as that of the role of the Arabs in the preservation of antique tradition, but because they are unhappy about the way in which history on the one hand and science on the other are being taught. History teaching still turns a blind eye towards science, the most exciting and noble of human ventures, and science and mathematics teaching is disfigured by the customary authoritarian presentation. Thus presented, knowledge appears in the form of infallible systems hinging on conceptual frameworks not subject to discussion. The problem-situational background is never stated and is sometimes already difficult to trace. Scientific *education* — atomized according to separate techniques — has degenerated into scientific *training*. No wonder that it dismays critical minds.

Now history-cum-philosophy of science has to show up science in history on the one hand and history in science on the other, and by doing this to exert an important *therapeutic influence* on both. If we fail to achieve this, we shall soon face a situation where an abundance of separate courses in history-cum-philosophy of science will turn the present two uncultures (to paraphrase Sir Charles Snow) into three, instead of helping to debarbarize both.

Now it seems to me that this therapeutic aspect has been narrowly interpreted. In the usual question, 'Can history of science give arts undergraduates a worthwhile insight into science?' the term 'arts' should be deleted. We cannot accept the present barbaric method of teaching science — not even for science students.

My third point is a minor reflection on the old plan of Science Greats. I think that to combine science and philosophy-cum-history of science at the undergraduate level would be very difficult. We certainly need intelligent people for many purposes who, while having all the advantages of the traditional arts education, will not be afraid of, or alien to, science. This could be achieved by developing a new honours school on the pattern of Literae Humaniores concentrating on the Seventeenth Century instead of on Classics. This is perhaps the last great epoch in the history of mankind of which a synoptic view may be achieved at undergraduate level.

A. R. Ubbelohde

Differences of approach are bound to arise amongst those for whom education is a by-product of the pursuit of knowledge, and those for whom new knowledge is a by-product in the primary pursuit of education. The view that the history of science is a branch of knowledge to be cultivated in its own right commands increasing support. But comments from Mr. Cohen indicate an important limitation. Even to scientists, anything like a general approach to science as a mode of human knowledge became impracticable towards the end of the nineteenth century, because of the subdivision into an ever increasing number of vigorous specialist disciplines. Beyond this limit, the history of general science is likewise no longer practicable with the pursuit in depth of selected aspects, that normally must accompany broad general perspectives if a discipline is to be academically viable in its own right.

If one accepts the view that with this limitation history of general science can constitute an interesting and viable academic discipline in its own right, this suggests answers to two other important academic problems. Adequate teaching of any of the specialist sciences requires some communication of its history, right up to present frontiers of knowledge. This is necessary both to give students some intellectual perspective, and because intellectual concepts tend to show spiral growth in which stages that have been left behind are encountered in modified forms, some way along the historic spiral. Such specialist teaching must remain a responsibility of the departments concerned; though useful support may be derived from those concerned with the history of general science, this consideration should not obstruct its primary objectives.

A second problem refers to the role of the history of general science, probably with some philosophy added as a means of correcting or curing the deficiency diseases that result from our modern extreme specialization of university studies. Those specially concerned with the history of general science in an academic community can usually make very useful contributions to the deficiency problem, for non-scientists and for scientists in rather a different way. But I think one should firmly oppose the assumption that teaching of the history and philosophy of science at a fairly elementary level can provide a unique or even an adequate remedy to specialization deficiencies. No single discipline in isolation can provide this service to academic education, though by their nature those subjects that give access to broad perspectives of human experience and human judgments of values may be expected and even required to make important contributions to general studies in the universities.

Requests by students for more teaching of the history of

science are an indication that they are aware of the deficiencies that result from the high degree of specialization of modern academic disciplines. Such requests should certainly be taken seriously as one more diagnostic feature of academic deficiency diseases, but the students' own suggestions about the remedies can only form part of the considerations about how to meet the problem. Like farm labourers visiting a country doctor, they only know the labels of most of the medicines.

D. W. Hutchings and J. Toulmin

We have come to the following general conclusions about the teaching of history and philosophy of science in the sixth forms of grammar schools in this country. The same principles might very well apply to courses in technical colleges and universities.

(1) There is no gulf between the arts and sciences, except an administrative one.

(2) When trying to teach this subject in schools, it is important that one should take the plunge and teach the arts students and the science students together. The difficulties which initially arise because of previous lack of contact between these two groups are very soon overcome, and the subsequent exchanges of ideas and discussions are well worth the initial efforts.

(3) One must assume that the arts people do not have very much scientific background and that the science people have very little sense of history or of logic; and that they have not developed their critical faculties to any great extent. It is of course so much the better if the arts people have done some science, and if the scientists have had discussion periods where they have talked about general philosophical or historical or critical problems in some degree. But, nevertheless, this subject can effectively be taught with these two groups of people, even if one has to start from scratch.

(4) We are assuming, and this is a very safe assumption, that the schools who are interested in teaching this subject in the sixth form have, in fact, only a limited amount of time at their disposal.

(5) We believe that the subject can be examined, and we firmly believe that it should be examined.

(6) While teaching this subject one should aim, we believe, to combine an essentially practical approach with a critical approach; that, on the one hand, there should be opportunity for putting the students in a 'scientific' situation, where they

can see some of the problems that arise when one attempts to test hypotheses empirically; on the other hand, we also believe that they should be given a certain amount of written work to do, that they can begin to think for themselves critically, and that they should also have an opportunity to examine at first hand the writings of scientists at a research level.

(7) We believe that this course should try to bring the students, to a great extent, up to date with regard to contemporary scientific *ideas*: it would be quite wrong to stop at the nineteenth century.

(8) The course should also be up-to-date with regard to contemporary work in the history and philosophy of science. This subject has been transformed out of all recognition in the last fifteen years and there are few, if any, textbooks suitable for teachers and sixth forms which incorporate this work.

(9) We feel that one should try throughout to place the students in the same kind of intellectual situation as scientists were themselves, trying to get them to understand why people found themselves in the intellectual positions they did, why they made the answers they did to the questions that they had selected.

(10) During the course some picture should be given of the social and historical backgrounds to the periods in discussion.

(11) The course should not devote itself exclusively to scientific problems but time should be taken out for periods on philosophical problems, problems of religion, problems of ethics, the tie-up between the arts and the sciences, etc. — all these should come in during the course as exclusive discussion periods.

E. Olszewski

In my country, Poland, courses in the history of science are now held in two universities: Warsaw and Wroclaw. They are offered to students studying at the department of philology who are training to become librarians. The two-and-a-half years of studies include 150 hours of lectures and 75 hours of seminars and finish with an examination. The Warsaw courses are conducted by two people.

What makes these courses different from similar courses in other countries is that they include the history of exact sciences and also of social sciences — economics, sociology, history, and so on. This is because of the requirements of the department of philology and the fact that in Poland history of science is understood very broadly. These courses include the whole history of science up to the present time, so that the last part of them is in effect a popularization of contemporary science.

Beside these courses we have in two technological schools chairs in the history of technology with optional lectures, and in medical schools chairs and lectures in the history of medicine.

A. P. Yushkevich

The importance of the topics which we have raised here is evident. The teaching of the history of science does not yet occupy the place it deserves in universities or in colleges of advanced technology. It is sometimes — indeed often — denied that the history of science is of value to students. The situation is, in fact, still deplorable.

I would like to emphasize that we ourselves, as the historians of science, have paid relatively little attention to this question. There is a great diversity in teaching methods, and in the courses available in different countries. In the United States — it would seem — the courses are, for the most part, on the general history of science. At the University of Moscow, on the other hand, there are courses in the history of mathematics for mathematicians, of physics for physicists, and so on. The course in the history of mathematics, for example, is a sixty-eight-hour one, and is obligatory. But the university curricula of Paris, Oxford, Harvard, etc. are almost unknown to us in Moscow, and those of the University of Moscow seem to be almost unknown to the scientists of France, England, etc. I do not wish to suggest that we should all follow an identical path; far from it. But I am sure that it is necessary to compare all that is being done in this field and to discuss the curricula, as well as the different methods of teaching.

A special commission has been appointed to deal with those questions which affect the teaching of the history of science. Unhappily, this commission only exists on paper. I think that it is time to begin the work of the commission by correspondence, by the gathering together of information and the publication of reports.

R. Taton

As Mr. Yushkevich has remarked, the section for the History of Science in the International Union for History and Philosophy of Science has appointed a teaching commission. This commission, which was re-organized in Barcelona in 1959, has, as its central objective, the collection and dissemination at an international level of all the information relating to the teaching of the history of science. If it is true that the activity of this commission is at the moment considerably curtailed, its members have nonetheless an opportunity of proposing to the President and to the Secretary of the Union the most efficient-seeming plan of action.* Moreover, it would seem desirable that our Symposium should adopt a resolution suggesting to this teaching commission that it should undertake an international inquiry into the teaching situation in history of science in different countries.

A. C. Crombie

We are all, I believe, agreed that the history of science has in principle the same claim to be included in the studies of an educated person as any other major part of the record of human thought and experience — it is part of *literae humaniores*. The practical problem we have been discussing — *how* is it to be included? — can, I think, be most clearly defined by looking at the content of the subject. As with other historical subjects this is defined by its sources: these are primarily surviving scientific and related texts, but also surviving instruments, machines, anatomical and chemical specimens and so on. The immediate problem, for both teacher and taught, is that of mastering the exegesis of these sources and this cannot be done properly without mastering the relevant context of thought, available techniques, social conditions, etc. By starting with the primary sources the student begins at both the central and the most concrete point — and this, to cite our local example, is how we begin studying the subject at Oxford, following the long-established practices of other, more experienced branches of *literae humaniores*. But to start at this point, whether in studying the history of pure scientific thought, of technology, of medicine, or of the history of institutions, is also to start with the major difficulties of exegesis and understanding and hence of the student's previous training.

I could not agree more with Mr. Briggs's insistence that knowledge of history and of the arts deployed by historians in wrestling with the complexities of historical explanation are as essential a part of the equipment of an historian of science as knowledge of science; I would only add explicitly (in agree-

* Correspondence on this subject should be addressed to Dr. R. Taton, Secrétaire Générale, Union Internationale d'Histoire et de Philosophie des Sciences, 12 rue Colbert, Paris IIe.

ment with Mr. Cohen) that the relevant history of philosophy, and also of other aspects of thought outside strictly natural science, should be included in this historical equipment. The chief task of the intellectual historian is to disentangle notions held by past thinkers about the cogency of arguments — a delicate question when these differ subtly from notions we may hold ourselves. I think that it may be claimed that some recent work in the history of science has itself made a notable contribution to these arts, and this has been done not only by paying close and detailed attention to available techniques, but also by showing in detail how general ideas of extra-scientific origin about the world can affect the notion held of a satisfactory scientific explanation and hence a whole range of scientific thought. Recent studies on Newton and on Kepler are only two examples.

To the practical question: what is the best previous training to equip historians of science to master the exegesis of their primary sources and the complexities of historical investigation? the answer clearly depends on the particular sources and periods. It is obvious that more demands are made on scientific equipment by later science — especially that of the past century and a half, and conversely earlier science usually makes more demands on equipment in languages and philosophical history. Previous training thus eases *different natural routes* into the study of different branches and periods of science. The history of science (and the same goes for history of medicine and of technology) is a subject much wider than science itself, and to understand any *period* of science historians need to become equipped to relate the science to the culture and society of the period. Until comparatively recently science was indeed a minority interest in societies where it existed at all, and to overlook this by concentrating exclusively on the science can only lead to distortion of the actual historical situation. Since 'science' covers as many different disciplines as 'history', there is no reason why these should not be combined in a variety of ways. It will come naturally, for example, to history graduates to relate science and 'scientists' to the social history and technology to the economic history of a period, and to philosophy graduates to relate certain fundamental, general aspects of scientific thought to contemporary philosophy. I agree with Mr. Wightman in doubting whether anyone without a fairly advanced training in, and experience of the *use* of the analytical disciplines of science — as distinct from simply studying the sources of its history — can ever really grasp the history of scientific thought technically in the concrete. I would go further and say that some experience of scientific or mathematical research, of the work-shop aspect of discovery (however modest), is at least an advantage to anyone hoping to understand the processes of discovery from the inside — that is, as they were seen by those who actually made the scientific history which is the central theme of our subject. This we should not forget, however necessary it is for us to relate this theme to the intellectual, technical, social, and other *conditions* for discovery if we are to have a proper historical understanding of it. Hence the relevance of studying the history of particular scientific problems and theories, as has been done for example in recent work on the history of mechanics, through different periods from start to finish. But if scientific knowledge is necessary, it is certainly not sufficient. As Herbert Butterfield has put it: "One of the greatest obstructions to the history of science at the present day is the fact that so many people, remembering what they were taught in their youth, think that they know the essential story already."[1]

Of course different people may have different reasons for studying the history of science, according to what they want from it. A scientist or a philosopher may not so much want history, as something from history. He may want to use history to throw light on some scientific concept or theory, or to provide examples of philosophical problems or situations in which he is interested regardless of their history. In Sir Walter Raleigh's phrase, his interest in history is really to use it "to teach by examples of times past, such wisdom as may guide our desires and activities"[2] in the present. These are perfectly legitimate uses of history, but they are always in danger of being perverted by using a version of history lacking the proper controls of historical scholarship. Conversely these controls to historical understanding may be just as misleadingly absent in the antithesis to the philosophical use of history — its use for mere antiquarianism.

One thing has been established beyond question by all the experience and publications that we now have to draw upon: history of science is not a field of inquiry to which scientists or historians or philosophers can assume, without risk of almost inevitable misunderstanding, that they can simply apply the

[1] *Harvard Library Bulletin*, XIII (1959) 334.

[2] *History of the World* (London, 1614).

skills they have learnt in their own disciplines. It requires training in the craft itself, in dealing with the documentary and material evidence as well as with the content of thought, which can be obtained only by experience with these particular sources and their individual problems.

It is just this understanding of past science in its historical context that cannot be taken for granted. For example, training in modern mathematics or physiology does not by itself equip us to understand the distinctive ideas and techniques of their seventeenth-century counterparts or to see the problems and the significance of discoveries as these appeared to the people of that period. Nor conversely does knowledge of Greek mathematics or physiology by itself equip us to understand the problems, achievements and limitations of the Greeks as these may now be seen in the light of our own more extensive knowledge of these subjects. The present throws light on the past just as the past may help to illuminate the present. The relevance works both ways because we are concerned with continuing as well as changing habits of thought, and the analysis of the *history* of science must at the same time involve an analysis of *science*. It is because different kinds of equipment complement each other in the exegesis of different scientific, technological or medical sources that the experience of working in the same seminar with people with different previous backgrounds can be so valuable a part of the training of historians of science, medicine and technology. Hence the importance of centres of postgraduate training and research. To cite our local experiences again, our programme of postgraduate training at Oxford is based on such seminars in which graduates in a number of different subjects bring a variety of scientific, mathematical, philosophical and historical skills to the exegesis of the same sources. About half of our postgraduate students have arts degrees and the experiment in bringing them together with science graduates is working very well; I believe the same to be true at Cambridge. The particular structure of the Oxford B.Phil. and of our Diploma makes this administratively simple and we hope gradually to be able to extend the range of subjects represented. This degree structure also makes it possible at least for arts graduates to study some aspect or period of the history and philosophy of science as a natural extension of their original subject in which their main work can continue — an arrangement of some practical importance when it comes to seeking an academic appointment.

I have concentrated on problems arising in postgraduate work in the history of science because we have devoted our main efforts at Oxford to building up a school of postgraduate training and research. But I should like to make two concluding remarks about the other aspect of the history of science as an academic discipline — the inclusion of it in the *literae humaniores* known to educated men. First, as we have been reminded, what happens in universities depends in part on what happens first in schools, and if the history of science is to be made interesting and relevant it is an obvious advantage if this begins in schools. Secondly, to cite one more example from local experience, we have found the co-operation of scientific colleagues of immense value — indeed indispensable — in dealing with the science of the last 100 years. For several years we have arranged a series of lectures each Trinity term on some definite theme in the recent history of science, for which we have invited different scientific colleagues to give separate lectures on their own special interests. One such series has been published as *Turning Points in Physics* (Amsterdam, 1959). We hope in future years to extend the themes and to include social and economic questions with which science, technology and medicine make contact.

Finally, I am sure that members of the Symposium would wish to co-operate in any inquiry taken by the teaching commission of the International Union mentioned by Mr. Yushkevich and Mr. Taton, and would wish to encourage the commission to take the initiative in this matter.

PART NINE

Problems in the Historiography of Science

27

Some Historical Assumptions of the History of Science

HENRY GUERLAC

I

History, of course, has something to do with the past. As we commonly use the word — neglecting such 'historical' subjects as palaeontology or evolutionary biology — we mean human history, the past of mankind, especially since the mastery of the art of writing.

But the word has a built-in ambiguity. It can refer to what Charles Beard called "history as past actuality", that is, the sum and total of everything men must have done in the past. Or it can mean written history: what men have thought or written about the human past.[1] The distinction is of more theoretical than practical significance. The past itself — history as past actuality — has fled forever; we cannot experience it directly; only our thoughts about it have any real existence for us. We can only construct an image of the past, or rather of selected parts and instants of it, by an act of mind, just as the scientist constructs a simplified model of the physical reality into which he cannot penetrate. We give the past, as Cassirer says, "a new, ideal existence" in our minds. Properly carried out, this ideal reconstruction is inferential in character — a "connaissance par traces", as F. Simiand[2] called it — based on our study of the documents, monuments and artifacts which have defied the erosion of time. It is the result of probable inference guided by our imagination, but not by an unfettered imagination. Our method is the method of Zadig.

History then, as I shall use the term, is a more or less disciplined inquiry into the past of mankind. Nevertheless we would not recapture, even if we could, everything we imagine to have happened in history as past actuality. Written history can only be highly selective, at best a mere sketch or outline of

[1] Charles A. Beard, "Written history as an act of faith", *American Historical Review*, XXIX (1934) 219–29.

[2] Cited by Marc Bloch, *Métier d'historien* (Paris, 1952) 21.

past reality. But what dictates our selection? An answer to this question could tell us a good deal about the objectives of the historian, his opportunities, as well as the restrictions imposed upon him.

Chance, to be sure, has played a major role in what we are permitted to know about the past; for though man is a record-making and record-preserving animal, he has set down only an insignificant fraction of his doings. And most of what he has recorded has, providentially, been destroyed and is forever lost. I say "providentially" because there is much about man's activities — one is tempted to say, by far the greatest part — which is so trivial and commonplace, so infinitely repeated without significant variation, that we would never think to dwell upon it.

But is there — has there always been — a criterion for what is not trivial and commonplace, for what has 'historical significance'? To a greater extent than we often realise, what we can know about the past is what our ancestors — the participants in events or those who came soon after — determined that we should know. They placed in the intentional record — in annals, memoirs and commemorative inscriptions — those men and events which appeared to them as exceptional, striking and wholly outside the ordinary dull routine of private existence. In the main, they singled out for preservation in the collective memory those events which they saw to have markedly affected the way of life, the thoughts and actions, of the larger social groups and political entities: a tribe, a city-state, a nation or an empire. So it is that the main scaffolding and framework of our view of history consists of those deeds, thoughts and productions which others besides ourselves deemed worthy of preservation because of their effect upon man in society. So it is, too, that early historians dealt for the most part with notable human actors and the part they played in political decision, war and dynastic struggle. It was upon such events — in the monarchies, oligarchies and feudal aristocracies of earlier time — that the destinies of men most obviously seemed to depend.

II
The broadening of history

From the beginning, then, written history focused on public matters. Individual actions were of interest only if they demonstrably affected the lives and thoughts of the social collectivities. And this, I feel, is still the characteristic of history, setting it apart from biography, romance and antiquarian curiosity. What has changed (for the writing of history has demonstrably changed in the past two centuries) has been chiefly the recognition of what varied and often subtle sorts of human action do in fact influence the fabric and the destinies of human groups.

What is most often stressed about the flowering of historical study in the nineteenth century — a new sympathy with neglected periods of history, like the Middle Ages, and the effort to make history 'scientific' by the systematic use of official and administrative documents — is perhaps not the most revealing. Fully as interesting is that the enterprise of writing history was broadened and deepened. When the historian relaxed his dependence upon what I called the intentional record — the annals, memoirs, and contemporary narratives — and turned instead to the unwitting testimony of official records and private correspondence, he not only demonstrated the bias and unreliability of his traditional sources, but he also caught a glimpse of a new and more subtle approach to the past. History was seen to consist not merely in the deeds of a few dominant personalities but in the largely impersonal unfolding of a nation's political and social institutions, in the cumulative action of many forgotten and often anonymous persons, and in the condition and aspirations of different social classes. The great European Revolution, which had cast up so many documents from their hiding places in looted chancelleries, confiscated estates and suppressed institutions, was itself a vivid demonstration of the complex forces producing historical change. Paradoxically, this greatest of all historical discontinuities — where venerable institutions were toppled, and pent-up energies burst forth to take command of men and events — made it evident that the historian could no longer neglect the hidden agencies, the gradual as well as the spectacular changes, which affect a society in the flow of time. A heightened sense of nationhood which the Revolution brought in its train, and the new democratic aspirations of which it was the expression, brought home the fact that history must be the history of peoples, not merely of their leaders. The slow, often imperceptible, alteration in men's lives; the change in their material condition, and in their ideas about God, Nature, Man, and the State: these were seen to be hidden stuff of history. This uniformitarianism, and this tendency to see history as social history, is already evident in the writings of Sismondi, Augustin Thierry and Michelet, with their picture of life in medieval town and country, and their attention to the role of the communes and to the rise of the Third Estate.[1] Something of the same sort is found in the Whig historians of Britain — Hallam, Macaulay and Grote — for whom history is the story of political liberty. Against this stream Carlyle set himself with his well-known, and quite reactionary, theory of the Hero in History. But Carlyle's was a hopeless stand. Opposing him were arrayed not only a new breed of constitutional and institutional historians, but the social philosophers, whose theories were destined to leave their mark on the work of the professional historian. Under the spell of men like Comte and Spencer, Hippolyte Taine and Thomas Henry Buckle made the first conscious attempts to write history in a societal, if not quite a sociological, fashion, and to give a proper place to social factors and to the role of ideas and ideologies. Buckle's admirer, Lecky, broke new ground with his classic study of the ideas of Western man which could be linked to the "practical, active and social" aspects of history.[2] And after Karl Marx, no historian, least of all men living in an age of rapid industrial and social change, could wisely neglect the role that class interest, economic institutions, and the changing modes of production play in shaping the human condition.

This expansion of the historian's canvas had clear implications. The most obvious was the need for specialization, for a detailed inquiry into those aspects of human history which had been largely neglected: for example, the history of commerce and exploration, of social customs and manners, of agriculture and village life, the rise of an urban middle class, and the condition of the labourer.

How, then, were these multiform aspects to be related one

[1] One of Michelet's most important innovations was the attention he paid (in the "Tableau de France" which opens the second volume of his *Histoire de France*) to geographical factors influencing the history of the French people.

[2] See Lecky's *History of the Rise and Influence of Rationalism in Europe* (1865) and his *History of European Morals from Augustus to Charlemagne* (1869). The phrase appears in a letter to Charles Hartpole Bowen apropos of Sir Leslie Stephen's *English Thought in the Eighteenth Century* (1876). Here Lecky wrote: "I hope we two may rather help than injure each other, he being concerned with the intellectual and speculative side, I with the practical, active, and social." See his wife's *Memoir of the Right Hon. William Edward Hartpole Lecky* (London, 1909) 133.

to another? Was it possible to delineate, in something approaching its living complexity, the temper, tone and cultural pattern of earlier societies? Here, I think, the work of the pioneer sociologists, and eventually the rise of ethnology, may have exerted a subtle influence. At all events after mid-century we encounter some bold excursions into historical writing that employed a new form and displayed a different texture.

With a few prophetic exceptions — like Voltaire's *Siècle de Louis XIV* — historical writing had been exclusively narrative, consisting of little but a running account of events and human actions. But the societal aspect of history demanded that the historian not only narrate the events transpiring in an early society, but display the pattern and structure of that society, the organic cohesiveness of its institutions, and the interdependence of its cultural elements. Only in this way could the events themselves be seen in their proper light, and their true character appreciated. Moreover, if the distant and highest goal of the historian was to study the development of societies in space and time — as Pirenne in our day has defined the purpose of history, and as Toynbee has sought to realise it on a panoramic scale — then the motion picture must perhaps be arrested, and its separate frames studied in detail. The solution was to make a cut through temporarily, and write what we may call 'horizontal' history, offering a kind of instantaneous photograph or portrait where the characteristic and stable elements of a society are singled out and described in their interrelationships. We find some early examples of this kind of writing — foreshadowed in Voltaire and in parts of Gibbon — brought to the fore in the famous third chapter of Macaulay's *History of England*, and in Taine's volumes on the *Ancien Régime*. But entire works, now classic, were written in this new form: Fustel de Coulange's *La Cité Antique*, for one, and a generation later Samuel Dill's *Roman Society from Nero to Marcus Aurelius*.

Specialization on the one hand, and attempts at cultural synthesis on the other: these have been the two polarities of historical writing during the last century and a half, two consequences of the expanded scope of historical inquiry. Both were — and are — essential. They should of course be related in an obvious way, with special studies providing the detailed knowledge and some of the insights necessary for intelligent and meaningful synthesis. Regrettably this is not always the case. Specialities, as we all know, acquire a life of their own, a jealous independence, a private jargon and an esoteric concern with the smallest technical detail. This has been true of those historical sub-disciplines which split off from history itself, and which — like the examples I have given — had as their original justification a deeper understanding of the processes underlying historical change. It is even more true of those quasi-historical fields, like our own, which had, as I shall now try to show, a different origin, and which dealt with human activities less obviously connected with those socio-political concerns that remain central to the work of the historian.

It is well to remind ourselves that the flowering of historical writing was an expression of a deeper and all-pervasive re-alignment of thought and method in the study of man and nature we see emerging at the close of the eighteenth century and the beginning of the nineteenth. Historical explanation as a mode of understanding through retracing a development (real or imagined); history, in the loose sense of genetic treatment of any subject, pervaded philosophy and social theory from the time of Turgot through Hegel and Marx, Comte and Spencer. With Thomas Wright, William Herschel and Laplace it entered into sidereal astronomy and cosmology. It supplied the geologists with their great explanatory principle. And it was applied — by embryologists, naturalists and anatomists — to elucidate the form and structure, the relationships and adaptations, of living creatures.

In what we now call the social sciences, the sciences of man, the same shift of attitude and method is to be noted. In the eighteenth century Age of Reason it has been customary to treat, in a theoretical and normative way, such problems as the nature of law or economic behaviour or the character of political institutions, by testing their conformity to some ideal plan, or judging them as approximating to, or falling away from, the dictates of the Moral Law or the Laws of Nature. This tendency was far from abandoned in the nineteenth century.[1] But 'historical schools' arose in the study of law — with Savigny and Henry Sumner Maine, for example — and in economics and in political theory.[2] The purpose was to illuminate the present by turning to the past, noting the con-

[1] The classical economists — James Mill, Nassau Senior and the rest — are well-known examples. In law and jurisprudence extreme cases are the 'analytical jurists', Jeremy Bentham and John Austin.

[2] Maine's criticism of Austin is enlightening on this altered approach. See his *Lectures on the Early History of Institutions* (New York, 1878), especially Lectures XII and XIII.

ditions which had given rise to particular forms and practices, and the changes these underwent. While such studies were clearly of value to the historians, with their heightened curiosity and expanded outlook, it was not always for or by the historians that they were written, but often by legal scholars for lawyers, or by economists for their confrères and for statesmen.

The same 'historical' tendency expressed itself in the study of man's artistic and cultural accomplishments: his language and literatures, his art and his music, his philosophic doctrines, his practical inventions and his scientific knowledge. Here too, the genetic approach supplied a new kind of understanding in areas which had been the special preserve of the theoretical and normative modes. Again, this was the work not of historians, but of specialists in the particular subjects.

It is important to emphasize, without depreciating their value, that these historical specialities, these genetic and developmental studies of special areas, lay outside the domain of history proper. The books of the pioneers — of Wincklemann, of Dr. Burney, of Tiraboschi and Victor Cousin — were intended to deepen the understanding of the student of art, of music, of literature or of philosophy. With few exceptions — and they came much later, like Taine's *History of English Literature* — such narratives bore the hallmark of their origin. They were often dry, sometimes technical, usually innocent of historical reverberations. The historical environment, the *moment* and the *milieu*, were studiously ignored.[1] It is hardly surprising that historians were slow to make use of them; slow, despite the example of Burckhardt, to consider the part played by art and letters in the social complex; slower still to appreciate the pioneer works in the history of science, which also were specialized works written for the specialist, when they were not popular introductions to the subject.

III
Some remarks on the history of science

We still consult today, and with profit, histories of science — or rather of the several sciences — written in the late eighteenth and early nineteenth centuries in the spirit, and with the

[1] A neglected early exception, and one of great interest, is Mme. de Staël's *La littérature considérée dans ses rapports avec les institutions sociales* (Paris, 1800).

limited objective, to which I have just referred.[1] It is obvious that Montucla's *Histoire des mathématiques*, and Delambre's classic volumes on the history of astronomy — like the books of Joseph Priestley — were intended for the scientific reader. So also were the books published at Göttingen, between 1790 and 1810, which seem to have been introductions to the several scientific fields taught there. Among these works are Gmelin's *Geschichte der Chemie*, Kästner's *Geschichte der Mathematik*, and Johann Karl Fischer's *Geschichte der Physik*. We know, too, that Johann Beckmann's pioneer history of inventions was based on the lectures he gave at Göttingen to his students of political economy.[2] Each subject, so it was felt, should be introduced by an historical conspectus.

This remained, I think it is safe to say, roughly the character of much writing in the history of science during the remainder of the century. With a wealth of factual detail, the several branches of science were traced out in their development by scientists and mathematicians — men like Sprengel and Sachs in botany, Thomson and Kopp in chemistry, Daremberg in medicine, Moritz Cantor in mathematics, and Poggendorff in physics. These contributions were notable, but the unity of science, to say nothing of the cultural environment in which it arose, was hardly suggested. This was also true of the ambitious work that has been described as "the first modern history of science", William Whewell's *History of the Inductive Sciences*, which is largely an assemblage of separate histories of the several sciences.[3] The unity Whewell was capable of giving the subject was obscured by his decision to treat "facts" and discoveries in this book, and to deal separately with "ideas" in his historically-oriented *Philosophy of the Inductive Sciences*.[4] His aim, at all events, was to throw light on the sciences through their history, and to provide "a basis for the philosophy of science".[5]

[1] For what follows, I have made use of my paper in IXe *Congrès International des sciences historiques I, Rapports* (Paris, 1950) 182–211.

[2] An amusing account of Beckmann's lectures on political economy, and their lack of relevance to the needs of future Prussian financiers, may be found in Karl Bruhns (ed.), *Alexander von Humboldt* (2 vols., Leipzig, 1872) I, 51.

[3] George Sarton, *A Guide to the History of Science* (Waltham, Mass., 1952).

[4] Or, as he put it himself, his *Philosophy of the Inductive Sciences* "contains the history of the Sciences so far as it depends on *Ideas*; the present work contains the history so far as it depends upon *Observation*" (*History of the Inductive Sciences*, I, 51).

[5] Whewell also had a practical purpose: "The present generation finds itself the heir to a vast patrimony of science. . . . The eminence on which

To all this work the general historian of the nineteenth century remained stolidly indifferent. Even Burckhardt, whose net was cast so wide, is a case in point. He virtually ignored the scientific side of the *Quattrocento*, said little or nothing of Leonardo da Vinci as a man of science, and cited only once, I think, and slurringly, Libri's *Sciences mathématiques en Italie*. When Buckle, under positivist inspiration, used some of the works on the history of science we have mentioned when he wrote his *History of Civilization in England*, and attempted to fit the history of science into modern cultural history, the majority of historians received his effort with almost total incomprehension.[1]

It is August Comte — for all the narrow rigidity of his thought — who first offered a new and more meaningful conception of the history of science. He believed, as his famous doctrine of the three historical stages amply testifies, that the true history of mankind is the history of the human mind. He believed, too, in the underlying unity, or unifiability, of the sciences, and in the possibility of what he was the first to call the *histoire générale des sciences*. As a perusal of his rather turgid writings reveals, he had a broad, if superficial, knowledge of the development of the sciences. And though he wrote no history, or history of science, he had a truly historical sense and came up with some perceptive insights. He saw the first anticipations of modern science among the Greeks of the Hellenistic period, though he had great respect for Hippocrates and Aristotle. With little knowledge of or sympathy for the Middle Ages, science to him really develops from a "révolution générale et continue" dating from the end of the sixteenth century, though prepared by workers of previous centuries, especially the Arabs. So far as I can discover, Comte was the first to conceive of, and to baptize, the Scientific Revolution. Like Whewell, he saw this revolution largely in terms of great men. It was set on its

we stand may enable us to see the land of promise, as well as the wilderness through which we have passed. The examination of the steps by which our ancestors acquired our intellectual estate . . . may teach us how to improve and increase our store . . . and afford us some indication of the most promising mode of directing our future efforts to add to its extent and completeness. To deduce such lessons from the past history of human knowledge, was the intention which originally gave rise to the present work" (ibid. pp. 41–2).

[1] See for example Bishop Stubbs, who remarked, "I don't believe in the philosophy of history, so I don't believe in Buckle" (cited by G. P. Gooch, *History and Historians in the Nineteenth Century*, London, New York and Toronto, 1935, pp. 345–6).

course, he wrote, by the new impetus simultaneously given to the human mind by the *conceptions* of Descartes, the *precepts* of Francis Bacon, and the *discoveries* of Galileo.[1] The sciences did not, however, emerge all at once. Indeed Comte's famous hierarchy of the sciences reflects his theory of their successive appearance: first mathematics, then astronomy and physics, and finally — in the eighteenth century — chemistry with Lavoisier and his paladins, and physiology (a term he used where we should use the word 'biology') with Haller, Spallanzani, Lamarck and Bichat.

Yet for all his emphasis upon outstanding creative personalities, Comte was — needless to say — not blind to social forces affecting the growth of science. Scientific progress, he argued, has never been due solely to man's rational faculties. It has been "heureusement accélérée par une stimulation étrangère et permanente", chiefly the "impulsion énergique qui résulte des besoins de l'application". While lending cautious assent to the view that each of the sciences had arisen from a corresponding art or craft, he gave this familiar speculation a special twist. In its infancy every science was nurtured by its close relation to some art or craft, which supplied it with positive data and impelled speculation into a real and accessible domain. Later, however, the rapidity of progress in any science depended upon its emancipation from its related craft.[2] Thus chemistry emerged as a science only when, in Comte's own day, it acquired a largely independent and speculative character. Writing in 1838, he believed that physiology had reached a point where it must cast off the bonds linking it to its associated art, medicine, if it was to become a science.

Comte was an articulate promoter of the history of science as a learned discipline. He urged upon Guizot, then Minister of Public Education, the establishment of an academic chair devoted to the "Histoire générale des sciences". And he influenced some work of real distinction in the history of science, for example Littré's translation of the Hippocratic Corpus — the chief work of ancient science recommended in Comte's *Bibliothèque positiviste* — and the study of Aristotle by Comte's English disciple, George Henry Lewes.[3] Buckle, another disciple as we have seen, wrote the first work of general

[1] *Cours de philosophie positive* (6 vols., Paris, 1830–42) IV, 217.

[2] Ibid. pp. 278–9.

[3] G. H. Lewes, *Aristotle. A Chapter from the History of Science* (London, 1864). This work is by no means wholly favourable to its subject.

history in which the history of science found a place — a brilliant and neglected pioneer effort.[1]

To see science as an historical phenomenon, responsive to, and influencing, the course of social change, one must view it, so far as the complexity and diversity of science permits, in unitary terms. It was through the logic and method of science, as well as its spirit and common purpose — in a word, through the philosophy of science broadly conceived — that a certain unification appeared possible. Men like Whewell, Mill, John Herschel and Jevons — according to their various preconceptions — sought to analyze the intellectual machinery which had brought science to the stable plateau of accomplishment they felt it had attained by the mid-nineteenth century. We are all familiar with their optimistic belief that they could set forth this method with convincing finality. But they could hardly foresee the profound changes, the deep insecurity, which settled over science — especially physics — near the turn of the twentieth century, and which impelled philosophers and scientists to a pregnant re-examination of the foundations of science. This effort to hammer out a new philosophy of science — by Mach, Poincaré and others — gave a powerful incentive to a more detailed, and an intellectually more sophisticated, inquiry into the past of science. This activity supplied new depth to the work of Paul Tannery, whom we all look to as the true founder of the modern history of science movement, yet whose debt to Comte is well attested.

It was his reading of the *Philosophie positive*, Tannery tells us, which first suggested to him what the history of science might become. Like Comte, he saw in the progress of science a key to modern history; and he discerned, more clearly than Comte, that a general history of science must be, first and foremost, a history of scientific *thought*, of scientific *ideas*, and not merely a chronology of great men, or, as in the books of Siegmund Guenther, a genealogical compendium of discoveries in the several sciences.[2] But, unlike the philosophers among his

[1] Henry Thomas Buckle, *History of Civilization in England* (2 vols., 1857–61 and later editions). The title, as has frequently been pointed out, was singularly inappropriate. Conceived as the introduction to a fifteen-volume history that was never written, the work treats not only England, but deals at length with Scotland and France, and more briefly with Spain.

[2] For Tannery's conception of the history of science see his *Mémoires scientifiques*, X, especially the "Programme pour un cours d'histoire des sciences" (pp. 1–9), "De l'histoire générale des sciences" (pp. 163–82), and "Auguste Comte et l'histoire des sciences" (pp. 196–218).

associates — André Lalande, Emile Meyerson and the rest — Tannery was sensitive to the *social* role of science. He urged attention to the history of technology in any course of lectures in the history of science. And he criticized Comte for ignoring the history of medicine, one of the earliest, and for long one of the most significant, points of contact between the man of science and the society in which he lived.[1] Considerations such as these contributed to his belief that the history of science belonged with history, not with philosophy. In 1900 he organized, as a section of a Paris congress of historians, the first international gathering of men working in the history of science; and between that year and 1905 he contributed articles to the newly established *Revue de synthèse historique*. Tannery's vision of an *histoire générale des sciences* was a giant step towards giving our subject meaning for the historian. How his heirs attempted to bring this vision to fulfilment, and how successful they were, is another question.

IV
The History of Science Today

The striking feature of work in history of science during the last fifty and more years has been its diversity. Much history of the older sort continues to be written, and of course should be written; for only by detailed study can the tangled skein of discoveries and influences be unravelled. But I think it safe to say that studies of this sort, under the influence of men like Tannery and George Sarton, have been carried out with a keener historical sense, a greater awareness of the complexity of scientific progress, and a real sensitivity to earlier modes of thought and to the context of contemporary ideas, than was the case before. We have had, it is true, our share of encyclopaedists and cataloguers, of happy dilettantes and popularizers, and of scientific antiquarians in passionate quest of the smallest technical detail. But if I were to single out the most notable

[1] Tannery objected to Comte's excessive preoccupation with the *sciences, théoriques et abstraites*. At one point he wrote: "En principe, si l'histoire générale des sciences doit retracer tout mouvement intellectuel scientifique, si elle doit s'attacher à mettre en lumière les diverses influences qui déterminent le progrès, elle ne peut évidemment écarter ni les sciences concrètes ni les sciences appliquées. . . . Les techniques les plus diverses, et non seulement les techniques proprement scientifiques peuvent obtenir, dans l'histoire générale des sciences, une mention que leur refuserait l'histoire spéciale" (*Mémoires scientifiques*, X, pp. 220–1).

achievement, it is the leadership of those men who have taught us how to focus upon the evolution of key scientific ideas and concepts. In this, Pierre Duhem is the acknowledged teacher of us all, whether medievalist or not. In this he has been followed by a number of our keenest minds — men like Burtt and Koyré — who have gone further and demonstrated the close relationship, during the formative era of modern science, between science and philosophy, and science and religious thought. Their contribution has been immense, and our debt to them is great indeed.

This enlarged and deepened conception of the history of science had brought us closer to the philosophers of science. Indeed it is men of philosophic training who have been chiefly responsible for, and philosophers who have been most responsive to, the notable progress that had been made. From the standpoint of the historian we may not have done so well. The newer history of science, with its strong flavour of idealism and super-rationalism, its often exclusive preoccupation with the genesis and development of key concepts, has about it the aura of a new specialism, a kind of meta-history of science.

We run the risk, in consequence, of seeing our subject spawn new sub-specialities, the history of technology affording a good example. The encyclopaedic range of George Sarton, some of us can recall, did not willingly extend into this prickly subject; he had little sympathy for it, and deemed it unworthy of his attention. He once replied by postcard to a distinguished medieval historian who had the misfortune to forward a reprint treating some aspects of medieval technology and bearing the title: "In Praise of Medieval Tinkers". Dr. Sarton's acknowledgment was brief. It read: "Dear Professor X: Thank you for your paper. I am interested in medieval thinkers, not medieval tinkers. Yours very truly, George Sarton." His attitude, I suspect, is quite widely shared. So much so — to refer to a current symptom — that the historians of technology in the United States have banded together and founded their own society and their own journal, just as the historians of medicine had done earlier. I think that Tannery would not have welcomed these developments.

At all events, the relation of the history of science to the growth of technology, and the debt that early science may have owed to the practical arts and crafts, are questions with a diminished appeal for many leading historians of science today. It is quite clear to me that the causes of this indifference are complex and deep-rooted. There is the matter of changing fad and fashion, but there is another tendency that, as a historian, I sincerely deplore. To discuss social influences, especially economic and technological factors, in the growth of science — or so it appears to many historians of science in Western Europe and America — is to assume a political and ideological posture. A short while ago I published a modest paper which sought to relate the rise of chemistry in eighteenth-century France to some aspects of French industrial progress. The somewhat teasing comment of one of my good friends and admired colleagues was that it was interesting, "mais un peu Marxiste". I found that remark quite revealing, for I doubt that an historian would have made it; certainly no good Marxist would have discovered much to applaud in my approach to the subject. In large measure, I share the impatience with much that English and Continental Marxists have written. I find a good deal of it naïve, rhetorical, unhistorical and crude. But I do want to be free to use, when I see fit, the insights these books and articles can provide me, and allowed to evaluate according to my lights the facts on which they lay so much stress. Take the case of Francis Bacon. A recent and often penetrating book on the rise of science, written in the idealist vein by an American scholar, takes a haughty line towards him, disposing of him with sneers. Yet scientist or not, profound philosopher or not, the historical influence of Bacon, in his day and long after, was immense. To cast him out — to view him disparagingly from the heights of the new idealism — is, very simply, to distort the history of science, to view it in only one of its aspects. Perhaps the reason for doing so is that Bacon is a special pet of Marxist historians. I am glad to say that such inhibitions are less evident among historians, the majority of whom (though they are not always the most unprejudiced of men) long ago made a certain accommodation with Marx. If we nurture such timidity, and even covertly feel that there exist forbidden subjects, and safe conventional attitudes towards certain great figures and events, we can hardly lay claim to the objectivity that should be our pride.

V
Conclusion

In this paper I have taken the point of view that historical writing, by its very nature, should be synthetic as well as analytic; that it increasingly involves the study of cultural patterns of past societies; and that its goal — admittedly a distant and perhaps unattainable goal — is the study of cultural and societal change. I have tried to suggest that one does not write history, or even necessarily contribute to its understanding, merely by studying in a quasi-historical or genetic way some selected and isolated aspect of human endeavour, however absorbing and valuable for itself. The history of science, like the history of theology, can be written — has been written — for its own sake. But from the standpoint of the historian, this is to write private, insulated history, and to treat science like a mere cultural embellishment, as remote from crucial human problems as the history of gardening, dress or cricket, subjects that nevertheless can be treated in what, to the historian, is a meaningful fashion. All that is required is that, in the specialization which is inevitable in all historical fields, the larger aims of history be kept in mind, and the special subject approached so that its place in the greater synthesis can be at least dimly seen. It is the specialist, no less than the generalist (the historian), who must be sensitive to the points of attachment to the larger cultural fabric.

How is this to be done? Obviously a broad knowledge of the period about which the specialist is writing is a pre-requisite. Beyond this, our problem is no different from that facing any historian of ideas, for I would hasten to agree that the history of science is primarily (but not exclusively) the history of *thought* about nature. But what is the place of ideas in history? Nobody, it seems to me, has given a satisfactory answer. Nor do I pretend to do so. But I can only insist upon one truth, or what I take to be a truth: that it is fallacious to make an arbitrary separation between ideas and experience, between thought and action, and to treat ideas as if they had a totally independent life of their own, divorced from material reality. Very possibly, indeed I suspect inevitably, the most abstract ideas — about God and Man and Nature — reflect or express, no less than art and music, the characteristic 'forms' of a given culture, and are shaped by them. Furthermore, abstract ideas of the more exalted kind have a habit of being transformed, indeed often debased, into ideas of cruder coinage and therefore of wider circulation and influence. It is these which men most readily translate into action or, sometimes, by a kind of historical 'Third Law', into justifications for inaction. I suspect it is these kinds of ideas that the historian, in contrast to the philosopher, finds most fruitful for his purposes. To study such operative ideas, it has been argued, is what we often mean, or perhaps should mean, when we speak of 'intellectual history'.

The intimate connexion between thought and action is a notable characteristic of science, the secret indeed — in the case of modern science — of its forward thrust and its immense power to affect our lives. I find the methodological distinction between 'pure' and 'applied' science, between science as thought and science as action upon material things, to be fundamentally deceptive. It forces a choice between viewing science as a kind of philosophy or as mere technical advance. Science is neither of these things, though it partakes of both. As a collective human endeavour — which is one of the ways the historian would like to see it studied, in terms, for example, of its recruitment, support and institutions — it has called upon the talents of many kinds of men, the lone thinker, the gifted experimentalist, the active physician, the skilled draughtsman, the instrument maker — men of peace and men of war.

No human intellectual activity less deserves to be studied in arbitrary isolation. None, unless it be religion, has played a greater social and cultural role. Yet it is these points of contact with the general flow of history that the historian can justly accuse many of us of neglecting. When we overlook the social connexions of scientific thought and action — and I am prepared to argue that no aspect of our subject is more in need of sophisticated treatment — we are not only raising a barrier between his work and ours, but we are in danger of distorting — and this is far more grave in its consequences — our image of science itself.

On Forgotten Sources in the History of Science

GIORGIO DE SANTILLANA

These are going to be some unsystematic remarks about changing fashions in historiography. The field is immense, and the changes in outlying quarters quite bewildering, as Miss von Dechend, my collaborator, might tell us on the strength of an impressive number of examples.

I am going to restrict myself here to one case history, which is within my personal experience, and belongs to the well consolidated field of Greek science. I take it as typical. The conclusions I should like to draw are based, however, on a fairly wide range of present-day 'revision'.

The case in point is the career of Eudoxus. Twenty years ago, I became interested in his relations with Plato, and I found that first of all I had to set his dates right. A great and scrupulous amount of work has been done on the subject since the time of Boeckh (1819). He fixed those dates astronomically, basing himself on the Octaeteris, but with an admitted uncertainty of several years. I started from the other end, Eudoxus's voyage to Egypt. I had to work my way, step by step, through the accumulated ingenious inferences of Unger, Susemihl, Wilamowitz, Hultsch, Wellmann, Tannery, Gisinger, von Fritz, Jaeger, Gelzer, and others. A well-worked territory. In the end I found sufficient evidence to shift down the dates by eighteen years.[1] My conclusions, as far as I know, have been accepted since. The dates stand now at 390–337 B.C. This explains many things. Eudoxus is a contemporary of Plato's old age; that is why Plato never became familiar with 'modern' astronomy. But the point of the story is this: I had been warned at the start by a high authority, who shall be nameless, to be careful and not put too much weight on that tradition of Eudoxus's stay in Egypt. What would he have been doing there, I was told, since the Egyptians had no mathematical astronomy that could be worth anything to him.

This is rather typical. True, Diogenes Laertius is our chief informant, and he is no great mind. In fact, no mind at all.

[1] G. de Santillana, "Eudoxos and Plato", *Isis*, XXXII (1949) 248–62.

But he need not be assumed to lie all the time; besides, there are many more references: Eratosthenes, Strabo, Seneca. It is Seneca who says, speaking of the planetary motions: *Eudoxus primum hos motus in Graeciam transtulit*[1] — Eudoxus was the first who brought those motions to Greece. Diodorus (I, 98) confirms it in different words. This is improbable, say our scholars. If he had wanted planetary tables, Eudoxus would have looked for Babylonian sources.

So Eudoxus went to Egypt by mistake. He did not know what he wanted, apparently. Still the facts are there. We are told in history that Pharaoh protected him on the strength of a letter from Agesilaus, that Chonuphis introduced him, that he made friends with the priests, learned their language, shaved his head and eyebrows and lived like them. Strabo was shown his house in Heliopolis, his observatory in Kerkesoura "where he determined certain celestial motions".

We are asked to admit, then, that the greatest mathematician of Greece learned Egyptian and tried to work on astronomy in Egypt without realizing that he was wasting his time; and when we consider the prodigious amount of creative thought and teaching he crowded into his short span of life, we are asked also to suppose that he spent bootless years in Egypt for some reason possibly of local colour; or maybe even for an interest in exotic literature, for we know through Eratosthenes and "others" that he composed certain "Dialogues of Dogs" translated from the Egyptian into Greek. Here the red pencil of the long-suffering philologist cuts in decisively. "Doubtless", says Hultsch, "we should amend this *kunōn* to *gymnōn*, and understand these as 'dialogues of naked priests'."[2] All right, then it cannot have been Egyptian priests, for they were decently swathed in linen. Or maybe, says Bissing — in fact, no, "beyond doubt" it was really "dogs", the usual animal fables. Eudoxus as an entertainer. We shall hear in a few centuries that Einstein learned Chinese in order to translate the Ching Ping Meh.

Yet, a century ago, a great Egyptologist, Heinrich Brugsch, looking at these data, suggested that Eudoxus must have translated texts from the *Book of the Dead*. There surely are, in those texts, enough dogs, wolves, jackals, dog-faced apes and dog-faced men, Thot the Time-keeper as baboon, and *latrator*

[1] *Nat. quaest.*, VII, 3, 2.

[2] F. Hultsch, in *Real-Encyclopädie*, ed. Pauly-Wissowa, VI, col. 949, sub "Eudoxos".

Anubis as Virgil calls him, who places him in the shield of Aeneas, to supply the title. There is also enough astronomical content, if we look for it, to make them relevant. There are dates of rising and setting of stars, ephemerids, conjunctions of planets, what is needed to give guidance to the soul in its celestial voyage. All this, however, is not in mathematical language as it would be in Babylon. It is strictly in mythical language. But the actions described are so weird and unnatural that, even before analysis, a one-to-one correspondence with something else suggests itself.

It so happens that we have the remnants of more than one cycle of Egyptian animal stories. Spiegeberg and Sethe have proved that the stories in the *Leyden papyrus,*[1] first discussed by Lauth, are tied to the myth of the Lost Eye of the Sun — the Eye that was stolen by Hathor as a cat and recovered by Thoth as a dog-headed ape. F. von Bissing[2] on reviewing the whole material concluded that the tales are authentically Egyptian, but that "it matters little whether they are connected or not with that myth", since they might be of independent origin. They ought to be, he adds, in the nature of a diversion or entertainment. There we go again. Why yes, they might have been so, hundreds of fables never written down must have been for sheer amusement, but in this case the idea is not specially plausible, if we consider (*a*) that the myth of the Lost Eye of the Sun is to be found in more than one civilization, and is a cosmological story; and (*b*) that in Egypt in particular, the Lost Eye of Horus put together again is a central *griphos* in which measure theory is worked out in detail. This insisting that they are "just animal stories" is Euhemerism at bay.

That Eudoxus was seriously concerned with Egyptian myths is sufficiently clear from a passage in Plutarch:[3]

> Eudoxus says that the Egyptians have a mythical tradition in regard to Zeus that, because his legs were grown together, he was not able to walk, and so, for shame tarried in the wilderness; but Isis separating his legs, made him able to move. This teaches us that the mind and reason of the god, fixed amid the unseen and invisible, advanced to generation by reason of motion.

[1] Spiegelberg, *Sitzungsberichte der Preussischen Akademie der Wissenschaften*, phil. hist. Kl., 1915, pp. 876 ff.; cf. idem, *Orientalistische Literaturzeiting*, IX (1916) col. 225–8.

[2] Friedrich Wilhelm Freiherr von Bissing, "Eudoxos von Knidos, Aufenthalt in Aegypten und seine Uebertragung aegyptischer Tierfabeln", *Forschungen und Fortschritte*, XXV (1949) 225–30.

[3] *De Iside et Osiride*, 376 C.

The interpretation is, of course, in the spiritual vein of Plutarch. The Egyptian original must have been more strictly cosmological. But the text is enough to show that Eudoxus the scientist did not take the subject frivolously. The parallel with the Daedalus myth must have been even clearer to him than it is to us. He surely knew of the ritual presentation of Ptah as a wrapped-up mummy, to symbolize the dead rulership. We might add to help him the unbinding of the legs of Saturn's image in the Saturnalia, to symbolize the ghostly return of the deposed ruler, and the binding-up again once his week was finished. The starting out of Zeus with his legs bound must have seemed to Eudoxus a very interesting variant of the general motif of succession of astral powers, well worth investigating. The loss of his works is a major tragedy for knowledge.

All this information has been thrown out of court and utterly forgotten by the Angry Young Men of modern Egyptology, who decreed that all of myth is either political allusions or sun cults, earth cults, the great Unconscious, and various forms of sexual pathology. I will grant that the mythical actions look unnatural enough to enter the great club of *Krafft durch Ebing*. If that is what you want to see.

There still might be brought to bear a few pieces of strictly documentary evidence. There is a well-known letter of Porphyry which says,[1]

> Chairemon the Egyptian and the others presuppose nothing that comes before the visible cosmoi, but they explain the gods of the Egyptians as naught else but the planets and zodiacal figures and their Paranatellonta . . . their myths indicate the periods of visibility and invisibility of stars, their heliacal rising, or the phases of the moon, or the transit of the sun through the positions on the sphere.

It is enough for the critics to see the name of Porphyry on this letter to rule it doubtful, late and out. As for Chairemon, there is a mention of such a name in Strabo, as that of an enthusiastic expounder of Egyptian antiquities whom the Prefect Aelius Gallus found too fancy for his taste. Prefects, especially imperial, are supposed to be men of sound judgment, so poor Chairemon got short shrift from the critics. They overlooked the fact that it is not he who is an author of that remark, but another Chairemon of a generation later, as we can see from the article of Schwartz in Pauly-Wissowa.[2] He seems to

[1] Porphyry in Eusebius, *Praeparatio Evangelica*, III, 4, 1–2; cf. Porfirio, *Lettere ad Anebo*, a cura di G. Faggin (Florence, 1954) (Greek and Italian).

[2] E. Schwartz, in Pauly-Wissowa, III, col. 2025–7, sub "Chairemon".

have been in the same tradition, and probably the heir to the earlier Chairemon's position. But he was himself a man of recognized achievement: Director of the Library of Alexandria, educator of young Nero in A.D. 49, a Stoic philosopher, a grammarian, and explicitly a *hierogrammateus*.[1] He wrote an important work on the hieroglyphic script, which was lost, except for the explanation of nineteen characters transmitted to us by Tzetzes. Those explanations turn out to be excellent by modern criteria, and most illuminating. Thirteen of those characters make astronomical sense. It is difficult to reject his testimony out of hand. Strabo writes that in his own time the Egyptian priest caste had died out, and that they had been uncommunicative to the last. Here is a scholarly Egyptian, their titled successor, who takes it upon himself to say what they had been doing in the past. How can we expect his testimony to be other than late?

These considerations are neither recondite nor peregrine. I used a modern tool like the Pauly-Wissowa to bring this subject to focus, but they can be found explicitly enough in Lauth.

It is refreshing, again, to find such a careful scholar as Lepsius (not, I admit, a contemporary authority) go into the actual symbols of Egyptian documentation available to Eudoxus, and trace there the origin of his models, like the nested spheres. If those are hypotheses, they are still relevant ones. But then his mind had not yet been arrested by modern interpretations.

If we rule out the evidence, then we are left with less than we started with.

We are told repeatedly that Eudoxus brought the planetary motions from Egypt. "Nonsense." It must, "doubtless", be wrong. But then why did he stay in Egypt at all? No answer. It is obvious, say the critics, that he got his data from Babylon, the same way as Hipparchus and Ptolemy did. This is strictly *a priori*, not a shred of proof. Meanwhile, the number of invalidations we have to go through becomes suspiciously high.

We might still get something out of the tiny fragments which have survived. There is one which says that Eudoxus called *beta* of Ursa Minor "the pole of the cosmos". Now even at the best period, about 1000 B.C., that star was only close to the pole, as Hultsch and Gundel remark, wondering why Eudoxus six centuries later was willing to content himself with such an

[1] See Tzetzes *Exeg. in Iliad*, p. 123, 11; *Hist.* V, 395. See also Birch, "On the lost books of Chairemon", *Rev. Archeol.*, I (1851) 16.

approximation. Pogo may have solved this in 1930, when he showed that the Egyptians found the meridian line by observing the superior culmination of *zeta* of Ursa Major before 1500 B.C., and of *beta* Ursa Minor thereafter. In any case, *beta* Ursa Minor was important since 3000 B.C., being used as one of the four points, together with Sirius and Spica, for dividing symmetrically the quadrants of heaven. What suggests itself is a re-examination of those critical words that we translate haphazardly one for the other: *polos*, *ouranos*, *aither*, *olympos*, *itys*, *kosmos*. It might be found that *polos* means a lot of things. It has the same connotations as the Egyptian *merkhet*, the instrument by means of which it was possible for the Pyramid builders to work out orientations with less than 3′ of error.

Since the time of Scaliger — a well-forgotten authority, but not forgotten by Ideler — it was known that *polos* was used as an indicator of time, *horologion*, such as the index of the sun-dial, a natural derivation from the general root *pel* — for turning over — but also relating to measure generally, and to moving alignments. Motion is of the essence.

To take quite another case, when we uniformly translate the Pythagorean doctrine as "transmigration" with chthonic undertones, we are certainly missing something: for the Greek texts have often *peripolesis*, which taken in conjunction with Macrobius's commentary makes pretty exact sense. And apropos of Pythagoreans, did they not in their ritual language call the planets the Hounds of Persephone? The shaggy family of Cynids seems to be dogging our footsteps. But let that be as it may.

The first thing would be to work out techical translations for technical terms, and not rely on purely literary knowledge of ancient languages to get us through. I have never heard yet of a publisher who would call on the same person to translate Agatha Christie and Wolfgang Pauli. It takes admittedly a specialized mathematicisn to translate Archimedes. Why should the criterion not apply to more ancient and obscure astronomical texts? I beg to be allowed to quote not even Vico, but Sir Isaac Newton himself: "It is only through want of skill therein that Interpreters so frequently turn the Prophetic types and phrases to signify whatever their fancies and hypotheses lead them to."[1]

It so happens that the fancies of the Angry Young Men of

[1] I. B. Cohen, "Newton in the light of recent scholarship", *Isis*, LI (1960) 500 ff.

modern orientalism run to earth cults and sun cults, to libido, incest, parricide, and other common tendencies. Hypercritical philology too often lends them a hand, by reducing subjects to intellectual insignificance. They treat texts as if they were written from free association or fortuitous reason, and cause nonsense to blossom forth in persuasive ways. Who knows what new fashion the next generation will bring?

Meanwhile, a prodigious amount of painstaking and penetrating work on archaic science lies under six feet of sod, scorned by successive generations, for debunking is as old as the Enlightenment itself. Where would we be, if we still stood by Voltaire's judgment of Dante? We do not. But in these remote things there is little reclaiming done. I have already mentioned Brugsch, now officially forgotten. The same in varying degrees applies to Boeckh, Ideler, Thimus, Usener, Lepsius, Seyffarth, Lauth, Schlegel . . . so many great and methodic scholars of a century ago. Because they made occasional grave mistakes, as who does not, they are ignored. Their successors try to avoid that risk, because their interpretations are not of the verifiable kind.

The deepest buried is Charles François Dupuis (1742–1809). He wrote before and during the French Revolution. His work contains practically everything that has been found out since on archaic astronomy. He had only the classical sources to work with, practically no correct Oriental texts, and about other parts of the world only the occasional reports of travellers, like La Condamine and Anquetil-Duperron. With these insufficient instruments, he worked out what seems to elude modern researchers. His knowledge of the pre-Socratics, as is also the case with Boeckh, is far more extensive than what can be derived from Hermann Diels, that bible of current scholarship; yet it remains this side of wrong guesses. His *Origines*[1] may be judged extreme, but it is sound, coherent and impressive. Yet he is not even named in Zinner's *History of Astronomy*, nor in Wolf's *History*. Mädler in his great historical work has a brief mention of his books, and adds: "His real merit, however, lies in the invention of the optical telegraph."[2]

But there is worse. The very men who rediscovered his results

[1] Charles François Dupuis, *Origines de tous les religions et tous les cultes* (3 vols., Paris, an III–V; vol. III, pp. 324–67 = *Mémoire sur l'origine des constellations*; Vol. III, Part 2 = *L'origine de la sphère*).

[2] J. H. von Mädler, *Geschichte der Himmelskunde* (2 vols., Braunschweig, 1873).

seem to be only dimly aware of him. The enormous pains taken by Boll and Gundel in reconstructing the different spheres are sheer duplication of effort. Yet Boll mentions Dupuis only twice with some disparaging words. Gundel, in his turn, is led astray by an impossible statement of Macrobius, where a look at Dupuis might have saved him, or failing that, a look at that other forgotten historian of astronomy, Bouché-Leclercq. It is only poetic justice. Such is the dread of loss of modern respectability that it can turn even strong backbones to water.

In very much the same way, in the matter of Chinese astronomy, some wild datings of Schlegel prevented Granet from paying attention to him, and he missed hundreds of good explanations for his collection of mythical material.[1] And now in turn I understand Granet is becoming 'old hat', displaced by Modern Philology. Even Sir James Frazer himself, that Ark of Knowledge, is half forgotten already.

Where would the physical sciences be if fashion compelled them to forget data every two generations? There was nothing wrong in Dupuis that some better information would not have cured. The intellectual achievement remains intact. If we realize that the man had to reconstruct Egyptian astronomy *before* Champollion's decipherment of Egyptian script, that he had to make sense only out of secondary classical — indeed 'late' and most 'doubtful' — classical sources we shall be able to appreciate this statement of his approach:[2]

> Macrobe nous assure, que les hieroglyphes avoient un sens [sc. astronomical]; et la connaissance que nous avons du génie Egyptien, plus encore que le témoignage de Macrobe, nous est un sûr garant; de manière que j'aimerois mieux reconnoître, que je n'ai pu en deviner le sens, que de supposer qu'ils n'y en attachèrent aucun. Les symboles tracés dans le Zodiaque se sont conservés, pendant trop de siècles, sans altérations, et se retrouvent chez trop de peuples, avec les mêmes traits, pour croire qu'ils fussent des signes arbitraires.

There is also, alack, another and more current way of going about it. Let me take as an example a commonplace of Greek mythology, eroded by frequent artistic use until it has lost any meaning. It is the story of Marsyas challenging Apollo to a musical contest, losing and being flayed alive by the god. It

[1] Marcel Granet, *Danses et légendes de la Chine ancienne* (Paris, 1926, Musée Guimet, Bibl. Etudes 64; reprinted 1959), Gustave Schlegel, *Uranographie Chinoise* (La Haye-Leyde, 1875).

[2] Dupuis, *Origines*, III, Part 1, p. 342.

stands there as an oddity, yet some research will yield the end of the story: Apollo was so grieved at what he had done that he broke his lyre, and a new kind of *harmonia* had to be invented. This corresponds to a tradition on another level, that there were two successive inventions of the musical instrument on different scales. Whoever knows the overwhelming importance that was given in archaic thought to measure theory will suspect here a *griphos* of the Pythagorean tradition telling us something about measure units fitted to moving proportions (see the initial meaning of *stoicheion*, not "element" but "step" linked with the *polos*) so as to "fit" (*harmozesthai*) the interlocking measures of the cosmos in motion. This is only a surmise and will have to wait. Very well. Now up comes another case in Mexican mythology. It concerns the celestial god Xipe Totec ("Our Lord the Flayed"), an alias of the Red Tezcatlipoca, in whose name the grisly festival of human flaying was celebrated each year. His other self, the Red Tezcatlipoca, was celebrated at another festival, the greatest of the year. His impersonator, the chief sacrifice of the day, had been kept playing upon the flute through the year of his impersonation. More and more curious, it was understood that the Red One had brought to an end the Golden Age reign of Quetzalcoatl by destroying his city of Tollan, and the means he had used was the flute, in the same manner as the Pied Piper. I am not saying all this is simple, I am suggesting that it might be considered intriguing. Still and all, you will find Xipe Totec presented in the manuals as a standard god of fertility. A distinguished historian of religion, K. T. Preuss, has added a fillip of his own.[1] Given the deplorable ways of those people, he says, the god Xipe "clearly" symbolizes sexual excess. And that is that. I wonder if the Assyrians, who used to flay captured chiefs as a choice form of death under maximum torture, were aware that they were granting them excessive sexual gratification. Either Mr. Preuss must dig up references out of medical literature, or he must tell us this is the way his private fancies run, or something. The inter-subjective element is lacking.

This, I would say, is a fairly typical caricature of the pseudo-Aristotelian or electric pig type of explanation. You dispose of the phenomenon by dropping it down a busy hole, or in any other way that can kill off the curiosity to investigate it.

[1] Konrad Theodor Preuss, "Phallische Fruchtbarkeitsdaemonen als Traeger des altmexikanischen Dramas [Vortrag, 1903]", *Archiv für Anthropologie,* N.F.I., p. 157.

Moving now to a more serious level, I should like to show that even there we find the contrasting approaches. Ludendorff, the profound historian of Maya astronomy, an eminent astronomer himself, has reconstructed the planetary tables of the Mayas. His criterion of interpretation I will give in his own words:[1] "In my opinion it is not permissible to approach these problems with preconceived opinions about what the Mayas can have known and what they cannot. We should rather try to infer what they can have known from the material provided by the codices and inscriptions."

A friend and distinguished colleague of mine with whom I was conversing the other day dismissed Ludendorff's conclusions offhand as "bilge". I wondered what were his reasons, since he has made no particular study of Maya documents. I found them in the pronouncements of the contemporary authority on the subject, Mr. Eric Thompson, a scholar of assured fame. Here is what he says:[2] "This investigation of the divinatory almanacs has established, to my satisfaction at least, that the supposed tables of the planets have nothing to do with the revolutions of those planets, but are merely the preludes to more divinatory almanachs." Mr. Thompson is at least careful, in that he asks us to take as a norm of the truth the measure of his own satisfaction.

The context is this: what Ludendorff had called the Mars cycle of 780 days (=synodic revolution of Mars) has nothing to do with Mars, because it is simply the sum of 3 Tzolkin/Tonalamatl calendaric periods of 260 days each. *Tertium non datur*. The mind is at peace.

This is far from being an isolated case. If you look into the official handbook of chronology, that of Ginzel,[3] you will find that the Egyptian Triakontaeteris, the thirty-year Sed festival, had nothing to do with astronomical phenomena, "auf keinen Fall". It so happens that this time Ginzel can be caught flatfooted by documentation that he had overlooked; it is all the more embarrassing in that his predecessor Letronne had explicitly suggested the link with Saturn. It was just to dispose of him that he had written: "auf keinen Fall".

[1] Hans Ludendorff, "Untersuchungen zur Astronomie der Maya, X" *Sitzungsberichte der Preussischen Akademie der Wissenschaften*, phys. math. Kl., V (1936) 85.

[2] J. Eric Thompson, *Maya Hieroglyphic Writing* (Washington, 1950, Carnegie Institute Publications No. 589) 293.

[3] F. K. Ginzel, *Handbuch der Chronologie*, I, 178.

I could go on with dozens of such examples.

This, I should like to submit, is a problem in philosophy of science, in the chapter on the reductionist fallacy. It is very true, we are all witnesses, that good minds can work themselves into paranoia, or at least paraphrenia, looking for complicated patterns that do not exist. Kepler is a borderline case, and a warning. We have to use our judgement.

There is a good rule for historians that I always treasured when I was working on my *Galileo*:[1] Never underestimate the power of foolishness and inanity in human affairs. It breeds situations which are almost impossible to unravel. True. We need only look at the historical scene today. Yet we see at work also a contrary force: prodigious amounts of intelligence and ingenuity which are often brought to frustration and ground to dust in the mill of the gods. This is historical reality. This is life.

Galileo established forever the principles of exact science against the Aristotelians, when he wrote that one necessary reason, once found, destroys utterly a thousand merely probable reasons. This idea is the cornerstone of physics, and we have done very well by it in the centuries that followed. But as soon as we leave the territory of direct and continuous experimental check — what Galileo expressively called the ordeal — and take this as a philosophical guide to explanation, dangers begin to arise.

The danger is clearly exemplified in Descartes, who thought he could proceed from absolutely clear, hence safe, scientific principles to build up a philosophy. We know how he built up a universe, from planetary motions and sunspots to the fabric of the body, by simple mechanisms. And since these, he said, sufficed to explain everything, you needed nothing else. *Frustra fit per plura quod fieri potest per pauciora*, everyone was agreed. I think few appreciate — and Crombie will bear me out — what a prodigious feat of intelligence it took. Nonetheless, it proved wrong. But something of it has remained in science: 'Let's try for the simple way', 'let us take apart the complex situation into simple elements'. It has bred that open catenary logic which carried scientific discourse right along into our own times, when it broke against the circular subtleties of organic systems, of feedback and end-point control. Our teleological mechanisms would have been the despair of Descartes.

[1] G. de Santillana, *The Crime of Galileo* (Chicago, 1955); also revised text in Italian translation *Processo a Galileo* (Milano, 1960).

To give a very early example of the conflict, Fabricius of Acquapendente observed the valves in the veins, and theorized that they prevented blood from accumulating in the extremities. His pupil Harvey discovered the circulation of the blood, and to him it became clear: the valves are there to prevent backflow. He considered Fabricius's explanation void and superseded. As it turned out, both were right. The explanations converged.

When the Cartesian procedure went over into the human and historic sciences, it wrought havoc from the start. That particular fallacy goes under the name of Cleopatra's Nose. We translated problems into simple elements without the check that natural science provides. The great equivocation between truth and simplicity was allowed to fester. When the scientist starts going wrong with his questions, nature has a brutal way of answering by short-circuits, explosions, lethal outcomes, queer behaviours; or simply by a stubborn non-response. But the material of the historian or philologist does not fly in his face in a blowing of fuses and a bursting of test tubes, with dying animals or spots going the wrong way on the scale. It bends hypocritically to his will, becomes as dumb or misguided as requested. With infinite perversity, it works up invisibly to delayed reactions which may bring whole edifices of theory crumbling down, but in such a confusing way that no one can figure out who made the first mistake. To be sure, revisions come in all the time, but for lack of any *experimentum crucis* they have to fit into the initial fabric. And so, now that refined philology has given us an imposing array of texts which are allowed to make so-called psychological sense or next to none, we go on adorning their authors with more traits of the so-called Primitive Mentality, to correspond. Still, that grand master of classical philology, August Boeckh, had warned us 150 years ago that if the ancients speak at times in strange ways, we should not conclude that their thoughts were so strange as all that.

The central and simple fact that we have forgotten is that the ancients, like the men of the Renaissance, thought in terms of different but convergent and continuously adjusting levels of truth. This is the presupposition of a Cosmos, that idea that was done to death by Descartes. Kepler was still entirely an ancient. Even Galileo came to grief by trying to fit into his new method the idea of perfect circles and circular inertia that he thought necessary to preserve the order of the cosmos. There was a Pythagorean in him that would not die.

The idea of a correspondence between various levels of reality, of a continually moving and shifting correspondence as the elements are carried along in the eternal circular motion of the cosmos — seems to strike our modern critics as outlandish and contrived. Yet it is the essence of that synoptic vision, as I characterized it years ago, which belongs to the archaic mind, and that the modern poet ingeniously disguised under the hieroglyph: seeing the world steadily and seeing it whole.

I have mentioned Galileo still fighting a rear-guard action, like Einstein, against the ideas he himself had unleashed upon the world. His perfect circles were, so to speak, residues of hieroglyphs. When you come to the first deliberate anti-Cartesian reaction, I mean G. B. Vico, you need only look at the frontispiece engraving of the *Scienza Nuova*, to see a pathetic attempt at reviving hieroglyphic symbolism to express a modern theory. There is an inherent logic in certain forms.

It should be the intellectual historian's task to grasp that synoptic vision, to etch it out in its full strength and almost obsessive complexity, guided by such evidence as that of Pythagorean texts, rather than wash it off into chains of almanacs. The acosmism which permeates modern thought brings such catenary notions even to the minds of scholars innocent of any philosophical inspiration. Let alone, then, to the technicians and dialecticians of what we like to call 'a growing world'.

And so, by way of these celestial loops, back to Eudoxus. Next to the homocentric spheres, his great achievement is the Octaeteris. This is currently presented as a good straight luni-solar cycle. But it would be wrong to tear it out of the context of that programme which is expressed in Plato's speculations about the Great Year. The early so-called Philolaic cycle of 59 years inscribed by Oinopides on a bronze tablet in Olympia was not very accurate as a luni-solar cycle, even making allowances for the state of the art. Boeckh was struck by this inaccuracy, but Kugler's[1] tables of planetary periods make it sufficiently clear that the 59-year-period already counted in Babylonian times as a reasonable approximation to two sidereal revolutions of Saturn. We might leave it at that were it not that Ludendorff has remarked that 59 years, neat, is the period in which the synodic and sidereal cycles of Saturn come

[1] August Boeckh, *Philolaos des Pythagoraeers Lehren nebst den Bruchstuecken seines Werkes* (Berlin, 1819) 136; Franz Xaver Kugler, S.J., *Sternkunde und Sterndienst in Babylonien* (2 vols., Münster, 1907–12) I, 43.

to a fit. This might be better and more architectonic, not at all excluding the other reason, and if we go back to Greece, we may find some more reasons. The bronze tablet of Oinopides with the 59-year *eniautos* or Great Year was set up in Olympia. Now Olympia is traditionally the place where the great struggle between Kronos and Zeus took place, and it is fair to infer that Oinopides had the Jupiter-Saturn conjunction in mind, the so-called Great Conjunction, which takes place every 59·5779 years and has been in the astronomers' mind forever. The 59-year cycle (if we take into account the lunations) has therefore a quadruple motivation, and this explains why a certain looseness seemed acceptable, seeing that it is so strongly fitted and counter-fitted.

The eight-year cycle that Eudoxus brought in, the Octaeteris, was really precise. Of its stemming back to Egypt there is no question. He actually fitted the beginning of his own Octaeteris to the start of the Egyptian Tetraeteris. Notwithstanding the calendaric importance of the Tetraeteris (cf. the Olympiads), it was the eight cycle that counted from the beginning. This eight cycle seems to repeat itself obsessively on all scales, with greater and greater 'years', up to the 11,340-year cycle which is made up of 8 Sothic periods, that is, of 8 Syrius cycles, as Julius Caesar Scaliger and then Ideler proved out of a famous passage of Herodotus.[1] Incidentally, I should like to challenge any one of my readers to write down a complicated piece of information that he cannot really understand with as much accuracy as did Herodotus. Let this be said *en passant*.

But why this obsessive eight, repeated in so many patterns, contexts, hieroglyphs, seals and cylinders throughout the Near East? It is here that Miss von Dechend, I think, has cleared up the matter for us. It is because eight civil years, or more precisely 2920 days, plus or minus one, are eight Julian years (as they were to be called), and at the same time the Venus cycle: 5 synodic and 13 sidereal revolutions of Venus, plus 99 lunations to boot, conclude themselves in eight years exactly. This made Venus into the great timekeeper: and not only in the Near East, but in many civilizations. Ludendorff's conjectures would seem then to be supported by circumstantial historical evidence. Modern critics who have never looked at the planets, and who certainly formed no synoptic view of their paths in

[1] Cf. Ludwig Ideler, *Handbuch der mathematischen und technischen Chronologie*, I, 137 ff.

heaven, may hold all such considerations as improbable and far-fetched. But look at the diagram subjoined (fig. 1), that I owe to Mr. Hinze, and tell me what ancient heart could have resisted it. We have here, limned in the skies, the original model of the Pythagorean Pentagram, which was the symbol of the Tetraktys. Moreover, as far as the Greeks go, the numbers 5, 8, 13 evoked the Golden Section, which goes into the building of the pentagon, as had been known since the early times of Pythagoreanism.

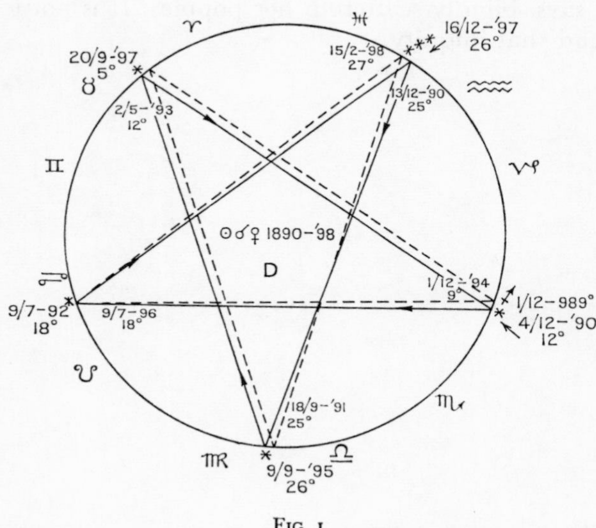

FIG 1

Shall we say that such things were utterly absent from the mind of Eudoxus, Plato's friend, as he was working on cycles? And that he found no help in Egypt?

Quite a number of years ago, I found out on incontrovertible evidence that something like it was certainly in the mind of Parmenides, as he set up his goddess of Truth, Aphrodite Urania, as the "Daimon who steers all things".[3] Parmenides, if you look in the philosophical textbooks where he stands as the inventor of the logic of implication, would not have been *prima facie* the most likely character for such thoughts. His mythological Proem is too often discussed as a perfunctory rhetorical introduction. It had been forgotten that he, too, had been a Pythagorean.

Cosmic and cyclic thought has its own methods of analysis,

but they are not ours. It has different objects of relevance, a deeper focus. We should not ask it to adjust to our own preconceptions about what Primitives may have seen or not seen in the multiple dial of the heavens. The men of archaic Greece thought of the sun and moon, surely, but they ignored our exclusion principle of 'This *or* That'. For them it was: "This, and all the more so insomuch as it is mathematically *also* that."

Let me suggest, then, that we look back into the great astronomical historians of the past, before we proceed on the way of interpretation. The iniquity of oblivion, as Sir Thomas Browne says, blindly scattereth her poppies. It is not for us to compound that iniquity.

29

Historiography of Science in Russia

V. P. ZUBOV

The history of science is sometimes called a young discipline. From one point of view this is true, but taken more broadly, the history of science has a considerable stretch of life behind it. It is hardly necessary to mention Eudemus: every scientist when tackling a new question will inevitably seek to know what has been accomplished by his predecessors, to know the existing material relating to his problem.

This interest assumes different forms in different branches of science. Mathematicians, physicists and chemists, unlike geographers, botanists or zoologists, do not feel the need for an exact knowledge of precise, dated facts relating to the more or less distant past. If the 'recipe' for obtaining oxygen is known, then the where, when and by whom this knowledge was obtained is of secondary interest. It was a very different matter when little-known areas of the globe were to be investigated; in this case it was necessary to have exact information about who had visited these lands, and when, and where, in order to plot out routes, to start off with the fullest possible knowledge about climatic and meteorological conditions and so on.

As far back as the eighteenth century, Russian historiography of science provides an interesting example. During the great northern expedition of 1733–43 the question arose whether climatic conditions permitted the journey to be continued in winter. It was settled by a study of archive material dealing with earlier journeys.[1]

The same thing can be found in the history of medicine. Here, too, there are many phenomena which can be studied only historically. This is the case, for instance, with epidemiology, in which neither experiment nor direct observation are possible, and the scientist can only investigate by comparative

[1] V. P. Zubov, *Историография естественных наук в России. XУIII в. - первая половина XIX в.* (*Historiography of Natural Sciences in Russia; Eighteenth and First Half of Nineteenth Centuries*) (Moscow, 1956) 5. For more detailed information on the period indicated in the title, reference should be made to this book. More precise references are given further only for the succeeding periods.

historical methods the incidence of epidemics over a long period. Since the question of public health is linked up with measures taken by the state, it has been necessary to turn to history every time the question arose of codification of reforms in medical administration and related matters.

It is therefore not surprising that the history of geographical investigation and the history of medicine should, in Russia too, have attracted the attention of scholars earlier than that of other branches of science.

In botany and zoology also, the historical point of view is essential. Here, it is not only bibliographical summaries that I have in mind, the need for which arose fairly early among systematists and morphologists, being dictated by the necessity of co-ordinating previous observations and of unifying nomenclature. Alterations in the composition of flora and fauna and the disappearance of some organic forms frequently make a certain work or a certain depiction of a plant or animal a unique and irreplaceable source. An instance of this is the notes of G. Steller (1709–46) on *Rhytina borealis* and his picture of it, found in the archives by P. Pekarsky (1869), when this animal had long ago been exterminated by Siberian hunters.

In the history of geology the best example is perhaps a large work by V. Obruchev (1862–1956), *History of Geological Research in Siberia*, published in Leningrad in 1931–47. The idea of such a work first occurred to the author in 1880, when he was engaged on practical geological work in Irkutsk. The book gradually expanded to become an all-embracing history of Siberian geological prospecting, extending far beyond the bounds of narrowly practical needs.

Even in its first stages, historiography of science was not limited to a mere registration of accomplished work in the interests of the further development of science itself. From days long past, the history of science has had the important educational purpose of showing, concretely and visibly, the strength and power of science.

It is noteworthy that when the St. Petersburg Academy of Sciences was opened, the two first speeches presented characteristically eighteenth-century purposes for the historiography of science: the first didactic and educational, the second concerning tasks connected with the needs of science itself. At the first formal meeting on 17 December 1725, G. Bülfinger delivered a speech which included a fairly broad historical section. Its purpose was to trace the gradual unification of scientific effort, the gradual change from scattered individual research to the solution of scientific problems by the combined work of large groups. At the second formal meeting (1 August 1726), J. Hermann took as his theme the history of geometry, regarding the gathering of knowledge of what had already been accomplished as the basic task of historiography of science: we must avoid the re-discovery of that which has already been discovered.

Finally, the need to include the history of science in the general historical picture of human progress was noted quite early, and very definitely. For Russia of the eighteenth century, too, the concept which characterized historiography of science in Western Europe at the end of the seventeenth century became a determining factor: the progress of modern science was sharply contrasted to the previous period of darkness.[1] Copernicus, Kepler, Huygens and Newton personified the first and real triumph of knowledge over age-old ignorance. Lomonosov returned frequently to this theme in the middle of the eighteenth century. I feel impelled to quote his eloquent words:

> Pythagoras sacrificed a hundred oxen to Zeus for the discovery of one geometrical rule. If his superstitious example were jealously followed for each of the rules discovered at the present time by clever mathematicians, it would be difficult to find sufficient oxen in the whole world.[2]

It is hardly necessary to state that such works as Diderot's *Encyclopédie* and Voltaire's works, specifically his *Essai sur les moeurs et l'esprit des nations* (1749) were well known in Russia.[3] During 1779–81, the journal *Academical News* printed an abridged translation of Montucla's *Histoire des mathématiques*.

The beginning of the nineteenth century saw a reform of higher education in Russia and the opening of a number of new establishments of higher education. To this period, too,

[1] Cf. my essay, "Les conceptions historico-scientifiques du XVIIe siècle", *Actes du Symposium international des sciences physiques et mathématiques dans la première moitié du XVIIe siecle. Pise-Vinci 16–17 Juin 1958* (Paris, 1960) 74–97.

[2] M. V. Lomonosov, *Preface to the Russian Translation of "Institutiones philosophiae experimentalis" by L. Tümmig, Полное собрание сочинений* (*Collected Works*, I, Moscow–Leningrad, 1950) 424. The Russian translation was first published in 1746.

[3] A. C. Crombie, "Historians and the scientific revolution", *Endeavour* (1960) 2–13 gives a very clear picture of the importance of Voltaire's writings for the history of science.

belong the first collected summaries of the history of various branches of science and technology specifically in Russia. Among them were historical summaries of Russian mining and Russian medicine. These were part of preparations for a reform in the mining and medical administrative bodies. Consequently, organizational questions held priority place in their contents. It may also be remembered that 1803 saw the beginning of a series of Russian circumnavigations, which attracted the attention of the whole scientific world of that day. It is therefore not surprising that the third sphere in which historical research developed fairly broadly, although not to the extent of publication of collective summaries, should have been the history of navigation.

It is important that even in those days, certain research works on the history of science were carried out jointly. A programme of such research was laid down in the new Medico–Surgical Academy (instituted in St. Petersburg in 1798 on the basis of the existing Medico–Surgical School). This produced articles on the history of medicine in Russia, a *History of Mineralogy* by A. Teryayev (1819) with a special chapter on Russia, and a *History of Entozoology* (i.e. parasitology) by I. Spassky (1824). The work of a group of scientists formed the basis for a monograph by W. Richter, *Geschichte der Medizin in Russland*, published in Moscow in German (1813) and subsequently in a three-volume Russian translation (1814–20).

Further attempts to summarize the work of Russian scientists in specific spheres were made by the botanist R. Trautvetter (1809–89)[1] and the zoologist J. Brandt (1802–79), who, however, limited his review to the activities of the St. Petersburg Academy.[2] These works were designed in the first place to satisfy the practical needs of science itself. Ch. Rouiller (1814–58) of Moscow University covered a much broader area in his "Appel à MM. les zoologistes de la Russie"[3] written in 1839, a paper containing a broad programme for the collection of material on the history of zoology in Russia. Some years later Rouiller paid considerable attention to the history of science

[1] R. Trautvetter, *Grundriss einer Geschichte der Botanik in Bezug auf Russland* (St. Petersburg, 1837).

[2] J. Brandt, *Versuch einer kurzen Übersicht der Fortschritte, welche die zoologischen Wissenschaften den von der Akademie der Wissenschaften zu St. Petersburg von 1831 bis 1879 herausgegebenen Schriften verdanken* (St. Petersburg, 1879).

[3] *Bulletin de la Société des naturalistes de Moscou*, XII (1839), No. 2, 308–11.

in the programme he drew up for a university course in zoology.

Rouiller linked up the historical approach to scientific phenomena with his general evolutionary concepts.[1] In the sphere of biology, too, he demanded a "historical" approach. From this point of view, his speech "On the animals of the Moscow area" is indicative. As an ideal, he demanded "the presentation of a living picture of the most ancient Moscow fauna and information on its movements, how and when one animal disappeared and another reappeared". The scientific ideal, he considered, was to be, to the greatest possible extent, a "duplicate and portrait of nature", that is to say, to reflect its movement and its unity. Science, Rouiller considered, is in constant motion, it advances from the perception of fragmentary, individual phenomena to the perception of the general connexion between them. It is the incompleteness and fragmentary nature of our knowledge which gives rise to a belief in the supernatural and miraculous.

It is not difficult to find much in common between the ideas of Rouiller and those of Herzen in his brilliant *Letters on the Study of Nature* (1845), in which he presented the philosophical problems of scientific evolution in the broadest sense and gave many expressive portraits of the leading thinkers and naturalists of the past.

In speaking of historians of science of this period, the astronomer D. Perevoshchikov (1788–1880) must not be ignored. This eminent popularizer of science made constant use of historical summaries as the best means to make the essence of one science or another clear to the reader or hearer. It was Perevoshchikov who translated (1861) the biographies of famous astronomers, physicists and geometricians written by F. Arago. He also engaged in research into the history of Russian science. His services in the study of the scientific work of Lomonosov are of particular importance. In the period 1829–65, Perevoshchikov called attention a number of times to discoveries by Lomonosov which had been either forgotten or insufficiently valued.

Beginning with the 1850's, the pedagogical importance of the history of science began to fill an increasingly prominent place. The demand that teaching be based on the "logic of discovery",

[1] In recent years the works of Rouiller have attracted lively attention among our historians of science, V. Petrov, S. Mikulinsky, B. Raikov and others. In 1954 the *Selected Biological Works* of Rouiller were published (*Избранные биологические произведения*, Moscow).

the disclosure of "the paths by which great discoveries in the study of Nature had been achieved", was the foundation of a textbook on physics for secondary schools written by N. Lyubimov (1830–97), a pupil of Perevoshchikov. It was first published in 1861.[1]

The same pedagogical problems led V. Bobynin (1849–1919) to study the history of science. Bobynin began as a teacher of mathematics in a secondary school.[2] He was almost the first scientist in Russia to devote himself entirely to a study of the history of his subject. His works deal mainly with the early period in the development of mathematics. He contributed a great deal to the study of the history of mathematics in Russia.[3] Bobynin was the first person in Russia to give a special course on the history of mathematics. This course was instituted in Moscow University in 1882–3, and he continued his lectures up to the end of his life. It should be noted that when he began them, they were an innovation, and not only in Russia.

The many years of devoted work done by Bobynin in publishing his historico-mathematical journal[4] provide eloquent testimony to the difficulties which had to be overcome in old Russia. This was the fifth journal of its kind in Europe.[5] Beginning in 1885, Bobynin financed it from his own limited resources and was its only contributor. After long and vain effort, he was forced to close it down in 1894. An attempt to revive the journal under another name in 1899 was also a

[1] Lyubimov wrote a *History of Physics* (*История физики*, 3 vols., 1892–6) which was not at all bad for his time. His *Philosophy of Descartes* (*Философия Декарта*, 1886) contains a Russian translation of the *Discours de la méthode*, with commentary.

[2] Cf. my article, "В. В. Бобынин и его труды по истории математики" *Труды Института истории естествознания и техники Академии Наук СССР* ("V. V. Bobynin and his works on the history of mathematics", *Works of the Institute of History of Natural Science and Technology under the Academy of Sciences of the USSR*), XV (1956) 277–322.

[3] Particular mention should be made of his excellent *Русская физико-математическая библиография* (*Russian Physico-Mathematical Bibliography*), which covers literature from 1587 to 1816 inclusively (3 vols., Moscow, 1886–1900) and his *Очерки истории развития физико-математических знаний в России* (*Outlines of the History of the Development of Physico-Mathematical Knowledge in Russia*), I, Parts 1–2 (Moscow, 1886–93).

[4] *Физико-математические науки в их настоящем и прошедшем* (*Physico-Methematical Sciences, their Present and Past*), 1885–94, 13 vols.

[5] *Bulletin de bibliographie, d'histoire et de biographie mathématique* began coming out in 1865, the *Bulletino* of Buoncampagni in 1868, *Zeitschrift für Mathematik und Physik* (Hist.-phil. Kl.) in 1871 and *Bibliotheca mathematica* in 1884.

failure; only one volume came out, containing 12 issues, the printing of which dragged out till 1905.[1]

Bobynin divided the historiography of science into several stages. The first stage consists, in his own words, in "descriptive history", when no noticeable differentiation exists between the history of science and of its auxiliary branches, biography and bibliography. As a final aim Bobynin regarded the history of science as a most important basis for the philosophy of science. Unfortunately, his own philosophical generalizations were insufficient and his main services lay in the sphere of "descriptive history". It must be said that Bobynin's main interest as a pedagogue was directed not so much towards concrete history, as towards mathematical psychology and its evolution; it was in the early stages of human development that Bobynin sought the key to the psychology of the child of school age. Some indifference to the concrete historical and philological aspects in the study of mathematical texts was particularly marked in his estimation of the work of the Russian historian N. Bubnov, publisher of the *Scripta mathematica* of Gerbert (1899) and author of a number of valuable papers on the history of medieval mathematics.

In speaking of Russian historians of mathematics of that period, one cannot omit A. Vasilyev of Kazan (1853–1929) and I. Timchenko of Odessa (1862–1939). The former did much for the study of non-Euclidean geometry and the work of Lobachevsky. He took an energetic part in organizing suitable honours to be paid to the great Russian mathematician on the centenary of his birth (1893), he worked for the establishment of a Lobachevsky fund to provide international prizes for the best works on non-Euclidean geometry, and participated in the organization of the *Bibliotheca Lobachewskiana* by the Kazan Naturalist Society, the purpose of which was to collect all the works on non-Euclidean geometry. Vasilyev himself wrote a number of valuable historical papers in this sphere, and in many other spheres concerning the history and philosophy of mathematics.

In Odessa, Timchenko collected a rich library on the history of mathematics, which included among others such bibliographical treasures as the first (*c.* 1477) edition of Richard Swineshead's *Liber calculationum*, which bibliographers of the

[1] *Физико-математические науки в ходе их развития* (*Physico-Mathematical Sciences in the Course of their Development*), I (the only volume, 1899–1904).

beginning of the eighteenth century called a book *corvo albo rarior*. It was with Timchenko as editor, and with his remarks and numerous addenda, that F. Cajori's *History of Elementary Mathematics* was published in Russian in 1910 (second revised edition 1917). The most important of Timchenko's historical works is a monograph on the evolution of the theory of analytical functions up to the beginning of the nineteenth century (1892–9).

Naturally, the work of zoologists and botanists begun in the first half of the nineteenth century was continued in the second. Suffice it to mention work done by the zoologist A. Bogdanov[1] (a pupil of Rouiller), the botanist V. Lipsky (1863–1937),[2] the zoologist Th. Köppen (1833–1908),[3] and many others.

Bogdanov deliberately took the line of collecting biographical material first. Believing that the historians of science still "remain at the stage of the past heroic period", he wrote: "Battles are of course won by generals, who play an important role, but shall we understand the very essence of the victory if, in studying the conditions which are the result of the battle, we look only at the general, honour only him and consider it unnecessary to look at those who helped him, who implemented his plans, who carried them out? What would happen to science if we were all generals in it, and there was no army doing the work?"[4] Bogdanov's somewhat one-sided concentra-

[1] A. Bogdanov, *Материалы для истории научной и прикладной деятельности по зоологии и соприкасающимся с нею отраслям знания* (*Materials for the History of Scientific and Applied Activities in Russia in Zoology and Related Branches of Knowledge*) (4 vols., Moscow, 1888–92).

[2] *Флора Кавказа. Свод сведений о флоре Кавказа за 200-летний период ее исследования, начиная от Турнефора и кончая XIX в.* (*Flora of the Caucasus. Collected Information on the Flora of the Caucasus in Two Hundred Years of Investigation, beginning with Tournefort and ending with the Nineteenth Century*) (St. Petersburg, 1899; Supplement: St. Petersburg, 1902). Lipsky also compiled numerous bibliographical summaries in the jubilee edition, *С. Петербургский ботанический са за 200 лет его существования* (*The St. Petersburg Botanical Garden in the 200 Years of its Existence*) (St. Petersburg, 1913–15).

[3] Th. Köppen, *Bibliotheca zoologica rossica. Literatur über die Tierwelt Gesammtrusslands bis zum Jahre 1885 incl.*, Bd. I–II (St. Petersburg, 1905–8). These volumes complete the "general section". The "special section" was not printed and is preserved in the archives of the Academy of Sciences. Köppen began collecting material as far back as 1875. In his bibliography he registered not only sources and historical articles, but even literature on folklore related in any way to animals.

[4] A. Bogdanov, *К. Ф. Рулье и его предшественники по кафедре зоологии в Московском университете* (*Ch. F. Rouiller and his Predecessors in the Zoology Chair at Moscow University*) (Moscow, 1885), 96.

tion on *dii minores* brought objections, from K. Timiryazev among others. But nevertheless, Bogdanov's book is a useful handbook still.

Another pupil of Rouiller, S. Usov (1827–86), like his teacher, approached the problem of history more broadly, organically combining a study of zoology with the study of archaeology and history. He had to turn to the historical aspect in 1860, when writing his *magister* thesis on the aurochs. He made a typical statement at an annual session in Moscow university, in a speech whose theme was somewhat unusual: "On Unicorns" (1877)

> Science has branched out and developed at the present time to such a stage that it is not possible even to be an encyclopaedist without extreme superficiality. Lacking the assistance of philologists, explorers and ethnographers (or their works), the zoologist has not the means to cope with even such a small problem as that of unicorns. We often hear that science is all-powerful. Yes, this is indisputable, but only when we understand by the word 'science' not merely some branch of human knowledge, but knowledge as a whole. In a specialist school my subject would be quite simply out of place. In the *universitas litterarum*, where the main branches of human knowledge are taught alongside one another, where the medical specialist every day meets the astronomer, the philologist meets the zoologist, the jurist meets the mathematician, it is quite another matter.[1]

It must, incidentally, be emphasized that in the second half of the nineteenth century the main stimulus in the study of more distant periods in the history of science and technology continued to come mainly from historians, historians of literature or archaeologists. For instance, a serious piece of research on astronomical phenomena mentioned in the Russian chronicles was undertaken by D. Svyatsky (1915) on the suggestion of S. Shakhmatov, a well-known scholar of these chronicles. It was also historians of literature who published works of research on the majority of ancient scientific texts. It is typical that the first summary on the history of science in Russia from the eleventh to the seventeenth centuries by T. Rainov (1940), who deliberately limited himself to the examination of published sources, without resorting to manuscripts, contains references to a large number of works by historians of literature.

In the same way, the main stimulus for the chemical

[1] S. Usov, *Сочинения* (*Works*), I (Moscow, 1888), 363.

investigation of ancient materials, specifically of colours and metals, continued to come from archaeologists and historians of art. One may mention, for instance, a valuable collection of quotations from ancient manuscripts with recipes for preparing colours and other technical instructions published by P. Simon (1906). The author himself regarded it as part of large-scale research into the history of books and libraries in Russia.[1]

The situation is somewhat different with the history of early Russian medicine; the physicians L. Zmeyev (1832–1901) and V. Florinsky (1833–99) published several texts and descriptions of early Russian manuscripts. The remarks of such a leading Slavonic philologist as A. Sobolevsky, however, disclosed obvious dilettantism in the work of Zmeyev. Serious attention was paid to the early period of medicine in general (and in particular to Russian medicine) by M. Lakhtin of Moscow (1869–1932).

It is not possible for us to dwell at length on the works of our orientalists. Here, first mention should be given to the work of the Rev. Hyacynthe Bitchurin (1777–1853) and in the second half of the nineteenth century to the well-known work of E. Bretschneider (1833–1901) on China[2] and various sources of the history of Chinese science, particularly Chinese astronomy, collected by K. Skachkov (1821–83).[3]

Among works dealing with research on ancient scientific texts, attention should be paid to the first publications relating to the Egyptologist V. Golenishchev's collection: by A. Bekström on the pharmacological papyrus (1903) and by B. Turayev on the mathematical papyrus (1917).[4]

For a long time a large number of research investigations (particularly into Arabic geographical work) were of an auxiliary nature to the general historical study of Eastern Europe, and specifically of Russia. In I. Krachkovsky (1883–1951), however, who made a study of Arabic geographical

[1] Laboratory analysis of ancient colours was subsequently undertaken by the chemists V. Shchavinsky (1935) and P. Lukyanov; cf. his monograph on the history of chemical handicrafts and the chemical industry in Russia, *История химических промыслов и химической промышленности в России*; the first volume came out in 1948.

[2] Especially his big *History of European Botanical Discoveries in China* (1899).

[3] In his lifetime Skachkov published only a few short articles on the history of science.

[4] The last-mentioned was subsequently published in full by Academician W. Struve, *Mathematischer Papyrus des Staatl. Museum der schönen Künste in Moskau* (Berlin, 1930).

literature for many years, up to his death, we have an example of the way in which the study of this subject too gradually became a field of specialized study.[1]

In the sphere of general philosophical problems, the ideas of the revolutionary democrats exerted a great influence on the history of science in the second half of the nineteenth century. Articles by N. Chernyshevsky and D. Pisarev drew the attention of the young to actual questions of natural history. Such scientists as K. Timiryazev and I. Pavlov subsequently spoke of their great importance.

It was these ideas of the 1860's that provided the inspiration for a series, *Lives of Outstanding Men*, which was undertaken at the end of the century by the popularizer F. Pavlenkov. This series included the biographies of such Russian scientists as Lomonosov, Lobachevsky, Kovalevskaya, Pirogov, Przhevalsky, and of a large number of foreign scientists. At the time, the series played a great role in enlightenment and education.

At approximately the same time (1900) the chemist V. Markovnikov (1837–1904), opening a meeting in celebration of the 150th anniversary of the first Russian chemical laboratory, organized by Lomonosov, said:

> To whom are the highest honours most frequently paid? To whom are monuments set up even during their lifetime? These monuments, sometimes built of guns captured from an enemy, usually remind one at the same time of tens of thousands of human lives. . . . But there is another type of public leader, outwardly more modest. Their achievements are not glorified by public celebrations and triumphal decorations. Often it is only future generations, comprehending all the fruitfulness of their work for the public good, and the power of brain and talent which was its motive force, who extend to them deserved gratitude. If the people will learn to recognize and honour first and foremost such heroes as these, then they will have the right to consider that they have reached the highest point in cultural development.[2]

It should be recalled here that thirteen years previously, in 1887, the Minister of Public Education, Delyanov, had not permitted a contributors' list to be drawn up for erecting a monument to the chemist Butlerov in Kazan.

In this connexion, interest attaches to a statement by another

[1] Krachkovsky's summarized research in this sphere remained unfinished.

[2] *Ломоносовский сборник* (*Lomonosov, Collected Papers*) (Moscow, 1901), 13–14.

chemist, N. Menshutkin (1842–1907), in the preface to his *Outline of the Development of Chemical Ideas* (1888), the first original summary in Russian on this subject. In his book, Menshutkin concentrated on the history of chemical ideas, beginning with the phlogiston theory, regarding the history of discoveries and the history of methods in experimental research as being more in place in a course of chemistry. Here, then, in the history of chemistry another tendency appears — to examine the history of ideas and problems apart from biographies.

A considerable number of papers on the history of biology came from K. Timiryazev (1843–1920), ranging from those on special questions, to synthetic pictures of the development of biology in the nineteenth century, and of science as a whole. Their specific feature is a deep interest in philosophical problems of natural history.

At the same time, Timiryazev's attention was always drawn to the personalities of leading scientists. He could justly be called a master of literary portraiture. Towards the end of his life he wrote:

> I have always been attracted to history. And my thought has always been especially drawn to the tragic greatness of fighters for truth and freedom in all its forms who were fated to fall victims in this struggle: the Gracchi, John Huss, More, Bruno, Galileo and Robespierre.[1]

Among Timiryazev's biographical outlines, the reader remembers in particular his brilliant characterization of Pasteur, Berthelot and Boussingault, and a series of articles on Darwin, including an excellent description of his visit to Down and his meeting with Darwin in 1877 (this essay was written for the centenary of the birth of the great English scientist, in 1909).

A convinced democrat, painfully conscious of the hard conditions under which science had to develop in Czarist Russia, Timiryazev was always able to give a propagandist edge to his literary portraits of Russian and foreign scientists, resorting to analogies or contrasts in sketching in the social background, compelling the Russian reader to ponder over the crying shortcomings in Russian life.

In an atmosphere of growing interest in the work of leading scientists, a more thorough study of the scientific papers of Lomonosov began towards the end of the nineteenth century. If one omits Perevoshchikov and certain others, the biography

[1] Timiryazev, *Сочинения* (*Works*), IX (Moscow, 1939) 281.

and work of Lomonosov had been studied in the nineteenth century mainly by historians and historians of literature. At the beginning of the twentieth century B. Menshutkin (1874–1938) began research lasting many years into the Lomonosov archives. For the 1911 jubilee he wrote a biography of Lomonosov, which ran into several editions. Before the First World War he had already prepared volumes VI and VII of the collected works of Lomonosov, containing the natural scientific works.[1] Menshutkin also did much to acquaint foreign scientists with the work of the eighteenth-century Russian encyclopaedist.[2]

In the history of geology, the impetus was given by an article written by V. Vernadsky on Lomonosov as geologist. Vernadsky (1863–1945) was one of those scientists who display an exceptional interest in the history of science. His friend and pupil A. Fersman (1883–1945) recalls his words when they were climbing the beautiful staircase of Prague Museum: "We natural historians must learn from historians the profound historical methods of understanding the past destinies of mankind."[3]

Already in his early lectures *On the Scientific World View* (1902), Vernadsky expressed a cherished idea, which he repeated insistently throughout his life: the history of science is something in constant motion, the results of each historical epoch are evaluated in the light of new scientific discoveries, enabling one to see in the past that which was not noticed or insufficiently estimated earlier. In his own words:

> The historian of science must always bear in mind that the picture which he presents is incomplete and limited; the sum of knowledge in the epoch he has studied conceals the embryo of future broad generalizations and profound phenomena which cannot be understood by him. The material he leaves aside may contain the most important thread of great ideas, which for him inevitably remains concealed and invisible. This is understandable, since he has to do with the incomplete — and perhaps infinite — process of the development or unfolding of the human intellect.[4]

[1] These two volumes came out only in 1934.

[2] Jointly with M. Speter, Menshutkin printed selected physico-chemical works by Lomonosov in *Ostwalds Klassiker der exakten Wissenschaften* (1910).

[3] *Бюллетень Московского Общества испытателей природы* (*Bulletin of the Naturalists' Society of Moscow*), New Series, LI, Geology Section, 21 (I), (1946) 59.

[4] V. Vernadsky, *Очерки и речи* (*Outlines and Speeches*) (2 vols., Moscow, 1920) I.

Like Vernadsky, A. Krylov (1863–1945) and S. Vavilov (1891–1959) were among those scientists a considerable part of whose work was done under the new conditions created after the Great Socialist Revolution. Both displayed a great and constant interest in the work of Newton. Krylov made the first Russian translation of Newton's *Principia*, printed in 1915–16.[1] Subsequently (1934) Krylov gave the proof of a theorem formulated by Newton without proof in a letter to Flamsteed, and found a method which formed the basis for calculating two Newtonian tables of astronomical refraction.

Vavilov translated Newton's *Lectiones opticae*, which has not been translated fully into any other European language (including, so far as we know, English), with explanatory articles and comments (1946).[2] He also wrote a biography of Newton.[3] Vavilov devoted close and constant attention to Lomonosov's work and was a skilful organizer of research in this sphere.

The new period, following 1917, was marked by the creation of scientific centres for systematic and collective research in the history of science, to which particularly great importance is attached in our country at the present time. In 1914 Lenin wrote: "The continuation of the work of Hegel and Marx must consist in the *dialectical* treatment of the history of human thought, of science and technique."[4] In our day the history of science not only stands firmly as a specific branch of historical knowledge, it has become an integral part in deciding large problems of a synthetic character. It is not limited to the plain registration of discoveries, or to the purely biographical approach in their study. It is not satisfied with a purely logical analysis of the connexion between theories and concepts in various historical epochs. Every phenomenon in the history of science is examined in direct connexion with conditions which gave rise to it, which made possible the discovery itself and its practical application. Increasing attention is given to the interconnexions present in the development of various disciplines.

In the Soviet period, the first centre of the history of science was the Commission on the History of Knowledge, formed in

[1] Republished in Krylov's *Собрание трудов* (*Collected Works*) (1936) VII.

[2] Previously (1927) Vavilov had translated Newton's *Opticks* (second edition 1954).

[3] First edition 1941; new edition including other works by Vavilov on Newton 1960; German translation 1951.

[4] V. Lenin, *Философские тетради* (*Philosophical Notebooks*) (Moscow, 1947) 122.

1921 under the Academy of Sciences. Its active organizer and chairman was Vernadsky. In one of his reports on the work of the Commission (1926) Vernadsky gave the following resumé of the advance in the latest historical research:

> Together with the history of the Mediterranean centres of culture, the history of the growth and development of *Homo sapiens* on our planet rises before us. Creative works by the great peoples of Asia which long ago began to appear — philosophical, artistic, scientific and in state-craft — are bearing fruit and becoming generally known, and alongside this light is being thrown upon the formerly unseen role of the 'non-historical' peoples. . . . The role of the East appears in an essentially different aspect, and the marvel of Hellenic science, its origins, are seen in a new light.

In the same report Vernadsky noted the "radical changes in our concept of west European medieval science".[1]

At present the Academy of Sciences of the U.S.S.R. has an Institute for the History of Science and Technology, formed in September 1953 on the basis of the former Institute of the History of Science, the Commission on the History of Technology and a number of other special commissions. In 1955 the Soviet National Union of Historians of Natural Science and Technology was formed, affiliated to the International Union of the History and Philosophy of Science.[2] The co-operation and constant contact among specialists in various branches afford opportunities for collective research not only in the history of the sciences, but also in the history of science as a whole.

The existence of the aforementioned centres has also made it possible to systematize the preparation of new forces working in the history of science. It has provided the possibility for the first collective general works on the history of science in Russia. Among such works, mention should be made of the *History of Natural Sciences in Russia* up to 1917 (three volumes, and a fourth, concluding volume being printed), a new *History of the Academy of Sciences*, and others. A large collective work is being prepared on the history of science in the Soviet period, with the

[1] *Известия Академии наук СССР* (*USSR, Academy of Sciences, Proceedings*) 6th series, XX (1926) No. 18, 1692–3.

[2] It is impossible to give even a moderately full review of literature published in recent decades. We refer to two extensive bibliographical indices for 1917–47 and 1948–50 (published in 1949 and 1955). *История естествознания. Литература, опубликованная в СССР.* Further registration is conducted by the Institute of the History of Sciences and Technology and the corresponding volumes are being prepared for press.

active participation of leading scientists in our country.[1] The history of science has been considerably developed in republics which form the U.S.S.R.[2] It is only now that a broad and profound study of the history of science in preceding epochs has become possible, specifically in the second half of the nineteenth and the first decades of the twentieth centuries. Collections of Russian scientific classics have been published with commentaries, for example the excellent, full and annotated collection of works by Lobachevsky, edited by V. Kagan and a number of other prominent experts; in 1954 a 25-volume edition of the works of Mendeleyev was completed; and from 1950–9 a ten-volume edition of the collected works of Lomonosov was put out. For the first time, the correspondence of our scientists has become known, giving a fuller picture of their own work, and of their connexions with other scientists within the country and abroad. A rather considerable number of biographies have appeared. At present, the Academy of Sciences has begun publication of a special biographical series, which includes the lives of the most outstanding scientists of all epochs and peoples.

Special mention should be made of the serial publication of scientific classics. In the Soviet period, several editions of this type have been undertaken. At the present time the *Classics of Science* series begun by the late S. Vavilov is being continued. The works of Leonardo da Vinci, Descartes, Newton, Euler, Lobachevsky, Aepinus, Lenz, Lamarck, Faraday, von Baer, Pasteur, Timiryazev, Butlerov, Dokuchayev, Pavlov and many others have already been printed. In contrast to *Ostwalds Klassiker*, the works are published in full. In Tashkent, the Academy of Sciences of the Uzbek Soviet Socialist Republic has begun the first complete publication in Russian of the classic *Canon of Medicine* by Ibn Sina (four large volumes have come out up to now). Among the publications of Arabic texts

[1] A large amount of data relating to the period mentioned is contained in the editions *Советская химия за 25 лет* (*Soviet Chemistry over 25 Years*) (1942), *Математика в СССР за 30 лет* (*Mathematics in the USSR over 30 years*) (1948), in analogous publications on geology (1947), astronomy (1948) and mechanics (1950), and in a later analogous series *Математика в СССР за 40 лет* (*Mathematics in the USSR over 40 years*) (1960, 2 volumes), *Астрономия в СССР за 40 лет* (*Astronomy in the USSR over 40 years*), and others.

[2] Out of a number of works already published, we limit ourselves to mentioning as an example the five-volume work by L. Oganesyan on the history of medicine in Armenia (1946–7): *История медицины в Армении.*

with parallel Russian translation, mention should be made of the mathematical texts of al-Kashi.[1] S. Sobol's many years of work editing the nine-volume Russian edition of Darwin's works (1935–59) is also worthy of mention.

Articles on the history of science are printed in large numbers in various journals, both purely scientific and popular scientific. A considerable number of them are to be found in the *Trudy* (38 volumes, beginning with 1954), published by the Institute of the History of Science and Technology, and in *Problems of the History of Science and Technology* (10 issues, beginning with 1956). The Publishing House of Physico–Mathematical Literature is putting out a series *Historico–Mathematical Research* (13 volumes, begun in 1948) and a series *Historico-Astronomical Research* (6 volumes, begun in 1955).

A number of Soviet museums, large and small, contain a great many examples of scientific apparatus of historical importance, but their study is only beginning. In 1947 a Lomonosov Museum was opened in Leningrad; in the future it will undoubtedly provide an increasingly extensive picture of the history of science in eighteenth-century Russia. In Moscow there is a museum for the history of microscopy, where thanks to the tireless work of the late S. Sobol, a large number of unique exhibits has been collected.[2]

One of the specific features in historico–scientific research in our country in recent years is the great attention paid to the latest period in scientific development. As an example I can cite collected papers and articles on the work of I. Pavlov and his school, on M. Planck and A. Einstein, general surveys of the modern development of different branches of science, and so on.[3]

In a brief survey, it is of course possible to cite only a few examples illustrating the trend of historico–scientific research

[1] Translated from the Arabic by B. Rosenfeld. Commentaries by the translator and by A. Yushkevich (Moscow, 1956): *Джемшид Гияс эддин ал-Каши. Ключ арифметики. Трактат об окружности.* (... al-Kashi. The key to arithmetic. On the circle.)

[2] Sobol has also carried out serious research into the history of the microscope and microscopic research in Russia in the eighteenth century (1949): *История микроскопа и микроскопических исследований в России в XУIII в.*

[3] Mention should here be made of the works of B. Kuznetsov on the history of the modern physics, and also the research work done by a number of young scientists, printed in *Trudy* of the Institute of the History of Sciences and Technology and numerous periodicals.

in the past and the present. Little or nothing has been said about many important phenomena and names. I think that it has been shown sufficiently clearly that the historiography of science has old traditions in our country and is very closely linked up with the solution of actual problems that concern science itself.

Commentaries

Commentary by Alexandre Koyré

Mr. Guerlac's very interesting paper, which is at the same time an admirable survey of the evolution of history in general and of history of science in particular, and a criticism of the manner in which it has been written hitherto, comes at the right moment. It is appropriate that after having spent much time and effort on the discussion of concrete problems relating to the history of science, we should look at it from another angle, and that, as historians, we should put ourselves, as it were, 'in question'.

Let us follow the delphic injunction of Mr. Guerlac. Let us ask ourselves: what is history? This term, as he reminds us, is properly applicable to *human* history, to the *human* past. But it is ambiguous: it designates, on the one hand, everything that has gone before us, that is to say all the actions, facts and events of the past (one might call this 'objective history' or 'past actuality') and, on the other hand, the *account* the historian gives of it, an account of which this past is the object. *Res gestae* and *historia rerum gestarum.*

Now the past, by virtue of being *past*, remains forever inaccessible to us, it is no more, we cannot reach it and it is only from its traces and *remains*, from its debris which are *still present* — works of art, monuments, documents which have escaped the ravages of time and of mankind — that we attempt to reconstruct it. But objective history, the history men make and suffer, is not concerned — or hardly — with the history of historians: it allows the survival of things of no value to the historian and mercilessly destroys the most important of documents,[1] the most beautiful of works, and the most impressive of monuments.[2] What it leaves, or has left behind, are mere

[1] As, for example, the writings of the pre-Socratics, of Democritus. On the other hand we have retained Diogenes Laertius.

[2] Sometimes, doubtless, it is to destruction and catastrophe that we owe these fragments, as in the case of the cuneiform tablets preserved for us by the sands of the desert but now, as Neugebauer has pointed out, deteriorating in our museums: or the admirable Greek statues discovered by submarine archaeology.

fragments of what we should need. Accordingly, historical reconstructions are inevitably fragmentary, uncertain, even doubly uncertain — poor little conjectural science, so has Paul Valéry described history!

Moreover, historical reconstructions are not only necessarily incomplete; they are also necessarily partial. Historians do not state all the facts, not even all the facts that they know or might be able to know — how could they? Tristram Shandy has shown us that it was impossible — but only those that are *important*. Thus the history of the historian, *historia rerum gestarum*, does not include all the *res gestae*, but only those which are — or seem — worthy of being saved from oblivion. His history, then, is the result of a choice, and even of a double or triple choice.

First there is the choice from the *res gestae* made by their contemporaries and their immediate or mediate successors, historians of the present or wardens of the past, who have noted down in their annals, inscriptions and memoirs facts which *to them* seemed important and worthy of being retained and passed on to their descendants, who in turn copied and preserved the texts which *to them* appeared to merit preservation. Then there is the choice made by the historian who, at a later time, uses these materials and documents which he has inherited and who, more often than not, does not agree with the contemporaries or with his predecessors about the relative importance of the facts and the value of the texts which they transmitted, or did not transmit to him.

But he cannot help it. He is reduced to complaining about our ignorance of a particular group of facts or of the date of a particular event which contemporaries had judged negligible but which seems to him of prime importance, or about not having at his disposal texts which would be of essential value but which his predecessors did not see fit to preserve for us.[1]

The fact is that the historian projects into history the interests and the scale of values of his own time, and it is according to its conception of history, and even to his special

[1] Contemporaries take note of things that touch them immediately, that is of unusual (mainly unpleasant) events; slow and deep processes escape them. Accordingly even among the 'important' events there are a great number which, at the moment when they occur, are, or seem, in no way important or remarkable and only become so at a later date, as a result of the effects which they later produce, such as, for example, the birth of great men, or the appearance of some technical invention.

and particular one that he undertakes his reconstruction. It is precisely for this reason that history is always being renewed and that nothing changes more often and more quickly than the immutable past.

In his beautiful account of the development of history — I refer again to the history of historians — Mr. Guerlac draws our attention to the widening scope of this subject in modern times, especially since the eighteenth century.[1] Interest turns toward periods and aspects of life previously unknown, misunderstood or neglected: it shifts from dynastic and political history to the history of peoples and institutions, to social and economic history, to that of customs, ideas and civilizations. Under the influence of the philosophy of the enlightenment, history becomes that of "the progress of the human mind": let us remind ourselves of Condorcet whom, curiously, Mr. Guerlac has omitted to mention. Thus it is natural that it should have been during the eighteenth century that history of science, a field in which this progress was incontestable and even spectacular, constitutes itself as an independent discipline.[2] Almost simultaneously, or very soon afterwards, especially under the influence of German philosophy, history became the universal method of explanation. It even conquered the world of nature: the principle that the past explains the present was extended to include cosmology, geology, and biology. The concept of evolution became a key concept and it is with good reason that the nineteenth century has been called the century of history. As for history more properly so called, that is human history, its progress during the course of the nineteenth and twentieth centuries was, and remains, overwhelming: the deciphering of dead languages, innumerable excavations, systematic research, and so on have added endlessly to our knowledge of the past. Also, every coin has its reverse side; and by extending and enriching itself, history has become specialized and particularized, has divided and subdivided itself. Instead of the history of humanity, we have multiple histories of this or that, partial and one-sided histories; instead of an interconnected and unified fabric, separate threads, instead of a living organism, *membra disjecta*.

It is just this excessive specialization and the stubborn separation of the great historical disciplines with which Mr.

[1] Contrary to widespread opinion which regards it as anti-historical, it is the eighteenth century that gave birth to our historiography.

[2] Like the history of art a century earlier.

Guerlac reproaches modern history, or modern historians, and particularly the history and the writers of the history of science. For these last, more than any others, are guilty of the two major faults that I have just mentioned. It is they above all who have practised this proud isolation from their neighbours, who have adopted an abstract attitude — Mr. Guerlac calls it "idealist" — of not taking into account the real conditions in which science was born, lived and developed. Indeed, if since Montucla and Kästner, Delambre and Whewell, history of science has made brilliant progress by renewing our understanding of ancient science, by revealing to us the science of the Babylonians and now of the Chinese, by resurrecting the science of the Middle Ages and of the Arabs; if, with Auguste Comte, history of science has sought, although without success, to integrate itself into the history of civilization, and with Pierre Duhem and Léon Brunschvicg to associate itself with the history of philosophy (a discipline almost as abstract as itself); it has nonetheless, and this despite Paul Tannery, remained a discipline apart, unrelated to general or social history and disinclined to be connected even with history of techniques and technology. It has vice versa, doubtless mistakenly, but not without apparent reason, been in its turn neglected by historians.

Mr. Guerlac maintains then that history of science, which has lately achieved some kind of liaison with the history of ideas and not only with that of philosophy, has nevertheless remained too abstract and too 'idealistic'. He holds that it must overcome this idealist character by ceasing to isolate the facts which it describes from their historical and social context, thus attributing to them, at least implicitly, some kind of independent (pseudo) reality, and that, to start with, it must give up the separation, in any case arbitrary and artificial, between pure and applied science, between theory and practice. History must grasp the real unity of the scientific activity — active thought and thinking action — linked, in its development, with the societies which gave it birth, which nourished or thwarted its development, and on the history of which it has, in its turn, exerted an influence. It is only thus that the fragmentation which increasingly threatens it can be avoided, and that it can find again (or for the first time) its true unity: to be a history *of science*, and not simply a juxtaposition of separate histories of the different sciences and techniques.

I am, to a great extent, in agreement with my friend

Guerlac — and I believe that such is the case of all of us — in his criticism of the excessive specialization and of the fragmentation which results from it in history of science. We all know that the whole is greater than the sum of its parts; that a collection of monographs, of local histories does not constitute the history of a country; and that even that of a country is but a fragment of a more general history — whence the recent attempts to enlarge the subject of the historical narration, to write, for example, the history of the Mediterranean instead of the separate histories of the countries along its shores. We are equally aware that the divisions which we establish between diverse human activities, which we isolate into separate realms (the objects of special histories, themselves separated), is quite artificial and that in reality they are conditioned by each other, interpenetrate and form a whole. But what is to be done? We cannot comprehend the whole without distinguishing its various aspects, without analysing it into its parts[1] — the reconstitution, the synthesis comes afterwards. . . . If it ever comes — an infrequent occurrence if we are to judge by the latest attempts to repeat the exploits of Burckhardt and to offer them to us under the impressive title of "histories of civilization". A juxtaposition of *histories* does not make *a history*. A history of mathematics, plus a history of astronomy, plus one of physics, one of chemistry and one of biology, do not form a history of science: nor even that of the sciences.[2] It is regrettable, without doubt, especially regrettable in that the sciences influence each other and are interdependent. Partially at least. But, then, once more, what is to be done? Specialization is the price to be paid for progress; for the abundance of materials; for the enrichment of our knowledge which increasingly extends beyond the capacities of a human being. Indeed no one today is in a position to write a history of science, or even a history of a science. Recent attempts again amply prove this. But it is the same in every field: no one can write the history of humanity, nor even the history of Europe, the history of religions, or the history of the arts.[3] As no one today can pride himself on a complete knowledge of mathematics, or physics, or chemistry,

[1] Our thought is abstract and analytical. Reality is one and the various sciences which study the aspects of it — physical, chemical, electromagnetic — are products of abstraction.

[2] A history of music in juxtaposition with histories of architecture, sculpture, painting, etc. does not form a history of art.

[3] Not even a single one.

or literature. Everywhere we are submerged. Therein lies our problem: superabundance and in its wake exceeding, yet unavoidable, specialization. But it is not only ours: it is a general problem. I do not know the way out of this predicament. Yet it may be that it is just this ever-growing specialization that ultimately will save us, enabling one specialist to rely more heavily, and with more confidence, upon the work of his colleagues specializing in other fields than his own. Some recent publications seem, indeed, to indicate that this may be the solution.

Let us now examine the second criticism that Mr. Guerlac levelled at us: that we are 'idealists', that we neglect the link between the so-called 'pure' and 'applied' sciences, and so misunderstand the historical role of scientific development. I confess that, sometimes, I did oppose them. Yet, I do not feel myself guilty — at least, not very strongly. As a matter of fact our 'idealism' — I will return to this point later — is nothing else than a reaction against the attempts to interpret, or misinterpret, modern science, *scientia activa*, *operativa*, as a promotion of arts and crafts, as an extension of technology, as an *ancilla praxi*. It makes no difference whether we praise and exalt it for its practical and utilitarian character and explain its birth in terms of the Faustian vigour of modern man — or of the rising bourgeoisie — in contrast with the passive spectator's attitude of medieval or ancient men; or whether we denigrate and condemn it as an 'engineer's science' which rates practical success higher than intellectual progress, interpreting it as *hybris*, as the product of the will to power tending to reject *theoria* in favour of *praxis* and to make man "the master and possessor of nature" rather than its admiring and reverent contemplator. In either case we have the same misunderstanding of the nature of scientific thought.

I am wondering whether Mr. Guerlac does not extend to all sciences, or to science as such, conditions prevailing only in *some* of them. Thus, for instance, it seems rather clear that the link between a theory and its application is pretty close in chemistry, or, to make a more modern example, in thermodynamics. Yet it is much less the case in physics, in rational mechanics; and it is doubtful whether there is any such link at all in pure mathematics; at least in some parts of it as, for instance, set theory or theory of numbers.

I am wondering further whether Mr. Guerlac's insistence on the connexion between pure and applied science and on the role of science as an historical factor is not, at least partially, a re-projection into the past of a present-day, or at least modern, state of affairs. It is certainly true that the function of science in modern society has in the course of these last centuries constantly increased its importance and that it now occupies in that society, and indeed in present history (*res gestae*), a central place, a place that is rapidly becoming preponderant and decisive.

It is also certain that its relation to applied science is more than close: the great 'instruments' of nuclear physics are factories; vice versa, our factories with their automatic processes are nothing but theories become incarnate, as are vast numbers of everyday objects, from the aeroplane that brought me here to the loud-speaker that amplifies my words.

All this, indeed, is not an entirely new phenomenon, but the result of a development, of a continually accelerating development whose origins are far in the past. It is evident that the history of modern astronomy is indissolubly linked with that of the telescope and that, in general, modern science would have been inconceivable without the construction of innumerable instruments of observation and of measurement which it uses. From the seventeenth and eighteenth centuries on, as Mr. Daumas has shown us, it was the manufacture of these that has brought about the collaboration between the scientist and the technician.[1] No one would deny that there is a distinct parallel between the evolution of theoretical chemistry and that of industrial chemistry, between the theory of electricity and its applications. Yet this interaction between theory and practice, the penetration of each by the other, the theoretical elaboration of solutions to practical problems (and during and since the war we have seen how far this can go), seems to me to be an essentially modern phenomenon. Antiquity and the Middle Ages offer us few examples of it, if any at all, apart from the invention of the sun-dial and the discovery, by Archimedes, of the principle bearing his name.[2] As for ancient technology, we

[1] This collaboration brought with it the rise and the development of a wholly new industry, that of scientific instruments, which played — and still play — the leading part in the 'scientification' of technology and the importance of which is increasing with every progress of science, at least of experimental science. How indeed could atomic physics be developed without parallel development of calculating machines — and photography?

[2] We may add the famous tunnel of Eupalinos.

have to admit that, even in Greece, it was a matter of trial and error rather than of 'applied science'. Surprising as it may seem to us, one can erect temples, palaces and even cathedrals, dig canals and build bridges, develop metallurgy and ceramics, without having any scientific *knowledge*; or at most, only its rudiments. Science is not necessary to the life of a society, to the development of a culture, to the growth of a state or even of an empire. Indeed, there have been great empires and impressive civilizations (we need only mention Persia and China) which managed entirely, or almost entirely, without science; just as there have been others (such as Rome) which, despite some scientific heritage, built little upon it. We must not, then, exaggerate the part science has played in history; in the past, even where science in fact existed as in Greece, or, generally in the pre-modern world, it was of minimal importance.[1] The real joining together of *techne* and *episteme* is a modern, and, in certain fields, even a contemporary phenomenon.

This brings us once more to the question of science as a social phenomenon, and to the social conditions which encourage or hinder its development. It is clear enough that such conditions exist and on this point I am in perfect agreement with Mr. Guerlac. How could I not be, seeing that I myself insisted upon it several years ago?[2] For science to be born and to develop, it is necessary, as Aristotle has already explained to us, that there be men of leisure; but this is not sufficient; it is also necessary that among the members of the *leisured* classes there would be men who find their satisfaction in understanding, in *theoria*. It is also necessary that the value of this exercise of the *theoria*, the value of the scientific attitude be recognized by society.[3] Now the realization of these conditions is by no means necessary for the life of societies. Quite the contrary, it is something rather rare; to my knowledge it has happened only two or three times. For, with all respect due to Aristotle, man, not even Athenian man, does not normally desire understanding. Societies, small or great, generally do not appreciate very

[1] Professor Otto Neugebauer has emphasized the small number of scientists in Antiquity.

[2] Cf. my article in *Scientific Monthly*, LXXX (1955) 107–11.

[3] Warring aristocracies despised science — accordingly they did not produce any: such for instance is the case of Sparta; the same is true of 'acquisitive' societies like Corinth. I believe it to be unnecessary to give more recent examples.

much the rather gratuitous activity of the theoretician.[1] For, as we must recognize, theories do not lead to immediate practical results, nor does the practical activity lead necessarily and at once to the formulation of theories. More often than not the contrary is the case: it acts as an impediment. Thus, it was not the Egyptian harpedonaptes, whose task it was to measure the fields in the Nile valley, who invented geometry: it was the Greeks who had nothing worthwhile to measure; the harpedonaptes contented themselves with rules. Similarly it was not the Babylonians, despite their belief in astrology and their consequent need to be able to calculate and predict the position of the planets in the sky, as Mr. van der Waerden has reminded us, who elaborated a system of planetary movements.[2] Once again it was the Greeks, who were not astrologers: the Babylonians contented themselves with inventing methods of calculation — rules again, even though very ingenious ones.

As a result, it seems to me that though we can explain adequately why science was not born and did not develop in Persia or China (the great bureaucracies, as Mr. Needham has pointed out, are everywhere hostile to independent scientific thought[3]) and although we may be able to explain why it was possible for it to be born and to develop in Greece, we still cannot explain why it did so in fact.

It also seems to me vain to attempt to deduce the existence of Greek science from the social structure of the city state, or even of the *agora*. Athens does not explain Eudoxus, or Plato, any more than Syracuse explains Archimedes; or Florence, Galileo. I even believe, indeed, that the same is true also of modern times, and even of the present century despite the so much closer co-operation between pure and applied science to which I have already referred. The social structure of England in the seventeenth century cannot explain Newton, any more than the Russia of Nicholas I can throw light on the work of

[1] It was practical results that Hiero asked of Archimedes. And it is for the (legendary) invention of war machines that tradition glorifies him. It was, equally, practical results that Louvois expected of the Académie des Sciences — and thus ruined it.

[2] Astrology, it is often forgotten, is only concerned with the positions of planets in the sky and the figures which they form.

[3] Even today they only seek practical results and if they sometimes encourage theoretical research — *fundamental research* — it is insofar as practical applications are expected of them. Thus, theoreticians as often as not follow the lead and, imitating Bacon, seek to persuade societies that sooner or later theoretical research will prove to be a 'paying proposition'.

Lobachevsky, or the Germany of Willhelm II enable us to understand Einstein. To look for explanations along these lines is an entirely futile enterprise, as futile as trying to predict the future evolution of science or of the sciences as a function of the structure of their social contexts.

Social contexts are, of course, not unimportant. We have seen that great scientific discoveries brought with them, eventually, practical results; we have seen — and see every day — applied sciences, just as Bacon and Descartes had promised, transform the conditions of our existence, the very world in which we are living. We have learned that, if science is not, in itself, power, it is the precondition of it. Accordingly the social appreciation of science — and of the scientist — has deeply changed in our century. We know — or we are convinced — that theory will automatically become *praxis* and that the purest of pure research — we call it 'fundamental ' — will 'pay off'. Indeed that is what scientists keep telling us in order to 'sell' themselves to the public. We believe them and are therefore prepared to give them support. Yet, even today, at least so it seems to me, it is not the practical orientation that explains the great scientific break-throughs. Applications result from the discoveries — they do not inspire them. Wireless telegraphy was not the goal pursued by Maxwell, though it resulted from his work. No more than the construction of the atomic bomb was that of Einstein and Bohr. It was understanding, not practical application that they sought. Thus, it seems to me — and if it is idealism, *tant pis* — that science, the science of our epoch, like that of the Greeks, is essentially *theoria*, a search for the truth, and that as a result of this fact it has, and has always had, value as an end in itself, and an inherent and autonomous — though not always regular and logical — development, such that it is only by the study of its own problems, its own history, that it can be understood by historians.

I even believe that it is just in the fact of this autonomous development — and not in the increasing influence of science on the concrete conditions of life — that lies the great value of the history of science, of scientific thought. Indeed, if humanity, as Pascal has said, is a single being, that lives forever and forever learns, it is with our own history or intellectual autobiography that we are concerned in our study. And it is also for this reason that it is so exciting and, at the same time, so instructive. It reveals to us the human mind in its most noble aspect, in its constant and persistent, always renewed, though never satisfied, pursuit of a goal which always eludes it: the search and struggle for truth, *itinerarium mentis in veritatem.* Now this *itinerarium* is not given to it in advance and the human mind cannot move along it in a straight line. The path to truth is filled with snares and strewn with errors; and failures are more frequent than successes. These failures, moreover, are sometimes just as revealing and instructive as the successes: it is through errors that the mind progresses towards truth. No, the *itinerarium mentis in veritatem* is not a straight path. It twists and turns, is occasionally blocked, and turns back upon itself. It is not even one path, but many. That of the mathematician is not that of the chemist, nor that of the biologist, nor even that of the physicist. We are therefore forced to pursue all these paths as we find them, that is to say connected or separated, as they occur in history, and to resign ourselves to writing histories *of sciences* before writing the history of science — into which they will finally join together like the tributaries of a river.

Will it ever be written? That, time alone can tell.

Commentary by J. A. Passmore

For two very different reasons, I find it hard to discuss Mr. de Santillana's paper: I largely agree with what I take to be his main thesis, and I am too ignorant to be able to dispute with him about his particular examples. Thus I agree with his general thesis that older works of scholarship often contain valuable material which more recent scholars are foolish to neglect; but whether this is so in the particular case of Egyptology I simply do not know.

I agree, too, that the historian of science should begin from the presumption that the texts he is discussing are saying something sensible. We can, in the case of any set of beliefs, past or present, distinguish three different abstract possibilities: (1) they are true; (2) although they are not true, they are plausible, that is we can easily see how a person writing at a certain time or in a certain tradition could come to hold them; (3) they are neither true nor plausible, but purely fantastic; explicable only as expressing a personal longing, whether it be an erotic longing, or a longing for power. As a matter of statistics, it might well be the case that most human beliefs fall into class (3), and very few into class (1). But even if this were so, a historian of science interpreting, say, a medieval text on proportions should begin by asking whether its author had in fact made a scientific discovery, should pass on to consider whether the text can be read as asserting what an intelligent man writing at that time would have found plausible, and only if this interpretation turns out to be impossible should he consider the hypothesis that the text is a personal fantasy, or an attempt to escape ecclesiastical censure at whatever cost to consistency, or an attempt to justify some extra-scientific doctrine.

At the same time, the historian's interpretation has to be defended by reference to the text; it has to fall within the range of philological possibilities. The text may force us to conclude that the author was not in fact sensible; that his doctrines were wholly fantastic. That ought not to be the first hypothesis we consider, but it may sometimes have to be our last conclusion.

Similar considerations apply to the interpretation of conduct. We know that Eudoxus was a very much cleverer man than we are; if the facts about his conduct are as de Santillana describes them — this I do not know — then certainly we should begin from the presumption that Eudoxus stayed in Egypt because he had something to learn there. But plenty of people have taken the trouble to learn a foreign language and to visit a foreign country because they *wrongly* believed that there was something they could learn there — and it is easy to see how Eudoxus could come by this belief. They have not always returned home immediately, whether through pride, or because they liked the country, or because they met a girl there. Even very clever men have been known to dally in Paris somewhat longer than their intellectual pursuits wholly justified. We have to remember that a scientist is a human being, even although our main concern is with what he contributed to science; we cannot rule out the philological evidence by some such general principle as that clever men never act except in a wholly rational fashion, even if our first presumption should be that they have acted rationally, if only because their rational conduct particularly interests us as historians of science.

Now for Mr. Guerlac. I want to begin by distinguishing four different ways in which the history of any form of intellectual activity can be written. I shall call them (1) doxographical; (2) retrospective; (3) problematic; (4) cultural.

Doxographical history dates back to Diogenes Laertius, and reappeared at the beginning of the modern period of intellectual history in the works of Stanley and Brucker. It sets out to tell us who a scientist was, when and where he lived, and what conclusions he came to. Brucker carries doxographical history to the extreme point; he sets out, say, Aristotle's views about motion as a series of separately numbered sentences. Doxographical work may be written at the fairly popular level, or, as in Brucker's case, with immense seriousness and solidity. But in any case it turns the history of science into a cemetery of dead opinions, which is not greatly enlivened even by the most elegant of funeral memorials.

Retrospective history begins from a great achievement and tries to show how previous scientific thinking led up to it. Thus it looks at fourteenth-century physics as a foreshadowing of Galileo, at eighteenth-century biology as an anticipation of Darwin, at Newtonian and post-Newtonian physics as an anticipation of Einstein. Unlike doxographical history, retrospective history begins from a problem and has a theme; but it tends in practice to exaggerate the degree of 'anticipation' in earlier theories, as also to leave the reader with the impression that scientific thought progresses in a straight line along a narrow path. Aristotle, one might say, invented the retrospective method. Macaulay's *History of England*, Hegel's *History of Philosophy*, and Einstein and Infeld's *Evolution of Modern Physics* exemplify it in different forms.

Problematical history is, I should say, the type towards which the history of science is at present aspiring. The problematic historian sees the scientist as a living, thinking being, confronting a problem, meeting that problem with certain expectancies about the form its solution will take and the method which will prove adequate to deal with it. In the case of 'moments of crisis' in science, he sets out to show how the intractability of a traditional problem, or the entry of a new problem, gave rise to changes in the scientist's sets of expectancies. For him, as Mr. Koyré has expressed the matter, science is "la recherche de la vérité", but he emphasizes that "la recherche" is a struggle, not a matter of cold deduction.

Cultural history is interested in science as a form of human endeavour, but in its conclusions rather than in its 'insides'. So far the cultural historian is like the doxographer, but unlike the doxographer he has a theme: the state of society at a certain time or its development over a period of time, and the place of science in that state or that development.

I want now to consider two remarks by Mr. Guerlac in the light of these distinctions. He urges upon us, first, the need for remembering that science is a unity and, secondly, the need for looking outside the history of a particular science to the history of the society to which it belongs. Obviously, both the doxographer and the cultural historian will be happy with these conclusions; the doxographer loves to leap from Galileo to Harvey, from Newton to Darwin, and his 'life and times' will often include a considerable historical excursus. As for the cultural historian, he, too, will think of Darwin and Faraday as different 'aspects' of nineteenth-century science, and it is his whole purpose to set the history of science within a broader social context. But doxography, it will be generally agreed, is unsatisfactory; and the worst thing that could happen to the history of science, I should suggest, is that it should be merged into some sort of general cultural history, which is interested in scientists only as 'expressions of their times', and in the most minor and major figures with a sceptical impartiality, preferring the former indeed, in so far as the minor figure is likely to be more 'characteristic' than the genius of his period. Relatively few historians have a real feeling for theorizing as such — just as very few theorists have any feeling for history — and that fact is only too apparent in most 'intellectual histories' of the 'cultural' sort.

What of the problematic historian? He is interested in expectations, in problems, in methods, and in the manner in which they have changed over a period of time; and I agree with Mr. Wilkie (above, p. 598) that he should look first *within science itself* for the explanation of such changes. But this again is a general precept; the historian must be careful not to force upon his texts an interpretation which they do not justify, in order to find within science the source of a new problem or a new technique which really arose outside it — say, in the development of industrial technology. So far I should agree with Mr. Guerlac: the historian of science should be alert to the existence of a world of philosophical, social and technological changes outside science. But it is quite another matter to suggest that he should incorporate that knowledge within the history he writes. The historian who tries to study the history of science 'as a whole' is, I wish to suggest, moving in precisely the wrong direction. What is needed, rather, are studies of *quite specific problems*, as in Miss Hesse's recent study of 'action at a distance'.[1] Science is a unity, in the sense that it

[1] Mary B. Hesse, *Forces and Fields*, London and Edinburgh, 1961.

possesses, in a large measure, a common spirit, a common method, but it does not follow that it has the sort of unity of development which makes it a suitable subject for a single work. And it is even less obvious that 'human culture' is a unity in this sense.

I cannot for the life of me see why to write history of science for its own sake is, as Mr. Guerlac suggests, "to treat science as a mere cultural embellishment", any more than to write the history of the British constitution for its own sake is to treat the British constitution as a mere "embellishment". I should rather suggest, indeed, that the attempt to write general cultural histories issues in works which show no real penetration into any *particular* form of human endeavour. But even if this is not so, there is at least no reason why *all* historical writing should be of this generalizing form, and very good reasons why the history of science should be written, at least part of the time, as "private, insulated history".

Commentary by Peter Laslett

This is to be the comment of an historian of society, not of an intellectual historian, least of all of an historian of science. I am incompetent to pass judgment on the content of these three papers in any other way.

I cannot, for example, offer anything other than an incidental reflection on the fascinating thesis about Eudoxus and the Egyptians which de Santillana has put forward. He must know that the rediscovery of what unfashionable predecessors knew is not a habit confined to historians. But he also knows that there is a particular temptation for us, especially those of us who happen to get the ear of the world outside the university, to retell the story of the past as our generation ought to hear it told (or wants to hear it told). This is, I suggest, one reason why it is that what is already known gets buried, why fashions of interpretations seem to proceed as if no one knew anything until this latest and most interesting of all points of view made itself manifest. We overlook what our predecessors discovered because we are so busy preaching our doctrine in opposition to the doctrine which they were preaching.

If he will allow me to be playful for a moment and make a reference, quite unfairly, to his own entrancing book on Galileo, I should like to ask a rhetorical question. Is there not something of this anxiety to tell our generation the history which they stand in need of being told in his repeated comparison of Galileo with Oppenheimer?

Guerlac's accomplished argument resolving the place of the history of science is beyond my competence likewise. I am on his side, perhaps on his side against Passmore, when he insists that we must look at what he calls cultural wholes. I sympathize too with his plea for a prolonged, unwinking stare at technology and its development, all over again. For my interest too is in the social origins and significance of scientific activity.

Even less can I hope to add anything to Zubov's paper. Its interest for me, if he will allow me to say so, was as much in what he did not say as in what he did. Surely the most extraordinary and most attractive of all episodes in the history of science will turn out to be what happened in Russia between, say, 1920 and 1950, the detailed, critical study of the relationship in those years between intellectual conviction, social and political organization, and scientific progress. I long to know more.

My comments, then, are to be parochial, the comments of an historian on one particular society, English society, at the time of the Scientific Revolution. And I start with this question: What did it mean to be a scientist in the seventeenth century? Science was not, for the men themselves, what might be called an activity in itself, and it is not to be made so by using their own term for it, the term natural philosophy. Rather it was what might be called a series of epi-phenomena, epi-phenomena of activities which were activities in themselves. Philosophy was the most important of them, of course, but the others were at a considerable social distance from philosophy, or so the exact and patient social historian has to suppose. Closest was medicine, but the technical activities of surgeons, or of wheelwrights, of millwrights, watchmakers, even of fishermen and butchers, were extremely remote, in sociological terms. 'Progress in scientific knowledge', we correctly claim, was an epi-phenomenon of the activities of all these people, but this does not mean that there was an activity called science in the seventeenth century. And it does not mean that we can in strict correctness talk of scientists at this time, not as we now use the word anyway. There were no scientists in Stuart England, and all the men we have grouped together under that heading were in their varying degrees dilettantes. In my view the established distinction between dilettantes and men of science proper, between scientists and amateurs, is deceptive.

All this may be obvious enough, but I believe it has to be said, because of what now follows. The epi-phenomena I have talked of are not to be made into a whole activity in itself by free use of the word anticipatory, with evolutionary added where necessary, by maintaining in fact that wherever we find that men were right (scientifically right) or on the right track in the seventeenth century, there we have the history of science. To do this is to commit the one and only error of general principle which the historians can commit, for it is to read history not forwards, as it happened, but backwards. It has been the great achievement of this generation, and here I have Koyré much in mind, to remedy this, and to reconstruct the true attitude of our ancestors to these problems, in intricate detail. To this important task must now be added the equally intricate, exasperating undertaking of finding where all these tiny little movements and reactions fit into the whole society. It becomes a question of minutiae, of residue as you might say. To the critical, sociological historian this is the project presented by the history of science in Stuart England, in the Heroic Age.

What then becomes of that large-scale, long-lasting, deep-seated movement which we call the Scientific Revolution of the seventeenth century? We must be a little leary of the word revolution, I think, because it seems to me to come from a model of societies and of social change which is not only crude and clumsy, but misleading in its implications. It would be convenient if another expression could be found as the title of that amazing transformation which can be seen in men's attitude to the physical world and in the degree and nature of their developing control of it. We want a title which does not invite us to put the Scientific Revolution alongside the Industrial Revolution and the various political revolutions (1640–60 in England, 1775 in America, 1789 in France) as if they were all strictly comparable, if not quite the same sort of thing, yet susceptible of being added together, or brought into play with each other. Above all we want a title which might make us pause before we so easily assume, as we always seem to do, that these movements in the last analysis, in some ill-defined but quite positive way, can all be referred to some more fundamental social and economic change, all finally 'expressions' of that seismic settlement in the underlying strata. To say this is not to play down in any way the importance and the extent of the change which we know as the Scientific

Revolution. Nor is it to deny that the social historian is committed to the task of finding the inter-relations between 'scientific' events and other events, for this is the process of historical understanding. Indeed the history of science is exemplary. It is a challenging succession of subtle problems in relating intellectual change with technical development on the one hand, effective social demands and imperatives on the other hand. In the world of historical minutiae which we are discussing, for I must repeat that 'scientific' activity in Stuart times was minuscule in scale, hidden within interstices scattered throughout the social universe, in that world nevertheless the most sophisticated historial analysis must be brought into play.

Let me invite a contrast of these assumptions about the task of the social historian studying science in seventeenth-century England with the assumptions which seem to characterize most historical descriptions of it. The coming of the bourgeoisie, the rise of the middle class, of capitalist economies, a large-scale, deep-seated secular movement affecting the whole social fabric of Western Europe, a distinct stage in the natural history of human society — this still seems to be the final reality appealed to. Because (and this seems to be the most obstinate *non sequitur*), because the Scientific Revolution was itself so momentous a change, it must necessarily itself have had momentous causes, can only be part and parcel of a general transformation of society.

Now the facts of the case quite apart from the logic of the inquiry makes this way of arguing extremely tenuous. Close study of the social world in which Bacon lived his life does not demonstrate that the generations which succeeded until, say, the time of Newton were generations of swift and total change, not even in isolated areas of English society. "There was no middle class in Stuart England" is a short and perhaps rather too dogmatic a way of describing the negative results of the task which historians of seventeenth-century society are now engaged in. Even when the traditional argument which links science with 'business' is traced in such a vital detail as the social composition of the early Royal Society, it is found to be unilluminating. In so far as the textbooks on the history of science refer the change to the growth of 'functional rationality' consequent upon economic rationalization they are in error. Inter-connexions of this sort imply a knowledge of the structure of society at that time which has never yet been available and is only now being painfully pieced together.

Naive sociologism is the expression which might be used for the tendency in historical explanation which I have been criticizing. It may be ignorance which leads me to suppose that it does in fact affect the thinking of historians of science, and perhaps I also exaggerate the extent to which they have failed to be on their guard against what we call the Whig interpretation, reading history backwards. But I think I can promise that by the end of the century the social historian will be in a position to offer a wholly subtler and more sophisticated account of change than is implied by the propositions to which I have drawn attention in these comments.

Discussion

J. Needham

I read Mr. de Santillana's witty and stimulating paper with the greatest sympathy, for our experiences have borne out so much of what he says. For example "if the ancients speak in strange ways, we should not conclude that their thoughts were so strange as all that". From the beginning of our project on the history of science in China, my collaborators and I declared war against the predilection for the quaint and the archaic which has bedevilled sinology for generations. Over and over again we have had cause to see how sensible the writings of ancient and medieval Chinese authors are, and with what clarity they often wrote. And as for accuracy, we know now how right Aurel Stein was when he said that whatever other opinions about Asian geography there might be, one neglects the statements of Chinese geographers at one's peril.

Mr. de Santillana also pointed out that we need "technical translations for technical terms, and must not rely on purely literary knowledge of languages to get us through". My collaborators and I could not agree more. When we come across an expression such as the "crane bird's knee" (*hu hsi*) we shall not get far if we miss the allusion to the flail, and indeed this expression was an eleventh-century A.D. technical term for combinations of chains and levers in mechanical engineering. So also, *chin chuang*, which might be rendered as "golden boils", in fact means lesions produced by metal weapons of war. Even Chinese scholars not *au fait* with specific branches of technology may often be led astray in such matters. Mr. de Santillana's words about "causing nonsense to blossom forth" are also a *cri de coeur* which finds response. The great sinologist James Legge, translating the *Lun Yu* (Discourses of Confucius) long ago, made him say that as no one would listen to his doctrine, he would "get on board a raft and float about on the sea". Legge thus made way for yet another unnecessary fatuous misconception of Chinese affairs, for he did not know of the *sailing*-rafts of the Chinese coast, powerful vessels of Antiquity like those of the Formosans and the Peruvians. What the sage meant then was that he would take passage to some other land where the people would be more willing to learn from him.

The burden of Mr. Guerlac's paper was that we must not

"overlook the social conditions of scientific thought and action". This indeed is the basic motivation of our project. When I was beginning research I was trained to be very careful always to do controls in my experiments. I remember a Lithuanian colleague whose English was slightly imperfect writing in his notebook "Flask 1: enzyme; Flask 2: enzyme + snag". Thus for us the Chinese experience through the ages is a control experiment for Europe — the climatic factor, for instance, which might make comparison with India difficult, does not enter in. Our two questions are (*a*) why did modern science not develop in China, and (*b*) why was Chinese culture more efficient than any other in the Middle Ages and Antiquity in applying science to human affairs? If the differences between bureaucratic feudalism, and the feudalism which in Europe succumbed to capitalism, have nothing to do with these differences, I am prepared, in the classical phrase, to eat my hat!

Mr. Zubov has told of the recognition by Vernadsky of the new light in which knowledge of the East makes us see Greek science, and has referred to the great work of the Russian sinologists in elucidating Chinese science. Mr. Guerlac has told how "our ancestors singled out for preservation in the collective memory those events which they felt had deeply influenced their life". We as historians of science are presumably still doing this. Here our own valuations come in question. We must record three types of achievement, those which directly led to the break-through of modern science (Mr. Passmore's retrospective approach), those that fitted in after that break-through had occurred, and last but not least, those that had no genetic connexion that we can see with modern science, but which form part of the ideal history of man's knowledge of nature and control over her. We should not think only of one long chain of continuous transmission of stimulating ideas, but also of achievements that for one reason or another had no succeeding links, at any rate in the light of our limited knowledge. Only so can we build a history of science truly oecumenical, the upsurge of all men in all times everywhere.

F. Greenaway

Mr. Guerlac is probably right in saying that the history of science is "primarily (but not exclusively) the history of thought about nature", but we must take care not to neglect his parenthesis. Much material exists for the recovery of the physical conditions of the experimental investigation of nature which is the distinguishing characteristic of most scientific inquiry. The enterprise of bringing into existence or representation the total experimental conditions of particular investigations or technical processes of important periods is probably best carried on in the few large museums of science and technology. University departments of the history of science are unlikely ever to have the peculiar and costly facilities required for this kind of work, and it is to be hoped that collaboration between them and institutions which do have will be fostered and increase. Museums have four functions: acquisition, conservation, research and display. There is a very interesting movement going on in which research and display are being combined to constitute a distinctive means of presenting the curator-historian's interpretation of history.

The curator has another role in the field of historiography, a service to the historian of the future. His policy of acquisition must look forward, guided by his own historical judgment. Modern records, particularly laboratory records, must be very much his concern, and it is to be hoped that it will be made easier for the curator to acquire important material. Without the record of experiment, and of the means by which it is done, even the historian of scientific thought will lack essential material.

W. Hartner

I cannot quite get myself to admit that our modern historians of science are as stubborn as they are denounced as being by my friend Giorgio de Santillana. Perhaps, in most of the cases he cites, he would do more justice to facts (which are known to be stubborn things) if he philosophized not with a sledgehammer but with a middle-sized instrument. It is indeed the fate of theories, of books, and even of the men who wrote them to fall into oblivion. Here as elsewhere, however unpleasant and unjust it be, it is not always quality alone that decides. One serious slip can be enough to doom a man and cause later generations not to turn to him again. Sometimes also — and this is worse — no other merit than a particularly high-pitched voice may enable a new Calypso to make the modern Ulysses forget the beautiful tunes that were sung in bygone days. Therefore, excavating what is good and leaving buried "under six feet of sod" what is obvious nonsense will in every case be a meritorious deed.

But let us be just: Boeckh, Ideler, Lepsius, Schlegel are not altogether forgotten, though the existence of later works on the same subjects (in Ideler's case above all Ginzel's *Chronologie*) may cause the uninitiated to deem it superfluous to have recourse to the older author. But who would ever dream of swearing to a theory just because it is from Ginzel, taking his work as a kind of verbal inspiration? He invested a tremendous amount of energy in writing his three volumes and did very well in many a respect, but in many another he could have done far better if he had not relied only on himself, not least in his chapter on China, which is simply wrong. But this deprecatory statement about Ginzel does not of course reinstate Ideler to the position of a prophet. He too made mistakes, some of which could have been avoided, others because he knew less about the matter than we do today. The prophets definitely belong to the past, and we should have learnt that by relapsing into past habits of uncritical belief or emotional rejection, we bar our way to real understanding. Nobody knows this better than the man who has written a really enlightening book on Galileo.

Charles François Dupuis has so far escaped my attention. I am anxious to know what he has to say about ancient astronomy and the pre-Socratics. Yet, however important things his book may contain, I cannot believe that it overshadows Diels's monumental work. Let us go ahead and dig out Dupuis and then profit from his learning as well as from Diels's! Boll and Gundel may have erred on some occasion or other (which of us is infallible?); should we therefore reject them altogether? I have had the privilege of knowing at least Gundel personally, and I remember him as a man who was not only ready but really anxious to correct, on the basis of better insight, whatever he might have said or believed in before. Bouché-Leclercq does not deserve the epithet "forgotten historian of astronomy". There is no better and more comprehensive work on the history of astrology, and I claim that all the initiated are aware of this. Festugière is unthinkable without him; I have quoted him innumerable times myself, and the same is true of Otto Neugebauer, who does not hesitate to call him a classic. Karlgren, owing to his unique range of competence in all branches of sinology, has indeed done important work even in the field so admirably treated by Granet. If on some occasion or other he has arrived at a divergent opinion, it will certainly not be without reason. But Karlgren himself would be the last to regard Granet as 'old hat'. Here too the right attitude is defined not by 'aut — aut', but by 'et — et', leaving aside what later research has proved untenable.

Proceeding from generalities to particulars, may I say that I do not believe that much can be inferred from Strabo's story that he was shown Eudoxus's house in Heliopolis, for the simple reason that the passage in question also mentions Plato, whose alleged visit to Egypt in Eudoxus's company is without doubt a fairy-tale. But re-reading the seventh book ("De cometis") of Seneca's *Naturales Quaestiones*, I have become convinced that his statement concerning Eudoxus ought to be taken seriously; it reads in full (Santillana cites it only in part):

> Nova haec caelestium observatio est et nuper in Graecia invecta. Democritus quoque, subtilissimus antiquorum omnium, suspicari se ait plures stellas esse quae currant, sed nec numerum illarum posuit nec nomina, nondum comprehensis quinque siderum cursibus. Eudoxus primus ab Aegypto hos motus in Graeciam transtulit. His tamen de cometis nihil dicit; ex quo apparet ne apud Aegyptios quidem, quibus maior caeli cura fuit, hanc partem elaboratam. (III, 1–2)

This makes far better sense indeed than Strabo's narrative. We may reject the *argumentum e silentio* that the Egyptians did not observe comets because otherwise Eudoxus would have mentioned it, but I see no reason to doubt the correctness of the preceding statement. For it says that Eudoxus brought home from Egypt *not* his theory of homocentric spheres, but only his knowledge of the planetary motions. In other words, since written or oral records available in Greece did not furnish him with the data or parameters necessary to devise his models of planetary motion, he went somewhere else to obtain the information he needed. And he chose Egypt for the purpose.

At this point I will be warned not to go astray and not to forget what our most competent historians of astronomy have established as irrefutable facts. If the Egyptians had made scientific astronomical observations, it would be expected that at least some of the records have survived. But apart from the meagre diagonal calendars on coffin lids, practically nothing has been found. More important still, Ptolemy apparently never refers to Egyptian observations, whereas he makes extensive use of those recorded by Greeks and Babylonians. It may be thought that these arguments have by now become commonplaces. Yet I venture to say that, to me, the problem does not seem exhausted: it rather starts to become interesting at this very point. Let us look at the type of ancient observations which Ptolemy found worthy of being used in his computations: if I am not mistaken they are mainly, not to say exclusively, lunar eclipses recorded with an accuracy of about one digit (one twelfth of the moon's diameter) and of one equinoctial hour or less. I believe that it would be preposterous to infer from the lack of written evidence that the Egyptians just did not care about eclipses and thus let them pass unobserved. But we are bound to accept the fact that they did not record them for whatever reason it may have been. As to other observations, we know at least that the heliacal rising of Sirius played a not too unimportant part in Egyptian history. They were the first of all of the ancient civilizations to derive from it (and its accidental closeness to the rising of the Nile) an approximate length of the solar year, namely 365 days, which they retained in their calendar (the only practical and really useful calendar to be found in Antiquity, equalled only by that of the Mayas) even long after they had recognized that it falls short of the true year by about a quarter of a day. During the Middle Kingdom we find those diagonal calendars already mentioned, which record *in toto* 36 constellations (including Sirius) more or less close to the path of the sun. By their heliacal rising, they served to indicate, with no great accuracy of course, the beginning of each of the 36 periods of 10 days (decades) comprised in one year (not taking into account the five epagomenal days), while at night their rising over the horizon marked the hours that had elapsed since sunset. Here again, it would be obtuse to claim that no constellations were known before the Middle Kingdom. In fact, there is ample evidence for their recognition and importance far back in Egyptian history, though we are not able in every case to identify them.

Who would claim then that the same Egyptians, however untalented, having observed already by 1800 B.C. the rising and the setting and heliacal risings of quite a number of stars, had forgotten completely about the planets, so that, by 400 B.C. or after, they were unable to tell a man coming from abroad about the main characteristics and periods of their orbits? In Greece, judging from what can be found in the pre-Socratic fragments and in Plato, there was little accurate information to be obtained. True, the man in the street, the farmer and the shepherd may have known more than the philosopher (remember that astronomical enlightenment has not even today percolated to all our modern colleagues in the field), but the deplorable state of the Greek lunisolar calendar evidently made it a difficult task to derive solar, lunar, and planetary parameters with even a modest degree of accuracy. The accuracy of information needed to devise the first model representing planetary motion was indeed far inferior to that required by Ptolemy. There can be no doubt that Babylonia could furnish more than Eudoxus wanted to know, but Egypt too could provide him with a good deal, and with an accuracy sufficient for his purpose. Here, I repeat, the advantage of the solar calendar should not be underrated; it makes up for quite a few insufficiencies, if there were any at all. The equation 25 Egyptian year=309 mean lunar months (as found in the Demotic papyrus No. 9 of the Carlsberg Collection),[1] representing according to Neugebauer[2] "an older Egyptian method probably uninfluenced by Hellenism", yields a value for the lunation of 29·53074 days (as against modern 29·53059), which is only 13 seconds too long. To give an idea of the accuracy achieved in this period, which served to regulate the intercalation of months and so to harmonize the lunar and the civil calendars, it may suffice to state that the error of 13 seconds per lunation amounts to 67 minutes in the period of 25 years, which makes $4\frac{1}{2}$ hours in 100 years, and less than 3 days in one Sothis period. The value of 29·5151 days for the lunation derived from the old octaëteris (99 lunations=8 Julian years or 2922 days) is 22 minutes too short, and that of 29·53085 days derived from the Metonic cycle (235 lunations=19 Julian years or 6939·75 days) still is 22 seconds too long. It follows from this comparison that the Egyptian value is by far the best, coming pretty close to the one attested in contemporary Babylonian texts and adopted later by Geminus and Ptolemy, namely 29; 31, 50, 8, 20 days and sexagesimal fractions of a day=29·5305941 days, which represents the optimum of accuracy.

In fact, not only Eudoxus could profit by becoming acquainted with this ratio; half a millenium after him, Ptolemy states (*Almagest*, VI, 2) that 25 Egyptian years equal a whole number of synodic months with a small remainder of 0; 2, 47, 5 days, corresponding exactly to the error of 67 months in 25 years as mentioned above. And it is by that amount of 0; 2, 47, 5 days that (*Almagest*, VI, 3, Table 2) the mean full-moons

[1] See O. Neugebauer and A. Volten in *Quellen und Studien zur Geschichte der Mathematik*, B, IV (1938),

[2] *The Exact Sciences in Antiquity* (2nd ed.) p. 90.

recede every 25 years from an initial date (Thoth 9, year 1 of Nabonassar), so that after about 1100 years the difference amounts to 2 days, the full-moons then falling on Thoth 7. In saying that Ptolemy *apparently* never refers to Egyptian observations, I had this particular case in mind because here, though not expressly denominated as such by Ptolemy, the debt to Egypt is beyond doubt.

As is seen from these longish arguments, it is possible to adduce at least some evidence of Egyptian astronomical knowledge by which Eudoxus might have profited if he really did go to the land of the Nile. To me it becomes more and more probable that he did, and going through what others have thought and written about it, I find that the older authors (Ideler, Boeckh, Hultsch) do not seem to have the least doubt as to the reliability of the tradition (indeed why should he not have gone to Egypt as many others did before and after him?), while those of the modern authors who take pleasure in denying it offer no other argument for their scepticism than "I just don't believe it". Neugebauer (*Exact Sciences*, p. 151) does not belong to this group. He states that he sees "no good reason to deny the possibility of his travels to Egypt", but then continues that it seems certain to him that "there was nothing to learn from the Egyptians themselves". For the reasons given, I am not quite so pessimistic because — if I may be allowed to repeat it — Eudoxus needed less, and another type of data than Ptolemy. Apart from the astronomical and calendariographic information, he may have found even such data of a purely mathematical kind — just enough factual knowledge to excite his curiosity and to stimulate his mathematical genius. I am of course thinking of the theorem that the volume of the pyramid is one-third of the volume of the cylinder with an equal base and height. In Egypt, this theorem appears as an empirical fact already in the Middle Kingdom. In Greece, we learn from Archimedes's *Method*[1] that Democritus was the first to formulate it without proof, while it was Eudoxus who proved it (in Heiberg's Latin translation: "Demonstrationem Eudoxus primus repperit, de cono et pyramide, tertiam scilicet partem esse conum cylindri, pyramidem autem prismatis, eandem basim altitudinemque aequalem habentium, haud exiguam partem tribueris Democrito, qui primus de figuris, quas diximus, hoc edixit sine demonstratione"). Now, of the little we know about Democritus' life, his travels to Oriental

[1] *Opera omnia*, ed. Heiberg, II, 429–30.

countries, among which Egypt is expressly mentioned, seem to be the only well attested facts. He could have obtained the empirical knowledge in Babylonia, in Egypt, or in both. It would then not be out of the way to assume that Eudoxus, having learned the empirical fact from his illustrious predecessor through whatever channels it be, was driven by curiosity to inquire whether more was to be found in Egypt about this and similar theorems, and that only after having recognized the vanity of his task, he devised his famous proof. But allow me to stop here so as to avoid the risk of being called the inventor of new fairy-tales.

May I say a few more words about the historical investigations of Professor Hans Ludendorff, with whom I had friendly contact until the last year of his life (and whom by the way I always found anxious not to be confused with his brother and his sinister philosophy)? He was not a man of preconceived opinions, and in his historical studies he proved true to the principles that had guided him through the many years of his activity as one of the leading German astronomers. To me, the overwhelming material presented in his twelve papers on Maya astronomy seems to prove that there is something to Spinden's correlation — to put it as modestly as can be done. Personally, after having invested quite a bit of time in dealing with this fascinating matter, I am convinced that much of what Ludendorff has derived from the texts and inscriptions will stand the test of later generations. I remember 25 years ago one of the few experts in the field giving me the advice not to place too much confidence in Ludendorff as he was just finishing a comprehensive analysis of his results to prove their untenability. A couple of years after, he told me that there still was some work to be done to furnish the final and conclusive proof; after that we stopped talking about the matter and, to the best of my knowledge, the paper has not yet been published. However, it appears that modern history, or philosophy, or sociology of science can do without the mathematical counter-proof of a qualified critic. For, obviously, looking out for an astronomical meaning of the Mayas' astronomical tables has been decreed démodé. Mr. de Santillana's quotation from Mr. Thompson's *Maya Hieroglyphic Writing* beautifully illustrates the changed situation: Spinden's correlation was compromised by Ludendorff's attempt to make it astronomically significant. Thus, astronomy having been interdicted by today's leaders, there remains only the other of the two alternatives: Thompson's correlation (against which I of course say nothing; it is in itself no less remarkable an achievement than Spinden's). Modern authors, such as Morley, do not even find it worth while to tell their readers in detail for what particular reasons they reject Spinden. The absolute anticlimax, eventually, is reached when the work of one of the greatest authorities is trampled under foot as 'bilge'. Dogmatism has conquered the field anew! In this instance, may I praise Mr. de Santillana's sledge-hammer as the appropriate tool.

H. Guerlac

The topic assigned me by our Director was a large one indeed. I chose to interpret my title, "Historical assumptions of the History of Science", in a particular way and to present some remarks on the historical relationship of the history of science to the writing of history during the past century and more. I should make it clear — as evidently I did not in the paper itself — that I have attempted to view our work in the history of science only as it might appear to the general historian. Because I assumed a particular posture, and emphasized a particular point of view, I should like to clear up some possible misunderstanding. First of all, I agree that the history of science must involve many different and highly specialized inquiries. I do not think my paper was a repudiation of specialization. Our central task is certainly still to reconstruct as accurately and painstakingly as we can, the developments of the several sciences. Moreover, I find the diversity of our activity in this respect to be healthy, stimulating and essential, whether we approach our subject according to the doxographical, retrospective, problematic or cultural modes described by Mr. Passmore. My chief point is that the last — the cultural approach — is the one which can best provide a link with the work of the general historian, yet it is the aspect which, I feel, in our present mood we generally neglect.

Secondly, I agree that the central core of our endeavour is the study of the development, growth and interplay of scientific *ideas*. As Mr. Hanson observed in an earlier session, the history of science is fundamentally the history of scientific thought. And I certainly feel, and tried to express in my paper, that the contribution of philosophical analysis and the work of philosophically trained minds have given our discipline a depth and sophistication which it badly lacked hitherto.

While I agree with Mr. Laslett about the dangers of writing retrospective or 'Whig' history, and have stressed the importance of seeing early science, good or bad, as cultural manifestations of earlier periods, I feel we have a legitimate right to be especially curious about those aspects of early thought which prepared the way for science as we know it today. In this connexion, Mr. Koyré chided me in his courteous comments for projecting the present condition of science into the past. By my stress on the relations of science to technology — which I intended only as a pertinent illustration of the way we tend to neglect social factors — I left myself open to his criticism. But if Syracuse does little to explain Archimedes, perhaps Greek culture as a whole may do so at least in part. And certainly, for the general historian, Archimedes does something to explain Syracuse. For earlier periods other cultural factors than the technological may well prove to be of the greatest importance, though I doubt if the technological factor can be safely neglected even there.

In the last analysis I tried to make a single and not very controversial point that I deem important. It is that if we concentrate exclusively on what has been called the internal history of science, on the filiation and unfolding of scientific ideas and technics, we may end up writing for ourselves alone, or for ourselves and the philosophers of science. We shall certainly fail to provide the general historian with what he requires: namely, some grasp of what the development of science has meant in its relation to human history. What I am urging is simply that we keep the general historian sometimes in mind, and do not neglect those aspects of the history of science of which he can make use in his difficult assignment of studying cultural and societal change. This may involve awareness of the material factors affecting or affected by the growth of science. It may involve a sensitivity to other kinds of cultural interaction, and even to 'intellectual history' — the historical role of lesser minds and lesser writings — about which Mr. Passmore made such an acerb commentary.

G. de Santillana

May I state, first of all, that my communication should be considered really as a joint paper written together with Miss von Dechend, although her modesty prevented her name from appearing in the title. I must underscore the debt I owe to her immense scholarship and implacable critical judgment, without which it would have been impossible to handle such difficult material.

I want also to thank the commentators for their understanding treatment of our rather hazardous suggestions.

To be sure there is nothing hazardous in insisting that the technical texts of Antiquity should be taken up again by translators who can understand the technical language. This is nothing against the philologists, if we understand philology in the classical sense of *ars bene legendi*, or the art of reading slowly. The chance I took was in suggesting that many texts hitherto taken to deal with some arbitrary form of prelogical thought are really couched in technical, albeit mythical, language, and should be explored for their scientific content. Neugebauer once said that before we go on digging the ground we might start excavating the museums, and this is only an extension of his remarks to an immense available amount of literature. There is a reasonable chance to be taken with that. If the enterprise pays off, the rewards might be great indeed. A whole submerged continent of thought might come into view.

Some very significant remarks were made by Mr. Needham and Mr. Laslett about the role of contemporary concerns in the historian's point of view. I hold that there are constant recurrent structures in history, which may be better understood by contemporary examples, and vice versa. When Edward Meyer wanted to understand the early Christian sects, he went to study the Mormons *in situ*. Of such structures are the great bureaucracies. They can be taken to have a fairly uniform behaviour, whether it be the U.S. Atomic Energy Commission or the Vatican at the time of Urban VIII, or the Egyptian administration under Rameses II. The study of one may clear up many aspects of the other. In that sense I believe in establishing parallels.

There are, on the other hand, certain historical phenomena which had best be understood by way of their difference from anything contemporary. Of such are medieval Christianity, or the cosmological thought of the ancients. There *is* a rational process in both, but it takes forms different from those we are used to. We should understand these complexes, then, in their *differentia specifica*. That is why I asked for an acceptance of the synoptic vision and the *Tertium datur*, even a fourth and a fifth level, of cosmological imagination. I know only too well that history remains, as Koyré has reminded us, "une pauvre science conjecturale", but we need not for all that see it in the too-frequent terms of "just one damn thing after another".

V. P. Zubov

In presenting my paper on the historiography of science in Russia, I made it my aim to give an account of the work done in this field, including such facts as are little (or possibly not at all) known in this country. In conclusion, allow me to summarize what the facts indicate. The development of the historiography of science in Russia is characterized by general features characteristic of all historiography in every country. Writings on the history of science arise in the first instance from the needs of science itself. But such a history remains necessarily pragmatic and limited: the first step in historiography is simply the compilation of a bibliography of scientific works, an inventory of known facts, or a catalogue of discoveries. As I have tried to show in my paper, the needs of the various disciplines differ in this respect: mathematicians, chemists and biologists each make a different approach to the past history of their own science. The second stage is to analyse the logical connexions between ideas and theories, without specifying the chronology of this connexion. Very often it is also dictated by pragmatic considerations. It is only when the chronological aspect of the connexions become significant, when the facts become localized in time and space, that the human factor appears and that one can properly speak of a history of science.

It is now no longer a question of the history of the sciences, but of a history of science. Since he is pursuing pragmatic aims, the man of science is only interested in the history of his own discipline. He becomes an historian of science as soon as he begins to consider the facts as an integral part of the history of human civilization. It is at this juncture that one must ask why each particular discovery should have been made in its particular social context. We cannot at this point go in detail into the question of how a man of science becomes an historian of science, that is to say, a philosopher and historian of human civilization; nor of how a philosopher and historian of civilization becomes an historian of science. Whatever road they travel, the result must be the same, for the goal is identical. As for the content of such a philosophical history of science and its methods, this basic historiographical problem could well become the theme of a further discussion.

Note on Scientific Manuscripts

Mr. R. N. Quirk was invited to raise this subject, speaking as a member of the Royal Commission on Historical Manuscripts; the Commission, established about 100 years ago, is an advisory body concerned with the preservation, etc., of historical manuscripts of all kinds (other than public records). The National Register of Archives, which is closely associated with the Commission, has available large numbers of reports and lists of documents possessed by private institutions and persons.

Mr. Quirk said that the Commission, which has so far not been closely concerned with the records of the scientists and of scientific research, was considering what should be their policy towards scientific manuscripts and records. In particular, he said that the Commission would be most interested in views on the following questions:

"Do historians of science attach importance to the manuscript records of scientists?"

"If so, would British scientific historians favour an initiative by the Royal Commission on Historical Manuscripts, directed towards preservation and identification of, and access to, scientific manuscript records?"

During a brief discussion, the consensus of opinion appeared to be that the answer to both questions was in the affirmative. It was felt that the preservation of scientific records was largely a matter of chance; that it was often very difficult to locate them; and that a more consciously thought out policy in this matter was needed. While the Royal Commission did not itself act as a repository of records, it would be helpful if reports on, and lists of, scientific manuscripts, for example in the hands of University Departments or Libraries, could be sent to the National Register of Archives. Reference was made to current inquiries in this country, and to the considerable activities of *Isis* in this field in the U.S.A.

As time was short, and as the matter obviously requires considerable thought and local investigation, Mr. Quirk was invited to provide a memorandum, which would be circulated to members of the Symposium and other interested persons and institutions, posing the problem as seen by the Royal Commission, and inviting comments, which he would be glad to receive.

Symposium on the History of Science
Oxford University
9th—15th July, 1961

Members of the Symposium

P. Alexander, *University of Bristol.*
Mrs. E. Heischkel-Artelt, *University of Mainz.*
W. Artelt, *Goethe University, Frankfurt.*
Sir Eric Ashby, *Cambridge University.*
John R. Baker, *Oxford University.*
Miss R. J. Banister, *Oxford University.*
G. Beaujouan, *Archives de France, Paris.*
Sir Isaiah Berlin, *Oxford University.*
D. Bohm, *University of Bristol.*
Miss M. L. Bonelli, *Istituto e Museo di Storia della Scienza, Florence.*
E. J. Bowen, *Oxford University.*
Sir Maurice Bowra, *President of the British Academy.*
A. Briggs, *University of Leeds.*
J. S. Bromley, *University of Southampton.*
G. Buchdahl, *Cambridge University.*
A. L. C. Bullock, *Oxford University.*
H. Butterfield, *Cambridge University.*
A. J. Cain, *Oxford University.*
E. F. C. Caldin, *University of Leeds.*
G. Canguilhem, *University of Paris.*
D. S. L. Cardwell, *University of Leeds.*
C. F. Carter, *University of Manchester.*
A. Clow, *B.B.C., London.*
I. B. Cohen, *Harvard University.*
J. P. Cooper, *Oxford University.*
P. Costabel, *University of Paris.*
A. C. Crombie, *Oxford University.*
H. L. Crosby, Jr., *Hollins College, Virginia.*
C. D. Darlington, *Oxford University.*
M. Daumas, *Conservatoire National des Ars et Métiers, Paris.*
Miss H. von Dechend, *Goethe University, Frankfurt.*
B. Dibner, *Norwalk, Conn.*
Miss D. Dyason, *University of Melbourne.*
L. Edelstein, *Rockefeller Institute, New York.*
D. Edge, *B.B.C., London.*
Miss D. Emmet, *University of Manchester.*
B. A. Farrell, *Oxford University.*
N. Figurovsky, *Soviet Academy of Sciences, Moscow.*

D. Fleming, *Harvard University.*

Sir Howard Florey, *President of the Royal Society.*

R. J. Forbes, *University of Amsterdam.*

S. Galin, *Hendon Technical College.*

B. Gille, *University of Clermont.*

C. C. Gillispie, *Princeton University.*

B. Glass, *Johns Hopkins University.*

F. Greenaway, *Science Museum, London.*

A. T. Grigoryan, *Soviet Academy of Sciences, Moscow.*

H. Guerlac, *Cornell University.*

H. J. Habakkuk, *Oxford University.*

A. R. Hall, *Indiana University.*

Mrs. M. Boas Hall, *Indiana University.*

N. R. Hanson, *Indiana University.*

H. R. Harré, *Oxford University.*

Sir Harold Hartley, *Royal Society, London.*

W. Hartner, *Goethe University, Frankfurt.*

J. W. Herivel, *The Queen's University, Belfast.*

Miss M. B. Hesse, *Cambridge University.*

M. A. Hoskin, *Cambridge University.*

P. Huard, *University of Rennes.*

R. W. Hunt, *Oxford University.*

D. W. Hutchings, *Oxford University.*

E. F. Jacob, *Oxford University.*

J. Jewkes, *Oxford University.*

S. Kapoor, *University of Hull.*

A. G. Keller, *Cambridge University.*

C. E. Kellet, *Newcastle General Hospital.*

P. W. Kent, *Oxford University.*

W. C. Kneale, *Oxford University.*

B. G. Kuznetsov, *Soviet Academy of Sciences, Moscow.*

A. Koyré, *University of Paris.*

T. S. Kuhn, *University of California, Berkeley.*

I. Lakatos, *University of London.*

P. Laslett, *Cambridge University.*

Mrs. R. G. Lewis, *Oxford University.*

B. J. Loewenberg, *Cambridge University.*

B. B. Lloyd, *Oxford University.*

C. A. Mace, *University of London.*

F. R. Maddison, *Oxford University.*

J. E. McGuire, *University of Leicester.*

W. Mays, *University of Manchester.*

E. Mendelsohn, *Harvard University.*

J. Millás-Vallicrosa, *University of Barcelona.*

L. Minio-Paluello, *Oxford University.*

D. Mitchell, *Oxford University.*

J. Murdoch, *Princeton University.*

J. T. NEEDHAM, *Cambridge University.*

L. NOVÝ, *Czechoslovak Academy of Sciences, Prague.*

R. C. OLDFIELD, *Oxford University.*

E. OLSZEWSKI, *Polish Academy of Sciences, Warsaw.*

C. D. O'MALLEY, *University of California, Los Angeles.*

G. E. L. OWEN, *Oxford University.*

J. A. PASSMORE, *Australian National University, Canberra.*

W. D. M. PATON, *Oxford University.*

Sir GEORGE PICKERING, *Oxford University.*

S. PINES, *Hebrew University, Jerusalem.*

M. H. PIRENNE, *Oxford University.*

M. POLANYI, *Oxford University.*

F. N. L. POYNTER, *Wellcome Historical Medical Library, London.*

D. J. de S. PRICE, *Yale University.*

R. N. QUIRK, *Royal Commission on Historical Manuscripts, London.*

T. RAISON, *London.*

J. RAVETZ, *University of Leeds.*

A. H. T. ROBB-SMITH, *Oxford University.*

V. RONCHI, *University of Florence.*

K. E. ROTHSCHUH, *University of Münster.*

G. E. M. DE STE. CROIX, *Oxford University.*

S. SAMBURSKY, *Hebrew University, Jerusalem.*

G. DE SANTILLANA, *Massachusetts Institute of Technology.*

M. SCHRAMM, *Goethe University, Frankfurt.*

R. J. SEEGER, *National Science Foundation, Washington.*

R. H. SHRYOCK, *American Philosophical Society, Philadelphia.*

H. M. SINCLAIR, *Oxford University.*

Mrs. D. W. SINGER, *Par, Cornwall.*

Miss B. SMALLEY, *Oxford University.*

W. A. SMEATON, *University of London.*

R. W. SOUTHERN, *Oxford University.*

D. SPEISER, *University of Geneva.*

W. D. STAHLMAN, *University of Wisconsin.*

R. C. STAUFFER, *University of Wisconsin.*

S. STERN, *Oxford University.*

B. STICKER, *University of Hamburg.*

Miss L. S. SUTHERLAND, *Oxford University.*

R. G. SWINBURNE, *University of Leeds.*

Sir RONALD SYME, *Oxford University,*

R. TATON, *University of Paris.*

O. TEMKIN, *Johns Hopkins University.*

G. TEMPLE, *Oxford University.*

J. M. THOMAS, *Oxford University.*

S. E. TOULMIN, *Nuffield Foundation, London.*

Mrs. J. TOULMIN, *Nuffield Foundation, London.*

H. R. TREVOR-ROPER, *Oxford University.*

R. A. TRICKER, *Ministry of Education.*

A. R. UBBELOHDE, *University of London.*

B. L. VAN DER WAERDEN, *University of Zürich.*

J. P. VERNANT, *University of Paris.*

R. R. WALZER, *Oxford University.*

G. J. WARNOCK, *Oxford University.*

A. WASSERSTEIN, *University of Leicester.*

L. WHITE, Jr., *University of California, Los Angeles.*

Dr. E. A. O. WHITEMAN, *Oxford University.*

D. T. WHITESIDE, *Cambridge University.*

G. J. WHITROW, *University of London.*

W. P. D. WIGHTMAN, *University of Aberdeen.*

J. S. WILKIE, *University of London.*

D. H. WILKINSON, *Oxford University.*

L. P. WILLIAMS, *Cornell University.*

T. I. WILLIAMS, *Oxford.*

L. G. WILSON, *Yale University.*

H. WOOLF, *University of Washington.*

WONG CHU-MING [HUANG KUANG MING], *University of Rennes.*

A. P. YUSHKEVICH, *Soviet Academy of Sciences, Moscow.*

V. P. ZUBOV, *Soviet Academy of Sciences, Moscow.*

Index